Intimate Communications

HERDT

Guardians of the Flutes.

Rituals of Manhood: Male Initiation in Papua New Guinea (ed.).

Ritualized Homosexuality in Melanesia (ed.).

The Sambia: Ritual and Gender in New Guinea

STOLLER

Sex and Gender: On the Development of Masculinity and Femininity.

Splitting.

The Transsexual Experiment: Sex and Gender—Volume II.

Perversion: The Erotic Form of Hatred.

Sexual Excitement: Dynamics of Erotic Life.

Observing the Erotic Imagination.

Presentations of Gender.

Cognitive Science and Psychoanalysis. (With K. M. Colby.)

Ritual talk: one-on-one backstage preparations.

INTIMATE COMMUNICATIONS

Erotics and the Study of Culture

GILBERT HERDT
AND ROBERT J. STOLLER

Columbia University Press
New York

Cover, frontispiece photograph by Gilbert Herdt. Ritual talk: one-on-one backstage preparations.

COLUMBIA UNIVERSITY PRESS
New York   Oxford
Copyright © 1990 Columbia University Press
All rights reserved

LIBRARY OF CONGRESS CATALOGING-IN-PUBLICATION DATA
Herdt, Gilbert H., 1949–
Intimate communications : erotics and the study of culture /
Gilbert Herdt and Robert J. Stoller.
p.   cm.
Bibliography: p.
Includes index.
ISBN 0-231-06900-6
1. Sambia (Papua New Guinea people)—Sexual behavior.
2. Sambia (Papua New Guinea people)—Rites and ceremonies.
3. Group identity—Papua New Guinea.
I. Stoller, Robert J. II. Title.
DU740.42.H445   1989
306.7'0899912—dc19
89-897
CIP

Casebound editions of Columbia University Press books are Smyth-sewn
and printed on permanent and durable acid-free paper
∞

Printed in the United States of America
c 10 9 8 7 6 5 4 3 2 1

CONTENTS

Preface *vii*
Acknowledgments *xv*
Notes on Dates in Text *xvii*
Introduction *1*

PART I. INTRODUCTIONS *13*

1. Clinical Ethnography *15*
2. Sambia Sexual Culture *53*

PART II. INTERVIEWS *85*

3. Interviewing Sambia *87*
4. Moondi's Erotism *101*
5. Tali and Weiyu on Ritual and Erotics *128*
6. Penjukwi: Portrait of a Woman *152*
7. Sakulambei: A Hermaphrodite's Secret *202*
8. Imano: Considerate Masculinity *246*
9. Kalutwo: Portrait of a Misfit *279*
10. The Interpreter's Discomfort *323*

PART III. CONCLUSIONS *347*

11. Summing Up: Clinical Ethnography
   of Sambia Erotics and Gender *349*

Epilogue. Training Clinical Ethnographers *381*
Appendix. The Editing Process *395*
Notes *403*
Bibliography *439*
Index *459*

Illustrations appear as a group following page 244.

PREFACE

Herdt:* Toward the end of my third and very significant field trip among the Sambia of Papua New Guinea, in 1979, Bob Stoller, a psychoanalyst and professor of psychiatry, visited my field site in the village of Nilangu. I had completed doctoral dissertation research among the Sambia between 1974 and 1976, two years' work on which I based my first book, *Guardians of the Flutes* (1981), that had been written in draft form in 1978, during a time of many dialogues with S. For the next two years, between 1977 and 1979, S. and I talked together, on clinical research, erotics, and gender identity issues, because I was fortunate enough to apprentice with him. When the opportunity came for me to return to the Sambia again in 1979, it was therefore natural for him to want to visit. He did so and the culmination of our work is this book.

Since that time, S. and I have collaborated but also continued our separate researches, which have led in several directions. For my own gender research I returned to the field for follow-up studies with the Sambia in 1981, 1983, and 1985, the total period of fieldwork being about three years. This work has been published in a series of books and papers, which the reader will find referenced in our bibliography, and the findings of which are distilled in Herdt (1987c). This body of ethnographic material backgrounds the present work that also presents a new contribution on erotics and culture, the theme that drew me to work with S. and that led him to the village as well.

Our study is motivated by the lack of material on sexuality across cultures and our concern to place erotics more centrally into anthro-

*You will find "H" or "S" at the start of sections that one or the other of us primarily wrote (though, of course, each of us corrected, added citations to, and edited all of the other's material).

pology (Herdt 1987c). We hope to explore and advance the study of subjectivity more fully by doing this. To do so we must study interviews on intimate matters and try to assess how the ethnographers' procedures help or hinder the process. In this way we try to deconstruct "sexual"—we shall use the more precise term "erotic"—meanings in cultures. We shall use data collected (almost haphazardly, because our original aim was not to produce a book) through individual interviews to show that it is only through dialogue, through interpersonal and intimate communication, that certain critical points of interest to the study of gender and erotics in culture are revealed. By use of this dialogic mode we are able to provide new kinds of cross-cultural data. Nonetheless, this mode is complicated, and we should note that this book took years to produce.

Stoller: By the end of that first morning in the village, I knew that we should write this book. The impulse still surprises me, for it was not even latent when I left Los Angeles. Though I knew H.'s findings in detail—we had been working together between his field trips—I am a psychoanalyst, not an anthropologist. I could discuss theory with him to help focus his material and could suggest questions to ask or point to hidden areas to uncover. But he is an ethnographer, not I, and these New Guinea findings were his, to be written up by him. That is still the case. The task before us, then, is not so much to describe the Sambia as to contemplate ethnographic method, which—it seemed that morning, and still does—can be strengthened by the techniques that the clinician (psychiatrist/psychoanalyst) uses: we want to report on the value of subjectivity in studying culture, erotics, and gender identity.

Many ethnographers still omit from their reports the fine details of field experience that make our behavior intelligible to ourselves and to those with whom we communicate.[1] How many ethnographic studies are there of "style"—of what is harmonious, ugly, bizarre, frightening, beautiful, exciting—in art, humor, dress, decoration, erotics? What a shame that these aesthetics are removed, for they form an unending flood of sharp and dim awareness shaping our perspective on reality, each waking moment. The psychoanalyst, living within his or her own skin and trying to do so with others, is surprised that colleagues in related disciplines do not believe such data are very significant. Erotics is a case in point (Stoller 1979, 1985a).

This, then, is a book about subjectivity in the study of people, their culture, and erotics. At its center are two principles: the way researchers experience themselves is a vital ingredient of their findings; and, equally, the way informants—subjects, patients, friends—experience themselves shapes what they communicate to us. If you know these perspectives are true, you may not believe anyone doubts them, while the doubters cannot take seriously the work of those who adhere to them.

Through our work with Sambia, we shall use our ethnographic dialogues to rethink method. We believe that these ideas apply to all disciplines that study human behavior: *what the observer feels and what is felt by those whom we observe is part of the research and not an interference to be washed out in research methodology.* The way we experience ourselves is, therefore, a necessary ingredient of our work, present whether we sense it or not. And to the extent we do not sense it, it creates even more of a mess than when we do. Such knowledge is one of the clinician's greatest strengths. Where does this knowledge lie? Whether in ourselves (intrapsychic) or between ourselves and others (interpersonal), it must be scrutinized, understood, and used if we are to understand our informants and ourselves. Unfortunately, such knowledge complicates our work, and perhaps—paradoxically—forever limits what we can know. For, of course, our understanding of ourselves will always be incomplete or biased, even for those closely connected to us, even for those who share our culture, let alone for those from other places or times. Misjudging what is happening inside another can also lead to wrong conclusions. H. and I, however, feel a new attempt can be made to study these problems. In fact we are driven to do so now, for each of us has reached a point in our separate investigations where we must more fully consider this aspect of our methodology—who we are as we do our work and who each person is whom we study—before going back to our own concerns.

If we were to practice what we preach, a good part of this book would be a description of each of us, not merely the usual curriculum vitae but a more insightful look at our personalities—at those of our attributes that influenced the way each Sambia responded to us. We have done so only to a limited extent, however. (And, without having tried, we do not know if we have the courage or the wisdom to do so.) Someday, if we are successful, books such as this—and better—will be published by others. But until readers are comfortable with a subjectively oriented report, they would fuss too much over the descriptions of each of us. Only when it becomes a given in research on human behavior can we demand that each explorer show us his half of the interpersonal equation. So let the following suffice to orient the reader; you will sense more who we are as you see the way we write and read the way we spoke in the field.

In 1975, while with the Sambia doing doctoral fieldwork, H. wrote to a friend at UCLA, also a predoctoral candidate, asking if the latter could refer him to a clinician familiar with contemporary issues in sexuality—erotic behavior and gender identity.* By coincidence, the student was at that moment helping me survey the comparative ethnography on sexual excitement. In our ensuing correspondence H. saw that I knew the field, and I found that he had gathered data on sexuality richer than any available in the anthropologic literature. In time, to further strengthen his capacity to collect and make sense of such data, and to increase his skills in using subjective information, he decided that he needed training in a clinical/research center after completing his doctorate. So, on being awarded a postdoctoral fellowship, he came to study with me at UCLA.

For my own work on the development of gender identity, H.'s findings on the Sambia, including those gathered before we met, have been among the few I have found rich enough—where the people are real enough—for cross-cultural comparison. When as an ethnographer you remove yourself (and thereby me) from your data and communicate only with normative descriptions, modal personalities, and statistics, there are no true grounds for this psychologically informed act of comparing. H. discusses this view in chapter 1.

Each of us learned about the other's literature, methods, and professional skills, our discussions built around reviewing and dissecting the data (in raw form embodied in memory, field notes, and audiotapes of conversations). Because predictions made in the office were borne out later when H. returned to the Sambia, and because suggestions for leads to follow brought forth new data, our enthusiasm persisted. So, of course, I went to visit the Sambia.

Regarding personality traits, H. and I share two qualities useful for our work. First, though each of us is "properly" (that is, classically) trained in our professions and not overly rebellious, sharp-nosed colleagues sense our territorial markers on alien hydrants. Second, for reasons probably hidden in the murk of early infantile experiences, we each need to get inside others' minds, to feel what they feel, and to know what they know (without having to suffer the misery of

---

*At all times when we write "sexuality" herein, we refer only to something in those two domains: gender identity and erotics.

really being someone else). That hunger (to use a word that points toward the primordial dynamics) underlies all rationalizations of the scientific value of studying subjectivity and guarantees the pursuit of our curiosity.

If an ethnographer and analyst work together, is it not more efficient to have them both in the same person? Though we believe it would be, as in the rare cases of Roheim and Devereux, we do not believe it easily can be. Nor have LeVine's[2] ideas about cross-cultural teams generated much enthusiasm. An analyst and anthropologist from the same culture may share similar cultural blindspots, but they have advantages as a team. Whatever similarities are shared by H. and me, there must be personality differences if we are each to fit the mold of our respective professions. Ethnographers, for instance, must want to live for long stretches in a foreign culture, should yearn to identify with people culturally different from themselves, must give up the middle-class comforts out of which they are likely to have emerged (if they are to have had the educational opportunities needed for becoming an anthropologist). The desire to stay put, to have a family, or to enjoy the pleasures of one's own culture cannot be urges in the ethnographer strong enough to disrupt his or her capacity to stay away from home.[3]

On the other hand, analysts should be, whatever else goes on in their lives, people who not only think about analysis but practice it (cannot bear not to practice it).[4] Since analyses take years and—to put it mildly—do not thrive on long, repeated absences by the analyst, we can expect that most analysts will prefer to stay home. Perhaps some day an analyst who likes to practice will find himself in life circumstances that allow him first to soak up a foreign culture until it is nonetheless his own and then to practice analysis there. (There was a bit of this process when European analysts, forced to flee, settled into new countries with new languages; but the cultural shifts were far less than what the classical ethnographer experiences.)

There are other reasons why the two disciplines are not easily combined in one person. Most analysts, with premedical training, medical school, internship, and three years of psychiatric residency before starting their analytic training, are rather aged by the time their seven to ten years of analytic training have ended and they are certified as competent to practice. To lay on top of that the requirement of a doctorate in anthropology is close to absurd. So far, almost no one has been able to combine the two disciplines; and if one should, there is the danger, as with other professional hybrids, that fellow anthropologists judge this colleague to be a lousy anthropologist but a good analyst, while fellow analysts judge him a lousy analyst but a good anthropologist.

So, since it worked easily for us, we recommend that a team—a compatible ethnographer and analyst/psychiatrist—work together.[5] When the ethnographer is accepted by people in the community in which he or she is working, the chances are good the colleague will also be. The two researchers as a team bring different personalities, life experiences, training, blind spots, and insights to their work. And, if personal and professional animosities (are they different?) are not present, the two will enjoy—as we have—how the strength of one repairs the weaknesses of the other and how what is background for one can be foreground for the other.

Hence by the time the helicopter delivered me into the Valley, except for and because of Herdt, I knew more anthropologically about the Sambia than anyone else in the world, including, in some ways, even the Sambia. And, whereas it would have been impossible for a stranger to drop in and be accepted, my arrival as the friend of H., who is so well regarded by his informants, was frictionless from the start. It was even easier, perhaps, than when I first meet a patient in our culture: the Sambia saw me so much as his extension that—as I felt and he confirmed—they spoke no less freely with me present than they had previously with him alone. (And perhaps, for some Sambia, my gray hair also made me seem safer, *hors de combat*.)

It was necessary that it be that way, for I could only stay ten days. One need be very, very cautious about the findings of an observer who spent only that fragment of time in a village (see chapter 1). (Certainly, those of us in Los Angeles are bemused by the standard East Coast journalist's report of Southern California culture based on watching the Beverly Hills Hotel poolside traffic flow.) But, after a couple of years of studying with H., I knew a lot about each of the people we interviewed and their culture. I was physically and psychologically at ease from the moment of entering the village; no barrier but language blocked communication between the Sambia and me, and with H. there, I did not have to spend years learning to communicate. (To confirm these declarations, there are our tapes.) Most important, I was not there pretending to be an ethnographer and was not aiming to discover new things about the Sambia.

What I did find, which has been well noted by others and does not require long field trips or an exquisite research plan, is that there are, in studying human behavior, many circumstances when we can neither ignore who or what it is we observe nor who or what each person is whom we observe. Psychoanalysis is, among other things, a certain kind of microethnography. [H: Well, at least the analysis that Stoller practices.] So the analyst brings a long preparation in clinical skills that lets him or her listen to others, as can any seasoned clinician, with heightened (though fallible) sensitivity.

In this work, as you will see, I was H.'s assistant; though on occasion, I could push the interview in new directions or take the lead when we were later exchanging ideas. If our experience as ethnographer and psychoanalyst working together was not a fluke of the circumstances and our personalities, we presume others can find a similar balance. What we did was certainly not psychoanalysis or psychiatry: it was Herdt doing ethnography—he has well named it "clinical ethnography"—amplified and illuminated by my suggestions about how to climb with sensitivity even further into our Sambia friends' minds. And it made us see that when ethnographers learn to use the clinical skills clinicians take for granted, anthropology is closer to the human minds it would study.

This account does not tell you who we were at *any* moment when collecting data on which we shall report: that challenge is not met by such a limited biography (of course, no biography is adequate for this task; all biographies are novels, none more so than autobiographies). We only hope you do not forget, as you read, that our reports and transcripts are not facts, hard as rock. All you will have is your impressions of our impressions. If you then carry the same skeptical but benign reading to all reports on human behavior, our book will have succeeded in one of its aims.

ACKNOWLEDGMENTS

H: One's work responds to many others, in part by context, in another part by dialogue. Stoller, both through our talk and in his work, has been the strongest consistent influence on my thought. Here in Chicago, however, the key context has been shaped by several of my friends and colleagues, of whom I wish especially to thank: Rick Shweder, Bert Cohler, Andy Boxer, and Julia Targ. In the dialogue on gender in Melanesia, and critically for anthropology as a whole, my work is responsive to Marilyn Strathern's, whose remarkable and pioneering insight has been a source of inspiration.

Anthropologists incur many debts in the course of doing field research and training. It is a pleasure to acknowledge here with grateful thanks all this assistance. For predoctoral (1974–1976) field support, Herdt thanks the Australian-American Education foundation and the Department of Anthropology, Research School of Pacific Studies, the Australian National University; and for postdoctoral funding, H. thanks the National Institute of Mental Health, and the Department of Psychiatry, Neuropsychiatric Institute, UCLA. The research reported herein is based primarily on 1979 work with the Sambia in Papua New Guinea, and H. especially wishes to thank Dr. L. Jolyon West, M.D., for the UCLA support that made this study possible. The writing of this book was made possible, in part, by a grant to Herdt from the Anne P. Lederer Research institute. Additional support came from the Spencer Foundation, which is gratefully acknowledged.

H. expresses sincere gratitude to the Department of Anthropology and Sociology, the University of Papua New Guinea, and to the government of Papua New Guinea, for research affiliation that facilitated this work.

H. warmly thanks the following people whose kind logistical and moral support made work possible: Ted Bickum, Robert and Sybil Stoller, Steven Alkus, Murray Fagg, Marielle Fuller, Clifford Barnett, JoAnna Poppink, and Lew Langness. We are also indebted to Louise Waller for her unending enthusiastic editorial commitment. Both S. and I thank again Mr. and Mrs. Dennis Best, of the New Tribes Mission, Papua New Guinea, for their kind hospitality.

Stoller thanks himself, Professor Herdt, his family, and his good luck—in ascending order of significance—for the opportunity to study the Sambia.

For their helpful comments and criticisms on parts of this manuscript we are ever grateful to James L. Gibbs, Jr., Waude Kracke, and Fitz John Poole.

We gratefully acknowledge the typing and transcription work on this book by Thelma Guffan, Jackie de Havilland, Ana Haunga, Flora Degen, Debbie A. Johnson, and Vincent Wang.

Finally, Sambia is a pseudonym adopted by Herdt to protect the true identity of these people. All names and places have also been changed for this reason. And we implore anyone having access to the true identities to protect and safeguard the trust of the people whose lives we describe below. Most of all, I regret that I cannot thank by name my Sambia friends who opened their homes and their souls to us, and trusted us to share their experiences. Perhaps someday circumstances will permit us to do so.

TEXT ACKNOWLEDGMENT

Parts of the following chapters have been excerpted herein with permission of the publishers:

G. Herdt, "Semen Transactions in Sambia Culture." In G. Herdt, ed., *Ritualized Homosexuality in Melanesia*, pp. 167–210. Berkeley: University of California Press.

G. Herdt, "Ordinary People." In *The Sambia: Ritual and Gender in New Guinea*, pp. 59–66. New York: Holt, Rinehart, and Winston.

G. Herdt and R. J. Stoller, "Der Einflub der Supervision auf die ethnographische Praxis." In Hans Peter Duerr, ed., *Die Wilde Seele: Zur Ethnopsychoanalyse von Georges Devereux*, pp. 177–199. Frankfurt: Suhrkamp Verlag.

G. Herdt and R. J. Stoller, Sakulambei—A Hermaphrodite's Secret: Example of Clinical Ethnography. *Psychoanalytic Study of Society* 11:117–158.

NOTES ON DATES IN TEXT

The events and ages of people (written primarily in the short biographic sketches of our case studies) in the following text were written up in the period of 1979–1982.
Introductory and concluding chapters were completed between 1985 and 1987. Final textual changes were completed in the copy-edit (1988). Unless stated otherwise, all ages and events refer to these periods.

Intimate Communications

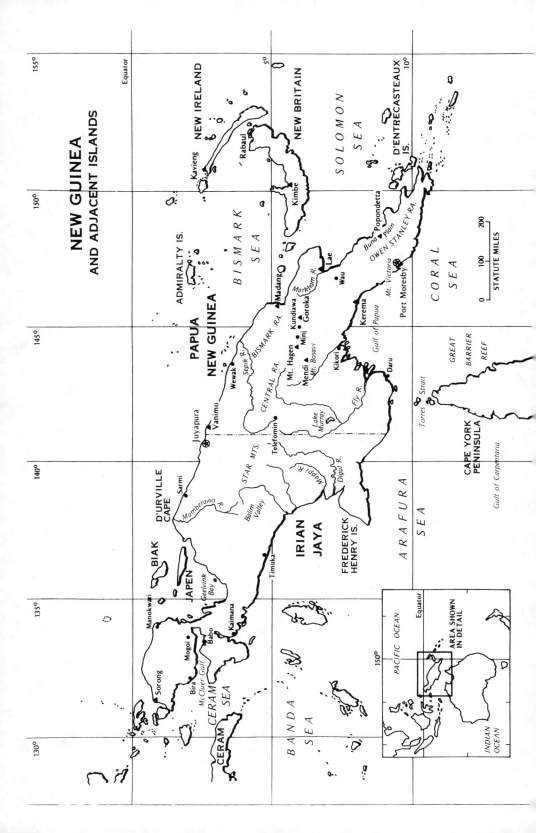

Introduction

H: This is a book that studies the personal meanings and private experiences of people in context to better and more fully understand culture. It also makes an argument for the collaboration of anthropologists and psychoanalysts, especially in the investigation of gender identity and erotics. We develop in what follows a kind of case study approach, which we call clinical ethnography.

Erotics, the study of sexual excitement, is still largely neglected in anthropology, the study of culture. Though great strides have been made in our understanding of gender—masculinity and femininity—in other cultures, erotic sexuality has been a less favored topic of study. We know about the cultural practices and symbols of men's and women's roles in other societies (reviewed in Atkinson 1982; Chodorow 1978; Herdt 1981; Ortner and Whitehead 1981; Rosaldo 1980; Rosaldo and Lamphere 1974; Rossi 1985; M. Strathern 1988). We know less about the people who embody these roles or purvey their meanings (LeVine 1982). Probably no one since Malinowski, in his *Sexual Life of Savages* (1929), has so much contributed to the systematic ethnographic study of erotics in another culture. And that was a long time ago.

Likewise, where a wealth of new material on gender in anthropology has appeared in the last few years, it seems to us that far less attention has been paid to gender identity. There is less concern with the subjectivity or phenomenology of real people's inner feelings, states of being—as in being male or female—and their related goals and representations of such. Far more has issued forth on gender roles, gender hierarchy, and the political economy of the sexual division of labor and female productivity (reviewed in M. Strathern 1988). We do not complain of this interest: does a dinner guest refuse the ap-

1

petizer? It has opened a remarkable new chapter in cross-cultural studies, whereby "gendered analysis is not merely a supplement but a *sine qua non* of social inquiry" (Atkinson 1982:256). Rather, S. and I miss more, and deeper, information on gender identity and erotics. Seldom have ethnographers pursued questions of gender identity orientation or development, as this is understood in contemporary sex research in the United States. Our work with the Sambia is a contribution toward this end.

The causes of this gap between past and present anthropology are not hard to find. On the one hand, sex has long been a tabooed topic in our society and the social sciences at large, the social context and mainstream of anthropology. Gender research has broken down this taboo, but only in part (Herdt 1984). Problems and reluctance associated with the cross-cultural study of homosexual behavior, for instance, reveal some of this old stigma and taboo (Carrier 1980; Mead 1961; Read 1980; 1984; reviewed in Blackwood 1986; Murray 1984). On the other hand, the detailed information necessary to study erotics and gender identity are usually omitted in ethnographies, at least until very recently. In part this is because of the general aims of ethnographic accounts, which are concerned with culture as a whole; and in another sense because of the theoretic treatment of gender as a cultural theme or mode, rather than as an individual construction. We shall discuss these issues later. Another cause of the gap is the sensitive, intimate nature of erotic feelings; for, as Mead (1961:1434) once said, "One characteristic of human sex behavior is the insistence on privacy." This is not quite true of all societies (Shostak 1981). Yet it is common enough that it has "serious implications for research in the field of sex" (Mead, *ibid.*). Special and sensitive attention to ethnographic rapport and interviewing is required. The overall frame of this we think of as intimate communication on sexuality.

Culture, gender identity, and erotics are our primary concerns; the Sambia of New Guinea provide our database. For this book extends the work of Herdt, the summary of which, on gender and ritual development, can be found in *The Sambia: Ritual and Gender in New Guinea* (1987c); it also continues and amplifies our collaborative work on erotics and gender identity (Herdt and Stoller 1985; Stoller and Herdt 1982, 1985); and it provides another context for Stoller's (1985a) work on the meaning of erotic excitement. For the moment we shall define our terms such that "sex" refers to biologic components, "gender" refers to masculinity and femininity, and "erotics" refers to sexual excitement.

We shall also critically examine our notions of "experience," "subjectivity," and kindred terms that emphasize the individual pole of the personal/collective spectrum in the social sciences. Our mode will not be philosophic or structural, for such formal analyses are available in the treatises of many fields, including, for psychoanalysis, that of Stoller (1979), and for anthropology, that of Herdt (1981). We prefer rather to provide an expository and didactic approach, through which we present our material as it occurred in the field. There is no hard and fast boundary between subjectivity and objectivity, and, indeed, many have rejected this dichotomy. But where such has been rejected—for reality/fantasy, and objective/subjective—the distinction between what is collective/personal has been less reanalyzed, except, perhaps, in those sensitive Third World psychoanalytic works (Doi 1973; Kakar 1983) where an awareness of the problematics involved in establishing intrapsychic meanings of cultural symbols seems more acute. These dynamic and oscillating boundaries will be charted.

For a long time, too, but often virtually in spite of itself, anthropology has pioneered the understanding of subjective states and meaning systems in other cultures. Progress in the area has been made, by design and by accident, though there is no universal agreement among anthropologists on what constitutes progress in subjectivity research. Interpretative approaches have emerged in virtually every social science and the humanities; and "experimental" ethnography is a controversial but popular genre in anthropology (see chapter 1). Some advances can be found in gender studies in this way as well, but we find, again—almost in spite of the efforts of anthropologists— that fine-grained studies of the subjectivity and meanings of erotics have been largely bypassed.

We are thus concerned in this work with deepening anthropology's long interest in the subjective dimension of people's lives. Many ethnographers have tried to reveal the thoughts and feelings of their informants, and among these workers was Malinowski, who explored the issues through his brilliant Trobriand works. British social anthropology did not, by and large, continue the effort. The approach in American cultural anthropology was more psychologic. Boas, Mead, and Benedict were pioneers in relating culture to personality orientations. Others such as Sapir, Kardiner, Kluckhohn, DuBois, Devereux, Hallowell, Spiro, LeVine, and R. Levy (to name a few) extended and enriched the psychoanalytic approach to the subjective dimension of cultural lfie. But with the eclipse of culture and personality studies and psychoanalytic interpretations in particular, anthropology withdrew its interest in culture and subjectivity. And thus the situation remained until ethnoscience and then symbolic schools of anthropology emerged in the 1960s. Now, in the 1980s, renewed interest can be seen in the relevant issues.

Ethnographers have shown a greater interest in their own subjectivity as a part of the total fieldwork project. Discussion of such concepts as "culture shock" indirectly expressed this concern, as we show in chapter 1. The design of interview schedules and questionnaires has also directly dealt with the problem of observer bias and subjectivity. The early genre of autobiographic accounts in ethnography expressed the field worker's involvement in other people's lives as well. These reports stopped short, however, of directly showing the ethnographer's thoughts and feelings during data collection. Rarely, for instance, did the ethnographer reveal his or her questions in the same context as the informants' responses, and when this was done, as in the cases of DuBois or Lewis, only limited information was reported on the fieldworker's responses to the native's responses at the time.[1] Such accounts used the fieldworker's experience, but in a chatty, peripheral way that generally humanized more formal ethnographic works published elsewhere. For S. and me, however, the ethnographer's subjectivity is of direct and nontrivial interest.

We wish to emphasize what LeVine (1982) in his well-known formulation has referred to as person-centered ethnography. As LeVine (1982:292) has noted, there is a

> growing recognition that biographical information collected in the field is inevitably filtered through the relationship between field worker and biographical subject, reflecting the personalities of both and the nature of their interaction, and that this process deserves explicit examination in research and subsequently in print.

This refers to the detailed and more personal meanings of people in society compared to the early, more normative and "nonexperimental" ethnographic accounts. Such studies are akin to what Kohut (1971) called "experience-near," or close-up, rather than impersonal accounts. They provide flesh to the skeleton of culture, subjectivity rather than the "machine" of idealized cultural actors. Our perspective is that ethnographers play a large part in constructing their accounts of a people—before and after the field: but most importantly while there and living with the Other.

Contemporary work in interpretive anthropology reveals a similar but different concern with field worker subjectivity. The goals, limits, and ramifications of this interpretive approach, perhaps best known from the works of Geertz[2] and his students, are presently the focus of hot debate in anthropology. How subjective and revealing can a fieldworker be and still remain rigorous, the authors of *Writing Culture* (Clifford and Marcus, eds., 1986), a major statement of this genre, seem to ask. Their answers are instructive. Take note, for instance, that Clifford (1986:6), who introduces the volume, lists six "determinants" of ethnographic writing, but no personal or psychologic factors are among them. The politicalization of the field is impressive, as is its debunking of the authority of ethnographic texts. How shall we evaluate these new "experimental ethnographies?"[3]

Our work shows the difficulty of drawing a hard-and-fast boundary between what is objective and what is subjective, a contrast that is becoming obsolete.[4] Depth interviews reveal better than other procedures the nuances and difficulties of showing how psychodynamic processes, such as projection, fantasy, and transference, occur across cultural boundaries. Where does projection begin and end? How can we tell someone's personal fantasy from a cultural belief? Are there no absolute boundaries between reality and fantasy? We shall try to examine such questions. And, following the leads of Devereux (1967) and LeVine (1982), we shall use a case method approach that reveals our questions, responses, and associations, so that we show how a question evokes an association in someone, which in turn leads to another question. This is not easy or apparent as a procedure in textual presentation.

We are motivated by a desire to escape pseudoscience, which still dominates many quarters of psychoanalysis and the social sciences, on the one hand, and our attempt to make the study of subjectivity more rigorous, on the other. For some, such as Tedlock (1983:322), ethnography is a "peculiar genre of fiction," the texts of which are a sort of comparative literature. Others go further and seem to suggest that ethnographic accounts should be humbled to the level (high or low?) of poetry. For us, this position goes too far. We want to find a middle ground.

S: Measuring the observer's effect on the observed and realizing that the observed affects the observer as well have, in this century, changed the nature of all research—from fundamental particle physics to my discipline, psychoanalysis. More than any other investigators of human behavior, psychoanalysts have been concerned with the distortions introduced by these subjective factors. In recent years, no clinical task has interested us more than trying to discover how aspects of the analyst's personality influence the therapeutic relationship: those that we are aware of and that can be used effectively, and those, coming from unrecognized forces within us, that produce uncontrolled effects (countertransference). H. and I believe also that these issues of self are just as important in writing reports of one's findings.

For studying human behavior, the primary instrument is not laboratory equipment, or random samples, or animals, or computers, but the researcher—ethnographer, psychologist, psychoanalyst, sociologist, or whatever. We should, therefore, know at least as much about the researcher as about the people investigated. (H: Only recently have psychologic and symbolic anthropologists emphasized this gap.) But rarely are we given that information, and readers do not much care, either. Mainstream concern lies elsewhere.

We think of Malinowski's diaries,[5] so scandalous to some anthropologists. It cannot be that his critics or defenders were surprised that, during his stay in the Trobriand Islands he was—without interruption—himself, that is, a feeling person with private experiences. In his diaries, he revealed, as he did not in his ethnographic works, that, by his own standards, he was racist, lazy, mean, tumescent with sinful desire, and under the influence of the rest of the ordinary day-to-day self-hatred that keeps ethnographers alert. Before the diaries became public, did anthropologists believe that such experiences were exceptional, that father-figures are the paragons their students fantasize, or that ethnographers leave their personalities home on setting out to the field? Do some imagine a way to study human behavior that does not filter the data through a sentient person at the time of collecting and at the time of reporting, that data are more objective—scientific—if we erase from the record the traces of the collecting process? It cannot even be that these critics did not know that the same is true of other ethnographers, at least themselves and everyone they know personally. Then surely it cannot be that these critics are unaware that this private life influences one's fieldwork at every turn and is even more pervasive when subjective life is denied or when it serves as a mat for the daily wrestle with the Devil. The critics' dismay at Malinowski's revelations marks an intuitive recognition of the same issue this book will examine more overtly and systematically: how subjectivity edits observation. We can regret that at times we participant-observers are too involved to see out through our own fog, but it is surely worse when that process goes unnoticed.

Perhaps it is too easy for those of us with medical training (forget, at this moment in the narrative, our speculative excesses) to appreciate the value of the hidden. For we benefit from innumerable advances in which the invisible was revealed. We expect that; it is our tradition. We demand that it always be part of our work. For instance, we know the uses of the blood sample, the biopsy, and the microscope in indicating the likely presence of unseen but vital physiology; or the power that comes with the capacity to project, in the mind's eye, the pathologic anatomy and hemodynamics of the heart from no more than the noise, interpreted as a "rub," we hear in our stethoscope; or the visualizing of a brain lesion revealed at first only in disordered speech; or the insight a reported fantasy can give into a person's hidden motives. That detective, the medical diagnostician, is forever on the edge of being wrong, for the manifest is so incomplete, so subtle, so complexly interwoven into itself. Still, if we considered only what we can see, hear, smell, and feel on the skin, we would not even be competent dermatologists.*

When it comes to the study of subjectivity—"who[†] am I," "who are we," "who are they"—the "social sciences" falter. They can mask that failure, it has often been noted, by trivializing until they find a statistically manageable task, or by analogizing on animals' behavior and brains, or by using culture-bound and oversimplified learning theory explanations, or by ignoring how fantasy moves behavior, or by denying that subjectivity even exists. (Statistics, animal research, and learning theory contribute powerfully and are invaluable for studying human behavior. I complain only of these misuses.)

We need not review here the advantages and limitations of experiments, those hallmarks of careful thinking. Right now, we shall note only that an experiment informs us more if the experimenter and his techniques do not contaminate the experiment. The laboratory ideal, however, is not only impossible in much behavioral research but, in the case of intimate communications, *cannot* produce the needed data. Only communication can do that, and communication requires a minimum of two interacting objects. Still, "social scientists"[‡] yearn to be scientists; science is the ideal.[6] (H: Should science aspire ultimately to explanation and, even more powerful, prediction? Or is it good enough, as Runciman (1983) has recently suggested, for the scientist to provide the highest quality *description* or, to paraphrase Taylor (1985), a better-than-average *understanding* in its own context?) Some things can be discovered—perhaps, like the Nile, can *only* be discov-

---

*A caution here as we praise the physician. Let us recall Freud's (1926) fear that medical training can threaten the kind of curiosity/empathy needed for exploring human behavior.

†Who, not "what"; "what" is a question better asked of a physiologist or computer and communications theorist.

‡This is the last time I shall use "social sciences" or "social scientists" herein. The continued use of quotation marks would make for a bumpy ride, but I would not be able to talk of the social sciences without using such punctuation because, for me, there is too little science in these sciences. So, for accuracy, I shall avoid "social sciences" and instead work with such circumlocutions as: "those studying behavior."

ered—without antecedent sampling methods, controls, statistics, or an *n* of more than one.

H: Anthropology, Sapir argued fifty years ago,[7] needs the psychiatrists' skills and insights into the range of states of subjectivity. In a way, my colleague, S., still argues for this basic position.

S: This attitude will seem especially strange to those who teach that my clinical disciplines of psychiatry and psychoanalysis never have said and never will say something useful, much less true, about human behavior.[8] H., however, since beginning his training, had felt at odds with that view. No wonder we hit it off.

Herdt's kind of clinical perspective approach can transform the practice of ethnography (as it also did for Malinowski and Mead and as it is doing now for Obeyesekere, Kakar, and others). When this is offered in the universities it will bring back to anthropology the students who thought that the discipline was less interested in humans than in Structure, Syntax, and Symbolism.*

But, to equalize my complaint, consider the comparable trend, in psychoanalytic theory, that only perfunctorily acknowledges cultural factors, and that has, in over seventy years, produced only two or three psychoanalyst-ethnographers and few ethnographic works by other analysts than them.

The nondeluded psychoanalyst knows that subjectivity is still beyond the reach of scientific method, that confirming and disconfirming tests cannot be applied. Psychoanalysts' findings are notoriously open to question but closed to inspection; one can never tell, even roughly, in reading analytic reports, what happened between patient and analyst. We analysts cover the lack of such crucial data with a storm of phrases such as "further analysis unmistakably revealed . . . ," "the patient's associations proved that . . . ," "from the analysis, it appeared that this represented a . . . ," "the literature confirms the finding that . . . ," "surely," "truly," "indeed," "certainly," "without doubt," "unquestionably," "the fact was," "positively," "inevitably," "decidedly," "absolutely," "unequivocally," "fundamentally," "assuredly," "definitely," "unmistakably." Of course.

And yet, as awful as this performance is, I think that the use of subjectivity is worth the risk. And the corrective is not to retreat to

---

*The road to charisma is paved with abstractions, mysteries, italics, exclamation points, and capital letters.

the easily sketched normative surface, or to the poetic stance that all culture is merely subjective. With "subjective" ethnography, one is in danger of being duped by the invisible; but with "objective" ethnography, one is at the mercy of the visible.

These issues were forcefully presented in detailed, intense, and scholarly fashion more than twenty years ago by Devereux.[9] It is hard to judge to what extent his ideas were ignored because the audience was upset or distracted and to what extent because the ideas were simply too new and took digesting. Whatever the reasons, Devereux's insight that research can transform anxiety into research method has caused no change in either ethnography or psychoanalysis, the two disciplines he practiced. As an analyst, I find it especially surprising that he did not move psychoanalysis, given analysts' concern with how the analyst's behavior changes what happens in the treatment. So it is disappointing that when analysts publish their ideas, they almost completely omit describing who they were when the treatment events published were taking place and who they are when reporting their conclusions. I am sure that analytic theory will improve and analytic research advance from its present rudimentary state when analysts acknowledge these factors.

This text is thus (1) a communication on experiments in ethnography, (2) in itself an experiment, (3) an exploration of a new way of teaching ethnography, (4) and a preliminary presentation of an alternative approach to ethnography. Let me begin with the book as a communication. It reports experiments* in which we tried out new techniques. First, from 1975 on—initially in letters, and from 1977 on in person—a psychoanalyst supervised an ethnographer to enrich the ethnography. Second, at the same time, an ethnographer taught an analyst ethnography to enrich the analyst (but not his analytic technique). Third, the two specialists worked together in the field, extending the ethnographer's interviews but also introducing a clinician (medical practitioner: diagnostician and therapist) into the final data collecting. Fourth, as the interviews unfolded, there were at the same time (both during and between interviews) continuous discussions of the clinical findings, techniques, underlying dynamics of the participants, and the processes going on among them. We also discussed their implications for theory in ethnography and analysis, and did a bit of theory-making and breaking (braking), and problem solving (therapeutics; psychodynamics; personal histories, e.g., data on gender and erotic elements; how to interview skillfully, etc.).

---

*Only in the sense of trying something out, not the experiments of scientific method.

Now, the interview chapters as experiment. We are trying to create a better method of reporting clinical data—data gathered from individuals talking intimately about matters important to them, particularly regarding erotics and gender identity. (1) At the risk of boring and then losing our readers, we have presented our transcripts in fairly unadorned manner (though—after an example in chapter 4 of how it reads before cleaning up—in more bearable form), and have preserved our original tapes should a colleague want to check the printed version with that from New Guinea. (2) We have discussed and exemplified ways in which, at every step in the reporting process, we changed the raw material. (3) We have kept ourselves present, as close to the way we really were as print permits. (4) We have added commentary to the transcripts to reveal what we think was occurring that cannot be recorded on an audiotape. (5) We both together wrote the book and have indicated the parts each of us wrote. Beyond that, we have told but not shown you—that would be too lengthy and dull—that we each edited and added to the other's writing, sometimes heavily, sometimes painfully, and always openly and without much defensive compassion. We tried to do that without homogenizing our styles too much. (You should know, however, that H. was more decent in doing this than I, accepting my nit-picking and complaints more congenially than I sometimes did his.) (6) We have put in asides to each other's commentaries so the reader can share in our disagreements. (7) We have tried to create in the book the ambience of uncertainty that is the reality of field work, thinking, and theory, for we feel most everyone ignores this uncertainty.

The next category of the book's functions is teaching. We have let you see how H. taught me ethnography and I taught H. about clinical skills and psychodynamics. We later discuss how these subjects can be taught in more formal settings.

And then the last category. We have begun to create a new approach to ethnography, which we have referred to as clinical ethnography (Herdt 1981; Herdt and Stoller 1985; Stoller and Herdt 1982). Our conversations on this subject are distilled into rudimentary suggestions as to how students could be trained in these skills and what the benefits would be for ethnographers and others who study human behavior.

H: In sum, this study results from our desire to infuse erotics and gender identity more fully into cross-cultural research and to explore and advance the study of subjective experience more fully by doing so. We are trying, in the latter sense, to deconstruct sexual meanings in cultural studies. We hope to show that certain ethnographic questions can be investigated only by searching deeply into the individual, and the more individuals, the better. Our data are interviews and observations and a close look at the personal meanings of Sambia sexuality that go beyond the structural factors of their great institutions, kinship and marriage, ritual and myth. In another sense, one might say that we have chosen to focus on erotics and gender as a way of providing a common language for critically examining the means—ethnography—whereby fieldworkers study and write about culture. Our purpose is not so much to answer all the questions we raise about the study of intimate communications as to urge colleagues to agree with us that these are fundamental questions that must be answered.

PART I

Introductions

CHAPTER ONE

Clinical Ethnography

> [Ralph] Linton once quoted to me the following remark of a colleague:
>
> > "My monograph about the X-tribe is almost finished. All I have to do now is cut out the life" (i.e., all references to real people and events).
>
> Devereux, *From Anxiety to Method*

H: What makes some anthropologists cut the life from their ethnographies? How is that stance embedded in our discipline's basic concepts and techniques? Is it not a contradiction to study Man but not *a* man? This chapter is concerned with the debate between those positions, and in it we extend our arguments for the need to develop an approach in anthropology—clinical enthography—that focuses on the reasons for and the methods of studying individuals intimately in order to better know cultures.

For almost a century anthropologists have studied the natives of exotic corners while other social scientists busily worked on pressing problems at home. Ethnography, as we know it today, emerged not by design but rather from the historical circumstances of World War I that led Malinowski to the Trobriand Islands, off the coast of New Guinea. From those years of living "as a native among the natives," as Sir James Frazer put in his preface to *Argonauts of the Western Pacific*, Malinowski defined the "subject, method, and scope of the inquiry" that was to become the classical mode of ethnography and anthropologic training. Shortly thereafter Mead went to Samoa. Other anthropologists followed. In the ensuing years Africa, Melanesia, Borneo, and the Amazon were to be sampled, bottled, and marketed at home under domestic labels. The subject was the natives' behavior; the product was the field report—the classical ethnography—about exotic places. Western civilization quickly transformed that subject matter and technique into a stable mythology about anthropology.

Since Malinowski, anthropology's supreme method has been participant–observation, a technique that structures the encounter between natives and ethnographer in a certain way. Is it an accident that Malinowski, the great ethnographer, was a poor theorist? No;

few are blessed with being great clinicians and great theorists. In no other field except, perhaps, psychoanalysis,* is theory and practice so intimately embedded in human relationships. And in no other discipline does research defy the application of objective measurements. In both fields as well, practitioners defend their methodology on the basis of special training, special talents, and special data—that "intensely personal form of knowledge"[1] characteristic of intimate communications.

The question of the relationship of subjectivity to the study of human behavior need not be restricted to anthropology. The pendulum that has swung away from psychoanalysis—the microscopic study of subjectivity—was carrying psychology, sociology, and psychiatry as well. And so these days, from a mixture of motives, many scholars in these disciplines still spurn subjectivity either as an explicit dimension of their methodology or as a subject for study. The scene is changing in anthropology, however. Interpretive approaches offer a new vision of how to handle subjectivity in ethnography. Yet, in the mainstream of anthropology, many still assume that the field worker is objective, as scientific as an experimenter in the lab. Recent statements on interpretive anthropology seem motivated by this view.[2] Other critics deride the study of individual natives in terms of their own subjective frameworks and have turned to other disciplines in trying to define the ethnographic approach.

Since its beginnings, anthropology has struggled with the question of the observer's role—of observer bias—in deciding what natives' behavior really meant. Whose interpretation (in what combination and situations) is right: the ethnographer or the native? The debate has taxed our best minds. The present consensus is: the ethnographer as observer. But even ethnographers' views are accepted only when we dress up our presence in ethnographic reports. One should, more properly, study the visible, the public, the normative; *kula* trading rings, totems,. garden boundaries, marriage contracts, exogamy, kin terms and kin groups, love potions, shamanism, initiation rites, economic roles, and on and on. And yes, life histories were collected and published. But did these not leave out the author? And yes, extensive interviews were done: but among this earlier generation who besides DuBois, Devereux, and a few other clinically oriented ethnographers published their questions and findings in detail? These exceptions, older and new, are admirable. The mainstream seemed, however, to lie elsewhere: in the direction of public knowledge. Objective facts.

---

*And related fields like clinical psychology.

Public meaning—shared, formal, patterned, standardized, homogenized, itself like "culture, this acted document," for Geertz (1973:10)—
is the proper stuff of the ethnographic report. Thus bent outward and
emptied of their privacy, the data of field research become objective,
valid. Scientific.

Participant-observation has emerged as *the* umbrella approach for
anthropologic fieldwork. There are new critiques of postcolonialist
anthropology and its servant, ethnography, which are reviewed in this
text. We recognize these criticisms and welcome the accounts of fieldwork that have addressed them. These critiques have questioned the
underlying model of scientific positivism that formed our attitudes,
assumptions, and procedures in doing and writing ethnography. Our
work contributes to this debate; we do not propose to eliminate participant-observation, only to question its antipsychologic framework.

Participant-observation is today best seen as an intellectual/sci-
entific ideology. It is the shingle we hang out, the advertisement we
make for anthropology's scientific status in the Academy and the
granting agencies. As an ideology—shared commitments to a guiding
image of research that is socialized through training—participant-
observation helps integrate a growing, disparate discipline; it bridges
a gap between the past and present ("intellectual history"); and it
creates continuity between our founding and present-day activities
(Ricoeur 1978). Every discipline has, of course, an image projected
for public consumption (viz., textbooks, granting agencies, University
Councils) and internal discussion (i.e., seminars, tutorials, and "private conversations" [Powdermaker 1966:9]). This is necessary. Freilich
(1977:19ff.) has written well about the process. He proposes further
that there are actually three cultures at work in the ethnographic process: the anthropologist's own "culture of orientation," "the native
culture," and "the fieldwork culture." This last mediating concept—
the heritage of modern anthropology—is Freilich's innovation, which
he sees as tacit rules and assumptions about doing ethnography. He
uses examples of how that cultural system permeates both professional circles (e.g., textbooks) and field research, though he concen-
trates on the former. Here we shall focus on the latter. We agree with
Freilich, though, that participant-observation is a rationalizing ideology that shields how we construct ethnography and live in the field.
A full analysis of this problem would require a review and interpretation of the signs, symbols, cultural categories, and discourses of
fieldwork culture—an enormous undertaking that would require a
book. In lieu of that, we offer only some first principles.

PARTICIPANT-OBSERVATION

From Malinowski on, participant-observation has been vague. The field worker's dilemmas are these. (1) *Be an objective observer* of a culture; but participate enough as a whole person that you understand all (including a people's aesthetic biases) and *become a friend.* (2) *Live with the natives* and press them enough so that their culture becomes a part of you who are alien; but in living there, *don't change them,* only observe the culture (as represented in native acts). (3) Become a *scientific authority on the culture*: in your writings don't show much of your self or your living in the field, *for that is personal, not scientific.* These dilemmas arose from the nature of anthropologic work and from our need (like psychoanalysts) to claim we are scientists. One of our basic points is that anthropologists *live* these dilemmas— in our heads, in the field, at home. The ad hoc method of field work culture developed later to help us live *with* the contradictions.

The untouched observer in this ideology is a scientist, but that kind of observer, by not participating, must observe less, possibly too much less. At the same time, the "social sciences," inventing from necessity, have wanted to be accepted as sciences less encumbered by scientific method: note such antipositivistic movements as humanism in psychology, ethnomethodology in sociology, or semiotics and hermeneutics in linguistics. Yet fieldwork *is* highly personal; without a particular fieldworker, one has no field data (Read 1965). The mythology of fieldwork culture provides recipes for "objectively" assembling and reporting fieldwork data: the ethnography. How much of the ethnographer as a whole person is admitted into one's published report?

Cultural anthropology is grounded in fieldwork: it is what distinguishes our discipline. Its methodology, participant-observation, lends itself well to anthropology's ambiguous status as one of the sciences* and also one of the humanities. It places anthropologists in the delicate position of being both a people's stranger and friend: detached, objective data-collector plus involved, trusted insider. That is how it was first heralded; only special people could manage its balancing act. However, those who pioneered field work—Malinowski and Mead, for instance—stressed, through the analogy of the laboratory experiment, the positivist science of participant-observation. Later workers

---

*In the United States, the National Institute of Mental Health classifies cultural anthropology as a "social science" and "health science," while the National Science Foundation classifies it as a "natural science." The National Endowment for the Humanities accepts anthropology also as one of its own.

such as social structuralists, culture and personality theorists, quantitative analysts and ethnosemanticists on the scientific side, and humanists, ethnohistorians, symbolists, and hermeneuts on the other, have tended to split apart this Janus. But none has rejected the ambiguity—participate but observe—of fieldwork. The fact that such divergent theoretic schools have been shielded under the same umbrella, which has also resisted change in its tried and true design, is important in understanding the mystique of fieldwork.[3]

One can see, however, important swings in the pendulum of ethnographic styles or genres. In the 1920s such fine, humanistic uses of the life history as in, say, La Farge's *Laughing Boy*, were published in the same period as material culture surveys, and institutionally focused normative ethnographies, such as Firth's *We the Tikopia*. After the 1930s, though, and such splendid rich studies as DuBois' *People of Alor*—which was published in 1944 and in itself marks a watershed of period clinical ethnography—a new trend can be noticed. Seldom do ethnographies of the 1940s and 1950s reveal much of the author. Only very limited exceptions, such as Mead's *Male and Female*, can be found, and these, by culture and personality hands, deal only very indirectly with the ethnographer's subjectivity. Institutionally focused ethnographies in the standard mode of normative social anthropology held reign until the late 1960s. Usually the authors of those texts mention individuals only in passing or in anecdotes. Usually they confine their personal experiences to a preface or the acknowledgments, or again to anecdotes. Later exceptions to this generalization are telling. A major text, Bowen's *Return To Laughter*, was published under a pseudonym, and as a novel. Read's *The High Valley* created controversy by being, in the minds of some critics, "too personal." The more recent and inflamed case of Castaneda's works has broken with past conventions, to be seen by some as a paradigm shift and by others as fairy dust. Since the 1970s symbolic and interpretive studies have brought a host of more subjective and humanistic ethnographies. These are more revealing of the author and his or her fieldwork conditions. These "experimental" accounts challenge traditional ethnography and raise new questions about the nature of knowing and the ways of interpreting ethnographic material. Yet these works remain controversial; and, as yet, they are still exceptional, not normative.

The original image of fieldwork was deceptively clear: "Living in the village with no other business but to follow native life" (Malinowski 1922:18). Within a few years, Mead (1977:4) notes, "Learning how to live in the field . . . became known as participant observation." The field was moved from the museum, armchair, or riverboat into the village.[4] The objective status of this knowledge—the ethnography—was controversial. But its aim was not, as set out in Malinowski's prospectus: "This goal is, briefly, to grasp the native's point of view, his relation to life, to realize his vision of his world" (Malinowski 1922:25;cf. Geertz 1976).

From the start this achievement was clearly difficult, requiring personal adjustment: be involved yet stay detached. Here is a textbook indication:

> A participant-observer, the anthropologist lives intimately as a member of a society. . . . He shares in the people's day-to-day activities, watches as they eat, fight, and dance, listens to their commonplace and exciting conversations, and slowly begins to live and understand life as they do. But he also remains detached from their life, at least to some degree. He is not living among another people to enjoy their way of life. He is there to understand it and then to report his understanding to others. Complete involvement, then, is incompatible with the anthropologist's primary goals, but complete detachment is incompatible with fieldwork. Successful fieldwork requires balance between the two, a balancing act which is every bit as difficult as it sounds. (Edgerton and Langness 1974:2–3)

As in any discipline, anthropologic fieldwork produces knowledge. Malinowski (1922:24) spelled out "three avenues" of this knowledge as goals for ethnography: (1) "the organization of the tribe, and the anatomy of its culture," using statistical facts; (2) "the imponderabilia of actual life," using "minute, detailed observations," a "sort of ethnographic diary;" and (3) "a collection of . . . narratives," folklore, etc., the *corpus inscriptionum* or "documents of native mentality." Eventually Malinowski attempted all these; taken together for a single society, they remain unmatched. He had no doubt that his work was scientific or that he made ethnography a Science.[5] Like Boas, Benedict, Mead, Radcliffe-Brown, and others, this ideology of science was meant to refute Social Darwinism, evolutionary speculation, shaky historical diffusionism, and bigotry in general.[6] And thus, these early workers shifted anthropology's laboratory from the museum to the village.[7]

How was the field of the village defined for doing ethnography? First, the dictum that one studied the whole tribe (its skeleton or anatomy) meant that native beliefs, behavior patterns, and social institutions were seen as parts of an abstract, functioning whole—"culture" or "society." These were to be laboratories,[8] the settings for field experiments.[9] Here lay the roots for functionalism (Malinowski, Benedict, Mead), structural-functionalism (Radcliffe-Brown, Evans-Pritchard), or modern structuralism (Lévi-Strauss). Second, this holism implied that ideally one studied in the round all of social life. "The ethnography," up until the last few years, should thus include pat chapters such as "Economy," "Religion," "Kinship," "Politics," etc. that claimed to represent the whole "culture" or "society." (We now find that effort too optimistic.) Third, present also in both Malinowski and Mead (1930, 1935) was "the individual," the study of which was contradictory. On the one hand it was easy to observe words and behavioral patterns; but on the other, it was almost impossible to study what natives thought, for they could not put their subjective states into words.[10] Therefore:

> . . . we have to study here stereotyped manners of thinking and feeling. As sociologists,* we are not interested in what A or B may feel *qua* individuals, in the accidental course of their own personal experiences—we are interested only in what they feel and think *qua* members of a given community . . . their mental states receive a certain stamp, become stereotyped by the institutions in which they live, by the influence of traditional folk-lore, by the very vehicle of thought, that is language. The social and cultural environment in which they move forces them to think and feel in a definite manner. (Malinowski 1922:23)

One abstracts "stereotypes" from observations rather than dealing with personal experience as such. And the empirical source of these social facts was clear.

> I consider that only such ethnographic sources are of unquestionable scientific value, in which we can clearly draw the line between, on the one hand, the results of direct observation and of native statements and interpretations, and on the other, the inferences of the author, based on his common sense and psychological insight. (Malinowski 1922:3)

Thus spoke Malinowski on methodology: aside from mentioning "psychological insight," his stance epitomized the mainstream in the positivist sciences of his time.

In retrospect these founding conceptions of the field were never fulfilled. (1) Few anthropologists claim to study everything anymore;

---

*Malinowski (like Mead) was slippery, sometimes claiming to be a sociologist, sometimes a psychologist.

field projects are problem-focused (as most granting agencies expect). (2) Functionalism has its limits;[11] that something functions or integrates does not make it adaptive (Alland 1970). (3) Malinowski, Radcliffe-Brown,[12] and others stressed function over meaning, despite Malinowski's pronouncements about "the native's vision of his world." (Only now is an anthropology of "meaning systems" emerging.) (4) The "functional field" of the village was defined as excluding external agents—colonial powers, missionaries, traders—even when they impinged on or devoured the natives.[13] (5) Whole segments or classes of persons and their meanings within a society, for instance, women, were virtually ignored (Ardener 1975). (6) Even granting Malinowski's dictum that we study collective categories of thinking and feeling, not personal experience, many subjects of interest have been largely ignored on those terms (e.g., the cultural context of gifts, myth, erotics or of "big men."[14] (7) Last—and of most significance—Malinowski never adhered to his own methodologic requirements. None of us has: not Malinowski or Mead, their contemporaries or students.

Had they done so more, ethnography today might be very different, nor would we be searching philosophy, semiotics, literary criticism, psychoanalysis, hermeneutics, history, etc., etc. so much for the guidelines on how to do our job: interpret our experience in other cultures, a task that we alone can tackle.

Participant-observation as a laboratory model failed, because the field is not a lab, we do not perform experiments, and tribesmen are interacted with as whole people, not experimental subjects.[15] Fieldwork was designed to make anthropology a science by ending speculation about *how* natives behave in the context of their own sociocultural institutions. (Only recently has the *why*—questions of origins—come back into cultural anthropology, but not without the criticism that this is unscientific and, the new primal sin, teleologic.) The laboratory model, even in Malinowski's works, removed the ethnographer from the native scene. Nor was it ever clear how the ethnographer was to use insight or empathy. This editing out not only removed the natives as whole people, substituting customs, institutions, and symbols in their place, but it attributed meanings and intentionality to the latter, as if such things were the people who gave them life. There are fine exceptions.[16] but they *are* exceptions.

RECENT INTERPRETIVE ANTHROPOLOGY

A flurry of critiques of cultural anthropology and its handmaiden, the ethnography that results from traditional field work in exotic cultures, has appeared in recent years. Malinowski's inheritors have been beset by various "ists": Marxists, materialists, symbolists, feminists, historicists, among others. We recognize their complaints and sympathize with some. For they have made us more aware of our colonial heritage, our disregard of the incursion of world systems into traditional societies, our not taking seriously symbolic systems or their connection to or mystification of social action, our androcentric viewpoint and sexist disregard of women, and our antihistorical (too "harmonious" and "adaptive") functionalism. Many other points could be added. Yet, until recently this intellectual debate largely stopped short of rejecting the old positivism of our umbrella approach, participant-observation, that imposes these dilemmas: be involved, but stay detached; study the Other, not yourself.[17] The same holds true for the fine anthologies on fieldwork of the past twenty years, which show anthropology's interest in reflecting on what ethnographers actually do in the field.[18] Though we applaud these efforts, they can be pushed further. For all have skimmed the surface of a basic psychodynamic problem—Devereux's (1967)—on how and why ethnographers interact with the natives.* For the reader to understand our approach to culture and experience and our handling of these issues, we shall sketch some principles.

Each culture has a somewhat unique symbolic system—signs, symbols, rules, values—that directs behavioral acts and makes for meaningful communications among its sharers. These constraints are reflected in or acted on, according to factors such as personality, sex, age, situation, and social controls. The question of how cultural ideals match actual behaviors is, relative to the person, the situation, etc., an open empirical matter.[19] The ethnographer's task is to discover those matches. In studying a native's experience, one can watch and also ask. But for many psychologic anthropologists and ourselves, depth interviewing is crucial if one expects to understand, from the native's point-of-view, how cultural ideas are perceived in his or her awareness, and how they relate to idiosyncratic ideas and feelings, or to reality. LeVine has argued such problems well.[20]

Each culture provides also a set of distinctive narratives—ways of talking—that guide who should say what to whom under what circumstances. A New Guinea big man's thumping public rhetoric differs from his private talk in a hut. Women's secret ritual talk seldom reaches the public, though its effects are felt there. A man's private

---

*In this book we follow anthropologic convention in referring to the indigines of any society (our own included) as the natives. The colonialist baggage of this term notwithstanding, 'native' helps keep us aware of who we are and are not.

feelings about his dreams and their implications may never ever be shared in public.[21] Recognizing the distinctions between these narratives (and all the knowledge to which they implicitly refer) underlies the ethnographer's interpretation of what people say. Yet, in the spontaneity of someone's communicating, these narrative distinctions may be blurred. People are different; they are idiosyncratic. So understanding those ideal types does not explain the meaning of an individual native's acts, words, or thoughts. It is thus not their culture, economy, or psychology that explains their behavior, but rather their experience—which subsumes all the above.[22]

To interpret these complex phenomena the ethnographer has only a hazy approach, participant-observation, which is vague enough to accommodate the behaviorists, ethnoscientists, marxists, feminists, symbolic and psychoanalytic-type theorists in the field. That stance seemed to work[23] in the past when those such as Benedict (1934) and Mead (1935) studied "whole cultures," or similar abstractions like "personality," "ethos," or "eidos." Ethnoscience made it work, as Geertz (1973:10–13) has argued, by ignoring the shared understandings that made the natives' mental schemas seem real. It still seemed to work for structuralists, political economists, cross-cultural psychologists, and others who, in repudiating each others' theories, seemingly accepted others' field data as scientific. But then the symbolists began to say they wanted another kind of science.

The interpretive anthropologists would have it work differently. By studying how cultural signs and symbols are constructed, and by describing how they operate in thought or are expressed in action, they hope to understand how humans construct meaning and so define their existence. Does the neologism—interpretive science—apply to what they do? In Geertz's style of this approach, culture becomes like a text in the hands of a literary critic. No need to worry over subjectivity ("mentalism," "subjectivism," "psychologism," "reductionism"), because what you see—public social action—is seemingly all there is (Geertz 1973:10). This philosophic behaviorism— "Culture is public because meaning is" (Geertz 1973:12)—has taken previous guises in anthropology to produce similar ends: configurationalism, national character studies, the life history approach, culture at a distance—that led to presumed group uniformity (the doctrine of experimental uniformity[24]). The reduction of human awareness to narrative texts—this new hermeneutics—is another maneuver by the sociocentric "social sciences" to create the illusion of objectivity without involvement (Crapanzano 1986).

Our approach differs somewhat in our interest in what flesh and blood natives do and think. We are not here mainly concerned with the cultural forms with which they think, though we shall discuss the relation between culture and experience as we go. We differ even more in attending to what the ethnographer does. The process and communications that produce ethnography are part of it, the more so when they are hidden in the final public document. To weave a culture in an ethnography by editing out the seams and stitches of its designer is to sacrifice craftmanship for mass product. When one is interested in people's meanings—not Meaning—ethnographic findings become privileged.[25] So, lacking description of what LeVine (1982:293 and also LeVine 1966) calls the "intercultural research relationship," ethnography provides the wall hangings for a mass Museum of Projective Texts. How lifeless.[26]

A variety of ethnographers is struggling to revise the fieldwork approach to give full recognition to the native's experience and the ethnographer's part in interpreting it. Ethnography is both process and product: while we are beginning to see the researchers' presence in reports, we still see little of them in the process leading to their published work. Recent works by Crapanzano, Kracke, Obeyesekere, and other pioneering clinical ethnographers provide critical and effective beacons to follow in the "experimental ethnography" genre (Marcus and Cushman 1982). Their works answer, in a sense, Sapir's[27] plea for injecting the clinical process into ethnography.[28] Here, we shall not examine further the implications for theory of our arguments. Yet we do think that the critical use of clinical ethnography will move us further in "the business of making anthropology out of fieldwork" (Bateson 1978:77).

To sum up: participant-observation commends us to study the typical, stereotypic, normal natives, and thus fieldwork is made to seem objective in the text, as if observer bias does not occur. The ideal ethnographer participates objectively, wary of real relationships with the people studied, as if the ethnographer's private experience were not what makes our field data possible. In this "public experiment"— a social contract with an implicit ideology, participant-observation— the signs of the ethnographer's and the native's subjectivity are removed. What actually happens in fieldwork is different.

THE ETHNOGRAPHY

The product of these endeavors is ethnography: fieldwork reports. The range of ethnography is enormous, in time and space, in subject matter, and in time spent in a place. In the Melanesian literature, ethnographic reports can be as brief as letters and anecdotal tidbits (Whittaker et al. 1975), as intensive as Malinowski's studies, or extensive as the many volumes of the *Cambridge Expeditions to the Torres Straits*.[29] They can come from short contacts over a few weeks' time, as with Haddon's (1901), Rivers's (1914), and Seligman's (1910) tradeboat surveys, or they may come from years in one place, as with Malinowski's (1922, 1929, 1935) Trobriand works. We have the uneven reports of missionaries, travelers, gold miners, and popularizers—with titles such as *Twenty Years in Savage New Guinea, My Father was a Cannibal, The Land that Time Forgot*, and *Adam in Oche*, some good, some bad. There are the great Papuan monographs of Williams (1936, 1940) with his biases intact, the product of a lifetime of anthropologic treks. Then there are respectable but often uninteresting monographs of the 1940s, 1950s, and 1960s on social structure, ceremonial exchange, big men, and ritual, most based on a year or two of intensive fieldwork, though a few are based on a weekend (Elkin 1953) or a few months (Blackwood 1979; Barth 1975; Fortune 1947). An overwhelming magnitude.[30]

Ethnographies are more than casual accounts of people's customs and cultures. We trust them. They are to contain little beyond objective truth.[31] Ethnographies are widely read and cited as scientific evidence in other disciplines and in anthropology, The Human Relations Area Files (established by that great quantifier, Murdock) accord ethnographies a normative, homogenized database allowing statistical correlations to be drawn from reports the world over. What do professionals think of the truth-value of ethnographies? The answer is instructive, and Evans-Pritchard once cautioned a critical attitude toward ethnographic reports.[32]

The fiction is that while anthropologists study whole societies, their reports—though only on a particular place—really concern the monolithic abstractions "society," "culture," and "personality," not the ethnographer or the natives as people. The themes and images of this fiction vary: tribal society is seen as good paradise[33] or bad paradise,[34] or degenerated paradise;[35] or it seethes with oedipal conflict,[36] or violence,[37] or paranoia,[38] or shame;[39] or it lacks oedipal conflict,[40] aggression,[41] individualism,[42] anger;[43] or it is harmonious,[44] in equilibrium,[45] gentle,[46] powerless;[47] or male dominated,[48] or female dominated,[49] or undersexed,[50] or oversexed.[51] And these findings are conveyed through different metaphors: society as a laboratory[52] or a clinic[53] or a stage[54] or a structure of Mind[55] or a structure of social roles[56] or a structure of livelihood[57] or a text for the literary critic.[58]

You name it. The "it"—society or culture—becomes the foreground; the author, whether male or female, young or old, novice or veteran, black or white, liberal or conservative, sexist or not, sinks into neutral ground.

In fact, of course, anthropologists do pass judgment on their colleagues and profession. And, for that matter, their own society.[59] We are able critics.[60] Certainly we are not a complacent group; one only need read reviews in the *American Anthropologist* or attend cocktail parties at meetings of the *American Anthropological Association* to find lively commentaries on intellectual works and resolutions about current political problems. Several kinds of criticism are made of ethnographic reports. They include questions about observer bias,[61] the competence of the reporting,[62] facts omitted or undue weight given to some facts rather than others,[63] and more than anything else, criticisms of the interpretations: theories, approaches, the style of data presentation (e.g., editing of data), familiarity with the literature, etc. What matters, for our purposes, is the human element involved in these criticisms of ethnography.

It is curious how many fieldworkers have avoided exposing themselves in their ethnography. The natives' responses, including experiencing the observer, are fated to obscurity. Seldom are the ethnographers' personal or cultural status accounted for in interpreting their findings. Some anthropologists have noted this omission,[64] but little has systematically been said about it. How odd that the highly personal knowledge of participant-observation makes so little use of one's involvement in presenting observations, through which the meanings and images of the culture of one's ethnography are also quietly voiced.[65] A few workers have used personal accounts of their experience to convey understanding. Please note, however, that with the exceptions of Lévi-Strauss's (1969) *Tristes Tropiques* and Mead's (1972) *Blackberry Winter*, our great anthropologists have not drawn explicitly on personal experience to write ethnography, nor have they published autobiographic accounts or diaries.[66] The rule in Malinowski's day was that a scientific authority edits him or herself out of the ethnography and removes other traces of life from the report.[67] This statement applies to other fields and psychoanalysis too. (Remember *The Double Helix*.)[68] Times are changing under the sign of interpretive anthropology. But not changing all that much.

What is the knowledge that claims to be ethnography? The problem may be broken down in three ways. What is ethnography? How do we know it is what it is presented as being? And what is its knowl-

edge good for? Classical ethnography* is a special kind of investigation. It is not a lab experiment. Whatever else it is, it is primarily
clinical: it studies people—flesh and blood people—with minds and
motives and feelings. And these people are studied by other people,
us ethnographers, who cannot search for ethnographic realities except through our motives and feelings. An ethnography that includes
experience as we observe others and what we know of interpersonal
interaction leads to better theories of culture and meaning systems
in action. But to include our experience requires us later to recon-
sider how Malinowski's "psychological insight" operates in ethnography.

What is ethnography *not*? Ethnography is unlike any other discipline. Its mode of knowing, form of knowledge, its problems of accountability, and its writings set it apart from other fields. It is similar to psychoanalytic research but it is not psychoanalysis, as Ann
Parsons once argued. We ethnographers are not trained to understand drives and intrapsychic conflict. We are not primarily interested in unconscious processes. (Some of us are not even trained to
talk to people.) The ethnography I have published on Sambia is not
applied psychoanalysis or transcultural psychiatry. Nor is it philosophy, biography, autobiography, diary, or novel, or the same as
cognitive anthropology, symbolic anthropology, or psychologic
anthropology. Ethnopsychiatry (Devereux 1980b) is similar, as are
observational psychology[69] and ethnographic psychology (Cole 1975).
Psychoanalytically oriented ethnography[70] is closer still.

Many styles of ethnography have emerged in anthropology over
the past hundred years. In fact, each worker develops a particular
way of doing ethnography, though the differences tend to be washed
out in written reports. The "life history" was well used by an earlier
generation of American students forced to do salvage ethnography
with the proverbial last Indian (Nabokov 1967). Culture and personality studies added new techniques: depth interviews, projective tests,
and questionnaires. Humanistic accounts—fictionalized stories and
novels—are an old genre coming back to life in ethnography. First-
person autobiographic accounts, such as Read's *Return To The High
Valley*, have provided personal records of doing ethnography. And these
have become even more frequent and visible, as the ethnographic papers in Clifford and Marcus (1986) illustrate this best.[71]

What these personalized accounts still lack, however, are *systematic* descriptions of natives interacting with the ethnographer.[72] Eth-

---

*By trained professionals, not laymen.

nographers from Malinowski on might allow a place for the life of the natives in sketches, case studies, "apt examples" (Gluckman 1967), "stereotypes" (Malinowski 1922), "fuller statistical documentation of empirical transactions" (Leach 1976), "biographies,"[73] etc., yet they generally avoided inserting their own lives into the reports. It was as if an unseen hand of Science authored the texts, rather than real people. "The whole temper of cultural anthropology," Sapir (1949:569) noted, "was impersonal to a degree." So impersonal that we rarely can picture even how the fieldworker lived. This, Crapanzano (1986) feels, still holds of even Geertz's classical ethnographic papers on the Balinese. The anthologies provide edited snapshots.[74] All the "other stuff" is put in a diary or never published.[75] (Although Mead[76] particularly described—made public—her field conditions.)

You get the picture: a powerful ideology is at work. Anthropology, in spite of its strong personal involvement, exerts a stronger pull to make research seem impersonal.

CLINICAL ETHNOGRAPHY

To give recognition to the clinical dimension of fieldwork, we suggest the term "clinical* ethnography" as a subtype and more precise form of participant-observation. Our scientific ideology can be shifted if not junked. But we cannot do without cross-cultural research, as Shweder (1984) has recently reminded us. Clinical ethnographies are reports that study the subjectivity of the researcher and the people who inform him or her. What matters are our communications with real people, one to one or one to many; people creating and exchanging meanings within interpersonal relationships.

The context counts, for cultural signs and symbols are embedded in situations. Contrary to contemporary anthropologists, we suspect that anthropologists rarely study in the field, let alone describe, whole cultural systems.[77] (At least not in one sitting.) Nor do we study only external social behavior, or its material manifestations, notwithstanding Marvin Harris. To understand meaning systems and the more private motivations and fantasies of people, we need accounts of the natives as individuals, not just as presumed spokesmen for their cultures. The natives are not slaves (i.e., "to custom"),[78] though neither

---

*The dictionary says, "*Clinical* . . . involving or depending on direct observation of the living patient; observable by clinical inspection; based on observation; applying objective or standardized methods (as interviews and personality or intelligence tests) to the description, evaluation, and modification of human behavior." The connotation of diagnosis and treatment—of the clinic—is not intended in clinical ethnography.

do they live beyond the citadel (of forces labeled "culture," "economy," "social structure," or "personality"). Other persons' meanings viewed thus in the round are our object.

How shall we use "subjectivity"? As one's private experience of experiencing—at all levels of perception, thought, speech, and action.[79] (We are not interested, for example, in sensory or motor functions, except to understand the *meanings* of a sensation or motor capacity for someone.)

We shall also stress what is true for ourself but too easily forgotten about our research subjects: barring torture, most issues with great meaning are revealed only to those one trusts, someone who will not harm you.* This desire to trust is no more a culture-bound artifact of western experience than is the capacity for insight (the power to harness subjectivity) or the need to share experience.[80] Rather, the seeds for "awareness of one's awareness—the knowledge that one knows" (Devereux 1967:23)—are essential constituents of being human. In clinical ethnography, understanding this awareness and how trust affects the study of it are crucial.

The cross-cultural study of subjectivity—a major aim of clinical ethnography—describes, interprets, and compares the ways people express feelings, beliefs, and motives. "Clinical" is meant to represent our interest in these processes—intimate communication, subjective meanings of self, others, cultural ideas and institutions, identity, and culturally patterned states of awareness. The subjective connotes skills familiar to the psychiatrist, analyst, clinical psychologist, and social worker for collecting reliable information. With the Sambia of New Guinea, our work is not therapy (though people felt better for having been able to talk in confidence); we did clinical interviewing adapted to the language and culture of Sambia.[81] To emphasize these issues in handling ethnographic data, we focus on but do not restrict our discussion to the clinical interviewing context, wherein we must accordingly interpret *all* experience. We shall argue that interpretation never stops, from home to the field and back.

Everything may potentially color the meaning of our data; so we must record as much as possible. Mead once referred to this ambitious stance as "disciplined subjectivity". At best, no matter how full our information, it is incomplete, for interpretation is always involved and is incomplete. In this process, psychoanalysis (at home) is aided by stable control of the office/analyst environment but weak-

---

*In chapter 11 we shall return to discuss interrelationships between psychoanalysis and anthropology, and in our Epilogue we take our ideas on ethics and training of clinical ethnographers further.

ened by the lack of observations of the patient beyond the office. On the other hand, anthropology (in the village) is strengthened by social observations, though we do not control the interview context in the manner of the psychoanalyst.[82] In doing clinical ethnography, therefore, time and repeated observation is a wonderful tool. Sometimes only follow-up can bring more complete data: clinical ethnography is like psychoanalysis, best done for years; and the more time one takes, the richer the observations and fuller the interpretations. A single interview, casual or not, is better than nothing. A week or a month or a year, talking with someone several times a week, provides more. But years of interviews are the test of "evidential continuity"[83] in an individual case study. What does a word mean? Why is he quiet *now*? Is that the same fantasy as two years ago? Why is she or he angry now? What about the dream fragment? Is this mood the same as the one I observed last month? Time shapes contexts and helps us interpret feelings and tacit assumptions, values, fantasy; as well as interpersonal relationships to significant others, including that alien other, the ethnographer. Clinical ethnography is not for the impatient. (Time is, of course, not time but mind. And mind, of course, is not the Mind but interpretations of subjective experience.)

There are, then, two interrelated perspectives in this clinical approach to ethnographic research. The situational one concerns the doing and reporting of interviews in longitudinal case studies. The global perspective concerns an attitude about all one's work: in order better to know what you know, study your own subjectivity and interpersonal relationships, from start to finish, that is, from the time you embark on the project until the end of your writing and editing. It may seem a paradox that the most objective means of doing this research is to explicate subjectivity. However, S. and I assume that since humans are not machines, we are biased. And so we "must use the subjectivity inherent in all observation as the royal road to authentic, rather than fictitious, objectivity" (Devereux 1967:xvii). We use our subjectivity best when we do not ignore or hide it; those deceptions distort our findings. We must, instead, show exactly who we were and are and what we did and do.

To sum up: in the "culture of fieldwork" fiction, the ethnographer is a finely tuned machine that serves as the representative of a culture of orientation to the representatives of the native culture. We shall suggest a better way: clinical ethnography. Let us now expand on this idea by looking inside the fieldwork experience to understand why we conceptualize this way.

TRAINING FOR THE FIELD

As is training in the laboratories and clinics a fundament for the medical student, fieldwork is the bedrock of training in anthropology. "Such fieldwork apprenticeship is so essential," Mead wrote (1952:344), "that I believe anthropologists should insist upon it just as medical men insist upon an internship before certifying a student as a full M.D."

But in training ethnographers, field experience has been seen as making the student totally responsible, in some intuitive way, for translating classroom theory and text into field method.

> At present we have no way of training a student to become an ethnologist other than by sending him or her into the field under conditions that make it necessary to take complete responsibility for the study of the culture. . . . On the whole the best method is to assure that a student who has had exposure to the literature and experience is to *send him into the field alone, with full responsibility for devising the appropriate applications of his graduate training to the culture of a particular people.*[84]

Whatever psychologic instruments or quantitative measures the student used, they were no substitute for "the bone-wearying labor of 'old fashioned' fieldwork" (Chapple 1952:342). And the responsibility for doing *objective* work was sacred. "The highest duty of every anthropologist," Chapple states, is in "securing accurate and objective data, as unbiased by the actions of the field man as possible."[85] But exactly how this occurred was not explained.

The result has been the tendency to see fieldwork as a magical ordeal[86] organized on a "sink or swim" principle. Nader describes it as "the principle initiation rite into the anthropological profession." Anthropologic folklore values those who have a rough time of it: "Supposedly one grows under stress, and the greater the stress, the more we grow" (Nader 1970:114).[87] Edgerton and Langness write:

> Many of the prominent anthropologists of today have criticized their professors for sending them to the field with so little formal preparation. Anthropologists have wryly recounted the frustration they felt when they asked their professors for advice [and were told] . . . "take a lot of pencils or send ahead a large supply of novels to ward off boredom." Even in more recent years some got the same sort of offhand answers to serious, anxious questions; Alan

> Beals illustrates: "In 1952, on my way to India, I asked a distin-
> guished British anthropologist to tell me his secret of success in
> doing fieldwork." His response was "Never accept free housing, and
> always carry a supply of marmalade." (1974:9)[88]

To sum up: "The student is thrown into the ethnographic ocean, and
nature takes it course. If he is worth his salt, he will return from the
field an anthropologist" (Nader 1970:114).

Sink or swim; nature takes it course: those who become anthropologists can adapt to other cultures. Anthropology celebrates the
ability of each generation of fieldworkers to rediscover for itself this
intuitive process with each culture in each "natural experiment" (Mead
1970). In the ideology of anthropology, fieldwork is a discovery process that defies formulas. Cultural relativism, a powerful piece of our
ideology, underlies this attitude toward training.

> There are dangers in being too explicit about how to do fieldwork,
> just as there are dangers in being insufficiently explicit. One cannot
> produce rules for doing fieldwork as if fieldwork were like a labo-
> ratory experiment. So complete and complex a human experience
> cannot be "programmed" in every detail. . . . An approach which
> might succeed admirably among gregarious Polynesians might
> fail altogether with the recalcitrant Nuer of the African Sudan.
> (Edgerton and Langness 1974:9)

Since we study whole cultures, not individuals as culture-bearers, there
are limits, it is felt, to the prefield training of fieldworkers. Namely,
we will not know until afterward what constitutes the experience of
Anthropology (i.e., the fieldworker) studying a particular culture (i.e.,
as represented by the natives, their language, and material culture).
That unique experiment in the special laboratories of human cultures
is the ethnography.

This training paradigm has, from the 1920s to the early 1970s, had
favorable but uneven results: relatively unconnected and basically
descriptive reports, few of which were concerned with field method.
Broad perspectives often stood in for theory, except in the grand sense
that culture or social structure determined human behavior. What
made ethnography useful was the brilliance and hard work of researchers who succeeded in bringing home remarkable truths of the
Other.

Yet we fear that our bureaucratic success undermined the training
of new fieldworkers.[89] "The Golden Age of American Anthropology"
(Mead and Bunzel 1960) in the 1960s and early 1970s witnessed a

surge of university jobs, federal grant funds, academic and public recognition, and student enrollments. This eventually slackened, but meanwhile, anthropology was almost popular, no longer a sport for the gentry. These changes democratized anthropology[90] but increasingly weakened the kind of training Mead advocated. How? Training shifted from carefully supervised apprenticeship to theory and textbooks; the teaching anthropologist became an authority and expert on a people, less a mentor and a socializer of new ethnographers. Professors had too many students and committee assignments and not enough time for individual supervision. And this bureaucratization in turn further strengthened the rise of participant-observation as a guiding fiction for the discipline. Anthropology is not to blame, of course; these structural alterations must be seen in the context of marketplace adjustments in urban America and academic life.[91] It became more difficult for anthropologists to do fieldwork. Paper work and university bureaucratic tangles grew; publish or perish pressures forced a rush to publication instead of slow immersion into one's place of study; ethnography produced few findings needed by technologically accelerating society; former colonies felt demeaned in being studied. Today, publishers have less reason to bring out large ethnographies for few readers. Ethnography, once the bizarre customs and bosoms were revealed, had as much allure as butterfly collecting.

We dislike the model of participant-observation that stands for the belief that the observer holds back participation so severely that he or she can observe only surfaces. Yet it is a fact—not a theory, a prejudice, or a fantasy—that ethnography occurs in a context of people who (just as you do now as you read) load the interaction with their subjectivity, that is, their private meanings. We also are uneasy that the culture of fieldwork ideology ignores how one's project begins at home, the instant one conceptualizes (imagines) a project. The field project is shaped by our personality, our daydreams, the texts and field reports we read, our professors' theories and anecdotes and advice, budgets, families, and friends: powerful images that move us long before we ever meet a native—and continue their effects to the end, as we make public our experience—ethnography.

The field project designed at home is obviously based on our selfhood, not just our theories or topical interests. First, of course, is the key question of personal and professional motivation: why *do* anthropology?[92] Training influences are extremely important; particular professors stimulate and guide us; certain university departments are associated with certain schools of theory or regions to be studied; and one's graduate student cohort shares interests and shapes knowledge. Then there are questions about the choice of field site: why go to the Arctic or the Amazon? How feasible or harsh and isolated is it (especially if one is Woman[93])? To match an area to one's topical interest restricts the available choices.[94] So do the needs of one's spouse or family. (Doing fieldwork can test a marriage to the limits; the many broken relationships prove the point.) Political factors are important: some Third-World countries are now closed to research; others require payments for research visas; funding agencies reward some types of research and punish others, or they rule out certain geographic areas; nor must we forget the old territorial game in anthropology, through which academic warlords claim a people as their own: 'That's Professor X's people, you can't study there.'[95]

Beyond these practical considerations, however, one's imagination figures actively in selecting a field area and subject. I chose exotic New Guinea because I wanted to study a living initiatory cult, not memories of one. We go to areas that intrigue and fascinate us;[96] perhaps the more rewarding our experiences there (research included), the more inclined we are to return.[97] Here one sees the seldom-discussed match in any field between character structure and professional research.[98]

So our work—fieldwork—begins in our heads, at home, not abroad. Vicarious participation starts there; we formulate images of the natives and of ourselves among them. Observation is grounded there: from ethnographic films or texts of related peoples, from correspondence with local missionaries or other residents in the native area, as well as (in some areas) films or discussion with professors, we take in hypotheses, field strategies, etc. (It surprises us that even clinically-oriented anthropologists ignore awareness of this prefield head work.[99]) Long before the field, an ethnography is biased, however slightly. How aware of these influences are we; of our motives and preconceptions carried into our work? Though we do not engage in old-fashioned natural history sojourns[100] (as did early European explorers[101] captivated by vulgar or romantic conceptions of "primitives") we still need to train students to be alert to this earliest fieldwork in the head.

Let us thus distinguish between several degrees of participating and observing.

First-order participation: This concerns direct interaction with others; eyewitnesses' accounts; observations of words, acts, affects—what Kardiner (1939:356) called "direct experience" in the field.

Second-order participation: indirect participation with others made while in the field; these include introspection and empathy focused on natives' experiences but going beyond what they say or do, as, for instance, when we remember the day's events and record or think about them. Here we observe our own impressions while still in the field. (Our day and night dreams in the field also belong in this category.)

Third-order participation: reading, thinking, and resonating to our fieldwork experience before and after leaving the field. How do we reach new understandings after leaving the field unless, in our heads, we are still participating in our field experience? These reworkings—interpretations—lead to our published report; they *become* the data. Without this hermeneutic approach, we forget how the acts of participating and observing begin inside of us, no matter where and when they become publicly visible.

Even in this crude schema we sense the difficulty of separating participation from observation[102] or of distinguishing between events in the world from those in the head of the ethnographer.[103] Not that there is not a vital difference between them, for there is; but it is their unity that deserves emphasis *contra* the ideology of participant-observation. To illustrate these impressions we shall rethink the field experience.

THE FIELD

Entree

What is our mental state on embarking? Are we excited and anticipating ("a great adventure"), anxious ("what will I find?"; "will I be competent?"; "it's hard to leave"), resentful ("why must I do this?"), angry ("why do they do this to me?"), or joyous ("at long last")? Or a mix of these? Shall we feel the same on stepping into the village? Why? Why not? Who helps or hinders us from getting there?

These transitional experiences modify our observations via our participations. Do we say so in our reports? Anthropology used to proudly deny that these events—this messy subjectivity—were pertinent. What do they have to do with "the culture"? ("Our subject is the village which stops at its gate.") Less so now. Mead (1977:5) wrote toward her end:

We knew that we had been bred in our own culture and could never lose our own cultural identity; we could only learn about others through the recognition that their membership in their culture and our membership in ours, however different in substance, were alike in kind. But we did not yet recognize that every detail on reaching the field and of interchange with those who tried to bar or facilitate our way to the field site were also part of our total field experience and so of our fieldwork.

What people help or complicate[104] our settling in: government bureaucrats, missionaries, patrol officers, linguists, native councilors, government translators? Even tourists?* How do we relate to them? What identity do we convey to each of these parties: subject, friend, student, opponent, playmate, sophisticate, fool, scholar? How are these identities conveyed back to the natives (by ourselves, by others)? Do their images make a difference in how they perceive us?

Few ethnographers will ever again work without these authorities being present, and some fieldworkers have noted their influences.[105] But in most *ethnographies* such authorities are often still absent. Why are they edited out? Perhaps politics prevents us from describing them.[106] A pity. For instance, despite rumors of antipathy between anthropologists and missionaries, field reports in New Guinea would be less advanced today were it not for the logistical assistance of various missionaries.[107]

In our first hours in the village we form and communicate indelible impressions; what do we experience and how do we behave in these initial contacts? Which people approach us? Are they friendly or hostile?[108] Who or what do they take us to be? Are we officially received by kings or chiefs? Who sponsors us? The natives press in; what motivates them: curiosity, influence-seeking, money, friendliness, anger, protection of their rights? Leaders present themselves and introduce us to their followers; or no one may come forth. Others may desire to work for us. Among the Sambia some young men and boys asked to work for me—to teach the language, to translate, to cut firewood, to cook. I hired no one at first: I didn't know what it would mean to hire them, or why they wanted to work, or how that role would alter them, or how I would or could pay them.   Only time taught me.† Textbooks advise us not to select overzealous people,[109] a preconception I remembered but which did not hold well for the Sambia, for some of my first contacts became key sponsors, teachers, translators, and friends.‡

*We are only beginning to demystify the extent to which tourism has thoroughly influenced certain ethnographic projects, as much as our view of ourselves (MacCannell 1976).

†The following allusions to my fieldwork cover my first visits (1974–76), when I spent twenty-two months with the Sambia.

‡These people included Kanteilo and Worangri, elder sponsors who were respected village leaders, and superb teachers and manipulators of me. Moondi, my best young informant, translator, and field assistant; and Weiyu, who got closer later than the others, became my best translator and closest Sambia friend. All are described in short biographies in Herdt (1987c), and see our interview chapters below.

Psychiatrists teach that the information in the first interview is very important (though we have to know ourselves well enough to trust our impressions and be practiced enough to know how to listen and observe). That first hour presents, in open or disguised forms, the characteristic elements of the ensuing interaction (i.e., treatment): signs and symptoms, moods, styles of communicating, uniqueness of personality, capacity to talk and interact, to trust and be trusted. For the anthropologist our first hours in the village reveal typical interpersonal issues that will immerse us from then on. It would be nice to have as detailed a record as possible of that time, including our personal reactions. Nicer still to place some of that diary in our later ethnography.

Culture Shock

On entering the village, we are to expect an attack of culture shock. The term conjures up images of confrontation with alien ways of life, unnatural practices: eating coagulated milk and cow's blood, women breast-feeding pigs, villagers refusing to tend their sick, infanticide, cruel treatment of women, statements that the ethnographer is a ghost or spy,[110] or that men fear their semen will dry up and they'll die. We may be stopped in our tracks, alienated, disgusted, enraged, fearful. And then we may shrink back. Depressed. We want to press down on this concept, because it is central to the objectified view of participant-observation, and because it is among the first experiences in the field. Bear with us in rethinking this problem for clinical ethnography.

Culture shock appears to be a common experience of anthropologists, however varied the specific events:

> The uneasiness brought about by living in an unpredictable social world, combined with the loss of one's comfortable social world, brings on a condition known as *culture shock*—the shock of passing from a familiar to an unknown culture. . . . In the face of culture shock the fieldworker often retreats for a period from any social interactions. (Edgerton and Langness 1974:23)

> Obviously the anthropologist in the field, especially in the early period when he is not yet sure of acceptance, is subject to extreme emotional pressure. Some field situations can be frightening, raising fears for personal safety, and at the very least the anthropologist knows he is undergoing a severe professional test in which he

must rely entirely on his own resources. . . . The common result
of this situation is "culture shock," the same psychological mal-
functioning as that experienced by most people who find themselves in strange settings, in which they recognize neither the cues
of the culture nor the appropriate responses to the cues. . . . In
greater or lesser degree all anthropologists experience culture shock,
at least on their first field trips and not infrequently on subsequent
trips as well. . . . (Foster 1969:62)

"Uneasiness," "unpredictability," "loss of one's comfortable social
world," "retreat," "extreme emotional pressure," "frightening," "entirely on his own resources"—culture shock. It is expected in all of
us.

Yet we are skeptical: Are we dealing with genuine anxiety or a
myth? (Or a catchy phrase that hides a lot of neurosis inside the claim
of appropriate fear. One person's fascination is another's fear.) If "all
anthropologists experience culture shock," then why does Malinowski
not describe the phenomenon? Nor do Mead, Bateson, Firth, Roheim,
DuBois, Evans-Pritchard or the six editions of *Notes and Queries in
Anthropology*, as far as we can figure out. What's amiss? Were these
pioneers superhumans who could not be shocked? Or did they, in
keeping with this book's critique, simply edit *that* life out of their
disturbances in the field? As, for instance, in the infamous case of
Malinowski's diaries? In both senses I think not.

Here are two other clues about our concept of culture shock. First,
in *exotic cultures*, the longer one remains (or the more one returns to
the same place), the less culture shock. The authors of *Long-Term Field
Research in Social Anthropology* hint at the normativeness of culture
shock and collectively conclude: "Not only is 'culture shock' mini-
mized . . . [in subsequent fieldwork] . . . but often the anthropologist is fully engaged in research within a few hours of arrival."[111]
Second, in urban settings—so-called urban anthropology—"culture
shock" is apparently absent; one finds few references to it.[112]

"Culture shock" is a fine-sounding pop-jargon phrase that should
make us cautious because of these anomalies. The idea has now been
imported into western culture.[113] This fact, together with the observation that the phenomenon has been little studied except anecdo-
tally since Oberg, even though "it" is still unselfconsciously referred
to as experience and as concept, suggests that "culture shock" is exaggerated in the culture of fieldwork. This should give us pause. If
one examines the anthropologic literature, allusions to the term do
not appear until after World War II. Someone[114] coined the term in

the late thirties or forties; by the fifties Oberg's paper helped to in-
stitutionalize it. Its origins are unimportant; what concerns me is its
ideologic and psychodynamic foothold in ethnography.

Ethnographers acquire the notion of "culture shock" (like that of
"informant," as we shall see), through professional socialization.[115] It
helps us to maintain that tenuous balancing act: participant-observation. We can do our job—like lab workers—no matter how uncomfortable our adjustment to alien situations. The experience we call
"culture shock" is thus a way of registering (objectifying) our belief
that this shock occurs to ourselves as scientists, not as private persons. Intellectually mystified and psychologically rationalized in this
way, it is then acceptable for the ethnographer to feel and think unacceptable things. But why use "culture shock" to cover danger, feelings of disorientation, alienation or loneliness?

First, there is our ideology. The traditional assumption is that anthropologists study primitive, static, closed systems. To adapt to these
harmonious, equilibrium societies, where everyone is related (or else
enemies) in face-to-face relationships, we must dislocate, even disrupt, a bit of their world. "We" penetrate, that is, some magical
boundary that represents "the culture" enclosing their village. Thus,
"culture shock": we are shocked in fitting in, they are jarred to accommodate us. This "we" that is shocked indexes more than the self.
It is the ethnographer, bearer of the culture of fieldwork, and representative of our cultural tradition; a "normal" scientist who reg-
isters "normal" emotional/cognitive reactions vis-à-vis the "normal"
representatives of the host culture. Since anthropology holds precious
the doctrine of cultural relativism—whereby all customs and meaningful acts are parts of a whole pattern ("their culture") that *is* human, worthy of respect, and adaptive in some sense—we, as cultural
spokesmen for the West, require some mechanism for communicating
(to our culture and ourselves) that these objectionable alien practices,
which we cannot object to, are understandable and eventually acceptable. Moreover, they will be made assimilable into western culture via the Science of Custom. So the ethnographer can accept (at
least intellectually) the aliens' way as relative: good, natural, and human. And for all these reasons the praxis of urban anthropology should
require no experience of "culture shock."[116]

On the personal side of selfhood, there are equally powerful psychodynamics compelling our use of culture shock. The mythology of
culture shock convinces us that we are unbiased. Since fieldwork does
not begin (as the folklore has it) until we set foot in the village, our
participation with the native does not begin in our heads but rather

over there; and we do not study ourselves beforehand. How we *usually* are, back home; why we unusually left it and are there; and all that transpired up to that first step in the village is ignored in the ethnography, counts as nothing. While participant-observation keeps us detached (not to be confused with objectivity), it also ensures that *we do not look inside.*

The idea of culture shock disguises our private experience in the field. "Shock" may be accurate if reality-oriented fears are involved. But if we are responding to something dangerous, such as an attack on our lives, our responses might be in the direction of, say, alertness, caution, or fear. Words like these come closer to naming our subjective states and pointing us toward knowing what we experience. But there are anxieties less immediate, with no direct danger, that more closely correspond to the popular category of culture shock. In this sense "shock" can also hide personal, idiosyncratic, neurotic* responses—legitimized as normal, expected, and nonproblematic (as in World War I victims of "shell shock"). Thus, I would rather say "I suffered from culture shock" than let myself or you know my biases, bigotries, and even racist impulses: distress that my moral, religious, or erotic sensibilities are being attacked. Or that my beliefs about what is proper demeanor or clothes or body form or personal hygiene or worship or whatever are being threatened. Here, the self's script and textual use of culture shock might be: *I did not come to this place to find (i.e., repeat) the anxieties that are so handy at home.*

Were it not for our personalities, interests, creative talents, and neurosis, we would not suffer culture shock but—in many circumstances—curiosity, delight, puzzlement, or surprise. Therefore, to place the responsibility for such experience outside of ourselves and onto culture (or nature, i.e., one's viscera) is to take a stand against insight. What we choose not to look at is a choice against learning more, ethnographically—against our recognizing that matters of taste, style, custom (to use a comfortably neutral vocabulary) may bother us a great deal and that our capacity to be bothered in such ways did not begin the moment we arrived in the strangers' land. Then, with practice, we may learn to what extent that which we feel is either our own invention or the results of outer stimuli or both.

Unless we accord personal motivation a role in the experience of culture shock we cannot account for the following folklore: that colleagues or co-workers of similar background in the same culture do

---

*By which we mean here: the invasion of one's contact with reality by unconscious conflict, either idiosyncratic or culturally shared conflicts.

not report similar culture shock; that others in our field—visitors, missionaries, traders, etc.—experience no shock where we do, or vice versa, or find instead curiosity or amusement;[117] or that, in some cases, the anthropologist's *spouse* is said to have had an easier time of it in the field. (Remember that the anthropology student is undergoing a "severe professional test.")

Some years ago, when starting work in Sambia, I experienced anxieties—shocks—of several kinds. I do not think of those experiences as culture shock, but in the old idiom they could be miscategorized that way. There was distress I felt in reaction to discrete events: helplessness at the screams of an older woman being beaten by her husband, others tensely watching outside their house—the screams intermixed with sounds of wood striking flesh, and her cries for a long dead mother. But "shock" is too vague. I felt helplessness, then pity, bitterness, sadness. (And even these words are imprecise.) Or the laughter of the initiates, who did nothing when a small boy fell from a tree on his testicles, splitting open his scrotum, blood everywhere. I was stunned for an instant and then enraged at what seemed dangerously callous complacency. Or Moondi's fearlessness, when he told me the secret practices of homosexual fellatio and thereby placed himself in grave danger. For days I feared for his life and mine, until the men accepted my knowing their secrets. Or, three months later, in the privacy of ritual initiations, when I saw the secrets become flesh in florid and open homoerotic play. I was astonished and embarrassed. (Herdt 1987c.)

Then there are emotions—they are cheapened by being called "shock"—that come from extended experiences: exhilaration with this New Guinea adventure;* loneliness for friends and family; mild depressions; malaise; sickness (malaria, dysentery); sexual frustration; rewards of friendships; and work that was an accomplishment. All these—disturbances or joys—*were* my work. I cannot afford to lose data and perspective by squashing them into the globbish "culture shock."† By staying awake, by not blurring my awareness of what I felt,[118] I sometimes found more of me and thereby allowed the ethnographer in me to find more of Sambia experience.

Malinowski, whatever else he may have felt, probably never knew of our "culture shock." He was not taught it. He did not have the luxury its distance provides, and we are unkind to forget this.[119] He was an explorer lacking the defenses of our ideologic armor. Perhaps

---

*"Culture shock" is negative. What about the wonderful surprises?

†One also loses a lot of data and perspective by the opposite extreme of going native, wherein we deny that the past is alive in our bones.

this is why his diaries revealed two people: Malinowski the Scientist, a myth his books created; and Malinowski the man, mortal as any other. The field notes and monographs were objectivity, the diaries were subjectivity. In the diaries we may have lost a hero, but anthropology gained a fuller ethnography. In the years following Malinowski, "culture shock" was created to mediate the same ideologic dilemmas that forced Malinowski into his diaries. By the 1960s, anthropology's golden age, many people, of diverse personality, social class, training, research interests, and professional motivations replaced the once small anthropology club. The pseudolanguage of culture shock allowed them to share seemingly common experiences without revealing their private biases and subjectivity. Were Malinowski alive he might now—in characteristic form—reproach us for not publishing our diaries. Either that, or better: put some of that insight where it always belonged in the first place. In our ethnography.

Identity Problems

We settle in, build a house, meet people, learn the language, learn names, make contacts, learn etiquette, learn the politics, find rapport with people, get comfortable, establish our role and identity as the anthropologist.

Supposedly, we are first like children, soaking up what is taught us.[120] Yet this analogy is flawed, for we have power—political, technologic, education—and we and our hosts know it. We know the outside. We are usually white and western, which have their power implications. Moreover, we transmit to the natives our sense of being superior, especially because we examine what they do and think and because *we* decide what about them we think is important for us to know. Thus we, going beyond their belief, believe that we become the final authorities on their reality.[121]

But do we not likewise structure the effects we have on our subjects or who they feel we are? The identity they give us, built from who knows what stories, experiences, and fantasies,[122] is confirmed and modified by our demeanor and our acts. Where do we build our hut? In the village? Away from it? Do we allow the natives inside? How do we acquire food? Do we share it? Do the natives share with us? What do we pay for? Do we work fixed hours? Do we sign off? (At night? On Sundays?) Do we establish taboos?[123] Do we make some areas off-limits: our sleeping quarters, eating quarters, toilets, storerooms, etc.? Why—what are we keeping separate from them? Do we let natives borrow? Do we borrow from them? How do we entertain ourselves when alone, with spouse, or with co-worker? How often do we travel in an area? Do we spend larger amounts of time with certain informants, friends, males, females, Europeans, on the government station, etc.? In what ways do we refuse to interact with the natives?[124]

And what meanings do people attribute to our acts? How can we unendingly respond to such factors throughout our lives at home and deny them in the field? For instance: "Though undoubtedly I feel a great debt to many villages, I thought it advisable from the point of view of academic objectivity not to get too involved in the lives of individual informants" (Epstein 1979:224).

Obviously we help shape our environment by what we do, say, and think, and our actions strongly influence the identity that the natives thereby ascribe to us. Once in motion, this identity "text" influences subsequent responses to us. A related point: do we notice if we set up modes of acculturated comportment (e.g., drinking behavior[125]) for the natives? Such issues lead to the question of who our informants are and how they choose us.

The Informant

The innocuous term "informant" emerged at the end of the nineteenth century as researchers moved off the hotel veranda to talk to "savages." "Savages" in turn became "natives," who turned into "informants." This shift was related to the emergence of the concepts of "culture" and "participant-observation." In the early part of the twentieth century the functionalists treated cultures as integrated wholes (while ignoring their own colonialist situation). The "informant" was a reaction to the early racism predating anthropology, and it represented as much as anything our intellectual progress. Where did it take us? Not too far; we did not escape our colonialist and positivistic heritage, for "the informant" is a notion that still embodies anthropology's contradictions.[126] Here, as with culture shock, let us question a key category in the culture of fieldwork.

Anthropologists know these cliches: "my informant said," "informants say," "informants argue," "informants believe," the informant stressed that," "informants could not explain," "informants denied," "it was pointed out by informants that," "informants were concerned to," "informants describe," "informants recalled." Yes: in this narrative form we see not this person in particular or that one, but rather nameless, faceless, sexless, ageless, colorless, impartial witnesses and specialists uncontaminated by who they are, precisely, or why they said what they said to us, precisely.

We needed a neutral term that made the sources of our cultural facts seem accurate and sound: objective. We needed a word to fill a gap: what does one call a category of people who tell us things and interpret them for us? They inform, provide knowledge, *become as spokesmen for their communities.* Here is a key: informants provide true knowledge about a culture that is supposedly custom-bound and homogeneous. It is not their private opinions or peculiar chunks of cultural knowledge that inform, but rather their capacity as funnels for revealing—to *anyone* who interrogates* them—the social facts as everyone else knows them, except, of course, the alien ethnographer.[127]

Anthropology's adoption of "informant" complemented the philosophic behaviorism of the time. We needed an analytic term that made our subjective data ring as scientific as that of our sister disciplines. The therapists had patients (in treatment); the academic psychologists had subjects (in experiments); the sociologists had actors and respondents (to questionnaires); the humanistic psychologists added clients; the hermeneuts use interlocutors (Reisman 1977). Are these comparisons apt? (Only clinicians—and their case is not comparable either—can claim the intensive, intimate knowledge of the ethnographer.) Only we have eyewitness accounts (Sontag 1966) coupled with the natives' point-of-view in context, the result of the live-in method that is not experimental, controlled, or abstractable. The informant, like the analytic patient, is $n = 1$.

And not only this: our informants, said Powdermaker, are thought to be friends. Here again the objective dilemma—be detached but friendly—emerges. On the one hand, our informants are like guides for the blind.[128] They are our spectacles, hearing aids, crutches, stomachs, spectographs, barometers, medical manuals, projective tests, culinary guides, drinking mates, history books, demographic files, guides in etiquette, lovers, baby-sitters, mountain-guides; they share with us their gossip, loves, hates; they interpret our dreams; become our watchdogs, cooks, servants, and even (dare we admit it?)—our sometime healers. All this humanness covered by the cold neutrality: informant. "Informant" thus admits such latitude in traditional ethnography that its promiscuous use is phony. When one term can erase the differences between individuals' age, sex, ritual status, social role, personality, context, mood, motivation, and—most important—the

---

*The dictionary gives this usage.

precise nature of one's relationship to that person, at that moment, that term is being misused (Herdt 1981). Few anthropologists operate as cold onlookers.[129] But in our ethnographic reports, in order to seem scientific, we traded one kind of racism, Social Darwinism, for another: cultural uniformity (e.g., blacks are . . . , Italians are . . . , Chinese are . . . , Sambia are . . . , doctors are . . . , farmers are . . . , ethnographers are. . . .): experiential homogeneity.

To call a person an informant is to press our audience to agree with us that we are scientific since our data are gathered in objective circumstances. But Malinowski is Malinowski: he smells of cigarettes, whisky, and concupiscence. Can we trust what he tells us about the sex lives of Trobriand girls? No, says the scientist, until his Malinowskiness is trimmed off. To the extent that you met him only in sentences that gave you no clues what sort of man he is, we could manipulate your attitudes about the validity of our ideas. Even a name, unless sufficiently foreign, can stir images; but "informant" is less likely to. The ideal informant is neutral, objective, and transmits a culture in its essence, passing the data through him or herself without the contamination of his or her subjectivity. Ideal informants selflessly tell us things, relay language and culture learning; they offer us facts, not their private interpretation of facts. This kind of informant makes us (H. and S.) flinch twice, first because no such people exist, and second because the idea supports the pretense that a culture exists in platonic forms.

Our culture of fieldwork assumes that informants yield up only true information, a belief particularly embodied in the subcategory, the "key informant." Here is, without doubt, a very close relationship. The key informant is someone known so well that his or her biography can be written.[130] But since these people are as fully subjective as anyone else, why should we assume that only truth—or the search for it—motivates them? Does truth rule out lies?[131] Don't we know that cultural knowledge is stratified, even in tribal societies, according to sex, ritual status, caste and politics? And how much more particular are the key informants' words?[132] Many of these relationships probably also contain deeper involvements—conscious and unconscious—including friendship, love, hate, attachment, and dependence: all the elements that make a relationship interesting, enjoyable, rewarding, and perishable. Are transference and countertransference involved?[133] If they are, how do we handle them?

Instead of "the informant" let us adopt the term "interpreter." After reviewing the fieldwork literature, we feel that the concept "interpreter" accurately describes and more closely approximates the methodologic role and meanings noted above than does "informant." Interpreters do nothing more than interpret things for us (which is quite a lot), offering their views and translations of their world and themselves.* Anthropology already recognizes this function in that those who inform about language can be called interpreters or translators. (See chapter 10 for a discussion.) Why should those who translate cultural conventions be more objective in doing so than interpreters of linguistic conventions? (Language and culture are equally open to interpretation; that we assume language to be more or less structured and objectively describable is another assumption of the culture of fieldwork.)

Aside from being more accurate, "interpreter" has two other advantages. One is that it is already used to describe the process of language learning. We do not need a different word to cover the process of culture learning. Moreover, the literature indicates that linguistic interpreters often serve as cultural interpreters too. (If we need to mark off these roles, we can use "linguistic" or "cultural" as modifiers, though often this description is implied in the narrative context and needs no emphasis.) The other advantage is that interpreter will sharpen the epistemologic status of our information. "The informant" carries heavy positivistic baggage; "interpreter" can hardly connote false objectivity. The term "interpreter" forces one always to be clear about what it is that is being cross-culturally negotiated. Including anonymity and privacy.[134]

What matters for ethnography is that the natives were portrayed as being disconnected from the ethnographers' experience (and vice versa). As some interpretive ethnographers have made clear, few texts reveal the native's words to us.[135] Forge (1972:296) stated this idea plainly: "No matter how friendly your informants may be, they can never understand you." No wonder some natives dislike being informants: we know[†] how it feels not to be granted that we have insight.

---

*The dictionary offers: "One who interprets or translates; especially, one who serves as oral translator between people speaking different languages."

[†]We can understand better the potential dangers for us of blandly inputting objectivity to informants when we reverse the business of being an informant. How do we perform as informants, and what do we make of our interrogators? Clifford Barnett (personal communication) tells me of anthropologists who were turned off when serving as informants to a medical research team. Why? Their interrogators only wanted certain information, not the whole story. [S: Who decides which story is the whole story?] Here the anthropologists were merely natives who could not know the whole picture and who could not therefore interpret their own experience.

Field Life: What are Data?

Having struggled with the anthropologist's dilemma in being a flawed instrument for measuring culture, we want now to ask what experiences in village living do count as data. Our answer is: all. That, however, being too much to contemplate, one must focus (and then pray that intelligence, good judgment, and originality—not to mention luck—bless our risky venture). On these terms universes of information go unused in traditional ethnography.

Example: living arrangements. I had the largest house in the village,* placing no restrictions on people coming and going. Indeed I encouraged them to. But the villagers did not want me to live alone: "You would be lonely." "Ghosts attack those who are alone." So the elder, Kanteilo, moved in. Then my cook, Kwinko, moved in. So did Moondi. And sometimes Weiyu. People called my house their hotel. So I was constantly surrounded by people. Little happened in the village that I didn't learn about eventually from people's constant talking, gossip, and everything else people do all day long. But this togetherness meant that I had no privacy. How did I experience it? I could never bear to eat alone in front of them, nor they, me; soon enough, then, the kitchen was open to food exchange.† For solitude I took walks, wrote, read, listened to the radio, sat on my porch and watched sunsets, tended my garden. Though in the swim of things, I also had ways to be by myself—pockets of aloneness, self amusement, and absorption—in this ambience of interpersonal closeness. For Sambia I was, in turn, a tourist-curiosity who became a resident; I was tutored and befriended, pampered, and deceived; I became a pseudo son, brother, and cousin, was thus fed and housed, politically and socially supported, lectured, scolded, exhorted, and extorted. I became a post office, first-aid clinic, bank, supply house—you name it. Still, I didn't merge with them; and Sambia, who are usually sensible people, probably would not have let me do so anyway.‡

---

*Sambia have small huts, and I wanted space. Did I need as much as I had? Did I need the biggest house? Did the village need me to have it? (I was and even when not there still am a political object my village uses in the local status game with its neighbors, former enemies.)

†I could afford to have large crocks of soup cooked every day, with canned meat and whatever vegetables were available. With this soup, I fed people who helped me. There was always enough for others who were around, and since food giving is so acceptable and expected, it fits my desires. (After two and a half years on soup, however, I rarely want soup anywhere, except in my village, where it is still tasty.)

‡Once, on an idle morning during a period of initiation, I was coaxed into trying on the garb of a warrior. (Until then I had never worn native dress.) I felt uncomfortable but kept quiet to get my male friends' responses. What a study in ambivalence. Some said I looked

Talking: who talks to me: Why are my friends the most verbal Sambia? Interviewing: who talks? How much, when, where, how loud or soft, about what? What topics (e.g., parents) are avoided? Does someone make eye contact? If a woman or a boy looks away or is bashful, how is this done: matter-of-factly, nervously, quietly, co-quettishly?* Why is someone quiet? What kind of silence is it—cold, warm, angry, or inviting? Why does someone only get quiet when angry? Why do I feel someone is talking too much or too little? What is the overlying mood of the interview: contentment, passivity, aggressiveness, brooding, fearfulness, or combinations of these? Joking: who makes jokes—men, boys, women? With me, too? When alone? Who laughs? With what kinds of laughter (amused, hysterical)? What do I joke about? How do I make light of events, of myself, of my anxiety? What amuses me? Appalls me? I sense someone is hiding something from me but have only empathy to go by: what are my associations (fantasies)? Do I forget names? Why don't I trust someone's dream reports? Resistance: why am I reluctant to ask something? Why do I consistently avoid some topics: What fascinates me? Bores me? Why am I afraid to ask someone about a particular experience? Why do some people altogether resist being interpreters?

Etc. . . . I need not list more in order to make the point that everything can contribute to shaping the data of clinical ethnography.

You might object that the anthropology student is ill-trained to undertake or understand this kind of interviewing. [S: It's too natural, unstilted, unscholarly.] Isn't the student in danger here, risking damage to others and him- or herself, particularly in sensitive areas such as sexual behavior, dreams, anger, and shame? Isn't fieldwork in an exotic culture demanding enough, under the circumstances of adjusting to strange life conditions—especially working alone—without adding the burden of intimate communications? Perhaps. If so, then we ought to invent training for clinically oriented ethnography and, as is done with psychiatrists, pick from our students only those most likely to be able to talk with others, and then develop the

---

"nice" and "strong" (a warrior); but others said "forget it," or "those garb are no good for you; they'll pinch and they've got lice." When I showed uneasiness, my friends told me to change back. I never wore them again.

*Sambia avoid direct eye contact with others who are defined as potential sexual partners, unless they (men to women, boys to bachelors, or vice versa) are purposely communicating erotic interest. I found that after talking with someone several times, their eye-avoidance diminished; eventually we would have regular eye contact.

seminars, practicums, and supervision that teaches students how to do such work and still comfortably live in foreign cultures.[136]

Our research aim is to understand others. Respect is a prerequisite of cross-cultural study, but where do we draw the lines for appropriate involvement with natives in the villages? When are natives, like doctors' patients, children, the mentally ill, the mentally retarded, and students, emotionally vulnerable to the fantasies they have due to our status? Mead's view (1977:7), by no means unique, is to avoid deep involvement:* "Immersing oneself in life in the field is good, but one must be careful not to drown." Ethnographers are not psychoanalysts, who, in order to allow their patients' minds full play, create a less active environment. How shall we study people's experience in another culture without ourselves knowing and experiencing the culture?

We have reached here a complex and ignored area in ethnography: the degrees of ethnographer involvement (participation and observation) with the natives and their institutions. It is amazing that these issues—psychologic, political, ethical—though basic to all fieldwork, have not been systematically discussed in the literature.

The spectrum of involvement with natives stretches from not being in the field (the armchair ethnologist), and from almost total detachment (sitting on a tractor measuring subjects' movements) in the field, to total merging into the culture (going native).

Let us take the detached fieldworker first. What is detachment? Removing one's true self from interactions? No intimate communication but only questionnaires, standardized impingements, formal interviews, structured tests, strict and technical work schedules? Is detachment avoidance? Perhaps one does not examine certain customs, behaviors, or attitudes; does not investigate beyond the limits of the village; does not look for native insights or interpretations, only for the surface of what is done or said to others; and especially, one avoids studying how the natives perceive you, what you are doing, and what your contacts with them mean to them. Such detachment is aided by believing that each native needs, hates, and loves his or her customs in the same way as others and that we should not ques-

---

*But those involvements occur. They are not reported. Even diaries are not published. [S: I wonder if the best ethnographic reports anywhere are not ethnographers' secret diaries. They may be full of craziness and human fraility, but less dishonest than the ethnographer's objective reports.] When ethnographers succumb [S: And sex is by no means the only sin; even the research as it is actually done—not the published deodorized account—may take cruel advantage of people; and are some missionaries guilty of soul-murder in the techniques they use to get conversions?] and edit these experiences out, are they not distorting data—on the pretext of doing science—and are their reports consequently less accurate than was the ethnographic reality?

tion what they experience. Detachment is also enhanced if one's spouse or children are there to insulate you, as does keeping your abode private. Detachment is maintained by myriad other things: language, dress, food choices, writing letters, field notes, diaries,[137] listening to music, sketching, smoking, interacting with officials, material comforts, frequency of field breaks, etc. The point is that nothing makes detachment out of these behaviors; rather, it is the ethnographers' subjectivity—a desire to keep distant—that does.

What about the other extreme, going native, becoming a pseudonative imitating native ways?[138] We have almost no accounts of this transformation, for it is a disgrace our profession says dishonors oneself, one's professors, department, and discipline. One has failed to master the passage to professional. Too much participation has corrupted observation,[139] similar to florid states of countertransference (e.g., sexual involvement with patients) that disgrace psychiatry.

What about milder forms of acting like a native, of subliminally accepting native ways and attitudes; for instance, never show anger or never hide anger; always share food or never share food. Some may recognize similar aspects in their work but not have thought of them as examples of going native, though we know that whole teams of fieldworkers have found it necessary to appear to be closely identified with the natives.[140]

How intimately must one live with natives to present their viewpoint? There are no simple answers, though most anthropologists manage to be both participant and observer, without going native. S. and I believe that good clinical training could prepare ethnographers to approach these issues in ways that would improve their coping mechanisms and the quality of their data.

Coping in the Field

How do most fieldworkers manage to both participate and observe without going native? We just settle in and adjust. First we take time out for recreation: read, eat, sleep, photograph, sketch, swim, make a ritual out of mundane activities such as cooking or bathing, listening to the radio, write letters. Visitors—fellow anthropologists, friends, government authorities—are successful distractions. (Virtually no ethnographers actually describe personal visitors in their monographs; some do not even mention spouses or families who lived with them in the field.)[141]

When coping weakens, distracting symptoms appear. Boredom is a fine example: it substitutes for anxiety and depression but is still a terrible threat to the integrity of one's data.[142] Then there are affect-deadeners. Alcohol, especially for older generations of anthropologists who did not have psychotropic drugs, relieved boredom, anxiety, depression, anger, guilt. Nowadays marijuana, tranquilizers, and antidepressants may be used. Still, as with coping devices in any circumstance, creativity can be preserved as well as damaged by these chemical defenses. One only hopes that these defenses do not lead to more guilt and more anxiety and then a blowout.

Sometimes we need a longer respite, appropriately enough called the "field break," by a trip to the patrol post or a town for a few days. (These interludes remind us we can escape from realities natives cannot.)

These experiences, we emphasize, are part of fieldwork. But they are usually ignored in ethnographic reports. Anthropology is like surgery; not just anyone can practice it. But in advertising this, let's also tell how we do manage to do it.

The problems raised in this chapter require a clinical training anthropology students do not really receive. Without that, three factors are at risk: the natives, the ethnographer, and the data. Something's got to give if insight is blocked. In our conclusions we shall take up training issues. Our purpose, however, is not to write a textbook of clinical ethnography but only to affirm that one is needed and to urge our colleagues in anthropology to work toward this end.

CHAPTER TWO

Sambia Sexual Culture

H: This chapter introduces the Sambia and their cultural attitudes toward gender and erotics. The title, "Sexual Culture," is meant to indicate our emphasis on erotics; only here, we show structural relationships between types of persons, types of sexual transactions, and fundamental categories of culture that Sambia bring to their encounters with one another. In this sense, the sexual is but one of many domains of culture, such as politics or religion, though it is, of course, highly open to personal meanings and innovations. Sambia, by nature of their emphasis on semen, have made themselves exotic in our eyes; this was not their intention, of course, and the reader should not be unduly distracted by the exoticness of their cultural system. Rather, we hope to provide here, and to a certain extent in the following chapter, the foreground and context whereby readers can place our case studies into the normative framework of Sambia society.

Every anthropologist has certain choices when he or she sets out to write an ethnographic piece. Whether we aim to describe a behavior or belief, an institutional pattern, or something as pervasive as an ethos, these require a cultural environment in which to make sense of them. But still, we have our options: how formal or informal shall the account be? Should we keep the language and entities confined to abstractions, jargon, technical models? What features shall we omit, emphasize, or color through concrete example or personal anecdotes? What time frame do we choose? Past perfect; present tense—as indicated, for instance, by data on social change and worries about ominous or benign implications of the present? Shall we

This chapter was previously published in a slightly different form in G. Herdt, ed., *Ritualized Homosexuality in Melanesia* (Berkeley: University of California Press, 1984).

write in the first person singular, or plural; allow more empathy through use of the active voice? Do we need tables, diagrams, maps and charts? How much literature should be reviewed to keep our colleagues admiring or quiet? Who is our audience? Do we invite them into our accounts or keep them in the shadows? What vision of the anthropologic enterprise is drawn on, hinted at, or promoted?[1] Each time I write on Sambia these questions buzz through me, and I must make choices accordingly.

This chapter is a more or less conventional ethnographic sketch. It outlines Sambia culture, and is, in the trade, a "set piece" that summarizes more detailed accounts to be found elsewhere.[2] I, the author, am virtually invisible from the scene, in keeping with respectable ethnographic tradition. (Multiply this chapter by a few factors— add chapter titles like "kinship," "religion," "ecology"—and you have "the ethnography," a recipe that still sells). The contrast between this chapter and the following case studies are like the difference between a skeleton and its flesh. Yet each type of account needs the other, is incomplete when taken alone. And the difference between them bears as much on ethnographic styles and methods as on theories of interpreting ethnography and culture.[3]

Sambia are a fringe-area Highlands people. They inhabit isolated ranges of the southern part of the Eastern Highlands near the Papuan border. Their high forest territory is vast, while the population (around 2300) is small, with population density between five and ten people per square mile. Historically, they migrated from the Papuan hinterland around Menyama about two centuries ago. Myth and legend relate that they fled after a great war. They share in cognate cultural traditions with other Anga tribes in the area, such as the Baruya (Godelier 1986), with whom they also warred and traded. But Sambia have also been influenced by Eastern Highlands groups, especially the Fore (Lindenbaum 1979), so their society and culture embody and reflect influences and transformations of imported patterns from both Papua and the Highlands.

Social organization and economy revolve around small sedentary hamlets built atop high mountain ridges for defense. Gardening and hunting are the main economic pursuits. Sweet potatoes and taro are the chief staples. Women do most garden work. Men do all hunting, primarily for possum, cassowary, birds, and eels. Pigs are few and are of little ceremonial importance. Descent is ideally organized on the basis of patriliny. Postmarital residence is patrivirilocal, so males grow up in their father's hamlet, inherit his land, and reside there. Marriage is by infant betrothal or sister exchange; bride-wealth was introduced only in the mid-1970s. Some men, especially senior leaders, have several wives. All marriage is arranged by elders, women being traded between exogamous clans, which tend to be internally organized as an extended family. Inside hamlets, nuclear (or polygamous) families live together in small separate huts; but there are also one or two men's houses wherein all initiated, unmarried males live. The hamlet tends to function as a corporate group in matters of warfare, subsistence activities, marriage, ritual, and dispute settlements.

Sambia society is comprised of six different population clusters of hamlets in adjacent but separate river valleys. These population clusters are divided, in turn, into subgroups (phratries) believed related by ancestry, ritual, and common geographic origin. Each phratry has between two and six hamlets, situated on ridges often within sight of one another. These local hamlet groups, known as confederacies,* intermarry and engage in joint ritual initiations every three or four years. But they sometimes fight among themselves. Warfare has indeed been rife throughout the entire Highlands Anga area, taking two forms: intertribal war raids to kill and loot; and intratribal bow fights designed to bluster and get revenge for perceived wrongs. In other words, within the Sambia Valley, my fieldwork site, hamlets have intermarried, initiated, and fought—sociopolitical dynamics of the behavioral environment that are crucial for understanding social and sexual life.

Relationships between the sexes are highly polarized. One sees this polarization in virtually every social domain. A strict division of labor and ritual taboos forbids men and women from doing each other's tasks in hunting and gardening. Women are responsible for food preparation and child care. Authority rests in the hands of elders and war leaders. Men are in charge of public affairs. The hamlet itself is divided into male and female spaces and paths tabooed to the opposite sex after initiation. Men's rhetoric disparages older married women as oversexed or lecherous and younger women as prudish or shy. Men fear being contaminated and sapped of their strength (*jerungdu*) by marriageable women.

Furthermore, male/female sexual relationships are generally antagonistic, and many marital histories reveal arguments, fights, jealousies, sorcery fears, some wifebeating, and even suicide attempts. Wives (much more than female kin) are stigmatized as inferior, as

---

*Confederacy here marks the same social unit as "parish" and "subtribe" in other New Guineast typologies.

polluting and depleting to men, because of their menstrual and vaginal fluids. Sexual intercourse is supposed to be spaced to avoid depletion and premature aging or death. (Couples may have sex every three to five days, or as infrequently as once every two or three weeks, depending on their ages, length of marriage, personalities, etc.) Prolonged postpartum taboos prohibit couples from engaging in coitus for up to two and a half years following the birth of a child. These generalizations indicate trends: but Sambia are polarized compared even with other Highlands groups (Langness 1967; reviewed in Herdt and Poole 1982).

How do Sambia understand the nature and functioning of the sexes? Male is the socially preferred and valued sex. Female is perceived by men as inferior, except reproductively. Infants are assigned either to the male, female, or hermaphroditic sex, and sex-typing of behaviors and gender traits is rigid from childhood on. Females, however, are believed to mature naturally, without external aids, for their bodies contain a menstrual blood organ (*tingu*) that hastens physical and mental development, puberty, and eventually menarche, the key sign a woman is ready for marriage and procreation. (Menarche occurs late in New Guinea and is now between ages sixteen and nineteen for Sambia.) At menarche a woman is initiated in secret ceremonies in the menstrual hut forbidden to all males (see Godelier 1986:74 ff.). Males, by contrast, do not naturally mature as fast or as competently. Womb blood and maternal care not only hold them back but endanger their health. Males cannot reach puberty or other secondary sex-traits (e.g., facial hair, mature penis) without semen; their bodies, their semen organs (*keriku-keriku*), do not internally produce semen, Sambia believe. Therefore men require inseminations and magical ritual treatments over many years to catch up with females and become strong, manly men (for details, see Herdt 1980, 1981, 1982a, 1982b).

Male development and masculinization after childhood are the responsibility of the men's secret cult and its initiation system. This cult is organized and perpetuated by the confederacy of hamlets. Boys are initiated at seven to ten years of age, when they are separated from their mothers, natal households, older sisters, and younger siblings. Thereafter, they must avoid all females for many years while living in the men's house. Avoidance taboos are rigidly enforced with shaming, beatings, and ultimately death (the last used to keep boys from revealing ritual secrets). Males undergo six initiations in all over the next ten or fifteen years. First initiation (*moku*) graduates are called *choowinuku;* second-stage initiation (*imbutu*) occurs between ages eleven and thirteen; and third-stage initiation (*ipmangwi*), bachelor-hood puberty rites, is for youths fourteen to sixteen years of age. These initiations are all done in sequence on large groups of agemate boys, who are from neighboring hamlets, thus making them members of a regional cohort. Initiates also become members of a warriorhood, which as local units are responsible for defending their own hamlets. Fourth-stage initiation (*nuposha*) may occur any time afterward. It is a public marriage ceremony associated with secret male rites and sexual teachings for individual youths to whom a woman has been assigned for their marriage. But genital intercourse does not yet occur between the couple. Fifth-stage initiation (*taiketnyi*) occurs when a man's wife has her menarche. The bride then has her secret initiation in the menstrual hut. Afterward, the couple can engage in coitus. The final, sixth-stage initiation (*moondangu*), is held when a man's wife bears her first child. She then undergoes a final women's secret ceremony too. Two children bring full adult manhood (*aatmwunu*) for males and personhood for both sexes.

The men's secret cult is ideally organized as a social hierarchical system according to ritual rank. Initiates are lumped into ritual categories: *kuwatni'u* is a category term for first- and second-stage prepubescent initiates (who may also be referred to as *choowinuku* or *imbutnuku,* ritual-grade titles); *ipmangwi* (or *moongenyu,* "new bamboo") bachelors are third-stage initiates of higher adolescent status. Pubescent bachelors dominate prepubescent initiates; older youths and young married men dominate them; elders are seen as politically and spiritually superior to everyone (Herdt 1982b). War leaders and shamans lead in fights and healing ceremonies, respectively. There is nothing unique about this ritual system, for many similar forms can be found in Eastern Highlands (e.g., Read 1952), Papuan Gulf (e.g., Williams 1936), and Telefomin (e.g., Barth 1975) societies. What is special, and what links Sambia and their Anga neighbors with Papuan lowland systems (e.g., Keraki, Kiwai Island, Marind-anim), is the widescale institutionalization of age-structured homosexual activities (Herdt 1984).

Sambia practice secret homosexual fellatio, which is taught and instituted in first-stage initiation. Boys learn to ingest semen from older youths through oral sexual contacts. First- and second-stage initiates may only serve as fellators; they are forbidden to reverse erotic roles with older partners. Third-stage pubescent bachelors and older youths thus act as fellateds, inseminating prepubescent boys. All males pass through both erotic stages, being first fellators, then fellated: there are no exceptions since all Sambia males are initiated and pressured to engage in homoerotic insemination.

The symbolism of the first homosexual teaching in initiation is elaborate and rich; the meaning of fellatio is related to secret bamboo flutes, and ritual equations are made between flutes, penis, and mother's breast, as between semen and breast milk (see Herdt 1982a). Boys must drink semen to grow big and strong. At third-stage initiation, bachelors may experience personal difficulty in making the erotic switch in roles (see chapter 4). Thereafter, they may continue having oral sex with boys until they father children. Essentially, youths pass from an exclusively homosexual behavioral period to a briefer bisexual period, during which they may have both homosexual and heterosexual contacts in secret, and finally to exclusive heterosexual relationships. Social and sexual inadequacies in masculine personhood are failures to achieve these transitions (see chapter 9).

SUBJECT AND OBJECTS

For the Sambia, who ritualize male obligatory homoerotic practices on a broad scale, it may be said that two forms of sexual behavior characterize their culture and developmental experience. For males, first sexual contacts are secret, transitional, male/male oral sexual behaviors; for adult males and females, the parallel form is initial male/female oral (the woman is fellator) sex in marriage. Later, heterosexual genital contacts occur. To my knowledge, no other form of sexual behavior occurs, including masturbation to orgasm. The rules and norms surrounding these two sexual modes are, in certain respects, both similar and different; I shall describe them below. But in both cases, semen acquisition is an imperative organizing principle of people's social interaction and sexual behavior. Its magical power does things to people, changing and rearranging them, as if it were a generator. They, however, can do little to affect this semen principle: it does not reflect on but merely passes through them as an electrical current through a wire, winding its way into bodies as generator coils for temporary storage. Because it is instrumental to growth, reproduction, and regeneration, semen (and its substitutes) is needed to spark and mature human life. Humans are its objects.

This view may seem upside-down to us, yet it is essential as a rational outcome of the Sambia point of view. By thus beginning with its novelty, we may hope to achieve a better understanding of the relative relationship between heterosexuality and homosexuality, subjects about which we Westerners assume so much. I shall first examine cultural ideas about semen and then study how these ideas influence sociologic types of semen transactions between males and males and males and females. Taken together, these ideas and social transactions form a system of objects of the semen. Though these two perspectives are conceptually distinct, their complementarity suggests how normative goals affect individual social action and the developmental cycle of the group. When we view all of the valuations based on this predicate, we are led to a systemic view of the structuring (but not the experience) of sexual interactions and erotism in Sambia culture.

Semen predicates two different sorts of relationships: *direct sexual transactions* between semen donors and recipients, either on the individual or group level (in the latter sense, I am speaking normatively); and *indirect semen transactions* that affect changes in a third party via the semen recipient, who is believed to serve as a transformer of semen (e.g., father to mother to baby). The concept "transformer" compares with Meigs's (1976) use of "transmitter," in which she argues that a person's body may store or deliver fluids (e.g., blood or semen) or essences to someone else. "Transformer" differs because of another dimension needed, transformation, that is, changing semen into something else, as medieval alchemists were thought to change lead into gold. I shall later disentangle these levels of description and analysis.

Cultural Ideas of Semen Value

Sambia have five main cultural categories of semen valuation. These include erotic play, procreation, growth, strength, and spirituality, all of which are connected with sexual behavior. The metaphoric and analogic uses in rhetoric and imagination of these categories can be found in other domains too (see Herdt 1981). Here, though, I shall explore their social significance for insemination.[4] The study of these categories will involve us in understanding how people (and in some ways, nonhuman entities) are represented as potential semen donors or recipients, transformers, or transmitters of semen value, in Sambia culture. This section is concerned with the cultural level of these concepts.[5]

There are two analytic senses in which I shall use the term "value." First, the anthropologic sense of conventional valuations in a culture: attributed or assumed meanings shared and assigned to people, institutions, and substances. Thus we can speak of the cultural regard for semen and the social esteem with which it thus endows persons and relationships. (There is also a libidinal value, present in conscious and unconscious thought, which will not concern us.)[6] Second, there is the Marxist sense of the value of a commodity, such as gold, which "when impressed upon products, obtains fixity only by reason of their acting and reacting upon each other as quantities of value" (Marx 1977:248).[7] Hence, we can analyze semen as a scarce resource that can be consumed and produced, conserved, invested, or otherwise spent. Persons and relationships may be valuated (as a means to an end) in regard to their status as donors or recipients of the commodity semen.

There are several tacit assumptions underlying the relation between semen information and the categories examined below, and I begin with them. (1) Semen is the most precious human fluid. Because it is believed vital for procreation and growth and is in short supply, semen is more precious than even mother's milk, its closest cultural equivalent. But precious does not necessarily mean powerful: menstrual blood is the logical antithesis of semen; it is dangerous and, in some rituals, is equally as efficacious as semen (Herdt 1982b; cf. Faithorn 1975). (2) Sambia are by character prudish people. (May I refer to them as "prudish lechers"? cf. Meggitt 1964). Semen, other body fluids, and sexuality are sensitive subjects: the data and viewpoints described below took years to assimilate, even though the presentation makes them seem obvious. (3) Sexual pleasure is seen by Sambia only in relation to another person; that is, there is no equivalent to the western category "sex" (used in relation to masturbation, pornography, etc. as an indefinite noun, e.g., "sex is . . . good, bad, fun, boring," etc.). Sex, in the Sambia sense, is only spoken of as: *duvuno* (pushing or penetrating into) a boy's mouth or a woman's vagina; or as the slackening of one's erect penis (lit., *lakelu mulu*, "penis fight") via "his bamboo orifice" (metaphor for boy's mouth) or "her thing down below" (euphemism for vagina). Again, the verb *duvuno* is not used for masturbation and only rarely for wet dreams in which the dream images concern copulating with persons (e.g., interpreted as spirits).[8] (4) When men refer to erotic desire (e.g., "I swallow my saliva [thinking about sex] with him/her") they tend to refer to their sexual outlets as if their alter's orifice (mouth or vagina) were fetishized objects like a commodity: "My penis is hungry" (i.e., they use "food" as a metaphor for their sexual needs). (5) All sexual intercourse may be defined as work (*wumdu*), play (*chemonyi*), or both. For example: it is *wumdu* to produce a baby by copulating with a woman many times; but it is *chemonyi* to copulate promiscuously with a boy once or twice knowing he will not procreate. Insemination is also an action that mediates (e.g., like ritual, *pweiyu*) between work and play, sacred and profane. Let us examine each category in turn.

EROTIC PLAY. When Sambia use *chemonyi* (play) as a noun in relation to sexual intercourse, they normatively refer to sexual release as erotic pleasure.* Semen is expended and orgasm (*imbimboogu*) achieved. I begin with this category not because it is most crucial—Sambia themselves would rank procreation first (Herdt 1981)—but because it is essential for understanding semen valuations and also because anthropologists often ignore erotic motivation as a native category.

The most general cultural attributes of erotic play may be sketched as follows. First, the factor of the sex of one's partner: erotic play symbolically typifies male/male more than male/female erotic contacts. Male/male sexual contacts are culturally defined as behaviorally promiscuous. Male/female contacts, normative only in marriage, are viewed (unless adulterous) as steady transactions aimed toward procreation. Erotic play is of course an aspect of all male/female contacts, but it is not their most important one. *Exclusive* sexual access to a person seems inversely related to erotic play: a man's wife, as his sexual property, as Sambia see it, is less exciting than a boy or woman taken at first (i.e., as a virgin), or only once, on the sly. Age is a contributing factor here: sexual partners are perceived as having more "heat" and being more exciting the younger they are. A second factor is reciprocity: the more asymmetrical the sexual partners (youth/boy), the more erotic play seems to culturally define their contact. (By contrast, I have argued elsewhere that the husband/wife dyad is the most symmetrical relationship in Sambia culture; see Herdt 1982b.) Third, sexual constancy, that is, greater frequency of sexual contacts, generally transforms sexual contacts from erotic play into something else. Husband/wife contacts are the most constant in Sambia sexual life.

Erotic play may be defined also according to the social purpose of insemination. Erotic pleasure is attached to male/male and male/

---

*There is no marked category for erotic play as such: it is signified in ideology and social intercourse by *chemonyi*, "orgasm," and several conditions of sexual excitement (e.g., erection). "Sexual" has a wide range of connotations in English; *erotic*, however, refers specifically to that which stimulates sexual desire, psychophysiologic arousal, so I prefer "erotic" in this usage.

female sexual contacts and to both oral and vaginal intercourse.* But only heterosexual genital contacts result in procreation; all other sexual contacts fulfill other quasi-reproductive functions (e.g., growth of spouse) or are for erotic play. Since homosexual fellatio cannot result in reproduction (marriage consummation), it becomes a demonstration of a fellated's psychosocial maturity, that is, of his power to masculinize a boy. But this valuation is significant only for donors: the boy-recipients value semen for their own growth. What donors value also is the fellator's mouth as a sexual outlet: the social purpose is sexual release.

Erotic play may be defined, lastly, according to the flow of a scarce commodity. Semen is viewed as a very scarce resource by Sambia, for, in reproduction, it is believed instrumental from conception to adulthood. It takes many inseminations to procreate: large expenditures of time, energy, semen. From this viewpoint, all male/female contacts may be construed as benefiting procreation (as we shall see next). Homoerotic play unevenly fits this paradigm. It is, after all, play, not work: procreative work is defined as producing babies. So how do they benefit the donor? Essentially, homoerotic play is culturally defined as an unequal exchange of commodities: recipients acquire semen, donors get sexual services. This exchange is unequal because (as Sambia see it) a man's semen is being depleted, but he gets only erotic pleasure in return ("which is insubstantial"). Homoerotic activity thus creates a dilemma for bachelors, which is perhaps why some engage in it less frequently as they approach marriage. Homoerotic play is, however, less depleting than heterosexual intercourse (work) which is, in part, why bachelors usually do not replenish the semen lost during their early homosexual activities.

PROCREATION. Procreation is defined as genital-to-genital heterosexual contacts that lead to the birth of offspring. Sambia regard vaginal intercourse as primarily focused on the production of babies. Oral insemination prepares a wife's body for making babies by strengthening her as well as by precipitating her menarche (if she has not already attained it). Fellatio also prepares her for lactation by semen being transformed into breast milk. Oral sexual contacts are not believed to make babies in anyone; only vaginal intercourse does that.

---

*All sexual contacts are symbolically defined by the norm of penetration and ejaculation into an insertee's mouth (initiate or woman) or vagina, insemination resulting from (the belief that) the full seminal emission ingested/absorbed by the recipient's body (mouth or vagina as entrance).

All heterosexual genital intercourse contributes directly to procreation in one's marriage, and *all* sexual contacts may be viewed as contributing directly to the recipients' procreative competence (wife or boy-fellator) or reproduction (wife).*

Procreation is jurally defined as resulting from genital-to-genital sexual contacts between formally married husband and wife. Since heterosexual contact is not morally or jurally allowed outside of marriage, privilege of sexual access to a woman's body is restricted by marriage; exclusive sexual rights belong to her husband. Likewise, exclusive access to a husband's body and semen, after birth of their first child, is his wife's right (which view is a key argument women use to resist polygyny). Traditionally, only infant betrothal and bride-service marriage (which was rare) required the transfer of goods or services to the donors bestowing a wife. Infant betrothal, though, required meat and small food prestations only, whereas bride-service required more wealth, in addition to the bridegroom's years-long work for his prospective affines. Sister exchange requires no exchange other than that of the women. Since infant betrothal is preferred and sister exchange marriages far outnumber those of bride-service, marriage transactions are not much related to bride-wealth in its usual anthropologic sense (cf. Collier and Rosaldo 1981).

Genital-to-genital intercourse creates a fetus by successively injecting semen into a woman's womb. After initial oral sexual contacts, a woman's body is viewed as ready to procreate. One instance of vaginal intercourse does not a fetus make: Sambia have no notion of conception in our western scientific sense. The womb is the container and transformer of semen. It changes semen into fetal tissue: primarily bone and skin but also muscle and internal organs. The semen coagulates inside the birth sac; this "biologic" process is central to fetal development, and its imagery is important in social thought (Herdt 1981:167–172 ff.). Womb and umbilical blood also become circulatory blood in the fetus; they do not produce any other parts of the child, which result only from semen. Social ideology thus defines procreation as productive work (not erotic play) in two senses: it is hard work to feed enough semen into a woman's womb to create a fetus; and it is hard work for the woman's body to change this semen into a fetus, sapping her own blood and carrying the child in her body for so long.

Blood and semen also differentially contribute to the sex of the offspring and his or her gender differentiation. First, both parents can

---

*Oral heterosexual contacts indirectly help procreation; see below under section on "growth."

magically influence the fetus's sex by ingesting various plants. They do this both because Sambia ideally prefer a boy as the firstborn and because they want to make the infant more attractive. Second, it takes more semen to create a girl than a boy. Two other beliefs explain why, and they pertain to the procreative/economic productive capacities of males versus females (i.e., in social reproduction). The most important is that females do more hard work (i.e., garden work) all the time; therefore, the female fetus pulls more semen from the mother to make itself. (A magical elaboration of this idea is that since females think about garden work constantly, their fetal thought anticipates and drains more semen strength in preparation.) The other belief is that a female fetus has a *tingu* (menstrual-blood organ), which makes the mother's vagina hot and therefore drains off more semen from the father during sexual contacts that create the fetus. During womb life, the sexes receive blood in differential amounts too. Essentially, girls have some of their mother's menstrual blood transmitted to their own menstrual-blood organs *in utero.* Later, during postnatal growth, this blood stimulates girls' psychobiologic feminization (sexual and gender differentiation). Boys, by contrast, have no blood transmitted to their inactive *tingus.* Nor do they receive any of their father's semen for use in their own semen organs: father's semen in both sexes merely creates fetal tissue. (Mystical aspects of these fetal processes are described below.)

Marriage is fully consummated after the birth of a child. Procreation results in final but distinct initiation ceremonies for the husband-father and wife-mother alike. The new father and his clan bestow a meat prestation on the wife's cognatic kin, especially patrilateral female kin, and her ritual sponsor, in public village ceremonies. Because procreation defines full adulthood for men and women, childless adults are not perceived as full persons. Nonetheless, all childlessness in marriage is attributed to barrenness in the woman or contraceptive sorcery by other men (usually thought to be envious fellow villagers who wanted the woman for themselves). Sambia men dogmatically deny the possibility of sterility in a husband (see also Read 1955); indeed, such is never discussed in social discourse, and the only category for sterility is "barren woman" (*kwoliku*). Childlessness is thus an acceptable reason for taking a second wife but not for divorce. Once a marriage is consummated, it is contracted for life; a woman is rarely taken back by the donor; when warfare occurs, a woman's ties with her natal group (i.e., enemies) are severed; divorce is thus extremely rare and usually instigated by a husband over his wife's perceived adultery; their children become jural members of the father's clan; and so only death breaks the marital bond.

GROWTH. Sambia believe that biologic growth in humans results from ingesting semen and equivalent substances (mother's milk, pandanus nuts). Sexual intercourse for growth is described as: *pinu pungoog-lumonjapi* ("pushing" to "grow" him/her, where *pinu* is an alternate verbal form of *duvuno*). This idiomatic form may be applied to both male/male and male/female sexual contacts.

The value of semen for human growth comes in successive stages, which differ according to the mode of semen transmission and one's sex. Initial growth for every fetus occurs through semen accumulations in the mother's womb. Postnatal growth in babies results mainly from breat-feeding. A woman's body is again treated as a biologic transformer of semen in this regard: a man's inseminations (especially oral) amass in and are transformed by his wife's breasts into mother's milk (*nu-tokeno*, breast food). After weaning, growth is aided by eating pandanus nuts, which are seasonal but are treated as nearly equal nourishment to that of mother's milk. (The productive source of this nut food is one's father's trees and his hard work in tending and scaling to procure the nuts.) Meat fed to children also contributes smaller increments to growth. Following weaning, though, girls continue to grow without further aids, whereas boys falter, staying weak and puny.

Male growth after weaning comes mostly from homosexual inseminations following initiation. This semen-nourishment form is male *monjapi'u*,* which men liken to breast-feeding (Herdt 1981: 234–236). Oral sexual contacts feed semen into a boy's body, distributing semen to his maturing skin, bones, skull and producing changes toward masculinization (eventuating in puberty). The bulk of ingested semen goes to the boy's semen organ, where it accumulates as a pool. This pool is drawn on after puberty for two purposes: it produces pubescent secondary sex-traits, especially muscle, body hair, and a mature penis; and it provides semen for later sexual contacts. (The first sign of surplus semen in the body comes from wet dreams.)

Girls require and are permitted no inseminations until marriage. Postmarital oral sexual contacts in cases of marriage before menarche provide a young wife's body with semen to stimulate the final

---

*Shortened by men from *pinu pungooglumonjapi*.

changes necessary for childbearing. Men also argue, as noted above, that women need semen to create breast milk. (Some women dispute these views and argue that a woman's body naturally creates milk; however, other women disagree).

In sum, semen creates biologic growth directly in initiates and wives through sexual contact, primarily fellatio, whereas it creates growth indirectly in fetus and newborn through being transformed by a woman's body into fetal tissue and milk. For spouses, then, growth and procreation are concepts that refer to different aspects of the same sexual contacts. For the offspring, as third-party semen recipient, growth is vital after birth, and long postpartum taboos prohibit marital sexual intercourse for fear the infant will be harmed (be stunted or ugly, an outcome that would shame the parents, especially the father, who would be viewed as lacking sexual restraint). In homoerotic activity, men offer boys the normative goal that semen "grows" them. But from the donor's standpoint, though initiates' growth does provide vicarious long-term confirmation of the fellated's manhood, a fellator's growth is not of direct importance to a bachelor's personhood. Rather, homoerotic play takes precedence as the fellated's motive; the boy's growth is a latent social function of the bachelor's behavior (and is, I think, often a rationalization on the men's part).

STRENGTH. Strength (*jerungdu*) is a key concept in Sambia culture; we shall here examine only its implications for semen transmission and thereby human maturation (Herdt 1987c).

Strength is absolutely derived from semen and its equivalents: mother's milk and pandanus nuts. But more than those latter substances, semen masculinizes a male's body; there is no substitute for it. Unlike procreation or growth valuations, strength can be obtained directly only through semen. In Sambia thought, there is a tendency to play down strength and stress growth as characteristic of the breast-feeding relationship. Suckling milk makes a baby grow, but it is much less associated with strengthening it. Semen in the womb forms the skeletal fetus; nursing helps create the baby's teeth, the hardening of its skin and skull. But milk is more for growth. The strong results of milk, Sambia believe, are transformations of semen: mother ingests semen, which her breasts convert into milk. The strong part of milk is also more crucial for male infants, but it alone will not masculinize them. Thus, strength is not intrinsically produced but is rather derived from the mother/infant relationship, itself a product of marriage. In male subjectivity, however, strength is a transactional prod-

uct that makes use of the father's secret sexual acquisition of semen
from other men, which he feeds to his wife, whose body, in turn, has
a natural capacity to store the fluid and turn it into breast food that
strengthens and matures the infant.

As with growth, a father can indirectly add small amounts of
strength over the years following weaning by providing meat and
pandanus nuts to children. Cassowary meat, too, which may be eaten
only by males, has fat (*moo-nugu*) that sometimes is treated as a sec-
ond-rate semen equivalent (Herdt 1981: 110). (Other kinds of fat, e.g.,
from pigs or eels, are never likened to semen.) But these are small
increments.

If one follows the semen cycle, we see a chain of links in which
men strengthen people: husband strengthens wife through initial fellatio; father strengthens baby through mother's milk; bachelor
strengthens initiate through fellatio. Symbolically, homosexual fellatio provides the key ritualized strengthening of boys' postpartum
bodies. As I have emphasized elsewhere (Herdt 1981, 1982a), male
insemination is chiefly seen as making a boy grow, the perceived outcome of which is strength. Culturally, the act of feeding/inseminating
is equivalent to the verbal category *monjapi'u*, male nursing, the so-
cial/perceptual outcome of which is the state of being *jerungdu*, as
seen in both its physical and psychosocial manifestations: large size,
attractiveness, valor, forceful speech, sexual potency, and many social achievements, including progeny.

There is another secret source of strength that is important in male
thought and that concerns the nonhuman sources for replenishing semen expended in sexual intercourse. Analytically, this semen valuation might be treated as separate from the "strength" concept because of its ontogenetic status in the male life cycle (adults give semen
away and then must replace it to stay strong). But Sambia do not
think of the matter in this way, for this replenishment is seen simply
as a further extension of strength-building. Yet, since this replenishment practice is learned later in ritual life and comes from trees, not
men, we shall here examine it as an auxiliary strengthening process.

In semen transactions, one person's loss is another's gain: semen,
which embodies strength, depletes the donor, whose strength therefore diminishes. Fear of semen depletion is an important theme in
male ritual discourse and ideology. (It is registered, too, in individual
gender aberrations [Herdt 1980]). Concern with too frequent semen
loss inhibits initial homosexual contacts, bachelors being cautioned
to go easy. (Here, again, fellateds and fellators are at odds.) Yet bachelors' fears are not great; and the early use of ritual mechanisms for

semen replenishment in fellateds is played down. Among married men, the situation is different. A key pragmatic focus of fifth- and sixth-stage initiation ceremonies is teaching about secret ingestion of white milk-sap from trees, which is believed to replace semen lost to women. (Pandanus nuts are another semen replacement, though of less importance because they are not always available.) This milk-sap comes from several forest trees and vines, and the sap is referred to as *iaamoonaalyu*, "tree mother's milk."

Trees are, in general, regarded as if they and their products were female, for example, as with pandanus trees. Myth also genderizes them this way (Herdt 1981). There seems little doubt that the imagery and symbolization of the adult man's semen replenishment is not, then, symbolic insemination but rather that of symbolic breastfeeding. This interpretation is confirmed by men's drinking sap from long aerial roots of pandanus nut trees: the trees are ritually referred to as "females," and the roots are likened to woman's breasts. We see, therefore, that semen comes at first from homosexual fellatio, later to be replaced by milk-sap (and, to a lesser extent, by pandanus nuts and cassowary fat); and semen, in turn, is transformed into milk and fetal tissue by women. At bottom, male ideology seems to postulate that these forest trees create *new* semen.

SPIRITUALITY. The final category of semen valuations I shall refer to as spirituality, though it is not a marked category in Sambia culture or language. Spirituality is, in our terms, an animistic composite of both natural and supernatural elements. These elements include most noticeably spirit familiars (*numelyu*) of various sorts, believed to be *transmitted* (not transformed) through semen for males (and through blood for females). The reproduction of spiritual elements in individuals and groups is entirely a social outcome of sexual intercourse over which individuals have little control.

Before describing spirit familiars, two other matters deserve mention. The first is the concept of soul (*koogu*), a spiritual aspect of personhood that is related to sexuality and parenting. There is no clearly formulated theory of the soul's origin in individual development. Some men attribute it only to the father's semen. Others say it is a combination of semen and material in the mother's womb (they do not specify which parts of semen and/or blood). Though the womb is important, some people attribute the birth of a child's soul not to fetal life but to postnatal socialization. Men normatively relate the father's semen to the child's soul in both sexes, especially boys. This ambiguity is no doubt an expression of all persons' normative blood ties to mother and matrilateral kin. Yet, since the soul survives death and becomes a ghost, forest spirit (big men), or hamlet spirit (prominent women) haunting its clan's territory, its patrilineal origin and after-life influence seem clear in sociopolitical organization. The skull and bones of the deceased also become powerful weapons in sorcery and are most efficacious when used by biologic kinsmen, sons especially. In both cases—souls and bones—spiritual essences of semen are thought to survive death. The other concept is "thought" or *koontu*, which I gloss as personhood. "Thought" is the totality of one's ex-perience, beliefs, and knowledge. Personhood is mainly a product of social training; its relation to body substance and biologic inheri-tance is less certain. Socialization is its chief source, however, and this means that both mother and father influence personhood.

Without question the most significant semen valuation for spirit-uality is the child's inheritance of spirit familiars. Transmission of familiars is ideologically clear and sex-linked. Boys inherit only their father's familiars via his semen. Girls inherit their mother's familiars through her blood. (Mother's milk, a semen derivative, is ignored in this domain.) Genealogic inheritance of clan familiars (i.e., totems) among males seems to derive from the semen that creates a son's body tissue. Later, males acquire other familiars attracted to them through ritual ceremonies: the nature of this attraction again implies that father's semen is instrumental. Shamanic familiars, transmitted through semen from father to son in the mother's womb, is a clear case of necessary patrilineal inheritance required for legitimate per-formance of the shamanic role (Herdt 1977), though some women shamans claim inheritance of father's familiars. Other familiars, both personal and clan-related, ensure longevity, spiritual protection, or strength. Male ideology generally denies women such blessings from their natal clan familiars. Men may have their familiars stolen un-wittingly by male children, which leads to sickness or premature death. Homosexual inseminations do not transmit familiars to semen recip-ients (cf. Schieffelin 1976, 1977). Finally, men's ingestion of milk-sap from trees is consistent with the perpetuation of their clan familiars (though this is not fully conscious in Sambia thought).

Semen Value in Social Transactions

Who may and should have sexual intercourse with what categories of persons in Sambia society? What are the principles of these social transactions? In this section I examine social action in relation to the cultural ideas of semen valuation already described. The sociology of semen transactions involves two viewpoints. First, there are direct semen transactions between persons resulting from sexual intercourse. Second, there are indirect semen transactions with a third party believed to occur by transforming semen into something else by a second party; whether the source of semen is human or nonhuman (i.e., trees), though the semen transformers are always humans. A subcategory of indirect inseminations may be seen as delayed exchanges between social groups, semen being returned to donor groups via former recipients in the subsequent generation. I shall study each of these types in turn.

DIRECT SEMEN TRANSACTIONS. All sexual contacts are restricted by exogamous taboos and social norms. Sexual contacts are permissible only between unrelated people; that is, those related through common cognatic links, especially agnates, are forbidden sexual partners. Marriage should be arranged between different clans, preferably of different villages. Statistically, though, up to fifty percent of all marriages are contracted within certain hamlets; father's sister's daughter marriage is normatively permitted in delayed-exchange marriage contracts; and mother's brother's daughter marriage, though frowned on, occurs rarely, when no alternate wife can be found (Herdt 1981). Homosexual contacts are likewise prohibited between all clansmen, matrilateral kin, age-mates, and with ritual sponsors. (Homosexual infractions occur, however, as between matrilateral cross-cousins or distant kin not normally encountered, though these are unusual.) Male initiates' ritual sponsors are called "mother's brother," a social title, since only some sponsors are actual or classificatory mother's brother. Nonetheless a boy's sponsor becomes, in effect, a pseudokinsman who combines both maternal and paternal attributes, making it very wrong for any sexual contact to occur between them. In general, all sexual contacts are highly regulated and tend to occur with people of other hamlets (who are potential or real enemies), so sexual contacts distinguish kin from nonkin and friendly from hostile persons.

In direct sexual transactions, all the above cultural ideas of semen value come into play, but the domain of erotic play is especially important. Erotic play is a social motive and goal that applies mainly to adult men. Their motive for erotic play is orgasm. Boy-fellators never have orgasms in homoerotic play. And men deny, in general, that women experience orgasm, though they believe women are lascivious and that some enjoy sexual play.

Men's enjoyment of erotic play changes through the life cycle. Some older boy-fellators do experience vicarious erotic pleasure from homosexual fellatio, as indicated by their reports (near puberty) of their own erections while fellating a bachelor, or by certain feelings or body sensations during fellation. Bachelors (fellateds) engage in homoerotic play to (in local idiom) "straighten their penises," that is, to reduce sexual tension/frustration, or to "feel *ilaiyu*" (here meaning pleasure) from orgasm. Men get erotic pleasure from copulating with their wives, first through fellatio, and then in genital-to-genital intercourse, which most men favor over fellatio. To repeat: male/female oral sexual contacts, like those with boys, are regarded more as erotic play.

Male social ideology defines both homoerotic and heteroerotic play as transactions in which the older male is *always* the inseminator. No role reversals are ever situationally permitted. The older male is viewed as the socially active party who should control the behavior interchanges that lead to the insemination. A man's control over sexual contacts is established by the social norms regulating the behavioral conditions of sexual intercourse. Men are physically bigger than boys and most women. During intercourse the man either stands over his fellator (who kneels) or lies on top of his wife (in the missionary position), methods that allow a man instant freedom to withdraw from body contact at will. Men are also usually years older than their insertees, either boys or women (even though, curiously, men regard younger wives as of like age and maturity; see Herdt 1981:177, 181). Again, these interactions are defined as asymmetric: women and boys get semen, men get erotic pleasure. Most men are (consciously) uninterested in the erotic arousal of either boys or women, so direct sexual transactions emphasize the sexual excitement of the inserter.

In spite of the men's view, the concept "erotic play" admits of some social reciprocity between all sexual partners. Men recognize that women have erotic interests; for instance, sexually experienced women are rhetorically described as lascivious harlots consumed by insatiable erotic appetites (Herdt 1981:187). Perhaps this dogma is the men's response to knowing that women favor certain men over others as mates. Men also know that boys joke about fellatio among themselves and that initiates favor some bachelors over others in regard to the amount and taste of their semen.[9] Bachelors likewise favor certain boys over others: those who are more attractive to them are either more or less sexually aggressive and/or willing to perform fellatio. These reciprocal aspects thus underscore the frame of play, and they are not found in notions of sex for procreation, growth, strength, or spirituality, all of which are passive outcomes of insemination.

Since semen is highly valued as a means to valuable social ends—personal strength, marriage, offspring, personhood—it should be conserved and wisely spent. Men assume that women and boys *desire their semen* for those social ends; no other motive is searched for in understanding why insertees engage in sexual intercourse. (*We* know the situation is more complex: for instance, boys must at first be coerced into fellatio; but men also know this.) The seeming personal conflict on men's part, at least in homoerotic contacts, is that *they get only sexual release in return for their semen.* They recognize this in idioms that depict the penis as having a mind of its own: for example, "that no good man down there [penis] gets up and we follow its nose" (euphemism for glans penis). Meaning: men inseminate from sexual impulse, almost against their will. Here, then, we may see a perceived conflict between private impulses and rational norms.

This conflict is felt in two other ways. First, women are prized as sexual outlets more than boys. Women are *owned:* this ownership is a contributing dynamic to the sexual excitement of Sambia men. Male/female relationships are, in general, filled with more power than are male/male contacts, for heterosexuality is more highly regulated. Sexually, women are also more powerful, for they can contaminate as well as deplete; and women deplete semen more than do boys. Moreover, sexual impulses leading to adultery are a tremendous social problem in Sambia society (see below). Second, when orgasm occurs it is treated as being beyond conscious control. Wet dreams are the best example.[10] For women, breast-feeding may also apply: some women report that they experience *imbimboogu,* which they liken to orgasm, when feeding, though it is not clear yet what this social labelling of their experience means (see chapter 6). All these points support the conclusion that individual sexual impulses are stronger than the need for semen constraint in heterosexual versus homosexual contacts. They also suggest that Sambia men are later motivated more toward heterosexual relationships.

Underlying this conflict is the fact that sex for erotic play is the only sexual mode that produces no social advantage to the semen donor. Because all ejaculation is debilitating and semen is a male's most valuable resource, all sexual contacts are viewed as a "careful metering of semen" (Gell 1975:252). Seen this way, erotic play represents what Gell (1975) refers to as a "nemesis of reproductivity": it makes no sense in the scheme of things, even though it is personally pleasurable. All other categories of direct sexual transactions may be defined as work, not play, for this reason: like other forms of work (e.g., gardening), sex for procreation, growth, and so forth produces social products. One's semen is spent to reproduce heirs and perpetuate one's clan. With this view in mind I will now contrast other cultural ideas pertaining to heterosexual and homosexual contacts.

The idea of procreation applies only to male/female sexual contacts. In native theory all heterosexual contacts, oral or vaginal, contribute to a woman's reproductive competence. In practice, however, only early marital contacts are treated this way: oral sex is infrequent after a woman bears children. My impression is that both men and women in later years prefer genital-to-genital contact (and I think most women always prefer vaginal sex). Though homosexual transactions are not procreative (but cf. individual boys' fears of becoming pregnant [Herdt 1981] and similar beliefs about male pregnancy elsewhere [Meigs 1976; Williams 1936]), semen in boys does assist in their reaching reproductive competence as adults.

The concepts of growth and strength are applied to both homosexual and heterosexual transactions. In theory, boy-fellators as semen recipients use sexual contact first to grow and then to get strong. Until third-stage initiation this norm holds; youths are thereafter accorded biologic maturity and may no longer serve as insertees. (By definition, a Sambia man who sought semen from another male would be terribly stigmatized as unmanly; and to do so with a boy—pederastic fellatio—would be morally unconscionable; see chapter 9.) Growth and strength apply differentially to women as semen recipients. Essentially, all heterosexual fellatio makes a woman grow and strengthens her until she is a mother. Later oral sex does not make a woman grow, for she is viewed as biologically mature. It does replenish her strength, however; a sort of perpetual fountain-of-youth men must give up after bachelorhood. Indeed, men complain that women are healthier and outlive them because of this ready source of orally ingested strength. (In this sense, a wife is like a boy-fellator.) Vaginal sex is generally believed to contribute neither growth nor strength to a woman: instead, indirectly, a man's semen creates and strengthens fetus and infant.

Finally, the concept of spirituality applies unequally to direct sexual transactions. No transmission of spirit familiars occurs between males and females. None is imparted to one's wife: she is simply *one* source of the transmission of soul and familiars to one's offspring. Again, men believe that only sons inherit father's familiars (either indirectly, through semen via mother, or directly, through cult ceremonies that call forth one's father's familiars after his death). A daughter's familiars come only from her mother; but her soul is linked (the notion is vague) to her father and his clan territory, though not irrevocably.[11] Moreover, there is absolutely no sense that a boy-fellator acquires his familiars from any bachelor-fellated; but the idea is neither here nor there, since Sambia never consider the possibility.[12] Conceptually, though, we should underline that their folk model of spiritual transmission keeps familiars discreetly in clans and firmly embedded in the genitor's procreative role. Here we see a firm separation between spirituality and sexuality, on the levels both of ideology and social action. The division between spiritual and material reproduction in marriage is especially notable (cf. Tuzin 1982).

There is one other notion, which we may define as spiritual, that involves direct homosexual transactions. *Kwolaalyuwaku:** a multivalent concept referring to masculine decorations and ritual paraphernalia (as a category term), which is also a ritual secret pseudonym for semen. (It is also close to *kweiaalyu-waku,* which literally means "sun's white grease," an alternate for cassowary fat [*kaiouwugu moo-nugu*]). The semantic referent of the semen aspect is esoteric, yet it clearly signifies a collective semen pool. This pool is perceived as the semen contained in the bodies of all men living within neighboring hamlets: it therefore reflects the ritual cult and the confederacy. The idea is that boys have access to this pool, which they can tap into through homosexual insemination, strengthening themselves. Symbolically, then, *kwolaalyuwaku* is a metaphor for the men's collective cult.

But on the individual level, the concept is bidirectional. I was long skeptical of men's statements that it *strengthened themselves* to inseminate many boys. How could this be? Men argue that just as a boy draws strength from numerous men, who deposit their semen in his reserve for future use, so men are kept strong by having their semen safely contained in many boys, who are likened to a sort of magical string of semen depositories for one's substance, spread throughout society. Should a man or any of his semen recipients get sick, other recipients remain strong and healthy. And since recipients harbor parts of one's semen (strength) inside them, so, too, one is kept healthy (in sympathetic-contagious magical thought). A woman lacks this protection: she is not a cult initiate, and her semen comes from only one man, her husband. Nor is a man likewise protected by inseminating women or creating children: the concept is not extended beyond homosexual contacts. Thus, semen not only bestows but maintains

---

Kwol marks male; *aalyu,* water; *waku,* a type of strong betel nut and a cover term for certain decorations. Sometimes the term is shortened to the secret name, *kweiwaku,* which men use explicitly to refer to "the semen of all men."

strength, the only evidence known to me that directly explains why homosexual insemination is felt to be less depleting than that of heterosexuality. In this ritual sense, homosexual practices are placed within a spiritual framework and are opposed to heterosexuality and marriage.

All the above sexual contacts concern normatively appropriate semen transactions between donors and recipients. *Illicit* heterosexual semen transactions (adultery) reveal the social boundary of ideas about exclusive jural claims over a man's semen. All adultery is severely condemned; a man may use violence against a wife suspected of it. Therefore, it is hidden until discovered, when the spouses fight. If a husband is accused of adultery or of wanting to take a second wife, the fight is called *kweikoonmulu*, literally "semen fight." Semen fights entail dreadful cursing and brawls. This adultery can be seen as "stealing another woman's semen," though it involves much more, of course. Accusations of a wife's adultery (which is rarer, for Sambia treat adulterous women harshly) also concern semen in two ways: fears that a husband's penis has been contaminated by intercourse with his wife's vagina after sex with another man (thought to bring him sickness); and questions about the wife's lover's semen contributions to a future child. In sum, adultery reveals that marriage bestows the right of exclusive spousal control over semen and insemination exchange as scarce resources.

What are the social effects of these direct sexual transactions on group relationship? Let us examine the most general latent and manifest functions of sexual contacts in the same generation. First, semen flow mirrors marriage transactions between groups. Semen may only be normatively transacted between persons of groups who can intermarry, that is, homosexual contact is forbidden with matrilineal kin and clansmen. The same clan that donates a wife thus has clansmen who are appropriate homosexual partners (cf. Kelly 1976). Affines of the same generation (e.g., brothers-in-law) are especially appropriate homosexual contacts. The paradigm of this affinal homoerotic bond would be a young man who marries a younger woman and who can inseminate her younger initiate brother, either consanguineal or classificatory wife's brother (cf. Serpenti 1984 and Sørum 1984). This man inseminates his wife to make her grow and strengthen her, and to procreate, and may (along with his fellow clansmen) inseminate her younger brother for erotic play, the effect of which is to help a boy grow and to strengthen him. These sexual transactions would define a man and his clan as semen donors, while his wife and brother-in-law would be recipients. Yet ego's clan is also a wife recipient from his younger homosexual partner's donor clan. This set of social transactions is common in Sambia life.

Second, marital/sexual bonds tend to create closer political ties between unrelated groups. Sambia generally engage in marriage and homosexual contacts with propinquitous groups in the same confederacy. One does not receive or give semen to intertribal enemies. Affinal ties, in particular, create closer political affiliations for mutual defense between and within hamlets. Affinal ties also establish marriage contractual obligations and sentimental bonds that persist in the next generation, influencing alignments among hamlets.

Third, semen metaphorically defines political power: inseminators are more powerful than recipients in virtually every sense. All male persons eventually serve as both direct semen donors and as recipients. All females are always direct recipients or indirect donors—to their offspring—whereas males constitute a category of both direct givers and takers. And their sexual status, of course, flip-flops during the male life cycle. Symbolically, I think, Sambia define the administration of semen as a masculine act, whereas the taking in of semen is a feminine act. One of the manifest functions of the secrecy of homosexual fellatio is to hide from women the shame men feel at having earlier performed in this feminine way (Herdt 1981: ch. 8). A latent function of homosexual secrecy is to rationalize and disguise men's use of boys as a sexual outlet. By the same token, the ritual secret of homosexual growth and strength unites all males as a category against all females. This social link, which also mystifies the nature of male/female relationships, politically reinforces male power and thereby perpetuates the men's ritual cult (Herdt 1982b).

INDIRECT SEMEN TRANSACTIONS. This mode of social transaction is based on the symbolic principle that semen is transmitted to someone whose body transforms it into something else useful to a third party. The paradigm is the nuclear family triad: father→mother→child. The alternative form of indirect insemination views men as replenishing their semen from tree sap, which their bodies turn into semen: tree→man→semen recipient. Having already described direct sexual contacts we can easily outline these semen transformations.

We have seen that sexual intercourse between spouses involves all the cultural meanings of semen value except spirituality. Now when we examine the effects of her husband's semen on her prospective infant, the woman's role as transformer is clarified at two develop-

mental points. First, to repeat, her orally ingested semen is transformed into breast milk. This milk is stored for the infant's nourishment after birth. Subsequent semen from vaginal intercourse is stored
and transformed in the woman, converted by her womb into fetal
tissue, as we saw. Both the intrauterine formation of the child, as well
as its postnatal breast-feeding, are indirect products of the father's
semen.

In this type of indirect transaction there is a subtle application of
cultural beliefs to action. Erotic play occurs between the spouses,
leading to procreation; but the concept is not extended to the transformative outcome, since the father never has sexual intercourse with
his offspring. Indeed the paradigm of sex as work suggests that woman,
as wife/mother, is *the means of production* men need to effect children's adult reproductive competence. Semen is indispensable for reproduction, yet so is a woman's body (breasts and womb). Moreover,
no matter how much the men attempt to claim procreation as solely
of their production, a wife is vital for social reproduction: she not
only gives birth but nourishes and cares for heirs, transforming semen into the strength of clans. She also transmits her husband's spirit
familiars to sons and her own to daughters. Both parents contribute
to the child's personhood or thought, but men believe only they produce its soul. Following weaning, a girl is believed to mature on her
own, but a boy needs more semen for growth and strength. Thus, a
boy indirectly taps the semen pool of his father through homosexual
contacts with other men who substitute, in his father's place, as ritual
semen donors, motivated out of erotic play. The sexual cycle is completed when this son becomes an inseminator, and his sister is traded
for his wife, sister and brother having reached sexual maturity.

The other form of indirect transaction consists in men ingesting
the white tree-saps. It may seem odd, here, to juxtapose this secret
ritual practice with reproduction. But Sambia male ideology treats
tree-sap ingestion as a part of the whole adult cycle of reproduction;
and, in my experience, men directly associate tree-sap drinking as
normal and regular links in a chain of psychosexual activities that
are as much a part of everyday life as their own erotism. Drinking
tree-sap is not actually taught until a man's last initiation, when he
is a new father. Thereafter, men regularly ingest it but always in
abundance after sexual intercourse with their wives. Men are thus
preserving their biologic maleness (semen) and restoring their strength.
Neither erotic play, growth, nor procreation as cultural ideas are applied to contacts with trees. Drinking tree sap simply regenerates semen and preserves health against depletion. So this ritual practice

may be considered a defensive tactic—and the more so because it is secret—yet it is more than that.

Drinking tree-sap also has a latent creative function: creating *new* semen that flows into the societal pool of semen. Sambia men do *not* view it this way: to them, drinking tree-sap merely replaces what they have personally lost. But, besides that, they see their society as a closed system, its resources limited for reasons I shall not here detail; suffice it to say that their religion is animistic and their ethos dominated by warrior values that recognize adulthood as a personal achievement that is, nonetheless, carefully nurtured through a strict ritual system that regulates people, marriage, sexuality, and semen. This view is predicated on a cyclical model of time (cf. Leach 1961b); seasonal movements, ceremonies, and customary transactions unfold in the round. Sambia do not recognize that their population is now expanding or that the concomitant stress on their resources (means of production) may be increasing; nonetheless, men believe that they expend semen and that they get more from trees. Let us now consider the implications of this view for their use of the concept of spirituality.

The trees from which men acquire sap are on clan territory. The land itself is one's main material inheritance from previous generations; it is held in agnatic corporate estate, though men own specific tracts of it from which they exploit resources (game, pandanus nuts, milk-sap trees). Land is coveted and defended against other groups; it is central to a clan's residential and territorial organization. It is guarded also by clan spirits. Ritual practices, too, are a social heritage, customs valued in themselves and for group identity, having been handed down from previous generations. It seems obvious, therefore, that the social ideology of trees provisioning new semen through the bodies of clansmen is a latent function of the regeneration of patrilineality.

Patrifiliation thus provides land and trees, ritual practices, and the social personae needed to transform tree sap into semen. Tree sap without an adult male body is just tree sap. The male body—the product of a long process of procreation with women and homosexual insemination from men, of magical ritual treatment making it fertile and procreatively potent—is the instrument that regenerates society. Tree-sap maintains maleness and masculine personhood. It regenerates one's clan, its patriline and hamlet-based warriorhood and thus the community itself. These social identities are conceptually placed, in time and space, through concentric social networks based on a magical notion of successive degrees of purest patrilineal substance.

Hence, male ideology claims that father, son, and clansmen are of one semen substance, one common origin place, one residential location—all elements of genealogic ancestry that fan out to embrace a pool of spirit familiars, ancestral spirits, and the semen sustaining all. Whether the trees are seen as beginning or finishing this process is beside the point: Sambia have a cyclic view of their system that makes tree sap pivotal in a greater chain of being. What is the nature of semen value in this whole system? This problem forms the last part of my chapter.

DELAYED EXCHANGE. The final category of indirect semen transactions concerns exchanges across generations between groups. This subject is very complex indeed, so I shall merely sketch contours of the system of intergroup relationships. What do groups give and receive? And do their exchanges of semen balance out across time?

The key principle of delayed exchange is that groups who exchange women also exchange semen through homosexual contacts. Group A takes a woman from group B. They become affines. Their initiated males of different cohort at different life cycle stages engage in homosexual intercourse both ways (giving and receiving semen). Children of groups A and B become matrilateral kin in the following generation. In delayed exchange (infant betrothal or bride-service) marriage, group A later returns a woman to group B. In direct exchange (sister exchange) they will not. Marriage between generation 2 of these groups is frowned on, except in the case of delayed exchange infant betrothal to father's sister's daughter, that is, a daughter of group A goes back to group B. Yet actual father's sister's daughter marriage (addressed as "sister" by her mother's brother's son) is also disliked; more commonly this woman is traded for another woman from a different group. Homosexual contacts between generation 2 are also forbidden. In effect, generation 2 shares ties of blood and semen: boys of group A were formed from the blood of a woman of group B, and their body tissue came from their father, some of whose own semen may have come from males of group B. These boys (of group A) must turn to a third, unrelated group, in order to take both a wife and semen.

What do groups A and B exchange? Group A gets a woman as garden producer and maker of babies. She reproduces heirs to perpetuate group A. Group B gets food gifts and a promise of a return woman (possibly her daughter) in the next generation. Boys of group A get semen from bachelors of group B and vice versa. Homosexual insemination ensures masculinization and adult reproductive competence. Boys of groups A and B may receive ritual sponsors from each other's group (in purest form, mother's brother). This man is the boy's guardian and teacher in sexual matters (remember they are forbidden to have sex). So each group provides boys of the other group with nurturance and sexual tutorship. In generation 1, a man may copulate with both his wife and her younger brother. The man gets a wife and another homoerotic transitional sexual outlet. His wife and her younger brother both receive semen: growth, strength. And the younger brother (or, if not himself, his sons or clansmen) will eventually receive a return wife, the brother-in-law's daughter, which the latter's semen created and nourished.

What does intermarriage do to social relationships? First, marriage transforms groups from unrelated enemies to less hostile affines. Where homosexual contacts occur with groups who are politically hostile, and between which warfare and masculine competition are common, marriage places affines in a set of productive relationships where none existed before. Second, they exchange women as resources. It is in the wife-givers' best interests to ensure that the marriage is productive in every way so that they receive a woman in return. Marital sex for procreation is productive social work; it outweighs erotic play in homosexual contacts and results in social sanctions against adultery and barrenness. Third, women and semen thus become circulating commodities. Unrelated groups exchange semen, on both sides, with the wife-donors getting a wife out of the bargain. The initiated boys of both groups require semen to complete their personhood, while the men need wives as sexual outlets and procreators to step out of the adolescent stage of homosexuality into the adult stage of marriage and family. Semen, therefore, though a crucial commodity, is secondary to women as a commodity: without wives men cannot attain full personhood. Even though semen is needed to attain manhood and it strengthens the new warrior recruits a village requires to protect and expand itself, this warriorhood goes for naught unless women are available for the group's economic and biologic reproduction.

Finally, the value of semen as instigator of social reproduction at both the individual and group levels pits males against one another in symmetric competition. This competition takes two forms, intragroup and intergroup transactions (Forge 1972). The one is intrahamlet individualized competition for homosexually procured semen in order to grow and have first pick of wives needed for reproduction later. Here, boys as age-mates try to out-perform one another in a contest to achieve maturity first. (In fact, older brothers encourage their youngers toward this end.) The other competition is between hamlets, and, in a wider sense, between a confederacy of intramarrying hamlets vis-à-vis the other confederacies of Sambia society. Men aspire to make their confederacy outdo others in war and overall productivity. Hamlets also act together to find women for their bachelors so as to produce more children—potential warriors and females for the marriage trade—compared with other groups. A race is on: its outcome is social reproduction. Conflicts within hamlets erupt over men competing with one another for wives and resources. Fights with peers over women in other hamlets also occur, sometimes precipitating warfare. But intrahamlet competition is overshadowed by the normative stress on achieving social maturity in concert with the best interests of one's own village group. Ultimately, social survival requires competing neighbors too, for they provide women and semen, and are the best defense—strength in numbers—against enemies elsewhere.

CONCLUSION

In this chapter we have explored Sambia semen valuations from several points of view: what seemed esoteric, vulgar, and trivial now seems complex and symbolically significant in understanding native concepts of sexual contacts and the structure of social relations and modes of production in Sambia culture. Erotics belongs to this symbolic field and cannot be understood, either subjectively or objectively, except in relation to the meaningfulness of this field over time.

Melanesianists have often ignored erotics and its meanings, especially in constructing comparative models of social organization and culture. Even heterosexual activities have, in general, been scarcely studied; and the meaning of the temporal and symbolic structuring of heterosexuality has not been accorded much analytic value beyond the vague category "sexual antagonism," which has been implicitly used to support whatever explanatory model an author advanced (Herdt and Poole 1982). But what matters more, for my purposes, is that the fluids of sexual and reproductive acts—semen, blood, and milk—have been too narrowly studied as entities or artifacts in exchange, or as parts of the growth process in reference only to individual development or societal functioning: they have been interpreted less often as symbolic objects and commodities, expressed through concepts and social transactions, whereby the natives reproduce the identities of persons, social roles, clans, and intergroup relationships across generations.

Past analyses of semen and blood as culturally constructed concepts in New Guinea belief systems, for instance, reveal this structural–functional emphasis. These fluids have long been viewed as important in native notions of sexual temperament and gender (e.g., Mead 1935). The great interest in procreation beliefs shown in the 1920s, first by Malinowski (1913) among Aborigines, and then in Trobriand descent ideology (Malinowski 1929, 1954), illustrates this interest. Writers questioned whether natives were ignorant of procreation and what such purported ignorance of conception meant (Ashley-Montagu 1937; and see Bettelheim 1955; Leach 1966; Spiro 1968b). We see now that denial of semen valuation in kinship and procreation belongs to a broader cultural discouse on social regeneration and reproduction (Weiner 1978, 1980). In Highlands studies, since Read's (1951, 1954) work, ethnographers have noted blood and semen as cultural signs of the body, sex, and gender. Accounts of the norms of sexual contacts, dogmas about conception, sterility, and reproductive competence, and ideas about exchange of menstrual blood and semen between people as patrilineal kin and affines, all illustrate how ethnographers functionally related body fluids to sociosexual relationships and the positioning of people in networks of social groups (e.g., see Berndt 1965; Glasse and Meggitt 1969; Langness 1967; Meggitt 1964; Newman 1964; Reay 1959; A. Strathern 1972; M. Strathern 1972; Wagner 1967). Preoccupation with the exchange of sexual fluids between groups addressed western individualist concerns with "discrete acts of giving and receiving" (Weiner 1980:71; cf. for example, A. Strathern 1969, 1972). Recent theorists have gone beyond exchange constructs, or structural models that view body treatment merely as reflections of society's divisions and boundaries (Douglas 1966), to interpret semen, blood, and other entities as the culturally valued materials out of which gender and reproductivity are symbolically perpetuated (Gell 1975; Herdt 1981; Lindenbaum 1972; Meigs 1976; Panoff 1968; Poole 1981, 1982b; M. Strathern 1978, 1980; Weiner 1980).

With the Sambia, we are dealing with people whose cultural systems use sexual relationships and fluids as objects and commodities to recreate social order in successive generations, for these are among the scarcest and most vital resources in this process.

Semen and other body fluids are not just things that *are:* they have a value beyond themselves for extending one's personhood—that is, existence—beyond the present. No doubt many experiences of these material things (e.g., fluids, sex, and others' bodies) entail this transcendent attitude. Sambia spiritual concepts speak to this issue directly, just as the conflict between sex as work or sex as play addresses it indirectly. "Religion is an art of making sense out of experience, and like any other art, say, poetry, it must be taken symbolically, not literally," Firth (1981:596) has said, a view germane to the ritual meanings of semen.

The social fact of semen for Sambia is that it is a scarce resource that circulates through time. Its material and phenomenologic attributes make it usable as commodity that can be consumed, stored, and given away. Its perceived use-value derives from the fact that (1) semen can be "contained" indefinitely in bodies and (2) then be seemingly passed, from person to person, without changing its essence or efficacy; (3) it represents an investment of labor (food, care, procreation of children) acquired through direct individual sexual transaction or indirect transformation (semen into milk), that can be given or received; (4) in being transmitted semen extends its transformative value to make the recipient more reproductively and socially competent; (5) these recipients, in turn, will produce more wealth and future individuals who will fill productive roles and fill out social groups; and (6) by so doing, semen transactions recreate social links between the living and the dead, the worldly and the spiritual realms, between ego and others, and between the divisions of the society.

In Sambia imagination, individuals are born and die, but semen flows through them (along with blood) to recreate society. Individuals pass on. Growth as an aspect of these individuals dies with them. But strength persists: in the form of bones and skin tissue in offspring; in spirit familiars; in ghosts and spirits; and in the deceased's bones, which after death may be used for sorcery. Erotic play passes on too, is useless, except insofar as it has effected growth, strength, and procreation. Sex as work is far more productive, if less exciting: family and heirs result. In this model, a woman's body as sexual-procreative property belongs to her husband, as much as his semen belongs only to her. Her blood, after marriage, belongs to his clan, through his offspring, which must be paid for in birth ceremonies. Both fluids are necessary for procreation, but it is semen that men own and control best. The natural fact that semen can be drunk (passed on) like any drinkable fluid sustains the view that it is a circulating, valuable, unchanging resource that must be, nonetheless, internally transformed in certain ways by certain persons to achieve certain ends.

The most powerful social fact of homosexual contacts is that they may only occur between potential enemies who may become affines (generation 1) and then kin (generation 2). Semen transactions not only define who is related and in what salient ways, but homosexual contacts predicate the partners' relationship as prospective affines in their generation, which makes their children matrilateral kin in their own. Structurally, social ties based on blood and semen should not be mixed via sexual relationships: semen relates nonkin, who in turn, through women as links, have descendants sharing semen and blood. (A male ego may receive semen from his brother-in-law, whose children, that is the ego's sister's children, possess her husband's semen and her blood.) Ties of semen and blood (via women traded) flow in the same direction. The seeming exception is marriage to actual (not classificatory) father's sister's daughter, a marriage Sambia frown on. Such marriages are acceptable only when this woman cannot be traded for another; but in these rare marriages spouses share no blood, though they may indirectly share semen via their fathers' homosexual contacts with each other's groups. Thus, the cultural principle not to mix blood and semen is contravened, and people resist such marriages. In general, this cultural linkage (blood and semen) makes heterosexual relationships more socially important and multiplex than homosexual contacts. Both men and women, their bodies and fluids, are needed to achieve biologic and social reproduction in this model (cf. Lévi-Strauss 1949; see Pettit 1977:70–72).

The practice of homosexual behavior is embedded in a cyclical tradition of semen transactions that made one's mother and father and will define one's own future relationships with boys and women. Identities follow from this semen flow. The tempo of such an ancient practice is to be found not only in this or that day's contacts but in the last generation and the next. The system sets rigid constraints, but individuals and groups follow strategies around broad time posts to maximize the value of themselves and their resources. Time does not forget who gave and who received semen.

This view does not explain ritualized homosexuality among Sambia; it merely elucidates the phenomenon in broader terms. For to seek causes, not just of the sociocultural system of values, but of individual acts of erotic behavior, we have to examine its individual subjectivity and developmental context, according them an analytic role I have here ignored. This is the concern of the following case studies of Sambia.

PART II
Interviews

CHAPTER THREE
Interviewing Sambia

H: What do the next chapters contain? How shall we think about their contents and how they represent the natives and ourselves? Remember that we did not originally set out to do research for this or any book. I was interviewing people I'd known for years; S. joined me for a few days in the village. Since I usually tape interviews, we had a record of what happened when S. joined in. After a day or so, when we decided to do this book, we were more aware about taping and interviewing as a team. Moreover, S. got involved and became a part of the sessions as he sat with me and others. Out of this fortuitous beginning the next chapters emerged.

These studies have an anomalous position in anthropologic research. They are not biographies of people in their fullness; they are not even biographic portraits.[1] Nor are they life histories, though we briefly outlined the essentials of each individual's history; or clinical formulations, though aspects of psychodynamic functioning and character structure are mentioned in individuals' profiles and then reflected on by us. These chapters are dialogues. Aside from editing for clarity, they convey conversations, fragments of broader case studies. Presented in translation, such texts are easy to read but harder to place in their cultural context, for, as Tedlock (1983: 323) has said, they preserve the "betweenness of the dialogue." Perhaps this interpretive problem confronts all cross-cultural work, but it is especially acute in cross-cultural clinical studies.[2]

Knowing what to say about a culture and how to say it across cultural boundaries is the classical problem of anthropologic epistemology. Strange or familiar,* people, places, ideas, actions must be described to others—readers who may not have a reference point (or worse, a false one) to think with. The question: "What is Sambia marriage like?" requires subquestions such as: "How is this institution—marriage—structured in Sambia society? What are its† agreed-on conventions, rules, and social trappings?" Such questions lead to a metaquestion: "How is Sambia marriage different from/similar to that of the reader's culture?"—where the *institution* (marriage) becomes the focus. They require cultural background and explanation. In a word: translation. Anthropology is translation, Evans-Pritchard (1962), Geertz (1973), and others have said. But translation is evocation only; translations are interpretations, editings.‡ Thus, in traditional ethnography, the normative perspective excludes much of life beyond the norm.

What is excluded may be of direct interest to the anthropology of self, gender, and dialogue. For some kinds of structural anthropology, the fine-grained, detailed utterances and contexts of intimate communications may not matter so much. They matter greatly to us: as S. has often said, without the *exact* details of someone's experience of erotics, your description hides more than it reveals. Thus, we have spent a great deal of time thinking about the process of writing and transcribing our interviews, and conveying them to readers. How does the editing process affect the meaning and interpretation of our interviews? To give full recognition to these oft-excluded matters we present, in the Appendix, a run-through of the entire process for interested readers.

Clinical ethnography raises special problems concerning what to say about a person's life and how to say it across cultures. The object is not the norm, yet norms must be understood in relation to the individual's thought and behavior. Here, as in what LeVine (1982) calls "person-centered ethnography," we must confront norms and rules as experienced, beliefs as internalized or deviated from in the individual's *concrete* norms. As we argued in chapter 1, clinical ethnography cannot ignore the cultural system or social settings of real people: that is the researcher's normative baseline. Yet this baseline can only be fully understood through individual case studies. How do *I* experience marriage and make it a fact in my life? The problem is

*We should be equally aware of the familiar: "To be 'self-evident,' a proposition or premise must be out of reach and unexaminable: it must have defenses or roots at unconscious levels" (Bateson 1976:58).

†Notice how easily we personalize social institutions in this mode of analysis: as if the institution had volition, goals—a mind of its own.

‡But there are better and worse translations. (Who informs or protects the reader?)

not quite Devereux's (1980a) problem of what is "normal and abnormal" across culture, but, more precisely, the issue of *what* a person experiences—and *how* that is seen by self and others, that is, as normal or abnormal, normative or eccentric; at different levels of awareness. Examples (from the text that follows): What does being a shaman mean to Sakulambei? How normative is his shamanism? How does Moondi feel shame and pleasure, and how much like our emotions are his? Does a hermaphrodite or a considerate man differ in masculinity from other Sambia males? What form does the verb *kalu* (sorrow, loss, sadness, depression) take in Kalutwo's feeling? And how does Penjukwi experience her femininity when with me? These questions, in short, require particular answers for particular people through particular communications.

Another background factor deserves mention. Our text often focuses on gender identity, the subject that first motivated us to work together, that led me back to the Sambia, and that took S. there. We know that our interest in erotics and in gender colors our data, writing styles, and interpretations; of course, this influence is true of all ethnographies. In the chapters that follow we talk with people I have seen primarily to study their masculinity and femininity.[3] Furthermore, some were seen because of anomalies in gender identity and sexual behavior, either as biologically intersexed (Sakulambei), as abnormal in Sambia eyes (Kalutwo), or as statistically aberrant (Imano). You may object that sex and gender are clinical subjects, and so, more than most problems that concern anthropologists, focus on individuals. Has our clinical approach made Sambia seem like verbal, self-conscious patients in the States? No and yes. No, we do not believe that these emphases on gender distort Sambia: the issues are important to Sambia themselves. To ignore sex and gender would harm one's ethnography in cultural domains as diverse as warfare, ritual, or family life. But yes, in my field house, I create an ambience for private reflection and discussion, an unprecedented experience Sambia had never imagined, that permits extraordinary communications and insights.

Throughout this book we call for renewed attention to the relationship between subjectivity and culture. We have criticized the positivistic ideology and rhetoric of those schools in anthropology that claim to do science without systematically using the subjective factors revealed herein. Our discussions of writing style, editing, jargon, doing long-term interviewing, substituting concepts such as "culture shock" for the observations the concepts summarize—this is our attempt to interject into doing and writing ethnography an awareness of how we think and feel. The object of the clinical ethnography we propose is the natives' experience of self as a lens we can use for seeing their relationships, feelings, and fantasies about others, institutions, and the environment.

So far, though, in debating these issues we have not discussed our image of self, as in "oneself" or "myself." When anthropologists refer to "self," "ego," or "person" they are in as much disagreement as their psychoanalytic colleagues regarding the connotations of these concepts.[4] Is Sambia selfhood different from other New Guinea societies? How does it compare to our own western conceptions? To ground the following material on interviewing we shall first examine psychoanalytic ideas and then those of Sambia.

S: Psychoanalysts have joined others who, over millennia, have tried to define self, that essential subjective experience. Yet there is still no agreed-on view. The problem, I think, is in part due to this subjective experience of self* being so dominated by our feeling of ourself, of being present. When we psychiatrists see states of self-fragmentation—dissociation—we recognize that this sense of oneness is made up of many parts fused in what one feels to be a seamless whole. Think of more ordinary matters like the right hand versus the left in playing the piano, where it seems that a product of one's creativity is not one's own but a gift (or curse); or enthusiasm, the god within; or dreams, those that are self-created, soft—no more than a signal— or roaring; or Fate—so often no more than the refusal to accept our own responsibility; or God, the gods, the Devil, devils, saints, spirits, ghosts, forces, Mysteries—fragments we chuck up in the process of denying the fullness of our self; or hallucination and delusion, wherein one's own mental work is projected onto the outside world and is then received back by oneself (which self; there are so many in there) as alien; or inspiration; or multiple personality, in which we divide our self into several parts, each with apparent autonomy; or works of art (most obvious in writings), wherein, somewhat as with dreams, we create innumerable personages, places, and plots from out of our own self; or schizoid states in which one feels like Kafka's creatures; or physical illness, where suffering can be so intense that one feels that a part of one's body is an enemy within or when we feel that our body—the equipment that we feel, when it works smoothly, is our

---

*Theorists carefully differentiate self from sense of or experience of self; the definitions are too exquisite for me. Even after studying the texts, I am no closer to defining self, though it seems so easy to experience.

self—gives out before we do; or states of trance, hypnosis, and possession.

But for most of us most of the time, the unspoken, unquestioned sense of "I" seems so spontaneously received, so much of one piece, that we consciously know nothing of the multiple "I's."

Tracking these complexities, Freud looked at the self—he called it "Ich" (mistranslated "ego") and found it an organized, dynamically energetic, tension-filled collection of mental parts and functions, sometimes conscious, mostly not, struggling—against impulses that would disintegrate us—for synthesis.* In time, his system for the structure of the mind† shifted from the clinical (that is, what can be observed directly or indirectly): conscious, preconscious, and unconscious mentation to theoretic structures: ego, superego, and id. (In this new system, "ego" took on quite different meaning: the ego was now an "it," not an "I."‡ The word "self" disappeared from analytic rhetoric and awareness, to emerge only when analysts were dissatisfied with the gap between their clinical work, which is a matter of one's communicating with another, and their theory with its structures that, as explanations, never capture that self-essence of our lives.

During the time when the dissatisfaction with ego/superego/id was congealing, the concept of identity was elaborated. Though many subheadings of identity were listed, the reality, in what one observed in others and in oneself, was, once again, too powerful for concepts to overcome. So this effort to corral the self experience also failed, though there were gains, since "identity" reached toward connotations different from those of "self." "Identity" implies mental experiences ordered around more or less enduring social roles (such as "I am a man; husband; father; son; doctor; American") drawn in from the outside world. One might say, then, that identity refers to the sense I have of aspects of my self, while "self" has the broader meaning: all that I mean when I say "I."

We are thus led to the problem, still unsolved by philosophers, psy-

---

*In doing this conceptual work, he was demonstrating, among other things, that the academic psychologists were naive and wrong to insist that what was mental was conscious and nothing else.

†In this realm of undefinable words, "mind" is sometimes used by theorists as synonymous with "self," but they are unaware they do so, thinking they have different meanings for each. When the hair-splitting is done, it is mighty hard to tell "mind" from "self." "Self" is more stylish.

‡The self had disappeared from analytic theory but not from the treatment. Freud knew that the subjective experience—conviction—of self was at one level a precious truth, its uncovering the goal of analysis. But at another it is an illusion of free will and responsibility: where the subject feels self, the observer sees functions, fantasies, dynamics, systems (most of which are far beyond the reach of consciousness). In this sense, "I" is an "it."

choanalysts, communication theorists, and computer scientists, of who is "I." The term has two quite different meanings: the subjective, immediate experience of myself, and an objective description—in many ways described better by others than by myself—of this person, this organism, this object for which I use the pronoun "I" and they use the pronoun "he." For instance, when saying that I dream, I refer to four different "I" processes. (1) I am asleep, in some way aware that I am asleep (for instance, I know enough not to fall out of bed) and am watching my dream somewhat as I do a theater-piece. (2) I am the person in the dream living in its actions. (3) I am the writer, director, and producer of the dream that is experienced by the first two "I's" just described; that version of my "I" plots the dream's course, introduces its characters and settings, decides on the feelings that the subjective "I" shall experience when I dream my dream. I do not know this "I." (4) I am an organism, a biologic machine, especially a brain, that exudes a dream.

No ethnographer, meeting a stranger at home, would accept as single-layered the sentences the stranger spoke. And the more intimate your relationship with someone, the more completely you know and can respond to the complexity of that person's communications. In speaking of these subjective layers and intersubjective complexities, I am underlining the need for the clinician's skill in getting people to reveal what they think and feel, to tell you what motives and meanings they attach to what they do and think others are doing.

"Layers" is a limited spatial metaphor. Better is that of a microdot (Stoller 1979). In World War II, microdots were used to hide large amounts of information in a tiny, apparently innocuous space. A full page of information was photographed down, in steps smaller and smaller, until reduced to the size of a typewriter period. That spot—microdot—was then pasted onto a letter whose overt typed message contained nothing secret. The secrets were in the microdot. With this spatial metaphor we conjure up the idea of many facts compacted into a tiny area. But we must add to it dynamics, movements—meanings, motivations, feelings, memories, fantasies, themes, scripts. Only then do we approximate what our waking lives consist of any—every—moment. Surely you do not think that right now I experience only the flow of words you read, and I do not believe that as you read, these words are your only thoughts. There is more: you are interpreting the words, arguing with them, forming impressions of me. You are under the influence of the place where you sit, the binding of the book, the hunger in your stomach, the time of day, the sound outside, last night's bad experience, tomorrow's responsibilities, the fate of your grandchildren born and those yet or never to be born, what your father said that Tuesday when you were three and your mother's style of feeding you when you were five months old. And what else, what else.

So keep in mind that in interviewing Sambia we shall be constantly thinking, without overtly stating it, that every moment of everyone's life is composed of mental processes that take the form of scripts and their interwoven affects. Our main theme is that the study of these mental processes in and between people *are* the practice of ethnography, not artifacts that obstruct.

H: Let us turn now to Sambia notions of self and personhood: first to background our interviews and then to foreground the discourse style of our clinical ethnography in the village.

Let me suggest that Sambia culture entails two distinct cultural worlds: the male and the female. I have analyzed this model elsewhere (Herdt 1987c) and will not repeat the argument here, but the idea of differing gender-related world views is crucial for interpreting dialogues with Sambia men versus women. These worlds are bound together in a synergistic way: all Sambia are reared in public situations, the norms of which are shared by men and women: public culture; yet men and women have different ritual secret domains of knowledge and discourse off-limits to the opposite sex. Though children are reared in public, boys must unlearn or negate feminine cultural attributes, rules, and behaviors (i.e., they are radically resocialized into the men's cult through initiations). Adult male behavior is based on the cultural discontinuity that, as boys, they shared in the female subculture, whereas as men they must demonstrate that they no longer abide by what they shared in as children.[5] The result is conflict—social and intrapsychic—between the moral rules and directives of the women's versus the men's worlds. This internal contradiction is never resolved, because it is basic to Sambia culture; and its conflictual effects can be seen in myriad expressions of men's behavior, including concepts of self and personhood.

To understand the construction of person and gender among Sambia requires a recognition—both historical and psychocultural—that *warfare* was the key behavioral reality to which Sambia had always to address themselves and their life designs. Until the 1960s, as we noted, Sambia and their neighbors constantly were at war. How is it possible, now, to reconstruct the conditions that led to day-to-day

decisions and relationships based on such conflict, let alone to conjure up in ourselves what the *experience* of such a life was like? We
cannot (Herdt 1987c; Stephen 1987).

But we can know this—the phenomenology of much of everyday
experience was the knowledge: a war is going on. No one was untouched by that deadly stone-age warfare with its severe test in man-
to-man, brute strength combat to the death. Sambia engaged in two
types of fighting. In the Valley, bow-fighting was frequent. It was supposedly bluster—a show of strength—through displays in which
warriors lofted arrows at each other from opposite mountain sides.
This fighting was limited to straight arrows. Barbed arrows and stone
clubs were ruled out, but people were sometimes wounded, and
sometimes the wounded died. Then a real war—no holds barred—
began, until blood revenge was obtained and a truce arranged. Intertribal war-raiding was for killing and was more deadly. Men and
youths from the confederacy would go on dangerous war-parties and
journey to distant places. Sometimes this was done purely to test new
third-stage initiates, to see what they were made of. Those attacked
did the same or eventually retaliated. War was a deadly pursuit, and
personhood was constructed in response to it.

Personhood thus has its roots in the public moral norms of the
village. Sambia are gregarious; they have a strong sense of sociality
and firm ideals about what is good (*singundu*) or bad (*maatnu-maatnu*).
For children and adults these moral norms are sensible: one should
be hospitable and share food (or consumables like tobacco); one should
not steal or destroy others' property; one should not physically harm
others or shame them; one should work to provide for self and family
and not be lazy; and one should converse with others, follow parents'
instructions, be true to one's word, and not meddle too much in others' affairs. For adults, moreover, the list includes more serious in-
junctions pertaining to ritual, fighting with or killing (except in self-
defense) one's kin or affines, and never engaging in heterosexually
promiscuous or adulterous behavior. All these norms, incidentally,
apply only to one's social world (from one's village to close neighbors)
in successively weaker degrees. Enemies are not human; therefore
killing, raping, or looting them are not moral violations.[6] All Sambia
share in these morals; that is what makes them Sambia. In some ways
people are always bound by these moral rules.

The full person is defined in public culture against the norms of
esteemed adulthood. Fully masculine people are those who have been
through all initiations, who are married and have at least two children. Furthermore, men must have participated in war raids, hon-

orably defended or killed; they must be good hunters and must provide well for their families through ample gardens. They should be actively involved in ritual activities, not spend too much time with women and children. As elders, they should be actively involved in marriage and land tenure matters and stand up to be counted through sensible rhetoric when necessary. Fully feminine people should have reached menarche, been initiated, married, and have at least two children. They should be successful gardeners and generous in giving food and consumables to others. They should maintain appropriate contacts with their agnates in other hamlets, which allows them to use some of their own clans' resources. As elders, they should be involved in female ritual activities and instruct younger women in matters like sex and marriage. These normative models provide powerful rules and images of how people *ought* to behave and what they *should* strive toward.

Yet these person categories do not define selfhood, because individuals uphold them only partially, and Sambia are, like other Highlanders, rugged individualists.[7] They recognize both moral and personal differences among individuals. Common expressions of this recognition are found in folklore and casual remarks: that Kanteilo is a good story-teller or a sayer of funny things; that men such as Mon are great hunters and fearless warriors, while others are rubbishy; or that some women, such as Penjukwi, are industrious gardeners and really generous with their food, while others are lazy or stingy. Why are people this way? Eccentricity, biologic inheritance, clan differences, bad spirit influences: the accounts and stories concerning these differences vary, but they all suggest underlying recognitions of selfhood.

It is one's thought (*koontu*)*—here close to our concept of self—that is responsible for such traits. (And this sentence reflects the syntactical construction these accounts take.) When saying why so-and-so has a particular behavior pattern people add: "That's just his fashion" (*gami pasen-tokeno*) or "That's his thought." Sometimes spontaneously and at other times after being asked, people will say, "That was his father's way" (or "her mother's"). Many behaviors are alternatively attributed either to custom (*pasen-tokeno*), ritual teachings (*pweiyu koongundu*), ancestral ways (*aiyungasheru*), or myth (*pasi koongundu*). Moral and personality nuances are products of one's *koontu*. In dream reports, *koontu* is a signifier both of one's conscious

---

Koontu may be used as a reflexive nominalized verb ("I myself *think* that . . . ") or as a noun ("I had the *thought* that . . . ").

waking personhood and of self, as I have shown elsewhere (Herdt 1987d). The personal pronouns "I" and "me" mark self, whereas *koontu* refers to the norms defining the person's social role. One's thought should reflect customary moral norms that define the good person, but they do not always.

If thought, and hence, self, have origins in childhood, then it seems obvious that selfhood includes aspects of the secular—that is, pro-fane—world of women. This view is implicit in men's *ad hoc* state-ments, but it contradicts male ritual dogma, and both initiates and men are ambivalent about it. (They are, however, firm in believing that one's soul, *koogu*, is mainly derived from one's same sex parent and is nourished and matured through initiation.) In private inter-views some men and initiates say they did learn things from their mothers, though others flatly deny such an idea. Even so no Sambia ever denies the fact of biologic heritage or subsequent maternal care; such personal statements are never expressed in public rhetoric. This maternal bond and female world signify the mundane morals and selfhood noted above. But men loathe to acknowledge it. Here, then, are foundations of concepts of personhood and selfhood among Sambia.

What remains is to identify the boundaries of culturally consti-tuted contexts in which communications about personhood and ex-perience are made to others—including the ethnographer—for these normative conceptions also shape the meaning of discourse types in Sambia culture.

We can argue, consistent with the above, that Sambia people op-erate in three different contexts with corresponding modes of dis-course noted previously: public, secret, and private.

Public situations are the most general context in which commu-nications are made. This discourse is bounded by the public norms sketched above. These communications occur in mixed audiences of men, women, and children. Daily events, economic activities, gossip, even dream sharing belong to this category of talk. Thus people are more rule-bound and conformative here.

Secret situations entail ritual secrets, names, and other informa-tion about activities hidden from the uninitiated and the opposite sex. This male discourse occurs only in the club house, in the forest, or, on those rare initiation occasions, in ritual cult houses, whereas female secret talk occurs in the menstrual hut. Yet there are layers of ritual secrecy stratified by initiation status.[8] Thus, at the elemen-tary level, all initiated males share in knowledge of first initiation, ritual flutes, homosexual activities, etc. More advanced secret knowl-edge is hidden from them until they achieve final initiations; this information concerns heterosexual purificatory rites and, ultimately, the myth of parthenogenesis—the greatest secret of all (Herdt 1981). At the highest level is esoteric ritual knowledge needed for certain ritual spells and paraphernalia; only a handful of elders—a very special audience—share in this most secret discourse (Tuzin 1980).

Finally, there are private situations, made of thoughts and activities not publicly shared but defined as not secret. Sexual activities of all kinds, because Sambia are prudish and regard them as shameful, are rarely told to others beyond one's sexual partner[9] though men brag of sexual exploits. Homosexual activities are private experiences not usually revealed except to intimates, certain agemates, and brothers. Likewise, heterosexual activities among spouses are *never* discussed with others, and adultery is carefully hidden.[10] (Children, in particular, should be kept completely in the dark about sexual activities.) Feelings of shame belong to this private domain. And so do daydreams, wet dreams, and any other nightdreams not publicly communicated. Magical knowledge about hunting, gardening, and sorcery, inherited from parents, is private information hoarded like money. Such private experience *is* selfhood; it may be shared with those one trusts most deeply, or it may not. When it is told in private situations, we may say that the communications are shaped by cultural norms and conceptions about what one *should* do, say, and think. But when such communications are made over a long time (such as to an ethnographer), these norms apply less and are transmuted by the individuals' idiosyncrasies and what the interviewer does in response to them. Thus the private domain permits the person greatest freedom of expression, of selfhood.

Let me underline the distinctive nature of communication in Melanesian societies that, like Sambia, use all three modes of discourse. In western culture, by contrast, our institutionalized secrecy is poor.[11] The institutionalization of public/private/secret in Sambia life, supported by norms and taboos, is, at the same time, an obstacle to the free exchange of information between people, an obstacle to easy ethnographic interviewing, and a phenomenon in its own right worth studying (one that, incidentally, defies easy study).[12] Those, such as anthropologists or psychoanalysts, whose task is to study people's inner worlds can best appreciate the convoluted forms of talking that weave in and out of these domains, or combine them in a single statement: metaphors, circumlocutions, lies, euphemisms, double entendres, slips of the tongue, puns, stories that are half-truth or pure fiction, fictions disguised to hide the truth; many ways to say what you want to say and not say, in whatever situation, to keep the social—and oneself—intact.[13] This matrix of public/private/secret is the full medium, a code, as it were, of interpersonal communication we must keep in mind to understand Sambia talking.

But this image of Sambia derives from the past, and does not embody the signs of social change, ever-present, that make this portrait possible, dear reader. For this we have to thank the end of war. And with pacification and a gradual lessening of the tensions of intergroup competition and sorcery, we see the signs of change in personhood. Sambia, who were ever sociable, can now be more gregarious and affable. They are glad that war is gone. Pacification has removed some constraints, created more freedom. People can travel more freely. Travelers fear less that they will be attacked; children play around the hamlet and down by the river, where they never could before; women go to gardens without armed guards; the secret cult has lost some of its grip—particularly since the late seventies, when an airstrip was placed in the valley—so women have freedom and initiations are less harsh. Things are changing; our presence in the village—like that of the nearby missionaries—was a sign of another world to be reckoned with and understood.

Our Sambia interviews must be understood in the context of this change. My presence changed things: I arrived and built a house. At first, in ignorance, I interacted with people in ways (subtle or overt) that made them compromise the public/private/secret distinctions in order to accommodate me. Examples: Moondi responding to my asking about his wet dreams and then, years later, his telling me his fantasies; or other initiates discussing their homosexual experience; or Moondi and then Nilutwo revealing the secret of homosexuality; or Weiyu talking about sex with his wife; or Nilutwo reporting dreams he told no one else; or Penjukwi discussing her feelings about her body. Sambia never asked each other such questions. Only I did; only the ethnographer's outsider status permitted such out-of-place, even unthinkable, questions. But I asked in private, in my house; and, after a while, unprecedented questions and responses were accepted. And then expected.[14]

What did my unprecedented questions do? They contributed in subtle ways to the breakdown of the public/private/secret divisions, for me to move, less earlier and more later (of course), from public to secret, or from secret to private, or whatever. I could do this switching of frames (see Goffman 1974) because I had seen the secret initiations and had worked a long time with Tali on what they meant to him, a ritual expert; I had lived with Sambia and knew enough about normative public rules to predict what people should do, say, or think; and by 1979, when S. came and we conducted the interviews below, I knew my informants well.

I created thereby a new fourth category of discourse: what people said to Gilbert when alone in his house. I did not intend to do that. Yet I wanted to understand my friends in that way, too, not just how they were in rituals or in public. I wanted to understand how they made sense of their lives for themselves—in private—as shared with me.[15] What they said was constrained by Sambia culture, their ritual experience, the time of day, what had happened at breakfast that morning, of course; plus, what they thought I expected to hear them say.[16] We shall get to that.

Because Sambia culture is built for males on a contradiction—be socialized in the female subculture but be accountable only to the male subculture after initiation—the conflicts in men's and women's lives were brought into my office. This aspect of our talking may have, in retrospect, fueled people's interest in talking with me. By the time S. arrived, I was so involved in these narratives that it was no longer easy for me to reconstruct self-consciously what had happened, step-by-step, in leading up to what we label "comfortableness," "impasse," or "ambivalence" in particular case studies that follow.

Who were our subjects? All live in my field village, Nilangu, excepting Kalutwo, from the neighboring village, but who is living in Nilangu's river settlement on the valley floor, twenty minutes away. This intimate contact in the same village, in eating, healing ceremonies, gardening, gabbing, and the grand rituals, brought me close to people, spoiling the setting as objective experiment but permitting me countless, rich glimpses and understandings of people's behavior out in the light of social day. For these people are not just informants. They are also: real cronies (Tali and Weiyu), seen by me, themselves, and others as such, making them allies; translators (Weiyu); or a boy who became a research collaborator and a friend whom I supported in school (Moondi); or a frightened acquaintance who has become a faithful, still distrusting, friend (Sakulambei, who nonetheless may trust me as much as anyone else); or a neighbor (Imano); or the wife of a neurotic informant/friend, who became an informant and even better friend (Penjukwi); or, as with Kalutwo, someone in a relationship so complex that it requires a string of adjectives and nouns (stiff-necked informant who wanted to be a friend and, even more, a patient).

I know Moondi, Weiyu, and Tali best—longest and most intimately—and have watched them change over the years. I have intruded into their families and become part of their histories. From the mundane to the ritual arena, in the village and on patrols to alien tribes and on to Port Moresby, I have seen them in varied circumstances and feel that I often know what goes on inside them. The following chapters present microstudies of our dialogues with them, our first effort to put clinical ethnography into practice.

CHAPTER FOUR

Moondi's Erotism

BIOGRAPHIC SKETCH

H: Moondi is an intelligent, articulate youth of Nilangu. The eldest child of a large family, he was born about 1960, so he was nineteen at the time of these interviews. His father is unusually mild, his mother an unusually strong, renowned shaman. They are a successful couple, and their marriage is among the most important in the village. Moondi himself is somewhat short (about five feet tall), stocky and tough; he is robust and, except for occasional bouts of malaria, healthy. Unlike his peers, he has been to grade school; moreover, unlike the one percent of Sambia boys who have some schooling, he has come back to the village. He is personable and impetuous, popular and well integrated in the community. Today (1987), he lives and works in Port Moresby. But it would not surprise me—and this speculation must be seen as essential to the meaning of Moondi's life, our relationship, and his sense of himself—if he one day returned and became a leader in his area.

I first met Moondi in 1974. He was just a kid, a second-stage initiate living in the men's house. He sought me out, wanting to work as a language informant.* He was anxious to be noticed, and ingratiating; Sambia are rarely pushy. Still, he wanted to impress me that he was smart and could read and write Pidgin. These traits plus his intelligence and tattered European clothes set him somewhat apart from his peers. His initial desire to be recognized and to please—as if someone's life depended on your giving him that certain job—made

---

*Several Sambia have served as language informants to a European missionary down the valley. Moondi did so briefly; that was his only model of how I could employ and work with him.

101

me uneasy. Nonetheless, Moondi's behavior defied textbook wisdom ("Never use those first, too friendly informants"). Within a month his special gift for translation had become invaluable. His demeanor then returned to normal. Even now, Moondi is the best linguistic informant and interpreter I have ever found. He is insightful and verbal too; so he became an excellent informant in general, and he was at times (1975, 1979) a crucial field assistant. Through the years I have followed him closely, periodically interviewing him and exchanging letters. I know his mind better than that of any other Sambia. And we are also friends.

Because of the length and depth of our relationship, I find Moondi's life more difficult to snapshot than anyone else's. My case study of him includes hundreds of pages and scores of tapes, not to mention his letters or my observations of him in many noninterview situations. These materials are fuller than for anyone else and they include: casual or offhand remarks (e.g., jokes); casual and structured interviews; observation of him being initiated (third-stage initiation, 1975); observations of his everyday interactions with significant others and strangers; of his being ill; of traveling with him and seeing him sad and happy, etc.; and finally, occasional dream reports collected over the years. Especially, I have studied his masculinity and erotic life. Beginning in 1979 after he finished grade six, I also taught Moondi some western concepts such as fantasy, free association, and guided imagery.[1] These tools enriched our work, allowing me to go beyond conscious, especially intellectualized constructions, and to explore aspects of Moondi's imagination and unconscious processes. But because they involved insight and exposed him to disturbances from sources unconscious to him, our talking relationship—which always had therapeutic aspects—changed. I turned the talking into a kind of supportive psychotherapy to let him feel comfortable enough to discuss anything he wanted.[2] Toward the end of my visit, this talking centered on his anxieties about personality change, his impending marriage, and his plans to move to Port Moresby and work there. The remaining facts of his life can be set out in three major periods: childhood, initiation and life in the men's house, and his late schooling.

Moondi's is the last generation to have experienced warfare in their childhood; that is important. He still has vague memories of actual events (the period 1960–1965), for instance, of his mother fleeing with him into the forest when their hamlet was attacked. But his *feelings* are even more intense: of faceless enemies and dangers and of his father's absence when fighting; real, dreadful fears that scar one's soul, that initiation later compounded, and that he can never forget. For such anxieties in traditional Sambia life touched every aspect of existence; and, without doubt, they will stalk him, ghostlike, forever, awake or dreaming.[3]

His father's circumstances and his parents' marriage were more than normally caught up in war. A fight broke out in his father's natal hamlet over twenty-five years ago. His father's brother was killed by his own kin; war was set off for blood revenge. Moondi's father fled to Nilangu, where he was sheltered and offered sanctuary by his betrothed wife's clan. Hence, Moondi's father settled in his wife's village. This anomaly has thoroughly influenced their remarkable marriage. His wife, Kaiyunango—Moondi's mother—is herself an anomaly: strong-willed, outspoken, and the most powerful living female shaman.[4] She is also the good-hearted, young-looking, and vigorous mother of ten children, eight of whom are still living. Moondi is her firstborn and her favorite son. This maternal strength and love are as much a part of Moondi's optimistic character as the unusual achievement motivation that has set him above many peers. When younger, his parents squabbled and fought, but then and now their marriage is more stable than most. Perhaps the matrilocal character of the marriage helped their children be unusually emotionally robust.

Like all Sambia males, Moondi was initiated into the ritual cult. His first-stage initiation, at age eight, was in 1968. He described himself (as do others) as immature and smaller for his age than most of his agemates. So he feels he was more the object of bachelors' hazing than other boys. Initiation was terrifying. He was shocked by the ritual secrets—ritual flutes, nosebleeding, homosexual fellatio. He disliked and feared fellatio with bachelors at first;[5] it was over a year before he himself took the lead in homosexual contacts. He was lonely and sad after initiation. In actuality then—and in daydreams still— he blames his parents for his initiation: they let him be initiated against his will.

As time passed, though, Moondi adjusted to the men's house life. In 1970 he was initiated as an *imbutnuku* (second-stage initiate). He did more hunting than before. He became a more enthusiastic fellator and was sought by many bachelors as a sexual partner.* Some of these sexual relationships were temporarily exclusive: Moondi would sleep with the same youth for only a day, because he considered re-

---

*Moondi is considered handsome by Sambia, and his personality makes him equally attractive. He was expert at playing passive and seductive, and bachelors favored his willingness to pleasure them.

peated contacts with the same person unmanly (a common feeling among boys). His life might have continued thus had Moondi not decided to go to school.

In late 1971, Moondi left the Valley and went to a mission station school a day's walk away. He became a nominal convert to its religion. (He was not, however, baptized.) He was among the first Sambia boys ever formally schooled. He learned fast and advanced. A year later he was transferred to an even larger school far away. At the end of his second year he returned home for the Christmas holidays. Then fate intervened and his life changed again.

While home in the village he became gravely ill, probably a combination of malaria and bad nutrition (at school). He lay ill for weeks, into the early months of 1974, preventing him from returning to school. He felt that he had lost his chance to go on.* So he fell back into village life, healthy again because food was plentiful, helping his parents, sleeping with the bachelors, and occasionally going on short patrols with local government officers. Then I appeared on the scene.

Moondi presented himself to me as a half-literate and likeable adolescent. He proved himself invaluable, since he could read and write, at tasks like census-work, which others disliked. I also needed a dependable young interpreter to help me interview boy-initiates— someone they could trust and with whom they could identify. (An initiate could not always trust older bachelors and men.)† Moondi was perfect. He could understand, for instance, that in keeping to a formal interview schedule I had to ask exactly the same question of a cohort of boys in as similar a way as possible. But almost from the start, Moondi also talked about himself, which I encouraged, for I wanted also to understand what made him tick. I urged him to express his goals, since I was intrigued about his schooling. Eventually I learned how illness had kept him back in the village. Eventually we made a deal: if he would help me in my work for a year, I would help him get back to school.

Meanwhile, in 1975, another initiation cycle began. It was time for

---

*Why did he go to school in the first place? His parents were against it, but he went anyway. He apparently wanted to see the world, to get outside experience. At the time he was too young to go to the coast and work, which left only school. He was intelligent. What role did that play? He had enough experience with the local missionaries to see what *they* had. Thus many motives—including a job, money, and escape from the bush—were involved.

†Some information (e.g., wet dreams) is shameful to discuss with anyone, but especially with adult men. Weiyu, my adult interpreter (see chapter 5), was no different from other men. Furthermore, boys are generally intimidated by men, who regard them as ritually uneducated children who should be seen and not heard. Moondi was also discreet, and, even more than Weiyu (cf. chapter 10), kept information confidential that initiates confided to me (e.g., on dreams and sexuality).

Moondi to become a third-stage *ipmangwi*, which he greatly resisted. He said he was "not yet grown," that he needed more time, and that once initiated his "thinking would be stymied." He'd never get back to school. He ran away, hid for a bit. Others coaxed and pleaded. He considered fleeing to the coast. But he gave in to the pressure and went through the whole initiation, as I watched (Herdt 1987c). Afterward, as a fellated, he was wildly involved with boys: I have never before or since seen him so different. His passion subsided after a few weeks, and he settled into new routines. Not long after, I finished the formal interviews with initiates; his new period of schooling took him away.

Moondi had assisted me invaluably for a year; he went back to a public school in late 1975. By late 1977, through accelerated advancements, he graduated from primary school. Unfortunately, because of local quotas on school returnees, he could not continue to high school. In the meantime we exchanged letters. He seemed to mature, enjoying life more and feeling more comfortable with himself. Since then we have been friends, as close as that relationship can be with people from different worlds.

When I returned in early 1979, Moondi was back in the village. He had grown up. I was happy to have his company—not just his assistance—for many of my friends from the mid-1970s were gone, struggling to live as itinerant workers on the coast. Despite the reunion and success of that work, a cloud thus hung over my stay: so many of our friends had left the village that it was not the same place. Indeed, I found it saddening to walk by the shadowy big old men's house* in Nilangu, closed up and dusty, due to the large number of initiates who had left.[†] It took me only a few days to realize, then, that Moondi was as thankful for my company as I was for his.

Meanwhile, some weeks after I arrived, marriage negotiations were held that determined whom Moondi was to marry. A sister-exchange marriage was agreed on between M.'s parents and those of the girl— a thirteen-year-old premenarchal girl of another clan in Nilangu. This event really changed Moondi. His heterosexual fantasies increased and he was thrown into a new era of almost adult existence. Some of the ensuing changes in him are described below.

Nonetheless, Moondi made it clear from the start that he was not satisfied with village life. He had already decided before my arrival

---

*Nilangu has two men's houses, and a few new initiates (since 1977) live in the smaller one.
[†]The exodus still continued in 1981, and, I am sad to report, the village was for me lonelier than ever.

to change his life again by moving to the coast. He agreed to work with me but asked that I help him leave for Port Moresby when I left. His fiancée was too young to formally marry yet, so, meanwhile, he would try to find work and make money outside. Thus, when it came time for me to leave, both Moondi and Kwinko (my cook, and Moondi's best friend, cousin, and agemate) left too. Port Moresby took them in. And there they remain today, both busy with new lives and adult jobs. Ten thousand years passed in half their lifetime—from stoneage war to city apartments. And the wonder is that so much change still lies ahead.

This chapter concerns changes in Moondi's erotism. First are narratives of his erotic daydreams and erotic looking. This work was central to my case study of M. in 1979, and it was nearing completion when S. arrived. I have also added the fragment of a session entitled "resistance," which concerns the collecting of this erotic material. On these tapes, Moondi talks with me alone. Then S. joins us. Here and in later chapters we present our interview data in the chronologic order in which it was collected.

INTERVIEWS

What is sexually exciting to Moondi? How does he have to restrict his erotic impulses? What do his erotic daydreams look like? These are the kinds of questions motivating this session. By the time it occurred, I had nearly completed my case study, M. had spent many hours over months discussing his sense of himself and his maleness through memories, attitudes elicited through my questions, his history of his erotic behavior, dream reports, guided imagery sessions, etc. Session I occurred with M. and H. alone. His family contracted a marriage for him as is customary. M. had had a role in these negotiations. His father approached him regarding the prospective match. Without going into the details here, M. "approved" of his marriage choice after some days of heated talk.*

I was lucky to be there when this all occurred. It provided me the opportunity to examine concretely the phenomenon of erotic looking, a subject I had studied for some time. Moreover, here was a chance to record how Moondi's erotic daydreams were shifting—one of the major shifts being from homosexual to heterosexual objects. But our

---

*These omitted details include such factors as: the social upheaval already mentioned that has changed marriage arrangements; Moondi's parents' marriage; Moondi's being the eldest son, which gives him more power to be involved; and his personality—intelligence and sophistication that helped him make the best deal possible.

conversations on these topics had to be done in secret (for the reasons noted above), so we talked when no one else was around. Consequently, a previous session on erotic looking had to be cut short because other people appeared unexpectedly. Here is the transcript of our first session.

FIRST SESSION: EROTIC LOOKING

HERDT:* Last time [three days before] you and I were talking about looking[†] and the custom forbidding you [all initiates][‡] from looking at the women.

MOONDI: Yeah [*apprehensive*].

H: And the women too, they can't stare at you. Now I want to ask you about this . . . do you still remember where it was we stopped talking about this last time? [Reference to the fact that we had had a session earlier but were forced to stop talking about this delicate subject because Moondi felt uncomfortable with others being present outside who could overhear him.] Do you, uh . . .

M: About that? It went like this—we were talking about how the women . . . . At that time we had to stop in the middle . . . break it [our conversation] off.

H: When was that? This morning we were talking, but there were plenty of people all around. So you said, "Wait till later on."

M: [*Cuts in.*] Yeah, later on. Because you were asking me, "At the times when you look intently at women, what are you thinking then?"

H: [*Quietly.*] Um-hm.

M: [And you also asked:] "Oh, when you look very strong at women but suppose the men are watching you, too, what can you then feel?" You asked me and I said, "Oh, *Maski!*" [Pidgin word with

---

*S: Each of us did our own editing of every bit of these transcripts, after H. did the original translations. Had only one or the other of us done that editing, the transcripts would be different, and though the essense of the interviews would still be there (says who?), the interviews now to enter your mind are no longer exactly the same as they might have been.

We begin with literal transcription—as literal as can come out of a typewriter—plus description of what is happening at that moment. At this point we shall leave intact the raw, at times awkward translations, that still hover between Pidgin and colloquial American English. Then we shall switch to our cleaned-up edited style so that reading will be more bearable. In this way, our editing becomes more visible to the reader.

†Whenever I use this term it will be translated from the Pidgin *"luk luk"* or Sambia *chemdu*, which have both social and erotic connotations.

‡Throughout these transcribed texts, [   ] will be used to mark commentary inserted after New Guinea, while editing; whereas (   ) will be used only to enclose material that occurred in the original session. All narrative text and footnotes are by H. unless otherwise indicated.

no real equivalent in English that here means something like "forget it for now."] Later on. And I said, then I said, "The times when I look [at women] and all the men look at me, then I think all the men can think of me like this: I'm looking to steal [their women] or something . . . [hard to translate but something like: looking and wanting to steal what I have seen] when I am looking strong at the women. Therefore: "I want to grease [butter up] the women"; that is what they all [indefinite] can think that I want to do when I am looking too strong at all women. All the men can think that [above statement] . . . and when I realize this, then I feel shamed* when I look into their [i.e., men] eyes.

H: When you were an uninitiated boy did you know about this [looking] then too?

M: At the time I didn't understand about it. You know [as a preinitiate boy] . . . plenty of times I used to talk with all the women and I didn't feel very much shame about talking to you looking at them [sic] . . .

H: But, towards all of the girls [tai] is that what you also felt?

M: About the girls . . . looking at them, I didn't feel anything in particular, no, I didn't. But [voice speeds up] at that period, we used to—I used to be around them a lot. We used to talk and run around together† . . . . So I didn't feel anything in particular about them. Nor about looking at the women or the girls [said simply and directly with no affectation]. So we would talk a lot together and I didn't feel any particular thing about them.

H: [Quietly.] Um-hm.

M:‡ When they performed the moku [first-stage initiation] on me, it was taboo to stare at women. They told us we can no longer get close to women. The big men made me afraid about that. But before, when I was a boy, I didn't have that fear. Only after the moku and then the imbutu and ipmangwi. That's when I got to be like this.

H: When you were a boy, you didn't play around [sex play] with the girls?

M: No . . . . Only because I was afraid. I wasn't afraid for no reason at all to play around with them. I was only afraid of playing around to screw them. But I didn't really understand how to actually

*What Sambia call "shame" (wungulu) is a far more powerful experience than that marked by our gentler verbs "embarrassed" or "ashamed." Therefore, to mark the difference, I use "shame" when translating directly from the vernacular.

†Sambia children can freely play in mixed sex groups until about age five when they are sexually separated.

‡We switch now to a cleaner transcript, edited to be more readable and bearable.

screw then, it was only my fantasy . . . and I thought: like our mothers and fathers do, that's how I thought of doing it. And I'd think, "If I do that, then all the men will get me," so I was afraid to do that.

H: But you didn't—or did you—look at the girls' or women's genitals when you were a boy?

M: When the girls were infants and didn't yet wear grass skirts, I saw their genitals.

H: And when they wore grass skirts?

M: Then I didn't look.

H: Is that tabooed or not?

M: No it is not taboo. But they must cover themselves. Suppose they simply went naked and the men saw them; then, in looking into the men's eyes, they would be shamed.* And it's the same with the women. We uninitiated [unclad] boys should not let women see our penises. The boy is also shamed if they all look and see him.

H: Would you have been shamed as a boy if you had looked at a woman's vagina?

M: [*Long pause; grin in voice.*] I've never looked at them. I never felt anything like that. It's their nakedness: it's not right that they should show it to you.

H: It's just down below [their genitals] that's shameful, isn't it?

M: Yeah. That part they must hide well inside their grass skirts.

H: I know that this doesn't happen here, but suppose, as a boy, one time a girl should secretly lift up her grass skirt and show you her vagina?

M: That girl [*tai*] is a real *pamuk* [whore]!

H: [*Chuckles.*] [I had never heard that word used for a girl before.] Oh, she would be a *pamuk tai*, huh?

M: Yeah. I could think, "Why is she showing me that [*a bit indignant*]? Is she a *pamuk* girl, or what?" But [*voice speeds up*] I could say to the boys [*lower voice*], "This woman, she showed me her cunt."† If I said that and the girl heard it, she could be shamed.

H: When she showed you her cunt, would your cock get tight?

M: [*Matter of fact.*] Oh, no. Not at all. I wouldn't be thinking about that with that girl. I could just say no to her, "You just don't have

---

*S: As with Americans and the interplay between a scantily covererd woman on a beach and her audience.
†This is the Pidgin term for vagina, which I leave in this form to convey its vernacular connotations.

any ·shame" [therefore, no self respect]. I wouldn't get hard. I'd just say, "You don't have any shame. You—you, ha!"

H: You could just rubbish her.

M: Yeah, curse her. Then she could feel shamed.

H: Mothers take care in fastening their little girls' grass skirts. [*Moondi looks away.*] You've got a lot of sisters and you know about this.

M: Yes. The mothers say, "You can't go and show yourselves to the boys. You must hide it [genitals] good. It is *your body.*" The mothers repeat that to all the girls and to the boys, too.

H: Now, what about the vagina: is it good or not good?

M: It's not a good thing. You [a female] could be shamed that they look at you. It's like this: they all know [*lowers voice*] that at that place [vagina] they all do it [sex]. It's not something all the men should be *looking* at. It belongs only to the two of them [spouses]. Only the man and wife should see her genitals. That's our custom. We must hide screwing. When I was a boy, if I didn't have a grass apron on, I would have felt shamed.

H: But it's your own body. Why should you be shamed by it?

M: [*Slowly.*] This is very hard for me to think more about. Why should I walk around without any clothes like a *long-long* [crazy] man?[6] They'd say to me, "You're not a small boy any more. Can you see your huge penis just hanging out there uncovered? Do you want to walk around naked like a crazy man?"

H: Now, what changed after you were initiated; what did they say at that time about looking [*purposely vague*]?

M: It concerned talking with women, and looking at women, and eating in front of women, drinking water in front of the women's eyes, eating sugar cane.* All of those things. That all changed. I thought: "Before, when I was a child, I used to just eat in front of women, but now . . . they initiated me and afterward they made me a different kind of person. They changed me and changed my thinking; and so now I can't look at women or talk with them. Or eat in front of women's eyes, either." And as I thought that, I feel afraid. It's the same as when the big men talk [exhort, threaten during the initiation]. They could hear what I said to the women, and the bachelors could come and rub stinging nettles on me [painful ritual punishment for breaking taboos].

H: And now [as a third-stage initiate]?

M: I can talk to the women sometimes. But before [pacification, when ritual was everything] we [bachelors] would have still been very

---

*These avoidances are all standard ritual taboos boys must adhere to after initiation.

shamed: we didn't do that. Now things have changed, and so we've got different ways.

H: When you were a first-stage initiate, you could not look at the women. Did you ever feel excitement when you were thinking about looking at the women?

M: No, I never felt that. Only about the bachelors.

H: Did you understand at that time that the big men were fencing you in?* That you couldn't look at the women, you could only look at the bachelors?

M: That's right. Now I can talk a little bit with the women. But I still won't ever look very strongly at them. [He does not add that he can only look at his mother, sisters, and kinswomen, and not at nubile women with whom he could have sex.] I can only glance at them, though; and talk a little bit and bow my head, and then talk looking at the ground. Before, I didn't do even that. But if you do it a little bit, more and more, some of your shame will go away. Years ago [after initiation], I used to be very ashamed of going inside my mother's house. But now I go and sit down once in a while. I want this shame to go away, so I can go and sit down sometimes. I might want to go inside of Mother's house, but if there are women inside, I don't go, thinking: "It's not good that I go inside and people all gossip that I want to look at them." Young women. (Not my sisters or my own clan, I'm not afraid about them.) Or the mother of my fiancée. They might think: "Why has he come inside here to be with me—inside the women's house? We didn't ask him to come inside here." There's plenty of people who would gossip like that if I went in there. I've heard such gossip. Sometimes when they [girls] walk around, some do this with me [*M. looks intensely at me eye-to-eye*; a seductive invitation]. They look right at me.†

[S: Does this text seem trivial, unimportant to understanding Sambia customs, subjective experience, erotism, ritual, adolescence, maleness and masculinity, styles of experiencing oneself and communicating to oneself, or capacity to communicate with a foreigner? In regard to ethnographic methodology, is this a useful way to gather data? How reliable are the data? What are H's responsibilities in regard to the transference reactions (e.g., dependency) such a conversation stirs up in Moondi, even more so since Sambia culture pro-

---

*This phrase—"to fence you in"—is a traditional idiom, the connotations of which here mean to sexually restrict, to ritually protect, and to keep women out of reach.
†See the third session.

vides no defense against such a powerful relationship? Are primitives'
minds primitive minds?]

Second Session: Resistance

What problems arise in interviews on intimate matters? When a subject like sex is so emotionally loaded, as among Sambia, how does
one deal with it? And how do its conflicts take form in the particular
resistance of one person's intimate communications? Here is our
starting-point.

This session occurred the morning after Session I. S. had arrived,
but he did not participate here. (He joined us later, that afternoon,
in the third session.)

Moondi and I are discussing the category *aambei-wutnyi* (gentle
man, which has feminine connotations: see chapter 8 for more detail).
Moondi is attracted to boys of this type. This subject, then, links his
gender identity to erotism, especially his shift from male to female
objects.

H: What about the *aambei-wutnyi*? What do you think of these men?
M: They don't say much, and they live peacefully. If you, a man, say
   something to them, they simply smile. I like that kind of man.
H: Can you also like this kind of initiate or like screwing with them?*
M: Yeah.
H: What kind of thoughts do you have when you think about him?
M: He doesn't say much. He just sits around. [*Pause.*] That kind of
   boy I can like. [*Longer pause.*] [S: H. is uh-hming: M's responses
   are awfully thin.] If I look at this boy, his kind of face is nice. I
   will like it. It's just like a girl's . . . [*pause, awkwardness*]. He
   doesn't have very much to say. He's not very strong. He's not strong
   in his ways. And when I see that [quality], I feel I like them all,
   that kind of man [*voice trails off*]. . . . He himself doesn't initiate conversation. He simply sits [passively].
H: Yeah, but what is it about his face that's nice, the same as a girl's?
M: [*Long pause. Searching around.*] It's like, it's not the same kind of
   face as other boys'.
H: Yeah. It's another kind.
M: Yeah, another kind.
H: What makes it another kind?
M: It's his looking. The way he looks at you. That's how; his way is
   like a girl's, he doesn't talk very much. Yeah, but even the girls—

*Moondi now takes only the fellated role in sex with boys.

they talk a lot—I know. [*Debating with himself.*] He just is the
kind who doesn't say much, just sits around, and when you talk
to him he smiles. [*Pause. Etc. This is getting nowhere.*]

This is resistance. Something in Moondi is gumming the works,
and it bothers me, for I do not know its source. We have talked about
this subject before, but Moondi is tense about it here. Others are not
around, which might otherwise explain his reluctance. Is he resisting
becoming *too* comfortable reflecting on these particular erotic feelings? Or is he struggling with emerging insight? He and I have discussed his sexual daydreams long enough that their covert features
are emerging into consciousness. Namely, the exciting personality
characteristics he attributes to his fellators are shared by his father,
who is a gentle man.* Perhaps this sharedness is now transparent and
Moondi cannot go further consciously without seeing the identification (thus, his resistance). [S: At any rate, observe H. as an ethnographer, with his thoughts on resistance; as he sits there with Moondi
on daydreams as significant experiences; on identification; on Oedipal matters; on insight and its vicissitudes. He worries if others are
around, unobserved, who might influence his informant's thoughts as
well as his own. Do other ethnographers wonder what their informants experience during such data-gathering? Do they think these
issues shape the data? Do they report these matters to us? Do they
regret it when they do not tell us just what was going on, or do they
believe that withholding information is more scientific or scholarly,
more honest or fruitful?]

H: Okay. [*Switching topics.*] When, before, you were sleeping [having
sex] with Weiyu, how did that come about?

M: [*A little anxious.*] I don't known . . . . At first, I didn't sleep with
Weiyu. It was only after I'd slept with others. I was an *imbutu*
[second-stage initiate]. [*Calmer*] . . . We were at Wopu [a nearby
pig-herding place]. They were performing the third-stage
[*ipmangwi*] initiations on Weiyu's age-set, and they were doing
the *imbutu* on us at the same time [in 1970]. They had done the
como eating ceremony . . . . You know, *inumdu* [a dark, shrubby,
green that is eaten].[7] We all built one great big hut. And we all
slept together there. The eight new *ipmangwi* and us, we just [sex-
ually] fooled around, back and forth. And at that time, Weiyu didn't
play with me. But after they performed the *ipmangwi* on
him . . . [*lowers voice here*] he was sleeping in another section

*See chapter 8.

[of the Wopu house] . . . he came over at night and touched me and woke me up. And [*very low voice*] I thought, "Who is that?" So I said [*whispering*], "Who is that, who is that?" And he said, "Me, me." And I recognized Weiyu's voice. He said to me [*whispers again, very low*], "Hurry up, come on. I like you. Let's do it." [*Pause.*] And then Weiyu screwed with me. [In this sentence the quality in Moondi's voice—I've heard it before—is: "Another man who sexually used me," a feeling that lingers despite M.'s belief he is strengthened by the semen.] I was a little afraid. I was a bit crazy. And he said, "Me, me." That's what Weiyu said to me [*M. chuckles*]. Then the two of us did it.

H: Did you feel that it was [morally] all right?[8]

M: Yeah, I felt it was all right. Afterwards, when I was an *imbutu*, I used to sleep plenty of times with Weiyu. Now, Weiyu is my cousin but he [says he] didn't know I was his cousin. He was sort of crazy. He knew, all right. [*Matter-of-fact.*] He knew I was his cousin, but he didn't want to think about it. [*Pause.*]

H: And you?

M: [*Defending himself.*] At that time I was very small and I didn't know—was he my cousin or not? [*Mask of innocence.*] But it was *him*: he came to wake me up first. He was big, grown-up. And he would have known about that.

H: Did you have it with other cousins?

M: Oh, many more! [*Raised voice.*]

H: Before, huh?

M: Yeah.

H: It's not really tabooed, is it?

M: [*Quickly.*] Cousins? That's tabooed [*with some indignation*]!

H: But you play around.

M: Yeah, that's right. [*Quieter.*] It's the bachelors' badness.

H: But [what about sex with] brothers and clan brothers?

M: Oh, no no, not them. [*Pause: Trying to reason himself out again.*] And now, Weiyu is [*lower voice*]. . . . I tell him (he's shamed): "You're my cousin, and you didn't think very well." So Weiyu gets shamed, and he doesn't listen to what I say. He'll just change the subject and talk about something else. [Not much different from western folks.] But sometimes when he really listens, he'll say, "I'm sorry; I am really shamed. You mustn't say anything more about that." But I still say, "Weiyu I was your cousin, but you didn't think." And he'd say, "That's true. I was just like a pig-dog man . . . exactly." And I'd reply, "That was your craziness."

H: You said that plenty of cousins play around.

M: Yes. They're all cousins; but when they see a boy that's really nice, they think that [as a fellator] he'll feel sweet. They know he's a cousin, but still they hide it and don't say "cousin" around him. They hide it and they think, "We mustn't call him 'cousin'." Then they play around with him like he was a *birua* [man from a hostile group: an appropriate homosexual partner] so he can sleep with us.

H: You too?

M: Yeah. I know that some are my cousins, but I—uh—feel shamed if I approach them. It's like—I think like this: "They're all big; they can think for themselves that we are cousins." It's their choice. And if they like me . . . if that's what they want to do [be my fellator], it's not important.

H: And do you feel excited then?

M: [*Dully.*] Oh, no. [*Terribly dully.*] They're my cousins, it's not right to do that with them. [*Low voice.*] I won't feel excitement. [*Pause.*]

H: As a bachelor, have you played with any of your cousins?

M: No. I never was sucked off by my cousins.

[S: Is this a wrong or a right way to learn about incest taboos? Would a more formal (i.e., structural analysis) technique to better? We change subjects.]

H: [*Pause.*] I want to work with you, to talk now about you and the girl they've marked for you [his assigned fiancée]. Can we talk as we were this morning? Now, you've had a kind of fantasy. I'm concerned that we not wait too long. If too much time passes, you might forget some of your thoughts: we have stopped talking [about this subject] for three days now.*

M: It's all right. He's [S.] come, and we're all simply happy.

H: Oh, no. I wasn't talking about him blocking our work. I was think-ing of how something has happened inside of you, that you're get-ting a new feeling, of being almost a man?

M: Yeah. I thought, "I mustn't talk too much." I must just sit down quietly.

H: But this [new manner of Moondi] is the same as your father.

M: Yeah, I thought that same thing. That's the way my father is, and now me too . . . .

H: Why should it come up now?

M: I don't know.

---

*When S. arrived, M.'s marriage concerns were temporarily forgotten.

H: Have you got some free associations?*

M: I'm not sure. I did hear that my father has gotten very sick over there, down below.[9]

H: Oh? [*News to me.*]

M: Sakulambei's woman told me. I was sorry. I wasn't just sorry, I thought about it very hard: "It's not good if he got very, very sick and he died." Around here, in these parts, we know that that is a bad place. There's lots of sickness there, and people die. My mother will go to him tomorrow . . . . She'll go to look after him.

H: Where is he?

M: At Erupmu. [*Quiet pause; then Moondi looks at me. I am waiting to see where he wants to go with this bad news.*] Oh . . . [*quickly*] that's all right. Let's go on and talk. [*Long pause. Soon after, many people enter the house. We feel it is best to stop at this point.*]

Third Session: Erotic Daydreams

The next session occurred later that afternoon, when it was quieter. At the start, S. is not in the interview, but he enters midway and joins in.

The immediate context of this discussion is as follows: during feast preparations that morning, Moondi's fiancée—accompanied by a gang of her young female friends—approached and reprimanded him in public. She had told him there was work to do (harvesting tubers for the feast?) with her parents. He felt shame and did not reply. In this situation, it is considered shameful for a youth to talk directly with his fiancée. We were never clear why *she* scolded him. But he still felt angered at being lectured—by her—in front of others. Later, Moondi mentioned that incident to Weiyu, who advised M. to talk back to her. Though seemingly trivial, this event is filled with important feelings for M: marriage, manhood, public social involvements. Here is where the tape begins. It led us into discussing his related fantasies.

H: This morning[†] we had to stop in the middle of talking about shame.

M: Yeah. It was about talking with the women.

H: Weiyu said to you, "Why don't you go talk back to her [M.'s fiancée]?" But you didn't. You told me, "I can't talk about that

---

*"Free association" is being used here as an English term; I taught it to Moondi with the concept "fantasy"; see note 1.
†Second session.

right now." [There were other people around, and he was afraid of being shamed.]

M: I thought: "It's not good that I disagree with her when we're not married yet."[10] Another thing . . . . If the men heard me being cross with that woman [fiancée], they could think: "That boy is fighting with her as if she is his *woman*," the woman who belongs to me, "as if arguing with a wife."*

H: You mean if you talk intensely with her, the men may think: "Moondi wants to marry that woman?"

M: Yeah. "He wants to marry her;" or they *could* think: "It's not time for him to talk to this woman. We [elders] haven't yet performed the *nupos* [fourth-stage initiation] on him that he can go and talk with women like that. So why has he scolded her?"

H: Is that why you get shamed?

M: Yeah. And I also feel shame when I'm near her mother and father . . . they could overhear me and think: "That boy wants our daughter too much," to screw her.

H: Would her mother and father really think that, or is that just what you think?

M: Just me. But sometimes it *is* true: people can say [*lowers voice*] "This boy is not married yet. He hasn't given a marriage feast for us. Yet he talks to her like that. Doesn't he feel shamed for talking like that?"

[*S. enters.*]

H: Let's go on to that girl they've marked for you.

M: Yeah. [*Pause.*] She really hides it when she wants to look at my face. I haven't seen her face very well, so I only can think of parts of it. I sometimes sit down and think: the nose of my woman is like this; it goes down and curves up a little bit. And I think, "Oh, that's really nice." And I think, "At night we would sleep together and do it, what all the *nupos* [married initiates] do. [*Very quickly.*] They screw in the mouth [*voice exhilarated*: the sense of a happy admission].

H: Are you talking about women? [I am surprised; I didn't realize Moondi knew the secret of the older youths: that they engage in fellatio with their young brides at or even before marriage (Herdt 1981:178–181).]

M: Of course. Weiyu told me. Though he's a little annoyed at me for telling others that he told me.

*Marriage always implies sexual intercourse.

H: Hm.

M: Yeah. Sometimes I think, "Suppose we constructed a house, a square house, the same kind as this one,[11] with several rooms and one bed. We'd sleep in it, and when I wanted to, I could shoot in her mouth. Because we would sleep in the same bed, I'd feel even *more* excitement. And she'd feel excitement from being with me.

H: In your daydreams* do you see her face or that of some other woman?

M: Hers. In the fantasy [M. uses this word, as taught by me, in the sense of daydream] she's got a towel and she covers up her face and her skin. She covers her breasts up completely. (I haven't yet actually seen them.) She hides them.[12] Sometimes I look at her and . . . she does that [hiding]. . . . I don't forget. So when I make up a daydream about her, I picture her face and her smile.[13] I don't forget. When I daydream about her, I imagine that.

H: When you do that, does your cock get tight?

M: Yeah! [*Said as "of course!"*] Whenever I think about her I get hard. All the time. [S: Those who believe homosexuality is caused by one's beginning erotic life with pleasurable homoerotic experiences will find this an odd homosexuality.]

Now, to see how homosexual desires compare with the heterosexual practices, I shift our conversation. I have relied on Moondi, more than anyone else, to investigate this issue, for I have watched him mature for five years (1979, by this interview) and, with our good rapport, have seen his heterosexual daydreams, underlined by the sincerity of the reported erection, overtake his homoerotic pleasures.

H: Now let us work the same way on your fantasies about X [a boy in the Yellow River Valley who used to fellate Moondi and about whom Moondi used to have daydreams].

M: Now when I'm with the initiates [potential fellators], I don't get fantasies. It's not the same as with the women, no, not at all. I'm talking only about the girl they picked for me to marry. Her only. When she is there, I feel happy about myself. When my girl looks at me, I feel she can think [*lower voice*] to herself: "My man. He's walking nearby and is seeing me." And she can look at me, and she can like me so much.

---

*I translate *koontu pookwugu* ("thought picture") as either daydream, or fantasy, depending on the situation and the speaker's meanings. Fantasies, sequences of mental images that have defined scripts, imply less recurrence and coherence than daydreams, though the two terms are experientially close. Moondi and I used only the word "fantasy," however.

H: When did you start having these kinds of feelings [a shifting from the homoerotic musings]?

M: When they chose me for marriage to her. That's when that day-dream began.

I was trying here to learn how Moondi's excitements toward boys and girls compared but didn't quite succeed. I felt he did not deal fully with his daydreams about boys because I was not clear enough.

[S: Yet the reader cannot tell that H. felt that until H. adds this paragraph above. It is in the nature of transcribed conversation that the participants' inner experience can only be inferred, and then usually not well. Novelists and poets have the advantage that they make up conversations so that the speakers reveal their intent. This is another example of our struggle with the problem of transmitting the data of subjectivity.]

H: Let's go back to your daydream. A square house.

M: Yeah. When we marry, we must build a house like this one* and construct it so one side has the fire for cooking and the other half is for sleeping. And on that side a little door. Inside is that bed; it's for two people. The two of us can sleep inside that bed.† And we can play around . . . hold her breasts. When I do that, she can feel something for herself, some kind of excitement to make her feel good. [*Pensive.*] Yeah. We can do that, and I can ask her, "Can we do it?" [have sexual intercourse]. [*He lowers his voice, which quivers slightly.*] And she says [*M. whispers*] "Oh, that's all right; we can do it." And I feel real excited; I really like sleeping with her.

H: Do you ask out loud or do you just whisper?

M: I ask her softly.

H: Because people are around or—

M: Oh, no. I'm just asking her softly, that's all. I just want to ask her softly. It's just the two of us, I shouldn't have to really make big

---

*See also note 11. A detail stands for so much. Moondi wants a square, untraditional hut: he wants change, a *new* definition of marriage, of masculine selfhood. (In fact, the pseudonym "Moondi" was chosen for this reason: it means "new [kind of] man", which is how I think of Moondi.) Does his fantasy concern identification with those Europeans who represent this change and transference to me ("similar to this hut")? Many questions that merit more data and more detailed study. But the main point is that no subjective element is meaningless.

†Extraordinary—I must repeat—to think a Sambia man will risk sleeping in the same bed as his polluting wife. What a fantasy.

noises [force her] in asking her. I just talk quietly. She's not far away. We're close together. [As he imagines this gentle love making, his voice is tender. This quality contrasts with Weiyu, who has also worked with me on his erotic daydreams. There's no tenderness there; just wham, bam, push it in: forcing a woman to have sex, a sort of rape. That's the excitement for Weiyu. Moondi, you can see, is different. Yet both are now heterosexual.] She says, "That's all right, we can do it." And when she says that, I feel my penis hard. [*Pause.*] I was thinking, "Why don't I get married quickly so I can do this." I think, "I want to sleep with her." And it gets hard.

H: In the daydream, when your cock is hard, is it [image of sexual position] in the mouth or down below?

M: [*Reflecting.*] Sometimes in the mouth and sometimes [*lowers voice:* a forbidden subject] down below.

H: Is it all right to have vaginal intercourse?

M: Yeah, she says it's all right. Then I get a tight cock in the fantasy and we screw.

H: And do you have a stiff cock while you're thinking that?

M: I get a tight cock, but for nothing. It doesn't do anything.

H: You just let it be?

M: Yeah, I just let it be . . . Oh, sometimes I have a piss, it's slack again. A fantasy does that. [*Pause.*]

H: The new kind of fantasy that you have, of women?

M: Yeah.

H: Now, the other one, about screwing initiates—

M: That belonged to before, when I was a new bachelor; then I used to imagine the boys.

H: Where is that fantasy?

M: I don't have sex much with the initiates any more. Before, yes. When we were down at Yellow Valley [during his bachelor initiation] I used to do it lots of times with that boy [X, above] who was sweet on me [the initiate with whom M. was infatuated, and vice versa]. But now? Not at all. I don't do it with the boys now.

Moondi's homoerotism has fallen off over the years. In 1975, he was regularly involved with boys. In 1976–1977, while at school, he had almost no homoerotic contacts. Since returning home, he has had infrequent homosexual play, in part, he says, because boys no longer excite him as much. He also believes he must not spend too much of his semen before marriage.

H: Could you?

M: I think that—[*pause*]. . . . No, not at all. I suppose if I felt I wanted to, I'd do it.

H: But when your cock does get tight, what do you do?

M: I just let it be, that's all.

H: Just let it be, huh? [*Long pause.*]

M: I just let it be, that's all.

Can we believe Moondi?[14] He has repeatedly denied over the years, both in words, fantasy, and actions that he masturbates. I tell this to psychoanalysts, who cannot believe it. [S: Me too, so far.] What do they doubt? That Sambia refrain? "It must be unconscious, they've just repressed it," an Australian analyst told me. [S: That's pretty silly.] Do they doubt the ethnography, or, the ethnographer's knowledge? [S: Not in H.'s case. I have pressed him twenty different ways and loaded him with my doubts so as to influence his interviews when he returned to his friends. At this point, I simply have no explanation, just doubts plus the expectation H. will someday find that some do masturbate sometimes—rarely—guiltily, secretly, never telling anyone else.] Why shouldn't they doubt? Show me one substantial report that tells what tribal people actually say and do about masturbation. [S: Roheim (1932, 1974)? Too much bend in his bias.] After seven years I still have no evidence of Moondi or anyone else masturbating to ejaculation. Here again are questions that demand in-depth clinical data. If an ethnographer says, "The Bongo Bongo do not masturbate," what are we to do with such a sweeping statement? (Beware of that weakness—few ethnographers mention masturbation in published reports.) Does such knowledge make a difference? Yes; learning about masturbation or the struggle against it can enlarge our understanding people's erotic behavior, gender identity development, self-esteem, empathy, moral outrage, religious rites, and capacity to identify with others (including those of the opposite sex). We need, in short, to study erotics, and to do so, we need deeper one-to-one study.

[S: It takes a certain innocence to think that public ritual must be more important to a culture or an individual than private fantasy. Any observer can trace the manifest content or effects of ritual. Do ethnographers know to—know how to—follow them into the individual's self-contained, secret or unconscious parts? Do ethnographers know that erotic drives, transmuted during their subterranean flow, can surface as ritual, war strategies, rules of politics, economic manifestoes, and decisions—even in Utopia—regarding woman's role at her man's side? The Leader's penis play can light the fires of crematoria and cities. And vice versa.]

H: I want to ask Dr. Stoller* if he's got anything to ask you before we stop, but it's up to you.

M: That's all right.

H: I will talk to him so he can understand. Oh . . . about S.'s work: you asked me this morning, "Does he [S.] follow your way of never telling other men about what I say?" and I said "Yes." So, likewise, if *I* talk to him, he will do the same as me [i.e., keep secrets].

M: Yeah.

S. has been sitting silently, listening. I sense both Moondi and Penjukwi as being natural and comfortable with S. I have achieved greatest trust with them: here they are generous—and courageous—with us in highly intimate interviews, like this one.

H: [*Turning to S.*] I didn't even tell you what we were doing.

S: [*Quickly.*] You were doing fantasies.

H: Yeah. This one is new during the last month—following marriage negotiations for his wife: he sees a new hut, and in the hut there is one bed. And he is in the bed with his fiancée. (She hasn't had her menarche yet.[†]) They are playing around, which he hasn't elaborated on yet, and he is excited because she has her breasts covered. He holds her breasts; and he gets more turned on; and then he gets a hard-on. And then he wants to screw her; and he asks her; and she says "yes"; and they *do* it. He gets an erection in the daydream . . . and in reality too, but he doesn't do anything with it, he says . . . I ask him, then, if this is different from the other [homosexual scenario] daydream he has, and he says it is. And I said, "Do you still have the other one sometimes?" and he said, "I do, but less and less all the time." I said, "How come you don't have sex with boys anymore?" He said, "Because I'm getting older, and I don't think about that much anymore." I asked[‡]

*Another detail: names and titles. Sambia call me "Gilbert," though recently (since 1979), Weiyu and Moondi have called me "Gil" (which my friends in the States call me). Before S. arrived, people asked me what to call him; Sambia are title-conscious. I told them his name was "Robert," or "Bob." Weiyu called S. "Bob." But Moondi and other called him "Dr. Stoller," apparently uncomfortable with the nickname. (And what else is involved? Power? Transference?)

†And so in reality they cannot yet be married or move further into the marriage process, that is, fourth-stage initiation, which extends over months.

‡This section has been edited for space.

if it was also because there aren't many boys available, and he said, "Yes." I said, "Is it both of those?" and he said, "Yes." I said, "Which is the most important?" He thought and said he thinks it's because there aren't any boys available. If there were, he would still screw them once in a while; but he doesn't now.

S: At this time, then, there is *no* outlet [no boys, no masturbation, no women]!

H: Right.

S: Is there an increase in the fantasy? I would think that with no outlet, it would [daydreaming] go on day and night.

H: Yeah. This is a new development: apparently he is doing it [daydreaming] quite a bit.

S: Well, it's not terribly important . . . .

H: He's hinted at this [heterosexual fantasy] to me several times before but I didn't recognize what he was talking about.*

S: Why is the girl premenarcheal? Does that turn him on?

H: Do you want me to ask him? I didn't check it out with him, since in the daydream, as in reality, she's premenarcheal.

S: But is it always a girl at that age level? For some reason that's a turn-on?

H: That's exactly correct. I hadn't thought about that. Since he thinks about screwing her in the mouth and sometimes down below, it means she's able to be screwed down below,† obviously, but I'd have to check that out with him to be sure.

S: By definition—or at least by permission—she has to be post-menarcheal . . . in order to be [vaginally] screwed by her lover. But in the daydream she's pre . . . .

H: Right. She's pre. That's very important.

S: I don't know that it is . . . it's the old story that every detail tells you something . . . but some more and some not so much.

H: This is a new version of the other daydream.

S: Why a new version today? Something about the *ceremonial* [marriage negotiations] of these past few days that you've mentioned.

H: No. [H: Yes; but I am referring to his tone. See below.]

S: Or because I'm here?

H: No. It seems related to his affect being different. We just went right into it . . . . There's something definitely different about his affect: and he found out this morning that his father is quite ill somewhere else.

---

*How much remains vague in an ethnography when the field worker—ignoring subjectivity—ignores informants' hints?
†That is, that she had her menarche.

S: Oh. And would this evening's activity [feast preparations] . . . ?
   If that didn't, then the news of his father would be more . . . .

H: Yeah. That's what he and I were talking about. When he first sat
   down, I could feel there was something different. He said, "I've
   been feeling different the last couple of days. Less aggressive." I
   said, "What does that mean? What about this afternoon?" [M.'s
   fiancée scolding him.] And then we talked about that. Then I said,
   "Does this have anything to do with you and me not having talked
   for three days?" He said, "No," and then he said his father is ill,
   which he found out this morning. That's how it went. [*Pause.*] So
   he and I will just continue on.

S: It's a different ambiance from the last interview. Now I'm just
   sitting in the midst of an on-going process and have no need to
   know anything. The last one [interview]* was [a tense] orientation; this one is just going—I sit and watch and it just looks very
   good. You get good information from both kinds, but there's more
   friction in the other one, which creates a different relationship.
   When there's less friction, you get frictionless information. They're
   both important. What is Moondi feeling now? My presence seems
   to have no [disruptive] effect. Was I present in any particular sense?

H: Well, *I'm* feeling something different in him. A flippant† quality
   that's not usually there but not necessarily because you're here.
   It may be what else is happening today. [*To Moondi:*] Dr. Stoller
   wants to ask you: He says that you and I are used to talking alone
   and now he's with us. How is that for you right now?

M: I think it's good he can listen and hear us so he can understand
   our talk. Your work is the same as his; when you gather secrets
   of one man—he [S.] won't tell that to another man. I just think
   it's good that he comes and listens, and if he wants to hear my
   secrets, that's all right. That's what I think. There's nothing wrong
   with it.

---

*With Kalutwo: see chapter 9.
†In the original 1979 session I said "flippant," but added: "that's not quite the right word."
The dictionary defines flippant as: (1) lacking due respect of seriousness; impertinent; saucy.
(2) obs. overly talkative. Now I think that neither of these connotations is apt; in fact, "lacking
due respect," "impertinent," "saucy," and "overly talkative" are all wrong descriptions of
what I felt in Moondi that hour. But over the course of editing, my doubts were removed, and
"flippant" stuck—until I checked the dictionary. I believe now—looking back over tapes and
transcription—that Moondi was lighter than usual—there was more lightness in his speech
and body language. My interpretation of Moondi that moment: he felt safe and secure, less
tense than normal. Somehow, our presence affected his lightness, but I cannot say quite why.
The point is that my original description now seems wrong to me, and all it took was that
one word. But who are we to believe—H. in 1979 or H. in 1982? I think I am more correct
now, having thought about that moment a half-dozen times over three years. Here is an example of retrospective reflection changing one's description.

H: I'll tell him. [*To S.*] He thinks it's good you want to hear how the two of us talk, and he knows that you, like me, don't reveal people's secrets. And he also knows that, by doing this, you'll be able to understand better that he and I have a certain kind of work, and that you'll understand his thoughts better by being here. And I think that's correct: I don't feel any hostility at all.

S: That has to be right. It's interesting that [*struggling*] there's an awareness of his own psychology available to him; self-awareness, not just experiencing. A revolutionary idea [for a Sambia]—that you can have your own psychology—

H: [*Cuts in.*]—thoughts [that one thinks, reflects, about oneself].

S: —and be interested in doing it. And that you would sit down with someone, that someone like Moondi can make that jump. He is experiencing discovering* what we—not everyone in our culture—but what we take for granted: the past is living [intrapsychically] in the present, and not in the sense of their [Sambia] ghosts. An idea like that was just not available [before, as a fully conscious cultural understanding].

DISCUSSION

S. and H: How is the erotic manifested in Moondi? What role has culture played? Can we say that Moondi's erotism is in any way eccentric or unique, a result of his life history and personal experiences? Sexual excitement is made, not born; some combination of personal and social factors create this.

Let us review and orient this interview.[15] We are talking with Moondi, a bachelor, who is moving toward marriage. He is male, the sex preferred by parents, since only males can defend the hamlet against the unending threat of destruction in war. At age eight, he is suddenly removed from his mother's doting attention and, via brutal and terrifying initiation rites, is resocialized by the men so that he will grow up to be manly, a warrior, a husband, and a father. The process begins with the first-stage initiation, when he enters the phase of semen ingestion. He has only a few years to do so, however, for with his third-state initiation at puberty, he may no longer take in semen but is to offer his penis to the next cohort of boys. At the same time the females are forbidden to him.

Whatever reverberations lie hidden within these overt experiences,

---

*S: I.e., meaning, interpretation, belief, synthesis; not conditioning, machinery, or acetylcholinesterase (even if it takes a bucketful of enzyme to get angry at women).

we know that from the start of their erotic lives and for the years of their peak orgasmic capacity, these young men are propelled into intense, obligatory, praiseworthy, powerfully gratifying homoerotism. At the same time that males are positively reinforced as the only sex objects, females are negatively reinforced. They are not just forbidden. The taboos are nailed down by the dread created as boys now learn how vaginal fluids cause illness (if not ritually treated) and eventual death—the consequence of being infected by even a droplet of menses. Yet Moondi, who at nineteen learns the identity of the girl he will marry, begins—without deprogramming—to create powerfully erotic heterosexual daydreams. And if he is like other Sambia men, he will desire women the rest of his life, without ever forgetting his homoerotic joys. In fact, by becoming initiators and teaching about homosexual fellatio to sons and other new initiates in later years, these men are reminded of and have reinforced for them the positive value of semen and homoerotic activities.

Probably if Sambia society allowed adult married men to be homoerotic, some, as in our society, would be bisexual. But those like Moondi would not; they love their lust for women. And it is that lust—with its depth and breadth—that behavioristic explanations would say ought not be there. As Moondi exemplifies and as hundreds of hours of interviews, gossip, and bull sessions with other men revealed, desire for women is—for all its vicissitudes—as gripping for Sambia men as it is anywhere else.

Could this just be bluster by men denying that they are "really" homosexual? We doubt it as we think of their desire for multiple wives, of the occurrence of adultery despite severe taboos, and of men's drive for intercourse, so strong that even the terrors of female fluids cannot halt the heterosexual tension. And finally, were that heterosexual need weak, it would be further subdued by the men's awareness that every ejaculation of semen advances the deterioration of one's manhood. (Remember that intercourse with women is thought to be more depleting than that with boys.)

In Moondi's case, then, we see a normative gender and erotic developmental pattern. What would seem bizarre and the negation of masculinity is, here, as in other instances of age-structured homosexuality (Adam 1986; Herdt 1987b), a particularly royal road to it.

What of aberrance? An example from Moondi's narrative returns us for a moment to our data. Even in the gay community in our society, we do not hear of men who fetishize other males' mouths, comparable to the fetishizing of women's bodies by heterosexual men. In fact, despite the importance of mouths as erotic organs among homosexuals and heterosexuals in our society, one does not hear at all of the fetishizing of mouths. Yet Sambia males, in erotic reminiscing, go on and on about the shapes and aesthetics of mouths. The same point applies to the emphasis on semen among Sambia, for, as noted in chapter 2, the quality of semen is a great factor in the fellators' experience. We do not find this same preoccupation in the West, however. And though there is an aesthetic of penis appearance among many (heterosexuals and homosexuals) in our culture, there is none with the Sambia. For them the penis is a semen conveyor, a vessel. It is at these points of precise observation, where technical vocabulary and theory give way to subjective reality, that we could find the proper proportions for mixing psychodynamic and learning theories to explain a piece of behavior (see Stoller and Herdt 1985).

Later, in chapter 9, we shall examine a man—Kalutwo—for whom erotic aberrance has become a way of life, and his case will, we think, reveal even more clearly the normativeness of Moondi's erotism.

Out of particular people, in particular cultural settings, one gets particular sexual excitement. The details of this phenomenon can only come from clinical ethnography. We hope to demonstrate this more in subsequent chapters.

CHAPTER FIVE

Tali and Weiyu on Ritual and Erotics

BIOGRAPHIC SKETCHES

H: Tali and Weiyu are my two most important adult collaborators.
They were essential to my research. They aided me in learning language and in understanding ritual custom, kinship, and marriage. Tali's
role as a ritual expert was crucial for studying Sambia initiation and
its meaning. Yet both men are far more than "informants." They are
also friends and companions, cronies who helped build my house, who
fed me, and became two more sets of eyes, ears, minds, and hearts.
This chapter is about these men, their relationship to me, and conversations they had with S. and myself.

The following texts present these dialogues. Unlike our other in-
terview-chapters, these data were not collected as part of individual
case studies. I was working with Weiyu and Tali on various social
matters, such as ritual beliefs and practices. S. joined in these conversations. He asked questions of his own that sparked unexpected
responses from the men. We shall examine the themes of our talking
later.

Both men have known me since 1974. Both live in Nilangu and
were my neighbors. Tali was then in his late twenties, though he looked
older and seemed widely experienced for his age. He was married and
had a two-year-old son. Weiyu was about twenty-two years old, still
a bachelor and living in the men's house. They were simply fellow-
villagers then, not especially close to each other. Their relations with
the outside world were as different as possible. Weiyu had worked on
coastal plantations for several years in the early 1970s, he spoke Pidgin
and Motu fluently, and he was relatively sophisticated (and saw himself that way) compared to his peers. Tali, on the other hand, was a

128

traditionalist who had never been outside the local area, spoke no Pidgin, and was naive about western ways. But because they shared many personality traits and were co-workers in my research, they eventually became allies and confidants.

I knew Weiyu first. His marriage ceremony occurred only a month after my arrival in the village. He stood out from his peers: he was taller, more verbal, gregarious and (by Sambia standards and my own) handsome. He liked to show off, to be seen as acculturated when it counted; when dressed in warrior garb (which was rare, for he usually wore western clothes), he cut a dashing figure. Women liked him and he knew it: he is still a ladies' man, a Don Juan. He liked sex with boys too; in fact, he likes sex in general. He's more blatant about that than most Sambia men, and his coastal experience was a big factor in making him more sexually aggressive. Weiyu and his cohort of three fellow initiates invited me (in December 1974) to join in their initiation festivities shortly after my arrival. I was thrilled, honored, surprised: I did not see then how that single event could get me so quickly involved as their ally.[1] This experience made me, by age (I was 25, about their age), subsequent identification by other villagers, and common interests (being bachelors), their agemate.

Weiyu's childhood is unusual. (Why is this true of almost all my Sambia colleagues?[2]) His true father was a renowned and feared shaman of Pundei village (Nilangu's sister hamlet). He was said to have been a physically powerful man, too—tall and strong, impressive and reckless. Some twenty years ago (Weiyu doesn't remember him) he was murdered by his own clan brothers in an infamous massacre that set off a war between Pundei and Nilangu.[3] Weiyu's father was simply too brazen and reckless: he openly flirted with women, let it be known that he was screwing other men's wives, used his powerful sorcery knowledge to keep men afraid of him, and—the unbearable and insane sin—claimed with pride responsibility for the (sorcery) deaths of several people. He was disposed of in an ambush—hacked to death by a gang of brother-warriors. As a result, his widow fled with her two children, Weiyu and his older sister, to Nilangu, where they were given shelter by their affines. Eventually, a Nilangu big man, Chemgalo, who was himself an older widower, took Weiyu's mother as his wife. He adopted Weiyu and, with unusual kindness for that day, gave Weiyu the advantage of full social rights in the village. Shortly before his initiation, Weiyu's mother died. He has been cared for since by Chemgalo's eldest daughter (his step-sister), and Chemgalo himself, who never remarried.[4]

The wound opened by Weiyu's father's murder has never healed.

His father's only biologic brother (himself a powerful shaman) also fled Pundei and never returned. This man (now deceased) used to mutter to me that the murderers would pay eventually (i.e., through his sorcery powers). Sambia is a society that honors blood revenge, yet Weiyu's father has never been revenged. So Weiyu grew up with a fantasy, sometimes quietly expressed today, that *he*, the son, carries the burden of knowing that there has as yet been no revenge. This awareness—and quiet, romantic identification with an amazing father cut down and never known—is burned into Weiyu's masculinity.

Weiyu's marriage was also odd. He and his wife were the first couple (to my knowledge) to have chosen each other. They were mutually attracted and went against others' wishes in marrying. There is also a sense that Weiyu's wife is socially inappropriate for him.[5] They have been at each other's throats for years. Both are jealous. Weiyu is also flirtatious and an exuberant fornicator. As a bachelor he loved screwing boys (was even sometimes unscrupulous, screwing his cousins such as Moondi, Chapter 4, who are supposed to be tabooed). He outgrew boys, though, and has since concentrated on women, whom he voraciously prefers. Weiyu is, nonetheless, more a fornicator than a lover of women: he is misogynous. He has had many fights with his wife; they constantly have terrible arguments. (I know he beats his wife, but I have never seen him do it. She has also clobbered him.) Though they have a house, gardens, and now two children, their marriage is not successful or satisfying.[6] (Weiyu's mother-in-law is always telling me "I told you so"; she didn't want them to marry by choice. The mother-in-law seems to feel that their chaos is the result of marriage inspired by romance, not custom.) Tali shares feelings of misogyny with Weiyu, and though Tali and his wife fight, they do not—nor do most other couples—persist in the vicious combat that characterizes Weiyu's marriage.

Tali is older and wiser than Weiyu. He is a thinker and a planner. His life is well organized: he knows what he wants and how to get there. He was the third of four sons of a prominent man, who had three wives. He grew up in Moonunkwambi, a neighboring hamlet (of the same phratry) that no longer exits. His upbringing was otherwise ordinary. Early on he showed himself to be a gifted hunter, and he still loves to hunt. First initiated about 1955, he has since been an active ritual cult member. He also fought in several battles before pacification and was considered a good warrior.

Tali had had, however, an unusually wide range of ritual training. He likes to travel and has been to virtually every dispersed Sambia group and all surrounding tribal areas. He has trading partners in other tribes. While still a second-stage initiate he traveled with several visiting Menya tribesmen back to their villages (near Menyamya) on a trading expedition. Through this experience he made contact with ritual experts and thereby with traditions of myth beyond any most Sambia *elders* know. He had also a distant older male relative and closer half-brother, who taught him many magical spells and special secret ritual techniques. Thus, by adolescence, Tali was already well on his way to becoming a ritual expert.

What kind of man was he to become?* First, he is a traditionalist. He believes in his heritage, its customs, beliefs, and conventional wisdom about the nature of man and woman, erotic and gender development. He followed all the correct formulas for his own development, from careful attention to being a homosexual fellator to gain strength, to following elders' instructions and regulations regarding his own sexual (insertor) contacts with boys and then women. When I first knew him he dressed only in native garb. He was not an imposing figure: medium height and build, average-looking, and not an exhibitionist. But in initiation he stands out: he is an organizer, quietly in command and competent in the public rhetoric. As he has grown older, he is more prominent and he keeps people and activities steady and working. He was married rather late, in the old way of infant betrothal—the most conservative marriage—to Nashu, a very traditional woman. Today (1982), in his mid-thirties, they have been married 10 years and seem content with each other. They have two boys, aged 7 and 4. They fight and squabble, but not as much as they used to; and they seem to me, now, to be happier and more successful than ever. They are generous, well-liked people.

My relationship with Tali and older men has always been simpler for me than my relationship with other interpreters, especially youths and initiates. This was, as usual, much of my own making. For a year (1974–1975) I largely ignored Tali, something I could not do with the initiates. Having come to investigate the boys' experience of undergoing ritual initiation, I felt it a duty to attend first to that neglected topic before others, and before it was too late (after the cult had dramatically changed following westernization). Working alone, classed as a bachelor, I was more identified with bachelors and had to overcome, as much as possible, the tensions, turmoils, and one-sided dominance of that social position in my dealings with young initiates. (With some of them I never succeeded; I remained either too threa-

*We acknowledge permission to reprint some of this biographical material on Tali (pages 110–111) from G. Herdt, *Guardians of the Flutes*, pp. 338–341. New York: Columbia University Press, 1987.

tening or too much a rich white European, to achieve trust.) With the bachelors, like Weiyu (until his marriage), the pressures were different, since I was perceived more as a peer (a colleague, a competitor). With women I remained a rather distant curiosity; benign, congenial, and eligible but much too roped off by the men to be very involved with them. With elders I was (at least with my sponsors) adopted affectionately, cared for, exploited and exploiting (e.g., I gave them canned fish and small gifts) but was still seen as immature and below them. Tali never got entangled much in these early scenarios; he was simply there, going about his hunting (he is still an avid and successful hunter), and mentioning that he had a lot to teach me.

Two things changed our relationship in late 1975. The first was my interest in ritual. Following the performance of collective initiations that year, I started to study myth and ritual. Before that I had interviewed initiates, for which Moondi served as the chief interpreter. Eventually, though, I needed to interpret the texts gathered from initiations. The men said that Tali was the one to ask. But, because of the stratification of ritual knowledge, I needed another interpreter—Weiyu—who, as a newly married man, could discuss such matters secretly with Tali and me (the initiates and Moondi were kept well removed at such times). Likewise, for fear of their embarrassment or shame, I had always to take care in arranging work with Moondi and other initiates, especially on topics like dreams and sex, when the adults were gone. I needn't belabor the obvious: that this dual secrecy presented logistical problems, conflict in interpersonal ties, and, after months, definitely changed my role to that of middleman-accomplice with initiates, who trusted me, on the neutral ground of my house. (My acquiring ritual secrets was, sadly, not complicated by deep involvement with women, since I remained until 1979 a spectator in relation to them.)

In these circumstances, Tali took to working with me frequently, communicating secrets about ritual and his opinions of them. He and his little son also visited my house to pass the time in the evening. I would offer him tea, or a cigarette, and a few disjointed pieces of conversation; but because I spoke Sambia poorly then, we usually said little, and he stayed only briefly. An accident then changed our relationship.

Late in 1975, I returned from the mountain patrol station to Nilangu, hiking through the mountains with some Sambia, including Tali. We arrived in the hamlet the day after his house had burned to the ground. (This misfortune is not unique, since grass huts are consumed in a few minutes, once they catch fire.) Tali was devastated:

all his possessions, including his ritual items and money, were lost. He was furious at his wife, whom he blamed. As usual, he handled this event with a flurry of emotion, followed by sullenness and then quiet depression. After a day or so of detachment, feeling sympathy for him and trying to bolster his spirits, I gave him a pair of my walking shorts (he had lost all his garments too), some tobacco, and a little money. (He could use the money to help him feel better; for instance, he would have to barter or buy ritual ornaments again, and he eventually did so.) He quietly accepted the gifts with thanks, was obviously moved, but otherwise said nothing.

Over the next year, those two events—our ritual work and those gifts—came back on me in unexpected ways. More than once when I least expected it, Tali spoke of his misfortune and my kindness. Once I needed a favor; he did it without my asking. Later he said I had also helped him. At another time, while I was on patrol (1976) among the neighboring Yagwoia tribe, Tali again was invaluable: he went among his cronies, found a bilingual Sambia, and then sent word to a Yagwoia man of a distant hamlet known to hold many myths. The man arrived near midnight the next evening, to my complete surprise. But since he had to return the next day, Tali led us that very night in setting about to collect as many myths as possible (acquiring them for his own repertoire too), till the wee hours of the morning. In ways like that he made me a friend.

But most impressive of all was what occurred one evening in late 1976, after a day's work with Tali and Weiyu on ritual matters. It was near the end of my fieldwork; men knew I would leave in a few weeks. And though I told them I would return, and though they wanted to believe this, life, they know, is filled with uncertainty. Around 8:00 P.M., Tali walked into my house with his son, and we began to chat. Weiyu also arrived. After tea and some jokes, Tali said he had thought about the *tingu** again and that he wanted to say something else he had neglected that morning. This afterthought surprised me, for it happened only once before. (That is, after an interview, Tali returned later wanting to clarify a specific point.) After he shared his thoughts, I thanked him, communicating my surprise. Then he added: "You really want to know about our lives. We thought you came just to learn about the ritual customs. [*Serious.*] But you want to understand us, don't you? That's why I thought about this and told you."

Over the years Tali has become a pragmatist. He was designated the first local *komitiman* of Nilangu by its people back in the early

---

*The menstrual blood organ, important in the ritual belief system.

1970s. Since then he has been a tireless hearer of local disputes. He has slowly learned bits of Pidgin (but is still not conversant). He nearly always wears western clothes now. In recent years, he made the unprecedented decision to send his oldest son out to a mission school, instead of initiating him and having him stay close. Today he sees the ritual cult as dying and feels that his son's schooling is a decision for his family's future. Nonetheless, he continues his hunting, has broadened his social contacts, continues to make arranged marriages through infant betrothal for his sons, nose-bleeds himself and follows customary ritual ways, and runs his household as a present-day form of the household he knew and loved in his childhood.

Weiyu and Tali worked well together. I liked Weiyu; and in our several years' talking, traveling—observing initiations, visiting neighboring tribes, going to the Patrol Post to resupply—and living close by, I got to know him for himself. As you would expect, Tali and Weiyu also became closer: they were no longer just fellow villagers and cultmembers; they were also co-workers for me whose social and economic interests were allied.[7] Both are self-assertive, gregarious, high in self-esteem, verbally articulate, curious and able to enjoy new experiences, misogynous, keenly interested in ritual customs and heritage, full of enjoyment of sexual behavior, etc. From talking constantly with me they share a store of experience and cultural knowledge (about Sambia and Westerners) unusual even for elder Sambia. And so they are now intimates, whom others identify with me.

The next sessions with Stoller must be seen in the light of this history. After several months, my follow-up work with Tali on Sambia ritual was done. I was finishing up and saying goodbye. These were men with whom I am so entangled that I think of them as among the people closest to me in the world. I was ready for more challenging dialogue with them than ever before, a new kind of ethnographic experience with one's friends; a mutual exploring of interiors so as to know each other better. Stoller was our catalyst.

SUBJECT I: WIFE-STEALING

This conversation occurred spontaneously between Weiyu and Tali, with H. and S., from 10:30 until 11:30 P.M. The tone is low-key, we are alone, late at night, a bull session. As in previous days, Weiyu and Tali have again drifted to the subject of Nilutwo.[8]

Nilutwo had an accident, soon to be mortal. While hunting he fell from a tree, breaking his back. He was flown by helicopter to a distant hospital, and returned, untreatable. His legs, paralyzed, gave him constant, terrible pain. His bladder was paralyzed. The skin of his legs had terminal trophic changes. He was episodically unconscious from uremic delirium. A once powerful, driven, warm, brave, masculine man—the greatest living cassowary hunter—was reduced to a dying, invalid ward of his wife and the village. Penjukwi, his wife, managed as best she could, but the ever-present conflict in their marriage erupted again. (Nilutwo, with the men's help, had stolen Penjukwi, shrieking in rage and agony, from her natal hamlet. She was subsequently, in effect, raped into marriage by N., a legitimate though rare form of courtship nowadays; see chapter 6). Tali, who was Nilutwo's friend, took over much of his support, and eventually Penjukwi and Nilutwo began living with Tali and his wife in their house. This placed Nilutwo squarely in Tali's life, and Tali frequently expressed frustration about it, as in the following session.

The men in the village were all wondering who would get Penjukwi after Nilutwo's death. By tradition, a woman may be inherited (levirate marriage) by her deceased husband's brothers or clansmen. Penjukwi was still young and attractive, and the men were very interested in her. But she was also independent and wise, so she had pointedly avoided situations that would have compromised her future choices. Tali was, in effect, her guardian. Weiyu, who loves to talk about semen and sex anyway, let it be known that he was interested in her, would perhaps marry her. I was aghast that the men were, in a sense, already drawing straws over Penjukwi before her husband's death. Though a friend of both sides, I felt obliged to help Penjukwi and thus put myself at odds with the men.

H. fills in S. on the above. Weiyu and Tali gossip.

HERDT: [To S.] Nilutwo now [finally] is totally at his wife's mercy. They're at each other's throats. He's been so difficult for her. But Tali probably won't do it. [Tali threatened to kick Nilutwo out of T.'s house, because N. is driving everyone crazy with his incessant demands, constant pain, and screams.] Tali has a good heart. He's just shooting off steam. [*Weiyu talks in a quiet voice to Tali. Then:*]

WEIYU: Nilutwo is thinking about his woman: "Those two [Tali and Weiyu], they're sitting and watching me. They want to butter her up for when I die." [*Tali chuckles. Then Weiyu snaps to T.:*] Stop that! This is serious.*

H: [*To T. and W.*] That's what you're thinking, huh?

---

*Only because Weiyu wants to steal Penjukwi.

W: Yeah.

H: Oh, yeah. Because he thinks you come around to butter up Pen-jukwi so you can screw her? Is that why Nilutwo is angry?

W & T: [*Enthusiastically*] Yeah.

H: Is this true?

W: It's true that that's what he's thinking. But we're not really buttering her up. That's just what he's thinking: "I'm just sick, I'm here, they think I'm sleeping, they [Weiyu] just think to themselves, 'He's an old sick man here, he's not about to watch and see what we do.'"

H: Is it true?

W: [*Broad grin.*] I'm a *man!* [Meaning: of course it's true. *Tali chuckles.*]

S: [*Quietly.*] So they would like it, huh? [*W. and T. laugh broadly.*]

H: [*Chuckles.*] So it's really true after all; it's not just his [N.] imagination?

W: Oooooh!

S: Why not, from their point of view? [*All half-serious and half-joking.*]

H: Exactly [*more serious*]. Why not, yes! [*Sarcastic.*]

W: [*Continues joking.*] When you go back to America and come back, you may hear that your friend [W.] did this and he did that [acted lascivious] to this woman.* Everyone will tell you the story. About me. [Tries to get more serious.] But listen, it isn't like she's a man, this woman. She can't just sit around here. She can't just be unmarried here. That's no good. A woman has no strength at all. Who's to help her work her gardens and build her new outhouse, and things like that?

H: [*Ironic.*] Who will help her by screwing her and screwing her?

W: [*Big laugh.*] There, that's it! That something of hers [vagina] doesn't have a man to boss it. Now me, I must be the boss of that particular thing of hers. [*Voice trails off.* He's a bit excited, horny, perturbed, and joking, all at once.]

H: [*To S.*] He says a woman shouldn't just sit around: just sitting there is no good . . . That [sex] is all she's good for.

S: Yeah.

H: [*Paraphrasing.*] There'll be no one to help her; women don't have strength of their own. Who will make gardens for her or help her out? And there's no one to boss her cunt.

---

*Penjukwi outsmarted the men; Weiyu never had a chance. See chapter 6.

W: [*To H., joking.*] Tali, he's a man of the law. He doesn't think like
     this.
H: Yeah, he's a good man. But *you* . . .
T: Yes, that's right.
W: Oh, I'm all right. I am a man.
[S: Pretty funny talk. But beneath the locker-room humor is a whiff
of death. Penjukwi is not just another local lady. As H. said above,
at 18 (she is now around 24), she was kidnapped and ravished by
Nilutwo; she was also uppity, known in the Valley for her looks, in-
dependence, and a spot of schooling (in a place of sophistication: a
village by a grass airstrip three hours away). Unlike the other women,
she has too much education and speaks some Pidgin. She also has an
odd tattoo on her face. (See chapter 6.) So when her husband—he
the great hunter, far too skilled to have such an accident—fell, the
men believed she had bewitched him to get revenge after all these
years. As soon as he died, they would accost her, beat her up.

   We were in a quandary. As much as possible, and slightly cowed
by the moral dilemma involved, we had at all times—H. for years, I
for these few days—obeyed our rule not to tamper with custom, settle disputes, teach new skills (other than the search for insight), or
practice medicine. Nonetheless, we broke this rule and, before leaving, warned all concerned not to harm Penjukwi. On returning in 1981,
H. found her alive, unbeaten, unraped, unthreatened, unmarried; de-
fiantly, happily alone. Sambia culture is changing. And she is perhaps—because the men are too dispirited to force her—among the
beneficiaries.]
H: Where and when should anthropologists intervene in such situations? We join others (see Epilogue) in our concern and perplexity
over such ethical issues. Still, we feel that ethnographers should in-
sert these ethical aspects *in* their ethnographies, rather than elsewhere in field method treatises or letters to the *American Anthropologist Newsletter*. Again, such editing restricts and distorts our work.

SUBJECT II: BREAST-FEEDING OR ORGASM?

We continue without break to a second topic in the same session. This
material arises from previous conversations on women hiding their
breasts and breast-feeding. As Chapter 2 explains, this topic is powerfully linked with sex—especially fellatio—though I did not con-
centrate on its private manifestations until S.'s questions prompted
me to.

H: [*To Weiyu.*] I was telling him [S.] about the way we all work.

W: Uh-huh.

H: Now, I was thinking about the times you've talked about the the custom of women hiding their breasts, that it's not good for men to look at them. Last week I heard that some women say they felt *imbimboogu* [orgasm] when they breast-fed babies. Have you heard this? [*W. and T. whisper for a minute.*]*

W: No. The women don't talk about this to us. But we think our wives have felt this. I can ask my woman and find out.

H: It's taboo to look at them while they're breast-feeding?

W: [*Repeats the teachings:*] You can't look at the mother feeding the baby and can't sit around with the mother and baby. Instead, you must stay with the men in the men's house.

H: Yeah, that's [breaking post-partum taboo] no good.

W: If you watched the baby with its mouth holding on to the nipple of the breast, I'd think of my wife's mouth doing the same to my penis. If you think like that [*voice speeds up*] you won't let her be. You'll want to screw her. Then you'll ruin your child.

H: Did we ever talk before about women having *imbimboogu* with breast-feeding?

W: No. [*To T. in Sambia.*] We didn't talk about that, did we?

T: No.

W: But it's true when they breast-feed that the fluid comes out of the breast, and when that happens they feel *imbimboogu*. I think they told you the truth.

H: Did you think of this before or only now?

W: Uh, uh. Only now. You mentioned it and that's it.

H: Hmmmm. I want to tell him [S.] about this. [*To S.*] I asked them if they had ever heard that when women breast-feed they have an *imbimboogu*, and he said, "No, we'd never heard of that before."

S: Had they never *thought* of it? I'm not correcting you. They'd never heard of it, but in addition it's not part of their fantasy system? Is that right? Or you don't know? Should you ask?

H: Well, now that I've said that, Weiyu replied: "I think that when their milk comes outside that they feel *imbimboogu*." So I responded: "What do you mean that you think that?" And then I clarify: "You mean now you think that's how it is? And he said, "Yeah, that's how I think."

---

*Why are they whispering? Because this subject is illicit, secret, and filled with power for males (and females). Here, then, is an example of what elsewhere I have called "whispering secrets."[9]

S: Do they think it's possible because both organs hang from the body, have a special end, and put out a fluid?

H: Well, that's—

S: You can't ask them that . . .

H: Sure, sure, yeah.

S: Well, how could you have an organ like that where you didn't get an *imbimboogu?* Now the next question would be: is that the same as ejaculation that *they* have, or is it just that it is the appropriate word for the fluid going out, not for the feeling?* The feeling that goes with it, not the feeling that goes with it coming out. And if they believe that, then how have they never seen a woman sense that?

H: Yeah, well, one answer would be that women always hide the act. [*Pause, seeing consternation on S.'s face.*] Women always hide breast-feeding.

S: But they don't hide. I've seen them.†

H: Well, that's what I just asked him. I said, how does it go, you know, with women breast-feeding babies? And then he said the ritual teaching goes that you're not supposed to watch your wife breast-feed, because you'll think of the breast as if it were a [your] penis with the baby [wife] sucking it. He made this motion as if breasts were the penis and the nipple—

S: So the ritual teaching very consciously links breast and penis, and milk and semen . . .

H: And the baby and the mother . . .

S: Yeah; so it looks like we are getting an amplification of a peculiar detail in the daydream [seen in Moondi's case, chapter 4] and what may be central to their culture.

H: Yeah, that's right.

S: If you want to try it again anyway, you can see if they think that the woman is literally having an orgasm in our sense of the word.

H: Yeah, yeah. I'm thinking now of various possibilities [for how to ask them to clarify their thinking. *H. turns to Weiyu:*] We have now heard you say that you've never heard the women talk about this.

W: Yeah.

H: Now when women . . . what do you think women are feeling when they give milk to babies?

W: Yeah, we don't ask the women that. But we think that their water [milk], it—the water of the breast . . .

*See chapter 6.
†Further discussed in chapter 4.

H: Yeah.

W: It comes outside and—

H: What do they feel?

W: None of us think about them like that. We don't think about what they feel when the milk comes out. They just give food to babies and we just forget about thinking about it, that's all.

H: Do the men ever talk together about this?

W: No, we don't talk about this. You mustn't [taboo] look too much at them [breast-feeding]. That's what the elders say. [*Coached by Tali, whose voice is hoarse from talking so much today:*] If you look too closely, what can you do? You have no outlet, no way: what can you do [if you get sexually aroused and you want intercourse, since this is forbidden].

H: Hmmm. [*To. S.*] Here's a problem in methodology: I've just asked them again something I have already asked them before: "Do you guys have any thoughts or daydreams about women giving milk to babies?" And there's just a blank.

S: What about using guided imagery? I'm not sure whether I mean guided imagery in the sense that you use it—the more formal technique—but could you improvise something whenever you get up against a blank that you feel has something behind it?

H: Yeah.

S: Could you have offered them the opportunity to have a free-floating visual experience?

H: That's what I'm doing with Moondi.

S: So, then, that's my answer methodologically. That's the exact place to try it: where you don't feel that it's a blank just because they've run out, or are bored, or tired, or something else.

H: Yeah. I've thought about that but never made this explicit; I can now. There is still another approach: I've asked them the straightforward question and know how to get at this from a different angle.

S: Yeah. Should you now go to a more roundabout question?

H: No, what I'm saying now is that I've asked the straightforward question and I know how to get at it from another angle. One angle is to bring up the question of why in the first-stage initiation teaching, the mother's breast is equated to the penis and why men go to the trouble of equating semen with breast milk. And by doing that, I set up a train of associations which will eventually lead to the same point.

S: Oh, I see. So that's what you should do, except that they're tired and—

H: Yeah, they're tired.

S: And pick it back up tomorrow. That's what we should do then.

H: [*Chuckling.*] Enough. [*To W. and T.*] We can all work tomorrow.

S: [*To H.*] Are you noting the time of day? It may not be important, but it's an easy thing to put down.

H: No, it is important.

S: Because material gathered between 10:30 and 11:30 at night will have perhaps no explanation except the time of night.

H: I usually note the time of day in my notes because it does make a difference.

But the men refused to quit, hyped on the conversation at the moment. So we went on. During this next part of the dialogue, we get into men's private experience of ritual beliefs. These beliefs concern semen depletion, such a widely shared fear among Sambia men. Specifically, we are talking of how men, during intercourse with their wives, picture the tree sap they will drink to replace their semen.

Unfortunately, our tape broke here, and we lost about three minutes of important dialogue. S., fitting into the situation, playfully challenged Weiyu and Tali's beliefs about the growth-power in semen. He testified that while he'd never ingested semen and has drunk no milk since childhood, he nonetheless has a wife and four grown children. How could they explain that? The men took the challenge and there were several rapid interchanges, each side determined not to give in. I was apart from this conversation, having never directly challenged the men's beliefs. This led us to discussing drinking tree sap. (You will see, later, how this dialogue may have dredged up latent thoughts in the men.) [S: My purpose in challenging them was not to get information on erotic and gender issues but to investigate the style and quality of their skills in argumentation, especially logic. I found that, given their first premises plus my having nothing but my mouth for proving my assertions—no appeal to authorities and information and no technology for scientific demonstrations—they were as smart as I. I had no advantages in the debate and we all had a great time.]

S: How do they experience drinking the tree sap? Do they picture the tree?

H: They talk of it as an image of the tree. [*To W.*] Do you have a thought-image of the tree?

W: [*Enthusiastic.*] I see that all the time. When I have sex, I think about the tree. [*Spirited talk between W. and T.*]

H: [*To S.*] W. says he sees it all the time. "I never told you about this; I don't know why."

S: I'd like to hear about that. He's really talking about the cult. And your main subject of study here all these years has been the cult.

H: Yeah. There's a simple explanation for this picturing the sap. (Well, not an explanation): the tree stands for their masculinity. The tree's got their maleness in it.

S: You're suggesting that it is defensive. (We should ask them.) I was thinking that it's not only that. You get it from your mother, from the moment you're born. It represents something inside you: it represents your father or what is taught you by your father, the most primal knowledge.

H: But how could it be taught like that? Because they don't know about this use of milk sap until they're fifteen years old and more. It doesn't have to be defensive unless it's defending them against something.

S: Well, I don't know what I mean. [S: I do now, but I'm still vague: the specifics, it is true, are revealed only in adolescence, but the power of milk/semen is in some way known to everyone—male and female—from infancy on. Every object in the real world and every function of any living thing—animal or plant—is believed to be saturated with the primal power of milk/semen. So, for instance, when a mother gives her milk to her infant, the mass of microscopic movements and behaviors we summarize with the word "feeding" is just a bit different from the way mothers nurse who do not have these beliefs. The teaching, then, starts at birth, long before the knowledge takes cognitive forms.] [*Persists.*] I don't know what I mean, but I'm not going to give in to what you said.

H: [*Also persists.*] It's secret knowledge until they're seven years old or so (and in different ways, until they're sixteen or seventeen).

S: You mean it's not till then that they hear about the vital function of semen? That's not what I meant but—

H: Well, they don't need replenishing [they need to be filled up first], and if they had that [tree sap] to start with, they might not drink semen.*

S: I've got it now.

H: I wasn't thinking of it as being necessarily defensive, though it could be, because the context in which he is saying this is: when he doesn't drink sap, he has trouble ejaculating. So in the very

---

*Boys who resist homosexual insemination might drink tree sap instead, no longer comforted by the rationalization that semen is their only source.

context in which those data have emerged it leaves cause for wondering to what extent is that a defensive image. Your idea is more like what I would expect an anthropologist to give! [*Chuckle.*] This need to replace semen is a religious experience, passionate (though not erotic), as in certain rituals. Passionate and not necessarily defensive.

S: Well, let's go back. He says it happens all the time, but he doesn't mean all the time. He means that, as far as he is concerned, it can happen at times when he has no explanation? Ask him to sort of like free associate to examine when thoughts of sap come up.

H: [*To W.*] Did you say: this kind of thought [the free floating image of the tree sap] or this kind of *koontu pookwugu* [image]—is it a thought or is it a *koontu pookwugu* [image] of that tree and its milk-sap?

W: It's only thinking* (*koontu*).

H: Thinking or *koontu pookwugu?*

W: *Koontu pookwugu.*

H: Do you see a picture of the tree inside of your thoughts?

W: Yeah, yeah, yeah.

H: Does this occur at other times?

W: *All* the time I get that. *All* the time.

H: All the time.

T: All the time. Before, when you asked me—and right now, we [W. and T.] were talking among ourselves, saying, "Oh, right now, as Gilbert was asking us about that . . . we didn't think to say it— to tell him so he would understand about that."

W: Only now; we just now thought about [reflected on and verbalized] this experience. [Weiyu is saying here that he and, he says, Tali, had felt this experience many times before but simply had never verbalized it. It's not that they were hiding it, they're saying, but rather they had just never reflected on it.]

H: Yeah.

W: [*Slight pause.*] You've asked us before: "When each of you ejaculates your water, what do you feel? What do the two of you think about?" You have asked us, just like that before, but we were just crazy [*long-long*]. We didn't think about it. [*T. agrees, wistful.*] You've showed us that . . .

H: You're talking about the *imbimboogu* [orgasm]?

W: Yeah, the *imbimboogu.*

---

*This expression—"thinking"—carries the sense of idea or mentation, not image or picture, as in *koontu pookwugu*, literally "thought picture."

H: . . . about the time when you ejaculate* your water. [*Said mat-ter-of-factly;* the locker-room atmosphere is gone.]

W: Um-hm. Um-hm.

H: Does this [imagery experience] sometimes come to you? Just any old time? When you're walking around or just sitting down or—

W: [*Spontaneous.*] At times when we're sitting and singing in a song-fest in the men's club house—and we're singing and marking a song about a particular [milk-sap] tree. And then, oh—[*voice speeds up*] I think, "I will think and go [i.e., in my thoughts] to that tree. Oh, this tree, it's got—"

H: [*Breaks in*]—That kind of something . . .

W: Yeah. It's got that something [tree sap, inside], and we sing about it [tree sap], and while we're singing we think: "Sorry, this tree, it's got that particular something, it [tree] gives it to me, and its [sap] comes and sticks inside of my own good body here."

T: [*Cuts in*]—and that milk-food, it comes to us.

W: Yeah. And [W. reports he thinks], "You, only, you're [tree] the guardian of our bodies, so we mark a song for you [the tree]." [See Herdt 1988 on Sambia song-fests and masculinity.]

H: You're talking about how it controls your *jerungdu* [strength]?

W: Yeah, yeah, that's it.[†]

H: When you actually drink the sap?[‡]

W: No.

H: When you urinate?

W: No. When I drink your [canned] milk, then I think "Gilbert, let me drink your milk.[§] It will go into my *keriku-keriku* [semen or-gan] here. Gilbert's helping me." [S: When I first watched these guys go for the canned milk, I did not know what was happening but nonetheless felt the power of their desire for the stuff. Polite and tense with *jerungdu* for *jerungdu*. A can, once opened, was

---

*Translation nuances: To be sure we were on the same track, I had used "orgasm" in the preceding sentence; its meaning is here unequivocal. But, in Pidgin, we rely on the verb *kap-sait* (to spill, pour out, etc.) to cover the ejaculation part of orgasm (*imbimboogu*), a term that covers both one's sexual arousal and ejaculation. Other Pidgin terms like *siutim* (to shoot, i.e., penetrate) are not used by Sambia to cover ejaculation. (Nor do Sambia use the general verb, *puspus*, "to copulate with.")

†I am surprised Weiyu could make all of this conscious. Not the thoughts about the tree sap, but that, while in the songfests singing about the tree, he can be thinking—fantasizing—about the tree and how its sap goes into his body to keep him strong. Though animistic and concrete, it still surprises me that Weiyu says he and Tali are thinking that in songfests. This statement shows, again, that Sambia social experiences have a reality unknown to the out-sider but obvious to the insider. How will one know without a technique for seeking, even when you do not suspect anything is there?

‡See Imano's account in chapter 8 about how it controls *jerungdu* [strength].

§Sambia prefer their hot drinks heavily whitened and sweetened. They would drink the canned milk straight if it were plentiful.

polished off as soon as we left the meal, one of the grand per-
quisites of helping H.]

T: [*Cuts in.*] Gilbert helps me [i.e., with his canned milk, a typical
construct like, "A man helps me be masculine and potent by giving me semen"].

H: [*Still disbelieving, to W.*] All the time? There's not one time when
you don't think about it?

W: There's not one single time when I forget it. Even when I sleep
in my house. When my wife and I screw. And when I come. The
same. The thought goes to the *itnandu* [a species of large wild
pandanus tree], the one that stands at the very top of the mountains. I think, "You, tree, you must come and hold me fast. It
would be bad if [during coitus] my soul went inside of my wife's
thing [vagina]. . . .

T: [*Cuts in.*]—the . . . uh . . . her . . . uh . . . vagina. [T. spits.
To say the word is to take its evil in one's mouth.]

W: Yes. That I know.

H: [*To S.*] As he describes it, it sounds defensive [i.e., drinking sap
defends maleness] sometimes. He has this thought when he's having an orgasm. The other time is during their songfest, when the
name of the tree comes up. He thinks then of that tree and how
he should go and drink some of its milk-sap so he will have tight
skin and stay strong. [H: That was a poor translation.]*

S: Why did you say it was defensive? [S: I do not understand now
what I was getting at, since the defensive aspects are so obvious.]

H: He also said, "There's another time when I think about this: when
I'm in my house and screwing my wife, I sometimes think about
the *itnandu* tree and how we place our head-hair at its base.† And
I think 'You, tree, you must keep me—that is, my soul—from
going into my wife's vagina when I am screwing her. Or else I'll
fall ill and die.' " [*Pause.*] This is new information for me. They've
just said, "We just never thought to tell you about this before . . . ."

S: They both have the tree come to mind when they ejaculate? Every
time?

H: That's what Weiyu says.

S: Do they believe that all the men have that same thought?

---

*I'm not sure what I'm saying here. Unless I'm talking about only the defensive function
of the fantasy. Because he has clearly said he has had pleasurable, metaphoric-type experiences in the men's house when singing about the tree. That is a positive, creative function,
not—at least not only—a defensive one. But in regard to his orgasms and the fantasy of seeing
the tree at that time, yes: the fantasy has defensive aspects.

†During later initiation rites.[10]

H: [*To W.*] Do you think that all the men have that same thought?

T: Not like that. [*They talk together rapidly about image-fantasies, about what other men had said about this, about secrets, about pandanus sap. S. and H. talk at the same time.*]

H: Well, there is some new information here for me. I think this is partly about masculine identity. They define masculinity as a system of beliefs we would see as largely defensive characture structure. They are taught: men are vulnerable since they cannot manufacture the semen they lose, the way women can with blood. But there is also the other quality you were trying to describe, a [psychodynamically] primitive sense of identification between yourself and a tree (which is so different from ourselves in that respect) with roots in early childhood and from gratifying sensual experiences.

S: [*Quiet voice.*] Can they tell us what other men have told them about this?

H: [*To W.*] Do all of the men think about that, or you two only?

W: All the *big men* [now elders]. They still think about that.

T: But the young ones have lost that kind of thinking.

W: But look: you just can't ask the men [*lowers voice*], "When you come, what do you think about?" You can ask if it feels good [*lowers voice*], but *not* about *ngoolu* [another tree sap] or *itnandu* treesaps. You can't talk openly about those thoughts. That's just for the two of us to tell you. And you must keep it secret.*

H: [*To S.*] He says they think the elders have the same kind of thinking as they do about it.

S: What do you mean: "it"? They have the same experience, in that "it" pops into their minds in the same way, or that they also believe in the milk sap? [S. keeps me from assuming what I think they're saying, keeps me focused so I ask *exactly* what they think rather than only hitting the general area. That technique distinguishes clinical from much of ordinary ethnographic interviewing done in anthropology.]

H: Are you talking about the men having images when they ejaculate with their wives?

W: Yeah, yeah; and it's not good they all know of this—

---

*All Sambia men have favored ritual techniques for preserving health. Some are clan secrets, others are private magical practices not shared with others besides one's son. Drinking the sap of the wild pandanus is a favorite of Tali's. His paternal uncle (substitute father) taught Tali, and he has taught Weiyu. When there are secrets and secret secrets, doing ethnography can get rather sticky. Typically, in New Guinea societies, one must proceed cautiously regarding secret knowledge when asking others questions so as not to tip off interviewees to what they may not know.

H: No, no. I'm asking if, when they screw their women, and are coming, do they then picture a particular tree and its milk-sap?

W: Yeah, yeah and [*lowers voice*] the *itnandu* too.

H: [*To S.*] Yes, the big men have the same experience of seeing the
tree and the image of the tree sap when they're fucking their wives
and having an orgasm.

S: Why does he say that? Because they have said it or because it just
makes sense?

H: [*To Weiyu*] Why do you think that all the big men think that?

W: [*A bit indignant.*] I've looked at their skins, and it *never* gets loose
and slackens. Their skin and their longevity too: they have all
been around here a *long* time. All of them think those thoughts.

T: [*Cuts in.*]—because they are still here; they haven't died.

H: [*To S.*] "When you look at old men and they are still healthy, you
know they have to be doing this to keep healthy." That's what he
said.

S: I'm not asking, "Do the men drink sap?"

H: Right. He understood that. He's answering you that they must
have the same image or else they would grow ill and die. Now
listen to the second part of what they said before. They said, "This
is our secret. We think the bachelors don't have this kind of thinking. It's our secret. So you can't go and ask the other guys, 'Well,
do you have this kind of thinking?' Because if they don't know,
they'll just get weak and die and that's their problem."

S: [*Immediately.*] Tell them of course we won't tell anyone.

H: We won't tell anyone.

W: Um-hm. Yeah. Yeah. [*Pause.*] Understand: T. and I are not purposely going slow—and hiding things—so that only now we decided to speak out about this. No, no, it's not that. We wouldn't
hide something from you, no, no. Only right now did we think of
this. [*T. agrees.*] He [S.] has come and started us thinking about
this. Now that it occurs to us we're talking about it.

H: [*To S.*] He doesn't want us to think, "We've been hiding this from
you all along. We haven't. We just thought of it now. All the times
you've asked us about this before, it just never occurred to us to
tell you." Somehow, your asking them about this has jarred
something loose. [H: But why didn't I ever ask them? S: Don't
make a big deal out of it. It's no evidence of great clinical skill
that I did. The trick is to not inhibit your curiosity. If you're not
suffering your countertransference, you'll be comfortable asking
whatever you're thinking. In fact, you'll often even know what
you're thinking.]

S: Well, I've got a response. I'm not quite sure what—a "thank you" response. Like this: "The four of us, sitting around talking, have something in common despite all the bantering arguments that went before." Is that right?

H: Yes! Of course.

S: What jarred it loose would be my saying things like, "I also have children and yet I don't drink milk-sap, milk, or semen" [reference to our earlier dialogue when S. baited them by saying that even though he never drank semen, etc., etc., he was still masculine and got a logic-intact argument from them showing how that could be.] But it's not that. I think what has loosened up the information is the way we're talking: I'm talking with them as equals, because I can't do anything else. It's not an act. I talk to them the way I talk to anyone at home; because I really enjoy being here. And maybe that frees them too . . . . I don't think they're trying to impress me.

H: Well that's an interesting explanation.

S: What is?

H: Uh. [*Pause.*] I'd have to go back and think about it. It's also possible that I simply never asked them, "When you're ejaculating, do you have other thoughts or other images?" Still, it seems odd, their over-concern to tell me that this is something that just popped out, something they simply never thought of talking about before.

S: Are they telling us that the thought, not just the sap in reality, is important?

H: [*Quickly.*] Yes! They are.

S: It's very important. And they're surprised they never mentioned it before?

H: Exactly. And *I'm* surprised. That's why I'm telling it to you. I mean, that's the sense of it. That's why I pursued it when you said we should drop it and go on. I had a sense something was floating around in there that I had not seen before and that if I asked one question, that would lead into it.

S: There were Greeks who believed trees had the spirits of women inside of them. For Sambia men this sap is equivalent to milk. What's the form of the woman in the tree? We know they think women are dangerous. So what happens to men when they drink all this milk? What about women's dangerous interior? How do the men deal with that? Why is vaginal juice terribly dangerous and milk-sap isn't? The answer isn't just that milk keeps you alive and tree-sap doesn't. Do these beliefs reflect ambivalence about mother's love plus her capacity to kill you, an infantile concept that later gets projected into all their defensive masculinity?

H: Hm. [S: Not a bad response to such high-tone theory.]

S: Do they believe in any other essence of womanness that is not contaminated with the paranoia—all the poison and—

H: No.

S: [*Struggling; puzzled.*] Milk is from women, and this sap is milk. Milk is good, like semen, yet all other aspects of female interior can kill a male. It's as if the *milk* doesn't have a sex but the *vessel* in which it's contained is a female. Is that your impression?

H: Mm—yeah.

S: What's the sex of milk? It may be a senseless question.

H: No, it's not senseless.

S: I mean to them.

H: They've taught me that all milk-bearing trees are female trees.

S: But that's not the same thing as the milk being a female substance. What's the *sex* of the milk? It always comes from females.

H: You know, all of these substances, such as pandanus-nut milk or tree sap are equivalents of and compared against mother's milk. That is concrete, conscious. But beyond that, what are milk's subtle qualities? It's as if that is the conscious frame—that's the frame—and all the other things are inside of it; the tree-sap and the pandanus-nut milk and the semen.

S: There's no gentle, tender aspect, no sense of beng *grateful* about milk? Only the strong, conscious "By God, we've got to get it!" quality?

H: Right. There's not.* A good point, obvious: there is no sense of thankfulness. Rather, a frantic urgency, a need to get it inside of you, when you've lost some, get some back inside of you as soon as possible, so you can continue to be healthy and don't die.

S: In our society, someone—poet or advertiser—tells you not only that the cow is feminine, but that milk carries her feminine qualities. I get no sense here that the milk that comes out of a woman is admirable; only a necessary thing.

H: But they do feel it nourishes you.

S: Yes, but do they feel tender or grateful toward milk? Is there any poetry that implies that?

H: There doesn't seem to be. It seems they look on milk the way we look on aspirin. You don't give it credit; it just does its job.

---

*Too quick; I was referring only to adult men. For boys—fellators—their experience is more complex (less repression), but that is another story.

S: Almost like medicine. Well, you better get back to them.

H: Have you any more ideas about this?

W: [*Quickly, dully.*] No, that's it.

DISCUSSION

H: Reflecting on this material, I find that both S.'s presence and his mode of questioning brought out this new information from W. and T. He jarred loose fantasy—imagery—that the men had known but never mentioned to me. How could I have asked about semen beliefs fifty times and never gotten this image? A partial answer is that, to the men, the image is—self-evident; their experience just is; it exists but is not reflected on. And because spontaneous, the experience is felt as apart from themselves. As with the Balinese trancer whose involuntary movements in religious trance seem like: "I see my leg move but 'I' did not move it" (Bateson 1976:61), the men recall the tree while singing, without feeling they willed it.

Two methodologic points follow. First, there are beliefs, fantasies, and shared images we ethnographers will never understand unless we push our interpreters. How did Tali and Weiyu say what they felt? S. *directly* challenged them, saying, "I don't agree that semen and sap are necessary for making men" and "Prove to me that you are right." Whether or not the point is proved is beside the point: it is the confrontation with another's reality that matters. But *the* crucial question is: Who is this other person who questions? The government, missionaries, tourists intervene; and the anthropologist can too, but supposedly should not. We are there to study, not change a society (chapter 1). A sticky problem arises. Perhaps only an anthropologist (like a clinician) is enough of an insider, is trusted enough to know how to press people to manifest their latent thoughts. Ethnographers do not dispute beliefs or practices, only record them. I never openly disagreed with the men on the unity of milk and semen, for it is essential to their way of life. We clinical ethnographers face a dilemma then: never probe beliefs and risk never seeing crucial (subliminal or unconscious) aspects of them; or, dare to confront them but risk causing personal and cultural dislocation. Should we take responsibility to help people through such changes? Are we then missionaries too?

Second, the meaning of some beliefs and practices can be discovered only by prolonged interviewing such as we did. Meanings are not isolates; they can be understood only in context, illuminated by associations. The affective dimensions, in particular, will be missed or misunderstood by piecemeal or checklist questioning that is hit-or-miss, and seen as such by interviewees. (Ever try to interview someone on the telephone? Would you hang up if someone tried it on you?) Some experiences and meanings are beyond us: "What is reported by East and West alike is that, in these special states of mind, the way of knowing is precisely *not* organized in separate or separable *gestalten*" (Bateson 1976:57). Clinical ethnography done in case studies seeing someone or several people for a long time—and allowing them to talk on their own terms—is the answer (our antidote) to this perplexing ethnographic problem

CHAPTER SIX

Penjukwi: Portrait of a Woman

H: What is it like to be a woman in a society like that of the Sambia, male-biased and ridden with sexual antagonism? How does a woman experience her femaleness—in dreams, erotism, marriage, childcare? What does femininity look like in someone who was literally abducted, forcibly married, and compelled to make a life in a place not of her choosing? These questions motivated my work with Penjukwi, my friend and best woman interpreter.

This chapter carries a heavy load. I did little work with women in my first fieldwork (1974–1976), and my writings to date have been based mainly on men's views of everything, including women. At S.'s urging I worked more with women, especially with P., when I returned in 1979. The effects were striking and important, the more so in 1981, when I worked more with women than men. In this book, however, this is our only study of a woman, and we use it to show how I—a white, young, male ethnographer—worked with a woman on such intimate matters as her sexual experience, and how S.'s presence affected her.

Penjukwi was born about 1955 in Kwoli hamlet, across the Valley from Nilangu. Her father, also born in Kwoli, was an ordinary Sambia man; he belonged to its leading clan. Her mother was from Nilangu hamlet, the daughter of a well-known big man and shaman. P. was their firstborn child, one of four children still living. P.'s mother is second in the area only to Kaiyunango (Moondi's mother) in being a leading woman shaman. P.'s parents had a good marriage. She reports that they liked each other a lot and seldom quarreled. She seems to have had a relatively happy childhood until her father died.

P.'s development is a fascinating combination of both traditional and socially changing circumstances. She grew up amidst warfare, which ended around 1964 when she was nine. Kwoli was the first hamlet pacified by government patrol officers. In 1963, a government rest-hut was built there, which the people burned down. Not long after, P.'s uncle (father's brother), Jemioko, a powerful big man and leader of Kwoli, was appointed the first *lululai** in the Valley. After the last war in the area other men were jailed, which led to total pacification. Two years later missionaries appeared and began working near the village. Other social changes followed, particularly in Kwoli. Thus, by the time P. was ten, her world was shifting dramatically.

P. had good relations with both her parents, but as she grew she preferred being with her father. By six she was steadily helping in the gardens with her parents. Her parents always slept together in one hut. P. loved to go with her father, whom she describes as a wonderful, warm man, on his daily rounds to gardens and nearby hamlets. Her mother was intensely involved in shamanic activities, did healing ceremonies "all the time," and frequently reported her dreams. P. was responsible for helping her parents by babysitting and related chores. But she preferred to roam with her playmates, a group of boys and girls of the hamlet. P. says she was aware of the difference between boys and girls at an early age. She engaged in surreptitious sex play for a time (which she enjoyed) with a boy of about nine years of age (before his initiation). P. describes herself as a "strong" girl, more so than other girls her age. For instance: she disliked gardening and babysitting until she was older; she liked to climb trees (unusual) and sometimes join in boys' games. Nonetheless, these attributes were not so marked that P. would stand out from other girls as she matured. And, by about age twelve, she was more fully involved in heavy and frequent garden work, because her mother told her that "men don't like lazy wives."

P.'s father died when she was twelve, changing her life forever. Her mother went into seclusion as a widow for a year, which dampened P.'s life. During this period, another uncle—Yanduwaiko, P.'s father's brother—greatly helped the family, and he and his wife became, in effect, P.'s guardians. Eventually, still another Kwoli man (another classificatory FB) grew interested in P.'s mother. He wanted to marry her and persisted, to some extent against her will, until she gave in. They were married, P.'s mother becoming his second wife. This man, P.'s stepfather, cared for the family and was a good provider. But

---

*Government-recognized local "head man," who was given a badge, a hat, cane, and some authority to arbitrate local disputes and keep the peace.

after their marriage, P. became increasingly independent of her parents. He and P.'s mother had many arguments. Thus, P. became unhappy living in their hut, and often slept in other kinfolks' huts in Kwoli. P.'s mother continued her shamanic activities. She and her second husband had two other children until, in 1979, he hung himself.[1]

Her uncle, Yanduwaiko, was the key influence in P.'s life from then on. Yandu is interesting. He became one of two official government translators around 1965.* He still works today at the distant patrol post in the same capacity. It was thus shortly before P.'s true father died that her uncle began living away from Kwoli, on the patrol post. This life was unprecedented for the Sambia at that time (only a handful of men were then absent from the Valley, working on coastal plantations). Few Sambia had even been to the government post. Yandu is a sensible, solid citizen, well-respected and liked, sophisticated for a Sambia man of his generation. Of course, in certain ways, he has had to toe the government's party line; has, no doubt, been privy to some awful colonial events and scenes, and has had to kowtow to European authorities, becoming a bit jaded. Still, he is no fool, nor merely a government puppet;[2] and he has influence back home. Yandu also has a good marriage (and several children) with a warm, lively, and intelligent Sambia woman, who also likes P. They too began living on the patrol post in the late 1960s. And, from 1966 to 1973, when P. was married, she had many short trips to, and several periods of living on, the patrol post with her uncle's family.

Through him, then, Penjukwi got to know some western ways, after a traditionalist childhood and being sheltered by her uncle and other kin in a place not so far from home. She saw Europeans; gained limited exposure to government station people; received western clothes, food, and other items via her uncle; and all this allowed P. more freedom and movement than Sambia adolescent girls ever had had in the past (though P. herself has seldom remarked on this and seems to take it for granted). Yandu's children and wife had even greater freedom. He expressed the view that his daughters should marry whomever they wanted,† an unprecedented attitude in those days (and unusual even now). And his wife was the only Pidgin-speaking woman in the area for years.[3] Furthermore, P. began to like the qualities and potentials her uncle had—she refers to him as a "new kind" of Sambia man—suggesting that such a man was what she

---

*No doubt in part through his older brother Jemioko's influence as *lululai*.
†As long as brideprice was paid.

wanted in marriage. (P.'s parents passively allowed these develop-
ments to occur.) Still, P. spent the most time in her father's hamlet.
She became a better gardener, was otherwise involved in village life,
and continued to mature. There was no arranged marriage for her,
and the question of her marriage was never explicitly discussed until
her menarche (1973).

Two other important things happened to Penjukwi in 1971–1973,
before her marriage.

First, she attended a mission "bush" school in the Valley for a few
months in 1971. From the late 1960s on, missionaries entered the
Sambia Valley. The Seventh-day Adventists became particularly active, sending native evangelists (from other parts of New Guinea) into
the Valley with the Word. They established two beachheads: at Kwoli,
a few hundred yards above the village; and at the extreme southern
end of the Valley, at a place called Kwapalaam, where an airstrip
was later built. They proselytized and won converts. But the price for
baptism was pretty steep: strict adherence to Levitical food prohi-
bitions (no pork, no possum: hence, no meat, except rarely from cans),
"tabooing" smoking and chewing betel-nut; monogamy, forcing men
to divorce second wives; and repudiation of ritual customs. Few
Sambia could stomach these demands; fewer still could live by them.
Nonetheless, P.'s oldest uncle Jemioko, the *lululai*, nominally converted, as did a few others of her clan (more women than men). P.
herself sometimes went to Saturday services ("holiday outings"), in
the local *haus lotu*,* but she never converted or adopted the mission's
taboos. What matters is that down at Kwapalaam a mission school
was set up in 1971. P., encouraged by others, went to the school several times a week. She learned a smattering of Pidgin (but never learned
how to write). It is extraordinary that some parents associated with
the mission allowed their children to live in two adjacent, sexually-
segregated "dormitories" for a time. Soon, word got out that boys
and girls were playing around sexually. A scandal forced the school
to close.[4] P. returned home to Kwoli more acculturated.

Second was P.'s meeting at the patrol post a young Sambia man
with whom she became infatuated. He was a distant relative of her
uncle, a bachelor, handsome, travelled (he had been to the coast
briefly). They liked each other. P. says he was kind, not strong or
loud-mouthed. They flirted and socialized, but their attraction never
went further physically. By the end of 1972, P. had seen him at two

---

*The Seventh-day Adventists celebrate Sabbath on Saturdays. *Haus lotu* is Pidgin for church:
a hut with pews and a plain wooden altar.

different periods. She was fantasizing about him. (See interview.) Encouraged by her uncle's open door policy on marriage, she began to daydream about marrying him. The interest seemed mutual, and enough contact was maintained between them that it became evident they might marry. Since this man was from a different valley—another phratry—there were formidable difficulties with such a marriage,* even were her uncle and parents to approve of it. Nonetheless, P. planned for it.

Sometime in early 1973, P. had her menarche—another sign of change in her life—while out at the patrol post. She could not, therefore, go through the normal secret menarche ceremonies back in the village menstrual hut. Her uncle paid for a feast at the post. Then, her menarche over and she sexually eligible for marriage, P. returned to Kwoli.

The circumstances of P.'s marriageability were odd. She had not been betrothed as an infant. She had no older brothers to push her into a sister-exchange marriage. Her step-father had no real claims or authority over her. And her uncle had said he would allow her to choose her own partner (so long as the groom settled in payment). Her clansmen—who were few—had no strategy in mind. Thus, she was able to pursue her fantasy about marrying her sweetheart.

The men over at Nilangu, however, had a different plan. P.'s mother was from Nilangu, and she had been infant-betrothed, though Nilangu's claim to P. was for several reasons weak. But they could claim—with some justification—that if P. was to go anywhere else for a marriage, then it might be back to her mother's natal hamlet. P. was also attractive: plenty of men had an eye on her. What's more—the real key—she was available. The rumor grew that P. was going to sneak off and elope with a man from another valley. Here is where Nilutwo—my cassowary-hunter friend—entered the scene.

Nilutwo was an odd, troubled man. Born about 1942, he was much older than P.—too old, in fact, by Sambia standards. He had had a woman betrothed to him from infancy, but he spurned her (and one other) as "too strong" (i.e., aggressive) for him. He gave her to Imano, who relished her (Imano's first wife: see chapter 8). Nilutwo's development was marked by conflict. His biologic father went crazy and died in N.'s infancy, and his step-father died before he was initiated (see Herdt 1981:ch. 5). N. had bouts of "crazy" behavior in his teens, and women had rejected him as a rubbish man. After a fight with his own clan brothers over one failed marriage negotiation in the late

---

*.999 of all Sambia Valley marriages are transacted within in the Valley.

1960s, he left the Valley in a huff, to work on a coconut plantation near Madang. He returned in 1972 to find his prospects no better than before: no woman available, no allies to find him one. He was often getting himself in trouble over his adultery attempts. He was on the verge of despair—considering returning to the coast again—when nubile Penjukwi appeared.

Nilutwo and Penjukwi were strangers. They were not well matched—by age, personality, or past acquaintance. Yet N. had a certain claim on her: she was his true father's sister's daughter, a respectable marriage coupling. N. approached P. several times. And each time she rejected him more vehemently. P. told me N. was too old for her: she never had considered him as a mate, certainly not over her sweetheart. In early 1974 (before I arrived) N. grew desperate: he heard that P. had wised-up and was planning to run off to the Wunyu-Sambia Valley, where her sweetheart was. Actually, it was Kanteilo who told him this. The old fox had got wind of her plans and went straight to the men's house in Nilangu. There, he got the bachelors worked up—Weiyu, others, and Nilutwo—saying that P. had better be taken before Nilangu lost forever what could be had. That night, P.'s abduction was set.

Nilutwo had to lead the action. Though reluctant, it was his prerogative, his show, his wife, his manliness at stake. At dawn, he, Weiyu, Kanteilo, and two other men crept over to Kwoli and surprised P. in her mother's hut. N. plunged into the hut and grabbed P., pulling her outside. Her mother began shrieking and hitting Weiyu. People screamed, babies cried, dogs barked: chaos. P. was dragged, screaming and fighting, outside the village. But N. got scared. Weiyu took over. He grabbed P. and literally dragged her down the mountain side, she losing all her garments in the process, exposing her. Meanwhile, the other villagers were held at bay.[5] She was hauled up the other mountainside to Nilangu, and imprisoned in a hut. Nilutwo was instructed to screw her into submission. They were guarded for days. Thus began P.'s marriage.

Even by Sambia standards, this was a dreadful start. Beyond that, the usual marriage ceremony was never held. Later negotiations gained the formal acceptance of P.'s people, who were paid a small amount of bridewealth compensation. N. was told to watch P. like a hawk until she got pregnant, for fear she would run off. And he did. Soon, P. and N. were settled into life together, seeming, when I arrived in late 1974, like a long-married couple. What I did not know then was P.'s trauma and humiliation, her having to give up the fantasy of marrying her admirer, and the less-than-ordinary life she had been forced into by Nilutwo. What was done to her, no woman in years had suffered.

In 1975, P. gave birth to their first child, a girl. Nilutwo was thrilled. He was closely attached to the girl. He calmed down. He was not a bad husband, P. says. He hunted and gardened a lot, was diligent in earning money, helped others, and seldom fought with her.

N. did his best, too, to make P. happy, I am convinced. It was not so much that he loved her as that he liked her. And needed her: for his acceptance by the village as an adult man with wife and child; for food, sex, and cooking—the affection she gave that helped him endure many personal conflicts.[6] For N. was a difficult and troublesome man, and he knew it; and he did his best to make a difficult marriage work.

I saw only Nilutwo's side of this marriage for a long time. But, in 1976, at N.'s constant encouragement, I worked briefly with P. as an interpreter, though it was difficult (my Sambia wasn't very good, nor was her Pidgin). Still, it was a hapless marriage: P. made the best of a bad deal, as is typical of her. Indeed, for someone who had been through so much, she seemed cheerful, warm, and lively.

I want to underline here that Sambia marriages are based on politics, not love; fortitude, not affection. Women's lot is not good. Even today there is not much choice in marriage. Perhaps Penjukwi knew that her fantasy about marrying a handsome, traveled youth from a distant place was just a pipe-dream. Perhaps not. Her abduction was ruthless; P. never forgave Nilutwo or the men for her brutal treatment and as much as is possible for a Sambia woman, she has never let them forget it. But we need to remember that Sambia expectations are different from ours, much less romantic and prettified. When one doesn't expect much, one is less disappointed.

P. had their second child, a boy, in 1978. I returned in 1979 to find P. and N. much as before, a bit more settled, a bit happier. Penjukwi seemed to be doing fine. Then tragedy occurred. In April, Nilutwo fell from a tree, breaking his back and transecting his spinal cord. He suffered in agony for months until his death (not long after S. and I left the Valley). Until his death in September, Penjukwi had to care for N. virtually as an infant. She stuck by him, beyond Sambia expectations of a wife, until his end. (Other women said, "If I'd been stolen like you, I'd never care for him like that.") She could not travel or garden. So P. sat for weeks with him, cramped in Tali's hut where N., legs paralyzed and without bowel or bladder control, was dying. When he was cranky and nasty, she ignored him or talked back. They had bitter arguments. More than once she told him to die and be done with it. "There's other men around here." Yet she said this in anger and frustration, when no one else could bear his pain, screaming, demanding. She stayed, I think, because it was her duty; P. is honorable.

My work with P. in 1979 went well. She was warm and open. We made fine progress during the first of my two field trips that year, January through March. Her Pidgin was passable but not great. (It was far better in 1981). Then, while I was back at UCLA, came his accident, in April. On my return (in May) we worked three months more; our talking concentrated on her having to tend N. and the resulting frustrations. My views of male–female relationships changed. But because of her onerous life, I spent much time with P. simply allowing her to express her frustrations.

P. and I worked alone some thirty times in 1979. There was a complementarity in it lacking with the men. Just as we would expect: that's in the nature of Sambia gender roles. But it was more than that. As with my other key informants, I liked P. and enjoyed being with her. Conflict *was* interjected into our relationship in four ways: by Nilutwo (who had his own reasons—namely, keeping P. away from other men); by the men (who were often jealous of P. and me); by P. herself (there were nonerotic and erotic aspects of her feelings toward me); and by myself (I never knew until I tried how much I could press P. for certain information, or how close I could get to her without her—and me—feeling uncomfortable).

By the time S. arrived, then, Nilutwo was dying and in great pain, which made P.'s life so difficult. She was also under growing pressure from the men, who, awaiting N.'s death, wondered who would get this prize, Penjukwi, as another wife, and how they would manage it. I let them know that I refused any part in these games. (See chapter 5.) An aspect of my work with her at the time, then, was anticipating what N.'s death would bring.

S. arrived and joined us. I felt no dislocation. However, toward the end, when we were discussing P.'s sexual excitement—a very sensitive matter—there were moments when I felt uneasy, we two white men alone with her asking such questions. She sensed my concern, and when we left a few days later, she went out of her way to say goodbye warmly to me.

I returned to even richer work with P. in 1981. She was alive, happy, independent, the best I had ever seen her, as she must have been before marriage. She was invaluable for my study of women and children. She seemed unscathed by those six years with Nilutwo, of whom she speaks honestly and gently. She had no husband and no plans for one, but neither would she deny the possibility. A lightness was in her.

S: This chapter, more than any other, is unbalanced as compared to what was actually said, for we have deleted two long sections; an account of an attempted rape, and a dream and its associations. These deletions intensify even more our concentration on the two erotic matters that now fill the chapter: an erotic daydream and the question does she have orgasms with breast-feeding.

It is obvious, however, that all our Sambia friends talked a lot about sex. We see three main reason for that. First (despite the paucity of such material in the ethnographic literature), sex—erotics and gender identity—is what many people think of regularly. Second, one of the main issues in H.'s research is sexuality. Third, S.'s studies are only on sexuality.

FIRST SESSION

This was our first interview together with P. She and I reestablish rapport after several days' pause following S.'s arrival. P. is at first focused on Nilutwo's pain. Then we discuss *imbimboogu*, a concept that involves us in understanding how individuals use cultural ideas.

The primary referent of *imbimboogu*, in males and females, is "orgasm." A lesser meaning is the tingling sensation in a limb that is asleep. In talking with P., I discovered that she used that term for sensual feelings she had when nursing her baby. Did her usage in that context mean that she was feeling an "orgasm" while nursing? I did not know. S. helped us find out. Early in this session, however, we discovered a man—a notorious womanizer—peeping. This had never happened before, and it angered me. When we kicked him out, P. then told how that man had accosted her three years before. We return in later sessions to the *imbimboogu* problem, which kept popping up.

HERDT We've lost quite a bit of time, haven't we? Three or four, maybe five days.

PENJUKWI [*Matter-of-factly.*] Oh, when do you leave the Valley for good?*

S: [*Enters with a kerosene lamp.* Though it is still dusk, we plan to have a long session and anticipate the darkness.] Let's put it far

---

*First P., then Kalutwo (chapter 9), open our talking with my departure. A sad feeling is in the air.

away because it's going to make a loud buzz. [*He moves across the room.*]

H: [*Echoing him.*] Yeah, as far away as possible. [*Turns to P.*] Some time yet. We don't know for sure just when we'll be leaving. A week or something like that. I've already told you about my boss, Dr. Stoller. I asked you before if it was okay for him to sit with us, and you said it is.

P: [*Raising voice, strong.*] Oh, I won't be afraid.

H: It's all right?

P: Yeah, I'm not afraid. I'm only afraid of the other men here [reference to Tali, Weiyu, and others]. Now you two have the same skin. I'm not going to be afraid of you [*a large smile in her voice that makes me know, listening to her in 1982, that she feels secure.*]

H: Good enough. [*Pause.*] Now today, what have you been doing?

P: Oh, nothing [*A little sadness in voice.*] I've just been staying in the house. My man, too [*pause*] he is in pain, and so I've stayed with him.

H: And so what if he—

P: [*Breaking in.*] What is it? He's got large sores [pressure sores] on both sides [of his buttocks], and so I've just stayed put. They [sores] aren't gone yet. They turned into really big sores, and he doesn't sit well. So I just stay around.

H: Are you getting around all right or not?

P: Me? Oh, no, no I'm not. [*Quiet, sullen despair.*]

H: How come?

P: Well, I can't go, can't walk around [to gardens, etc.], and so I have to sit around grouchy [*nervous chuckle*]. I don't sit easily; when I am able to get around then I'm fine. Whatever I need [food] I fetch and can be fine; but just sitting around the house I'm not happy. So I'm not doing well.

H: I heard that this morning the two of you [P. and Nilutwo] were sort of cross at each other. When I came along and S. was following me, [*pause*] you and Nilutwo . . .

P: Oh, not really, he wasn't cross. It was just tiredness [the sense that the argument was nothing].

H: Does he do that [*frequently*]?

P: [*Pause.*] I told him, "This master* [S.] wants to come and ex-

---

*P. uses "master" in the same way as Sakulambei, and the usage is interesting. Tali, Weiyu, and our other male subjects used it only rarely in relation to S. Saku did much more so. Why? Two things come to mind. First, P. had worked less with me in 1979 than the others. Second, women have had much less direct interaction with whites than men (many of whom have worked on the coast). In a general sense, then, the colonialist power structure is more distant

amine you. You've got to stay quiet [don't be cantankerous]. You must [*sort of smiling in her voice*] settle down so he [S.] can come and look at you."

H: Did he listen to you?

P: He didn't talk, he just listened, that's all [*amusement in her voice again*].[†]

H: Do you have any preference for what we could work on or shall I [choose it]?

P: [*Pause.**] This man [husband] doesn't sleep well. His sides have sores, and he turns and moves around all the time. He doesn't sleep well at night. He keeps turning at night and keeps getting me up . . . and the others did a song-fest. So we didn't sleep well [a song-fest was held last night in Tali's house, where P. and N. are living]. We were there, and so I didn't sleep well.

H: In Tali's house?

P: Yeah. Soluwulu's [Tali's brother] child wasn't well. N. told me that there wasn't anything we could do to stop the song-fest, be-cause it wasn't our house. It's Tali's hut; so we just had to put up with it and not sleep well. Besides, they had to heal Soluwulu's baby. And Soluwulu kept going in and out, the child crying on and on; it was crying and it couldn't even take breast milk. And she [Soluwulu's wife] is pregnant again; so her milk is dry and she didn't have any to give the child [to quiet it.]**

H: Is that why it was crying?

P: Yeah [*smiling*]. An older child would simply stop, but he's too small. A child so small doesn't think. He'll just cry and cry a lot.

H: For milk?

P: For milk, but there isn't any.

H: What is it now? Has she just weaned it?

---

and more mythologized as a formal barrier to women. I would argue also that women's suppression by Sambia men is shared more by Saku, in whom hermaphroditic stigmata (and perhaps more or less conscious feminine identifications) have perpetuated distrust of whites and alienation from power figures.

[†]Here and elsewhere P. refers to Nilutwo like an ornery child to be humored and scolded, which her amusement signifies.

*In 1979 P.'s Pidgin was still not strong and at times like now she paused out of awk-wardness as to what to say next. It was easier for her then to follow my lead. She was also, I think, intimidated by S.; she assumed S. spoke Pidgin. (What a surprise for her to find untrue the colonial stereotype that whites are omniscient.)

**This child, a boy, had always been very underweight and sickly. He was over three years old. Several months later Soluwulu's wife had another baby who was extremely malnour-ished, even though the mother did her best to feed him. He died in 1981 despite our attempts to save him. The local medical orderly said he had died of spinal meningitis compounded by pneumonia (not an easy diagnosis to make without proper training or a laboratory). I add this note to remind readers of the dreadful health problems that still take Sambia lives.

P: Just now. It's dried up [milk], but he's still crying for it, still sucking. But there's no milk.

H: Hmmm. And does the mother let him do that or not?

P: She just thinks, "It's not very big. So he can just suckle without
[getting any milk]; that's all right. It's not so big that I should
keep it off the breast."

H: Boy, but that's a pretty big child!

P: Oh, not really. That's a firstborn child, and so it doesn't grow very
quickly. When it's matured and is big, then [*pause*] . . . they
should not have started working yet [having sex again to make
another baby].

H: Have they started walking around together yet [euphemism for
having sex again]?

P: Not yet.*

H: Let me ask you about something we were talking about last
time . . . about breast milk and about giving breast milk to your
baby. [*P. immediately hides her face, embarrassed.*] You've got a
baby now, and you're breast-feeding him. I was [began to say
"surprised"] thinking about your saying that when you breast-
feed him you feel *imbimboogu*.† I thought very hard about that. I
was wondering, does it feel the same as when you are screwing
with your man or is it another kind [of experience]?

P: [*Matter-of-fact.*] The same.

H: The same? Truly? [*Still surprised.*]

P: Just the same. [*Pause.*] When we two screw, it's the same as that.
It's just the same.

H: But do you feel [with a man] hotter when screwing or when you
breast-feed your baby?

P: When my man screws with me. It's only then that I feel hot.

H: Now, what about with your baby?

P: My baby, too, when it drinks milk then it can [*pause*] create that
[feeling of being] hot too.

H: The same?

P: Later it can feel like [*she smiles with a nervous laugh*] *imbimboogu*.

H: Painful or sweet? [*Imbimboogu* covers both the pleasure of sexual
arousal and the strange sensation of a limb "asleep."]

P: (*Quickly; natural.*) Oh, it's sweet only.

H: Is this hotness inside your breast or . . . [*voice trails off*]?

---

*P. was either ignorant or evasive here, for I had the impression from the men that Soluwulu's
wife was pregnant again.
  †By which I here meant orgasm.

P: Inside the breast.

H: Deep inside, the breast nipple, or what?

P: Around the nipple.

H: Can I tell Dr. S. so that he can ask you about it?

P: [*Slight anxiety, then relaxed.*] You can tell him. That's all right.

H: [*To S.*] We have been talking as we had the last two times before you came. She tells me that she *feels* the same feeling, using the term for orgasm, when she is having sex (when she is screwing with Nilutwo) as when her baby drinks her breast milk. And so I've been asking her, uh . . . how she feels *that;* and I keep asking her what are the differences, and she keeps telling me it's the same.

S: (*Quietly.*) It's been reported.

H: Really [*surprised*]?

S: It's not universal, nobody knows how often, but it is not at all unusual. Some American women [this is not to imply it happens to American women only] report that at times, when they are nursing the baby, they are not only hot and have orgasms but . . .

H: It is possible . . .

S: What I don't know is how fast does it happen, how often does it happen, where it is felt. Because there is a lot of different places: clitoral, vaginal, pelvic: how does it feel when nothing is inside of her, or when she's having coitus, etc. . . . Does she have it all the time, part of the time? Some women feel very *guilty* about it— "*Oh, my God,* what's happening?" Then try to make it into a psychological statement with their infant (just a contamination of psychoanalysis—not that analysts have not said that). At any rate, it would be interesting to find out how often; with all the babies; was it the first time: get the history of it. (I don't think it's terribly important but it's kind of: "what the hell, if that's what you're talking about.") How did the subject come up? Had you talked with her about that particular thing before or just now?

H: No, I brought that up because I wanted to ask her about it. It was, uh . . .

S: No, she told *you* because you had never heard of it before. When did she first tell you?

H: Let's see. In the last several days.

S: Another question that would be related to it would be: what happens when a man—and there's been only one man—sucks, touches or whatever [her breasts]. Could it [*imbimboogu*] happen to her with just foreplay? (I don't know whether there is any [foreplay] in her life or not.) Because there are women, who, when their breasts are stimulated, have orgasms. Whether those are the women who have it with their babies or not, I simply don't know.

H: Those all give me some questions to ask her. [*To P.*] I've been telling him, so he would understand what we're talking about this . . .

S: [*Cutting in.*] Had she heard about this from anybody else? Probably not, because they don't talk about sex.

H: Well, see, all the men believe this; all* the men say that the women feel this. That's one reason why I wanted to check it out.

S: Find out from her does she know if other women have this or not.

H: Yeah. [*To P.*] I want to ask you now about the time when you have this feeling—when you give breast milk to your baby and you feel *imbimboogu*. I was telling him about this and he was telling me his thinking about it. I want to ask you if you've heard of other women who feel *imbimboogu* when they give breast milk to their children?

P: [*Spontaneously.*] Oh, they feel that too, all of them feel that. It's not just me. I think all of them do. [Society is a useful foil even among Sambia.]

H: Do they talk about that?

P: They all say, "I give milk to my child and then I get an *imbimboogu.*" Also, I see someone's water [milk] simply fall out from nothing [full breasts between feedings]. I think, "It's the same, with me." But the only time when they all get *imbimboogu* is when the baby is feeding. When my baby doesn't drink milk, then I don't feel it. At times when I leave my baby and go round the garden, don't come back quickly, when I come back slowly, then my breasts are swollen and I can get an *imbimboogu.*

H: Oh. [?]

P: Then my baby thinks, "My mother doesn't bring back my milk quickly, so I am crying and crying waiting for her." He cries and cries and waits. And when he thinks that, then my breasts have to have an *imbimboogu.* [The magical construction here is the baby wants milk, thinks of it and cries for it, and when he thinks that, it makes P.'s breasts feel *imbimboogu*, because of his thought at some distance away.] I think that when I go round, he's thinking of me like that, and so I have it.

H: You're saying that at that time, that's when you're feeling *imbimboogu*, when you walk about?

*H: That's exaggerated; see chapter 5.

P: Yeah.

H: On the path?

P: I've finished gathering food and I'm ready to come back; so at the time, when I come back walking on the path, this time it can happen [*slight laugh*]. At other times, when I don't come back quickly and I'm in my garden standing there working, I can feel *imbimboogu*.

H: When you get *imbimboogu*, you feel hot in what place [of the body]? Where do you feel hot?

P: [*Pause.*] I'm hot in the nipples, inside. That's where I feel it.

H: Down below, inside your cunt, what do you feel there?

P: Oh, no. Inside of there [*smiling*] I don't get an *imbimboogu*. At times when the two of us [husband and self] play around, that's when we [women] feel that.

H: Hmmmm.

P: And in my breasts it comes when my baby drinks from it—

H: [*Butting in.*] Wait. [At this point H. gets up after hearing a noise that suggests someone in the next room is leaning against the wall. Until this point it was absolutely quiet. I go outside into the next room, our kitchen, and am astonished and angry to find Gam-bakutu. He is an older, married man with two wives and many children, Nilutwo's older clan brother. He is a notorious adulterer and has for some time had his eyes on Penjukwi. It is rumored that when Nilutwo dies, he will try to take Penjukwi as another wife. Though he cannot speak Pidgin, I am outraged that he has stayed in the house, violating the confidentiality of the session, after I had asked everyone to leave. The many references to *im-bimboogu* were a give-away. So I tell him in an angry but con-trolled voice to leave. I come back in the office to contain my anger.]

S: Why did you get up? You heard somebody?

H: Yeah [*still fuming*].

S: It was somebody who didn't belong, who shouldn't be hearing this?

H: Yeah, right. Somebody was here. That's what we were trying to avoid.

S: Should I look [to ensure that he's left]?

H: Yeah, you should.

P: [*Barely audible.*] Somebody's there in the kitchen.

H: Yeah.

S: Nope. He was just looking back to see if we were looking. Because he wants to find out what's happening here? Or he knows?

H: Yeah, he's probably ashamed now that I caught him doing it [being a voyeur].

S: Had she known he was there?

H: No. [*Turning to P.*] Did you know that he was there?

P: Who's that?

H: Gambatkutu.

P: [*Stunned.*] Oh, not at all. Didn't he go to his house [before we started]?

H: I just now removed him.

P: Oh, you go get rid of him.

H: I've already done it.

P: He shouldn't be standing there eavesdropping.

H: Yeah.

H: [*To S.*] Well, it was just—I'd have to give you the details—especially about *him*. He shouldn't have been hearing that.

S: You don't know that he did hear it.

H: Oh, yeah, I know that he heard it because that's what gave it away. He was sitting there all the time.

S: Does this damage her?

H: Well, that's it—I mean it's absolutely awful. He's been trying to screw her for months and months and we're talking about orgasms and he's probably sitting there getting a hard-on.

S: Well, I'm—now I'm just being me—but I'd kick his ass around for that,* I mean, I wouldn't just leave it at this.

H: Yeah.

S: That may not be the right thing for you [as an ethnographer] to do, but, I mean, that's just despicable.

H: It's understandable, and it's less despicable here because they think she's shit anyway, but even so—

S: I'm just being personal. So—

H: Yeah.

S: He should have been told to go, but somehow maybe you shouldn't. You'll know what to do. Is she now at risk because of this and is she now going to be troubled about this?

H: Well, yeah. [*To P.*] I've been telling him about this bad thing that he's [Gambakutu] done, sitting there listening to our talk. I always kick all the men out when you and I work. So I'm wondering whether you have any worry because he sat there and listened to us.

P: Oh, that's his way.

---

*As I would do at UCLA. Or is it none of our business to bring our morality into the ethnography, even if our beliefs are the same as P.'s?

H: Uh-uh. I'm asking you does this worry you or not? I'm saying it's not good if you're afraid he heard us talking . . .

P: Oh, no, no. He wouldn't have heard us talking about that.

H: Huh? [*Disbelieving.*]

P: No, I'm not afraid of that. I'm not afraid.

H: [*Sort of making an admission.*] Nilutwo told me that some times he [Gambakutu] comes and wants to butter you up. [We delete here—it is too complex and tangential to the chapter to follow here—a long account by P. of how Gambakutu once tried to attack her. This peeping incident led her to talk about her bad feelings regarding him. We continue from that point.] All right. I want to tell him[S.] a little bit.

P: O.K.

H: I always knew that he had at some time or other—

S: [*Cutting in.*] You mean Nilutwo?

H: No, the man who was in here, who is Nilutwo's elder brother, clan brother, and who has a claim to her after Nilutwo is dead, I knew that he had at some time tried to screw her; you know, adultery.

S: The minute you got up, that broke the discussion on breast-feeding.

H: Yeah. This is a good point to stop. Is there anything you would . . . I doubt if she'll mind if you want to ask her anything.

S: No need to keep her any more. [*To P.*] O.K., that's enough. Tomorrow. . . . [Break. H. physically accompanies P. to her house— wary of Gambakutu for her—and returns. Then:]

H: We face problems [re P.'s talking about *imbimboogu*] about semantics of the language and the culture. Do you see what I mean?

S: No. What problems?

H: This question of—you're suggesting that the women and the men (not necessarily in the same sense) believe that women have orgasms with breast-feeding; that women actually experience this— let's say "orgasm" in quotes. They use the same term for the experience in coitus and with nursing. And that men *know* that women have this experience, and that this therefore focuses men's erotism on the breast, breast-feeding, breast milk . . . you have a part of it in the public culture associated with women, and the public culture associated with men.

S: What do you mean "the public culture"?

H: The secret culture is associated with homosexuality that only boys and men know about, and which women are not supposed to know about and probably don't. There is also a secret culture that women have, in which there are ritual secrets that are hidden from men, only the women wouldn't kill the men if they were found out: what to do about breast milk, breast-feeding, and stuff like that. So you've got these different pieces of a whole phenomenology. The semantic problems would run like this—I asked her again and again, "Is it the same experience? When you're having this experience [breast] that you call orgasm what are you feeling inside your vagina?" She said, "I don't feel anything down there." And then I said, "Well, where is the heat that you're talking about?" She gave me the same answer as before. "It's in my breast." And I said, "Is it way inside, or is it at the nipple?" She says, "It's at the nipple." And then she starts to tell me this story, which is impossible; I can't believe it. When she's been in the garden all day and she hasn't breast-fed her baby and her breasts are *very* full and she feels there's a need for the breast milk to come out, she starts thinking about how she will breast-feed the baby. And as she's walking back to the hamlet, she has this experience she's calling an orgasm. I mean, it doesn't, can't . . . sound believable. I'm not doubting that she's having what she's said—the question is, what does it mean? The answer is that I need more data.

S: We'll just have to get that out of them, by some good questions, which may not succeed; you've tried for two years. If you're on to an . . . unspoken, powerful (partly because unspoken, unacknowledged) erotic communication system between the sexes, then you should investigate it further. (That's what you're doing.) If the men believe that women get erotically turned on—in our sense— by breast-feeding babies. . . . [See chapter 5 on this point.]

H: And it looks as if they are—

S: No. You're saying something different: I'm not concerned with whether the women *are* or not. If the men *believe* that, and are sending out their knowledge of this in this *particular*, complex way—of never talking about it, of sitting in corners and just snickering about it, and getting hard-ons about it, so that the women are receiving the men's knowledge from *that* complex way— then the women *must* be sending back some signals. If all the men are looking at the women's ankles, as in the nineteenth century, then the women have to find clothes in which they hide their ankles *in a certain manner.*

H: To be erotic—

S: In a manner so that when the wind blows and you step off a trolley . . . by mistake . . . In other words: it will have to be *in*

kind that the women repond with one of these hostility mechanisms which create erotic excitement.* That's what you want to
be looking for, in this. Unrelated to what we are talking about
now, you said the other day that you had once heard a very strange
[*to H.*] detail—that came up in the middle of the erotic fantasy
of a man [Imano: chapter 8] who has been defined as heterosexually mature, sexually competent—this centrally important item,
for which all the rest of the daydream is almost foreplay: [he pic-
tures] a baby at the breast and at that point he has his orgasm.[†]
Right?

H: Yeah.

S: All right. You may now have a piece of information that explains
that . . . [a fantasy] which would be impossible for a nonpsy-
chotic man in our society to have had. And you say that if you
told that to ten men here, all ten would get turned on.

H: Hm, yeah.

S: One of the *major* clues may be this potential [suggested] mechanism of the men talking about the women getting turned on: and
the women responding to that in some way. Now one of the responses the women have, is that they may in fact, a hundred percent of them, she says a lot do, but we don't know what the word
orgasm means—they may in fact get turned on by the babies. And
one of the reasons they all may be turned on in reality by the
babies is that they know that the men find it a turn on. They may
be *trained* in erotism.

H: Oh . . .

S: They've got a nipple which has some capacity—and they may be
heightening its capacity because of all this *silent*, but not absent
silent, just subtle noise—communication—going on [between the
women and men]. That would explain, in good part, why that man
[Imano] had that fantasy. Now, you may have essential pieces of
information that may be related.

H: Is it possible, that women could be having a *genuine* . . .

S: Women in our society report genuine orgasms with suckling.

H: Orgasm where?

S: Orgasm where? If you mean orgasm, there's no problem with the
word. It only has one meaning. (Unless it's misused by analysts,

---

*I believe that, rather as you need at least a whisper of hostility (to hurt, to harm, to put
down, and humiliate) for a joke, so it goes with erotic excitement. The skeptical reader will
find the argument at length in Stoller (1979 and 1985a).

†This session occurred before the one described in chapter 5, where Weiyu himself relays
this daydream.

who talk about gastric orgasms and bowel orgasms, [i.e.] some kind of excitement with explosiveness.) In the sense that these women are saying, women have reported that they put a baby on the breast and the baby sucks and they have a genital orgasm.

H: Genital orgasm . . .

S: That's the only orgasm there is. All the rest is fantasy.

H: Yeah, exactly. But *she's saying that she doesn't feel anything* [in her genitals].

S: Well, now—we've got to find out what she's saying.

H: Right. It's not clear yet. Well then, this is worth talking about with the men. We could talk about this tonight, because I'm going to be talking to them.

Later that night we did the main interview work in chapter 5, on men's beliefs about breast-feeding and ritual.

A LATER SESSION*

This was the longest session. [It is followed by another, starting page 192.] It lasted almost two hours. At first P. is in the next room. The previous session (unreported) ended early when men began gathering noisily in that outer room.

H: There are two things I want to ask you about. There is a dream, and then there is a daydream she has had.

S: I want some orientation. Why do you want to tell me this *now*? Then I can ask the next question. Might it not be worth the extra effort to *not* tell me, and have her review it again—and she's telling it to a new person. Perhaps it would be better for me not to have heard it before so I have nothing in my head until you translate it. And then maybe what I ask will be different than what I would ask otherwise. [*H. leaves room and brings P. in.*]

H: [*To S.*] [I'm always fascinated by] the little ways—some conscious, some unconscious—men have blocked me from working with her.

S: That would be very interesting. That belongs in methodology. That is, the ways in which—not just the translator, not just yourself,

---

*Again, unfortunately for space, we must delete our second interview with P. She began by telling a long dream about gardening, which had some anxieties in it. That led to her associating to menstrual blood; and then I asked her about the sources of semen and blood. Though valuable, these data deflect from our present focus and will be reported elsewhere. Just remember that many discussions have occurred with P. on many topics, before and after the following session.

not just this, not just that—but the ways in which *the people* will prevent you from getting data. Not just secrets; that's another story. But just because women are to be put down, and this one in particular.

H: Yeah, exactly. I thought of it now because of the guy who is in the kitchen there, who doesn't want to leave. He's lingering.

S: You're going to keep an eye on it, and if he doesn't leave, throw him out? Or he'll leave?

H: I've got to throw him out. [*H. calls out:*] Moondi, Moondi— Moondi . . . [who didn't want to be displaced.]

M: Huh?

H: Are you outside or inside?

M: Outside . . .

H: All right . . . [*To S.*] this will be difficult for her, if I ask about her daydream, because it will be with two men [H. plus S.].

S: It had gotten to be easy with you?

H: It was easy, but still difficult. [We hear Moondi leave at this point.]

S: Difficult, but her relationship with you made it possible. And now, all of a sudden, there's a stranger. But not "a member of the society" so it would be bearable. A stranger.

H: Yeah. It will probably be [awkward] for a few minutes and then pass.

S: Could you tell her anything about me to make it easier?

H: I was thinking of how I could do that. . . . [*To P.*]. We are talking about our work, and then I want to ask you about some things—

S: Tell her that you and I have shared our information for years. Not about her, but just . . . and that we are *comfortable* with each other, and keep secrets. Emphasize the sharingness so that she feels that she can share with me.

H: Um hm. [*To P.*] I want to ask you about something. But first, I want to tell you: well, you know, Dr. S. is, like my boss. The two of us share in each other's work and exchange understanding; he talks with me, and I talk to him. Even the secrets of men or women, we share those secrets too. We both follow the same rule, that you can't tell others about this; that's forbidden. You have to keep quiet, listen, and when they tell you their secrets, that becomes your secret too. I am happy that he follows this rule of mine. We're the same in that way. [*Pause.*] I want to ask you about something from before. When we started, before, on your first fantasy, you told me [some time ago] of an image you have in which you play around [sexual play] while still a *tai* [girl]. You and that *kwulai'u*

[boy] you used to play around with.* Is it okay if we talk about this?

P: Yes, that's okay.

H: When did it [daydream] first begin?

P: Oh, I was married; we were married [the abduction], and then it began.

H: When you and your man were first walking around [metaphor for sex]?

P: It was then. At the time I saw it like this: me and that boy [from her childhood], the two of us were little and we did it like this.

H: You did it like what?

P: We were together. "[I would imagine] We used to do this . . . ".

H: In the image, what can you see first? Like, his face . . . or a place, close to a tree, or see the earth or sky . . . ?

P: The edgeland forest. Close to the huts.

H: Now this place, does it have things—grass, flowers . . . [*soft voice*]?

P: [*Soft.*] Uh, huh. Grass, flowers, bamboos, pandanus fruit. And we played there [*smiles*].

H: Is it a nice place or a bad place?

P: Oh, it's a nice place.

H: And is it morning or night?

P: [*Thinking.*] Oh, morning.

H: Is it just you two, or others too?

P: Some small boys are there, and we're all carrying firewood. And we say to them, "You boys stay here; we want to go over there." Near the bush.

H: Close to them or a way off?

P: Farther away. We can't hear them. It's a long way off—we can't see them. No. Just us two. We say to each other, "We don't want them to see us. We've got to go hide in the grass." And so we go.

H: Does the boy lead or do you?

P: He pushes me [to go].

H: What does he say? He's just asking for nothing [playful foreplay talk]. Do you respond to him?

P: Yeah, I respond. I say, "We didn't come for just anything?—no; we came to search for insects and for young fern sprouts.† That's what we can find." [*Smile.*]

---

*The nine-year-old boy described in the introductory biographic sketch.
†Children and older adults eat these foods.

H: Um hm. When you say that, do you smile at him?*

P: Yeah.

H: Does he look strong† at you?

P: Yeah.

H: And when he looks strong at you, what do you feel—in the day-dream?

P: I think, "He wants to ask me about doing what I've heard our mommas and papas do." He mustn't want to do this. [*Smiles.*] He shouldn't look strong at me so much. So I just smile.

H: Then what happens in the image?

P: We don't talk. He says, "I want to screw you with your [P.'s slip] cock." [*Chuckles.*] . . . *He* says that: "You look at my cock"—

H: *His* cock. And what do you feel?

P: We both want that, and he's asking me . . .

H: Um hm. What do you feel inside? Happy? Afraid?

P: Just happy. [*Pause.*] Then—

H: When do you picture this? Only when screwing [with Nilutwo]?

P: At that time.

H: When you see his [Nilutwo's] face?

P: No, when I see his cock. Only then.

H: First he himself removes his trousers or grass sporran—?

P: [*Cuts in.*] *He* does that.‡

H: And when you see his *laakelu* [penis], you recall the fantasy of you and the boy playing around.

P: Right.

H: Now I want to look closer at the fantasy. The boy says, "Look at my cock." You like that.

P: Yeah.

H: Then what? Is he then forceful? Removes your grass skirt? Or what?

P: He may be forceful and . . . remove my grass skirt . . . and then we don't have . . . [*mumbles*].

H: What?

P: We do it, just play at it [screwing]. [*Smiles.*]

H: Do you see his cock in the image? His boy's cock. . . . What do you feel?

P: Happy.

---

*Implying seduction.

†See chapter 4, on erotic looking.

‡P. is underlining that Nilutwo makes the overture, not she. The attitude is: only a whore initiates sexual foreplay, even in marriage. And by clarifying what I had said, P. distances herself slightly from the sexual excitement that might threaten our interview. Perhaps the potential tension between us needs defusing here, keeping the talk less active, more intellectual.

H: Happy. You're not afraid of his* cock?

P: Oh, when it was new, I was a little afraid. But when he stimulated† me a bit then I was really pleased. [*Chuckles.*]

H: You're talking about stimulated in your cunt or outside, the lips of your cunt, or where stimulated?

P: Just outside. Not really inside.

H: Within this fantasy can you feel *imbimboogu?*

P: No. Only when we're done, then we feel *imbimboogu.*

H: With Nilutwo.

P: Then I get *imbimboogu.*

H: And what about in your fantasy?

P: That's . . . just my *koontu* [thought].

H: [*Surprised.‡*] What?

P: It's just *koontu.* Just thought.

H: So in your fantasy the boy stimulates the sides of your cunt with his cock; and in truth [at that moment] Nilutwo puts his cock into you. Is it the same moment when the boy does it and when N. does it, that you feel *imbimboogu?*

P: The same time.

H: You won't have the fantasy *after* you feel *imbimboogu?*

P: After the fantasy I feel *imbimboogu.*§

H: Can I tell S.?

P: [*Smiles.*] You can tell him; I'll listen.

S: [*Quickly.*] Her style: when she smiled, shyly, and kept her hand so she just barely looked at me . . . I would read it the same as at home.

H: I think she's comfortable telling you; I think she's a bit excited about sharing it with you; interested. And a little . . . fear, about me telling you. But she's comfortable enough. It's fear in the form of embarrassment, being shy, very soft, "feminine": in another

---

*I am vague here, for I was not sure how much P. was marking off her daydream from her intercourse with N.

†*Sigerup*, the Pidgin term, is so vague (see chapter 4). Could be: aroused, buttered-up, scratched, touched, vibrated, etc. "Stimulated" roughly translates this situation.

‡Fascinating that for the first time, here, P. refers to her experience as *koontu.* I've argued [chapter 3, and in Herdt 1987d] that *koontu* is a metaphor for "self," specifically the public social norms that keep people in line. May we interpret P. as meaning she has a socially acquired script about what she *should* feel regarding orgasm with her husband, as opposed to the private scripts she may tell no one (may not completely know herself)—except, perhaps, me?—and that may differ from what orgasm *should* be? Thanks to S., I am alert to that possibility, and if lucky, I may learn if it's true.

§S: Our same argument put this time as rhetorical questions: is a woman's daydream to be counted as a fit subject for ethnography; can one learn about culture this way; is the private daydream less revealing than the public myth (which probably started as a private daydream); can humans understand each other across cultures?

Sambia woman her fear would take a different form at this moment.

S: She's never looked at me, but I've never had the feeling that she was consciously cutting me out. Instead, she didn't look at me because nothing counted but you and her. And I was safe enough that she didn't even have to think about me. The pleasure she has in being with you and talking with you is the style I felt. She was concentrated on you. Not "I refuse to acknowledge the presence of this other person." It was that I wasn't important. But [she is] not hostile. Because she's so absorbed in the pleasure of being with you. And I don't even mean the affectionate but rather I think she likes the task. Okay.

H: So, I've been asking her about her favorite erotic daydream, the only one, as far as I know, she has now. This is the daydream. She's a young girl of, say eight to ten, eleven; not yet to puberty. And she is with a boy her age. They're near the village where she was born. On that side of the village there are flowers, bamboo, and grass—it's a nice place. And they've been playing with some children in the morning. They tell these others to occupy themselves while P. and the boy go off to do something. At this point she does not know what is going to happen—

S: But she does know. In this society everybody knows about sex, at an early age.

H: No, no they don't.

S: Children—

H: No.

S: They do not know about intercourse?

H: No. The implication is that the boy is stronger than she is and knows more about sex than she does. And so they go off . . . And it's the two of them alone—

S: [*Hears someone in the kitchen.*] You'd better go out there—

H: That's the old man [Chemgalo]; he's all right.* This is based on reality—

S: It sounds like it.

H: This happened several times with a boy she grew up with. And so they go out to collect ferns and insects to eat. But the boy has something different in mind. He begins to look at her sexually. That is, he is looking at her intensely, which means in this culture that he wants her, desires her.

---

*We've grown more cautious since Gambakutu's secret listening. But Chemgalo (Weiyu's step-father) is ancient, and hard-of-hearing.

S: [*Interrupts.*] This has nothing to do with her daydream but with the culture: he looks where—face, eyes . . . ?

H: At her face—

S: She knows he's looking at her face and she turns her eyes down. . . .

H: And smiles—

S: Because at that age she recognizes what that look means.

H: In the daydream.

S: Yeah.

H: And she smiles.

S: What smile—what kind of smile?

H: Well, I imagine, a charming smile.

S: Shy, innocent—understand, but doesn't understand.

H: It means, "I accept your desire."

S: "I do understand"—?

H: Yeah, that is, "I will be your desirable object." She started having this daydream when first having sex with her husband. She was very afraid. When she saw his penis she was very afraid. It was so big—

S: That was the first one she'd ever seen? Like that? [*Pause.*] Not crucial—

H: Yeah, I don't know* and I'd have to think it out . . . That's when she had this daydream. And in it she sees a little boy's penis. First she's a bit frightened . . .

S: A little boy's erect penis?

H: Yeah, a little boy's erect penis. The boy looks at her strongly, and she smiles in response. Then he says, "Look at my penis." She looks. He removes his grass skirt and she sees his erect penis . . .

S: And she sees one then for the first time.

H: For the first time. And she is frightened at first, but then feels okay. . . . Then, in one version he pushes her down, lays on top of her, puts his penis partly in her still immature vagina. In another version [these have been told in earlier interviews] they lay down together and it's a little less rough. The story line is that she wants him, but he's also very firm and he's pushing her. But it's not a rape, not that. She wants him [to do it that way]. And in reality she is using the daydream when she sees the [Nilutwo's] erect penis. In the past she associated to this daydream two erotic night dreams in both of which she saw a little boy's penis, not a man's penis. And in one of these, mine [a night dream seeing me]

*I'm 99 percent sure that as an adult woman, P. had never before seen an adult erect penis.

was the same way. It was me, my body, my face, everything was the same, but it was a little boy's penis and not a man's penis.* And *that* gets her more turned on: having this daydream when her husband is about to enter her, gets her more turned on; and the daydream is gone as soon as she has her orgasm in reality.

S: What happens? They're lying down, and he pushes in a little bit. Is there anything about a hymen?

H: That's one of the things I haven't asked about. She's a virgin [in the daydream].

S: It all seems unfinished. He *begins* pushing, he doesn't get very far. There are daydreams in which that would be the end?

H: Yeah.

S: Another thing I'd like to know, that you can't probably find out, is about women in general in this society. Here's a story. A young woman gets married in Los Angeles. And has had no real sexual experience. (Comparable to P.) She's about to have intercourse with a man who has, pretty much, raped her; that is, he has stolen her from her home, ruined all of her plans, taken her to a new place where she's got no right to do anything at all. She's never seen an erect penis on a man before. She's perhaps going to have a physically painful experience (which it is for some women).

H: And she said it was.

S: And she has an orgasm. Now it's not unheard of, but the larger question is: are the women in this culture, generally speaking, highly arousable? This would indicate it, if you were to extrapolate, like a crazy-man, which you have the right to do. But there are cultures in which women expect to have orgasms and always have orgasms. At least so it's reported (and God knows how accurate those reports are).

H: Yeah.

S: But does she represent that even in a traumatic [experience]. . . . Is she representative of all the women? Does she talk with her friends? And does she get the feeling that women expect to have orgasms always?

H: Well this is a highly personal subject. [*Sober.*]

S: Sure it is! [*Laughs.*]†

---

*I didn't deal directly with such sensitive transference reactions in P. until I returned in 1981, mainly because I wasn't able and ready to. They were worked through then in what I think was a mutually respectful way. I shall report that elsewhere.

†I want to underline here that our emotional cues to each other—my soberness, and S.'s amusement—indicate better than our words the momentary gaps between us, in our different professional experiences and emotional understanding of Sambia. Is S. not used to sexual openness in Los Angeles culture? Am I not more reticent for the Sambia?

H: She's never told this daydream to anybody else.

S: But do they talk about their experiences? People will talk about experiences sooner than they'll talk about daydreams.

H: Well, I have some idea about that, but I can ask her.*

[*To P.*] Dr. S. wants to ask us† about when you feel *imbimboogu* when screwing. He wants to ask if sometimes you talk with others about this; do you hear others sometimes talk about having *imbimboogu* with screwing? Do they talk about that?

P: No [*serious*]; they're not about to talk openly about that.

H: Women—

P: Women; no.

H: With your close friends—Nashu [Tali's wife]?

P: Not her either. She's not going to talk about *that* [*whispers*]—I've told you: only when we're asleep, and our legs are turned so that we feel *imbimboogu* [limb "asleep"; a totally different meaning of *imbimboogu*], only then can we say, "Oh, I felt *imbimboogu*." Now this other [erotism]—no, no, not at all.

H: Do you think other women feel *imbimboogu* when they play around with their men?

P: Oh, sure, only they won't talk about it. We all have *imbimboogu*, but they just don't talk about it. That would be shameful.

H: Did your mother talk about it to you?

P: No, no, she didn't ever talk about that. But I think it's not just me who gets *imbimboogu*. All of us women do. We just don't talk about it. We hide it, that's all. [*Smiles.*]

H: [*To S.*] She says what I expected (because we've talked about this before): she's never heard any women, including her best friend, tell her about having orgasms. But she believes that all women have orgasms the same way that she does. But it's *extremely*—this is a very prudish culture. People just don't talk about it. Even her mother; I asked her if she'd talk about it and she said "No."

S: The question is, "Why does she believe that they all have this?" It may just be, "Since I have this, how can anybody else not . . . ."

H: That would be the most obvious answer.

S: But they really do not [talk about it] at all. That doesn't shock me, I've heard [of other instances] before. Okay. So the other

---

*I know now (after another trip) that in general neither Sambia men nor women talk about orgasms, even in private with their closest friends.

†I do say "us" on the tape. Why not "you" instead of "us"? It was subliminal until now (1983): I am identifying with P. verbally, and thereby marking us off as a couple of insiders, vis-à-vis S. By doing so, I imply to P. that I will protect her self-respect should S. go too far in his probings.

question is whether the daydream goes any farther, beyond the point at which she's lying down and the boy begins to push.

H: Yeah. Now I have not asked her about the details of her orgasm. This is difficult . . . because of the terminology. I haven't asked her where . . . I have the sense that it's [orgasm] way inside, that is, it's vaginal—

S: Vaginal, not just clitoral.

H: Not just clitoral, if in fact that's possible.

S: What?

H: That she could have a clitoral orgasm.

S: Well it gets rubbed indirectly during intercourse and participates in women's orgasms. It either participates or it is the main part of it—depending on what's touched. It would be interesting to know—is it vaginal and to what extent. She says it is, is that right?

H: She says it is—

S: [Cutting in.] Is there a vocabulary for the anatomy, is there a word for clitoris?

H: There is a word. Boy, I tell you, I never got that from men!

S: You mean they don't know about the clitoris?

H: They know about it. But they don't want to think about it. [Pause.] It took me a long time to figure that one out.

S: Why don't they want to think about it?

H: The answer—you won't believe the answer: I can't answer you in any simple way. It would take a long time to fill you in. But [in a nutshell], my last view is that men think of it as a kind of penis.* [S: not just Sambia men.] I never got that before; I just worked on it the last few weeks. But at any rate men don't have a term for that. Now, Penjukwi gave me the term for it—

S: The women's term, or everybody's?

H: The women's term. It was a *big* secret. There may be something in that that I haven't mined yet; I think there is.

S: How do they know about it [clitoris]?

H: [Pause.]†

S: Well, I'll give you the answer: because they have experienced the sensations of it.

H: Oh.

S: All right. I mean, how else would they know of it? They're not sitting around with mirrors.

H: Yeah, obviously, sure. [To P.] First, I want to ask you: in your

---

*My genuine naiveté—I hail from rural Kansas—is not only a character trait but a valuable ethnographic tool.

†Another example of an obvious question I had never thought of before.

fantasy, when you see this boy, and you're playing around, and he gets on top of you, does he get on top of you while you're lying on the ground?

P: [*Pause.*] Yes.

H: Now when he puts his cock inside you, not too far inside but a ways, after you're finished, what will you both do? Inside the fantasy? Or is that the end of it?

P: At that time, I just think, "It's done."

H: It's done. After he inserts—

P: His cock—

H: Inside a bit in your cunt. And then it's done.

P: It's over—

H: Now, in truth, you feel *imbimboogu.*

P: At the same time.

H: Now I haven't asked you this before: in the fantasy you're a girl. Now in a girl, the cunt isn't opened yet.

P: Right.

H: Inside it, the opening is covered by some skin . . . covered by skin [hymen]. Does the boy break the skin and go inside?

P: [*Quickly*] Oh, no; he doesn't go completely inside. Just a tiny way.

H: This far—? [*Gestures with hand.*]

P: Yeah—when we're big, then [*pause*]. I've already told you when my breasts are still small, it's [vaginal entrance?] the same.

H: The same.

P: Yeah. When the breasts are big and mature, close to turning downwards, then at that time it [vagina] can open [i.e., menarche].

H: That was the first time, when your man screwed you—

P: Yeah, it was him, he's the one who messed me up the first time—

H: He broke it [hymen]?

P: Yeah, he broke it. It was painful then. There was no blood. Just pain.

H: Yeah. [*To S.*] She says that's the end of the daydream, the point where the boy penetrates . . .

S: Somewhat—

H: About an inch.

S: Is it stopped by her hymen?

H: [*To P.*] In the fantasy, what keeps him from going deeply inside?

P: My skin—

H: Far enough for you to just feel him, that's all?

P: I just feel him.

H: Truly inside, or just at the surface?

P: No, just the surface. We're just playing at it, that's all.

H: I've forgotten the name of it, where the skin layer is [hymen] atop your [vagina] . . . What is that—I forgot—

P: Oh, uh . . . [thinks] Wait . . . [she's forgotten, too]. . . . Lakandiku.*

H: Lakandiku. In your fantasy, too, can you feel that inside it, there is heat?

P: Oh, not at all.

H: [To S.] She says that it's her hymen that prevents him from going inside. She also told me something that I guess I forgot or didn't know exactly. That she was a virgin when her husband stole her, and he was the first man who penetrated her. It was the sweetheart she had, who lives in another area, who she'd wanted to have sex with, and she was thinking of him—at the time when Nilutwo stole her.

S: Wait a minute. But not the fantasy you just told me?

H: No, no. That's about the little boy.

S: So she was not having the [little boy] fantasy when Nilutwo first came at her—

H: Oh, yeah.

S: But the sweetheart?

H: No, no.

S: What are you telling me about the sweetheart? You said it was the friend that she had in mind—

H: Oh, I'm sorry. At the time she was married, she did. She was abducted, and she wanted to marry her sweetheart—

S: Oh, I see—

H: And I had the impression that she may have had sex with her friend, but she didn't.

S: But she wasn't thinking of him; I thought you said she was thinking of him [sweetheart] when Nilutwo came at her—

H: She was about to marry him—

S: Not thinking of him at that moment—

H: Oh, no, no, not when they were having sex.

S: Okay. This was not, when she first used it, an erotic fantasy. It was a defensive fantasy—to make an erotic experience less dangerous. Do you know what I'm saying—?

H: Yeah, that's—

S: Not used for sexual excitement at all [at first]. It was used to mas-

*I had only heard this word from P. It is never used in any kind of public discourse, and not by men at all. Apparently women use it rarely in private. But at this point, I am still confused and do not realize lakandiku means clitoris (see p. 183).

ter an unmasterable situation. But it became an erotic fantasy—

H: Became erotic later, yeah. Let me check out one detail. [*To P.*] At first, when Nilutwo seized you and they put you in that hut, the *first* time, (when you felt pain as he went inside you) did you have this fantasy? The first time, or was it later?

P: No, it was the first time.

H: The first time. At that time did you feel *imbimboogu?* Or not?

P: Yes, At that time I felt *imbimboogu.*

H: The first time?

P: Yeah.

H: But you felt pain?

P: I felt pain; but when he screwed me the next time I had [*smiles*] *imbimboogu.*

H: Oh. [*Pause.*] The same night, or the next day, or—?

P: The next day. When he first did it, it was very painful, I didn't feel *imbimboogu.*

H: And the second night?

P: Then I got *imbimboogu.*

H: And did you have the fantasy then?

P: Yes.

H: And the first time with Nilutwo, you didn't have the fantasy?

P: Oh, no, I didn't. This here [*lakandiku*] is just the surface. Now deep inside we call it . . . *lakwuku* [vaginal vault].

H: Yeah, now when you felt *imbimboogu*, did you feel it inside the *lakwuku*, or where?

P: We feel it deep inside.

H: Where?

P: Deep inside.

H: Deep inside—in the skin . . . ?

P: There.

H: On top, where the skin is, or below in—

P: No, on top—

H: On top and inside—

P: There—

H: At the very back— . . . And when you feel your *muguchelu* [vaginal fluid] come, do you feel it in the *lakwaku*—

P: There, right there [i.e., "yes"].

H: Now, Dr. S. wants to ask you, have you ever felt *imbimboogu* in your *lakandiku* [clitoris; I finally realize P. was referring above not to the hymen but to the clitoris].

P: [*Sweeping gesture.*] *All over.* My *imbimboogu* is in all of it [genital].

H: *Lakandiku?*

P: There too. Both inside and outside.

H: Do you feel it inside first or outside first?

P: No, inside first we feel it and then outside.

H: [*To S.*] Well, this is new information to me. Let me tell you what she just said. She told me she feels her orgasm inside (and this is another term men don't have)—must be the back tissue of the vagina, the very deepest part—

S: The depth—probably nearest the cervix. What some women in our society called "deep vaginal orgasm," when there was a time when that was the measure of whether you were feminine or not, in the late fifty's and early sixty's. It was kind of joking and yet serious that you "weren't really there" unless you were capable of that. It is deep, as deep as you can get in the vagina, and it gives a whole pelvic quality to it. Not just a sharp, localized clitoral type thing—

H: Yeah. Well, it's important that this [anatomy] has a cultural category for it, that it's linguistically marked.

S: You mean this anatomical area is different from the vagina—

H: Yeah, it is marked.

S: It [vaginal vault] has no [common] name in our culture—

H: Oh—

S: It's just called vagina—

H: Well, you see, the three parts are marked. Inside this part—where she says she feels her orgasm first—she's feeling it first inside in this place. And then she feels it outside, at the clitoris—

S: What about lips?

H: [*Pause.*]

S: Do they have a name for that?

H: Yeah, they have a name for it—there's a name for it [*mugu laaku*] but this is not the same, but let me ask her. [*Turns to P. and they talk.*] The impression I get is that she feels it inside, it's not clear to what extent she's feeling—after she feels it—feels her orgasm deep inside, to what extent it becomes a generalized orgasm for everything—

S: But it spreads to all—?

H: It spreads to all. She says that she feels it first more intensely in the clitoris before she feels it on the lips of the vagina, but it seems as if it subsumes the whole area; so she's feeling generalized sensations.

S: Is there anything that sets it off besides just: the time has passed and rubbing has occurred? Is it that he or she is responding to anything [specific] that's going on in him, or is she responding to a private fantasy, or is she responding to neither of those but just to "after you rub for a while it comes," or something else?

H: [*To P. They talk at length. Back to S.*] She has an orgasm when his cock is inside of her and specifically—which she didn't tell me before—she starts to come when he has ejaculated, when she can feel the semen inside. There must be several moments when she can feel the semen start to slurp around. That's when she has her orgasm.

S: This is a statement that's a question: The thing that is exciting enough for her to finish her excitement is that he has ejaculated *his semen*, not just that he has ejaculated. That's not the same thing. Do you hear what I'm saying? Maybe—it could be the "convulsive activity" that would be the turn-on, or it could be "I possess the semen," I don't know which of those it is.

H: I think I know what it is, but let me ask her.

S: This [society having a] semen cult, it's a worthy question.

H: [*Talks with P.*] Well, *she's* putting the emphasis on feeling the fluids [hers and/or his?] or the semen inside of her. I didn't get that sense before. This is really very rewarding for me, because I *know* I've got the right terminology.

S: You never had it before?

H: No. But now I've got it, [a term] I've never used with her before: there is a category for excitement.

S: Different from the word for orgasm?

H: No, not orgasm.

S: Excitement?

H: Excitement—(the category *kalu mundereindapinu*). I've never used this term with her before. I use it with [some] men (e.g., Moondi) all the time. I ask them, "Are you feeling excitement?" It's a proof that I've got the right cultural connotation, that I can use it for the first time with her and I asked her, "When do you start to feel excitement?"*

S: It's not "excitement"—our word is too vague. We have to add "erotic" or "sexual." This is a word just for genital excitement, not any excitement?

H: This [term] is for excitement [a noun modified by various adjectives to fit the person's experience to the situation]. I say, "When you start feeling excitement, is that when he starts to ejaculate?" She says, "No, not then. It's when he starts to butter me up to

---

*Lest the reader be confused, this summary refers to material that was deleted above for space.

screw me that I start to feel excited." See, that's the correct sense of it. The correct sense—you don't get excited when he's inside of you. (It might be possible for that to happen.) But *she's* getting excited when he starts to seduce her. He wants to be inside of her, and that's when [why] she starts to get excited.

S: That's the foreplay.

H: Yeah, that's the foreplay. Then I said, "When he ejaculates, are you more excited?" and she said, "Yes." And I said, "When do you stop being excited?" "When he takes his penis out." So that's exactly what I would have predicted, but I've never [with P.] used that word [excitement]. So it's a good test that I've got the right sense of it that I can use it with her for the first time and she confirms—it's very important semantically that I've got the meanings right.

S: We've gotten quite a bit [of information]. The kinds of things if you had enough time you'd want to find out. Here's something you take for granted: She says to you, "What makes me have my orgasm is the presence of the semen in my vagina, and what gets me excited is the fact that he shows that he wants me." Those are self-evident, right?

H: Yeah.

S: No.

H: [*Laughs in surprise.*]

S: Behind those are I-don't-know-what-fantasies and life experiences. I could imagine another culture, I could imagine certainly other women, in fact I *know* of women for whom the semen is so disgusting inside of them that they can't bear it.

H: Oh, really?

S: The question is [not only why is semen disgusting for them but] just as much why *is* it not for her. Therefore, don't take anything for granted about sexual excitement. Got it? Once you've got that clue, you'll never forget it except you always forget it and you keep getting into [twisted up by] your own definitions of normality.

H: I just recalled that every last man I've ever worked with here always says that women spit on any man who doesn't have semen. The men say that unless the women can see and feel the ejaculation—

S: All right. That's strictly not to be taken for granted.

H: I've always regarded that as a piece of men's [identity]—but now I think—

S: You don't know; you've only got one [woman's statement]—

H: But a possibility is that in many women here it [ejaculation] really is part of their excitement: it really is necessary, and if a man doesn't have a big seminal emission, it's a big deal. I never thought about it before.

S: Could this—it doesn't have to be—could this be now some of the evidence of the—you can't call it the semen cult—but the importance of semen . . . this would be the form maybe in which you get your first clue of how it shows up in the women. They may not know there's a semen cult [homosexual activities], but they may have learned that semen is big stuff, not just to produce babies. So a clue like this could be (at this point, you're just speculating wildly) your chance—you muddle along and all of a sudden you discover a doorway where you didn't know there was one—

H: Yeah.

S: And you now open that door, and it opens up into female reciprocal—reciprocating—the reciprocal of the male semen cult. In what form does that present in the women's lives? That's the way you are going. (It might not be a door.)

H: There's a whole subject that she and I have never talked about: the men's belief that women like to acquire semen either through their mouths or through their vaginas—

S: [An acquisition] which devastates the men—

H: Which devastates the men but also excites them.

S: Oh, sure.

H: And, but especially through their mouths, because it is believed to strengthen the woman's body, her tissue, her bones and to provide breast milk.

S: Are the women told this,* or is this one of the secrets of the men?

H: This is the men's belief, not necessarily a secret; it's supposed to be a public thing.

S: What do the women believe about it?

H: See, that's what I never asked her.

S: Well, ask her what do women feel—what does semen do besides—

H: I want to see if there is somebody inside here. [*Goes to check.*] I thought sure I heard some talking. He's just in there by himself [Weiyu's stepfather, Chemgalo who, uncomprehending, is sleeping out his last days in the safety of H.'s fire].

---

*Probably yes, in their secret menarche ceremonies.

S: But he's been muttering in there to himself—I saw him talking like he wasn't facing anyone else. He just shouldn't fall into the fire—

H: [*Talks to P. telling her what happened. To S.*] I was just noticing she is *so* feminine.

S: Even in our culture she would seem so. I mean, she is as feminine as any women I've ever seen in any part of the United States; Paris, France; Bergen, Norway; Rome, Italy. How come?

H: I don't know.

S: She's never learned that from the other women here. [H: She would have; there are others as feminine in demeanor.]

H: I was just noticing what she was doing with her hands and . . .

S: Her whole everywhere, those facial expressions . . .

H: Her face, and her eyes . . .

S: The sound of her voice . . .

H: Her smile, and the softness in her eyes . . . [We are enjoying ourselves.]

S: But she's very feminine by the standards here.

H: Right. Yeah, this is one of the things about gender identity. It takes you [ethnographer] so long to pick up the subtle things. Then they take on meaning. I mean the way she . . . you see the way she's using her hands [i.e., small expressive gestures]. No masculine man ever uses his hands that way.

S: But Kalutwo—

H: Yes, that's right and the other guy [Imano].

S: Up the hill—

H: Yeah. [These circumlocutions exemplify how we avoid saying people's names in front of other people, in order to preserve confidentiality.] He especially, he's [Imano] a very emotionally expressive man; that's a feminine quality.

S: Men are expressive with their hands, but it's more [*thrusts arms out, slashing at the air*] . . . fists, and uh, sharper.

H: But less than that.

S: I've seen some men doing it.

H: Weiyu will do that.

S: Yeah, that's who I was thinking about. That's who I've seen do it. He sat there gesticulating with his hands . . .

H: Yeah; but now, that other guy up the hill [Imano], he's in that [gentle masculine] category. He's an especially expressive man with his hands in a feminine way. He has soft gestures, the way he touches his face . . . (details, that are in my field notes). Like the way he'll touch his cheeks is unusual . . . . But anyway, she was saying that [collecting my thoughts] . . . I was asking her about the . . . what was the question we originally got on? I was asking her about . . . drinking semen, and she says that she thinks . . . . There for the first time, there was a little disgust in her voice. Some disgust about orally ingesting semen . . . . She said that, uh—

S: [*Butts in, lowers voice slightly and sensitively says*] Well, did she do it in her uh, uh [*groping for words*] . . .

H: She's done it a few times, and she doesn't like to do it. She thinks it's boring. Here's a fundamental difference between the men's and women's views: She thinks* it's basically baloney that semen is necessary in order to strengthen a woman, to prepare her for child bearing, and so forth. She has mixed feelings about what it is that produces breast milk. She holds out the possibility that semen *may contribute* to it, for the simple reason that she has noticed in her own body that there's no breast milk before the time she had started having sex with her husband. And she is again approaching now that period when she's about to have babies.

S: [*Inserts.*] Whoa! That might be right, but she hasn't had sex for a long time and yet she's got lots of breast milk, doesn't she? Is she feeding now?

H: Yeah, she's feeding now.

S: Where [does she believe] is it coming from?

H: Well, uh . . .

S: [*Continues.*] Other semen from other times?

H: She's got mixed opinions. She's saying that inside she feels that her breasts are making it, that there is something in her own body that's producing it. One part of her says that that part of the story is baloney too. She wouldn't reject that, but what she does specifically say is that she dislikes fellatio, and her husband has too often wanted to have fellatio with her. She will often say, "No, I don't want that, I'd rather have it down below."

S: She doesn't say why? She doesn't know why he wants it, he just wants it?

H: No, she told me why. She says that [rough translation] the old men say in the ritual teachings that the man mustn't have vaginal

---

*Now, as an adult woman. Her feeling was not as clear when younger. We ethnographers cannot be too conscious of the fact that people's gender identities and erotics may alter, as they move through the life cycle, experience more, and change.

sex too much because it is harmful to his health, and he should have fellatio more often.

S: Did the men tell the boys to tell their wives that? Or is she just inventing it?

H: No, that's true, it's a true story.

S: They did say that [*voice rising*], you mean they really do believe it?

H: That's part of the ritual teachings!

S: Oh, I thought it was "What are we going to tell the women to make sure that the women don't discover what we really do."

H: No, they [the men] really do believe that, which goes along with the view that coitus is more threatening and damaging than is fellatio. It's [coitus] closer to the source of the uterus, she's saying, (this is interesting, I hadn't thought of it like this), "Forget the mouth. I'm a bit disgusted at having your semen in my mouth. I don't believe your stories. If you want to give it to me, let's have sex in my vagina, where it's closest to my womb."

S: Also, she doesn't get any excitement from it [fellatio].

H: Yeah, exactly, but the point is that with this comment she associates sex with the womb, having semen "fed" into her womb. That's very important, because the man's view is that coitus is the most depleting act. Fellatio is definitely less depleting and dangerous because you're physically farther away from the vagina and womb. (See Herdt 1981.)

S: [*Pause.*] We don't have to give up the idea yet that we're getting the reciprocal of the men. But there's a lot more about semen in these women than in other societies' women. At least in conscious awareness.

H: Yes.

S: You want to keep looking for that. . . . You taught me that typically when the man starts into marriage, he begins fellatio with the girl as a bridge for himself toward the dangerous vagina, from the safety of the boys.

H: Right. . . . I forgot to tell you about something you asked about a while ago. When Nilutwo abducted her, and they had sex the first time, it was very [emotionally] painful for her. But she is very precise that the first time that he started to enter her, when she saw his penis, she was frightened: *that* was the first time she had the daydream. But she had *no* orgasm that time. It was the second night that she had an orgasm. She had the fantasy at the same time, and she continued to have it frequently, although not every time for the first six or so months.

S: Probably she had it frequently, meaning every time she was more frightened.

H: Yeah.

S: And less excited.

H: It's such a transparent daydream. [S: Only to us.]

S: You get what I meant when I said that is was not an erotic daydream [the first time she used it]. And it may never have been when used with her husband: [with him] it may have been an anxiety-reducing daydream. But if she's lying around all by herself and staring at the ceiling and avoiding masturbating [since Sambia all allege no one ever masturbates], and she has it, then it's an erotic daydream, and you have to understand the difference. There'll be something different in some detail between the two, says my prediction. You never did find out about another piece that we picked up. You were interrupted when we were finding out whether the word for orgasm had the same meaning as breast-feeding, and so, keep that in mind. You may want to go back.

H: Yeah, that's right.

S: At any rate, what seems more exciting [for H.'s research] than where she feels her sexual excitement—you could be on to something big, though not as big as your original discovery about the semen cult—is the ways the men's cult presents to [is filtered through] the women. It cannot present as a revealed secret. How do they absorb it [the secret], and how do they absorb it into their understanding of what it's like to be a female and a woman in this culture. Now that is probably more important in the remaining time you've got than to find out much more about what's the nature of her orgasm.

H: That sounds right.

S: So there you have some more about the semen cult, [though] we don't know *what* you've got.

H: Now that you've brought it to my attention, it seems obvious, but I wouldn't have thought of it. That's quite a thing. [*Pause.*] Well, I think we'll quit. It's been almost two hours.

S: Yeah. She's been a good help.

H: Yeah. [*To P.*] Oh, I think we'll stop now, we've finished two hours' worth now.

P: Okay.

H: I think tomorrow too, I'd like to work quite a long time with you. Is that all right?

P: Yeah, that's all right.

H: Okay. Suppose in the morning, we'll kick everybody else out and just us, we can work. Is that all right?
P: Yeah, that's good.

LAST SESSION

H: I think this is the last time that you and I will be meeting together [*quietly and slowly*].*

•   •   •

P: There's lots of people around. [*Pause.* We don't know where we'll go with the interview. So S. suggests we talk about her plans for protecting herself after Nilutwo dies. How will she escape another forced marriage? Will the men beat her up? Could she be killed? We get depressed. We talk with her about her plans after N's death. Then:]
S: If we're in a lull, then you can ask her about the tattoos. If you're not in a lull—
H: [*Depressed.*] No, I'm in a lull. [I felt down thinking about P.'s plight. We are trying to think what to do next. S. had earlier asked why P. had a light tattoo on her face, unlike other women in the village. At first—several years ago—I wondered about P.'s tattoo but had grown oblivious to it and had never asked her about it. S. reminds me now.] Dr. S. wants to ask you about that mark on your face.
P: Oh, Yanduwaiko's people—his wife—they put that on me.
H: Did you ask her for it, or did she just do it?
P: Oh, no. She did it. She said, "I want to decorate you with that" [*smiles*].
H: And you let her?
P: Yeah, I let her [*chuckles*]. She is just like my mother. I used to sleep curled up in her lap. It wasn't just me. It was Gam's wife too.
H: Do you like this?
P: [*Laughs.*] Oh . . .
S: [*Laughs.*] She covers her face with her hands. That's the first time she's done that.
H: She used to do that all the time.
S: Oh, really? Is it because of me or because of the subject? And me, or not me, or the subject, or all of us?

---

*Again we must delete a long dialogue here on sexuality to save space.

H: It's all that. [*To P.*] Do you like that mark? [*Soft humor.*]

P: Guh [*chuckles*].

H: You like it?

P: I like it.

H: What does it do for you?

P: This woman said: "We all do this. And you should have one too."

H: [*To S.*] She says it's her aunt who did it. The government translator's wife at the patrol station. She's like her mother. And at
one time her aunt wanted to do it to her and to her other aunt.
But then I asked her, "Do *you* like it?" And she said, "Yes, I like
it."

S: But none of the women in this hamlet—

H: No.

S: None of the women in her hamlet—just the women at the patrol
post. What does it mean?

H: [*To P.*] Does this mark have a meaning for you?

P: Um—no, not for me [*raises voice, squirms, chuckles*].* That's just
that woman's idea. I don't have any idea about it.

H: But you like it, don't you?

P: [*Smiles.*] That's just that woman's idea. It wasn't mine.

H: Not yours?

P: They all said, "We want to put this on your skin . . . So you have
to do it." That's all.

H: [*Chuckles.*] Ohhh. [*To S.*] I'm getting all kinds of new thoughts.
She's very embarrassed; she wants to deny that it was her decision, "Just my aunt's." But I don't believe that.

S: Is this vanity?

H: Yeah.

S: She's caught being vain.

H: Yeah: see, this is a sign that she's a different kind of woman [from
the rest in the hamlet]. She is; she regards herself that way. She
speaks Pidgin and stuff like that. There's a sense that she's a little
bit freer—

S: To have done this?

H: Yeah. Yeah—for sure. I'd never really thought about it much—
but you see this is what women of a tribe† in the Central Highlands do. I don't want to say their name because it has a negative
connotation here. They're regarded [here] as sort of promiscuous—

---

*This response, and this effect, are typically feminine, and unusual for P. with me. She
seems here to resort to the womanly script, "I'm innocent."

†Chimbu. Sambia have encountered Chimbu who have body tattoos.

S: This is a custom of theirs—

H: Yeah.

S: How did it get down here? [H: It hasn't; just in P.] This is contact?

H: A lot of contact at that station. [Outside New Guineans are employed at the patrol station.]

S: And it indicates? Erotic promiscuity? A different relationship to the world?

H: Not necessarily. A different relationship—a different kind of femininity: more open. See, they kiss there; they're open about holding hands. They're more aggressive. You know the Sambia boys are afraid of those women—in Goroka and other places. [And they detest the thought of kissing.] I never thought of it before, but it matches her personality that she did that.

S: When? When was it?

H: [*To P.*] Did you have this done when you were a young woman [*chenchorai*]—

P: I was a *tai* [girl].

H: Oh, still a *tai*—were you very little, or bigger? Same as—

P: [Says a seven year old girl's name]—bigger.

H: Oh. [*To S.*] She was a girl still, hadn't had her menarche yet, but was within a year or two [c. 17–18 years old] of it.

S: What about the one on her arm?

H: Her arm? [*Surprise.* I hadn't even noticed that one.] . . . [*To P.*] Now what about that one on your arm?

P: [*Laughs.*] No, that's nothing! [H: Does the laugh signal a real choice which P. made, not the coercion she earlier described?]

H: [Another interruption from outside. This conversation is very public. Did this change P.'s behavior? *To P.*] There's chaos out there. What about your hand?

P: A small boy and I had them put them on us.

H: When you were still a *tai?*

P: Yeah, I was a *tai.*

H: Oh.

P: One of my [classificatory] sisters put it on us—Gam's people. I just let them.

H: [*To S.*] She did it when she was still a girl. She said she wasn't thinking; did it with her clan sister.

S: This is . . . most unusual.

H: Huh?

S: Most unusual.

H: Oh, it *is* most unusual. I never thought about it. She's really embarrassed about having it.

S: You mean, beyond the men?

H: Oh, yeah, I don't know why. I can see that she got a little angry about being asked about it.

S: Do you think it's all right [to ask about this]—I really don't know what I'm doing [*laughs*].

H: Yeah, I think it's all right. [*To P.*] When I asked you about your arm tattoo I looked at your face and I thought you felt a little anger. Why was that?

P: No—

H: You said, "No, I'm not cross about that." But I see your face, and I think there's a little anger.

P: [*Laughs.*] No, not really. It's just that you're asking me too much [about this] and that's no good.

H: Really?

P: Yeah, that's true.

H: Oh, this talk is no good?

P: Um-hm. It's not just me who's done this, plenty of other women have. I don't want to talk anymore. [*Angry.*] I'll go . . .

H: They have too; oh, yeah. [*To S.*] That's the first time in all our work she's ever done that. She says, "Don't ask me any more or I'll go outside." I don't know what it means.* First time she's ever said that.

S: The first time ever? The question is why she's so upset. . . . I guess we should quit. [Tape unintelligible for a few moments.] All right.

H: [*To P.*] That's it. . . . We want to say thank you for all you've said and for your help. We're really pleased. [*Warm smile.*]

P: Me too, I'm really pleased. It's only right now, you two have asked me too much about this [tattoo: covert way to say, "I was angry"]. So that's all—

H: Well, that's okay. We didn't know about that, and so we asked . . .

P: Well, that's okay, but you've asked me too much about this. I didn't mind until now. [H: for the first time P. wants to argue with me. She won't give it up. We really touched a sensitive spot.]

H: I can understand that. But we were just asking. You know. Dr. S. doesn't know about things here, and he just wanted to find out. You, too, do you have anything you'd like to ask him?

P: Well, I just don't understand why he kept at that. That's no good.

---

*I think that I do now (1988). Sambia never had tattoos traditionally and in 1979 only P. and her aunt did. We asked about it in a context of sexuality, and P. seemed to feel her character—moral rectitude—was challenged. She *could* get angry because S. asked the question and she felt close enough to me not to hide it.

AFTERWORD

We ended this long session in a wash, interested but tired and ready to have a break. P. had been angry and almost broke off her talk with S. Only later did I wonder if we had created in her—consciously and unconsciously—fears, doubts, and desires regarding all this sex talk, which were transformed toward the end into an angry response at S.'s surprising question about her tattoo. Unwittingly S. had pushed a button that rubbed against those anxieties, by committing a faux pas: don't ask about the aberrant (related-to-erotic) tattoo. Still, we said goodbye cordially.

And the next day, true to herself, my friend Penjukwi seemed her usual self, comfortable.*

DISCUSSION

H: This chapter illustrates the rewards for and problems in doing clinical ethnography. The rewards comes from better understanding P.'s sense of self, her view of her life experiences, and her thoughts about her sexuality. The problems include the issue of discussing such intimate topics with a woman in a male-dominated society. P's bravery is remarkable, for not only did she overcome her fears and doubts about working with two white men, but she persisted in the face of Gambakutu's ugly peeping and worries about her husband's approaching death. I underscore here again my uneasiness about the focus on erotism in this case study. Though in other chapters—on Moondi, Sakulambei, and Kalutwo—sexual and gender issues are critical, the potential for sensationalism and charges of sexism are greater here: shades of two white masters questioning one poor woman. Then, too, this chapter has been drastically shortened; the omitted materials would have decreased the artifact.

These dialogues, then, must be understood in their narrative context. Interviewing people of the opposite sex on erotic matters requires skill: trust is essential. Even that is not always enough. Many periods of interaction, sometimes therapy, may be needed to build trust before discussing sexual excitement. Respect and consideration for the other person's privacy is ever crucial. The interviewee must know—consciously and then intuitively—that the researcher is not sexually interested in the subject. Otherwise, trust is impossible, for at some level (perhaps unconscious) he or she will fear being used and therefore harmed. The researcher must know this; and that

*After a while she wrote to me[7] in the States, saying that things were going fine.

awareness must be made clear, explicitly or implicitly, perhaps many times. The power differential between two such people is great; only time and rapport, plus continuing respect, make such investigations possible. If this is all true for people interacting in the same society, how much more so in another culture, especially one such as Sambia, where women do not talk to men of their sexuality!

Because it has taken me years to know the importance of this last statement, I do not advise the beginning student to undertake such research prematurely. One needs beforehand so much self-under-standing, cultural and linguistic competence in the culture, and rapport with the community. In my case, I never attempted such sensitive interviews with women my first two years in the field. Perhaps the men would not have permitted me to do so anyway. Even now, as you saw, they throw up obstacles to my work with the women. Why?

We can identify these factors clearly. (1) Men never talk to women in a one-to-one, reciprocal way. (2) Women and men do not discuss their sexual experience together, and, as P. pointed out (and as we know of our own society traditionally), Sambia women do not even share with each other feelings about such intimate matters as having orgasms. (3) I suspect that men are highly interested, even jealous, of my contacts and relationships with women, though to say this is almost impossible for them. (Note Moondi's reluctance to leave us. Are the men conscious of this jealousy?) All three factors set up a context of power and status in my talking with P. This condition, and the ever-present potential for intimacy in discussing deep needs and feelings, enhance the possibilities and shape of P.'s transference. This means, for instance, that certain expectations (of her father and mother, or others) can be projected onto me, though the true source of these is not myself. The clinical ethnographer, to pursue sexuality as a long-term issue with another person, must be aware of such transference. Clinical training is necessary to attain this understanding. (See the Epilogue.)

In these sessions with P., despite the misunderstandings and the lack of more supporting data, we move closer to knowing her view of herself and her sexual experience. The link between breast-feeding sensations and genital arousal raises important questions: about the universality of certain female sexual experiences, the role of semen and milk in women's thought, and so on. We do not fully understand these experiences or their correlates—either in P.'s life history or in Sambia culture (chapter 2)—but we have more clues to follow; these are what clinical interviews can provide. Moreover, we often sense in these dialogues a pervasive *discourse* on the nature of female and male sexuality as interrelated phenomena in Sambia culture. Social reality too can be studied in a unique way via such interviews. And without the resulting dialogues, in spite of their shortcomings, an ethnographer can report on sex and gender or male/female relationships in a society, yet miss domains of information, not to mention the problem of inadequately understanding the native's viewpoint.

With subtle and intimate topics such as sexuality, surface behaviors—gestures, words, feelings, what-have-you—can mask other things. They are microdots: for instance, P.'s tattoos. What do those tattoos mean to her: femininity in general; her sense—modern, not old-fashioned, of her femaleness; sexual freedom; modernization, including travel and exposure to western ways; her social role that, in its normativeness, makes the tattoo highly visible and yet a symbol of her private self; identification with her aunt, her uncle, the customs of other New Guinea peoples; her feeling she is daring; her defiance of the men's power over women; her desire to live her own life, in spite of her fate—including the fantasy of marrying her sweetheart had it not been for Nilutwo's abduction; scripts about what men and women like and don't like; feelings about who she is and who she can never be. All compacted in a tattoo. When S. asked about it, those scripts (i.e., she—for she, her self, is those scripts) responded to S.'s question with shyness, anxiety, then anger. Her self filled the tattoo, becoming, for an instant, more important than anything—and P. was P. but not the normal P. Microdots contain all that we are and are not. Clinical ethnography is the means for studying such details.

We cannot yet answer these questiosn fully. The results of our work will, however, eventually bring more answers. In the meantime, our aim is to provide a means to discover better questions, and thereby enhance the discovery process in anthropology.

S: More important for me than anything else we could discuss regarding P's case is a necessary weakness in any ethnography: there is always another informant who would give more facts, a different slant, or total disagreement. Beyond that, as we emphasize, no matter how we select informants and how rich a report we generate, the story (in anthropology called "the ethnography" and in psychoanalysis "the case report") is filtered through the investigator's personality. To improve the findings, then, we would need a swarm of ethnographers. And even that would not quite work. The problem becomes worse to the extent that the above weakness is ignored.

Our interviews with Penjukwi highlight this argument: to talk only to males distorts one's view of the culture. But how does one get the women's view? Especially if you are a male ethnographer? If we recognize the inadequacy of our ethnography, at least we can imagine improvements.

Though H. sensed these issues, I hounded him, throughout the two years of our almost five-days-a-week-discussions, before we were together with the Sambia, to make the most of his good luck in having one female informant, even if that good luck was colored by her aberrance compared to the other women. He did so.

Could H. have found his ethnography in the earlier years using a woman ethnographer? Perhaps, but it would depend as well on *her* personality, skills, and relationship with H., ability to carry on in that physically hostile environment, and permission (in the subtle things, not just a gross okay) from the people—male and female—of the village. It would be as difficult to find such an ethnographer as it would have been if someone had been searching for a Herdt before 1974. The odds are not good.

Let me now underline a few points related specifically to P.

First, there is the problem of the unnatural effect the ethnographer has on the culture, especially when, with his wealth in money and technology, he introduces a community to desires never imagined. What other effects, also powerful but more subtle, do we produce when these people, unsophisticated in our ways, find themselves, like a population that has never known measles, mortally infected with a disease to which, because of their awe, admiration, envy, and love of us, they have too little resistance? What wild transference notions must inhabit them. And then this magical person—who to his colleagues is not amazing; just another ethnographer—can come and go from their land, regardless of what they want.

When planning my trip, I made up a little emergency kit, to permit, if necessary, fragmentary first aid for Gil and myself. I had wondered if I should be prepared to help Sambia as well, a problem with untold dimensions. (From H.'s teaching, I knew that one could bring in a hospital and stay busy.) Within moments of stepping off the helicopter, I learned that a man a few hours into the jungle had put a spear into his wife's back to remind her of the rules governing Sambia marriage. So I, nakedly naive, asked if I should take off down the path, cute little kit in hand, to determine whether the spear had, for instance, penetrated the peritoneum, stuck itself into a kidney, ruptured the intestine, introduced infection, could be removed without killing the woman—all this not only without my being an emergency room physician or a surgeon but without my even knowing what it mean to trot on down a path in the jungle. Had I made that house call, what promise would be in it for everyone in the valley, not just Gil's friends, about medical care? And had I done well, what goes on in people who get a glimpse of such medical care and then lose it shortly thereafter?

In P's case, we wondered, before we left the Valley, whether, when her husband died, some of the men, within the bounds of their customs, would kill her for being an uppity, disruptive female. Was it our business to prevent her murder, and, in doing so, inflict on these people our alien morality? When we decided to hell with it—we were going to protect her by warning them not to kill her or even beat her senseless—we knew we were indulging ourselves. In doing so, we perhaps saved her but pushed our friends one step further on the road to unforseeable cultural change.

Second, what about our confusion with *imbimboogu?* Is it good ethnographic technique to press so hard and so long to understand a category? Is it proper for two men to push a vulnerable woman regarding intimate experiences, especially in a culture where men and women never talk together about such matters? Is it worth reporting even briefly, much less in so much detail, the travails of our inquiry; is this a contribution to the practice of ethnography? Is our theory strong that nonerotic psychocultural factors make up what becomes the erotic and that therefore the study of erotics is a powerful way to study a culture? If so, does it warrant what we did to P.; do we even know what we did to P? Is the absence in ethnography of reports on erotics a legitimate omission? Necessary? Worth the price? Are we correct in accusing colleagues of neurosis (countertransference) when we wonder why such data are not present in ethnography and scarcely found anywhere else in the "social sciences"?

We believe that getting details about sexual life—about any and all intimacy in individuals—is not a detour from the great issues of anthropology but is, rather, an ideal way to bring the researcher to the center of a culture. Therefore, anthropology's lack of such data, especially if it has occured because the subject is exciting, disturbing, guilt-producing, or repugnant to the ethnographer, puts the lie to anthropologists' claims of being scientists, objective, or open to understanding the people they study. This failure is thus a crime of the mind. (And no less so if ethnographers have gathered data on intimacy and then suppressed the material. Likewise when editors do the same.)

Our purpose in presenting this material, then, is not simply to inform the audience about odd Sambia folks or how odd Sambia folks are related to other peoples, but to emphasize the value of a methodology such as ours for studying people, individually or *en masse* as a culture.

CHAPTER SEVEN

Sakulambei: A Hermaphrodite's Secret

BIOGRAPHIC PORTRAIT

H: In a society that prizes maleness, in which men emphasize phallicness and exhibitionistic performances, and where ritual and myth give highest value to penis, semen, and many progeny for admission into adult masculine personhood, there could hardly be a condition more anomalous or sensitive than hermaphrodism. When I began fieldwork among the Sambia I did not know that. Nor did I know that there are intersexed Sambia: hermaphroditic males who are treated differently from birth, who are said to have microscopic penes, and who apparently suffer from 5-alpha reductase deficiency, a rare hormonal syndrome.[1] Sakulambei is such a person. This chapter reflects on his life, its public and secret stigmata; especially the private secret he never dared share with anyone, and the relationship with us that let him share it.

By 1979 Saku was in his late twenties, already established as a powerful shaman. He was married but childless. I have known him since 1974, when he was just an acquaintance who looked and acted a bit odd in the first months of our relationship. In 1975, I interviewed him several times on his shamanism. He was warm, knowledgeable, and articulate, but I felt there were things he was hiding. I was not then interested in his hermaphrodism and did not discuss it. Soon thereafter I saw him belatedly initiated into third-stage bachelorhood, years behind his agemates. A few months later he was married, surprising everyone. In early 1979, I began interviewing him in depth to understand his gender identity. After four months' constant work, we were joined by S., which produced dramatic results.

I am uneasy condensing Saku's biography. He and his history are complex and easily distorted. As with other of my friends, my materials on Saku are rich and cover years. I worked alone with him, without an interpreter. As with Nilutwo, I studied Saku's dreams, which facilitated the strong transference attachment he formed to me.[2] Saku liked me, and I, him; over the years my respect and admiration for him grew as I learned more of his struggle to be himself. He had never completely trusted me, though in his distrust, I sensed a desire to trust that was missing in, say, Kalutwo.[3] It was not until these two following sessions with S. that I understood his mistrust.

Let me now sketch Saku's history and discuss the progress of our work in 1979, when S. entered the picture.

Saku was born about 1953. Warfare was still raging throughout his childhood. During our 1979 interviews I did not know the details of his birth. I did know that, though reared in the direction of the male sex, he was sex-assigned a hermaphrodite at birth. He was so touchy discussing the subject that I could not learn the particulars from him. But once he opened up to S. and me, I was later able, in 1981, to investigate the details of his birth and even interviewed the old woman who served as midwife and who made the sex assignment.[4] He had been born with a tiny penis and an odd-looking scrotum. As are all male hermaphrodites there, he was assigned as a *kwolu-aatmwol* ("turnim-man") because people knew that sexual differentiation in the genitals would occur around puberty.[5] Hermaphrodism is a mystery to Sambia. It has magical associations. But mysterious or magical, hermaphrodites are stigmatized. No different in appearance from other hermaphrodites at birth, Saku has made himself different. He is a powerful shaman. I know of no other hermaphrodites, past or present, who became shamans, let alone great shamans. Saku's achievement is unique.

It is Sakulambei's fate to have been the son of the greatest living Sambia war leader. Mon, his father, died in 1983. But until his death, in his late sixties, he was rough and tough, and still acknowledged as *the* leading elder of Pundei hamlet. Mon killed at least eight men and was involved in countless battles. He married six times (outlived three of his wives) and fathered more than twenty children. Before his death, Mon was among the three or four oldest living Sambia in the Valley—survivor of wars, epidemics, and famines, and the last of virtually all his brothers, agemates, friends, and enemies. To the end, he was the ruthless, cold-blooded warrior, for some forty years holding leadership through bluster, guile, intelligence, threat, and his special warlike skills. For instance, he proved himself a master of treachery, not above killing a clan brother.[6] At one time he held shamanic powers, and throughout his life practiced sorcery to support his leadership. But Mon was never a successful shaman and had not practiced his arts for years. Still, longer than anyone, Mon firmly controlled his world—for nearly half a century.

Saku was the third and last child of Mon's third wife. She was much younger than M., and through a sister-exchange marriage had been traded from a distant hamlet at the other end of the Sambia Valley. Her brother, Yumalo, also a fight leader, was even more important as a great shaman. He became crucial in Saku's development. Saku's mother died many years ago, when he was five. We know little of her, except that she was frail, was a minor shaman herself, and was well liked. Her marriage to Mon was apparently not happy. She never adjusted to living in Pundei. She bore a daughter, a son, and then Saku, all of whom are still living. (From what is known,[7] all except Saku are anatomically normal.) The parents fought a lot, and Saku's mother was often ill. When she got sick, she would return to Yumalo, to be treated through his healing ceremonies. She died and was buried there in her natal hamlet (c. 1958).

In early childhood, Saku thus had an almost nonexistent relationship with his father, and his mother died early. Because of his stigma, we can presume his life would have been a disaster were it not for his maternal uncle Yumalo, who stepped in at this point. Even before his mother's death, Saku spent most of his time in his uncle's household, Yumalo already functioning as a substitute father figure. After she died, Mon ignored Saku, which was apparently fine with Yumalo, who cared for him. By that time, Saku's brother, of more interest to Mon than was Saku, had been initiated. Age was not the only reason, though; it seems that Mon saw Saku as an embarrassment, rejecting him for years.

Saku took his mother's death very hard. He says that after her funeral, her ghost came to him more than once. And something else: a few months later, he was playing alone in a garden when a young boy—a spirit being—came to him to play. The other, who looked older than Saku, befriended and talked to him and performed amazing feats. This being[8] became Saku's first and most important spirit familiar when he later practiced shamanism. A figure in Saku's dreams as a child, Saku still sees this being in his trance states now. Next to Yumalo's spirit familiars, the child familiar (who grew in imagination as Saku grew, but who manifests normal masculinity) has protected him through thick and thin. But Yumalo sensed something wrong, and when Saku told him of the child spirit's visitation, his uncle wisely told him not to pay much attention. (But not to ignore him, either.) From then on, Yumalo took an even closer interest in Saku, who became, in effect, his adopted son.

Yumalo was a curious figure. I knew him before he died, an old man, in 1977. He was a contradiction: vigorously masculine, with two wives and several children, he was nurturant and sensitive. He was a traditionalist, yet he wore funny western clothes, easily able to accommodate the accoutrements of both worlds. He was considerate, generous, never querulous—a fine, proud old wizard. Yet he was feared, some say hated, by his enemies, because of extraordinary shamanic powers and sorcery magic that surpassed others in the region. Though he liked women and had good marriages, he had his own hut apart from them; yet at the same time he felt no stigma in planting and harvesting his own sweet potatoes (female activities). In short, Yumalo was a bundle of both feminine and masculine features somehow balanced through his shamanic identity.

Saku is clear he would not have become a shaman had it not been for his uncle. True, he had all the right social ancestry to become one,* but that might have gone for naught without his uncle. From earliest years, Saku had had dreams. These dreams were crucial to his calling as a shaman. Many were prophetic. Saku gives examples of dreams he claimed to have had when only six or seven—before initiation—that people believed foretold the future. His uncle did more than encourage these dreams: he discussed them with Saku, taught him how to interpret them, and explained that they would enable Saku to become a shaman. Yumalo did not in the slightest way disparage Saku for his hermaphrodism. And because of this tolerance and his uncle's special attention to his growing preshamanic skills, Saku adored him. In short, largely due to Yumalo, Saku longed to become a great shaman like his uncle, which identity/role is laced into Saku's very being and enables him, against great odds, to surmount a difficult fate.

Saku was initiated with Weiyu's[9] age-set around 1964. He was older than the other boys, which probably helped him through the ordeals. Yet by age ten Saku was already toughened. He had been taunted by children who said he was really a girl, not a boy, or a boy who didn't have a penis. His older brother didn't help him much, but Weiyu— his cousin—always stuck up for him. There were several times when Saku got into a fight and Weiyu defended him. They were friends, not just cousins. (Years later, when Weiyu was close to death from

---

*Saku's father, father's brother, and mother were all shamans, in addition to Yumalo; and their shamanic familiars all had long genealogic validity. Thus, Saku is a primary shaman, compared to a Kalutwo, whose claim is secondary and largely contrived (see chapter 9).

malaria, Saku sat with him, performed healing ceremonies, fed him for weeks, and nurtured him back to life.) Only one thing—but an odd one—stood out in Saku's first initiation: he did not bleed when the men plunged cane-grasses down his nose.* Saku says he felt the nosebleeding was silly and not necessary for him: he would grow to be masculine quite nicely without losing any of his blood.[10] He has never bled his nose since, either.

He underwent second-stage initiation normally too, about three years later. At his first initiation, his father took more interest in him and even tried to persuade Saku to return to Pundei and live there. And though Saku did begin to spend time there—his natal hamlet and clan—he continued to spend more time at his uncle's.

Meanwhile, Saku was growing, and he was involved, like other boys, in homosexual activities. Two things should be stressed about this. First, Saku has always been known as an enthusiastic and skillful fellator, wanting to get as much semen as fast as possible. On the other hand, though, Saku (who had no trouble discussing it) told me he always felt that fellatio was a little silly. (But not silly enough not to do it.) This view, as with his refusal to nosebleed himself, carried with it the sense that his body was relatively self-contained and needed no help to mature. I didn't believe him.[11] Second, Saku's gender identity and erotic life are aberrant in that he has never been fellated. Saku did not talk about this, because he could not discuss his hermaphrodism (not just his anatomy) with me: he could not tell me that he is terrified of others seeing his genitals. Only Imano (chapter 8) resembles Saku in never having been fellated. However, their reasons were quite different: Imano wanted to save his semen for women, whereas Saku is terrified of others seeing his genitals. From all indications Saku was simply so ashamed that he could not be a sexual inserter.[12] I do not know how strong Saku's sexual impulses are, but he claims to have had several wet dreams. At the same time, he continued to be a fellator well after the normal period.[13] In part, this abnormality stems from Saku having had no third-stage—puberty—initiation until 1975 (whereas Weiyu, his agemate, had undergone that ceremony in 1970).

The main reason Saku was not elevated in the initiation cycle was his father's (and other men's) attitude that there was no sense wasting time on him. Third-stage initiation meant (among other things) that one was biologically mature and ready for marriage. "Why waste a good woman on a flawed hermaphrodite!" I have heard men say.

---

*I doubted this story, but Weiyu and others confirm it.

This attitude so hurt and enraged Saku that he finally left the Valley and went to work on the coast around 1970. He has never forgiven his father or clansmen.

So Saku left his own land. He was in Port Moresby for a while: cheap plantation labor. His dreams and some trance experiences continued. Then he moved near Goroka, the provincial capitol, where he lived on a coffee plantation for three years. He now became more sophisticated about the white man's world, seeing things he both liked and disliked. But after four years, disgusted with life there, he grew tired and homesick. He returned to Sambia to find that little had changed: he was trapped by his anatomy; to some he would always be just a freak. He worked hard, planted coffee trees, made as much money as he could (most of which he gave to his uncle and aunt), and eventually built a tin-roof house: *the* sign of westernization. He took up his healing practices, too, with more fervor, though he still had not gone through the shamanic initiation. A little later, in late 1974, I arrived on the scene.

Saku did not stand out from the crowd in those days. He alternated between traditional garb and western clothes (and still does). His height was normal but his build slight. He lacked the burly anatomy of those Sambia who look like New Guineans in racial characteristics, and his light brown skin, fair complexion, and brown frizzy hair made him look Papuan.[14] By Sambia standards, he is handsome. Closer up, though, his face is unusual.[15] I now see that it matches his personality: androgynous. His broad, intelligent forehead is faintly creased by fine horizontal worry lines. He also has creases vertical to his eyebrows, which are oddly bushy and thick on an otherwise sparsely bearded face.[16] His high cheekbones and long square nose (unusual in Sambia) give him, to me, a graceful, proud countenance. His lips are thin and gray-red, his teeth stained bright red from constant betel-nut chewing. But what strikes me most are his eyes. They are liquid, darkly beautiful, but sunken and a bit close-set. They are— I can think of no better word—chameleonic: they can seem to reflect whatever they see, and yet be expressive or dull, shallow disks, mirrors. They can be happy and sad, proud and despairing, warm and cold, dark and bright, open and mysterious. They can make him seem to be waiting, wary, suspicious, always searching for the slightest sign of disapproval or rejection. I was, consequently, more sensitive and careful with Saku than with others, as if handling crystal.

As I got to know Saku, two themes emerged. The first I observed a hundred times. His responses are highly situation–specific: Saku becomes what others do or expect him to do. He reflects his environment. (Human chameleons are hard to detect and harder to study.) For instance, it took me a long time to know that Saku makes sexual allusions or comments only in public. At first I found that, like other men, Saku made sexual allusions about women to me in private. But I felt it was contrived: there was no hostility in his slurs. (How different from the natural spontaneity with which men, such as Weiyu and Tali, frequently and vigorously insult women.) When I did not respond, did not reinforce that behavior, it stopped.

The other theme reflects a truer sense of self: "I am the shaman Saku." The shamanic identity—the trance states, dreams, identification with familiars—all are woven into himself—his core. (Cf. chapter 9.) When he was most comfortable with me, alone in my house, I saw subtle behaviors remarkable for a Sambia man. Examples: a passivity that waits for me to make a move; a quietness—quiet voice, low affect, a chronic despair—with secrecy and shame behind the quietness; an embarrassed smile as he turns his head from me, more like an initiate or woman; a way of moving his whole body when speaking or looking out the window, coupled with controlled gestural use of his hands; an almost dainty way of holding cigarettes (between the second and third fingers of his left hand), his hand propped up on his arm, the cigarette jutting out, in a way that is neither masculine nor feminine, but odd; and finally—this one baffles me—Saku is the only Sambia person I have ever seen who crosses his legs, one over the other in the British style (where did he get that!).* The sum of such traits is neither wholly masculine nor feminine; and when I am with him, his presence is unobtrusive to the point that I can feel almost alone. Strange but not unpleasant.

Saku must have known he was getting nowhere with father and clan: no woman—no masculine adult personhood—was being given, and none was in sight. His father as much as said he would not waste a woman on Saku. In 1975, this trend reached a head, and Saku disappeared. I did not know what had happened until I heard he was being initiated third-stage with distant kin of his uncle over the mountains in the Yellow River Valley. When I arrived there with friends to see their initiations, Saku stood tall in his best warrior garb. We heard a rumor that he had arranged a marriage and would return soon with his new bride. Everyone was amazed, as was I, but I was happy for him. Looking back, I believe Saku grew tired of being nothing. Something seemed to have snapped in him. So he swallowed his

---

*Perhaps from me, I'm not sure.

pride and went out to make a new life for himself—wife included—without his clan's help. He turned from what could not be—a perfect male body—to what he could have.

His uncle helped Saku again in two ways. Yumalo arranged to have his younger classificatory brother's daughter (Saku's mother's brother's daughter, a marriage frowned on by Sambia) marry Saku. Saku asked *her* for her personal permission, too—a rare gesture to a girl who had recently reached menarche. She agreed, knowing he was a hermaphrodite. Saku made bridewealth payment, equally as rare. They returned to his hamlet and took up residence. People said the marriage would never work, and they made cruel jokes about it.[17] About the same time, initiation for Moondi's cohort was held in the Valley, and a new men's house was built in Nilangu. This was a great event. A shaman's initiation—the last ever performed—was held in the new men's house. Saku was then formally confirmed as a shaman, his uncle attending the ceremony. The story of that experience is told in the session that follows.

Saku seemed happier. On returning in 1979, I wanted to get him to talk. We discussed many things, spent long hours on his dreams. But I could not get him to broach his hermaphrodism, which I wished very much to learn about as another way of understanding the origins and dynamics of Sambia gender identity. As I struggled to allow Saku to tell me—in his own way—about his early experiences in relation to being a hermaphrodite, we bogged down. He was very scared when I approached the subject, nor could he tell me details of his erotic life, for that, too, impinged on his anatomy.

By the time of S.'s arrival, we had reached an impasse, though quite different from, for instance, that with Kalutwo (see chapter 9). Saku did not resist me by staying around yet being hostile, by wearing me out, as did Kalutwo; but rather by exiting, sometimes for a day or two, or for a week. He always came back; I never scolded him. He knew, I think, that I was a friend and that I could be counted on: he wanted to trust. But I felt he had been so traumatized for so many years that it would take something great—such as patience—to lift him out of his reluctance, pain, and fear. My skills were limited.

What I could not know was that behind Saku's open secret—his hermaphroditic body—lay a deeper secret. When Stoller came, and helped Saku tell me in two hours what I had tried to have him say for years, we learned of another terrible trauma, one that had inhibited him as much as his childhood. A white man, a strange European, had years before photographed Saku's boy's nude body—in front of others—and had then left, Saku's fragile pride carried away in that photo. Since then, a humiliated Saku had despaired at what had happened that afternoon. He lived in fear that the man would return and repeat the unbearable trauma. He lived in fear of his own rage at what he would do. This is where S. helped out Saku—and me.

To conclude this introduction: Sakulambei is remarkable. His unique developmental history explains, *because* of his hermaphrodism, how a courageous person managed to survive and even prosper despite great obstacles. In creating himself, he has shown how one can, when loved enough, overcome the most terrible traumas and defy what fate seems to have in mind. But Saku's fascinating story should not obscure a point more central to our undramatic thesis: ethnographers who ignore the intimate circumstances of their work and of the lives of people with whom they work, searching for cultural structure and ignoring the aberrant are dehumanized also.

FIRST SESSION

In 1979 Sakulambei had been talking with me for several months on shamanism and its relation to other aspects of his life. I wanted also to study his gender identity. Being a hermaphrodite and so identified in the community, he provided a unique chance for understanding variations and vicissitudes in the development of masculinity. Though I several times approached the subject, he had great difficulty talking about it. I was pushing him as hard as possible, aware of his shame and anxiety that people might talk behind his back and make fun of him. In fact, people did. I was proceeding slowly and cautiously. A few days before S. arrived, I had broached the subject again, and, as he had before, Saku again exited. It wasn't that he *really* had left; he was avoiding me to avoid talking about his hermaphrodism. Since I had a lot to do and was preparing for S.'s arrival, I simply let him be during this period. But knowing S. had arrived and was important to me, Sa. returned after I had sent word that S. wanted to join me in our talking.

Saku and I were right then at a point where the information I was trying to elicit, but that I had been denied for almost five years, was most important. S.'s arrival put life back in our interviews.

The transcript begins in midstream, after I had first given S. some background and then had described the impasse in Saku's and my relationship. Saku begins by explaining how a dream of his foretold Stoller's visit.

SAKULAMBEI: No one said, "Gilbert's big man [S.] has come." The men didn't tell me. I was down in the Moonagu country.* I saw the helicopter from down there and on my own I thought, "He's [S.] come now. He's come to him [G.H.]." Then I returned and slept in my own house. I dreamed. And inside my dream I thought, "How has he come here?" And I thought, "You [myself] didn't go and see him. I hid and watched you from a way off." My body was completely shaking, and I was thinking, "How did he come here? By plane or water or what?" And the two of you, you just stood away, looking at me. You didn't come close to me. Then I went up to the master [S.] and asked him, "Where have you come from? Where have you come from?" But he didn't talk to me. He just stood there looking. So then, I said to him, "Let's go up to Nilangu and see Gilbert." I said that to him, and the man, he didn't talk, he just looked at me with his eyes, that's all. [*Ominous.*] "All right," I said to him, "you stay here. I'll go to him." And so I went and I came up to the bridge and then, after that, you called out to me. You said, "Come." And you said, "The Big One has come. I told you about him, that he would come eventually, and he's come now. Haven't you heard the news?" That's what you said to me. My response was, "I didn't know he was here." Then we shook hands. I told you that my body was very afraid and we shook hands. Then I said the same to him [S.], but he doesn't understand Pidgin. I was crazy inside my dream. So I was talking without any effect.

   A little later I saw Moondi over near the bridge, and I said to him, "What are you doing here? Come on translate for me! I've never been to school." [*Through all this, Sa. is anxious, is trying to please, and feels inferior, qualities he has always had with me, though gradually less so.*] "You've been to school. What are they saying? Can you hear some English or not?" And Moondi says, "Yes, I can." Then he said to him [S.], "This man Sa. doesn't understand English; he's afraid, his skin's afraid," and I felt afraid. Then we wanted to go to Nilangu Village, but as we were approaching the bridge, the *kaunsalman's* wife called out to us. Then people woke me up and I told my wife, "I dreamed of Gilbert's boss. I saw him." I told her, "I think tomorrow he'll [S.] come," and she said, "Oh, no, he's already here. He's staying up in Ni-

---

*Moonagu phratry hamlets lie a day's walk south of us and are a different political unit from ours. Saku's wife and distant matrilateral relatives are from there.

langu. Go and see him." So I thought to myself, "Why did I stop working with Gilbert? He wants to go away now. I've got to go back." And I didn't just think that, I told her: "It's your fault. You're sick, and that's why I had to stop working." [Saku was healing her through ritual.] She said, "You're right. It's my fault." So I came back up here to see you, thinking to myself, "I'm sorry I lost my work. I'll go see him. You can see. He'll feel sorry for me. Will he take me back or not?"

H: Can I ask you about this dream? When you woke up, what did you feel?

Sa: [*Very quickly.*] Well, I hadn't seen him yet. And I thought, "He wants to kill me."

H: He wanted to *kill* you [*incredulous*]?

Sa: Yeah, that he wanted to kill me. I didn't understand him; I don't know English. Then you said to me, "That's my boss there. Why are you shaking?" A little later I shook hands with him. "I don't know you and so I was shaking." That's what I said to him.

H: In your dream what kind of face did you see?

Sa: The same as his is. The same. I had told Kerutwo's [local *kaunsalman*] wife,* "I've already seen him in my dream. His hair is white." And she said, "That's true."

Remember that Sa. is a shaman who is expected to have prophetic dreams. He is an avid dreamer who can spin long accounts of his dreams. Here he's saying he had a visionary dream before ever seeing S. In the dream he says he saw S.'s face exactly as it is. He tried out this vision on the people after he awoke from the dream. Because Sa. began this session with a dream report—one that he feels is so important—and because I feel that he is communicating his apologies and guilt, and more subtle things about what he can and cannot say and do (transference), we continue on in great detail, going over the dream. But because of lack of space, pages of the report have been cut here. We pick up where H. asks Sa. what he feels now about S.

H: Now that you're truly seeing him, what do you feel?

Sa: I'm very happy, for he didn't come here for nothing. He's the very man who sent you here. And you've come and worked and given us good food, soap, tobacco, other things. We're very happy with you. I'm very happy. Him, he alone sent you, and in that way he's really helped us. Our bodies . . .

*A minor shaman.

Tape runs out. While H. turns it over, S. asks him if Sa.'s full re-
galia—more stylish, clean, and orderly than anyone else's—indicates
Sa.'s pride in being a shaman.

H: [*Pointing at Sa.*] These are the decorations of a true shaman.
Sa: That's right. [*Wistful?*]
H: And dreaming that way happens only to a shaman.
Sa: Right.
H: And now you've come and you are wearing the decorations of a
　 true shaman.
Sa: Right.
H: [*Turns to S.*] He says, "That's right." I hadn't paid attention to
　 it, but these are the decorations shamans used to wear all the
　 time. That goes with having the kind of dreams he has. So, on
　 coming to tell us this dream—
S: —he dressed appropriately for it.
H: Yeah. [His dress is his armor for today. Somewhere, conscious
　 and unconscious, Stoller has the power to destroy him, he thinks.]
S: And in addition, he's the carrier of the past? He's the carrier of
　 power of being a shaman?
H: Yeah.
S: Now, you told me that he's a very good, strong shaman and knows
　 it.
H: Uh-huh.
S: How did he get the power?
H: I know the answer, but I'll ask him . . . again.
S: I'm looking for something else [his feelings about his her-
　 maphrodism]. He might give it to us.
H: [*To Sa.*] Dr. S. doesn't know about your shamanism. [The word
　 I translate as "shamanism" is *kwooluku*, which has several mean-
　 ings: the role of the shaman, the person enacting that role, and
　 the powers of the spirit familiars that invest the particular per-
　 son in that role (see Herdt 1977). So, when, in Sambia, I say,
　 "your *kwooluku*," I can translate it as "your shamanism"—where
　 "shamanism" here implies all three meanings.] He wants to ask
　 you how its *jerungdu* [power]* came to you.
Sa: The power came as follows: shamanism doesn't come from noth-
　 ing, just any old way. We put on all our decorations, and we sit

---

*Here and below, *jerungdu* has the usual physical and phallic connotations (Herdt 1987c)
plus—for shamans—the resonance of power to control spiritual forces unavailable to other
men.

down inside of the *narangu* [ceremonial cult-house where sha-mans are initiated (see Herdt 1987c)] and do the ceremony. It's as if we were almost dead [in a trance]. Shamanism doesn't come from nothing: if your father had a *kwooluku*, then it can come to you. And when he dies, his *kwooluku* (familiars) go to nearby spots and wait, like the base of a clump of bamboo, after he's dead. If we're still small when he dies, it won't come to us yet. It [spirit familiars] will come close to us, and watch over us and just stay there. As we grow, it is inside of the grass around the base of a bamboo clump or in a pandanus fruit tree or in nice flowers one's papa himself had planted. Now, when we're grown and we stay inside the cult-house [after initiation], then it will come back to us. Sometimes we can feel it and see it in dreams—see papa, or see him acting as a shaman. It comes up inside of us. And then we feel it. We know. We think to ourselves, "Now I'm a *kwoo-luku*." We hear it cry [the whistle sound the shaman emits as a sign that his spirit familiars have come inside of his person when, during a trance-state, he wants to perform as a shaman]. And that's it.

H: [*Back to S.*] Well, a pretty big mouthful but a great synopsis of the shaman's calling. He says that the decorations belong to the kind of person who becomes a shaman. The identity is associated with the decorations.

S: Does he make his own? Or did he inherit them and has he fol-lowed the tradition? Or was he *given* the tradition?

H: Let me ask him. Did you make these decorations yourself?

Sa: These here [chest band of shells] I made myself. And these [feath-ers], my mother's brother [Yumalo] gave them to me.

H: Oh-h. [*Surprise.*]

Sa: It was Yumalo [Saku's great shaman-uncle]. And this ass-cover, Yumalo himself made it, too, and gave it to me.

H: I hadn't realized that.

Sa: I only put it on to show him [S.]. When I'm done I'll put it back in my house.

H: Can he look at them? [*S. reaches out and touches the shell deco-rations draped across Sa.'s chest.*]

Sa: Yeah.

S: Are these bird-of-paradise [feathers]?

H: No, those are another kind . . . . Oh, yes, those ones there. [Sa. has several different kinds of feathers in an elaborate headdress.]

S: And he did this.

H: No. It's very interesting: his maternal uncle, the one who gave him his shamanism, gave that to him.

S: So it's giving, in a material way, not just a ceremonial tradition. OK. I interrupted you.

H: [*Repeats Saku's report.*] And that is how you are able to receive your shamanism.

S: Why is he better, stronger than other shamans?

H: Dr. S. wants to know why your shamanism is stronger than others. He heard from me that you were the strongest *kwooluku* in the Sambia valley.

Sa: You already know all that: this *kwooluku*, it doesn't belong to me. In ancient times it came to some man.* When he died, it went to another man who took his place. And he would have it, and be old, and then he would die. And so it went, until Yumalo got it. He had it. Then he died, and now I have it. It is passed along, just like that.

H: Just like that. [*A beautiful description. Repeats this for S.*]

S: [*Softly.*] Tell him something like this for me: "I am very strong, so I want to know more." Does that make sense to you?

H: Say a bit more so I get a better sense of it.

S: "There are other things, secrets." Let him know I am strong. *I am.* So I know something about secrets . . . . I can also *withstand* secrets. . . . I can also *keep* secrets. So I want to know more. But don't tell him that if it's not the right thing to say.

H: [*Reflecting.*] Um [*back to Sa.*], Dr. S. wants to tell you his thoughts before we finish: he says *he's* a strong man. He himself says this. He says he's truly pleased and fascinated with what you said, but he thinks there is more; he says, "I think this *kwooluku* also comes from something else."

Sa: Uh-huh.

H: He heard your story, but he says that he thinks it has another meaning, too, a secret [*ioolu*] that belongs to it [i.e., the hermaphrodism]. I, myself, don't know what he [S.] is pointing toward. But he says he really thinks that.

Sa: Uh-huh.

H: He thinks there is a secret in your *kwooluku*. This secret [going very slowly and carefully here] somehow helps . . . you to . . . to get some of the thinking which belongs . . . to . . . your . . . shamanism. This is what he says. He also says that in

---

*One of Yumalo's patrilineal putative ancestors, therefore a matrilateral ancestor of Saku.

his . . . very own . . . kind of work . . . he . . . he works with secrets all the time. With men and women in America. That's precisely his work. [For several years, S. worked with biologically intersexed patients, including some with hermaphroditic genitals, in studying origins of gender identity.] And he says that . . . he, himself, is not afraid of secrets. He has no fear of secrets. And he also says that he has strength of his own and he wants to hear more about the ways of secrets in your shamanism. Is this clear?

Sa: Uh . . .

H: Because, for myself, I'm not really clear what he's talking about.*
The secrets.

Sa: Secrets here?

H: Yeah.

Sa: The secrets of a shaman? You know, there are none.†

H: No.

Sa: No. We men talk about it openly here.

H: But he doesn't mean only secrets of *kwooluku*. He means also secrets of your own. And he says he himself is not afraid of secrets.

Sa: [*Quiet, serious, apprehensive.*] Um-hm. [*A little stronger.*] I wouldn't . . . hide . . . [*Voice trails off.*]. There are no secrets in my shamanism. I'm not clear what he means.[18]

H: [*To S.*] He understands but says shamans have no secrets. Then I said, "I don't think he means just your shamanism. I think he also means you." And he said, "I have no secrets." Then I told him that you study secrets and are not afraid of secrets. Then he said, "I'm not sure that I understand what he means." It would probably be good enough to leave it at that, but you can say more.

S: Yeah. Well, that's good. Thank him. Will we be seeing him again?

H: Yeah. [*To Sa.*] Can you come back tomorrow?

Sa: [*Quietly.*] Uh-huh.

H: He says he'll be back tomorrow.

S: There may be secrets in him that he doesn't know about yet. Or something like that. Let's see if he can discover his own secrets. That'll give him power.

H: *Oh!* Yeah. [*To Sa.*] Oh, now I understand Dr. S.: He's pleased to

---

*I want S. to carry the ball.

†Even in the most superficial sense, Sa. isn't being straightforward here. Shamans are secretive people, more than any others. They have their own tricks of the trade to hide. (S. doesn't know that.) Sometimes, for their own safety, they must be sly: they have shamanic opponents who try to do them in.

talk with you. He wants to see you again, to work with you again. He says that we all have secrets in ourselves. He says that if we can find our own secrets, it can give us more strength. If we can get to the bottom of our own secrets, it helps clear away things that have a hold over us.

S: [*To Sa., via H.*] It may just come into his head, or it may come in a dream or it may not come.

H: [*To Sa.*] He's helping us some more. Saying, "This kind of secret, it can come up just any old time in thought. Or another time it can come up inside a dream. Or sometimes it won't come up at all."

S: We'll just have to watch and see.

H: [*To Sa.*] He says, "We'll just have to look and see what happens." Is that all right?

Sa: Yeah, that's good.

S: I don't know . . . but what does he feel? How does he . . . what's his experience been like with us today? What's he doing now and what's it done?

H: [*To Sa.*] He wants to ask you: all three of us have been talking. As we've been doing this, how do you feel now that we've been talking like this?

Sa: Oh, us talking here?

H: Yeah.

Sa: Oh, it's good, good. My thinking is that it's good [*a little bit forced*].

H: He says that it's good.

S: [*Quickly*] Good.

H: Did you hear him, Saku? [*He shakes his head.*] He said it's good. Well, that's it. Have you got something you want to say to me?

Sa: Only that I'm hungry for tobacco.

H: I'm sorry, but I can't help you. I'd give you some but mine's all gone. You can ask everybody else.

Sa: Yeah, they told me the same.

H: I wouldn't hide it from you if I had some.

Sa: Yeah, of course, I know. I was just asking, that's all.

S: Is he going to dress this way the next time?

H: [*To Saku.*] He wants to ask you will you be decorated the same way tomorrow too?

Sa: [*Lightly.*] Yeah, I won't change, I'm not going to change it.

H: He says—

S: I like it, I want him to wear it again.

H: [*To Saku.*] He says he really likes that a lot.

Sa: I'm not going to change, I'll go to the songfest* just like this. And tomorrow morning I can come; is that okay?

H: All right, fine.

SECOND SESSION

H: Yesterday Dr. Stoller talked to you about the kind of work he does. He said he was pleased to be with you and he was very pleased with your decorations.

Sa: [*Quietly.*] Uh-huh.

H: Yesterday he told you about his strength [*jerungdu*], which all three of us use in our work. This morning, too, you saw him use it with Nilutwo.†

Sa: Uh-huh.

H: What did you think of that?

Sa: No thoughts. Whatever he says, I can follow that. That's all. [*The resistance stiffens.*]

H: Hm.

Sa: Yeah. Whatever he wants to talk about is all right.

H: [*To S.*] He says he'll do whatever you want.

S: OK. Well, let's move into this, respecting the fact that he's a good shaman. I would like his impressions of my shamanistic number with Nilutwo this morning. And I don't know if I can expect this of him, but I would like the truth rather than have him butter me up or be nervous with me. You see, my view of that performance is, "Oh, God, it didn't work." They may not see it that way, but I wouldn't want him to say, "Oh, you're a great magician," in order to make me feel good. . . . I don't know how you can play that with him.

H: He wants to ask you about shamanism, his and yours. He's heard me say that you are a big shaman in this Valley. He'd be pleased to learn about your shamanism and your spirit familiars. He wants to ask you first: what do you think of what he did with Nilutwo?

Sa: I guess he wanted to look inside, to see inside his liver or something. Is a bone broken inside there? He wanted to look inside

---

*A songfest for a marriage ceremony to be held in Kwoli hamlet that night. The whole village piled out for it.
†S: Nilutwo is dying, in terrible pain because he cannot change position, is exhausted, cannot sleep, expects his friends to steal his wife when he dies, and is enraged at fate. To relieve him, I tried, before a tense audience, to hypnotize him this morning, acting like a hot-shot UCLA wizard and hoping, for his sake, that my sense of being a damn fool didn't show. He did not bat an eye. So, an honest failure, I finally stopped. No sooner had I left the hut, however, than he fell asleep and slept many hours.

of him* [S's hypnotic technique interpreted as shamanic divination for diagnosing illness].

H: What did you think of that?

Sa: It's good. It's very good. Truly good. We don't know how to do that. He was looking hard at him.

H: Yeah. He's not a bad man [S.]. He's not someone from the ghosts.[19] He's a good man.

Sa: Yeah, that's right.

H: So he knows how to do that kind of thing.

Sa: Yeah, that's really good. I was watching what he was doing to Nilutwo, and I thought, "He wants to look at all of his bones or whatever is inside of him." He looked in, and that was good.

H: [*To S.*] He thought what you did this morning was good. He watched you carefully and felt you wanted to get inside of Nilutwo just like a shaman divinates while in a trance. It has a magical meaning of what shamans do here.

S: So my performance is in a realm that he's familiar with.

H: Yes.

S: And I was competent, not in my results, but as a performer of it in my own style. Is that what he's saying?

H: Yes. He said it was good and he was very glad that you did that.

S: All right. Now, let's move into his shamanism: what's it feel like to be a shaman? How has it changed over time? What's his sense of his power—now as compared to when he first started? Is that enough to start?

H: Yeah. Some of these questions we've already gone over.

S: Then don't spend much time on them.

H: I don't know how this can be done, but I want to ask him the question [I tried] before he ran away: his hermaphrodism.

S: OK, go to it. Maybe we're in good enough shape now.

H: Uh—I'm trying to think how to do it best. You've reinforced the part in him that's most sensitive. He's not as afraid. So I've got a good start. We were working on how he first got his powers from his maternal uncle, the man he mentioned yesterday.

S: What do you want to know that will be difficult for him to answer unless we help him respond safely?

H: What is his sex life now?

S: You might not get that so easily.

H: [*Exasperated.*] I haven't *been* able to get it.

---

*S: I kept telling Nilutwo to stare into my eyes as I stared deeply into his. God knows what that act means to a Sambia man. With us it means, "You are being hypnotized. So go into a trance like you know you should."

S: He turned you away? Or you haven't dared ask?

H: I was just preparing to move into these sensitive areas when it stopped.

S: I see. Could you—uh—

H: —if somehow I could shift some of the responsibility to you . . .

S: That's what I was going to say—

H: —but do it differently—

S: —but do it differently—try this on: tell him that I put my power into you. Would that make sense? Not just taught it to you, but [*S. makes a noise here like an electric drill—"bzz": the feeling is implanted in me*] put it into you so that he is safe when he talks to you about these things. [*Emphasizes.*] "*I* will protect him because I put into *you* the capacity to protect him."

[S: By injecting my power into H., I not only let Saku know that H. now possesses my shamanic powers but I also get H. to feel it. In politer circles this is called "identification," a process we all know helps form identity—converts students to teachers or healers. It brings to life the business of education, making organic the formulating of techniques.]

H: [*To Sa.*] Do you want to say anything to him? If not, I have something to ask you. Is that all right?

Sa: Yeah. [*Quiet and a bit depressed.*] You talk. I have nothing in particular to say. [*Quiet. I feel he's holding back; he's worried where we're going.*]

H: All right. [*To S.*] To do this we need privacy, so I'm going to get rid of everyone in the house.

S: That's what he just asked you?

H: No, it's my idea. It signals him that I'm going to ask about important things.

S: Proceed, and make him know that you are *lovingly* protective. That really *is* what you're doing. Make him as comfortable as possible, and let him see you recognize how difficult this is for him. Anything you can do to make it possible, that's what you want to do. That's what you just expressed now, in fact. [H: Such simple wisdom put into practice provides a context in the field otherwise impossible to achieve but utterly essential to a Saku-lambei.]

H: Yeah. [*To Sa., H. summarizes S.'s message.*]

Sa: That's your choice.

H: Is that all right?

Sa: [*Almost inaudible.*] That's all right.*

 H: I don't want anyone to hear something that belongs to you only, or to your shamanism. I want to protect you.

Sa: [*Almost inaudible.*] Uh-huh.

I get up. Lots of noise, people milling around. I chase them out, fasten the door, come back into the room, and talk again.

 H: He [S.] says this: he's got this strength, a power, a good power. And he wants to encircle you with protection so that, inside, you and I can talk about your shamanism and your experiences without your being afraid of me. [*Pause. No response. Now to S.*] I've said it as clearly as I can.

 S: OK. Now we just have to go and see if he lets us. If he *sort* of lets us, then we can amplify.

 H: You have a pretty good sense of him, his childhood, his development. But I know nothing about his sex life, and he and I have *never* discussed his hermaphrodism.

 S: Well, why don't you now do it.

 H: I want to ask you about your shamanism.† I want to ask you some things I haven't asked you about before. About the time you felt the spirit familiars come inside of you. Those of Yumalo. In the *narangu* [shaman's initiation] of Nilangu hamlet [1975], you still didn't have any of Yumalo's familiars, right?

Sa: Uh-huh.

 H: And Yumalo told you, "I must not fall sick. If you entice my familiars away from me, I might die."

Sa: Uh-huh.

 H: But later his familiars came to you, and he hadn't died yet.

Sa: Yeah . . .

 H: [*Pause.*] Now, when Yumalo's familiars came to you, what did you feel?

Sa: [*Confident.*] "This mother's brother of mine, he's going to die. He's not walking around much. He just sits around his house." His familiars came to me. He wasn't visiting his gardens or anywhere else. He'd just sit around his house. And by and by he would die. He spoke out to me.

---

*S: I felt pain for him here—and more as we proceeded. I didn't want my first great shaman to be just a kid decked out in his best feathers. He was scared-trying-to-be-brave and trying to honor his identity. Quite different from Kalutwo, whose pain/resistance took the form of sullenness.

†I begin with this subject for two reasons, as I now realize. First, we are comfortable discussing it; it opens rapport again. Second, because Sa.'s sexuality is so bound up in his shamanism, which centers his identity.

H: You mean he pointed to you [the accusing finger: because Saku had taken his spirit familiars, it meant Yumalo had fallen sick].

Sa: They performed a *narangu* here and he told me, "I won't come to you now. I won't be able to stroll around from now on. This soul of mine, soon I'll give it to you* and I'll die."

H: But when did his shamanic familiars come to you: then or later?

Sa: Later. When we performed that *narangu*—

H: —Yeah—

Sa: At this time—the shamanic familiars of Yumalo—*he* sent them. He himself said he thought his familiars were choosing to go to me. So he sent his familiars to me. But I thought, and then I said, "Don't give them to me; you will get sick and die. Don't just sit around the house." I told him that. And then he said, "Oh, that's all right. I shall just become inactive." [His aged uncle was saying it was all right if he now died.]

H: Now at this time they came inside of you in the *narangu*?

Sa: Yeah—[*His voice warms; he's reaching out to try and help me understand.*]

H: I thought that it happened but you sent them all back.

Sa: Yeah, at this time I spoke out to Yumalo, "Why don't you try them out on me. Try me." [The idiom here, "Try me out," means a "test." Shamans test each other to see how powerful and disciplined they are, and so he's suggesting that he told his uncle to test him and see if he was enough of a shaman to be able to handle his uncle's spirit familiars.]

H: "You can just take back your spirit familiars afterward?"

Sa: That's what I said. [*Pause.*] And then he said, "That's all right. If I die, say, or if I really get a big sickness and can only sit around the house, then you must come and visit me." [Saku lives below, down at the river, whereas his uncle lived in a village about an hour's walk away. He's suggesting here that his uncle was saying, "It's all right for you to take my spirit familiars now, though that will eventually make me sick. So when I get sick, since you have the healing power now, you must come and perform healing ceremonies on me."] Like that. So, when I saw him afterward, I didn't just sit around [ignore and forget my uncle]. Instead, I went to him all the time. I bought fish and rice and got other foods and gave them to him. So [*voice trails off*] . . . at the time that he looked at me when he was close to dying [late 1977], it

---

*Metaphysically true, in that the spirit familiars are part of the entity of the soul, Sambia believe.

was only then his spirit familiars came to me for good. [We skip here details of Saku's shamanic trances and identifications with familiars, since this material leads us from the main course of the chapter.]

H: What do you feel then?

Sa: I feel at those times that my mother's brothers' soul hasn't gone away, not gone away.

H: It's still around. He's still around with you. He's fastened to your skin, huh?

Sa: Yeah, that's how I think; I think like that.

H: All right, I want to tell this part to Dr. Stoller so he understands, all right? [*To S.*] At the time of his shamanic initiation in 1975, his uncle's spirits wanted to come to him of their own volition. But that would have killed the old man; it would have robbed him of his soul. So Saku sent them back to him.

S: Why was his uncle willing to do it?

H: Because his uncle thought he was going to die. He was an old man. I knew Yumalo: he was a . . . strong, kindly, masculine; a presence. In some ways he resembled—had the same habits as—Saku; imitation [by Saku] mostly, I think. When he has trances now, he often sees his uncle's face. [Saku trances frequently.]

S: [*Interrupting.*] Benign?*

H: I haven't asked him that yet. Uh . . .

S: Can I ask—for orientation; it has nothing to do with the present subject but it will help me. Did he do the initiations?

H: Yes, but I don't know the details yet, because we haven't worked on that.

S: What happened when he was a [fellated] bachelor?

H: We haven't done that yet.

S: But there must be someone here who was his age.

H: Oh, yeah, I know what *they* say, but I don't know what *he* says [i.e., about screwing boys].

S: I see. Because he has testosterone, without question, in him. Do you understand what I mean? He's got appropriate facial hair and muscular build.†

H: Yeah.

---

*A question I might not have asked, at least not then. Perhaps I would have asked it later. But it seems an important point, one that might make the interview go differently now and save time later.

†Saku's facial hair only began appearing in the last several years, which is abnormal for Sambia.

S: So his testes are intact. Now does he produce—you can't answer this—does he produce semen . . . and are they [boys, women] taking it from him, or . . . ?

H: Well, the closest that I know, is rough. But pretty reliable sources say he *never* did screw any boys. The boys always wanted to, because they were curious and wanted to find out . . . but he would never do it.

S: I see.

H: But he has told me that at least once, possibly twice, he had wet dreams.

S: So that as far as you know he has only had a couple of ejaculations in his life.

H: As far as I know, right.

S: Okay, you don't need me now.

H: I've figured out a way to ask about his sex. But it would be better if you asked him. . . . This may be premature, but we don't have very much time. So, if you can somehow convey the message that *kwoolukus* are . . . if somehow it can be conveyed that strong *kwoolukus* are also masculine shamans . . . and masculine men . . . who have erections, inseminate women, who produce babies . . .

S: [*Spontaneously.*] Tell him: me.

H: Yeah.

S: Is that the approach?

H: I'm thinking now that that's how I can do it.* [*To Sa.*] Dr. Stoller wants to ask you more about your shamanism. He says, "The way of our shamans—he's talking about himself—is that a certain kind of shaman becomes a certain kind of man." [*Slowly.*] Now this kind of man develops just like everyone: first he's a child, then he grows up. Then, he [S.] says of himself, "I found a way that I became a man." And he wonders whether it was the same for you, or if it was different for you?

Sa: This shamanism here . . .

H: Yeah [*softly, almost a whisper.*]

Sa: Oh, this . . . I don't know. [*Sa. is engaged here.*] Before, did Yumalo do the same? I'm not sure.[†]

---

*Why could I think of that at that point? S.'s presence changed something in my relationship to Saku. Perhaps, again, as with Weiyu (chapter 10), S. put a friendly and supportive presence into our talking that gave *me* the space and perspective to free Saku from ambivalence.

[†]Fascinating that, in responding, Sa. has here referred us to his beloved Yumalo. This is not only defensive. Sa. modeled himself after Yumalo, using the latter in order to know what

H: [*Enthusiastic.*] Oh, but he isn't talking just about familiars, he's talking about his body too.

Sa: This *kwooluku?*

H: No, no—of his very body. [*Spontaneously to S:*] I'm going to do something that's not quite ethical, but I'm going to leave the language vague enough so that he may suspect that you are . . . you may have some hermaphroditic qualities . . . [*pause*].

S: Good. [I do, in the sense that I can work with hermaphroditic patients in such a way that a few thought I was a hermaphrodite. That is why I said "good" and felt that was not unethical.]

H: But I'm going to let him project it, if he can do it.

S: Fine.

H: [*To Sa.*] His appearance is real, but when he [S.] was born, they looked at his body and wondered: "This baby, is it another kind, or . . . ." They didn't know for sure. Now, when you see him, you see that he's become the same as a man. But now he's become a shaman. And now he's a man, too. He's the same as *you* . . . but when he was born, they thought he was a different kind. And so he wants to know if it was the same with you.*

Sa: This . . . I don't really understand you. [*Pause. Silence.*] My *kwooluku* . . . when, before, my mother gave birth. I don't understand well. [He understands precisely but is dodging. Still, compared to my earlier sessions with Saku, he is not now frantic. Rather, his voice is calm.]

H: Um-hm. [*To S.*] He says he doesn't understand.

S: What did you ask him that he doesn't understand?

H: I said, "You [S.] are now a man and a shaman; but when you were born"—and I used the neutral term for "child," not "boy" or "girl"—"they, those who first saw you when you were born—said you were a different kind." That's the language. But I left it so vague—

S: That he doesn't understand it. Or—

H: He just may be resisting—

S: He chooses not to understand it.

---

to feel and believe. Hypothesis: Sa.'s identity was not finished at initiation, unlike other males. It is still not finished. His hermaphrodism forces and allows him to pick and choose, because his aberrance has always placed him outside norms.

*I'd repressed this, until translating the tapes in 1981–82. It amounts to a lie; I as much as said S. was a hermaphrodite. I don't think it was harmful; the circumstances of the interview were extraordinary. I never lie with informants but fudged in this instance. I think it helped; but readers may disagree with this tack. [S. One should never, in doing research, lie in order to get information. Supervision corrects such mistakes.]

H: Yeah.

S: Okay, skip it. You've done what you can. Ask him what he was like when he was born. And using the same word "they" may give him a chance to get out if it's unbearable.

H: Yeah. [*To Sa.*] Now, Dr. S. wants to ask you: "When you were born, what kind of child were you?

Sa: At that time?

H: Yeah.

Sa: I don't know [*uninvolved*].

H: But, you know, what did they say . . . when you were born? What kind [of person] were you?

Sa: My father . . . mother?

H: Yeah.

Sa: I don't know—

H: You haven't heard the news [meaning: what local belief is]?

Sa: Um-hm. [*Straightfaced* and *calm.** *Pause. Silence.* Saku differs from Kalutwo in that he cannot bear these silences. I know if I keep my mouth shut—something I am learning to do better—he will break the silence. He wants to please.] I heard nothing about that.

H: [*Quickly.*] You didn't hear about it. [I feel compassion for Saku's pain on this subject and try to comfort him, supporting his attempts to bridge the silences with communications.] [*Pause.*] Uh . . . [*to S.*] First he said he didn't know. And then he said he wasn't around at that time. Then he said his parents never told him.

S: About what? I'm sure you're paraphrasing him accurately. But I want to sharpen it up. They didn't say "what" about "what"?

H: [*To Sa:*] He's asking if you said, "You didn't hear well what they said?" Is that it?

Sa: I said, "That's the choice of all mommas and papas" [plural indicates all classificatory kin], that's what I said. You said to me: "Is it the same as a boy child or a girl child?"

H: Yes. [*Grateful*: breakthrough: *we're finally on the same wave-length.*]

Sa: They all said, "It's a boy child."

H: A boy child. that's what they said. [*To S.*] He said—

S: It's a male, boy.

H: A male, boy, yeah.

S: Like every other boy?

---

*Saku (like other Sambia males, who learn to lie to hide ritual secrets) is a good liar. He is more accomplished than others, because of his shamanism (doctors don't always tell patients the truth) and probably because of his hermaphrodism.

H: [*To Sa.*] He asks: "The same kind of boy as all the boys around . . . "

S: Yeah, the same.

H: [*To S.*] He says, "Yes, the same kind."

S: Now?

H: [*To Sa.*] He says, "Now too?"

Sa: Now, too, all the same.

H: He says, "Now too, the same." My feeling is he's a bit angry about this, but I think he's willing to talk about it.

S: Keep going.

H: Yeah. He's more willing to . . . you're dragging answers out of him. He's letting . . .

S: He's letting us—

H: Drag questions out of him.

S: Yeah. Should we give him support now and tell him that I'm glad he's talking with us?

H: Yeah.

S: And that I appreciate this . . . and he's helping me, who came from such a long distance, who wants to know about a shaman here.

H: Yeah, that's good.* [*Summarizes for Sa.*]

Sa: That's all right. [*Low; down.*]

S: All right but not all right.

H: Yeah. [*Pause.*] There is a danger that if we press him too much, he might get scared.

S: Yeah. [*Quiet.*]

H: There is also danger that if he's willing to answer questions we don't ask him, we may never get another chance. So it's a risk either way.† That's *always* the risk I feel about him. And I'm willing to either way, because at this point, I will do nothing to harm him. So whatever happens, I will protect him. The research comes first, and that's okay, because I *will* protect him.

S: Try this: shamans are . . . I'll just talk: this isn't what you should say; you and I know in reality that shamans the world over are different from everyone else.

---

*Understatement. One of the most important things I have learned from working with S. (and translating these tapes) is the value and need of giving support and reinforcement—especially when someone is in pain—in my talking relationships, which I'm more conscious of now.

†The first, not the second risk, seemingly endangers Saku. The second risk seemingly endangers only our research, right? Wrong: if Saku wants to unburden himself of his pain and we fail to help him do that, the chances are he may bear it alone—unsupported—the rest of his life. We would be cold not to appreciate the dual risks of this sensitive juncture.

H: Yeah.

S: He should know, and perhaps he would be interested to know, that shamans all over the world—even in my country, namely the Plains Indians, or the southwest desert groups [e.g., Devereux 1937], and the people in Siberia—all over the world, shamans are different. Nobody except someone who is different is *allowed* to be a shaman. And he should know that I come here with the information that *everywhere* shamans are different. And that's the only way they can do what they do—because they're different.

H: Yeah.

S: Start with that and then—you don't expect an answer yet—and then I want to study—and this is true when I am studying him: is he different? And if so, instead of his being afraid of it, can you let him know that he should be proud of it because he couldn't be a shaman unless he was different? Then maybe we can approach how he is different.

H: Yeah. [*To Sa.*] Did you hear him? Saku? He's been giving me knowledge: I also have never heard him say this before. He's got white hair and a lot of knowledge. [The traditional Sambia metaphors for wisdom.] And so he's told me this: he wants to talk to you about this knowledge. He says he knows about shamans in all places. They aren't the same as just plain old men and women. They're another kind. He says: "Our shamans in America aren't the same; they're not just men and women. They're different. [*Elaborates.*] Dr. Stoller is not frightening or shaming you but encouraging you to be happy about yourself. Because these powers of yours, from the *jerungdu* of your *kwooluku*, come from your being different. That different kind [of person] and your *kwoolukus* come about only from that body of yours. [*Pause.*] When I hear him say that, I feel he is only expressing his happiness toward you. He says: "I want to help you with your own thinking about yourself." And this, too, I've never heard it before. You know, I'm just a kid; he's got white hair, he's not newborn, he's old and knowledgeable. [*Pause. Long silence.*] This boss of mine, he's got friends with whom he works [i.e., patients]. Now these people, are, too, a kind of shaman. They're the same body [type] as you exactly. When they were born, people looked but couldn't make sense of their [the infants'] cocks or cunts [exact translations of the Pidgin words]. And they said: "This is a male, but it's not the same as a boy, it's another kind. It's a boy, but at the same time it's a different kind." Now this boss of mine has friends who are the same as that; they're the same, the same as you. [*Lowers voice.*] He's not afraid of them; he's not shamed for them. He's only happy about them. Why? Because they all have their own *kwoolukus*. And so he comes and is happy with you in the same way. And I have now told you all about that, that knowledge. Me, too, I don't know about this. Now he's come and taught me. [*Pause.*] Now, what do you feel when you hear this?

Throughout this long monologue, Saku and S. are silent. My speech is clear and quiet. I am trying to give a point of view radically different from that of Sambia culture. I am softly impassioned in a way I seldom am in public and have been only rarely with Saku, since I dislike monologues.

Sa: [*Quickly.*] But this is no good. [You have to hear the tape to appreciate Saku's voice, so different from before: weary, intense, and highly strained—as if these five words resonated from within the very center of his skull, uttered through clenched teeth that shred each word as it is spoken.]

 H: [*Steady.*] Do you feel it's no good because of this kind [hermaphrodites] or because of this kind of talk?

Sa: The talk. [*Sullen.*]

 H: Just the talk. Do you want me to say that to him?

Sa: That.

 H: You want me to tell him? [*To S:*] I told him that in America you have friends who are the same kind as him. I told him they believe themselves to be males, but they're not males in the same way. They're different. And when they were born, the parents saw them and didn't understand. And that he is the same kind as them—

 S: You told him, or he confirmed that—

 H: I told him that he is the same kind as that. And I told him that although they're like that, you aren't afraid of them, nor do you have any feeling of shame.

 S: If you try something—perhaps—this is for you to say to him, but for a beginning, for me to think. Is there any way you can find out, when he came back today, what was he hoping for . . .

 H: Oh, yes . . .

 S: What would he like to get? And is there any way we can open that door? Does he want to ask *me* things: I'm asking him: and he's free to. It wasn't that he came here hoping to ask me questions; he probably never thought of such a thing. What did he hope for? And what does he feel now that he's hurt and it's not going the way he'd hoped? He's been hanging around all this time

because of something he wanted. What does he want? And can
we help him with that?

H: Yeah. [*To Sa.*] Dr. S. says this: he sees you and thinks, at first
you came back to work with us. He saw you and he was happy
with our talking. And he thinks, at this time when you come here,
do you yourself want to get some knowledge or understanding
or feeling. . . . And now he's said to me: "I've sat here and asked
you plenty, hammered your ear that way. Do you want to ask
me anything?" He doesn't want to sit down and just ask you: not
good that you think hard [i.e., worry] about him—

Sa: Ah, I'm not going to think hard about [fear] him. It's all right.
[The first hopeful sign he's back with us, some warmth again in
his voice.]

H: And he's thinking, "When you first came today, did you want to
find out about something, or some feeling or such?" He wants
to ask you about that.

Sa: Oh, yeah. That's clear. For myself?

H: Yeah, for yourself.

Sa: I want to say this: I'm not going to be scared or anything. And
by and by I can talk to him. You know . . . here . . . they gave
birth to us . . . I want to speak out to him. . . . * [Strong voice.]

H: Um-hm.

Sa: This kind here [vague], do they [whites] all understand them all
completely too . . . ?

H: Yeah—[*soft*].

Sa: He wants to know—

H: Yeah . . .

Sa: So I'll tell him about it.

H: Yeah.

Sa: They all looked at us[†] at first—"I think it's a girl," that's what
they thought. And then, later, they all looked at us and saw that
we had a ball . . . they looked at us, at our ball [testes], and
they all said: "I think it's a male."

H: Oh-h.

Sa: They all say that. [*Pause.*] And, likewise we've got cocks . . . and
we've got balls.

H: Um-hm.

Sa: But, our water [urine] we all lose it in the middle [extreme hy-
pospadias: urinary meatus in female position, not at the distal

*S.'s last comment via me turned the tide in Saku's fear and resistance. Asking Saku what
he wanted acknowledged him.
†Sa. uses the plural throughout this section to refer to himself.

end of glans penis as in normal males]. Now, all the same, could they—would they fix it? [*Voice almost cracks from strain, he sounds close to tears.*] Or . . .

H: Do you want me to ask him—

Sa: Yeah . . .

H: You want me to ask him?

Sa: Yeah.

H: [*To S.*] Boy, that's really something. Whatever it was I said, it turned him all around.

S: What did he say?

H: I said . . . I gave almost a literal translation of what you said. And as you can see he loosened up and got less uptight . . .

S: Yeah.

H: And he said, "I want to tell him [S.]: 'I know you want to ask me about this, and you've come a long way to ask me about this, and so I'm not afraid, I'm going to tell you.' " I mean—that takes a tremendous amount of guts. So he says that the first time when they looked at him, they said he was a girl. Then they saw he had a penis and testes. And then later (he keeps using the first person plural to refer to himself) he says, "Now we have a penis." But also saying there's something wrong because the urine comes out wrong. I'm vague about that, what that means—

S: That's all right. . . . It's out; he's opened it up. He finally said it.

H: Now, he wants—he asked me something which astonishes me. He wants to know if you can fix . . . him. If there is something you can do, if there's some way you can fix him.

S: The chances are in reality I can't. If I were practicing medicine, even here, the thing I would have to do, before I could answer him (I'm not telling you to tell him this) is I would have to know what more is the matter [i.e., do a proper examination to arrive at a diagnosis]. It probably is something anatomical and beyond repair; I would have to determine first what is to be fixed. Is the "fix something" to make a bigger penis, to make a more naturally male appearance, or to get an erection, or is it to ejaculate or what—you know I don't even know. But before we did any of that, I would say to him what I'd say to anyone else: tell him he's brave to have said this.

H: Yeah.

S: Tell him I know that and appreciate it and respect him for what he just did.

H: [*To Sa.*] He wants to tell you about this [request]. But first, he says that you've got a lot of strength to talk out about this. Why? Because about this something many people could be afraid. You are brave to think and talk about this. And now he wants to talk to you about what you asked about. "Can this something be fixed," you ask him that?

Sa: Um-hm. That.

H: Before he answers, he must ask you more to understand what it is you want him to fix.

Sa: Yeah. . . . Before, when we were still very small. . . . [*His voice changes: quiet anger for the first time.*] Then, who came here? Gronemann. Gronemann came. They [*vague*] came and looked at us [*me*]. He looked at us [*me*] for nothing. And he didn't say anything [*low, quiet voice here*]. . . . They all looked inside us [*me, looked at his genitals*]. But you two talked [*to me*] and so I am telling you. [*Quiet rage.*]

H: Oh. [*Amazed.*]

Around 1965 a government patrol passed through the Sambia Valley. It was one of the early patrols, designed to assert an Australian government presence (which led, several years later, to final pacification). Gronemann, a German businessman, not a government official, accompanied this patrol. (We are not sure why he was permitted in.) He took a sexual interest in some Sambia initiated boys (prepubescents), which extended, in Saku's case, to wanting to see his genitals. He photographed Saku—a deeply humiliating experience, for Saku was ashamed of his ambiguous genitals; Sambia never appear nude to others, and the shame was compounded by others (natives?) having witnessed the photographing. Word got out about the incident, and the resulting traumatic stigma was in Saku all these years.

I did not know until this moment about the photographing. I had heard stories of Gronemann's sexual exploits with boys, but that's all. Nor did I know until two years after this interview—1981—that Saku had had sex with Gronemann *before* the photographing (Saku sucked him). All in all a sad story.

Gronemann's business interests in New Guinea enabled him to return to the area over the years. Saku, aware of this, never felt free of threat.[20] (Discussed in the following.)

Sa: And, we [I] thought, "Later, if Gronemann comes back, we [I] want to ask him about this: 'This something here [flawed genitals]—would you [Gronemann] care enough about us [me] to . . . do something, about this [*purposely vague*]?'"

Then . . . but . . . [*scowls**] Gronemann he took our [my] picture and he looked at it, and he didn't—talk [explain why he'd
done what he did: look at and then photograph Saku's geni-
tals] . . . . So we [I] were just talking nothing about him helping us . . . . [In the last sentence, Saku seems to say—in words
and intonation—that he was a stupid son of a bitch to ever imagine being made whole by Gronemann in return for being shame-
fully photographed in the nude.]

H: Oh-h [*low*].

S: Oh, that's sad [*pain in voice on seeing Sa. now*] . . .

H: Do you want me to tell him?

Sa: Yeah, you can . . . no reason not to . . . . [Near tears.]

S: Oh—he looks like to wants to cry almost. Is that right, or am I
reading that in?

H: Yeah, that's right.[†] And that's not all. Do you know who he's been
talking about?

S: Why?

H: I've never before gotten this [secret] part of the story. Here's what
happened. Apparently, Gronemann was part of the first patrols
that ever came here. Someone must have told him of Saku.[‡] And
he must have looked at Saku and taken pictures of him. I don't
know the details. There was a hint from Saku that he hoped
Gronemann could do something to change him. But then "this"
was done to him—and I say it that way because it would have
been a terribly humiliating experience [to be photographed in
the nude[§]]. He took the picture, and—left. So here are my
thoughts: we are here, now, duplicating a similar situation; he
was humiliated before [ten years old]; he's about to cry; he had
this hope back then, that was raised and then dashed. And the

---

*Saku's present complex state—anger, fear, humiliation, confusion, hope, trust, distrust—
must be underlined. First is his puzzlement now, as an adult, as to what motivated this awful
stranger, Gronemann, then. Second is his still-remembered puzzlement when, as a child, he
could not understand what Gronemann was doing. Third is the mix of fear, envy, and disorientation, the result of the white men's automatic sense of superiority, even to their rights to
invade and seize Saku's body and its secret.

†Within a few moments, he did silently cry, tears falling down his cheeks, but no weeping.
I want to witness that Saku is no crybaby: in all these years I've seen him cry only once in
public, when he was deeply insulted by a clan brother. He may cry in private, because, I think,
he is compassionate (some Sambia men do not ever cry). But he is also tough; his crying here
was deeply moving: a twenty-year secret, shared. For myself, I am angry and shamed for Sa.

‡I later learned that Gronemann also interviewed and photographed other boys in the
nude.

§Sambia are prudish about exposing their genitals. They never do so, not even to bathe.
To be stripped nude and photographed in front of Europeans or other New Guineans would
have been, for a ten-year-old boy, catastrophic.

guy didn't have enough . . . compassion . . . to at least say something to *calm* him, and apparently just walked off.

S: That—we're not going to do.

H: Yeah.

S: Now the question, What's wrong?, is not an anatomical dissertation . . . . At the start tell him that; we are not going to *take* anything *away* from him; we are not going to take advantage of him. He doesn't have to answer anything. I'm not going to take any pictures of that part of him. And so forth.

H: Yeah. [*To Sa.*] Dr. S. says this: he hears this story about what Gronemann did. He's never heard this story, and I haven't either. He hears this, and he feels sorry. He wants to talk with you about your asking him if we can fix this something. But first before that he wants to say this: "Now I've come here and we're talking. I'm not going to take anything from you; not at all. I'm not going to take your picture; not at all. I'm not going to take your thoughts: if you don't want to talk, or respond to me, that's okay." It would be no good if you think he'll do the same as Gronemann before: he won't do that. He hears this and he thinks: "Oh, Gronemann didn't understand; he stood and took a picture thoughtlessly, that's all."

Sa: [*Quickly.*] And so—like this: he took our picture for no reason, and he didn't pay us for it. . . . He didn't give us good pay or anything, like clothes.

H: Yeah.

Sa: And so, I've got an angry belly about him. [*Rage.*]

H: Yeah.

Sa: Now, if he comes and asks me again—

H: Look out! huh? [I am so relieved to see Saku's anger.]

Sa: Yeah. Because before he took my picture for nothing, gave me nothing. "And you: [to Gronemann] You bring down big money in your work"—you know, that kind does.* Wait, later, the future, that's how I'd cross him.

H: Yeah. [*Thinking hard.*]

Sa: [*Reflects.*] I'm talking about Gronemann, I'm not talking about you two.

H: Yeah.

Sa: And [*raises voice, kinder*]—you can talk to me. That's all right;

---

*By talking directly to this imaginary Gronemann—who lives everyday in his insides—Saku shows he has over the years, constructed a scenario of what he would do and say to get revenge on this white man. And he knows enough of the outside to imagine that Gronemann was wealthy.

there's no shame in it. [How very different is his assurance from his mood when we began over an hour ago. He has not only revealed his secret, taken us into his confidence, and expressed his turmoil, pain, and anger, but now he says: "My anger isn't for you. Don't be afraid of the shame." He here returns S.'s earlier gift. In other words, beneath Saku's turbulence lies a warm and well-put-together man, who did not let fate burn him up.] [*Smiles.*] You know, the men who go round the coast . . . they [vague] see the cocks of Europeans.*

H: Hm. [*Pause.*]

S: [*Interrupts.*] I've really got to say this here: don't say anything; let him say everything he has to say.

H: Yeah. [*Quiet.*] Um. [*To S.*] He's very angry about what happened to him with Gronemann. I knew that's what it [emotion] was . . .

S: You knew—today?

H: Oh, no, I mean, right now. Before he said he was angry I could tell he was angry. And I said the right things to allow him to express his anger. He said he's very angry about what Gronemann did. He just took the picture and took off.

S: He's angry like you would be, and I would be, if someone did that to us. And he's in worse shape because he could never talk to anyone about it.

H: Yeah [*depressed*].

S: Till this morning.

H: Well, the most important message he left me with is that he's willing to talk with you. He's not ashamed to talk with you. Is there some other assurance that I can give—aside from all I have translated for you—that this isn't going to happen again? To make him comfortable—

S: There's no such thing as "I give you my word"? Or the equivalent?

H: Yeah, there is something like that.

S: First of all, I've got to know what word I give, because it's important to me to be honest to my word.

H: What I can do is say you will make a promise that you will not do so and so.

S: Well, what won't I do? I will *not* take a photograph; I will not ever humiliate him; I will not ever let anybody know about *him*— I might let them know about *somebody*. [And that, reader, is, in

---

*Not clear what Saku is referring to, but it may relate to stories men tell on returning from the Coast, regarding sex with white men in coastal cities.

reality, all you have been told.] That is, this story that we now have, as a piece of our methodology, might be described. There's no way we can tell him that it won't make a difference. But I promise *him*, that I will not—the most important thing—ever humiliate him.

H: [*To Sa.*] Yeah. He wants to say this to you and me. First he wants to say: he's heard this story and he feels truly sorry about what Gronemann did to you. Then he said to me, "You've got to tell Saku: I'm never going to shame Saku. I'm not going to give him more shame. I heard this story, and I'm really sorry. I won't shame him. You [H.] must tell him. I won't take his picture. I'm not going to shame him by telling people about him. I'm not going to make public some pictures or stories about him. All stories and knowledge of Saku belong only to him and to us, and I'm not to go talking around about this." And he says: "This is my promise."

S: Now after that is something positive: that he may feel better to have told somebody he trusts the terrible story he could never tell before. It may offer him some *relief*—of this burden—right now.

Terrible noise from kids screaming in the background. H. drives them off. Then:

S: This guy's been carrying an agony around inside himself. And we've got to, if we can, free him, so that he can at least go back to the starting line of what he's got the matter with him [an incompetent penis].

H: Yeah. [*To Sa.*] Dr. S. says: he's heard this bad thing Gronemann did, and he thinks, "This shame that Gronemann made in you— is connected to your fear that came from when you were first born, when your momma and papa didn't understand about how they marked you [made sex assignment at birth]—this shame has carried to the present and is stuck in your thought, and it screws up some of your thinking."

Sa: Yeah, that's right.

H: So he wants to say: you must know that he and I won't shame you or screw up your thinking; if then you can talk about it to us, then Dr. S. can expel that shame. That can make it better. You can get rid of that shame, and get rid of that bad thing Gronemann did to you before. And you can live better.

Sa: Yeah. Now I can tell you about this: if I was big, like now, and he tried to do that, sorry! He wouldn't make me shamed. But, I was just a small boy. I was the same as J. [a first-stage initiate in our village, a boy about ten years old]. They had initiated me, but that's all. I had no thought. Suppose he comes back later, I've got to tell you two. If Gronemann ever came back, I'd have said to him: "Before, you put a great shame on me. I'm not happy with you." [*Steady voice. He's back to his normal intonation now.*] Now, if he had paid me for that, paid me a lot, then I wouldn't be so angry at him. Had he done that and looked at me . . . but he didn't. He did wrong. This master.* Me, myself, from my own strength I did things—I planted a little coffee [trees] and got a little money. Now I've built my own tin-roof house. Now I work for you and make a little money. My stomach is still hot from this [*lowers voice, angry again, voice almost breaks*]. I'm just sitting down now. If you want to ask me something now—that's okay, I'm not going to get shame. I can talk.

S: The only thing I would say: you've got to give him *all the space.* Ask him the right questions . . . I don't know what to tell you: you're going to have to be a good clinician. Don't take the time to tell me what he said—just let it go. Let him run.

H: Yeah. [*To Sa.*] Do you think I should keep talking to Stoller?

Sa: [*Firm.*] You shouldn't worry; don't be afraid. You must tell him. It's my choice, if I want to tell him. So, you can go ahead and tell him [*level-headed*].

H: [*To S.*] He's identifying with me. He says you should talk with him: don't be afraid or ashamed, just tell him. [*To Sa.*] When Gronemann first got you, you were a *choowinuku* [first-stage initiate].

Sa: Yeah.

H: You didn't see him later as an *imbutu* or *ipmangwi?*

Sa: No, I didn't. [*His whole body is trembling.*]

S: Is he shaking now?

H: Yes.

S: Does he want to cry? He may.

H: I thought he was about to, on the verge.

S: Does he . . . he . . . want my permission? Is it the wrong thing to do in this society?

H: It *is* the wrong thing.

S: It's all right *with me.*

---

*Note how Saku shifts back here to the Pidgin "master," where before he used "Gronemann." He has objectified Gronemann's status to be the all-powerful white man, and he implies in this projection the reality and fantasy of the endless power-plays of life under a colonial regime.

H: It might be all right with you.

S: I'm telling you to tell him it's all right with me. But he doesn't *have* to. Can you tell him that?

H: [*To Sa.*] I was telling him [S.] this and he stopped me half-way to say that he's seeing you and he thinks that when you expressed this shame that Gronemann made in you—he sees your eyes and hands and thinks you're close to crying. You want to cry about what he did back then?

Sa: [*Quickly.*] Yeah.

H: S. says, his own way is that if you want to cry it's all right, there's nothing wrong with that. He's told me to tell you if you want to cry, it's okay.

Sa: It's like that. When I was still very small, I thought: "What does he want to *do* that he's taken off my grass sporran?"

H: He himself took off your sporran?!

Sa: Yeah. He told one of his men to do it. And at that time I thought, "He's looked at me. He wants to put nice new [western] clothes on me." But, he didn't put them on me. Now I'm big and I think to myself, "Sorry. Before, he really rubbished me, fouled me up. He took a picture of me, and maybe he showed it around to other masters." That's what I think. So, now, I think bad of him.

S: He's just shaking . . . shaking all over.

H: Yeah, I know. I think it's probably reassuring for him for us to just talk—

S: Yeah, yeah, yeah. That's what he needs [*intense whisper*].

H: So he said when he was a first-stage initiate, without his permission, an older man—not one of his kinsmen—took him to the place wherever Gronemann was, which was probably in a tent or something, and they removed his grass sporran to look at his genitals. And then, it's not clear if it was against his will—he was just ten years old—a picture was taken, and he's got a fantasy (I think you were right) that that picture is now being seen by others. And people are looking at it. And the meaning is that he was humiliated, because against his will they did something which is morally wrong here, they exposed his genitals and took the picture. So part of him is out there—floating in space. He said, tell him that—tell S. So, this is all news to me; I never got this story before.

S: I might do something, but I've got to know more. What's he feeling now? He's shaking from what?

H: Well, I can feel inside of *myself*—*I* am shaking.

S: Rage, humiliation, fear. What I want from him now is to get it out. Not to hold it with a shaking, but to feel free to say what the shaking is saying.

H: [*To Sa.*] I told S. what you said. He says: "I hear this, and I am thinking about this." But he also says that he sees you and you are shaking some.

Sa: Body-shaking. [He uses the Sambia, not Pidgin, word for it.]

H: Yeah. Yet he thinks that it's not good that you hold onto this shame. You must expel it, expel it through talking. Whatever you feel—anger or what—you've got to talk it out.* Talk it out to him.

S: Now what he should do is talk. To me, to you. Get it out.

H: [*To Sa.*] He says, "You talk, talk to us."

Sa: He looked† at me. I think about that, and I'm afraid of him. I'm not happy with him. [*Low, quiet voice.*] I'm not too afraid, but I am unhappy with him. He didn't think enough of me to give me something. That's all, that's what . . . I shake for . . . [*voice fades out*]. I'm not happy about that. I know—before, when I was small—he looked at me, but he didn't pay me for it.

H: Um-hm.

S: [*Directly to Sa.*] Talk—talk to me. Is that clear?

Sa: Yeah.

H: He says talk to him.

S: Turn to me, talk to *me*.

H: Turn around and look at him.

S: Tell me what you need to tell me.

H: Tell him what you must talk out about to S.

Sa: [*Flows.*] That's all, what I said to you. Before, he looked at me, and he didn't pay. So I'm afraid of him; afraid of only this Gronemann. This kind [of man] is no good, here. . . . He looks inside of their sporrans . . . at the pubic area of *men*. That's an altogether different kind of man‡ [*tiredness in voice*]. So I've been afraid of him. If he had done good for me, I wouldn't think like this. Suppose he had said: "I want to do such and such, and so I'll pay you for it. And if you shake, then we can stop." If he'd said that, it would have been okay. But he looked at me, and this picture he showed to all the masters: "Here's a different kind of

*Talking out anger is what Sambia customarily do in moots; thus, Sa.'s talking is appropriate in that way too.

†Here and above, Sa. uses the term that can mean erotic looking. (See chapter 4.) It is a complex thing, this looking, which here carries the sense of: "I can't shake the feeling of Gronemann and others staring at me, exposed, so cheapened."

‡Saku suggests that Gronemann gets his kicks by looking at male genitals. Sa. feels that it is not right, that it is, as we would say in these circumstances, *using* the natives, perverse.

boy to look at." He thought that, he showed the picture to his friends. And so, I'm angry at him, heavy in my stomach at him. [*To S:*] I want Gilbert to understand: "Before, you [Gronemann] made me afraid and I didn't like it." So I didn't talk out to you [H.], but now I've told him all. [*Long pause.*]

It is so important to me, and to our joint work, that Sa. has acknowledged here his hiding and evasion of the subject of his hermaphrodism. This was the healthy and truly *human* thing to do. It was a way of acknowledging my struggle to reach him, and the ambivalence I felt in trying to open up this area in our dialogue. He acknowledges, that is, the open secret we could never discuss, by telling me that the dreadful secret—of Gronemann's picture-taking years ago—was a secret he could never broach. Thus, Sa. has directly responded to S.'s move above—"talk to me"—while also indirectly telling me with kindness that I am there, and that what I had tried to do was too frightening to talk about before. Not "H. is frightening," but "this deeper secret was too frightening." This acknowledgment and honesty startles me, as I think of it now (1982). Kalutwo never did that; perhaps he *cannot*. This acknowledgment is for me a sign of Sa.'s greater trust and care, of his healthy core personality.

S: What should I know?

H: He says most everything I've said before. Except he's added that he's never stopped being afraid of Gronemann . . . afraid that Gronemann will do the same thing. And in saying that, there's the sense that he didn't have the power to say "no" to Gronemann.

S: That's what I was going to say before. Now I'll say it again. [*S. repeats to Sa.*]

H: He said he was afraid to talk to me about this before, when I brought it up. But now he's told us both. [*H. repeats S.'s words to Saku.*]

Sa: I think, when I say this, I won't be afraid. If I curse him I think [*lowers voice*] I won't be afraid.

H: And you won't forget?

Sa: No. Now, what I said to Dr. S. I can't forget. [*Stronger.*] I have to put it on the front of my face [remember it easily]: I won't forget about it; I won't forget about this. I put it on my face now and I can watch and wait. I won't forget about this. [*Long pause.*] You know. When he came here and made us afraid that's not good. That's something truly no good. I always thought, suppose he would want to come here and take away [study] our customs or—that's all right, there's nothing wrong with that. But [*almost inaudible here*] when he came and did that—[*pause*] *makes us afraid* in your [sic] balls* [*sad chuckle*], that's not a good thing. So when he came here and made us afraid . . . [*pause*] that's very bad. That's what I think. You know. You masters have another kind of—a big kind of—

H: Power. [*Despair in voice.*]

Sa: Yeah. A big kind of power. Yeah. But us here—

H: You don't have any.

Sa: That's right. We don't have any [power]. [*Sad undertone throughout all this talk.*] And when he came and shamed us, that's no good, that's something that's very bad.

S: [*Cuts in.*] Is this unusual for him? What he's doing? [At this moment, Sa. is visibly shaking, his hands clasped to hold himself together. He is terrified.]

H: Yeah. Yeah, it's rare for him.

S: For him?

H: Yeah. For him.

S: And for the culture, too?

H: *Yeah. He's really tense.*

Sa: I'm really pleased with the two of you. [*Sa.'s voice breaks at this point. Pause.*]

S: [*Low voice.*] I want to hear him think out loud. Can we get him to do that now? If we can get him to, it will help me if I can know what he's experiencing.

H: [*To Sa.*] He asks what are you thinking, so he can understand. It helps him to know about you later.

Sa: [*Voice quickens.*] Oh, I am thinking he is helping me, helping me truly, I'm thinking like that. And another thing is that I'm very pleased with you. [*There's a smile in Saku's voice here. This is hard to translate. His voice is low and his words vague.*] And I was thinking no good about him [Gronemann]. I wasn't thinking good things . . . and he came along here and did that bad thing. And another [S.] has come along here to help me. And I'm very happy about that.

H: [*Repeats to S.*]

S: [*Quiet voice.*] Does he feel inside that he will be able to sleep tonight?

Sa: Well, when I go home I'll get a good sleep.

---

*An idiom: a little fear is "fear on the skin"; a lot of fear—fright—is "fear in the balls" (genitals), an allusion to the retraction of male genitals under extreme anxiety (e.g., in war).

H: You'll get a good sleep, huh?

Sa: Yeah. I think bad about Gronemann; but now he [S.] has helped me and I can forget thinking about Gronemann and all these other things, and I can go home and sleep good. And I'm very pleased with him [S.]. Very pleased. And I'm very pleased with him. That's all.

H: [*To. S.*] He says that before he was very afraid and ashamed about this and now you've helped him. And all of these feelings have gone outside of him and now he thinks that he'll be able to go and get a really good sleep.

S: That's good. If he wants to say any more, that's fine. But we don't have to have more. If he wants to do it he can tell it for *his* sake. He could—whatever the word is—deposit inside of us whatever he has to.

H: [*To Sa.*] Now, this is for later. Dr. Stoller says he is really pleased that you have talked to us and you have told us about this. That you have shared this with us. Now, suppose you want to finish here with this talk, that's all right, it's your choice. Or suppose later you want to say more, that, too, is your own choice.

Sa: I can come back later [*lower voice*] and talk.

H: Tomorrow?

Sa: Yeah. Come back later and finish with this.

S: What he tells us from now on is for his sake. We don't need more. Before, he was coming in here because Gilbert was doing research. If he wants to come in here now and talk about anything he wants, we don't need it. I don't mean "Fuck you! We don't need it." I mean he now has an opportunity to come in here and talk about *anything* he wants. He can bring it to us for his sake. And if he doesn't want to he doesn't have to.

H: [*To Sa.*] Dr. S. says: "I was working with you to get your thoughts. I, too, wanted to know about you. From now on. . . . We won't ask more about that. But if you, for yourself, want to come and talk, well, that's your own choice. We would be pleased to do that with you, to help you lose your fear. So that you won't be afraid or ashamed of this anymore."*

Sa: [*Low voice, exhausted.*] That's all right.

S: I guess that's enough work for today. Unless you've got something else that you want to ask him.

Sa: Hm. [*Long pause.*] Now what? Is that all? Is that all? Him,

---

*And this offer, this supporting relationship, I have continued with Saku ever since, across field trips in 1981, 1983, 1985, 1988.

Gronemann, that master, that's all I worry about. He shamed me, and that's it. So, I've told it *all* to you now. That's it. I wanted to tell you [H.], but I forgot about it. I wanted to say that he [Gronemann] made me shamed before, but saying that scared me. I was shaking. And so, now, I'm really happy about the two of you. That's all for now.

H: That's it. Tomorrow you must come and we'll talk again . . . .

Sa: All right, tomorrow I'll come. [*H. accompanies Sa. outside.* They say goodbye. Sa. leaves, H. returns.]

H: I was just thinking as I went out the door that I always have a compelling need when I have finished here [inside room] to go out and say a few words with the person that I have worked with to let them know I know there is another existence outside that's different from inside here, and that I am *also* out there with them, too. And that it's not good enough for me to say goodbye inside here. I have to go outside and say goodbye, too. You know, I've run that thought through my head hundreds of times—every single time I go outside that door.

S: But you would specifically *not* do that in a psychoanalysis. For different reasons, for some other thing that has to flow. [*Pause.*] *Everything* is important [*emphatic*].

H: Yeah.

S: Everything is important, including why you do that here and why I don't do that at home, with an analytic patient.

H: Well, this to me is why we are here.

AFTERWORD

The next day we were to see Saku again, but he didn't show and he sent no word. The day after that, I saw him near his house. He said he was "very sorry" for not showing; he was drained but okay. I think he was overwhelmed by our last session, needed a breathing spell to work through what happened. He offered weak excuses for not showing, which I accepted, but we both knew why he did not return. We said goodbye and kept in touch through occasional letters.

Looking back now, I realize I could never have foreseen what Saku was hiding all those years. I thought he was just ashamed of his hermaphrodism. Had I known of the trauma with Gronemann, I would have proceeded differently. But I could not know that, until S. came along. Perhaps it is a measure of how much Saku trusted me that we got as far as we did working alone. I lacked the skills to go further then. I've changed. Working with sensitive people like Saku has shown me: take nothing for granted; understand as much as possible before believing in your guesses; be supportive, and be patient.

Saku's life is better now; he is not as weighted down. In 1981, I returned to the Sambia and worked more intensely than ever with him. He was far less secretive and in two weeks was completely open. He told me more of his story, this time with less shame.

This study of Saku underscores the power of clinical ethnography for studying others' lives. A more sensitive case than that of Saku-lambei can hardly be found in the ethnographic archives. Empathy and trust made our work possible. Clinical skill helped us understand Saku's secrets. What is this skill? Why was I short on it? Did we press Saku too hard? What are the ethics of bearing down in interviews to discover something? Let me briefly review these issues.

First, to state the obvious: this material could not have been collected without remarkable trust between Saku and myself. Such rapport takes a long time to build.

Second, rapport by itself does not bring the data we collected here. That requires other clinical strengths that use focused empathy to work through someone's defenses, past their pain, if they wish to do so. You saw how S. helped Saku to feel his way through painful past experiences, sharing these with others for the first time. I could not do this before; was not experienced enough to keep Saku from getting lost in the avalanche of pain. S. got us through Saku's anxieties, to see more clearly the turmoil to which they pointed. He helped Sa. see that learning his secrets did not frighten or destroy us, and, therefore, him. S. supported Saku more tenderly than could I. With the secrets in the open, Sa. could see himself anew.

Third, training and experience create clinical technique. S.'s thirty years [1979] of interviewing and treating and formulating patient cases are available here. *That* does not bring empathy, however; empathy is more: self-image, motivation to understand other people's motivations, and interest in others are some of its characteristics. S. supplemented me here; my cultural knowledge of Sambia and my work with Saku complemented his clinical experience. Either alone could not have produced this chapter.

Most students, on beginning fieldwork, cannot undertake sensitive and intimate interviews. I could not have. Too much prior ethnographic background is required. The interviewing skills take time to develop, nor do they come naturally. Such supportive understanding requires special training. But this *can* be acquired with training. The first fieldwork is the first step.

Nilangu village. Photograph by Robert Stoller.

Nilangu children at play. Photograph by Robert Stoller.

Anguished child searches for his share of feast. Photograph by Robert Stoller.

Bridge off which Penjukwi tried to kill herself during abduction. Photograph by Robert Stoller.

Nilangu men: afternoon gossip. Photograph by Gilbert Herdt.

A shaman leads parade of initiates. Photograph by Gilbert Herdt.

An elder teaches in Sambia male initiation.
Photograph by Gilbert Herdt.

Sambia warrior. Photograph by Gilbert Herdt.

Two men unearthing mumu feast. Photograph by Gilbert Herdt.

Nilangu women and girls in repose. Photograph by Gilbert Herdt.

Women and children around
a fire. Photograph by Robert
Stoller.

A pig kill in the bush near Nilangu. Photograph by Robert Stoller.

Feast preparations in the village. Photograph by Gilbert Herdt.

Small boy near a water pool. Photograph by Robert Stoller.

Intimate communications. Photograph by Robert Stoller.

S: Our discovery of Saku's secret overemphasizes Gronemann's badness. As victim, Saku experiences Gronemann as consciously malignant, while Gronemann, as is so often the case with colonialists, executives, teachers, parents, doctors, politicians, and administrators, does not realize how different it feels to be the one who delivers the power versus the one who receives it. Gronemann would probably have been surprised had he known that his whim had been an unending, awful presence for Saku. [H: Bob is being kind.] To what extent does ethnography inflict similar, though less severe, effects on the people studied? To what extent is the process by which we take information from people natural/benign/helpful and to what extent does it damage? To what extent do we researchers act in innocence and to what extent not?

Being a clinician—more precisely, a therapist—I see my work with patients as worth the pain it inflicts because the goal is therapeutic, and the intention—from moment to moment, depending on my knowledge of myself—more for the patient's good than for mine. Patients do not always experience it that way. Does this therapeutic quality hold in the ethnographer's work? Our argument is that it should, not to the extent that we, as ethnographers, are trying to remit pain, remove symptoms, or help people find happiness, but that, from moment to moment, whatever we say and think, as is true for the physician (however much it may be breeched in reality), the rule should be *primam non nocere*.

Did we press Sa. too hard? How clear are the ethics of clinical ethnography? Are they taught, practiced, monitored? Should ethnographers be as aware of the issues as, say, psychotherapists, or can the rules be as relaxed as for newspaper reporters? You saw us struggle with these problems in our interviews with Sa., where the interplay so resembled a piece of therapy.

Though not needed for every undertaking, clinical ethnography provides a way to uncover such information as Sa. gave us, with the bonus of helping people feel better about themselves.

CHAPTER EIGHT

Imano—Considerate Masculinity

H: It is well known that "strong" men are prominent in normative male comportment in Melanesia. Penetrating portraits of these are available in the literature (Read 1959; Watson 1972). "Big" men are a key to New Guinea Highlands social organization as we also know (Sahlins 1963; see also Brown 1978). And protest masculinity, in the generalized sense of defensive male-posturing to ensure against internal fears or external accusations of softness, is omnipresent too (Herdt 1987c). There has been much less attention directed to what is commonly known in Melanesia as rubbish men, antiheros who fail to live up to ideal standards of masculinity. Even here, however, there are hints of such figures around (Watson 1960). Far less is known of what Margaret Mead (1935) once called "gentle" males in New Guinea. Here, it would seem, is a very rare species indeed. In this chapter we provide a detailed report on such a man.

BIOGRAPHIC SKETCH

Imano is exceptional, perhaps the most gentle and kind Sambia man I know. Indeed, if you interview his contacts—wife and children, age-mates, extended family, friends—he emerges as one of the most considerate people in the village. What is this gentleness? I began research with Imano to understand questions like that. Why he is so considerate at first glance seems trivial but is really as important and fascinating as any manifestation of Sambia culture and erotics.

Quiet, sensitive, and intelligent, Imano is a married man in his early thirties. He is slightly older than Tali, though he looks younger and is far less socially prominent.[1] He is married with two wives; they have borne five children, of whom two are living.[2] He is a good

246

provider and able gardener. His is the second-most numerous, politically important clan in Nilangu. His father's nuclear family, moreover, is very prominent, his father having been a big man and war leader who was socially and economically very productive and lived to ripe old age. (Both parents are now dead.) The third of four sons in a family of eight children, Imano grew up well protected and strongly integrated into his natal family. This social heritage gives Imano biologic brothers and many classifactory kinsmen who are natural allies and supporters. Imano thus has lived in Nilangu his whole life, in customary arrangements that suit every ideal of masculine culture: patrician affiliation, inheritance and ancestry, patrilocal residence, and marital status. If ever one were to search for gender aberrance, you would pass Imano by; right? Wrong.

On closer examination Imano reveals—by Sambia standards—marked gender aberrance. As a child he had no wish to be a fierce warrior. When initiated he disliked (silently laughed at) homosexual practices, and compared to peers, he participated in them far less and experienced them in a different way. But his greatest aberrance is that he never served as a fellated, has never copulated with a boy. He married as quickly as possible and then took a second wife. He enjoys his wives and loves heterosexuality. Thus, Imano has deviated from several cherished social norms; and in normative terms, his form of masculinity is odd. To the western reader Imano may seem normal. But to Sambia he is almost (though not quite) as aberrant as Kalutwo (see chapter 9); Imano is to exclusive heterosexual behavior as Kalutwo is to exclusive homosexual behavior: an extreme case.

During 1974–1976 I knew Imano only slightly. He was a pleasant neighbor. I had congenial but superficial contacts with him and no special reason to interview him. It was not until 1979 that I began working with him and several other men like him to understand quiet masculinity. I did it then because I discovered belatedly that I had overlooked an important cultural category (namely, *aambei-wutnyi* "gentle" or "feminine" man) of male personhood.

In my original fieldwork I elicited, recorded, and studied the major and minor categories of masculine personhood and their symbolic attributes; so I thought. This set includes elders, war leaders, strong men, rubbish men, bachelors, initiates, and uninitiated boys.[3] (There are some similar, not identical, categorical status differentials among females.) In the 1979 work, though, I uncovered another small group of men who are quiet, married, acceptable but seen as "weak" (*wogaanyu*) compared to their showy peers. I had considered them ordinary (not average, and not rubbish, men, who are different). They were the men I had imagined to fight in the rear ranks during battle, compared to the rubbish men (who are said to be cowardly and, if charged, would run). Both in identity and in behavior, these gentle men reflect a masculine style that looks and feels different from, say, Weiyu, Tali, Moondi, or even Kalutwo (who is a rubbish man). Men like Moondi's father (see chapter 4), and perhaps Sakulambei (chapter 7),[4] fit this mold. They are "deviant" in Mead's terms,[5] but not so different that their presence shouts at you. Their fellows pay them no notice. A good clinician might have attended; the ethnographer didn't.

I can understand why it happened: they stay in the background. Stereotypes and category terms depend mostly on cultural context and interpersonal focus, wherein people are labeled, responded to, are given attributions, or make claims about themselves. These men are not only quiet, they are sometimes absent. Usually, men respond to others' absence—in rituals, for instance—by impugning them as weak or *wasaatu* (rubbish men). If forced, men might label as rubbishy, absentees such as Imano. However, that seldom happens; and the sense of *wasaatu* has another connotation when used for someone like Kalutwo (chapter 9, and in the following). On the other hand, *aambei-wutnyi* are not impugned, probably because in one domain that really counts today—reproductive competence—they are, if anything, eminently successful.[6] By 1979, when I began asking about the range of masculinity and femininity among Sambia, these gentle men looked different to me.

*Aambei-wutnyi** is one of those native concepts the anthropologist finds hard to translate. One rarely hears the word in everyday speech. In general, *aambei-wutnyi* is a mild slur, not used much mainly because it refers to only a few males. *Aambei-wutnyi* includes: being quiet, unshowy, socially awkward, not physically big or powerful; someone who avoids public ritual displays; who spends too much time with women and is gentle with children, liking women and family life more than do most men. It would not be quite right to gloss this noun as "feminine man" (and certainly not as "effeminate"[7]), for men such as Imano are more masculine than those Americans call feminine.[8] It was to understand the origins and dynamics of this gentle masculinity[†] that I began interviewing Imano in 1979.

---

*Aambei-wutnyi: aambei is a transfix of *imbei*, which means "young adolescent female cassowary" and is a general metaphor for women and cassowaries; *wutnyi* marks masculine person.

†Whenever used, this term will be the translation of *aambei-wutnyi*; it comes closest to the meaning held by the Sambia themselves.

Let us compare rubbish men (*wusaatu*) with gentle men (*aambei-wutnyi*), for both are clearly set apart from that glorious identity, war leader (*aamooluku*). *Wusaatu* is an immediate, damning label, showing that one is weak, cowardly, irresponsible, *unmanly*. Take note that women also use *wusaatu* in reference to men, whereas *aambei-wutnyi* is used much less frequently.[9] The contrast active/passive is helpful here. The rubbish man acts as if big and showy, yet fails. Rubbish men are *wogaanyu* (weak, unmanly), a public term. *Aambei-wutnyi*, by contrast, is never used in public conversation or oratory: it is whispered. To do so would shame the men so labeled. But there is another (subliminal) reason it is not used. *Aambei-wutnyi* is a sign that a man is comfortably quiet, is more feminine than he should be; whereas *wusaatu* means that a man is uncomfortably failing to perform as masculine. *Wusaatu* is also a strong verbal social sanction to push men—the men who *can* be pushed—into being more masculine; *aambei-wutnyi* is never used that way. That difference raises a final contrast.

As stereotypes, both *wusaatu* and *aambei-wutnyi* are also social identities, stigmata. But they differ in how consistently and permanently people apply them as labels. Since the performative contexts of masculinity range so widely—from war to ritual to sex and on and on—a man's manliness may be judged according to the situation. He may be a failed warrior and a superlative hunter. A few men are *wussatu* across the board: consistently unmanly.* For others, though, *wussatu* is situation-specific and can later be cast off. As an identity-type, however, *aambei-wutnyi* seems invariant and predictable, Sambia say, based on personality configurations constant from childhood to old age. Yet remember that there are few of them—the label is less negative and symbolically charged than *wusaatu*; and these men—unlike rubbish men—are not out to prove anything to anyone, so they are seen less.[10] Besides, they are nice people.

I worked with Imano for a few weeks, for about twenty sessions of an hour or more each. (I also interviewed three other *aambei-wutnyi*, two adults and a pubescent initiate, but they are not discussed here.) I found Imano amazingly open; able and willing to discuss intimate feelings many Sambia men could not after months or more of interviewing. (Compare Kalutwo, from whom it took years to collect similar information. And that was like pulling teeth.) I found his frank-

---

*Kalutwo (chapter 9) is a *wusaatu* but he was not when beginning his social career twenty years ago.

ness, friendliness, and comfortableness refreshing and warm. Though I do not know Imano as well as others like Moondi, I feel my impressions are reliable. (But not complete.[11])

Weiyu, whom Imano trusts—they are close kin—always served as my translator since Imano cannot speak Pidgin. (In chapters 9 and 10 we show how Weiyu's dislike, while interpreting for Kalutwo, changes the situation.) I also interviewed Weiyu in private about his views on Imano's interviews[12] and cross-checked aspects of Imano's case study with others in the village who knew him well.

Today, Imano presents himself as an ordinary, relatively happy, traditionalist-type man. He still wears customary garb: sporran, bark cape, colored beads (but interestingly enough, he never wears the warrior's belly- or waist-bandoleers). He wears no other decorations, keeps his hair short-cropped and beard cleanly shaven (all traditional features). He has (like his brothers), an unusually high hairline, a broad forehead, bright expressive eyes, fine features, and is of medium height and build. Up close one can see fine horizontal worry-lines in his forehead, which contribute to his looking sensitive and intelligent.[13] He smiles a lot and has marked smile lines around his mouth, is fidgety and always working his hands.

Imano has told me of his development, especially childhood, in good detail. His story is confirmed by others. By any measure, whether one is Sambian or an anthropologist, what stands out is the character and presence of his father and the kind of marriage his father made. Imano describes his father as tough, fearless, a warrior quick to rise— a heavy. He was feared by men and ruled unquestionably over his wife and family. He was a main war leader in Nilangu. His speech was garbled;[14] he was a "man who didn't talk much." Even so, his children never feared him, he never hit them, and he and his wife rarely fought. The parents were often together, more than is usual. His mother was a kindly and much-loved woman, and a prolific gardener.[15] Imano's father was faithful to her, and he never took a second wife (which is extraordinary for a big man). Though he fought many battles, Imano's father was apparently not a man's man: it is said he never slept in the men's house.[16] In short, the image I have is of a tough, strict father, who was nonetheless loved and loving, who had a peaceful marriage and provided a bountiful and mostly harmonious home life.

Imano's first memory is of being breast-fed.[17] He was close to his mother until about age five. But after his mother had a new baby (he was about three), he crossed over the boundary stakes of the women's space and began sleeping closer to his father in the men's space in their house. He loved and admired his father more, as he got older. Still, he can remember in childhood being scolded for not being forceful in games and hunting. He sweated over that: his father compared him to his next older brother. (On telling this experience, Imano turned tense and looked both pained and guarded.) But he said he told his father that that was all right: his brother could be a great fighter if he wanted to while he, Imano, was different. (This remark may seem hard to believe—a five-year-old standing up to his father this way— but it is true that Sambia children have license to talk like this.* Imano reports it as a real event.) On the other hand, his mother defended him, he says, retorting that "quiet men live longer." Imano still remembers many intervillage battles of his childhood, when he hid with his mother and other children in the back of the hamlet, in fear of enemy assaults. He says he cried for his father, wishing that he would return home safely, which he always did.

Imano was glad to be initiated. He was older—ten—than his fellow initiates. He said he was happy to be "sent to the men's house" by his father, for he wanted to "grow and mature quickly." He didn't miss his mother, he said, for "I was already big and grown." He was afraid during some of the ritual ordeals but not abnormally so. His father stayed near. His response to the idea of the homosexual teaching is pure Imano: he silently laughed at the ridiculous idea of sucking another's penis.[18] But privately, he felt shame. He was afraid of fellatio, avoided it for months, being more ashamed than afraid. He sucked only two men in his life: one of them (assigned to him at initiation) once; the other—a bachelor of whom he was very fond—many times over a period of several months.[19] This fellatio, because minimal, was aberrant.

Perhaps the greater indicator that Imano's gender identity is different is his never having served as a fellated. When he first told me this I did not believe him. No man ever said that before. Imano almost boasted of it, with no shame or regret, though I checked many times. To my knowledge, no other Sambia man[†] has not been sucked by boys, for this means he is not ritually complete, has not demonstrated he is fully masculinized (Herdt 1980; 1981). But I am now convinced it is true; two other men have confirmed it of him. Though he had little homoerotic interest in boys, he was "proud to be inter-

---

*Sambia children are rarely punished, for fear it will stunt their growth. Fathers, unlike mothers, do not reprimand their children, a fact that enters into the ordeals and submission expected from initiation.

†Excepting Sakulambei (chapter 7).

ested to be initiated a bachelor" since it meant "I could marry a woman." From puberty, then, Imano has preferred women and could survive the resulting lack of sexual partners till marriage.

Imano married young, at an appropriate age, after serving two years on the coast as a plantation laborer. The experience seems to have changed him little; for example, he speaks no Pidgin. On returning he married, right away, a strong woman whose fiancé—Nilutwo—could not abide her sharp tongue and aggressive ways (see chapter 6). They have had sex a lot, more often, I think, than is usual. He enjoys this heterosexuality and is attached to his first wife. He took a second wife, another virgin, a couple of years later. This caused strife in his household, for his first wife fiercely resisted sharing him. They are all still married; but his second wife sleeps elsewhere to avoid squabbles (to be described in the session that follows). He definitely prefers his first wife sexually and otherwise.

Being a quiet man also means that Imano still attends to private ritual practices in normative ways. On the one hand, he avoids public ritual displays, seldom nosebleeding himself with the other men. On the other, it is believed he is a faithful *private* nosebleeder, regularly purging himself after his wives' periods.[20] He privately drinks milk-sap to replace semen after sex, though not always. (Indeed, he rationalizes his lack of screwing boys by saying that giving his semen to them would have used up his semen too fast. So he reserved it for women.) In short, he follows ritual procedures *after* sex to a tee, allowing him, we may speculate, more sensuous relationships with his wives (i.e., closer identification with them via these culturally-constituted defense mechanisms). The details and implications of these points are elaborated below.

How did Imano present himself during our interviews, how did he behave? First, he was often embarrassed, at times bashful, talking of himself. Other men do not express shame by bashfulness. Especially when talking about sex he was overly self-conscious.[21] After a couple of sessions, though, his shame faded, leaving only bashfulness. Once he felt easier, he alternated between being bashful and open, between uneasy and contented: smiling, with hands folded in his lap.

Second, another unusual gender trait: he expressed his emotions far more than most Sambia men. In an hour he could laugh and joke, look happy, turn somber and reflective; and these emotions moved easily on his face and body.

Third, he had lots of nervous energy, mild anxiety beyond that usually seen in men (or boys). He constantly fingered his face, touching his chin, lightly pinching his cheeks.* He shifted posture, some-times putting his head in his hands, leaning against the table, or thoughtfully looking out the window, searching. He has an audible, soft, automatic cough, nervously clearing his throat as often as three or four times a minute. He used these anxious gestures in social in-teractions too.

Fourth, his habitual stance with me was: "I want to please." He smiled constantly. Even on raising his voice he smiled. He never showed me anger or disgust. He strained for approval, attentive to my questions and movements. He was affable. I never felt him to be hostile even in his anxious gestures. He thus made me feel a need to reassure him, to respond frequently, to let him know I felt him to be a good person. It was not usually that way with the other men with whom I worked, though it was when working with Penjukwi, Saku-lambei, and several boys.

On the other hand, unlike the latter people, Imano did not seem fragile or easily hurt. He spoke fluidly in our interviews, and when we were done, he left easily, without loose ends. (I did not worry either that he would take what I did or said with him outside my office, because he was self-contained. That contrasted with Kalutwo, Pen-jukwi, and Sakulambei, with whom I did watch my behavior. For what they needed from me was never finished in interviews but spilled into other situations.)

Imano, in brief, was different, gently masculine, a personality like many of my students, colleagues, and friends in America.

THE SESSION

We interviewed Imano together only once, for an hour one morning. S. was present and fully involved. The complete edited transcript of this interview follows. What was the context of our talk?

Before S. came along, Imano was describing his life and his mar-riages. Because of his peculiar masculinity I was particularly inter-ested in his heterosexuality and erotic excitement. At the start of the interview we discussed an argument he had had with his wives: just one small event out of many that reveals his considerateness. In the latter part, we turned to his sexual excitement, and he discussed day-

---

*This is another idiosyncracy I have never seen in other Sambia men but have in children and some women.

dreams, replenishing his semen through drinking tree-sap, and aspects of his sexual foreplay with his first wife.

Though this range of topics may seem broad for an hour interview, it is rather typical. Readers who have done open-ended interviews know how many topics can enter an hour. Sometimes I tried to keep my interviews more focused than this one, by often returning to earlier comments of the person. Here, though, we were exploring; and our discussion opened up aspects of Imano's erotism that I had not known.

WEIYU: Imano says, "Yeah. There is a lot still to talk about, about when my [first] wife and I first started walking around" [metaphor for screwing in the forest].

HERDT: But still they argue?

W: [*Quickly.*] Yeah, yeah. The two of them do not talk any differently to each other.

H: She still says Imano's just a rubbish man, a soft man?*

W: Yeah, yeah, yeah.

H: And she fights with him?

W: Yeah, yeah.

H: Yesterday?

W: Yesterday. The two of them fought. Kwinko and I saw them. They had just finished fighting. Over their hand pouch [wallet] and also over . . .

I: . . . a long pair of trousers. . . . [Imano knows some Pidgin words.]

W: A long pair of trousers that was cut into halves, sewed up, and made into *bilums* [carrying bags]. Imano had given one to his other wife.

H: To the daughter of Kanteilo? [Imano's second wife is Kanteilo's daughter, and the old man really favors her.]

W: Yeah. Gave it to her, and so that woman [Imano's first wife] said, "Hey, does that belong to you that you are giving it away to her? That belongs to me. [The first wife had made two tote bags from the old trousers, and Imano gave one to his second wife without the first's permission.] What you own she does not look after very well."

H: What did Imano say?

W: [*He turns to Imano and asks him; I. replies:*] I told her, "You are big and adult." [*I. talks to W., who reports:*] The first wife told the

_____

*When couples fight they say horrible things to each other never said otherwise. We may see his wife's epithets in this way.

second, "That bag does not belong to you. It belongs to me because my Imano gave it to me. He came back from his coastal work and gave it to me, at the same time, with some money." Now this woman [the second wife], she does not sleep there in our house. She sleeps elsewhere.* So it is not good she should lose her money. She's got to have something to put it in.

I: It's been that way.

H: Doesn't the other woman, the daughter of Kanteilo, put her money together with Imano?

I: No, no [*a feeling, half-feigned, that she is more than he can handle*].

W: Yeah, yeah, they put it together.

I: Just like that.

H: But you're saying that only the first wife and Imano put the money inside the one bag?

W: Yeah, yeah. That belongs only to that first wife—only her.

H: What of Imano?

W: He divides his money up for the two of them. He doesn't keep any for himself.

H: None? [*Surprise.*]

W: Yeah. He's a middleman, that's all. He doesn't hold it himself. When he works for money [on government patrols], he gives it to them.

H: But where does he store it?

W: He splits it down the middle and gives it to them both. He holds none at all.

H: Oh! [*Surprised throughout.*] I want to tell Dr. Stoller. Here's a good example, and just a mundane detail, of his kind of masculinity.

S: I was on the same track.

H: It's so typical. He had a fight with his wife yesterday. Kwinko and Weiyu broke it up . . . Just a yelling session, though. They had picked up sticks and were starting at it. His first wife was there when he gave a tote bag to his second wife. The first wife got jealous, typical when there's two wives. This discussion led to information that each wife has her own place for cash. Unlike most men, who hold the purse strings and dole out only pennies for their wives, he has given the money *to his wives*. When he needs money, he *asks* the wives. That's really an atypical pattern. Weiyu would never do that.

S: Why did he? When did it start? Go back to the beginning. If you want to know why, start with the first thing a person said.

---

*Because the two wives fight, they cannot live in the same house. Imano prefers to reside with his first wife.

H: [*To W.*] I want to ask him, when did he first start doing this?

W: [*For Imano.*] When he married his second wife. He used to do that with his wife and did not think more about it. So when the next wife came along, he thought to himself, "Eeegh! If I continue to give money only to the first one, the second might argue, fight with her or fight with me. It's no good to cause trouble over this."

H: But he started it when he was *first* married?

W: Yeah, the first wife.

H: All right. Let's ask him about when it all started. [*Weiyu and Imano engage in heavy conversation. Meanwhile, H. remarks to S.*] There is a really big difference between them: Imano uses his hands in a feminine style.

S: Yeah. I could see that.

H: Watch Weiyu, he doesn't use his hands to gesture the way that Imano does. You'll see it [style of mannerism] later on this afternoon when we talk with Penjukwi.*

W: [*Tugs at H.'s shirt.*] When they were first together, he wanted to butter her up—his first woman. He showed his money to her saying, "Look, look, I've got something here. You must hold onto this really good." Imano thought to himself, "I've got to give her something or she won't want me and will run away with another man." So he kind of tricked her [to get sex and to keep her]. And then she concentrated on the great pot of money he'd given her. So she really stuck close to him.

I: [*Breaks in.*] There, that's it. True, true.

W: He still thinks this way. He hasn't changed.

H: [*To S.*] This is really interesting. . . . It started when he was courting his first wife, who [formerly] was Nilutwo's fiancée. Nilutwo was trying to get rid of her and give her to him.† Imano *wanted* to marry her. He really wanted to marry her. He thought the best way to be sure that she would say yes—meaning, this is not the best way typical men[22] do—was to show her his money and say, "Look, here's what I've got; this is what I'll give you." And he gave it to her. And ever since, she's just been a great wife. Not great in that they have not fought, but—[right for him]. Still, he was afraid that if he didn't share, she would spit on him and go to another guy. This is unusual in several ways. First, rather than just saying, "You are a piece of my property; we're going to be married and that's it," he felt compelled to want her to *desire*

*See chapter 6.
†Nilutwo was Imano's classifactory clan brother, that is, his true father's brothers' son, making them parallel cousins, a close relationship.

him, to be attached to him. He did not just force her. That would be a major difference in masculinity compared to other men. Then—as almost no other man would do—when he married the second wife, he anticipated jealousy between the two wives *over money.* So he simply sat them down and said, "I'm going to divide up my money equally and give it to both of you." Whereas most men would hang onto it and dole it out as needed.

S: Our word—not theirs—he would be "considerate." In our society, although that [above] would not be considered nonmasculine, the phallic man is partly defined by the fact that he doesn't give a shit about other people. [*Pause.*] Having two wives is unusual?

H: No.

S: Why did he want to?

H: That's a good question; let's ask him that.

S: He loves intercourse?

H: Right. . . . [*To Imano.*] Dr. S. wants to ask you something.

W: Uh-huh.

H: Why does Imano want two wives? Why wasn't he worried at all about their having arguments?

W: [*W. and I. talk.*] He can tell you why [*smile in voice*]. Here's what he says, "If you have only one wife and she gets pregnant and has a baby, then, if you screw her, you'll harm the baby [a belief that reinforces the postpartum taboo]. Your child will be skin-and-bones and look like a flying fox [a bat: skinny, with misshapen black face, pushed-in nose, big teeth: the epitome of an ugly, nighttime creature: the dreaded ghost itself].

I: Yeah.

W: So he married both. When one has a baby, he can still screw the other. He can still screw the other one. And also, he thinks, "This one wife works hard making gardens, while the other, the second wife, is lazy."

H: [*Back to S.*] A common description and an honest answer. The post-partum custom is that when you've got a wife and screw her while she's breast-feeding, you will spoil the baby, because it's taboo. . . . It will die, it will be sickly, etc. You've got two years or more of taboo. Who are you going to screw? So: "I took another wife." And that's correct, because he really does *love* . . . heterosexual screwing.

S: Is it all right to move into that area?

H: Sure.

S: Does he do it *well,* by his standards? Does he do it well by each wife's standards? "Well" would include: hard enough (I presume);

and I don't know what else—foreplay may or may not be a part of it—you just climb on and screw and get off? Then I presume one of the criteria for the women is that it lasts long enough, etc. He's a soft man with a hard cock.

H: But he's a hard cock; that's the description [in previous work] he gives us.

S: But what is the wives' version?

H: We haven't talked about the second wife, only the first. (It would require a whole lot more work; I won't get into that.) I know the answer for the first wife: she loves screwing, and he loves screwing, and they enjoy it together even after they've had an argument, which is part of it . . . and . . .

S: What do you mean part of it? It is a turn-on?

H: I think it *is.* I think that's part of it but not the only part. He . . . says he is able, unlike some men [e.g., Weiyu]—for instance—to postpone ejaculating long enough that his wife can have an orgasm. He does that consciously because she asked him to.

S: He has no trouble doing it?

H: He doesn't seem to; most of the time he can, and he seems to enjoy prolonging it. He has made a point of telling us, many times, that when they were first married, they would screw two or three times *a day*—which is unheard of . . . *

S: Is it?

H: Yeah.

S: Why is he concerned with her pleasure? Is that typical?

H: No. It's extremely deviant.

S: Is that "considerate" again?

H: Oh, yes—it's extremely deviant.

S: Are women concerned with the men's pleasure?

H: By the men's definition.

S: But is her definition that she just spread her legs, or . . .

H: By just spreading her legs, just by allowing herself to be screwed—that is "concern" with the men's pleasure.

S: Well, he seems "concerned" in a more artistic way. Like some western men . . .

H: Oh, yes, by far. That's one of the reasons I like him. His concept (not in all of its totalities) of being with his wife is the closest thing to a relatively considerate heterosexual relationship in our culture, with give-and-take between the husband and wife, during

---

*For Sambia men, women's bodies, especially secretions, are so polluting that the danger hems in the pleasure.

sex, and where they are also. . . . He says that they talk while making love . . . about . . . making gardens, about the kids and stuff. Sometimes about erotic things.

S: At the moment they are screwing, they are talking about the gardens? [*Impressed.*]

H: No—after sex.

S: You've had the impression in the past from the men that the women don't have orgasms.

H: Yeah.

S: You seem to have a totally different body of data now.

H: That's right, because it's deeper and better. In the past I confined myself to several guys only. Now I sample different types of males.*

S: Were the first guys just holding something back from you?

H: No, no. It just happens that my two best adult informants [Tali and Weiyu] just don't recognize—in quotes—orgasms in their wives or any women. They don't; they're just phallic and that's what you'd expect.

S: Are they phallic and they also come much too soon?

H: They come very quickly, like in his [*points to Weiyu*] case. He says all the time that his wife gripes about it—that he just can't hold it, that it's just like that [*snaps fingers*].

S: Is that the cultural standard for a masculine man?

H: That's normal.

S: It's not premature ejaculation?

H: No, it's not. I checked that out, though there are a couple of men I have heard of on that level. But T. and W. do not think themselves premature ejaculators, even though they get it in and within 60 seconds [sometimes longer] they can have an ejaculation.

S: That's it [*confidently*]: "healthy attribute of a man." When they sit around talking to each other, no man who does that feels he has anything wrong with him.

H: Oh, no. The faster you get in and out, the better you are.

S: You mean, in that way you don't get poisoned?

H: Right.

S: Yet Imano's not concerned that he's in there longer than any other man in the hamlet?

---

*Studying aberrant men like Imano was important in this way. What I learned from their exceptionality gave me clues in looking again at normative men. The range of normative variation in Sambia society is thereby clearer. (I shall describe this variance elsewhere.) Warning to ethnographers: don't exclude anyone—especially deviants—from your field of study. Normative isn't all. [S. I suspect that when it comes to psychologic things—motivated behavior, affects, fantasies, etc.—no *individual* is normative, except to gross inspection. Everyone is odd around the edges.]

H: Right.

S: That means he's not concerned that what the other men call poison—intercourse—he's perfectly happy to have.

H: Right.

S: I mean: he's not worried about poison?

H: No, it's not that simple. He's also . . . he does all the ritual procedures to cleanse himself.

S: He's worried about it [*pause*], but he's not *that* worried about it?

H: He's worried about it but he still does it. Furthermore, take a for instance: the usual procedure is every time you have an ejaculation, you should go into the forest and drink milk-sap [e.g., from certain trees].

S: He does that?

H: Not always. So that's an indicator he doesn't have as much anxiety as you would expect for someone with that duration and quality of sex with his wife.

S: The hypothesis would be that he doesn't have that much anxiety because he doesn't have to prove that much about his masculinity, maleness.

H: As culturally defined and subjectively defined. That's correct. [*To Imano.*] I want to ask you about your other [second] wife. Is she happy when you put your cock inside of her? [*The two men whisper about sex and happiness.*]

W: [*Quickly.*] She'e also happy about it.

H: What is she happy about?

W: He says, "Happy with my penis" [*chuckle*]. It's big enough for her.

H: Because of its strength or its heat?

W: Its heat and [a word here I can't figure out] of it too. It goes deep inside, and her pathway [vagina] is completely filled. Big and long, up to here. She feels it, feels its sweetness; that is enough for an *imbimboogu* [orgasm]. She feels sweet. She says to him: "You can't pull it out too fast." . . . When she says that, he just lets it stay in.

H: And he, too, feels happy about letting it stay inside?

W: Yeah, yeah. That's it.

I: Happy, that's all. . . . [*to H.*]

W: [*Chucke.*] That's how it is.

I: [*Chuckle.*] True, that's the truth. [*Imano interjects in Sambia, with an expressive voice.*] Joy. . . . [*and then goes* "whoosh," *as if to say,* "It is so pleasurable, you almost want to cry."]

H: That's true, huh?

I: That's the truth [*a little giggle*].*

H: [*To S.*] I ask him, how is your sex life with your second wife, and he says, "She likes my cock, it's hard, it's big, it's enough for her. I put it inside, really inside, she likes it, she likes me to stay inside." And I asked him, "Do you keep it inside?" And he said, "Yes, I keep it inside." And I said, "Does she have an orgasm?" And he replied, "Yes." And he said, "Yes;" and I said, "Does she usually have an orgasm?" And he said "Yes;" and then I said, "How do you feel about being inside her that long?" And he said, "I like it." And then you saw what the last response was—"I enjoy being inside of her long enough for her to have an orgasm."

S: Is her orgasm a turn-on for him?

H: That's the question I've never asked.

S: Or is it just, "I'm glad that she could have an orgasm"?

H: When your wife has an orgasm, do you also feel bodily excitement? [When I say that, Weiyu, because he and I have worked on excitement, says *"kalumundereindapinu,"*† which here refers to the erotic. He uses feeling in his voice, and expressive gestures for what those feelings would be, to also indicate having sex. Imano cues to that and responds. They set up quick exchanges that are not just words, but involve gestures and sounds associated with excitement leading to orgasm. (Incidentally, Sambia men communicate this way between themselves, too.)]

W: That's just how it is. His wife feels an orgasm, and then she says to him [*voice speeds up*]: "You mustn't take it out." And he's thinking to himself, "I want to feel the same for myself" [*excitement in Weiyu's voice*]. *Ilaiyu* [verb for pleasure, joy, happiness]!

H: I don't mean just "happy," I'm talking about feeling more. Does *he* feel more pleasure in his penis when *his wife* has an orgasm?

W: [*Coughs, embarrassed?‡ Clears his throat.*] You're asking does he feel happy?

H and W: [*together.*] . . . about his wife's orgasm.

W: Imano says, "It's very good to get an orgasm. She must get an orgasm too. [The next phrase—*hap i dia i stap*—is very hard to

---

*How very different from T. and W. (and many other men) is the tone of this talk. Despite all the sex talk, there is no dirty locker-room atmosphere. Another meaning of considerateness.

†*Kalu* is a polysemic word: as a noun, it means "liver" (body organ) associated with powerful feelings, just as we use the word "heart;" as a verb it means, sad, lonely, longing; in this construction it roughly means "liver get up," in sexual excitement. (See also chapters 5 and 6.)

‡Weiyu, my phallic friend, is unused to such a question; more important—here I speculate—he is embarrassed by such an alien thought.

translate. It connotes being overcome with the experience of *ilaiyu*, too impassioned, half-faint, spent. *I stap* means "is happening, is being;" so the whole phrase suggests "something that leaves her happily spent."] Then I'll shoot her again, more and more, and continue it more until she's finally exhausted."

H: [*To S.*] I hadn't thought of it, but it makes sense that it's a turn-on for him when his wife has orgasms. When the wife does so, he gets more excited. "When she has her orgasm, I want her to be spent and I can screw her more, and that makes me more excited. And then I want to screw her more and again and again." Now, see, that's just so peculiar. [*To W.*] You've heard about Imano's way; it is very much his own, huh?

W: Yeah. When he was talking, my thoughts went to my wife. My woman, does she get that kind of feeling? And he's talking about that, huh?

H: But you don't help your woman to have orgasm?

W: [Interesting quality in his voice, as if defending himself against the thought that he would be the kind of—gentle—man who would want to give his wife pleasure.] I don't think about *her* having to feel that. No, I don't feel like that.

H: When you shoot your water, do you want to screw her more?

W: [*Emphatic*] Uh-uh! No. [*Then—ambivalent.*] When the cock is loose, when I've done it, it's [sex] done. A little later, when it's tight again, [*excitement in voice and he snaps fingers*] I want to put it in and lay her back [get her worked up, and then after it's done, she'll just lay back].

H: [*Pause. To S.*] I asked Weiyu, since I hadn't before, "How do you feel about what Imano said?" He said, "I don't ever think about my wife's orgasms. That's the way he [Imano] is." I said, "Would you think about screwing her again after you've come?" He said, "No, I just pull it out." What he'll do (he has told me before) is ask her to hold his penis for a couple of minutes. That's apparently enough to get him excited again. Then he'll put it in again. And that enables her to get turned-on again, enough that the second time she may have an orgasm. [Though this isn't clear from Weiyu: he's not sure himself.] But he's not thinking about her pleasure when he does that, he's thinking about him coming again. That's a fundamental difference between him and Imano. These data are believable, I couldn't pick just anyone here off the road and ask those questions and get reliable answers. But if he (W.) says that, I believe it, because I've known him a couple of years.

I talk with him so much that when he gives me an answer, I can know if it's real. I feel it.

S: There's no reason why he should be superficial with you?

H: Right. Yet these are subjects that are normally difficult to talk about, and these are prudish guys.

S: But not in here; they're just not prudish.

H: Because it's an artificial environment. So, there you are. It's a great "natural" difference between the two of them.

S: I think you know the answer: if you ask Imano how many men are like him [*pause*] . . .

H: His answer is that he's one-of-a-kind; there's no one like him. Everyone else says the same about him; and remember he falls into the category of [*aambei-wutnyi*] gentle man. In this hamlet, there are only two other men who could be said to be that.

S: His concern for his wife is part of the proof that identifies him with that diagnostic category?

H: Yeah. It would be, but the others don't know these erotic details [and still they categorize him thus].

S: He's identifying with the woman (we would say), and the men somehow know that, even if they don't have the words?

H: Exactly. [Here I spontaneously shift topics. In previous sessions, Imano had alluded to having erections in relation to drinking tree-sap. It had not been clear to me when or why he got hard, and I wanted to clarify this. Since Sambia intensely focus on semen, in and out of sexual intercourse, and because men identify milk-sap with semen, I wanted to be sure that Imano's sensuous feelings were not fetishism: that the tree-sap, in itself, did not arouse him. (Information on semen and tree-sap in other males made such fetishism a possibility in Imano too.) So this conversation provided an opportunity for me to explore Imano's erections in this regard.] [*To Weiyu*]. I want to ask Imano about the custom of drinking milk-sap from the trees. The last time we talked, we discussed how he would go to the trees and drink their sap to replace his semen [as all men do]. First, he drinks the milk of a tree; afterwards he goes to his house and at night, when he remembers he drank the tree-sap in the afternoon, his penis is tight. What makes his penis tight then? That he drank the milk-sap, or that he is thinking of his woman?

W: [*Mid-sentence.*] . . . And he goes and drinks tree milk-sap and after that he comes and sleeps. Then he thinks to himself "Oh, I've gone and drunk the tree-sap and my water [semen] has gone to my woman. That water went into her vagina, and so I went and drank the tree-sap. Then, when he thinks this, his thinking goes to his mother [euphemism for penis] [S: *!!*] and it just gets up [erection]. And then, when he thinks that, his thoughts go to her [wife] and—

H: [*Cutting in.*] He goes to—

W: He wants to touch her [get her aroused].

H: [*Echoing Weiyu.*] He goes and wants to touch her, huh? Does he know what causes his erection?

W: Yeah, yeah. It doesn't get erect from nothing when he drinks [tree-sap]. He doesn't think of himself that he drank tree-sap and now he's got an erection. [I. thinks:] "After I've drunk the sap—did I drink it for nothing or what do I do then?" [*Weiyu whispers here, but then raises his voice to emphasize.*] "Oh, I screwed my wife's cunt and that's why I've gone and drunk it, huh?" And so he thinks this and his bugger [penis] gets tight.

H: And that's what he says just like that, huh?

W: Yeah. [*Imano agrees with W. at this point.*]

H: Now, at this time he knows that this [erection] is not simply from having to urinate* . . . . He's thinking that it's that he's seeing [fantasizing] himself drinking tree-sap—because he will later want to screw his wife. So then it gets up [he has an erection]?

W: Yeah, yeah.

H: This [erection] isn't from simply urinating?

W: Uh-uh, no, it's not from that.

H: [*Quickly.*] Now suppose he doesn't have his wife available to screw? What does he do then?

W: If he has an erection? But his wife isn't there, huh? [*Imano adds something.*]

H: That's right: she's not there or it's forbidden because she's menstruating or something.

W: Yeah, it's taboo or because his wife has a baby [postpartum taboo].

H: Yeah. [*W. turns to I. and asks him; they talk for a minute and a half. During this talking, I. clarifies what he does when his wife has a baby, is breast-feeding or otherwise caring for a baby.*]

W: He says that; "Yeah, I'm married to two women all right, and so I do that kind of thing. . . . When a baby stops me [prevents him from having sexual access to wife] and my penis is tight, then I

---

*Sambia men associate morning erections with the need to urinate. They also use urinating as a way to get rid of unwanted erections.

think to myself, 'My penis is tight here, huh? Well, I can go to the other wife who has no baby. This one here, she's got a baby and it's not good that I harm it.'" So he thinks about going to the other wife. Then, when he thinks like that but he is still sleeping in his hut with the other one [with the baby], and he gets an erection, he simply stops it, lets it be. [I. motions showing how an imaginary erection can be placed underneath one's waistband so that the penis is strapped against the abdomen and it can't move around.] And then when he's sound asleep it goes away [erection is forgotten]. He sleeps like that. In the morning he gets up and thinks to himself. "Oh, last night my cock was tight and there's that other woman who has no baby." He takes her and [they go to the forest] and he shoves it inside.

H: Oh.

W: And that's how it goes. But here's another point: suppose both of them [wives] have babies but it is still tight. When this happens he knows to come and sleep here in your house.*

H: Oh. But suppose I'm not here, then what does he do?

W: [*W. turns and asks I. and they chat. Then W. quickly says:*] Well, the men's house is always here.

H: Oh, he sleeps in the men's house, huh? [*I. is improvising: if he does sleep in the clubhouse, it's rare: I've never seen him do it.*]

W: Yeah. [*I. talks to W.*]

W: Sometimes he just goes to sleep with lots of [kin-related] women, a lot of people who are all sleeping in the same house. When he does that, he's not going to think of it [sex]—and so he can sleep peacefully.

H: Oh.

W: Now, ooh, if he and his wife sleep [*raises his voice in amusement*] in their hut, he's not going to be sleeping very well. If he sleeps alone and his cock is very, very tight, he's not going to sleep well. His cock really spoils him, spoils him greatly [he's horny]: that's the way it can harm his baby [he'll be overcome by sexual desire and want to screw his wife, which will harm the baby].

H: Okay. Now when he's talking about "all the women," who is he really talking about? Old women?

W: Oh, any of the women, the old women and his sisters and his in-laws and [I. adds "in-laws" again] . . .

H: Suppose his penis is erect for no reason. Does he simply let it alone or does he go and urinate?

---

*Imano did this only a couple of times I remember. Others did it many times.

W: [*Asks I. They talk. W. turns back and says dolefully:*] He just about comes close to hammering [hitting] his own penis [*a small chuckle in his voice*]. If his penis stands up and simply stays erect, he goes and runs away to the bush, [to hunt], that's all.

H: Oh.

W: And now when the cold gets to it, it will become slack and go down.

H: He doesn't urinate then?

W: No, he doesn't do that.

H: All right, I understand. [*Then I. begins to talk about the fact that there is very little you can say at times like this (when he has an erection). H. adds:*] Oh, sorry, there's something else, another thing I wanted to ask [choppy as if remembering something important that he had forgotten]. I need to stop here and ask . . . when he's finished drinking tree-sap and then he goes back to his house and sleeps and he has thoughts of the milk-sap of the trees . . .

W: Uh-huh.

H: [*Continuing.*] His thought then, it [semen] can go to his woman. Now sometimes can he think of—

W: [*Butting in, very firm voice*] First, he can think of the tree-sap. He can think "Oh, this tree-sap . . . here I've screwed with my woman and I screw with my wife and so, because of that, I had to go and drink, huh? Her cunt is like this [the sense that while thinking about this, he has an image of his wife's vagina] and when he thinks of that, his penis gets up.

H: But I was wondering if he sometimes thinks about his wife's breasts?

W: [*Quickly turns and immediately asks I.*] That's it, it was like before when he was younger, he would think of her papayas [a joke, a metaphor for women's breasts] and then it would be tight without any other reason.

H: Yes, but at those times when would he drink tree-sap?

W: He says at those times he doesn't think about that. He thinks to himself, "Oh, I've sent my water to my wife and so now I'm replacing it [with tree-sap]."

H: And he can also think of his wife's cunt, huh?

W: Yeah, that's right.

H: All right.

W: When he was younger and he looked at her breasts, then he got hard like that. [*I. coaches Weiyu, listening to what he is saying in Pidgin, and then adding things, which W. immediately translates.*] When he holds them [breasts], his cock is simply tight. It is tight and he thinks about this. [I. means that when he looks at her breasts and gets aroused and thinks about screwing with her, this is the image he has when he's drinking the tree-sap; and that is *what the sap is for.* I.'s voice is so heavy here that I barely hear W. I.'s voice rises to a crescendo, and he keeps repeating "my young woman, young woman"—meaning before she had her first child. This experience most aroused him—seeing her breasts. His voice has a strange quality: insistent, excitable, an intense whisper. He seems different from his usual self, with a frenetic voice, saying over and over again: "She was in this virgin period" or "She was a virgin." This thought thrills him.[23]]

H: [*To W. and I. loudly.*] Okay.

W: Uh-huh.

H: [*To S.*] Well, I'm done. If there's anything you want to ask . . . .*

S: I don't know about the last couple of things—if you could just give me a couple of sentences (so I'd know what was going on).

H: We've been talking about heterosexuality, and we have worked on this aspect before: how he goes to the forest and drinks milk-sap. He's one of the people with whom I check out the experience of how the milk-sap drinking goes. [Cf. chapter 2.] He doesn't get a hard-on [while at the tree] and there is—what he does is he drinks the sap and that night, when he goes home and is just lay-ing down, he can daydream; he gets a hard-on but it's not just any hard-on—it's a "hard-on-[concerning] the milk-sap." You see, here is where I haven't got it right yet—the sap, you see, it's like getting an injection . . . of semen, and it's inside of you—so now you can screw [because] it's inside of you. It's when you get a hard-on you've got something to give, something to ejaculate; and [he's] thinking about the sap that has gone inside of him and is, literally, [believed to be waiting] in the area of his penis. He then thinks about his wife's vagina.

S: [*Interrupting.*] Well, what form does he think about it—not pic-tures?

H: I don't know.

S: [*Continuing.*] Maybe it is, I don't know.

H: Well, he is picturing it, I mean, that's the closest I've got.

S: (*Persisting.*) Picturing what? I mean, does he say he goes around picturing her standing there—in which case he would just be seeing pubic hair or picturing her legs apart, external lips, or the whole deal [*emphasis*]? That's a different thing.

*S. was a patient listener in these sessions, and he blended in so well that at times I forgot he didn't speak the language.

H: Yeah. I haven't asked him, you see I haven't asked him those specifics.

S: [*Continuing.*] Is he picturing her doing something or is he just seeing the anatomical parts protruding or something [*voice trails off*]?

H: Let me ask him. [*H. to I. and W.*] Sometimes at night after you've taken the tree . . . . sap and at this time he thinks of his wife's cunt, his cock gets tight.

W: Uh-huh.

H: [*Continuing.*] What kind of image of his wife's cunt does he have so that his cock gets tight?

W: [*Grunting.*] Uh-huh. [*He asks Imano.*]

H: [*To S.*] *Koontu youtnu* is the native category for daydreams or fantasy. It seems to be a close-enough equivalent to our concept. He says that he thinks about her cunt, about the surrounding area of the cunt [the word W. uses means edges or sides, suggesting the lips], and inside there is its heat. And when he thinks about that, then he gets hard.

H: Does he see a picture—or?

W: [*Asks I.*] Picture, Oh, yeah, picture, a picture.

H: Now does he see the sides and its [lips] . . . at that time is his wife standing up or does he see all of her or does he just see her thing [euphemism for the vagina]?

W: [*Quickly.*] Just her thing. He just sees it, he doesn't see her face.

H: Only that [vagina]? And does he see her pubic hair?

W: Yeah, yeah, that too.

H: [*Being sure.*] Her pubic hair?

W: Yes, that.

H: And the lips of it?

W: Yes, and that too.

H: How is that—she doesn't have her grass skirt on?

W: Yeah, it's like he thinks about when they're having sex and "that's what she does to prepare for me—she makes it very easy for me," huh? That's how he thinks.

H: Yeah, now he won't think about this area here [*H. points to torso*]?

W: No, uh-uh.

H: Or about her face?

W: [*W. asks I.*] No, not that.

H: Just her thighs around the vagina, huh?

W: Yeah, he says he only thinks about that part. [*Pause.*] And also about her hotness [the heat of her vagina] . . .

H: [*To S.*] He says that he sees a—and this sounds right—he sees an image of the vagina, the lips of the vagina, the pubic hair, and the sides of the legs where they meet. He doesn't see the face, he doesn't see the lower part of the legs, he just sees that; he just sees that, sort of dislocated, and he thinks of the heat inside the vagina and that's what is exciting.

S: That's the turn-on?

H: Yeah.

S: What about the breasts?

H: I already asked him that. He says no.

S: They are not exciting?

H: [*Quickly.*] No, no. I'm sorry: breasts are exciting to him. They used to be more exciting for him when his wife's breasts were very full and tight.

S: Yeah.

H: He told me now—I asked him, "When you're getting this same image" (we were talking about when he drinks tree-sap) "Is this also [images of the breasts] exciting?" And he says, "No. Definitely not." It's only her cunt, it's not the breasts. In general, at other times, he is excited when they were full, tight breasts; whereas now, his wife is getting older.

S: Do women have—this is a gender question that applies to men and women—are women's breasts erotic to them [the women themselves]? All of them, sometimes; all of the time, some of the time?

H: [*Sigh*] Oh, boy!*

S: Do they want to be touched, kissed, fondled, or whatever on the breasts?

H: Oh, you see, I've never asked any of those questions [of I.]. I know subliminally what I think some of the answers would be, and they would go: 'Oh, women don't want to be, they don't want to have their breasts touched. It's off-limits, taboo. But you see the question is: what does that mean? It's a turn-on, subliminally: women's breasts are exciting by being hidden. [*To W.*] Are you sure this [statement] concerns only the two of you? Do you think that your women really want you to try to hold their breasts when you're screwing with them? Would your wife sometimes take your hand and put it on her breasts?

W: Uh-uh, no. [*Ambivalent.*] Yeah, a whoring woman would do that.

---

*Do you agree with me that S.'s question seems simple but is difficult to answer without extensive and intensive data? If not, how would you answer for American women? How would ethnographers answer for other societies? Sometimes, like here, S. posed questions that require years to answer.

H: Yeah, but what about your own woman?

I: He means our own [women].

W: No, not at all. Yours, yes. [W. implies white women enjoy their breasts being fondled. How does he have that fantasy?]

W: About me, holding it, like that, huh? Yeah, if you do that she can go "Aye" [raises his voice, feigning a smile and hostility]. "Why are you holding it like that? What are you holding me for? Do you want to screw that you're doing that or what?" And she says that to me, then I would. . . . [I. is distracted and W. scolds him.] Aye, cousin, you listen to this. [Then W. talks to I., telling him to pay attention.]

I: I'm listening, I'm listening, why are you saying that to me?

W: [Speaking for him.] "I'm listening!" You are thinking.

H: [Very quickly.] What's he thinking, what's he thinking about?

W: [Talking for himself without checking it out with I.] He's just think-ing about what he can say next, getting ready his answers if we ask him. That's what he's thinking.

H: Is that what he's really thinking? [To W.] Right now is he day-dreaming?

W: [W. asks I.] Yeah, yeah. [Somewhat confused.] Oh, he was day-dreaming.

S: Let's get it! We can go to the other thing some other time. How come, right here in front of us?

H: Because we were talking about it and he was thinking "What would I say . . . ." [I. then says, "I'm listening to them."]

S: "What would I say" if what?

H: "If they asked me, what would I say if they asked me"—

S: "If they asked me, what would I say"?

H: [Halting. Saying to W.] Ask him now, right now, what's he having a fantasy about? [W. & I. exchange for a moment.]

W: He was thinking about his wife's breasts.

H: His wife's breasts?

W: Yeah. "When I hold them my wife says to me 'Aye!' [in the playful sense, stop that!]. My wife says that to me . . . [but it's] just play—giving me a line: 'why are you holding on to me? You're just fooling me'" [seductive, a little hostility, the sense of an am-orous game].

H: Ohhhh.

W: [Continuing.] "Aye, you're just playing, fooling me!"

H: Playing around?

W: Yeah. He's just [wanting to be] fooling around and she's [feign-ing] disinterest about him trying to hold her hands . . .

H: Well what's the fooling storyline in it?

W: "You mustn't hold [amorously] me."

H: Is it that she really feels sweet about it?

W: Yeah, feels sweet, but she doesn't want him to know that she feels sweet about it, so that 's how she acts. Yeah, yeah, she [pretends] not to look and understand, not to understand it. And when she says that, you must go hold her hand and when you do, then, after that [she'll say]: "Do you want the two of us to screw?" [*Said in a light voice, as if entirely able to take the woman's line in this little drama.*] So you say, "Yes," you say it like that, and so you do it. That's what he's [I.] talking about, that's what he's picturing.

H: [*To W.*] Okay, we're just chatting. We're really happy to be talking, just talking about our work. All right. Next time, when we're working, we can go back and talk a bit longer about what you were telling us about your fantasy concerning your wife's breasts.

DISCUSSION

H: [*Echoing W.*] Oh, that's what he's thinking huh? [*To S.*] Did you get that?

S: No. I know it's about breasts and loving them or whatever it is.

H: [*Chuckle.*] He was thinking about his wife's breasts and [what happens] when they're together; this is different from what happens with Weiyu.

S: Yeah.

H: When they're together he grabs hold of his wife's breasts.

S: [*Continuing.*] Even though it's not as exciting?

H: As exciting.

S: Yeah.

H: But he holds on to her and she goes into this number where she says, "Oh, stop doing that." [*In the background Weiyu is laughing at my caricature.*] And he's getting more and more excited as she does that. And the more she does that, the more she [subliminally communicates she] wants it. The term he uses is, "She's faking at it." [*In the background I. is chuckling to himself and then begins his nervous cough.*]

S: Faking—not wanting it.

H: She's faking that she wants it. [H: That's a slip: faking that she *doesn't* want it.] And I. knows that she's faking, and she knows that I. knows that, and that's part of the game.

S: Wait a minute. She is faking that she wants him to stroke her breasts and she really doesn't want him? [H: S.'s confusion is my fault. I got it backwards.]

H: She really wants him, but she doesn't want him to know.

S: Oh, all right, it wasn't clear. She's faking *not* wanting it?

H: [*Echoing*]—Not wanting it.

S: But in fact she is getting more and more excited.

H: She does want it. Her breasts are erotic.

S: Good. And you didn't know that?

H: No, no. I did know that, but not in this way.

S: What do you mean: in what way *did* you know it?

H: I never asked him that question: "Do you . . .

S: Well, what did you know?

H: I knew that her breasts were erotic.

S: For her.

H: For him.

S: Now I'm asking . . .

H: Right. I didn't know that her breasts were erotic for *her*. I did not know that, that's right.

S: Or for anybody in this society, you didn't know that?

H: Not in this way. I knew that—

S: Well in what way did you?

H: I knew that they were erotic because they're being hidden and because—

S: No, I meant that . . . you touch them and it feels more like a "hard-on-as-you-touch-it," and feels more.

H: Right, I didn't know that.*

S: Okay. Now you still don't know if it's for anybody else except his wife.† So your next question would be, is it [that way for] two women? And if it's two women instead of one, then you begin to wonder if there aren't other women.

H: [*Quietly.*] Yeah, uh-huh.

S: So she really likes it . . .

H: Yeah, that's right. And so as she is pretending to resist him touching her breasts and getting a little bit more excited—

S: And he's getting more excited as she's excited.

H: More excited; and he has a hard-on now she's resisting him, then he holds on to her hand and says to her, "Let's screw."

---

*Here is another example of where S. helped me—through his interrogation—to clarify what I do *not* know, in order that I can ask new questions. Not only did he ask people new questions through me, but he asked me questions that brought new awareness to me, and hence new interpretations of previous data.

†As reported by her *husband*.

S: They, this couple, have foreplay.

H: [*Pause.*] Yeah.

S: That's foreplay.

H: [*Thinking and then surprised thinking it.*] That's foreplay.

S: They have foreplay and you don't know if there are other people who have foreplay.

H: No, I don't.*

S: Well, I'm also talking methodology now. It takes two of us to get this information.

H: Yeah. And that is foreplay; you see I knew that, and yet I really didn't know it, until you said, "That is foreplay." I know it [holds] for myself but I didn't think of *that* as foreplay.

S: But I'm talking about something else at the same time. I'm talking about you and me doing research and the advantage of the two of us doing it.

H: Exactly. Because you think of questions that fill out the things that are obvious, and what *you* get, you see, is what he just told *me*. What I couldn't have done was that. I asked him, "What happens when you get a hard-on and your wife has got a baby or she's not there?" [He said:] "Well, I take my cock and put it underneath the waist-bandoleers and go to sleep. In the morning I go to my [other] wife and screw her." And then I said, "What happens if you can't do that, what happens if both of them have got babies and you can't [screw them]?" And then he said, "I will go and sleep with the women." And then I said, "What do you mean by that?" And he says, "I go and sleep with the women and I don't think about it." And I said, "What women?" And he said, "My sisters."

S: So you mean he leaves his own house?

H: His own house.

S: [*Continuing.*] Because he's got a high level of horniness and he gets rid of it by [being near] forbidden—totally forbidden . . . women who are most likely to dampen his sexual excitement because he just wouldn't be excited by their breasts. They're his cure, they're his hot-cold showers.

H: Right. And that's another thing he says. "Well, sometimes I go to the men's house or sometimes I'll go and sleep with the women, namely my sisters, etc." Now that seems to me probably a normal thing to do although . . .

---

*Now after other field trips, I think Imano's kind of foreplay *is* unusual and few other couples do it this way.

S: You mean "normative"?

H: Well, certainly normative to do; it's something most men *could* do and probably don't do very frequently. I mean I need to find out about that.

S: Need to find out if he's the one that invented that technique and nobody else does it or have others done it? That's what you want to find out? Now this question you may not and shouldn't ask, and that is, does he ever want to put his hand on his cock when it's tight.

H: Now I know the answer to that. He told me and this surprised me. He told me that he would sometimes put his hand on his cock or in the area of his cock, and he said it in such a way as if to suggest that he is not masturbating but doing something similar to that. But anyway, that's the sense of it.

S: But the hand on the cock is not eventually going to start moving?

H: Right. It's going to in some way, perhaps, help him get rid of his need. . . . [*Weiyu, Imano, and I make a couple of grunts to each other without saying anything, to acknowledge each other's presence. And I say to W. and I.:*] He's [S.] pleased to be talking with you.

S: One question. In this society watching women nursing seems to be a turn-on. Now I'm not saying that idea is wrong. I'm just saying I have a feeling that there's something more about that, because I've seen women sitting around here nursing all day long. And it's not appearing to me to be something that they are hiding particularly; or as if the men are going to peek-a-boo, like if a naked girl walked down the streets in Los Angeles. So what's the story on that with him?

H: We've already gone over this: it's definitely erotic. It's a turn-on for him to watch his wife's breasts, so he leaves the house or she figures out ways to hide from him sometimes.

S: Well, what about the women sitting around [he sees] from time to time nursing?

H: I've been thinking about that.

S: [*Cutting in.*] What happens with that?

H: I've never really thought about it; but the more I do, the answer is obvious. When we were there the other night in that house—

S: [*Inserting.*] She covered up . . .

H: She covered up.*

_____

*Before a healing ceremony, in someone's house, we were in a crowd where several women were nursing, one of these being Imano's first wife.

S: [*Adding.*] Sort of, but she wasn't breaking her ass to do it.

H: Yeah . . . I saw her the other afternoon—you'd have to . . .

S: [*Emphatic.*] I've seen women breast-feeding. I've been taking pictures of women breast-feeding. They're doing this whole "big thing" with these cute little babies just tugging away.

H: Let me give you the possibilities as they come to me as flashes. Number one: it's okay to breast-feed with your brothers and fathers sitting around. It's not going to be a turn-on to them. Second possibility: you know it's a turn-on and you're out in public doing that, and you *are* turning men on by doing it.

S: I can't believe that other women would let you do that.

H: Why not?

S: That the women would let you turn on the men that grossly? I mean hard-on turn-on? If that's true, then there's a whole other piece of the culture I don't know about.

H: It doesn't sound right to me either, but I can think of some of the contingencies. Maybe there's no men around. Maybe there's no men who would stand around and stare at him. [H: Slip, it should have been *her*].

S: Yesterday.

H: Yesterday?

S: At that *mumu*, there was a mob of men; as to whether they are all brothers or not [I don't know], but they couldn't have all been.

H: Yesterday; but you see I can't answer that either.

S: Is it that you only do it in a certain place? I'll give you an example.

H: [*Butting in.*] Oh, that's it, that's it exactly, that's part of the *context* factor. It means different things if you're doing it in the shopping center and different when you're doing it in the home of a man. There's going to be a couple of men sitting down there who have got their attention freed and who can watch you do this. And if there is just casual conversation you can get turned on just thinking about it, but they [women] can't give you the signals or anyway any overt signals.

S: Let's see if I've got it right. I'll translate it into our culture. A woman dressed up with, let's say, fetishistic shoes—high heels— it depends on [*chuckles to himself*] the season and fashion, with a feminine skirt in a living room, is with the men and the women after dinner. And a little bit of her thigh shows. Now the same woman, and the same people, the next day, are sitting around the swimming pool, and she's right up to her crotch with her bikini. Well, nobody's going to think [then that the thigh is erotic] though that's the same tissue. Have you got it? In other words, it's not the anatomy that's showing; and it would be a bit vague to say that it's even the situation. She is going to be sending physical signals about the skirt part of her and those signals are even better than—it's not ESP—it just happens to be her crossing her leg and moving around, and the fact that she is subtle about it makes it even more exciting. If she was gross about it, everybody would throw her out of the house. They would throw her out of their circle of friends. Is that what it is?

H: That's right, exactly, that's what it is. I never thought it out like that, but what you're saying is within certain contexts, that is— culturally defined situations—the act is subliminally loaded so that it becomes erotic.

S: Okay.

H: People are doing it. Even the word "act" is too vague. People are willing: they are willfully doing it—that is, they know what they're doing even if it is subliminal.

S: And you mean you were telling me that there isn't much about this in the anthropological literature?

H: [*Pause.*] Not in these terms, no.

S: Okay. Well I'll say no, no, it isn't true.

H: But it is true.

S: [*Still astonished, perseverating.*] But that anthropologists have never either known it or admitted it? Now that's a discovery. Why can't a discipline know that it can be done. Because therefore [if anthropology paid attention to such details] it can better describe what it is doing. It's the thing we keep talking about: what is it that you *can* measure. . . . And what are you failing to measure? And always tell people [e.g., your readers] that.

H: That is what some anthropologists said. Remember Victor Turner's argument: "We can't do what the psychoanalysts do." We can't penetrate the hoary caverns of the unconscious because we don't have the expertise.[24]

S: But I'm saying something different than that. It [listening as a psychoanalyst does] can't be done [by H.] even though you could have done it. But that's not what I was talking about. What I was saying was that even the anthropologist can't [in reality] do what the anthropologist could [in theory] do, because he'll never have enough time, because every question should lead to—well, [*gestures*]—there's the point of the pyramid: I don't know how far that pyramid spreads; not because you [anthropology] can't deal with unconscious processes, not because you're a biologist or some other discipline, just simply that every question should ask so many other questions. (But if you just stayed on the surface, it can't be done.) There isn't enough time in a lifetime. And if you could do it [describe subjectivity] with one person . . . you'd never know about the other one. That's why when you start using a word like culture or some other generalization, in some way it seems to me that you're saying it *can* be done. You do it with words that [you imagine] really encompass it all. And [then] you'll be satisfied with those words, those generalizations. What I'm saying is "No, it can't be done." Now if you really genuinely believe that, then you'd have a different anthropology.

H: Imano told us, "When I've done the thing with the tree-sap and I think about my wife's vagina, I get excited,"—and all you did was to ask him, "What do you think about then?" Such an obvious question. I should have asked that, and maybe in another six months I would have. He could respond so easily.

S: I'm just being a naturalist.

H: And it's an authentic daydream because he [Imano] was sitting there doing it just then, before us: that's an observation. It was here; he was doing it. And he was able to just say, "I see not her face, not her breasts, not her feet, but her vagina. And in seeing that I think about how inside it is hot." Now I could give you some more content which would make that more meaningful: how it's hot, and why that heat is important, and what's done with that heat, and how the heat is different from outside where your cock is and you put it inside, and stuff like that. But the central part is there. And it's still conscious and quite available. . . . And anthropologists don't ask for that data! It's just right . . . on the surface. But—it's too easy to say—it's taken me two and a half years of knowing these guys, the culture and the language and everything, to be able to sit here and just ask him that question, "What is that?" And they can just answer. It's too easy to say "no anthropologist"—there may be a few anthropologists who have my experience and my rapport and so forth. And yet *you* [not I] asked that question.

S: I think that they would ask if they wanted to be ethnographers in the best sense of the word.

H: But many were not really interested in sex and gender identity and eroticism . . .

S: But they haven't done it about *anything*. How many people have sat for two and a half years trying to establish a relationship of trust?

H: [*Yelling in background.*] Did you hear that?

S: What?

H: That loud yawning [*some muttering here between S. and H.*] Do you know what that was? That was our next subject [Kalutwo] who is giving us the signal that he is tired of waiting [i.e., two minutes]—which is typical of him. That's one of the ways that he can be overbearing. That's what I meant when I said he did that thing at the door one afternoon. The door was closed but not locked, and he comes up and interrupts a session when I am talking with somebody else. And he knows if he did that—if someone did that to him—he would be annoyed [but] he interrupts us. So he yelled out to us and says, "Open the door," and made a big deal out of it; a sarcastic joke about it, to be precise; the content was "Why are you locking me out"? And he said that in a funny but hostile way—

S: But he took some of the heat off by making a joke?

H: A joke, right. But the door was *unlocked* and he hadn't pushed it to see if it would open, which is typical of his way of dealing with me in this situation.

S: Talk about anthropology . . . and let them come in. That little insignificant detail is just as important as anything. Why should you just spend your time collecting lizard songs and ignore that? Who is to say that what he just did and your description of him is of any less importance to an anthropologist, that is, the study of the psychology of mankind, than anything else? Who arbitrarily decided that that grunting yawn was to be ignored by an anthropologist, that the words to the songs are more important? What is the theory of the difference that excludes that thinking and says it's not important or "just let psychoanalysts look for it"? But— it *isn't* psychoanalytic work at all.

H: And the next question is: how is it that I, sitting here, was aware what that [yawn] indicated [whereas other] anthropologists would have missed that?

S: Right. That's just a matter of personality, what's different about you. We're talking down anthropology! Cross-cultural psychology or something [as if these things were not] related to the practice of ethnography.

H: He's very anxious so I better start. If you saw him he can't (*too much static on tape*) . . .

S: Am I a shaman from overseas?

H: My hunch is really fearful, that there's going to be fireworks going on inside of him when he is in here talking with us.

CHAPTER NINE
Kalutwo: Portrait of a Misfit

H: Kalutwo is an unremarkable-looking Sambia man in his mid-thirties whom I have periodically interviewed over the past five years.[1] He was reared as, appears to be, and lives as a biologically normal male. People first mentioned him as a man with a troubled marital history, a minor shaman of a neighboring hamlet. But marital problems are common among Sambia, and while men make fun of him, K.'s peers still acknowledge him. My first impression of K. was that as an adult he spent too much time with the small initiates around the clubhouse.

I first began working with him in 1975 on his shamanic activities, while studying individual shamans. Even then I sensed he was odd; he was sheepish when discussing his healing activities, and he avoided his own history. Those interviews unearthed fragments of his childhood and marital background. Though K. was technically married four times, each marriage prematurely failed, and he was increasingly stigmatized for those failures. The elders and his peers, as usual in such matters, tried displacing the blame onto his wives and their greedy lovers, who supposedly stole the women away.* Later interviews (in 1979) showed that such views were rationalizations: K.'s unmanly avoidance of his wives drove them, one after another, into other men's huts. This perspective led me to reconstruct more carefully K.'s family background and childhood, which began looking bizarre. I finally became aware that K. not only feared women but still preferred erotic contacts with boys. Unlike other Sambia,[2] therefore,

---

*Despite the fact that the men recognized then, and even more so now, that none of their other peers had been given and had lost four wives, without consummating a marriage or having a child.

Kalutwo comes closest to being like a homosexual in the old sense of that western label.

In the late 1950s, well before pacification, Kalutwo was traditionally reared and initiated into the male cult. He still lives in that traditionalism, which has two aspects: he was initiated into the male cult, and he is a shaman. But some pieces of his developmental history and identity in these regards are deviant. As an initiate he was a bit small for his age. Later, he fought in several battles but stayed in the back lines, no fighter. (Nor, he admits, did he aspire to be one.) He is indifferent to hunting, which adds to setting him apart from other men. Instead, he prefers gardening, a respectable pursuit, but more for middle-aged men and, of course, women. Yet he is lazy, so his gardening is lackluster. More recently (since 1975), he began assisting in shamanic healing ceremonies, which he explains he does because they help people. His involvement in gardening and healing, though, has decreased in the past few years, a period in which he has become more glaringly deviant (being unmarried and childless). He is also sadder. Since his enthusiasm for other male activities and social relationships has also decreased, his peers disparage him even more.

Still, K. presents himself as tough, stiff-lipped, a traditionalist-type: old-fashioned masculinity. He wears a grass sporran, warrior bandoliers, and bark cape, the ancient insignias of a warrior. In a time of increasing social change, he has never worked on the coast and does not want to; nor does he speak Pidgin. (By contrast, half the adult male population has now served as contract plantation laborers on the coast; they sometimes wear western garb and many speak Pidgin.)[3] Besides dressing conservatively, K. is, like Imano, scrupulous in keeping his beard shaven and hair short-cropped (both traditional masculine features). He is physically plain, short, stockier than most Sambia men, and, some say, ugly by Sambia standards.* He is stiff, distant, and uncomfortable in public; is known by his peers to be secretive; dislikes children; is often quiet, emotionally flat, and brooding; though he is watched for his sharp tongue and sarcastic wit. These traits are aberrant but not out of the range of traditional Sambia masculinity.

Below this sullen masculine appearance, however, is greater aberrance. First, he has no manly achievements: no battle scars or heroic deeds, no impressive hunting record, no female conquests (not even

---

*Sambia consider his snub nose unattractive. He told me he felt both his parents found him ugly.

one) or wives with many babies, no oratorical skills or powerful ambitions. Kalutwo, now more than ever, is shiftless, going nowhere. Second, his marital status is abnormal: in a society anchored in its valuing marriage as the bedrock of adulthood, he is an unmarried, aging bachelor now and has no erotic relations with women. Third is his physiognomy: a face controlled but deeply creased with the heaviness of worry, suggesting that pieces of himself are at odds with each other, making him look older than his years. These are matched by body movements that are slow and slumped, as if he carried a weight alone. His eyes are sad. Yet, despite this agedness, one senses something oddly unfinished about his eyes, as if a boy lives imprisoned within. (We cannot publish our photographs of K. but believe most readers would see these qualities.) And finally, there are his personal ties: a few companions and supporters who see him as a social failure but not an outcast; no immediate family except for a close relationship with his only remaining blood sibling, a widowed older sister on whom he is dependent emotionally and for subsistence; and the boys who fellate him, a pleasure difficult to arrange as he ages and boys tire of him.

In short, K. imitates a tough warrior, but he cannot bring off this performance since his own needs undermine it. So he is disparaged as a rubbish man (*wusaatu*)—and not always behind his back—for, in Sambia society, merely seeming tough does not prevent a man from being stigmatized as a masculine failure when he cannot demonstrate masculine achievements.

How did I reach these impressions? Kalutwo did not figure in my initial research project, for that was focused on the initiations. Nor did I use him as an adult interpreter to retrospectively study men's past ritual experience. Though we met on the day I arrived in the Sambia Valley (November 1974), he was only a face in the crowd; I ignored him.[4]

Later, after interviewing him regarding shamanic healing (1975–1976), my attitude changed; but only in 1979, while actively talking with him for three months—mostly on erotism and his gender identity—did I try harder to understand him. Then, my empathic communication shifted greatly: Before, among the other men, I had chuckled when they gossiped behind his back about his disgraceful marital failures and rubbish ways. Seeing his face visibly contort with pain as he told me of his childhood, my unthinking disparaging diminished, and I changed, for I understood better his sadness and the helplessness he had endured alone.

The greatest methodologic problems in working with K. involved language. Like Imano, he speaks no Pidgin (though he can pick up fragments in conversation), so I had to use an interpreter. But unlike Imano, the presence of a third party (interpreter) has in part biased my data. Though K. was eager to work,[5] and such interest indicates trust, the translator's presence inhibited him. Our work would have been better, I feel, had we spoken alone. (See chapter 10.) To lessen this distortion, I have deployed the following procedures. When working on public matters (e.g., shamanic healing) where precise meanings counted, I used on different occasions one of two different interpreters. For private matters, K. himself chose Weiyu, my best translator, with whom he was cordial and felt pretty safe.[6] When possible, I cross-checked my own impressions by talking with him about the same matter at different times and from different angles. And finally, when it did not violate his confidentiality, I have sought corroboration from his friends and relatives, such as concerning his childhood circumstances. Using a translator is nonetheless a poor alternative to working alone with him, for, on the most sensitive matters and despite our rapport, K. still hides from me.[7] Here is a sketch of his masculine development.

By almost any indicator Kalutwo's childhood was unusual compared to other Sambia men. His parenting was, by Sambia standards, bizarre. Little is known about his mother, who died twenty years ago, except that she was a conscientious gardener who shunned crowds. She later avoided contact with all men. She had had three children by her first husband and was an older widow by the time Kalutwo arrived. Two of these children died, leaving an eldest sister (still alive) as her mother's chief companion. Later K.'s mother began an illicit liaison with a married man of a neighboring hamlet. (It is difficult, here, to reconstruct what such an affair entailed, but it may have involved only flirting and having had sexual intercourse several times secretly in the forest.) That man—Kalutwo's biologic father—subsequently rejected her, for reasons still not entirely clear, though he was married and already had adolescent children. This kind of rejection seldom occurs, since the product—a son—would normally be desired and claimed by the father, not left to become a fatherless bastard. (There is not even a category term in Sambia for "bastard"; that absence reflects the strong cultural basis for heterosexuality in marriage, and the wish for heirs, including adoptees.) So Sambia, who are prudish, prize virginity, expect faithfulness in marriage, and outwardly condemn promiscuity, came down hard on K.'s husbandless mother when her pregnancy became noticeable. She protested, pointing to the father, and appealed to him for marriage. In such circumstances, it would have normally been appropriate for the man to have taken K.'s mother as a second wife, but he did not do so. He disclaimed involvement or responsibility, an ominous rejection, for it labelled K.'s mother as immoral, and it meant she would have no economic support in rearing the boy. She was condemned by all, including even her brothers, who should have helped her. Instead they publicly insulted and beat her. She thus left to live in isolation with K. and another widow at a pig-herding house well removed from the hamlet.[8]

This history—of a liason that led to a morally offensive birth, humiliation, banishment, and bastardization—dominated K.'s childhood. He grew up without a father or acceptable substitute; his mother avoided all men. Unlike what should have occurred, none of his mother's brothers became substitute paternal figures. In fact, to worsen matters—and here we see how familial guilt and conflict were built into the child's environment—K. was told his father was dead, and the man's true identity was hidden from the boy. It became a family secret. Having been treated shabbily, his mother not only was bitter toward men, but withdrew from community life, including all contact with men. K., the "cause" of this unhappiness, and a male at that, became her only remaining joy (and not much of a one). Years later K. consistently described his mother to me as a whore.

K. participated, as prescribed, in all early initiations, but his response to them was strange. He feared and resisted first-stage initiation. He says, for example, that he faced the rituals wishing he had been born a *girl*, a desire unheard of from Sambia men. Though his first response to doing fellation was fear—that is how most boys respond as we have seen—within a day he was enjoying it, his pleasure made up of shame, a sense of danger—and sexual excitement. Despite his fear, K. had an erection with his *first* fellatio, he says, a remarkable response no other Sambia male has ever reported to me. He became an enthusiastic fellator for years. When, in puberty, he was initiated a bachelor, after initial embarrassment he eagerly switched to being fellated, and enjoyed copulating with boys and daydreaming about them. He did not stop using boys. He never has.

Some years later, K. was married. He was not active in the arrangements, though by custom and personal motivation he should have been enthusiastically interested. He would or could not consummate the marriage, fearing his wife sexually, even after months passed. Bored with the long wait, this wife left him (or was stolen by another man, depending on one's perspective). Three additional marriages over a period of years, went the same route, two of them to the same woman.

Only in one marriage did he have sex, and that by fellatio, at his wife's instigation.

In the mid 1970s I watched the next-to-last marriage fail. K. avoided the woman as he had his other wives; eventually an older man with other wives took her (this man was, in fact, Weiyu's only living biologic brother, much older than he was), and they married. He died in 1980. In 1981 K.'s agemates tried again to persuade him to remarry her, for his bachelorhood was an embarrassment. The couple tried; after some turmoil they had fellatio. However, by the time of my departure, the marriage ended miserably, the woman breaking away exasperated.

This one heterosexual experience so filled him with shame (a truly unmanly response for Sambia), that through a combination of self-inspired, pathetically comic circumstances, he was jailed, humiliating himself and his wife and thus rupturing the marriage. This outcome ensured bachelorhood for life.

Without question K. wants the trappings of marriage as a social institution—a wife, children (heirs), a hearth, and estate. It is just that sexually and psychologically, he cannot bear intimacy with a woman. It is not wild guessing to presume he does not like coitus (and—different from all other Sambia men—he dislikes discussing the subject).

Before 1979 I worked with K., trying mainly to glimpse the strands of his gender identity and erotic behavior. Then, as now, I thought of him as an unusual test case for understanding the origins and dynamics of Sambia masculinity. His aberrance—exclusive homosexual behavior in defiance of social norms—could shed light on the nature of Sambia heterosexuality in family and individual functioning. He was never at ease discussing his homoerotic behavior and history. Only with discomfort could he describe the type of boy who turned him on (small, unrowdy initiates with hairless upper lips).* It was harder for him to describe his erotic feelings about women, though he slurred them as dirty and dangerous. It was harder still for him to discuss feelings about me. But he could not bear discussion of— even allusions to—his rumored desire for prepubescent boys: he wanted to suck them.

I learned of this rumor only when two initiates mentioned (inde-

---

*This erotic choice in boys is common among bachelors (see Moondi, chapter 4). However, as K. gets older, he has to be less and less fussy about his fellators, whom he sometimes has to pay to service him (which is, in fact, the way in which this payment is culturally interpreted by all the parties). At thirty-five, disparaged and without the liveliness of the bachelors, K. now takes what he can get.

pendently of one another, on their own) that K. had tried to reverse fellatio roles with them. I doubted this. It is strongly tabooed but not unheard of for a married backsliding adult man to have a boy drink his semen. I know of several married bisexual men who enjoy boys, one of which cases I have substantiated.[9] But erotic reversal is fundamentally wrong for Sambia, or, to be exact, crazy.[10] No one performs fellatio on prepubescent boys; and for an adult to go for boys when they have only begun producing semen is to steal the semen society reserves for those boys, who can grow strong and manly only by its ingestion. For an adult to try and suck on a boy is simply shocking. So Kalutwo fiercely avoided this topic with me and, when I indirectly mentioned it, he fled.*

This chapter in many respects is about how K. communicated with me, how he wanted me. Not "wanted" in an erotic sense but rather a complex of needs he had—unmet by anyone else—that he came to recognize through me and then to need more. Needs like understanding, compassion, someone to talk to, someone to get sympathy from— approval that he was socially recognized and valuable because Gilbert spent hours talking with him. He needed all that plus the small amount I paid him,[11] and toward the end of our talking he could say it. But these needs were met only by revealing secrets and allowing me to ask questions that were sometimes unbearable for him. So he had profoundly ambivalent feelings toward me, far more so than that of Sakulambei (chapter 7). K. *resisted* me, then, not wanting the pain but wanting the other good things of our relationship.

FIRST SESSION: ALONE

The following text was my last session alone with Kalutwo, on July 1, before S. arrived. By persisting in asking K. about his sexual experience, I encountered more and more resistance. K. would agree to be interviewed, but when I reached into such subjects as his erotic fantasies about boys, he would clam up, turn cold, and refuse to talk. We had reached such an impasse on a couple of occasions before S. arrived. Yet K. persisted, always came back, wanting to talk again, even if he would not let me probe further. The following interview was the most intense of the final exchanges. I present it to orient the reader to the second interview, done jointly with S. five days later.

---

*The first time in 1979 I hinted at it, K. panicked, rose, and said he had to leave, which he did. (He had never done that before.) The second time, some weeks later, he left tensely, after a few minutes, when he tried to make it seem he was not running away from that subject. In subsequent years he never could discuss it.

It also provides a contrast in style to what it was like for S. to be with us.

HERDT: Last time you were telling us [H. and W.] about that first time, when you were a *kuwatni'u* [first-stage initiate, seven to eight years old], inside the cult-house, the men marked a bachelor who was to shoot [orally inseminate] you. That first time, you said, your penis was tight.

KALUTWO: [*Through W.*]* They'd put it in my mouth and I got hard.

H: What were you thinking?

K: I put it in my mouth and got hard. I put it in my mouth and it was hard.

H: Yeah. And what were you feeling? [*An effort to push through his wary perseverating.*]

K: That in the future, when my turn comes, I'll do this to boys. Later, when I'm big, they'll give me boys. Then I'll have a hard cock like now [that first time]. My cock back then was showing me what to expect later.

H: Did you have a fantasy when your cock was hard, when you were an initiate in the cult-house?

K: Yeah, that when I have a mature cock, I'll have erections just like the bachelors did when I sucked them.

H: But that first time [during the initiation, after the men told the boys about the need for boys to ingest semen], were you already thinking that later you would be able to shoot the initiates?

K: The big men told us about that: "Your turn will come. When you grow up you can screw the boys the same way the older youths had screwed you."

H: At that time was your penis tight—the first time when you held their penises,[†] or the first time they put their penises inside your mouth, or what?

K: [*Much tiredness in translator's voice.*] Oh, the first time that they put their penises in K.'s mouth. Then.

H: And when you held them [the bachelors' penises], was your own cock tight then?

K: No.

---

*From here on "K" indicates Weiyu translating K.'s Sambia into Pidgin. Throughout, Weiyu sounds tired, dragged out. K., on the other hand, is energetic, a bit harsh—a loud defensive, raspy whisper—as he talks of his early homosexual experiences, which he wishes to conceal from others outside the house.

†Since K. was using the plural—"Their penises, the men"—we followed him. But he did not fellate more than one youth at a time.

H: [*Perplexed. K. is giving contradictory accounts.*] Now, when they put their penises inside your mouth, what did you feel then?

K: The first time when it was new for me I felt pain on one side, inside my mouth.

H: [*Surprised.*] Pain? I think if you got some kind of pain like that, if you were to think about it, your penis wouldn't get tight. Is that true? [*Voice raises.*]

W. translates to K., and then there's a pause as K. looks for an answer. K.'s remark is the usual response men make about fellating the first few times, especially if the fellated didn't ejaculate quickly. Recall that K. was initiated small, around eight years old, so his mouth was small. And how rough or gentle was his first partner? In any case, what is striking was K.'s—the fellator's—erection.

K: [*Pause.*] The first time you do it, it can be painful. What got my cock hard was when their semen shoots in my mouth. [See Penjukwi, chapter 6.] It wasn't hard for nothing.

H: What did you feel?

K: [*W., translating, is indignant toward K.*] Well, what should I feel?* I swallowed it and I was hard, that's all.

H: [*Persists.*] What were you thinking?

K: The bachelor's semen went in and I was hard.

H: [*Irritated.*] What did you think or feel?

K: When we're done, I swallow it.

H: [*Impatient.*] Yeah, yeah, I know, but after you swallow the semen, and your cock is hard, what do you feel?

K: [*Pause.*] That in the future, I can get an erection just like any bachelor does. I'll touch the initiates, play with them. I'll be allowed.

---

*Affectless responses—"I felt nothing," or "What should I have felt"—were common for K., especially in our later work. They wore Weiyu out; they eventually wore me out. Sometimes they were said blankly, as if K. was genuinely unsure, as if he had never been taught what to feel or could not trust what he had felt. The more threatening the experiences being reported, though, the more he would turn blank, then cold. Sometimes, I think, K. consciously hid what he felt due to the translator's presence (discussed in the following). But at other times the dynamics were different. How can this difference be measured? It is true that Sambia seldom ask one another explicitly how they feel about the interior of selfhood. Even so, my observations and other men's comments about K.—in ordinary settings—confirm his low repertoire of emotional expression and his need to shy away from disclosures that reveal any of himself. On such occasions and in his relationship to me, he was more than passive; he also seemed genuinely to feel nothing, as if he were consciously empty. Interpretation: K. was subliminally aware that sometimes he must avoid probing (disclosure, insight) because it made him anxious; so he consciously resisted discussing some subjects (associated with repressed and denied conflictual feelings and their old traumas). Such interchanges in ethnographer/native awareness and their methodologic implications for transference/countertransference dynamics will be discussed further in chapters 10 and 11.

H: [*Cuts in.*] When you thought about that with a boy, did you picture their faces?

K: [*W.'s voice now is soft, sullen, downtrodden.*] I was small then. I don't remember well.

H: All the same, what made your cock erect? The cock doesn't erect by itself.

K: [*Immediately: without reflection.*] The semen goes in. That's all.

H: [*Persists.*] Well, what did you think about their semen that it made your cock hard? [*To W.*] I think he's got some thoughts about men's semen, but he's not thinking about those thoughts now.

K: My skin* isn't hard when the semen is inside. No. It's when he puts it in and the semen goes in. And that's what I'm thinking of.

H: Is it the hardness of their erections that makes yours hard?

K: When theirs is hard, then mine is [i.e., there is no other reason].†

H: Are you thinking of the whole appearance of the erection, or just its size, or the glans, or what?

K: No. It's just hard.

H: You were saying that each time they come in your mouth, you have an erection.

K: Yes, that's how it was.

H: Does it make any difference if it's a big penis or a small penis?

K: The men around here—it's small. It's [penises] small.

H: [*Puzzled.*] Huh?

K: I don't stay erect all the time, only sometimes.

H: Huh? I wasn't talking about you; I was talking about the bachelors.

K: Oh, I see.‡ The bachelors all have very, very big cocks: they become very big.

H: [*Impatient.*] I know; I know about them. You don't understand, huh [*to both W. and K.*]?

---

*K. nearly always uses euphemisms for body anatomy and fluids, more than other men. A sign of his greater prudishness?

†S: Resistance. Such resistance is fear, resentment, stubbornness. No one else was so closed off. Yet, as H. noted, K. kept returning for years, needing the love. Every psychiatrist is familiar with this opposition and the patience and insight required to hear it and then turn it to use. But what about the ethnographer without clinical skills? Does he or she record the resistance-soaked words as a true story or omit them as meaningless? Other informants, equally stiff, quit, some even the moment they are asked to help. The data they will never give may count as much as those of their garrulous colleagues. Why did K. persist? A good clinician can sometimes spring loose the information frozen in the resistance, freeing the person (patient or otherwise) and giving new dimensions to our understanding of our interpreter and of his or her culture.

‡It was not clear here if this misunderstanding was the interpreter's or Kalutwo's.

K: All the bachelors are the same. They get big, very big, like that, all of them, they get big.*

H: Uh-huh.

K: Every cock, they all do the same thing.

H: [*Disbelieving.*] They're all the same? You say they're all the same?

K: No. Only when I'm sucking them. It's the same with all of them. It happens every time.

H: [*Several further exchanges follow in the same vein; then:*] What was he thinking? There's something here that doesn't make sense to me.

K: No. There's nothing else [i.e., "That's all I have to say."] . . .

H: Me too. [*Pause; thinking hard.*] When your cock is hard, what do you feel? Happy? Angry? Do you complain? [I have the sense of butting up against a brick wall. I can't get any feeling out of him.]

K: I wasn't happy about that. [*Clears throat;* a sign, I came to know, that he is indignant.] [A moment's loss of recording here from broken tape.]

I'm really pushing K. here, belligerent. Rarely am I belligerent with Sambia or anyone else. Lest the reader become too critical of my sex questions, I offer two observations. First, no Sambia man I ever interviewed had such trouble saying why he got aroused. Second, K. himself had much less difficulty discussing screwing boys (though he resisted providing details of his excitement). K. was aberrant. I see now why I resisted translating these tapes:[†] such resistance (K.), such frustration (H.). My annoyance increases until it breaks through here and stymies the dialogue.

[*Kalutwo breaks in, louder than my voice, and talks for about thirty seconds. Weiyu asks him questions. This goes on for about a minute, and they halt. Then, to break the heaviness, I offer them tobacco. We all light up and continue.*]

H: Now, when was the first time—he was big, or a little older, or a little younger—that he started to think about [fantasize about] the faces of the initiates—about when he could start to screw them? Was that when he was a first- or second-stage initiate or what?

---

*S: Is he, in this obtuseness, playing at being the village idiot, and if so, is he conscious he is? Pseudostupidity is a technique the weak use to disarm the powerful, a masochistic gimmick that works best when it is so habitual that it is unconscious.

†More than with any other tapes, I labored over these for Kalutwo, feeling tired and bored.

[*W. translates to K., who clears his throat again. The tape is turned over and Weiyu says:*]

W: He was second-stage.

H: When did you begin to imagine the faces of the boys you could screw?

K: When the hair under my arms and the pubic hair began to grow.

H: What were you imagining about shooting the boys' mouths?

K: Nothing. It got erect, and I thought, "It gets erect."

H: [*Small voice.*] Oh. [*Pause.*] Did the bachelors ever touch your penis while screwing you?

W: [*Puzzled; doesn't know what I'm driving at: won't let himself dare to think it.*] About . . . what?

H: Did bachelors ever touch K.'s [fellator's] penis?

W: You mean, did he get hard if they touched him?

H: Yeah.

W: Do you really mean that?

H: Yeah [*nonchalant*]. I've heard that some do that sometimes. The bachelors.

W: When K. was an initiate?

H: Yeah, either younger or older.

K: [*Looks stunned, then appalled.*] No. Not at that time, no. [*Long pause. Silence.*]

I am approaching asking him, but not directly yet, about his desire as an adult to suck boys' penises. I hoped, if I touched on subjects close to that one, he would drop a hint, a signal that it was okay for me to ask about his sucking or touching boys' penises. His "No" here—with grunts of moral indignation—turns off that effort. So I search for a way to proceed. Impossible, on this dread subject, with a translator present.

H: Later, when you started to shoot the initiates . . . you knew what your penis was doing [what his erections meant]. You knew why your penis was erecting, huh? The penis got up at the [thought of] mouths of the initiates, didn't it?

K: Yeah. When older, it would get up; but I didn't know why.

H: [*Consternation.*] I'm not sure. I would like to know. You say that as a second-stage initiate your penis would get up and you didn't know why. You got an image [fantasy] of the faces of the initiates, and then your penis would get up for no reason. I'm thinking that when you got to be a bachelor you knew the reason why your penis got up.

K: Yeah, when I was a bachelor, yeah. My penis would get tight when sleeping* with the boys. Tight.

H: Oh, yeah. But before, you told us that you would get a fantasy about screwing the mouths of [fellators] boys.

K: I think about their mouths, and my penis gets tight. [*K. says this like a declaration. He starts talking to W. again. W. concludes:*]

W: Yeah. [*Quoting Kalutwo.*] The tree's way is to stand up. But you and me, us men, we're different. When we think about something, then the penis can get up, that's all.

H: That's it! That's what I'm saying. You and I have talked, on and on and on and on . . . and you say your penis just erects for no reason, at least when you were an initiate. And now what are you saying?

K: When I think about the mouth of the boys, then my penis gets tight.

H: Is that it?

K: [*Angry.*] That's it. That's all that happened. It [the penis] just gets up by itself. At that time [when you are an initiate], no, no, you won't think about anything. It just gets up by itself. [*W. chuckles.*]

W: It's just tight for no reason at that time [*chuckles again*].

K: Oh, you [W. and H.] you go back, you keep going back to where you had started talking before. [Apparent allusion to me asking him about his erections in his first fellatio experience, which he didn't like.] [*W. chuckles again.*] And so I think I'm going to go now. Tomorrow I'll come back. [Again, Kalutwo is saying, "I don't want to work on this; so if you do I'm going to leave. Beware, any time in the future, any time you bring this up, I won't talk about it, I'll leave."]

W: It's us, the two of us, we're strong . . . strong . . . strong . . . [Weiyu's stuttering here[†]].

K: I've told you I can only work when I have nothing else to do. Now I have to go; there are other things to do.

So K., who must be panic stricken, tells us that he wants to leave; he's had it. He's insulting to us in his affect, makes faces, but he doesn't just leave; that would be too rude. Weiyu jokes; he is terribly embarrassed. As a last resort I confront him with my reality assessment:

---

*This euphemism for screwing (common among Sambia) K. used frequently; but I have always felt that for him the literalness of sleeping-together-skin-contact mattered more than for most Sambia homoerotic partners.
†Whenever Weiyu becomes very nervous he stutters.

"Are you afraid of me; are you running away?" I am a bit surprised that he agrees almost spontaneously; so I repeat: "Is there any way I can help you feel better?" He tries to accept that plea, recognizing somehow that I am giving him back control; he must sense that beyond his defenses I really care. Finally he says he'll leave and come back later in the afternoon, when he'll feel better about working, a positive sign. I agree; then, another odd turn. After silence he asks me what my last question was, fifteen minutes ago. I am surprised; he really doesn't want to leave. I repeat the question in context without hostility and he begins to respond, but, taking his lead, I ask another question, and he draws back again. Then he insults us by asking us if we heard he said he wanted to leave! I say yes, unsmiling, and he departs, leaving us alone; it's bizarre. He's running because I was too close.

A side note, a difficult but important methodologic issue. K.—who started working for the money—is now fleeing because, perhaps, like Galako, my other failure,* I was too close to home, confronting K. too much with the conflicts he has so long avoided, rationalized, hidden from. He knows this; except that with K. there is a translator—which makes it doubly unbearable. He must sense it better than anyone but we two. No amount of money now can lure him to reveal more unless he decides to do that for himself and me. He surely won't. How does the tired rhetoric of participation-observation explain that? At this moment I am intensely aware that I am doing unconventional ethnography.

SECOND SESSION: WITH STOLLER

The session opens with the four of us—Kalutwo, Weiyu, S., and H.—seated at the table in my house. It is mid-afternoon, we are alone. We are all within reaching distance. Except for W., we all look at each other. W. is staring out the window when we begin, seemingly bored. But K. watches us, especially me, intensely, more searching than usual. We are looking at him. I feel awkward, somewhat embarrassed because of the previous impasse with K. and because I do not know where to begin. S. and I talk about K., orienting the interview. K.

*Galako is now [1979] a bachelor—Moondi's agemate—whom I studied for a few weeks. His intense attachment, as fellated, to a small boy was striking and unusual. I had tried to get him to discuss this for weeks, seeing him on a regular basis. (I interviewed him three years ago, too, while he was still an initiate.) He got scared and left, and would not be interviewed again. In 1981, frightened still, he refused to be interviewed but would sit and gab with me publicly. In 1988 he lived unmarried in a coastal town.

knows this, and the more we discuss him, the more he stares at us. S. is heard first, describing his impressions of K. at this moment.

S: [*Looking at K.*] . . . and it's among the saddest faces I've ever seen—on anyone* [*pause*]. But it's not just sad, because his eyes keep turning up to look at me, to wonder what's happening. But this man—but he's not—he hasn't been able to get rid of it. Some people, when they're chronically depressed, are doing other things to their depression—to schizify it . . . so that you don't quite feel its intensity. His brow looks like he's in *today's* pain. Not just old pain that he's gotten used to. Chronic depression can take so many forms. His has taken no other form except—and it isn't depression—it's sad, hurt . . .

H: [*cuts in*]—Despair—

S: —Despair: "My God, can't you help me? What are you going to do to me next"—in the sense of a kid who is going to get hit, pleading. And now he lowers his eyes to drink his coffee and it's: "Oh, Jesus, nothing good is going to happen." All of those [*lowers voice*] looks in a *terribly* sad face. And he doesn't change? That's not a hundred percent of the day?

H: That's a lot of it [*quietly*]. Not a hundred percent, but ninety percent.

S: All right. A hundred percent is a different condition.

H: It's ninety percent. Some days maybe seventy or eighty percent.

S: That it shifts has another whole psychiatric meaning than if it's permanent. *Almost* permanent is existentially different than if it were totally permanent. And it's worse to be able to *feel* the differences [*perhaps*] in a way, than to just have made it fixed unchangingly like a manic-depressive depression that lasts for three years. God knows that's awful, but you learn ways of living with that. This man isn't able to live with what's happening.

H: In a sense the pain is more conscious.

S: Yeah. He's really living the true pain, not a distorted version of it.

---

*S: By saying, "*It's* among the saddest faces I've . . . " I was subliminally expressing an impression different from, "*He's* among the saddest people I've . . . " or, "*His face* is among the saddest I've. . . . " The way I said it implied more starkly that Kalutwo does not, for all his anguish, offer himself to us. We do not so fully receive his pain that we want to reach out to help him. Instead, his pain also shows anger and withdrawal—a demand for help that contains refusal at the same time. He withholds his face from us. He is doomed, for he has doomed himself. Without insight, he will never find the script in his lifelong attitude (character structure) of making demands on others, in order to test their commitment, that they will never fulfill. I am familiar with that technique in our society, where that silent, hidden demand is assuaged by daydreams of some wonderful, loving, understanding, caring person—heavenly or secular—who ends the pain. This mechanism prolongs masochism to eternity.

H: And that's the story that he gives. He doesn't put it in those words, but that's what he—

S: You mean you have data that confirm my impressions as I look at his face?

H: Yeah. [*To K. and W.*] Dr. S. and I have been talking about our work. That's all. He [S.] doesn't know about your life. Let us see how our work goes. The two of us have been talking, that's all. Now we've finished, and I'm simply letting you know, that's all. [*To S.*] I don't know where I'm going. I'll just have to do it as I go along. Because of the situation I told you about. [Reference to the above impasse in my interviewing with K. before S. arrived.] I shall try to feel him out to see how much he can talk about without getting frightened. I'll do that: I will respond to the affects and ask him accordingly. So I don't know quite how I'll go with it.

S: What about trying this route: he keeps looking at me. To go back to where you were before I arrived would be to lose an opportunity. [On the other hand, opportunities are the last things we want with certain people, because it's too much for them.] Might you not be able to work your *way* into it by finding out more: what does he feel about me being here—instead of going instantly back to the place. One other thing. . . . W. is sitting here in a completely different posture.* The two of them are parallel now, instead of facing. Is that because he simply hasn't gone to work yet, or is that a response to this man?

H: Yeah. [*Cautiously.*] He is responding to him. That's how he usually sits here with K. [Listening to the tape now, I remember the suspicion growing in me that crystallized when S. asked me about Weiyu's posture. I knew something was different in Weiyu's behavior all along, but S. made it—W.'s resistance to translating for K.—fully conscious and thereby available for me to use in later work. My initial caution here—I tell W. that S. and I are talking only about work—reflects a concern that in this exchange they would sense—W. sometimes picks up on my English—that W. was resistant, which would shift his subsequent behavior.]

S: But not with others?

H: No, not with others.

S: OK. Consider this possibility: K. is aware of this totally different, unbelievable experience now there's two of us here. I'm known in

---

*Note how S. immediately picks up the body language messages of Weiyu, which I had virtually ignored: see the next chapter.

the village in some way. You might do better—wherever you're trying to go in your work with him—acknowledging that new event. Asking him what does he make of this. The more open-ended the question about my presence, the better the information you'll get.

H: Yeah. We've stopped working for four or five days. And now the three of us are talking again. But it's different; it's not just the three of us. [*To K.*] S. has come and is sitting with us. What do you feel about this? [For the first time in this session W. perks up. I think he sensed a bit of a challenge here, which interested him.]

K: [*Pause. Smile in voice.*] Nothing in particular. I'm just waiting for the two of you, that's all.

H: OK. [*To S.*] This is a typical response. He said, "I don't feel anything." He's saying, "Whatever you want to do . . . I'm just following you guys."

S: Fair enough. Caution and depression and a lot else. But I won't give up yet. I want to know who he thinks I am . . . and not just a label.

H: [*To K.*] Dr. S. wants to ask you what kind of man do you think he is?

K: You are the kind of man that would come to a place like this; you've come to watch Gilbert work.

S: Still evasive. Again: what kind of man am I? Not label, not profession, but things like "good," "bad," "interested," "kind," "dangerous," "a mixture of." I'm really pushing him for a—

H: —And he's really bad about questions like this, because I ask him all the time.

S: Maybe I shouldn't do it—

H: [*Cuts in.*]—Uh-uh! I ask him all the time, and he's just very [*searches for a word*] unresponsive. Let me ask him.

S: Also, tell him I don't want him to be unresponsive. [*Laughs.*]

H: [*To K.*] Dr. Stoller knows you don't know about him, but he still wants to ask you about your thoughts about him. What kind of man do you think he is? Is he a good man, or is he no good; is he a man who does bad, a man who talks too strong, a man who holds a grudge, a man who makes you afraid, a man who follows other men: what kind of man? Think clearly and say whatever comes up. [*I finish and W. starts to translate. W. clears his throat taken a bit aback by the questions we pose.*]

K: No, this man . . . our good man [uses first person plural] . . . has come into our hamlet. What kind of badness could he have? He has no badness. He is nice (*singundu*).

H: [*Responding immediately.*] What kind of *singundu?*

K: *Singundu.* [*No elaboration.*]

H: His skin? His habits? His meanings? Or what? On his face or in his liver [his true feelings]?

K: Uh-uh. What kind of something could be in his liver? [*Voice trails off.*]

S: [*Quietly, the objective physician.*]* He is not in as much pain as he was.

H: Yeah, I can see. [*Pause.*] But I don't know why. [*Small chuckle.*]

K: This place is the deep forest . . . and yet he's come. He is a good man, not a no-good man. I won't worry over him about anything in particular. I think only that, "Ooh, he's come along inside this great forest. He's a good man to come here to see me. This place doesn't have a road for a car or for going all the way to America or Australia. . . . Flying—and then landing here [helicopter]—that's the only way you can get here."

H: [*To S.*] You probably understand most of that. He says you're a good guy; it's really special that you've come to a place like this in the middle of the forest. And he says, "Why shouldn't I think you're a good guy. . . . You're nice, you haven't done anything bad so far, you've come to be with this other guy who's good, and . . . you know he thinks it's—

S: —Is this superficial or b.s.—or safety—or does he feel, "There's something in that face [S.'s] that shows curiosity and involvement with me?"

H: It's not just bullshit, but it's superficial, the kind of answer he usually gives. I've been working with him for months this visit, right? I rarely get more affect than that. . . . I know [hope?] there's more there . . . but it's so deeply hidden . . . that it's very hard for him to dredge up much more than that. It's genuine, but it's not the whole story. And it's also phony, in a way, because he's not telling you what he really feels, and both I and the interpreter know that.

S: Yeah. [*Quiet voice.*] That's great. And we're working out a way of talking with him as we're doing this. [*Intensifies.*] He came in so troubled and worried. Now he's engaged (though we don't know what it means that he is). And he now has a different look. The sadness is still there, but his head is both pulled back—"I'm being

---

*S: That's too ironically polite. I was just warming up before the game, a curious observer with someone I didn't know and had barely started to identify with. As yet no love, no hate, no commitment, no defenses.

so careful" and pushing forward—"I want to get into this more."
[*H. agrees.*]

H: Now he's given you a piece of himself; he's offered you his opinion of you. So now he wants a response.

S: Here's my response (but I don't know how you're going to do [put] it): "I'm glad that he is responding, but I want more."

H: Dr. S. says this: He's happy to hear your words. He feels good that Kalutwo is expressing his ideas. Now he wants to hear more about K.'s feelings about himself. [*As W. translates this, K. smiles and looks up at us. Before that his head is mostly low, in his hands, his eyes looking at the floor.*]

S: There! Look at that. Now, that was an odd smile . . . shy and—

H: [*Breaks in*]—a nervous smile—

S: Yeah . . . but not a total push-me-away smile.

H: No . . . warm . . . it was a good smile.

S: Nervous, yeah; because he's wondering what the hell is going on . . . what game am I [S.] playing. But it still seemed a little relieved. . . . Don't let me say these things if you don't agree.

H: Yeah, I know.

S: We're dropping bit by bit down to something more workable.

H: That's right. [*Pause.*] Kalutwo, have you more thoughts about Dr. S.? [*Said quietly.*]

K: No, I don't have any more thoughts. He [S.] is our man. He is our visitor, a nice man. [*Slowly.*] He is like our Gilbert here. . . . He's a good man, not in a small way, with his gift of the sheep and tinned fish and rice [S.'s gifts to the village for a feast]. Only Gilbert's kind of people care and look after us. He visits Gilbert, and he has given us sheep and a huge bag of rice and fish. But it would not be good if he came here and buttered up Gilbert . . .

H: [*To S.*] He's warming up. He says you and I are different in wanting to come inside of a jungle like this. But, he says I'm afraid you're going to steal H. away, and take him back with you to America. It's very nice to talk with you, but you're going to steal away this man who's working with me.

S: The look he had before was of a dog that had been badly whipped. Then someone petted the dog for a moment, and the dog felt a bit better—without trusting, with good reason: one pat doesn't make a whole new life. But now here's something to be stressed, that you haven't quite told me. He seems to be saying, "I love Gilbert. You're [S.] coming here, that's very nice, but I'm really frightened that you're going to take away this person that I love." If he feels that, then how the hell does he deal with the fact that he has love for—nonerotic love [*H. agrees*]—has love for, can't do anything about, has feeling for—someone you can't control, who has different skin, clothes, and comes and goes. . . . What's the point of getting yourself attached to someone like that who in the past left you, *before* the man from overseas came to take him away, and now is even *more* likely to leave.

H: That's correct. It's in his ambivalence: even when I was really pressing, half of him wanted to stay [when he would start to flee]. And now he's back.

S: He couldn't leave! Why, he's the one person who's hung around your place more than anyone else—never said a word, face to the wall, not communicating with anyone—including himself. Yet he's always *here*. He's so desperate to be attached to someone. Fill me in for one or two words. (I'm sorry it breaks into our present discussion, but I'll need it.) What whipped him, or who whipped him?

H: Briefly: he never had a father. His natural father's identity was kept a secret from him because he was a bastard. The mother hated the father. The mother brought him up feeling that he should be afraid of men, and he was brought up so that the mother didn't like him very much, either. She had a lot of resentment because it happened to her, that men (her brothers) had treated her the way that they did when she had the baby, and the father wouldn't accept it. He grew up thinking that the father disliked him. He told me that when he was going to be initiated, he said, "Why wasn't I a girl?" [*Silence.*]

S: Proceed. [*Pause.*] That's a terrible tragedy. I feel sad when I hear it. When I say, "Proceed," I'm trying to cut off my feelings, which I shouldn't do.

H: Yeah, it's just—

S: —his face looked—

H: His whole life is like that. But saying that makes it seem like it's been done to him. And it has, but the last twenty years he's done it to himself.

S: Of course. That's the story of mankind.

H: Well, I'll move it along now.

S: And I'll hang back.

H: [*To K.*] Now, before, the two of us were talking a lot about our work and about the meaning of your—what you feel about us— What does it mean—that? . . . And *now* the two of us are sitting here and talking, wondering how we can find a way of interviewing good. So that our work can go along a straight course . . . and come out on top. Now he [S.] knows what it's like [to interview] in America; and I know what it's like here, inside Sambia. But I don't know what it's like [interviewing] in America. So now the two of us have combined it. So we're just telling you. [*To W.*] Now, I'm thinking of K., and I'm thinking if, from before, if there's something—if he's got anything he wants to ask S. about, at this time, he should just talk. I'm not talking about only now, I'm not saying that I want to push him—I'm not thinking about just now. . . . Later, if he gets some thoughts and wants to talk about them or ask about them, he should just talk. He can ask him [S.]. He has white hair: he's our elder and he has a lot of knowledge and if he [K.] wants to ask him [S.] something later, that's all right. It's his choice, whatever he wants . . . and I'm not just talking about now, I'm talking about later, too. And all later times, too. [*To S.*] You're going to be his father.

S: [*Quietly.*] That's what I was thinking before.

H: That's exactly what it's going to be.*

S: This is very hard.

H: That's exactly right.

S: It must be terrifying for him. You're his father, and I'm your father.

H: Yeah. My first thought was to say to her [a slip—I meant "him"]—but I couldn't figure out how to say it—"If you ever have something you want to *ask* Dr. Stoller, ask him." But I couldn't say that to him; it puts too much of a burden on him, and he's too passive for that. So, I tried to do it by saying you're a wise old man, and you and I are trying to find a way to do this work here: I constantly ask you questions, and he should too. Part of the problem is his worry I am leaving.† And now the news has just been brought that . . . and with that clear to him, his affect will change because he is going to be aware that I am dealing with the transportation problems, that I'm probably getting what I want, and that I'll be going soon.

S: So he'll have to pull back to spare himself another agony.

H: Yeah. [*Pause.*]

K: [*Spontaneously talks about two minutes. Weiyu translates to H., who translates to S.*]

H: He says he used to think, when I first came here, that I'd probably be here a year or two and then I'd go away and they'd never see me again. But when I left, I sent letters to the people who worked

*S: It wasn't. Perhaps there was too little time. Or perhaps, in another sense—fear and resistance, cold anger—it was. H: More the latter, my heart says.
†We have decided that when S. goes out, H. will too, for a spot of R&R.

for me and I'd tell them how I was, and sometimes I'd send a bit
of money. He watched this and realized he had been wrong; that
when I left I *hadn't* forgotten the people I was with; that I didn't
abandon them. So, now that I'm working with him, he's saying,
"I'm sitting and I'm watching and I'm wondering; since I'm working with you, are you going to be like that with me? Will you
write letters to me when you leave?"

S: What are you going to say?

H: I don't know. I'm going to have to answer.

S: No, I'm asking *you* to tell *me*. I want to know what *you* feel.

H: I feel that he has made the relationship more than I expected it
to be. He has responded more than I expected. And he has shown
me more care and openness than I expected he would.

S: Than you thought he had in him?

H: Yeah. Than I thought he had in him. [Surprised at the thought.]

S: You thought he was so damaged that he would never *dare* allow
himself to try again?

H: And *not interested* in trying. Yeah.

S: OK. So what's your answer . . .

H: My answer is that I am going to write him.

S: You mean he reached you?

H: Yeah. [*In Pidgin to K. and W.*] I've listened to him, and I'm really
happy with what he said. When I leave I won't forget. I'll send a
letter back to him. Weiyu, you can tell him, too, that I'm not a
man who lies. I tell the truth.

W: [*Lights up on hearing that and says to K:*] He's not the kind of man
who doesn't tell the truth. He *does* look after his work-friends.
He's not lying. He's telling the truth. He's not full of empty talk.
He says what he thinks.

K: Yes. I've watched you, and I know you tell the truth. Some
European men would think, "Well, you're not my baby. I don't
have to care for you and think about you, send things to you as
if you were my child. Did I give birth to you? Did you come from
my semen? No. You're another man's child, not mine. I'll help
you only while I'm here, only then. But I'm not really your father.
Rubbish! I'm not your father. I won't send you letters." Some men
would think like that.* But you think differently. Your thinking
I like. [*Long pause.*]

---

*Kalutwo shows us in this vivid narrative a well-etched script about how he expects peo-
ple—he says "men"—react to him. He implies a wish for the father he never had.

H: He says like this . . .

S: Excuse me. . . . Look . . . he smiles. You look at each other with full contact . . . *totally* different from the start. OK, go ahead.

H: When I told him I was going to write to him, I said, "You know I'm not a person who says things he doesn't do." And he said, "Yes, I do know that." And he says, "I watched you. Some Europeans would think like this: you're not my baby that I should send you letters or money. You're not a child—I didn't carry you, I'm not your mother—" these are his words—"some men would think like that, but you're different. You remember the people you knew before. That's a very good way to be."

S: So much for the "noble savage," or the "ignorant savage," or any other racist beliefs like that. We're doing the same psychological. . . . I don't mean the cultures are the same or the identities the same. . . . I know that they have fundamental aspects of their identity that we'll *never* comprehend, that are different from us. But the dynamics—and I'm not talking about psychodynamics— just the dynamics of our relating to each other—are no different than what happens in my office. As he sits there, his face is not alien to me. Now, there are alien looks I would not understand . . . of course. But we're working here with a different style [from what ethnographers report]; the way I work with people at home. By "work," I don't mean something cold . . . distant . . . objects. I mean a human experience with form, not just appearance. We have a whole other task here: to find what's happening beyond the words. Because the translator's (Weiyu's) experiences are also part of the ambience and help create the questions and the answers—

H: —Exactly—

S: —Not just the words he [W.] chooses. His choice of words is part of it. *But there's nothing that's not part of this.* The coffee we were drinking at first is part of it. (But not to anthropologists, apparently.)

H: He's given us a signal. He's telling W. something to say to us. And every time he does that, he responds more and opens up more and feels more—

S: —Wait a minute. He *said* this? Or you just caught something subliminal—The *word* "message"?

H: —The *behavioral* message—whether it's conscious or unconscious—is, "I am opening up and I'm feeling nice."

S: Yeah, but he didn't actually say that in words, did he?

H: No. I don't know the precise content of the message yet.

W: K. says, "Your country has good food.* But you don't think (if you come here), 'What will I be short of?' You don't think like that. You think, 'That food [etc.] can just stay there ["I won't miss it"]. That's its place.' And you come alone inside these parts where we [Sambia] are as possums, sitting in tree-holes. [This jungle place is hard to live in.] The patrol officer comes and he says to us. 'Come on, give us your tax money.' 'Oh, sorry. We don't have any.' And we say that to him and he just jails us. And you? You come along and you help us and you give us money. And the officer comes to us and he asks us about throwing away our tax money and you pay us and we give it to him. Therefore, I'm very happy. It's so good that you've come to live in our hamlet."†

H: And I am happy to be here in this place. [*Pause.*]

K: You're a very good man. You come here. You don't come and take our food from us. You bring your own, you cook it, and give us some, even though we have our own food. You do that. You're a very good man. We're so very pleased with you. [*Pause.*]

H: [*To S.*] He's just going over the same theme, telling me what a good father or mother I am.

S: It's probably the theme of his life. But airing it has put it into that form. Do you want to say more about this? Is this defensive repetition?

H: No. [*Thinking about this now, H. agrees with S. He doesn't know why he didn't agree then.*] This hasn't happened before. I guess your arrival provided a convenient way for him to say things he has wanted to say to me before and that may also be an effort to repair what happened when I talked with him last time.

S: Yeah. It's *got* to be repaired. He feels something terrible happened—that he had to *run*: if you're panicked, you do terrible things; and after, you think, "Why did I do that?"

H: I've felt the same, that he saw this happening but couldn't prevent it. . . . I haven't given you all the details. I'll tell you after it's done. I don't want to go on much longer; it's getting late. We haven't done *anything* [*laughs*] except talk about him.

S: What have we done for him? We should do something. Does he measure what's done for him by the amount of time you spend with him?

---

*Because Sambia use food as a metaphor for relatedness and nurturance, you may interpret these remarks of K.'s as suggesting that I have forsaken the nurturance of my own land and people to come here: an act of courage he finds difficult to comprehend.
†S: What a run of thoughts, so much easier—almost manic—than before.

H: Partly. This was enough time.

S: We took a lot of his time by our talking to each other. Can he be told that all our talking was for him, not just for us? It really was, though we were doing our own research. It's for his sake that you want me to understand him in the way you do.

H: OK. Now it's clear. I can get that across. [*To K.*] We should finish up, but I want to say this: Dr. S. and I have talked a lot, but we weren't just talking about nothing. I am trying to teach Dr. S. what I know about you so that he can help me help you, not just for our work.

K: All right. [*Pause.*]

S: One last question. How does he feel about what we've done here today?

H: [*To K.*] Dr. S. asks, "What do you feel about our talking today?"

K: We've sat down and we've talked. I'm just pleased, that's all.

H: [*To S.*] Same as before: he feels fine, it's been good. There's a positive feeling there. No harm done.

S: Good.

H: [*To K.*] He's pleased with talking with you. OK. That's enough. The two of us [H. and S.] haven't eaten yet.

FINAL SESSION

We met with Kalutwo on the afternoon of the next day from 1:30–4:00 P.M. The four of us gathered, sat down, and sipped coffee. We exchanged greetings and small talk. Before interviewing, S. and H. discussed where to go in this session. S. suggested that he carry the interviewing. His idea was to ask K. to teach him about his shamanism. This approach was similar to our work with Sakulambei (chapter 7), only here we used it to learn more about K.'s shamanic identity, since direct questioning on K.'s sexual behavior would be too painful for him. In the midst of this questioning, K. searched for security again—referring back to the previous session when he asked me to write letters to him. Then we went on talking about his shamanism. In order to orient the reader, I add a few words here about Sambia shamanism and Kalutwo's brand in particular.

Like the rest of his development, Kalutwo's history of shamanism is splintered and convoluted. It contains too many contradictions to be considered only a role performance or dismissed merely as a defensive maneuver. Examples: K. had his first trance experience around puberty, but he did not begin serving in healing ceremonies till recently. (That fifteen-year delay is too long and therefore culturally aberrant.) He lacks the genealogic ancestry to properly claim inheritance of shamanic spirit familiars (usually inherited from one's father or father's brothers). His trance states—which I have observed in healing ceremonies—seem shallow and forced compared to those of other shamans (Saku especially, a fact his peers recognize by disparaging K. as a weak shaman); and he cannot exorcise objects (the performative feat *par excellence* of a strong shaman). Nonetheless, K. was ritually installed as a shaman in a *narangu* shamanic initiation in our village in 1975. One suspects that his marital problems and the failure of his last marriage must then have been on his mind.

Kalutwo's shamanic status does seem to help bolster and defend his identity in several ways. The shaman's role makes him stand out somewhat from the male crowd. His spirit familiars also provide him with spiritual powers others should take note of, even if they don't fear them, as they do with Sakulambei. During healing ceremonies K. is more aggressive—exhibitionistic (what Price-Williams [1975:88] refers to as "psychopomp"). K. has several familiars, some female, some male; and these figures—voices that he experiences during trance states—seem to appeal to K.'s dimensions of female and male identification, of which I believe he is more conscious (like other shamans) than most Sambia adult men. K.'s shamanism, then, helps him to sustain, against formidable social pressures, his sense of self—especially of maleness—while lacking other manly achievements.

But Kalutwo, as I mentioned, is not a great shaman in Sambia eyes. This means that his personality does not show the spectacular intrapsychic fracture lines that I believe underlie the trance and possession episodes that get things done (and sometimes, great things *do* get done) in the leading Sambia shamans' (e.g., Saku) healing performances. Ironically, however, the same dynamic structure that can do those creative things (i.e., heal someone) and which K. lacks (his shamanism is more mechanical), places these fragile shamans at greater risk of psychotic-like episodes and grandiose behaviors (sometimes leading to personal disasters, as in the case of Weiyu's father). K.'s personality is stolid and less grandiose than those latter shamans, who seem able to *become*, in trances, the fantasized masculine and feminine figures (shamanic spirit familiar personalities) that mobilize events during ceremonies.

Indeed, people disparage K. as a weak shaman, and, compared to Sakulambei—who is more unpredictable and fragmented (i.e., recall his chameleonic trait)—K. is a no-account, insignificant healer. I have always felt that K. was rather a fraud; other Sambia suggest as much, but only in gossip. His trance-states are not quite believable; the performances seem trumped-up. Because K.'s shamanism looks and feels more artificial, intellectualized, and less integrated into his personality, I interpret his shamanism (as an identity and as a role context) as more of a conscious cultural defense than, say, Sakulambei's. Take away K.'s "secondary" shamanism and you have a loss of self-esteem, social status, leaving perhaps depression. But remove Sakulambei's "primary" shamanism and you have nothing—obliteration of self, nonexistence. Those are two very different sets of dynamics and character structure.[12]

We begin with H. talking about the affective tone of interviewing K. following yesterday's positive start.

H: Your presence has put life back into the interviewing, but just where we're going, I don't know. I know what I want in the interviews with everyone else, but I don't know what I want with him.

S: That's because *he* hasn't given shape to your work together. It takes two people to give shape to a relationship.

H: That's right: he firmly said "No" to where I was going,* but he still wants to work. Yet he hasn't given me a signal.

S: [*Cuts in.*]—He hasn't told us what *he* wants. He's only told us that he doesn't want to go the route we were talking. Where did we break off yesterday, and what broke us off?

H: Only time. We had just established rapport. And there was that response to your white hair and you being someone who might answer some of his questions . . . Remember that he too is a shaman; a weak, minor shaman. He wanted it [the shaman status], and he practices it, but he does it without enthusiasm.

S: Does anyone want it from him?

H: Probably not.[13] Unless it's his sister. His sister is his mother-substitute for his mother. Now, I know what I can do to get him talking. I can just say, "I'm going to ask you about your shamanism." That's not what I really want to know about, but I don't think I'm going to learn about that. . . .

S: Tell me in two sentences what you really want to know about.

H: I want to know about his [erotic] relationships with boys. That's what I want to know about.

S: And how much do you know?

H: Not very much. I know—

S: —You know *something*. You know he has them and desires them. . . .

*Study of K.'s sexual excitement, especially its pederastic component.

H: I know he has daydreams, and I know he desires boys—I know that it still continues and basically it's—now he wants to be married. And he's got two reasons: one, because he wants children; the other reason, because boys aren't willing to go along with him anymore. [*To Weiyu*] Let's ask Kalutwo: does he have something he'd like to talk about?

K: If I do ask him [H.] for something, or if I worry about it, I can't talk out. I'll be shamed: he's [H.] not like my kinsmen that I can say just anything to him. I might cry and make him feel sorry for me.

H: What's he talking about?

W: I think he wants to ask the two of you for something.

H: OK. Ask him what it is.

K: When you go away over there [America], will you help me with a letter?

H: Yes I will.

K: I've watched others who worked with you. You don't forget them. If you did that for me, I'd get some money like you send to the others who worked for you. While you're here, I won't ask you for something: This is my country, not your own (where you've lots to give away).

H: What would you want me to give you?

K: Could I ask for something . . . like an old blanket or something like that?*

H: OK. Well, we've already talked about that; when I go out I'll send you back letters.

K: All right. That's nice. That's nice [*matter-of-fact*].

H: Now, is there something you would like to talk about, about yourself?

K: What about my shamanism?

H: I, too, was thinking about that. [*To S.*] He'd like to work on his shamanism. That's a good idea. I know that pretty well. He—it turns out he cares more for me than I thought he did.

S: I knew that right away yesterday.

H: I didn't know it. Now, whether it was because it was so guarded, or it was me, or it's the relationship; or what is it?

S: I don't know. My impression is that it's not a defect in you that

---

*What will a few dollars or a blanket add materially to K.'s life? Something, to be sure, for K. has no means of cash income (aside from the odd government roadwork or periodic census patrol labor, or others' gifts). I don't underrate that. Yet such gifts—from me—have an added significance: security, feeling wanted. You can count dollars, hourly wages, and measure blankets; but how do you measure security? Gifts between ethnographers and their friends are a complex thing: another piece of fieldwork culture that merits attention.

you wouldn't pick up. It's just that it's easy for a third person to see. Maybe the geography—you two facing each other and I as the third point on the triangle—may let me see him differently. I seem to hear him telling you . . . doing the best he can to tell you that you're—I don't like intellectualizing,* but you're his attachment object. He's never *found* one before. And it isn't all transference (in the sense of fantasy). The fact is that you *have* served him and nobody gives a *damn* about him here. He's just rubbish, right?

H: Yeah, that's right.

S: You haven't treated him like rubbish. How could he *not* feel that— because of some reality in your relationship—for the first time in his life he's got someone. And there's no way he can articulate it—to anyone.

H: Hmm. That makes sense.

S: So, to me, it's obvious. The pain there in his face is the pain of loss; since earliest childhood, a terrible sadness. He's so desperate to get close to you; but you set the rules of a game he can't understand. All he knows is that, in order to get close to you, he has to find some technique. And it's to sit down and be interviewed. I mean [*chuckles*]—I mean, it doesn't make much sense here. It makes sense in Los Angeles. But here, he has to make sense out of a totally incomprehensible way of reaching the beloved lost mother, father, object—whatever it is. And you were there sending out clear-cut signals that you would function in that way when nobody else had.† Yet he couldn't find the path through the forest to get there. And he still doesn't know how. But sometimes he's known that he's had to do it in a way that he didn't want to do it. Sometimes you touched on things so awful to him to talk about that the hope he would get good feelings from you was nullified. So he's left at a zero-point, and he just walks away—for a while— from the whole thing. Now he's in a terrible bind, because [ground down by his resistance] you withdraw. He knows you do that, and he knows that you come back . . . but will you send him letters . . . that is, will you still be there? You said you would. Nobody's ever come through before—but you're more likely to; I think he probably does believe that. And he's not into the "miss

---

*S: The circumstances—jungle, rain, mosquitoes, dinners of taro and sweet potatoes, muck— were conducive to more modest—or is it "more honest"—discourse; so we rarely intellectualized grossly.

†Right. The special—odd—discourse I mentioned in chapter 3. Only, with people like K., who need more, the therapeutic dimension of this talking is more evident, like a fire that will not burn without kindling.

you" part of this. . . . You have him available to *you*, but he's not doing what, say, Penjukwi does: she's doing it for herself. She's getting a joy out of it. The same for some of your other friends. For him, though, it's desperate, primeval.

H: That's helpful. . . . So, he says he wants to talk about his shamanism. That is as good a subject as anything else; at this point, I don't think I'm going to learn what I want to learn. [*To K.*] Dr. Stoller and I want to learn more about your *kwooluku* [the spirit familiar that makes one a shaman]. [*K. whispers to W., again on the subject of the letter.*]

W: He's talking about the letter. He says he can't get it at Mountain Patrol Station [a few days' distance].

H: Then we'll put his name on a couple of envelopes, and they can go straight to him. When S. goes back to America, he'll send a picture inside of a letter back to Kalutwo. [*K. smiles broadly and gurgles.*]

S: Hm! Biggest smile yet. How come he understands the Pidgin? Does he want a picture of the two of you? Or is that too powerful?

H: No, it's not. Do you want a picture of the two of us?

K: All right. One of me and one of the two of us?

H: Yeah.

K: All right.

S: And I can use that as an excuse for getting a picture of this room, which I really should do anyway, with the two of you talking.

K: And if you do, I'll be very, very pleased.

H: [*To S.*] He says if we do that he'll be really pleased with us.

S: Right now?

K: Yes.

S: [*Takes snaps.*] Tell him it takes a few months and I'll send it to him.

H: He says in about two moons or three moons, he'll send them along to you.

K: Fine!

H: OK, that's all. Now, Dr. Stoller would like to say this to Kalutwo: Stoller, too, is a kind of *kwooluku* [shaman].

W: Yeah, one kind of *kwooluku*-man. I thought the same thing. I thought that about him down below there. When for—

K: [*Interrupts*]—Nilutwo. We all saw him.

W: That's right. I watched him and I thought [when S. was trying to hypnotize Nilutwo]: this man, he's a *kwooluku*-man.

H: What do you think he was doing to Nilutwo?

K: The way he was looking with his eyes at N., I thought he was acting like a shaman. And that if he looks at N. like that, N. will fall down dead.

H: Dr. Stoller would like to know about Kalutwo's *kwooluku*. How does he experience it inside himself? What changes did it cause in N.? [*K. perks up, sits up a bit; has some of his old life in him.*]

K: When my familiars come to me, they come inside, and at such times my feeling is entirely different. . . . At that time my walking is—is like speeding—running . . . like a shooting arrow and very happy. You won't walk about easy, then, you just shoot along—one, two, three . . .

H: And he's talking about—?

W: —The time when the familiars want to come inside of his body.

[We discuss K.'s shamanic calling and bring up his initial trancing.]

H: But at first, when he went and lay down in his house, did the familiars come and whistle?

W: They shake around. When he [K.] starts to shake, then they all come and whistle.

H: Had you been through the *narangu* [shaman's initiation] yet?

K: No . . . the first time, I didn't see it in a dream. I started shaking and while there, it whistled. They all whistled. And then I thought: I can become a shaman. A familiar has come and stuck itself onto me, and it's making me shake. So I can become a shaman.

H: And inside of your dream, at that time, they showed you a leaf or something?

K: Yeah. Leaves, cordyline, *pit-pit* [a tall grass].

H: [*To S.*] He believes you're a kind of shaman who wants to learn about *his* shamanism. Here is what he has chosen to tell you; he's never told me this before, and I'm trying to find out what it means. He says that when he was a third-stage initiate, which would be after age sixteen, sometimes he used to walk around and go to the gardens. Sometimes, when doing that, he'd feel a bit strange. He was usually with a kinsman and his son. They went to the gardens. Then he went back to his house and lay down and started to shake a bit. At this time there was the sound of his familiar— the whistling sound you heard the other night*—which emerged

---

*S: We were in a healing ceremony, forty or so of us crammed in a hut, while K., assisting a stronger shaman, did his number, whistling, chanting, and sprinkling us with water from sacred leaves. No one took him very seriously, but they all joined in with boisterous pleasure, especially when he spritzed H. and me. I guess I was cured, but of what I never found out. (It started hours before we arrived. We squatted there from seven to midnight and then quit. The rest carried on till dawn. I was not in a trance, say I, but the hours passed outside of time; I don't know where they went.)

of its own volition. And he knew this meant that his first spirit-familiar had come to him.

S: The whistling sound the other night at the healing ceremony was not ascribed to a person but to a familiar?

H: Yeah, a spirit-familiar. Let me give you more details. . . . The setting for this first spirit-familiar visit [trance] is: he's just reached puberty; for the first time he's expected to perform as a bachelor—that is, to screw boys; he's approaching marriageable age, is having to think about sex and women; he's on his own, his mother and [biologic] father having both died within the last two or three years; he's pretty much alone in the world except for an older sister. . . . And he is reporting a trance (or pseudotrance) experience not overtly associated with anything in particular. It just happens to him; it's happened several times. He *chooses* to interpret this experience as meaning he is being selected as a shaman, even if he is without the necessary ancestry. Something in him is choosing to be a shaman.

S: Would you say this: a man who is psychologically unprepared for the tasks ahead—that is, for enthusiastic heterosexuality—at this point chooses a different route? Is that what you mean to say?

H: Right.

S: What were his responses to this first experience: honored to be chosen? frightened to be chosen?

H: First, probably scared. Then less and less scared. [*To W.*] The first time his familiar came to him, what did he feel?

H: [*While W. asks, H. says to S:*] We have gone over this material before, but there's something special about it now because he has chosen to tell *you* about it. [*As K. answers W.*] I hear what's happening here. K.'s responding as he typically does when defensive, when he doesn't want to feel. He says, "What should I feel? What do you expect me to feel?" My question "What do you feel?" is always too direct. He really has a problem feeling. That's one of the issues here.

S: You mean that the feelings are too much for him? He hasn't enough resistance against feeling? That is, his feelings are too intense, and so he must use a blunter defense, rather than just, say, a schizoid defense in which he consciously does not feel?

H: That sounds right. He hasn't enough resistance against feeling.

S: It's a possibility. It fits.

W: He says the first time he felt the familiar and it whistled, he was frightened. And that special time—not just any old time—it shows you the leaves and such like [i.e., items used in healing ceremonies]. But when he heard the whistles again, he was only pleased, not afraid. "I can," he says, "remove people's illness."

H: [*To S.*] Here's what is happening: K. has just now rolled a cigarette, he smokes (remember: the thing that induces the trances is smoking) as he starts to talk about his trance. He says that when he first started shaking he felt afraid, but when he *knew* he was being possessed by a familiar—that is, as distinct from just the shaking—he felt joy. "Why," I asked; the standard response he always gives—he "would be able to heal people."

S: Look at his stance now: he's turned away. He's blocked his own head so we can't see it. He's in contact with us, but in a negative way, not out of contact.

H: So defensive.* Yet, this subject of shamanism is his baby. He says he *wants* to talk about this.

S: Would he be willing to teach me anything? I mean *anything*. About shamanism. He could be generous if he would teach me. It's really true that he could teach me. Would he be willing to put into me some of his information? *Not* so I would be a shaman like him, I don't want it for that. I just want it in order to compare it to my shamanism . . . called psychoanalysis. It would be helpful to me and generous of him, like giving a feast. I'm asking *him* for some generosity.

H: Dr. S. says this: he's come a long way and he has his own familiars, but his familiars are of a different kind. He would be very pleased if Kalutwo would teach him something, the same as if K. were to make a feast for Dr. Stoller. [*W. gets enthused now, for he's got the flavor of what S. is trying to say through me.*]

W: Dr. S. wants you to teach him something! To tell a story about what you know.

K: [*Quietly, puzzled.*] Story about what? Say what to him?

W: Well, it's for *you* to say. It's your story. What do you want to say to him?

K: [*Cold silence. Looks at us. I sense he is bewildered, for he is so rarely asked to share his knowledge. He shares only by performing healing ceremonies.*] No.

H: No?! [*Amazed. To W.*] Ask him why.

---

*K. was saying he is pleased to be a shaman because he can help people. The shaman wants to help people, but people also fear shamans' greater sorcery power, especially in trance states when the spirit familiars take over the shaman. I see therein a defensive maneuver the shaman (this applies to Saku too) may use, a socially accepted device for controlling people at a distance. In addition, K. can be connected to others in healing ceremonies without giving of himself in other social contexts. This shaman's (K.) succorance is, then, *also* a means against being close to others in everyday life.

K: Talk about what to Dr. Stoller?

H: That's for you to decide. It's your story.

W: [*Amused to K.*] There, I told you! Say what you want to.

H: Can you teach him one little thing about getting a familiar or not? [*W. beseeches K.*]

K: [*Cold, flat.*] No.* [*Weiyu starts again, consternation in voice, which then falls off, somewhat in despair. He gives up. Long silence.*]

S: [*Quietly.*] There's no way we can get from him an explanation why—or did you even ask him why?

H: I did ask him why, and he just said "No." He's closed. And you see I'm at a loss. I don't know what's going on inside him. This is the first time since you and I have been working together here when I feel like I'm floating, lost. It's overwhelming for him. He can do it, but he doesn't want to do it.

As we tried to decide where to go next, we paused. K. and W. rolled cigarettes. We picked up the conversation, but a technical failure occurred; the batteries in the recorder had worn down and we missed about five minutes of the conversation. During these minutes our strategy changed. Faced with the failure to get K. to teach S. about shamanism, S. asked him about something else. Out of nowhere S. asked K: "What do you feel about your semen organ (*keriku-keriku*) and menstrual-blood organ (*tingu*)?" K.'s response surprised the hell out of me: he more or less denied that he had a semen organ the way other men do.† When translated to S., it didn't surprise him at all. The tape picks up here.

K: [*Low, gruff, angry voice.*] Yes, I would teach Dr. Stoller about my shamanism. But he changed the subject and asked about my *keriku-keriku*. And so I was [*stumbling*] . . . wrong, and shall shut up. What do you really want to know? [*K. whispers keriku-keriku to W. as if it were a secret. He usually whispers about the keriku-keriku.*] That's all; I don't know what to do now.

H: Do you want to talk more about this?

K: No. It's unpleasant.

---

*The reader need not fear that K. is simply protecting his shamanic secrets of the trade. Having interviewed over a dozen shamans and K. on this very topic, I know another motive is at work.

†Sambia believe all humans have such organs (see chapter 2). Their functions are quite different for the sexes: females get life and strength from the *tingu*, but it is nonfunctional in males; males draw all strength and masculinity from their semen organs, which, in women, are nonfunctional. For a man to assert that he has no semen organ is madness, shocking. No one had ever done it before to me.

H: I want to finish talking about this now. But first I want to understand why you don't want to talk about the *keriku-keriku*.

K: It's something that . . . the *keriku-kerikus* won't help us with our gardens; they won't go with us when we walk around. [Note the odd but not unique construction; he has animated the *keriku-keriku*.] I don't want to talk about this. Now if a man makes something, yes: then I can talk about it, but not about this, which I haven't made. [*We do not understand K. here. So W. asks him to clarify. K. shakes his head.*] Oh, yeah, yeah. The time when you, a man, make it, then I can talk about it.*

W: Oh. [*Turns to K. for clarification. K. responds curtly.*]

H: What did you say? If you make [sexual?] movements, then it [semen organ] can do something?

K: It can't do anything by itself. It won't. You, a man [the possessor] only you could control it. You, a man, that's all, can make it do something. By itself, it can do nothing.

W: [*To H.*] Now, I think you have asked him too much about the *keriku-keriku* and he wants to leave. So he's acting this way. [*Weiyu is amused and smug.*]

K: [*Exasperated.*] That's enough work for now.

H: All right, that's good enough. Now, we [H. and S.] want to say this: we ask you about the *keriku-keriku* for a good reason; we want to understand more about you and Sambia. We know it is hard for you to see what we are trying to learn. We don't want you to think we are just rambling or that we just want to give you a headache from all our questions. We need you if we are to understand.

K: [*His typical passive surrender:*] It's my fault; I don't understand. [*Long pause.*] Tomorrow he [S.] must also ask Sakulambei about the *keriku-keriku*.

H: But this . . . [*pause*] . . . it. . . . [*Pause. I am puzzled. Why does he refer us to, and link Saku with, the keriku-keriku?*] Why should we ask *him*?

K: All the shamans have *keriku-kerikus* here. You are asking about that, and so I am telling you. [Apparently, when S. asked about the *keriku-keriku*, K. took this to mean, "Do I, a minor shaman, know something special about the *keriku-keriku*?" That subject upsets K., and so he refers us to Saku, a big shaman.]

---

*S: This disordered sentence seems a combination of an unclear statement, a thought that lost its anchor when deprived (by writing it down) of its inflections, a garbled translation from Sambia to Pidgin by Weiyu, and a final translation—to English by H—cut to death by the earlier confusion.

S: At this point I break off editing the transcript of H.'s translation of the proceedings and shall use the interruption to note a few issues about editing.

Why do I now stop giving you (my edited version of) our transcript, which covers, so far, about an hour's conversation?

1. It is, in total, almost incomprehensible because of the way the participants were having trouble understanding each other.
2. K. continued to be devious, pseudostupid.
3. Background noises overwhelmed the voices so that pieces are eaten out of some sentences, spoiling the meaning on into the following intact talk.
4. The tape machine fouled up for a few moments and then worked again; perhaps we changed the batteries. (I no longer remember.)
5. Though a lot of the discussion comes through clearly on the tape and in translation, there is so little substance that I dare not risk the reader's boredom by sticking to our resolve to approximate the microscopy of our ethnography. (We comfort our scientific consciences with the thought that the transcript, in all its frazzlement, is available to colleagues, as are our original tapes.) The discussion could have been useful. It was an effort to see how Kalutwo saw himself vis-à-vis Saku, a hermaphrodite [i.e., someone with a genuine semen organ], the most respected shaman in the area. Do they both have the same kind of aberrant *keriku-keriku?* Does K. feel he is a psychic hermaphrodite?
6. As usual when confronted with K., H.'s translation powers weaken[14] as he listens to the tape and tries to render it all into English for me.]

H: So we should ask Saku? Saku understands?
K: It's hard for you to understand. So ask Saku. He will say, "This man [Kalutwo] doesn't understand. I know what you want to know and I can show you." Saku will know.
H: Oh, yes. I've heard some say that before.* [*Weiyu breaks in:*] "True, that's true" [*agreeing with K.*]. You tried to show me in the past but I didn't understand: do you think that your *keriku-keriku* is the same as Sakulambei's?

This was a tricky question. By referring us to Sakulambei, K. was (consciously? unconsciously?) comparing himself with Saku, who is

---

*That is, Saku is enormously knowledgeable about shamanism.

friendly to him. What did that comparison mean? At some level, K. is identifying with Saku. On the surface, K. suggests we should ask Saku because the latter is a powerful shaman. On another level, though, every Sambia man knows he possesses a semen organ, and most could tell what it does in their sexual development. (Compare Weiyu, for instance, in the next chapter.) I was wondering at this moment, then, if somehow K. was identifying himself not just with Saku's shamanic role, but with his hermaphrodism too. Few if any Sambia men—shamans included—would refer us to a hermaphrodite to clarify questions about (normal) male sexual functioning. One might argue that K. believed this was an appropriate and efficient suggestion because he knew we were interviewing Sakulambei at this period. I disagree: the fact remains that K. resisted describing his own views about the semen organ; he was trying to fob us off by saying, "Go ask Sakulambei," and he implied thereby that Saku knew the truth we were seeking about the semen (his) organ. Other men would say that hermaphrodites are so flawed that they could say nothing about maleness (semen organs). In all these respects, K.'s presentation of himself differs from other men's.

K: They're not different. [*Now Weiyu breaks in, saying,* "They're (semen organs) the same." *K. becomes expansive.*] Everywhere, America and wherever, it [the *keriku-keriku*] is the same. There aren't other kinds.
H: Oh, he thinks that he and Sakulambei are the same? [W. translates; and as K. talks, W. lets out a great belly laugh twice; apparently Kalutwo has finally tuned in on me. He starts to whisper. Then W. adds: "Oh, you're [H.] all right," sensing the odd comparison with Saku.]
K: Now I understand a bit. I know you're asking me about—

After K. has referred us to Saku for the facts on the *keriku-keriku*, he realized the implications of his comparison: that I suspected he was comparing his maleness with that of a hermaphrodite. Now his voice changes, and he visibly struggles to clarify what he was trying to say. He whispers to W., who replies in a gruff, grudging voice, "Oh, I understand" (speaking for K.). W. to K.: "That's all right; I know." K. breaks in again here and starts to whisper to W.

K: [*Whispering now.*] Are you asking about the penis or . . . ?
H: I didn't ask you about that; I asked about the *keriku-keriku*; is it the same as his [Sakulambei] or not? [*While saying this Weiyu nods his head saying,* "Yeah, it's the same keriku-keriku; yeah, I

know, the keriku-keriku, *yeah.*"] Is that [*keriku-keriku*] the same as yours?

K: [*Emphatic now.*] No, it's not the same.

H: [*To W.*] But he first said that I must ask Saku about that. [*Weiyu breaks in and starts translating rather nervously to K. Then, in an angry voice, K. responds.*]

W: K. was just talking about him being a shaman, that's all. He's a man-shaman and you asked me [about that].

K: About me. A man, yes: the *keriku-keriku* is the same, that's all, but now we're talking about shamanism.

H: Yeah.

W: Sometime in the future, S. can ask Saku about all this.

H: What does he mean. . . . I don't understand.* [*K. breaks in and starts talking louder.*]

W: What was it? Yeah. [H:? I'm lost.]

Throughout this period K.'s voice has been soft, a gruff whisper; his voice has a lot of movement, different from before. We got him worked up asking about his semen organ. He became angry, and some of that anger was in his voice. But the quietness, the tenseness in the whispering is about the secret—the shared secret—of Sakulambei's hermaphrodism, with the implication that it is shameful for people to talk about it. Especially, one should never speak of it in front of Saku, who would be greatly shamed and humiliated, which could set off an explosion. Note, too, that Saku and K. are on good terms—shamans and members of the same great-clan—and they both have aberrant marital histories. Their identification with each other is perhaps closer than anyone has said. But we then hear denial in K.'s voice, when—at the end—he realized what he implied: that he was like Saku in his anatomy, that they both had the same *keriku-keriku*, or that K. was different from other men and more like Saku. K. continues talking louder, a bit frantically, with a new quality in his voice. (I've listened to the tape several times to get it.) The sense is that K. is scowling: "nasty" best describes that scowl. It is as if he is talking to spit something out (perhaps the identification with Saku).

---

*There was no input by S. in this segment until the end. I thought perhaps he had gone out, but I double-checked and he was there. S: I was. But K. included me out, never looking at me, never even pointedly not looking. He rarely looked at H., rarely at Weiyu. Mostly his eyes look down, his face wary, sad, angry, accusatory, with sudden, appropriate moments of smiling when sharing a light remark with W. He surprises me deeply that such bone-aching misery—his face has been sculpted by it—can pass for a moment. I have no sense that his depression is just dependency, manipulation.

W: [*Emphatically.*] You and me, us men. . . .

K: Yeah, the *keriku-keriku*, yours and mine, it's the same in all of us. [K. uses the word "penis" here and also "*tai*," meaning girl, pointing out the contrast between the two sexes. Here, the external anatomy is the visible sign of the inner state being discussed via the *keriku-keriku*.] We are talking about the shamans here. I'm not the same as a man. Shamans with their ability in a trance state can [like X-ray vision] see what is inside someone. I can't see inside his body. Ask *him* [Saku, what he has inside].

H: [*Silence.*] All right. [*Quiet voice.*] Good enough.

K: Can we see what's inside me?

W: [*Animated, mocks such magical power.*] Something inside there? Some betel nut inside? [He points to a net string bag as if one can as easily see inside the body.] There's betel nut inside of there? Let me have some! [*Otherwise*] . . . you should put it away in another place. Now, this something [semen organ] belonging to all of them—you and me, we don't know. Have they [hermaphrodites] got one? We don't know. [*Going over the same ground.*]

H: All right.

W: That's *enough*, let's stop. [*Anxious to finish.*]

H: [*To S.*] This is . . .

S: He's [W.] dying. I mean this man [K.] is tearing at the interpreter's inside. . . . We'd better close things off.

H: S. is very happy, pleased that you have told us these things. We'll work again . . .

K.'s great reluctance to leave is described above and in chapter 10. For several reasons, S. and I never did work again with him. In 1981 I found K. much the same, though sadder. And ditto in later years.

KALUTWO—FINAL THOUGHTS.*

K. was terribly difficult yesterday. Our session was long, frustrating, exciting, tedious, revealing. It taught me more about resistance, especially K.'s resistance to me and W.'s resistance to translating. And about the translator's role, how unconscious forces can constrain his behavior and ultimately the information collected in any domain, es-

*Written the day after this session; I usually write process notes of some kind after interviews; periodically, I review notes in the field to write summary formulations on each person studied closely.

pecially those troublesome to the translator, thereby influencing the meaning of fieldwork data.

Before Bob arrived, K. and I were at a standstill. I wanted data on K.'s homoerotic relationships with boys, and why he needed them, but he pulled back. I treated him better than anyone ever had, and K. wanted unendingly to be with me. But his way of wanting me—his prickly passivity—confused and exhausted me; so I would give up on him. (Even now—1982—immersing myself in this material for over three hours while translating, it tires me to review K.'s material as it does no other.) And, as Bob says, more than K.'s sexual aberrance, there is his interpersonal aberrance—which other people dislike. He is hostile, and people not only pull back from him, but, like W., they respond to him with hostility and humiliating putdowns. K. is doomed to his terrible self-fulfilling prophecies (a sad merry-go-round he can't get off). For all that, Bob claimed he could see in K. how much K. loved me.

Bob said to me: Is it necessary that every Sambia hamlet have a rubbish man like K.—whom men can humiliate and treat like this? I responded with Levy's (1973:471–473) suggestion about the Tahitians: the *mahu* (transvestite) is present in every village as a sign (for other men) of how *not* to be masculine. Bob then says that while K. has developed and is being perceived in this way, no one set out to do this to him; once stigmatized, however, he became a convenient target for men. Kalutwo's pain, embarrassment, and need to explain himself again—when we misunderstood K.'s statement about the hermaphrodites—results in humiliation on K.'s part because K. didn't communicate clearly that "I am a man." So, in having to clarify, he subordinated himself to W.

An important contrast can be made between K. and Imano here: though men clearly assign Imano to the category of gentle man (as they don't with K.), the passivity of each is fundamentally different. Imano communicates to me about himself without hostility; in fact he's one of the least hostile Sambia men I know. He likes himself, enjoys his life and his wives; he knows who's boss when it is necessary; he allows them to push him around in little ways and sometimes in big ways. He can laugh at himself and take other men's jokes; he will even make himself the brunt of their jokes, for example, in admitting how he likes to spend so much time with his first wife. K. could never do this; his only humor is sarcasm, which he can aim only at others. He is passive but resists being passive. When describing himself, he sees himself only as the object of what others have done to him; his marriages were disasters because his clan brothers

sneaked around and "stole" his wives, or because the wives committed "adultery" and humiliated him. Yet, by Sambia standards, he
was worse than a terrible husband; he was no man at all.

Bob asked K. how he felt about his semen organ: where did S.
pluck that question from? It was the right button: K. smiled, got embarrassed, became defensive, then hostile, and so did W. This led to
valuable information, though not so much in what K. said, as by what
he denied. I was startled that K. denied that he had a semen organ;
what a remarkable answer, even if by misunderstanding. His ambivalence, confusion, and associating to his spirit familiars, including
the way he said it all—"unmanly," in Bob's terms—was extraordinary. But the session came to a dead halt when K., stated he would
talk no more about the semen organ. We said that K. was so uptight
in this session, but he was also concerned and interested. And he
wanted something more, especially a promise that I would send him
letters when I left. Bob says that this—trustworthy love—is what K.
really wanted.

S: All of H.'s interpreters became very attached to him. Undoubtedly, he chose them and they chose him because there existed from
the start the *anlagen* for strong attachment. The form these reactions
took in his friends we can call, for the sake of this discussion, "transference." For the nature of his interviews with each of them was so
intimate in content and feelings that a therapy-like atmosphere was
established. As different from anyone they had ever experienced, he
wanted to listen to them, to understand them, and therefore they felt—
in fact, they *were*—important to him, in ways they had never been
with anyone before. He was benign, giving, and insightful, and this
was coupled with his—to them—highly aberrant state of being an
outsider. So they were more vulnerable to his presence—less defended against it—than they had ever been to anyone before. Nothing
in their culture gave them defenses in advance, the way we would be
equipped in our culture. As far as I can tell, the only advantage he
got from this was better data. (I wonder—we can never know, since
the reports are silent—to what extent other ethnographer–informant
relationships become intimate and lead to nonresearch payoffs.)

As we saw, however, Kalutwo's case teaches us that transference
reactions not only can lead to deeper, truer information but they can—
probably must—lead also to resistance about giving up one's interior
to another. In the transference situation, advantage and disadvantage
are not only inextricably mixed but disadvantage—if one is able to
look well—is hidden advantage. For, as every analyst knows with his

or her patients, in the resistance is information about how one has dealt, from infancy on, with certain situations.

H. has been immersed in this transference from the start. Then, especially but not exclusively with my supervising, he became—in my view—better able to use that situation and less at its mercy. He came to see that content is shaped by relationship, and relationship is part of content. So, since the culture both *is* and *is in* the interpreter, the relationship offers the ethnographer, at any moment, a biopsy of the culture, both its structure and its specific content.

The problem for the ethnographer in dealing with transference reactions is that, so far, most ethnographers have no sense of the concept as theory or as living experience. They are, then, as Devereux (1967) says, at its mercy, unable to deal with it and therefore prone to countering it with their own distortions (that is, countertransference). In this way, they may not only lose information but increase the resistance, so that information will be more actively withheld and even more distorted. We saw that effect in action with the translator's pain in dealing with Kalutwo's unmanliness and other aberrances.

We should not avoid these issues simply because they complicate the education of ethnographers and their data collecting.

We find another example of the value of clinical experience in H.'s coming to see Kalutwo as having a homosexual orientation and thereby different from the other men. When H. and I began working together, early in those two years before I joined him in New Guinea, he knew of no one he would label as "a homosexual." In good part, he thought this because he found no one who seemed a homosexual by the criteria of our culture. My first position with him—based on simple ignorance plus statistical inference—was that there had to be homosexual Sambia men. As he began to fill me in on his friends, K. certainly stuck out as aberrant but only in his being chronically depressed, without friends, not interested in the things that were so important to the other men. Only gradually, on absorbing H.'s reports—this, remember, being before I met Kalutwo—did I suspect that K's aberance was gender/erotic as well. Then H.'s observations fell in place, and we both saw that K.'s erotic attachment was to males, not females (in fact, to boys, though I do not believe this should be called pedophilia, since the loving of boys is not aberrant but a necessary part of Sambia culture).

H.'s technique of data gathering has the strength that one can better find what goes on inside his interpreters; in that way, he has entrée into forms—external and internal—of the culture not available to an outsider. On the other hand, his method is so slow and so dependent on the relationship between ethnographer and interpreter that one may never get an adequate account of the degree to which the *meaning* of something, for example, an erotic practice or a ritual, is shared among all the people of a community. Good ethnography, if aimed at understanding the whole of a culture, needs both the interpersonal/dynamic and the normative/statistical techniques of cultural study.

POSTSCRIPT: 1987

H: It is now many years since my study of Kalutwo was begun and ended. Nothing has changed in K.'s life since that time. He is still a gender misfit, but he is also, by Sambia lifespan ages, an older, nearly aged, man. During my last visits (1985, 1988) I found him still unmarried and unhappy. My occasional letters to him—promised years ago—have not kept us in touch, for he cannot read these without a translator, and he has never responded to them; but at least we have had contact. He seemed still shy and awkward and obtuse and trying-to-be-close to me, however; and I seemed more respectful and understanding of him and the turmoil to which I subjected him. We could be cordial with one another but nothing more.

S.'s discussion of transference and countertransference is entirely appropriate and illuminating in the case of Kalutwo. Editing this chapter one last time has been painful to me, in part because of how much better I now understand our interviews. I have always felt that alone of all the several score people I have interviewed and tried to understand, my attempts with K. were a failure.

Only through training with S. did I come to see *through* K.'s words and roles—and in this sense, his defenses against his own gender aberrance and erotic problems. And only later have I come to see better how at the time I lacked the psychologic skills to be of more help to him and to my work. This pain and feeling of failure has made me at times want to edit out whole pages of the text in which I felt I looked and acted stupid, insensitive, and uncaring. I have even felt like cutting the whole chapter and throwing it in a drawer marked: "Not to be opened until retirement."

It would of course be dishonest to do so and my integrity—not my common sense—has kept me from committing this act of ultimate censorship. Yet this is only the negative side of what I learned working with Kalutwo. The positive side is how I grew and desired never to repeat such mistakes. For we learn in this way too—looking back with more experience and perhaps, sometimes, with wisdom as well.

Unless we ethnographers are willing to make available to readers (especially our students) our failures as well as our successes, we shall profit little as a discipline from our human studies; moreover, we invite being treated badly by the next generation, who will find it hard to believe we could have always been so infallible and, in that way, inhuman.

CHAPTER TEN

The Interpreter's Discomfort

H: Usually we* think of interpreters as technical aids, language machines. Interpreters don't make waves. Even anthropologists tend toward this view. Field interpreters are not judged as whole persons but rather as: competence, reliability, and usefulness; defined as: language skills, intelligence, and facility for translation.[†] Though we know there are other problems, the technical view holds by and large; the other problems have often been ignored.

We know, for instance, that people vary in their capacity to learn languages and translate from them across cultural or ethnic boundaries. We know also that translators and informants may face what—for lack of a better term—one might call "identity problems" in their work. Textbooks used to recognize these problems by advising discretion in choosing interpreters corrupted[2] by too much western experience.

Most anthropologists want to work in the native language without interpreters. A few do not. (I think one's wanting to learn a foreign language measures desire for empathy and identification with those people.[3]) But probably many fieldworkers in exotic cultures rely on interpreters, for, obviously, ethnographers vary in their language-learning capacities. Language families also vary in complexity. In a place such as New Guinea, with over 1,000 languages, most of them unwritten and unrecorded, there is great variation. Malinowski quickly became proficient in Kiriwinian, because it is a straightforward Mel-

---

*S: We who are not interpreters.
[†]One should distinguish between *interpreters*, who change verbal statements into another language, and *translators*, who are also responsible for deciphering and setting down written texts in another language. The latter task Evans-Pritchard saw as *the* problem of anthropology.[1]

anesian language with a written grammar available. Mead usually used Pidgin, not the vernacular, in New Guinea, for she worked for brief periods among groups with difficult non-Austronesian languages.[4] Therefore, many New Guineast ethnographers have worked in trade languages or *lingua franca*, at least at first, or when working with certain subgroups (e.g., women), or on particular topics (e.g., religion). Interpreters have been widely used, probably by most of these ethnographers, for significant periods. The extent of this reliance is belied by puny acknowledgments: a sentence or two soon forgotten.[5]

More important, we have not studied the personality or motives of the interpreter in the ethnographic project. Obviously, if one is simply trying to record objective, shared patterns (norms, values, etc.), using language machines—the false idea of the anthropologist-as-scientist and his interpreter and/or informant—subjective elements such as motivations play no part. *If* ethnographers act differently, their reports should behave differently: all but a rare few reports do not.[6] This chapter concerns such neglected factors. We want to look inside one interpreter to understand better the interpreter's interpreting. Our object is Weiyu's discomfort in working with Kalutwo.

Let us begin with the way interpreters are depicted in most ethnographies: nameless, voiceless, noiseless.[7] A worse lot than the ethnographer, who is at least heard (but not seen). What of the interpreter's age, sex, intelligence, incentives, life history, social or political status, temperament? Or degree of familiarity with the ethnographer: are they (like the faceless informant) strangers or friends; how long have they worked together; under what circumstances and for what purposes? These factors influence the interpreter's interpreting. Most ethnographers recognize such factors, I suspect, in choosing interpreters, but they do not say so in print.

Distortions also occur when interpreters try to normalize or screen out what they either cannot understand, empathize with, are troubled by, or feel would embarrass the interviewer. With psychiatric studies, this translation-distortion problem is acute.

Clinician to Spanish-speaking patient: What about worries, do you have many worries?

Interpreter to patient: Is is [sic] there anything that bothers you?

Patient's response: I know, I know that God is with me, I'm not afraid, they cannot get me. [*Pause*] I'm wearing these new pants and I feel protected, I feel good, I don't get headaches anymore.

Interpreter to clinician: He says that he is not afraid, he feels good, he doesn't have headaches anymore (Marcos 1979:173).

What suffers in anthropology is the ethnographic description, our main concern here.

Perhaps it is unfair to Weiyu, subjecting him to such scrutiny in his interpreting for Kalutwo, a man so frustrating that he drove us both crazy. I might have chosen to scrutinize the process with Moondi or Penjukwi.[8] But only with Weiyu did S. and I work for any length of time. So in keeping with the book's emphasis, Weiyu will serve as our subject. I believe, however, that if we were to dissect any text produced by an interpreter anywhere, we would discover similar subjective factors—more or less overt—permeating its interpretation. Besides, Weiyu himself started the dialogue. He would let me use him here.

Weiyu and I have taught each other about interpreting. Though illiterate and limited in his knowledge of western experience, he was not a naive interpreter, as chapter 5 makes clear. He was highly motivated, enjoyed interpreting, and fitted it easily into his daily routines (e.g., gardening). He had earlier worked on coastal plantations, where he learned Pidgin and Motu, for four years in the early 1970s, before marrying. (He is more fluent in Pidgin. He also speaks a little of two language groups bordering Sambia; so his linguistic range is equal to, or greater than, mine.*) His language skills are not unique; many Sambia speak several languages. Tali, for instance, is fluent in two other Anga languages besides Sambia, and younger men speak Pidgin too. Their Pidgin, though, is colloquial (bush Pidgin), picked up through informal contacts. It is sufficiently different that you must learn each local form from scratch or miss important idiomatic variations, such as in lexical meaning.[9] The more Weiyu and I worked together, the more familiar we became with each other's personality and speech styles. [S: What a huge difference in ease and accuracy must be there when translator and ethnographer are close.]

After months of work, and wanting richer interviews, I realized that I had to teach Weiyu how I wanted him to interpret for me, a procedure that John Whiting et al. (1966:156–159) has recommended and carefully discussed in his early methodologic work. I learned this skill earlier with Moondi, when doing detailed interviews with initiates. (I had never done research in another language and had never

*I'm not great at learning languages. I can read French, but years of classroom Spanish are almost gone. I speak, read, and write Pidgin fluently. My Sambia is conversationally equivalent to Weiyu's knowledge of the neighboring languages of Sambia.

used an interpreter. During training, I never learned that one has to coach interpreters, much less that one has to teach them to be effective. I might not have known to, had I not worked in a psychiatric setting some years before and seen diagnostic interviewing done.) At first, I was concerned mainly with getting the interpreter to render as exactly as possible everything said. But here, both Moondi's and Weiyu's translating sacrificed *completeness*: errors of omission (leaving out words, sentences), of substitution[10] (e.g., inappropriate words or concepts or—more gross and this happened less—substituting their view for the interviewees'), and condensations (glossing whole statements with a word, odd constructions, or rendering an ambiguous construction as simply "good" or "bad," "yes" or "no," etc.).

And then of course informants—suggestible—take cues from the interpreter.* The more Sambia I learned, the more these errors decreased. My questions sharpened; I knew the areas to watch carefully; I picked up errors more quickly. I found myself pleading or demanding that Moondi or Weiyu say exactly what they felt they had heard, no matter how meaningless to them. They found this at times tedious and frustrating. So I praised their faithfulness to the translation, let them know I understood how the work could make them tense, and sometimes debriefed them after sessions.[11] I was careful but, at first (1974–1976), not dedicated enough, which led to inaccuracies in those original data.

In 1979, though, I approached the interviewing differently, less concerned with general cultural patterns and more focused on individual expressions. I tape-recorded nearly all important interviews. I had learned from S. to go for details; had learned that often, in areas such as sexual excitement, moods, or fantasy, without details, you have little useful information.

By this time Weiyu and Moondi had worked with me a long time. I knew their personalities and speech styles well and they mine. We were research collaborators, and, in our closeness, our interviewing was raised to new levels of subtlety. I concentrated on exploring meanings, as in the connotations of verbs and nouns, going for depth of a person's experience and sacrificing breadth to do it.† For the first time I also imported western concepts, like "fantasy," and uncovered

---

*I don't know that this effect has been studied in ethnographic work, but I found the following statement by a linguist: "Despite taking some precautions, in some cases I have detected an increase of up to twenty percent in the number of words cognate with the interpreter's language due to the suggestive effect the interpreter has on the informant" (Healey 1964:5).

†I could afford this loss after spending two years on more sociocultural matters.

native equivalents to ideas such as "excitement." Once Moondi and I agreed on meanings, he helped teach Weiyu (see chapter 4). So, for instance, after a few weeks' work with Kalutwo, I could use Weiyu to question K. in detail about his erotic fantasy and related sexual excitement and be reasonably sure—after a few sessions—that I knew how Kalutwo's experiences, via Weiyu's translations, were connected to my questions.

[S: We cannot be sure H.'s concern with subjectivity brings truer data than the objectivity of a pigeon-training behaviorist, but we know everyone believes it *can*—even the latter scientist when he listens to music, enjoys Shakespeare, or loses his appetite to a surly waiter.] Validity does not, ultimately, rest in those tapes. It is in me, in Weiyu, and in the particular constructions I make in the text. [S: In other words, nowhere.] If you question the validity of these texts, you should. That is the point. All texts should be subjected to such scrutiny.

This chapter consists of an interview we had with Weiyu. It follows immediately on the last session in chapter 9. (These two sessions are separated by only a couple of minutes.) After we worked with Kalutwo, Weiyu arranged to get K. out of the house so W. could talk with us alone. Why?

Chapter 9 shows how frustrating it was to work with Kalutwo. He was temperamental, touchy, ambivalent, secretive, passive–aggressive, dependent, irritable. But he would stay with it, even allow more. It was tiring: an hour with K. was more than three with Imano or Penjukwi.

Weiyu's resistance to interpreting for K. grew with the weeks. Still, Weiyu was patient.[12] He never refused to work with K., for in his status as my assistant, a man like W. could not quit. And he did other interviews for me without difficulty. But in interpreting K., he could not deny his boredom, frustration, short temper, lateness for interviews, greasing me for extra tobacco or coffee to get through it; and then immediately afterward changing the subject or heading off somewhere else. Though barely there at first, by S.'s arrival these tactics were glaring.

Meanwhile, my impatience and frustration with Kalutwo had also increased. I'd pressed him and got nowhere. To press K. was to press Weiyu. Reviewing and translating the tapes these past two years, I am surprised how hostile I was to K. (but sparing W.). Sometimes it is subtle, but S. picked it up easily. No other interviewee made me do this. (In retrospect, the tapes have taught me that only tapes give good enough records to see more fully one's own subjectivity.*) Even after months of close interviewing, you see, I was not in touch with my total experience. I did not know I was responding from unconscious sources (countertransference) to K.

S: Partly, only partly. When someone's life work is to drive others crazy, only countertransference, culture blindness, or organic brain disease could keep us who interview him or her from a spot of irritation. I would judge H.'s response to be countertransference only when he took advantage of K.'s vulnerability.

Note to psychoanalytic colleagues: I think it is a mistake to call all the therapist's/researcher's resonses countertransference. It's true we forever pack our pasts with us and therefore transfer those old times into the present. Still, there are times when our behavior is dominated by such distortions (neurotic perceptions), and times not. Roughly speaking, I'd say that, when treating patients or listening to interpreters—where the task, scientifically and ethically, is to hear what the other tries to communicate—countertransference is neurosis that spoils our sense of the other. If we call everything countertransference, then we have no measure of where we end and the other begins. And that is indulgence.

H: Into this complexity stepped S. He could not know the subtleties. Yet his arrival changed the behavior of all three of us. Kalutwo, frightened and angered, ran away, then returned, wanting to talk again. My hope for working with him was renewed, and S.'s presence helped me be more empathic again.[13] In those sessions, however, Weiyu did not noticeably change, until the end. His reaction to K. after finishing was climactic. He came to us, then, cursing, expressing how he really felt about K.—months of accumulated frustration spilled out. S.'s presence allowed Weiyu to do that. His response is psychodynamically and culturally complex. It differs from an earlier session (chapter 5) in which Weiyu and Tali loosened up, challenged by S.'s questions on their beliefs. Instead, indignant at Kalutwo's responses to S., Weiyu demanded to speak with us and set the record straight. I had held Weiyu back, discouraged him from discussing K.'s aberrance. He had had only me with whom to share his frustrations, and I hadn't listened.[14] S. made Weiyu's silence more unbearable, so he spoke up.

The episode begins here, as K. leaves (p. 330).

---

*I can agree with Healey (1964:18) who remarks that "Listening to such recordings is a kind of shock therapy."

H: This is a real—a real . . . [*much confusion*] discovery for me: another dimension of my relationship with Weiyu, the meaning of an interpreter, and the meaning of the data I've collected from Kalutwo. I didn't have that before now . . . . It's the right question—and now it's so obvious to me . . . it's so obvious . . . so even if the whole session came to no more than this—which it didn't—it produced something important . . .

S: . . . It's a study of the methodology of anthropology, in which we were trying to demonstrate how crucial is not just the information, but the interpreter as well.

H: And not just in general about the interpreter but specific issues about the interpreter: it's so obvious that Weiyu's hostile. Why didn't I see it all along?

S: I swear, he [W.] could not look at that man [K.] . . . and for all these hours. At times he was ready to laugh out loud and had to put his hand up like this* to prevent the—whatever it is you intend when you put your hands up to block someone out . . . . [At other times] he put his head in his hands and couldn't even go on; he couldn't translate right; he couldn't talk . . .

H: It's so obvious; why didn't I see it?† I've been hammering my head against him for two months [*S. chuckles*]—a *long* time. And it's so obvious, now that you've said it . . . . It's been very difficult.

S: This man [K.] is tearing at the interpreter's whole life: the ritual cult, the initiations. This guy stands as proof—threat—of what can go wrong, what the whole culture is structured to prevent, to deny.‡ In a different way from the way a woman [for Sambia men]

---

*We were all seated around a table in my interview room. I sat on one end, Weiyu sat next to me on the adjacent side, K. sat next to him, and S. faced them (on my right adjacent side). We were all within four feet of each other; W. was seated about two feet from me, and a foot from K. W. faced S., though during the session he became increasingly worn down and would sometimes look down at the table or at the opposite wall. Half the time he sat up. During the last half he leaned against the table with his elbow propped up on it, his arm supporting his head. This was his left arm, the one closest to K. His arm was a partition between them; most of the time K. could not see W.'s face because of the arm, nor did W. turn to look at him. I don't think W. was conscious of this body language. Nor was I. But S. was.

†I'm being unfair to myself. I did know both consciously and subliminally that Weiyu was hostile to K.; there are many examples in my notes before S. came along. But I did not know the extent of W.'s hostility, nor did I see the gross form we are about to see. S.'s presence did something to the situation that spread the hostility. He asked K. about the semen organ, and this, I think, set W. off. My interviewing and observing many others besides K. disturbed my focus then (in a way as they would not now, because I am more aware via S. of this aspect), and perhaps I needed those others to defuse my hostility too. (All that is aside from the facts of the rain, malaria, and my too many other projects.) Last, I would add—apropos chapter 1 and what I have written elsewhere—that living in a tribal village somehow blunts certain subliminal awareness, keeping them from reaching full consciousness. We discuss this point in chapter 11.

‡Aberrant people constantly do that to us. Perversion is subversion.

stands as proof of what goes wrong. This—K.—is another whole category. This is a category of: a-man-doesn't-turn-into-a-woman, a-man-turns-into-*that*. Is that right?

H: That's right.

S: And Weiyu is terrified by the "nonsense" of this failed man.

A baby screams in the next room at the top of its lungs; a horrible noise. Both K. and W. rise to leave. We agree to work together again tomorrow afternoon. K. asks us if we are going to Wop, where a feast will be held soon. I say that only S. will go. K. still tarries. Silence, Then W. says, "Enough. That's enough for now." But K. is not budging. I tell W. that I want to work with him further, a signal for K. to leave, getting us all off the hook. Another silence, and then the door creaks.

S: He's still not going out the door. [*We watch.*] Is that amazing or is it amazing? Is that the way he usually leaves?

H: No. It is amazing. [*It was five minutes before K. left.*]

S: That's not the way he usually leaves?

H: I'm drained: he's just a mass of ambivalence.

W: [*Rises.*] I'll go look—

H: [*Cuts in.*] Yeah, you go look [if K. has really gone] and come back.

H: [*To S.*] He [W.] just winked at me as he went out the door [to indicate that he'd see about K.].

S: Look for what?

H: He just winked at me this moment as he went out the door; Weiyu; now, just now, this moment. [*The baby screams again.*] Hey, what's going on out there?

W: [*Thinking I am talking to him.*] No, all the others—they've got to go first—we can't talk with all this clamor.

By now my house is filled with people. Imano has his baby, who is distressed for some reason. Two small boys are raising hell amid a group of oldsters gabbing and lounging on the floor. Kwinko (my cook) is tearing out his hair trying to get some order. I shoo the boys out, leaving the elders (who understand no Pidgin) alone. K. finally leaves.

S: A complex game is being played. K., in a maneuver parents and psychiatrists in our culture would recognize, both wants to go and wants to stay. He will not continue the conversation, so he leaves the room but then hovers in the adjoining room (where before he has remained for hours), jealously concerned with the conversations that continue behind the closed doors.

But he will not stay today, for the conversation is to be about him. W. wants to unburden himself about the effort to work with K. So K.—poor, tenacious, angry, deprived, suspicious, intelligent, self-destroying, sensitive, helpless, yearning K.—must be pried loose from the hut.

H: [*To S.*] Weiyu was just doing a number so he could get rid of the informant* and we could work again. He did that as an excuse.
S: Did what?
H: What he just did. It's too complicated to explain. But—
S: The baby screaming?
H: The baby screaming is—do you want the whole story? The story is this: Imano has been waiting for his interview with us. He's got his baby with him. W. and Imano cleverly agreed to kick the baby out so it would seem Imano could be with us. But that was just a ploy to fool K. into leaving so we could talk about him. This was a conspiracy between Weiyu and the next guy to get rid of the informant [Kalutwo] who has now just left.
S: How did that get rid of the informant?
H: By making it seem like we were going to work with the next guy, when we were really not going to yet.
S: Then otherwise K. would have just hung around by the fire?
H: Right.

Let us review this scenario. For Weiyu to talk with S. and me, he wanted K. away. But K. wouldn't budge. (Did he suspect we would talk about him?) So W., on his own (without talking to me), decided to get rid of K. by making it seem we were to work with Imano, whom we were to see next.† Part of the ploy was to separate Imano from his baby. That's why the baby started screaming: the child didn't want to leave his father. Now W., S., and I are alone.

S: Where are we? We are about to sit down and talk to Weiyu. And he wanted this. He needs a session after the translation? Was that your impression?
H: Well, he's the one who got rid of everyone. We'll ask him.

---

*"Informant" is the word, not "Kalutwo," so that the latter will not know about whom we are talking.
†Imano left and returned later for an interview.

W: This work with K. on the *keriku-keriku*: [*low, embarrassed laugh*] how could I know?

H: Do you, for yourself, want to talk about that?

W: Yeah. Let's not work on anything else. Let's talk about *that* man. [*Lowers voice, with emphasis.*] What kind of thinking does he have anyway?

Note to myself, 1981, on hearing the tape: There's a vengeful quality in his voice. I hadn't realized what it meant until just now. When I allowed him the chance to talk about other things, he said, "No, let's talk about that man and what kind of a mind he has." I see S. was right: at this moment, W. needs to talk this out. K. is a thorn in his side, this man who is so aberrant.

W: [*Mimicking K. disparagingly.*] "What kind of work?" What kind of talk is this of his? What kind of *jerungdu*? [*Then regular voice.*] He doesn't have *jerungdu* [courage, prowess, balls]. This kind of thinking. It's like women's! Myself—Weiyu—yes: I understand the semen organ. I've got *jerungdu*. And yes, it's [semen organ] got its *own* strength; only it can strengthen us and make us strong men. That's it. [*He is frantic in voice to get it out and to say it as strongly as he can. He has held it in so well, during the long chore of translating.*] We don't have something else. The *keriku-keriku* is our boss. That's all there is to strengthen us so that we can say, "I'm a real man." That's how I grew up. What about him? What do you two think of him?

H: Yeah.

W: You two interviewed him about his *keriku-keriku*. I'm still thinking about what you asked him; I haven't forgotten.

H: Now, you're thinking that the *keriku-keriku* makes men strong.

W: Yeah, that's it. It's for making us mature and grow strong. If he [a male] grows up with that, he will be a strong man. When he grows up, it strengthens him, his bones. That's the function of this *keriku-keriku* [*whispers that word*]. When I go to make a child,* only that one thing growing inside will strengthen its bones. It controls that process. And later it will be inside of him, strengthening him.

H: OK. I'm going to tell Dr. Stoller now. [*To S.*] He says, "This guy's

---

*A baby is created from the substances. The father contributes semen: after many ejaculations, he has stored enough in the woman that the process begins. The semen gives the baby (male or female) strength, which is nontangible, but also bones, muscle, and the *keriku-keriku*. The woman contributes blood, which becomes the soft anatomy and, in males, a constant remnant of femaleness that personifies the unending struggle [S: to which Kalutwo succumbed] against bisexuality.

thoughts are just screwy; he talks like a woman." [*S. whistles low.*] Then he says, "Kalutwo doesn't know what he's talking about. You and everyone knows what the *keriku-keriku* does. It gives you strength; it gives you bone; it gives you manliness; it gives you semen; it's what produces babies."

S: What does he feel Kalutwo said that was like a woman?

H: [*To W.*] You said that K.'s talk is the same as a—

W: [*Interrupts*]—the same thinking as a woman's. [*Excited.*] The women don't understand much when you ask them about some things. All they say is, "Uh, uh" [*motions as if women are dumb and don't know what to say*] . . . . Only when you show them "Here, here, this something" [*he points*], only then will they understand. Only then they'll understand. [*Letting off steam.*] You two worked hard with K. asking him, asking him hard about the *keriku-keriku. And he didn't understand!* . . . I don't know. Does he understand, or doesn't he? First, he said he doesn't have a *keriku-keriku.* Then he turned around a little later, and you [H.] said, "All right, if you don't have a *keriku-keriku*, if you think you don't have semen, then . . . [*Weiyu emits a little sound and kicks, as if kicking a dog away:*] Get out! Fucking! I'm tired of this little dog here, this kind of dog! [*He scowls.*] It's not good. It doesn't make sense at all, that kind of dog! Sorry, he's just a different kind.

H: [*Confused by Weiyu's pejorative analogy.*] Huh?

W: No. I'm still thinking about that man [Kalutwo]. That man—his talk, it's not straight . . . . [*Shakes head and voice trails off, with depair.*]

H: [*Quiet voice.*] What are you sorry about, Weiyu?

W: I'm sorry about one particular thing, something.

H: Weiyu?

W: I was thinking of something you said . . . that his talking was . . . . You keep asking him . . . . He said, "I'll be sorry when you go away over there, I'd like it if you sent me a letter." Not any old letter but some particular something [*means money*]. He was thinking about this, that's all. [*Weiyu means Kalutwo was playing on our sympathies, while all he really wanted was money.*] That's all . . . a letter. Like that. That's all. I don't have any more to say. That's all. [*Pause.*]

H: [*Clears throat.**] Now, in your thinking—

W: [*Breaks in.*]—We don't want him to think, "I'm sitting out here,

---

*I am a little startled at Weiyu's bluntness and his sophistication, which he didn't show with K. A good actor.

and they're all in there saying bad things about me." [W. is imagining what K. might have thought had we let him stay in the other room while Weiyu spoke in private with us.] So I got rid of him. He understands Pidgin; he could be shamed.[15]

H: [*Straightens up. To S.*] Weiyu got Kalutwo out of the house so that K. wouldn't be ashamed when we were talking about this. And he says that Kalutwo's thinking is just not right . . . that he just doesn't understand what the *keriku-keriku* does. . . . That Kalutwo's thoughts about this are like a woman's. Like a woman, he says one thing and then he says another thing; first he says he doesn't have the semen organ, and then he changes his mind. And when he talks about semen, he says, "Oh, I don't want to talk about that; that's an awful subject."

S: He's saying that's typical of the way women communicate?

H: Yes, and he is also saying that Kalutwo's whole attitude toward the subject is like a woman's.

S: In what way?

H: When I asked him about semen, he said, "Forget this; I don't want to talk about that anymore; I have had enough of that." That's not the response a man would make.

S: But Weiyu knows that this is not a man who is uninformed? He's a man who went through the initiation. Therefore, Weiyu would feel K. has no right to be this way. Am I right?

H: Let me ask Weiyu. You know K. knows about this. He's been initiated. He's a grown man.

W: [*Inserts enthusiastically.*] He's a grown, older man. He even knows the married men's stories about intercourse with women.

H: Does he know about the *keriku-keriku*?

W: The *keriku-keriku*? [*Whispers.*] I think he doesn't know about it. He knows it exists but not how its tubes, its pathways go, he doesn't understand how it works.

H: But you and I, all of the rest of us men, we know about the *keriku-keriku* . . .

W: Yeah, yeah. That's right. That's it. Nothing else controls you and me. Yeah. You two talked to him on a subject, but he'd only say, "Oh, you're talking about this subject, huh? I'm trying hard to understand that. All right, this subject there? All right . . . this subject?" He didn't respond to us [meaning K. didn't engage us in a dialogue; he kept asking us to clarify further our questions, which were already clear]. I was just babbling idly about women. [W. is chastizing himself: a new feminist.] Even if you talk to women, they'd understand. Women have got their own thinking;

their thinking is clear. Only *he* doesn't have any. His thinking is really another kind. A woman will understand your questions. She'll show you. Now, Kalutwo, not at all. He doesn't have any . . . of his own; he doesn't have any at all [*lower voice, frustration.*]*

H: Doesn't he know about his own *keriku-keriku*?

W: He knows, he knows but . . . . He knows that in our insides, se-men comes through the *keriku-keriku*. It's that which I think he doesn't understand. But knowledge of the semen of possums and other animals, he knows about that. He knows *only* that [that animals also have semen].

H: [*To S.*] He is clarifying his comments. He says, "I, Weiyu, really used the wrong analogy. Kalutwo is not like women; his thinking is not like women's because women also—if you ask them to tell you about something, they will tell you about it—they won't squirm out of it and go along a different path. They will tell you about it; and we men are also the same way." So K. has got his own special way. So I asked him about that. He said that K. knows—this is important—he knows he has a semen organ inside because all of us men know that the only function of the se-men organ is to supply semen to the cock.

S: —And he knows he has semen.

H: He must. Well, that's not what he says.

S: I'm saying if he's having relations with boys, he knows he's got semen. Therefore, he's got a semen organ. Or he has disconnected the concept in some way that men never do, because, we might say, of his identification with women?

H: Weiyu is saying that K. is disjointed. He must know what all men know, because he's had all the teachings that there is about that thing inside . . .

S: So his answer "no" and his answer "yes" is an approximation of fact. The answer is: "Yes, I do have one; but no, I don't have one in the sense that mine is like other people's or has the same function as other people's. There is something wrong inside of me so I can't be defined as a normal male."

H: Yeah. We were intellectualizing more or less about the semen organ until I asked him about semen. Then he [K.] got uptight; he had anger in his voice. Weiyu noted that: he said K. wasn't doing a very good job of talking about this until you asked him about

---

*Weiyu implies that Kalutwo's—in our lingo—erotic neurosis has ground K. into such a mass of ambivalence that only confusion remains. Even women are better than that, the misogynist admits.

semen, and then he just said, "I don't want to talk about that," as if to say: "That's awful." Now, a normal man should say, "That's my semen. I've got lots of semen! What do you want to *know about it* [*showing off*]?" It's something a man should be proud of. But that's not K.'s affect. W. is telling us that Kalutwo's attitude toward semen is not a *man's* attitude. There's something disconnected in K.'s feelings about semen. W. is not that way.

S: Why did W. have to talk with us now?* In order that we be clear [see the failure in] what this man [K.] was doing?

H: Yeah.

S: What else does Weiyu want?

H: He wants to do something else, and here's where you've got it right. Now I see that. W. wants to tell us what the real function of the semen organ is.

S: That we not be left with the wrong impression?

H: That's not the only thing. There's another sense, too: W. knows so well about the semen organ that it's easy for him to talk about it. He doesn't have any trouble talking about it. *"That comes easy to me:* let me teach you about it; it's easy for me."

S: He wants to give us the right information.

H: There's also an emotional dimension too: "You're barking up the wrong tree with this guy. So let me tell it, it's so easy for me."

S: Is there some intensity, an "Oh-my-God-I'd-better-get-this-to-them?"

H: Yes. Here's how I would have read this before, if you hadn't been here and I had had the same session with Weiyu, and I hadn't been thinking the way I'm thinking right now. Weiyu would have come in, but I wouldn't have known why he got rid of Kalutwo. Then it wouldn't have happened the same way. Maybe he would have come in and said: "I'm going to tell you about the *keriku-keriku* now." And I would have said, "I know all about it."

S: You would have put aside your question, "Why in the hell is he so insistent about telling me what was already done ten, twenty times, and I know it cold?"

H: Yes, exactly; and I would have ignored what *he* wanted to do. Because the meaning of it, I think, is that this isn't for me, *this is for him.*

S: He's *got* to have this session with you.

---

*Throughout these dialogues S.'s ability always to bring me back to the interpreter's immediate subjectivity shows a clinical attention that was missing in me.

H: Exactly. I wouldn't have thought of it before, but it's so obvious now.

S: I've suddenly got a new anxiety: I look at that dwindling pile of tapes, and I look at the calendar.

H: I told you so. [S. felt his two-dozen two-hour tapes would never be used up.]

S: I didn't believe you. We should do it for his sake, but I would also like, if I could, to probe his scornful laughter, his head down, his refusal to look at the man, his anger—

H: Will you ask him about that; it would be easier for you?*

S: Sure.

H: Ask him the questions, and I will too, as ideas come to me.

S: Do we have to release him from his pain regarding Kalutwo?

H: [*To Weiyu.*] Do you want to tell us more about the semen organ?

W: No [*emphatic*]. The two of us have completed our work. I've taught you that. It's done now. It's inside your books now. Now I just want to [*whispers*] say [my] bad feelings† about that man [K.]— and so I came to talk with the two of you. You mustn't think, "He [Weiyu] wants to come and tell more about the semen organ." [*Shakes head.*] No. There's no more talk about that. I've already taught you.

H: [*To S.*] I said, "Do you want to tell us about the semen organ? And he said, "No, I don't really want to tell you about that. I just wanted to talk about these bad things about K. I just wanted to get him out of the house so I could say bad things about him." Now, I'm thinking, it's crazy. It's getting so thick for me that I'm starting to forget pieces . . .

S: You can't hold your questions together?

H: Yeah. Weiyu's [stated] purpose in doing this was to tell us about the semen organ. But that's not really what he wanted to do. He wanted to say bad things about Kalutwo. It's more conscious than I thought, his—[*pause*]

S: —Disgust, anger, rage, whatever. Those are all so conscious and have been all along. They *are* this very minute; look at his face.

H: Something is more conscious than I had thought it was [*pause*] . . . . I know what it is. He was going to come in and give us a lecture about the semen organ to explain its function.

---

*After months of work, and so many things to do before leaving in a few days, I am feeling swamped, no longer as focused as in chapter 4. That, too, is an unspoken aspect of field method.

†In hundreds of interviews over many years with Sambia this is only one of three times I ever can remember someone saying this about someone else.

But he changed his mind and said, "Look, I have already told you about that. I don't have to go into that again. What I really want is to say bad things about Kalutwo." Now that seems bizarre. Has Weiyu ever done that before? In a thousand sessions? Well, maybe a couple of times.

S: Is he concerned that we didn't recognize it so he had to make sure that we do?

H: I hadn't thought of that, but it's so obvious, that's why he did it.

Searching my memory now, I recall at most three or four times in the last two and a half years that Weiyu, having been the interpreter, returned to talk privately about a session. And it is rare for him to say he thought someone was full of bull. Remember the powerful constraints of shame in Sambia culture. To have said such things in front of K. would have shamed him greatly; thus, it would have shamed Weiyu also to have said them. Unless you want to stir up a fight, you do not insult someone.

I think now that what wasn't quite conscious in Weiyu's thinking is this: he had never before directly communicated that he thought K. was unmasculine, an incompetent male: that is the bottom line. A man should be able to talk about his semen organ and semen without shame; but K. was embarrassed discussing both subjects. (As he had been before.) And I was amazed Weiyu could verbalize with disgust, frustration, and anger his unequivocal opinion: Kalutwo is a failure as a man.

This points up a detail about clinical technique. Why didn't I check all that out with Weiyu? What S. was saying was, "I think it's quite conscious; look at the expressions on his face, etc." S. said, "Ask him if that was the reason he returned to the subject." Here is an important difference between how I operated as an ethnographer and how S. was as a clinician: it isn't enough to presume the ideas were conscious in Weiyu, as I had thought; S. wanted to *know* if they were conscious or not and what was their exact form. Details count: God lives in details. The clinician is more a detective of the individual. Where the ethnographer is satisfied—with appearance, with the outward forms of the behavior—the trained clinician (when competent) is not.

S: OK. [*Looks at W.*] What's he thinking? Is he just waiting for us to stop talking? Does he want to say more?

H: No, I asked him. He said "no."

S: OK. He's comfortable with what he said.

H: Yeah.

S: Is he concerned we didn't recognize it so he had to make sure we did?

H: I hadn't thought of that. But it's obvious in all of his comments that that's why he did it.

S: [*Very quiet.*] Not necessarily: he may know that we know it and yet he must say it anyway.

H: Oh. [*To W.*] We are wondering why you came here to say bad things about K.?

W: [*Impassioned.*] The two of you worked so hard, and you've only gotten a headache from Kalutwo's evasions. That's why. K. knows . . . . He knows, but he doesn't talk straight.

H: [*Cuts in.*] Why doesn't he want to talk straight?

W: That's it! That's what I mean! Why *doesn't* he want to talk openly? [*Raises voice, animated, excited, exasperated. Then lowers voice.*] He's shamed. Here. [*Motions to side of abdomen.*] He's thinking, "It's no good if they ask me about that something [semen organ] inside me. If I talk I'll be shamed."

H: [*With consternation.*] What do you mean? Doesn't he have one? Or what?

W: It's not that. He's got it, but he's shamed . . . of talking about what he actually does [in sex].

H: Of what?

W: Shamed of [*drops voice*] the women, or something . . .

H: The women!

W: [*Low voice again.*] Yeah. The women—and the boys too. He sleeps with them and so . . . [*pause*]. This is a new man [S.] here. So Kalutwo's shamed.

Let me underscore two background points. First the difficulty experienced when, on beginning fieldwork, I found the secret cult. The men hid it from me. Only two people, Nilutwo and Moondi, were then my interpreters on secret matters. In time, I was accepted, but even then, when men talked of homosexual practices, semen beliefs, and sex in general, they were reluctant, hidden, secretive, and ashamed. Eventually, the secrecy lifted (Herdt 1987c). The men trusted me and became open to the point that they were able to be themselves with me. But Kalutwo here reminds me of that early period, when he and others resisted talking about these sexual matters. His present resistance is a biopsy of the greater problem I've had in getting K., as compared to other men, to talk about these things.

Second, why was K. the most resistant of my informants—always resistant, not just now? No one else, except Sakulambei, who did open up to us in the end, had K.'s sort of resistance. Was this a piece of character structure, a defense to protect gender disorder: heterosexual inhibition and homosexual preference? If the latter (though we think both hunches are right), then this poor devil, in his aberrance, points up currents—anxieties and their resolutions—the rest of the people ("the culture") handle more efficiently (e.g., with repression). Thus, in this case study, we have uncovered the Sambia man's key problem of psychosocial adjustment.

W: He's shamed of this . . . of speaking his mind . . . about women. He was married before.

H: He lost his wives?

W: Yeah. He lost them all . . . . Some* of them he screwed, but he hid it from us when he was talking. [Weiyu is upset at this reference to the further evidence of K.'s unmanly way: "What man would deny he's screwed his wives?"[16] In K.'s only admission— fellatio with his second wife—he claimed she had initiated it. Weiyu never believed it. I do.]

H: [To S.] More details. He thinks Kalutwo felt ashamed because we're asking about women and boys, about having a semen organ and screwing. Weiyu says that . . . uh—

S: —that he's a New Guinea transsexual.[†] [Pause: H. looks baffled.] You didn't understand me? He wants to be rid of his male [semen] organ.

H: [Consternation.] Go on, I'm sorry.

Stunned. Thinking, "My God, that can't be true." But on hearing S. label it, something crystallized I had known a long time, and then, I thought, "Yes, there is something in that, but he's not a transsexual. He is more masculine than a transsexual." [S: Right.] What does W. allege is different about Kalutwo? K. knows the semen organ is inside him, yet he's hiding information about it from us. He wasn't really telling us what he feels about it; that's what W. means. I asked him, "Why?" W. said, "He's afraid that you [S.]—a new presence here—

---

*Whose version is true? Weiyu's? H.'s? Since K. told us he screwed only once, we must presume people have different versions of K.'s story.

†I wasn't being literal here, only playing with an idea to stimulate my own thinking, to get myself, in an instant, to play off present observations and intuitions of this man in this culture against what I learned in ours. What I meant then is that, though transsexualism is an impossible clinical concept with the Sambia, he was the closest to it one would find. [H: Sakulambei may be closer, at least he would have been a few years ago.] It would be more accurate to think in terms of transsexual impulses and their degree of consciousness rather than trying to apply to Kalutwo the diagnosis of "transsexual," which implies an identity, a powerfully motivated commitment to become female and live appropriately as one. [H: Right. I argued something like this statement of Stoller's elsewhere.[17]]

are going to ask him about screwing boys and women." So what is different about K.? "He's got the semen organ, doesn't he?" and Weiyu said "Yes." "And he's got semen, doesn't he?" and W. said "Yes. He's got that." So I repeat, "Well, what's different?" and W. says, "It's the way he's *talking* about it. He doesn't want to talk about semen because he's shamed. He's shamed because S. is asking him questions, and K. will be shamed if he tells about it: how he used to be married, how he probably screwed a couple of women in his marriages . . . . (But I wonder.) He's shamed of telling us that." At one point K. bragged to some men that he had had sex with one of his wives twice, though K. has never told *me* that. W. thinks K. fears that we shall again dredge up this whole story—that K.'s ashamed of. Weiyu's overall message is that K. is ashamed about his masculinity, maleness . . . that's why this is bizarre for W., who is *so* heterosexual.

I don't feel I sufficiently communicated to S. my sense that K. was hiding because he was afraid I would ask him about his present homosexual relationships with initiates; that I would pursue the rumor that he has tried to suck the penises of the boys; and that this may have appalled K., who wouldn't have been able to bear the shame of talking with us about that subject now. Maybe in a year or two from now he could do that, but not yet. [In 1981 he still could not.] And he couldn't do it except under *exactly* the right circumstances. Not here, with an interpreter there, in front of whom he would be deeply ashamed and whom he could not trust. Weiyu might blab it around the hamlet. Kalutwo was not just reluctant to talk about his semen and maleness, but more: he didn't want to discuss his particular form of homosexuality.

What does K. do? Though *he* has not spoken of it, it's more than rumor. To repeat: two boys told me he tries to switch roles with them; he, an adult, wants to suck them, an incredible affront to Sambia males' masculinity. K. may have been terrified we would bring that up; he fled shortly before S. arrived *because* I was finally aiming to explore. Related to this interview now is Weiyu's marked heterosexuality. In saying above that W. is *so* heterosexual I mean also that Weiyu is extremely masculine by Sambia standards. W.'s earlier enthusiasm for boys was masculine too. When I first met W., he was in the overtly bisexual period, had just married, and was not yet—his wife had not had a baby—exclusively heterosexual. From the start, he was open and almost exhibitionistic in reporting his sexual exploits, buttering the boys up and appropriately screwing them. For a Sambia, taking pride in having been an inseminator of both boys and women is masculine. And W. was extremely proud. The differ-

ence in gender identity between them permeates the interview. It makes
K. uneasy with W. and makes W. despise K. Kalutwo has never felt
at ease inseminating boys and was quite put off by screwing women.
The contrast with W. couldn't be greater; W. with his enjoyment of
homosexual relationships, which he then gave up simply because
women were a greater pleasure.

S: Our focus should still be on Weiyu. He was deeply disturbed by
this interview, which—is this right?—is the most intense of all
the interviews that he had to translate with K., though this problem was present each previous time. It was worse for W. this time.
Is that right? He's been able to put up with your asking these
questions over a long time. But K. is constantly busy refusing the
full masculinity of his culture. He is trying to confuse *you*; even
his not talking clearly to you was a furtive expression of the failure of his masculinity. K., in a roundabout way, is expressing a
dreadful possibility: a male might be unmasculine and deny his
maleness, and then, as if that weren't bad enough, the son-of-a-
bitch—to paraphrase the way Weiyu feels about it—does it in an
unmanly way! [*Laugh.*]

H: That's it exactly. He is talking in an unmanly way.

S: About an unmanly subject that goes on inside him. That just makes
it worse. So this was a very hard time for Weiyu. He just couldn't
bear it after a while. Not only that, he had to get K. off the porch,
as if to say, *"Get out of here!"*

H: Right, because he has never done this before—

S: He threw him out of here!

H: —He's never physically removed him before. *I've* done that a couple of times but only because I wanted to work privately with
someone else.

S: This interview was unbearable for the translator, is that right?

H: Yes.

S: I don't know how much time he can spend, but maybe it will be
cathartic for him to now be free to say what he does think of
having to work—not what does he think of this *man*—but what
does he think of having to put up with *this* translating, what was
he suffereing that he had to bear somehow by laughing, by putting his hand up, by refusing to look at the man, by facing parallel
with him rather than face-to-face with him, by all the twisting
and turning, the mistranslations, the refusal to repeat the translation properly, etc. What was he having to put up with inside
himself?

H: [*To W.*] Dr. Stoller wants to ask you about your feelings when you translated for Kalutwo.

W: [*Somewhat fatigued.*] No, look, my friend. This here—I want to talk to him [S.] about it: I didn't feel anything in particular. I only talked to him [K.], that's all. I only waited for his words. I waited and waited . . . Ssh! [*disgust*] . . . I waited and waited. It was a pain in the ass [*scowling, frustrated*]. But about him? Nothing! He didn't answer me straight. "Oh, yeah, it's all the same, it's all the same," like that. He just worked at keeping his mouth shut and then later would go back and say something about what went before. I'm tired of this kind of talk. But I didn't feel anything else. This kind of man, his talking, I don't like it. I've been sitting too long. He's given me a backache. Yeah, this kind of man . . . . His style of talking. I have a backache from sitting with him so long. Now [*brightens up*], when I'm translating for Tali or with Imano, this doesn't happen.* I'm pleased with someone like that. You ask him, "How about that?" and he tells you [*sharp, strong, punctuated voice*]. So I translate quickly; that's really good. It goes quickly, quickly! I like that kind of man.

H: Yeah. [*To S.*] He says he's tired. He's tired of Kalutwo's . . . [*searching for the right word*] . . . style. You ask K. a question, and you sit and wait and wait. Finally he gives you an answer, and usually it's not right . . . . And you wait and wait some more. "I'm tired of this kind of man because he just"—

S: —He's not a man—

H: [*Echoes S.*]—He's not a man. Then he said, "This is no good . . . it's not the same with Tali. Ask him something [*H. snaps his fingers*], he'll give you an answer just like that. Or look at Imano: whatever you ask him he'll give you a straight answer just like that. It's always straight."

S: And is that correct?

H: Yes, even in Imano's case. He feels that with that kind of man, a quiet man . . . the message is (I still haven't worked this out) that Imano is so comfortable with his wife and is a [gentle] man, and yet he is so *open* about his sex life and his—

S: —But, W. feels, he's [Imano] a man, a male. He's different from the rest of us but he has his organ and he has his semen and he uses it appropriately and uses it with women. He enjoys that but

*W. subliminally tells us here that it matters not whether you are a tough (Tali) or soft (Imano) guy; they're fine people. It's the bogged-down obtuseness of K. that bothers him. (And K.'s fear of marriage too.) W. isn't just being a macho bigot who hates "homosexuals." I think it's Kalutwo's depression that has Weiyu so worked up.

he's still within the category of male (this is really a question), while the other guy is acting like he's in a different category by the way he behaves and by the way he answers quetions—especially by the way you can't get a straight answer.

H: Right.

S: It's very, very painful to have to deal with someone like that and be nice instead of throwing him out at the start.

H: Yeah, that's right. And I have to say that he [W.] has got—

S: —Forbearance.

H: That's right [chuckle]. Far more than other men. That's why I tried to be as patient as possible. I guess I realized that all along. Subliminally he has taken a lot. [Pause.]

W: You know, you've been working a long time, and I am the big gainer. I understand translating now and don't have to work hard to understand.

S: Tell him: I'm indebted to him. I understand what it is like for him to have to sit here and help Gil translate and to try to make it as accurate as possible despite what Kalutwo was saying. I understand the gift that he gave us by being willing to translate for us for our research.

H: Yeah. [To W.] Bob says this: He knows you've worked hard at helping me translate. And he knows you don't much like to translate for K. So he's very happy you have worked hard on the translating. It has gone fine; he knows that, and he knows you have done good work.

W: [Quickly.] I wanted to show K. what you were aiming at. But that's not how it was.

H: We know. But we're pleased with you because you tried so hard to gather knowledge about this kind of man . . . . He's got a different kind of thinking, and we know it's hard for you to try to get that thinking.

W: You too, sometimes, you got a headache . . .

H: Yeah, you're right. [To S.] He says, "You got some headaches too." [Chuckle.]

S: You bet! [Laugh.] I know what poor Gil has put up with!

H: [To W.] Yeah, the two of us, it's the same. All right. That's enough.

W: Okay. [Leaves. Smiles goodbye.]

H: The least pleasure I've had is from working with Kalutwo. It has been the most difficult. For the energy invested, it has been so hard, uphill every inch. Anyone else, even the shaman [Saku]—it's not true of anyone else. Even the [evasive] shamans; I enjoy working with them, almost always. Sometimes Saku is very sensitive, but the sensitivity I don't mind because I usually know where he's at. Whereas what you were saying about him, the informant [K.] is correct. [There are now people talking in the background, where Weiyu has gone for coffee with Moondi or Kwinko. So I monitor my words—it is automatic now—using "informant" instead of "Kalutwo"; I know they're there and can overhear us.] Sometimes I feel he willfully sets out to exhaust and confuse me so I will just give up.

S: The diagnosis for him at home is "passive-aggressive," the way you get at somebody by a passive technique, not by going directly at them. You exhaust them with your passive resistance. In one sense he was not a good choice if your main purpose was (and it was) to collect data—not in the superficial sense—on maleness and masculinity and sexuality. Yet he was a fine choice, because he is the most aberrant person in the society. Therefore, anything you got was worth more, because you got the most aberrant person, even though, in his aberrancy, he brought resistance with him. If you wanted to measure something in this culture that nobody in the history of the world has ever done in an alien culture, that is, how does a person resist, then you could not have picked a better case. You have now something most anthropologists don't [don't know how to] pay attention to: psychology; the inner psychology or character structure of a human being and how it colors his behavior. And you also get a glimpse into how he maintains aberrance, not just the gross aberrance of the sexuality. For they [Sambia] respond even more to his social aberrance. You couldn't have picked a better person. You may suffer from his resistance, but your suffering—not *"you* suffered"—your suffering was your organ for *measuring* aberrance. It's a more real way of measuring it than are his words. The words do not measure his aberrant personality. Our only measuring instrument is ourself, not our cognition, but our feeling: "I can't bear this." In that sense you could not have picked anyone better. But you weren't picking him for that. You salvage something additional for your research when you recognize your suffering was a piece of anthropologic research using the only organ available. You can't measure with a tape recorder what he is doing to you [and therefore who is this conglomerate of resistances, defenses, memories, fantasies, desires, affects—this person—Kalutwo]. And you can't measure it by sitting on a tractor and counting (see chapter 1). That anthropologic methodology [ours] has never been paid attention. [Not quite. See Devereux (1951, 1978), maybe Mead (1935) too, but she was rather rudimentary clinically.] Instead of *using* their suffering, anthropologists do the same goddamn thing your tractor-sitting friend does, ignoring the internal tension his informants' resistance causes, treating it as noncommunication, as not significant, not useful, not ethnographic, as epiphenomenon, working around it, changing it into something else. Shaping their research so that they didn't have to suffer. [H: Ignore it and, exhausted by ignorance and the anger plus self-hatred, it causes you, if you are committed to learning about humans, to lock yourself away at the end of the day—as if the work was so painful it couldn't go on twenty-four hours a day, blotting out how ethnography should be in the field. And get drunk or read novels or take tranquilizers or get depressed or go home and never return or be unable to write up your data or become a department chairman or university president.] You couldn't do that. You didn't have enough sense to ignore your work and to do something superficial.

H: Right. I mean—this is also really an educational experience. That all makes so much sense to me, but I never thought of it in that way. You see, Nilutwo is like that—Nilutwo had terrible, terrible—oh, my heavens!—resistance and suffering. [But we managed to work through some of it.]

S: What we're measuring is that anthropology has made a mistake. It refused to look at the individual and thought it could get away with measuring the general. There's no such thing: there are a bunch of individuals. [Mild oxygen deficiency, marked education lack, jungle madness, beginner's enthusiasm, but—I still think—more correct than ignoring individuals and their subjectivity.] Now, the majority of those individuals agree about the *tingu* and the *keriku-keriku*, but each one is an individual still, and anthropology—I have said this to you since the first day we talked—makes a mistake ignoring the individual's psychology. If they say, as [Victor] Turner (1964) did, "It's beyond me," that is *not* a mistake; that's the right thing to say. To say, "We don't want to deal with this, and we'll pay the price," is fine. But to say it's not a part of anthropology, not part of the study of Man, that's a mistake, a historic mistake, a *great* mistake. You cannot back off from mistakes like that. Mistakes like that eventually cut your throat. Let's do something else.[18]

PART III
Conclusions

CHAPTER ELEVEN

Summing Up: Clinical Ethnography of Sambia Erotics and Gender

H: In this book we have provided our closest look at Sambia erotics and gender identity. Previous works have charted the construction of gender and sexual excitement in Sambia culture in formal and certainly more conventional accounts of these phenomena.[1] This study, by contrast, is our most exhaustive effort yet to provide the reader an experience-near[2] narrative examination of Sambia sexual culture.

To be successful, a close-up, experience-near account should make a native's world come alive to the reader. More important, it should show how the culture is experienced by its purveyors; how interpreters not only sense but act on their meaning systems. To do this without demeaning the natives or oneself in the study of erotics is not easy: sex is still a dirty subject to some. Perhaps this difficulty explains in part why anthropology—which has led the way in pioneering gender studies since the 1960s—has avoided erotics as much as any other social science, the sexologists and psychoanalysts excluded of course.[3]

We have sought to present our interviews with Sambia pretty much unadorned. Sometimes these dialogues speak for themselves, sometimes not. What is between ourselves and Sambia—our culture and theirs, sometimes a language or an interpreter as well—harms communication but not insurmountably. This inbetweenness makes for distortion but also discovery.

Our use of narratives—more often dialogues—is pathbreaking in cross-cultural studies of sex and gender. Our texts show Sambia subjectivity as well if not better than our friends' myths and rituals; but these symbolic forms (available elsewhere to the reader) are a background for these texts, which poke their heads through in the words and idioms of Sambia everywhere, both by what is said and not said.

349

Subtleties permeate this process, for there are many ways to mis-translate words or translate too literally and miss the speaker's intention. Then there are differences, some substantial, between the meanings of our interpreters qua individuals: not semen as such, but what this body fluid means to Moondi and not Kalutwo; to Saku who lacks it, Penjukwi whose breasts exude it, and Weiyu who is concerned about its conservation. Here are great problems in the interpretation of culture and particular persons; no wonder the book took us so long to do.

Sambia is not only animistic but a dream culture and not just a society enmeshed in war but one in which gender roles and erotic experiences are built in and through conflict and dramatic rites of masculinization. Ritualized homosexuality is a part of the heroic culture complex war leaders and great shamans created and sowed to make their neighbors respect and fear them. The self in such a culture is not our nomad individual or a lone child. Selfhood is constructed in relation to others, and *only* by relation to these others does the experience of self make sense as a construct. This "relational self"— here is another popular concept[4]—is manifested in erotics and gender too. For gender, masculinity and femininity, as Stoller (1985b) has written [S: not quite], is not born but made; it is in its essence, convention. It is also more than that, because its definition is subject to the great and sometimes humorous, othertimes dastardly whims of fate, of biology and history. Who could not feel as much in the sad fate of Sakulambei? And yet, to reflect on the issue another moment, one can see gender and erotic variations as well in Moondi, in Penjukwi and Kalutwo. The "accidents" of their lives, as Freud referred to this, exemplifies a primary goal in this book: to show that those who study this domain of culture—erotics and gender—must study culture close-up, through people's subjectivity.

We never planned to do this book: Rather, it emerged from interacting with Sambia. I hesitated when S. suggested doing it. What was worth publishing? After all, I, the ethnographer, was doing what I had done in the village for years. S. dropped in for a few days. We turned on the tape recorder; our case studies were simply another week in many interviews and observations. Nothing special except our excitement in doing this together. Stoller and I complemented each other; even our disagreements enhanced our work. Our interviews were not intended to underscore this interpersonal issue or that. Yet a week of talking with people provided a range of experiences in enough depth and breadth for us to feel, at the end, that we had something to say, with examples that brought our method to life. The book has now emerged as I could not have pictured then. It results from improvisation, for we had no precedent to follow, and the product is neither an ethnography nor a textbook on theory or method.

We mention this background because the book is unconventional. Our writing style is informal; we retain the form of our dialogues in the field, and we have not dressed up our narratives with formal theory or jargon. Though I followed Stoller's lead here, I felt at times uncomfortable: we weren't scholarly. The text seemed plain—though it was often difficult to translate our transcripts from foreign languages into ordinary English—for my colleagues in anthropology. Now, however, at the end of the years-long writing process, Stoller's aesthetic position seems correct. My resistance to his style derived from my identification with the overly formal discourse style of anthropology, compelling me to feel that unadulterated language is common and reveals you have nothing upstairs; and a subliminal feeling of propriety that some of what we revealed (e.g., ourselves) should remain invisible.

Unconventional, too, is the way we preserved the dialogic character of our work. S. proposed that we not blend ourselves in writing the book, as is typical of co-authored works. Moreover, we have reported our parenthetic remarks, doubts, misunderstandings, slips-of-the-tongue, and speculations. Each has responded to this metalanguage of our interactions, as well as on our observations about interpreters' body-language, affects, etc. This noise, normally edited out of published accounts, we left in to show that it is part of ethnography. In this way, readers see our separate ways of thinking as anthropologist and psychoanalyst.

There is discussion today about deconstructing these fields. Anthropology and psychoanalysis carry a lot of intellectual baggage. Postmodern accounts of culture try to work through this, shedding false assumptions of the Other. Analyzing Freud has also become popular. Some of the anthropologic accounts are fine endeavors, conveyed with high-sounding language. Far too seldom, however, are we shown *what actually happened* in the investigator's encounter with his or her interpreters. The accounts provided for us, from the standpoint of genre, are indeed different from those of Malinowski and Mead. But when they omit the details and interpersonal processes that made the product possible, we are still at the impasse the old positivism of participant-observation bequeathed to us from the Victorian period.

I do not dislike the positivist ideology of fieldwork because it fails to yield "psychologic data." That is not its aim, and this paradigm has not completely hindered the production of sensitive accounts of culture. Rather, I object to how it renders a field study, disguising the psychologic reality of that study, regardless of what actually occurred in the field. This is faulty science and bad method. For it blurs who did and said what; why they did so; and these distortions prevent us from being close enough to unpack the ethnographer's interpretations. Malinowski's ghost is still with us: ethnographers (and psychoanalysts) still tend to omit the subjective and intersubjective dynamics of field dialogues, behaviors, and the representations of such in the writing-up process. I know that many of us in the social sciences feel interpretive anthropology has liberated us from the dead hand of experimental/biologic models in science. One marvels at the difference in ethnographic accounts in the *American Ethnologist* compared to ten years ago. But this conceptual change in our presentations of cultures has not fully reached into our field methods. Not really. It *does* make a difference that clinical processes are left out of the training for and practice of ethnography. We still rarely see the steps—*any* of the steps—that led from the field events to a report. This is a pity, for ethnography is about people's lives and real-life problems, not just about stories.[5] And some of the excesses today not only deprive us of these real-life details in context; we are given stories of stories: the nihilism of the art critic who cares little for the opinions of his subject. And unlike works of art our ethnographies are supposed to be about the real lives of real people.

We are not implying that clinical ethnography will remedy all these problems. Let the reader be skeptical about our rhetoric on the scope of clinical ethnography.

Cultural anthropology needs clinical ethnography today more than ever. When we began this project I could not imagine the upsurge in hermeneutics and interpretive ethnography. We have seen major advances in the study of culture since then. These changes entail risks, for instance, a sliding back to epistemologic relativism, as Spiro (1986) has warned. We still so little understand how people experience their traditions and how such subjectivity interacts with the public meanings of others to produce specific outcomes. We need better ways to account for and understand stability and change in human development and group functioning across societies (Spiro 1986:278–281). We need, that is, the bifocal vision of which Sapir[6] spoke long ago, a focus on individual and group simultaneously. For the study of erotics and gender identity, cross-cultural data are still too impoverished and decontextualized to truly compare masculinity and femininity, sexual excitement, and the fantasy constructs of people from different cultures. Clinical ethnography will not do this work. It is a method for making better—richer and deeper—observations. But without that method we will lack the data necessary for enlarging our understanding of these issues.

We divide our summing-up into two major areas: the study of Sambia erotics and gender, and the nature of subjectivity in other cultures, especially as discussed by anthropology and psychoanalysis. We shall conclude by discussing transference and countertransference in the study of culture and erotics, the key issue of sex talk for clinical ethnographers.

SAMBIA EROTICS AND GENDER

"Erotics" and "gender" should be dealt with separately (Stoller 1968), but it is hard to do so with our Sambia material. This problem is revealing, theoretically and methodologically. Does one's gender identity always predict the direction of erotic excitement? Dichotomous cultures, to use Carrier's (1980) term, are built on opposition between masculinity and femininity—their exaggeration, polarization. Sambia culture is like this. Thus we should expect to find this manifested somewhat in the production and performance of sexual behavior too. Culture helps structure this. It also conditions dialogue or talk about erotics and gender, but the individual contributes too, and certain differences between our interpreters above—such as Imano's gentleness, Penjukwi's tattoo, or Moondi's erotic daydreams—are impressive.

Culture will not, ultimately, predict these differences,[7] for these are not its concern, nor are they even intended consequences of socialization. That Sambia provides its great stereotypes, war leader versus rubbish man, is of supreme developmental significance for masculinity to emerge in Sambia males; but these stereotypes alone do not determine who achieves or fails in a lifetime. They do not explain Imano's softness or Weiyu's hardness. Only the boundary conditions are thus explained. Structuring of gender and erotics by culture is therefore conditional. This seems obvious to many of our colleagues in the psychologic sciences [S: "sciences"]. The shallow concern with intracultural differences is one reason that some outside anthropology mistrust its findings.

Stoller can speak to this issue better than I.

S: In recent years the study of gender identity led me to take up the old question how masculinity and femininity relate to erotic excitement. You might have thought, as I did, that anthropology would be full of the precise data one needs for comparative study. Yet I was not able to find a single report in which one learned exactly what turned a person—a particular person—on. (The word "exactly" is a crucial redundancy, for, in the case of excitement, if you do not know *exactly*, you hardly know at all. People can hide the secrets of their erotism in every detail of their behavior and fantasies.) Dozens of papers and books in the literature took for granted qualities such as "attraction" or "beauty," as if these aesthetics were givens, rather than their being for research *the* challenge.[8] There was no awareness indicated of what inner forces make an object beautiful or exciting or disgusting or frightening. Ethnographers tend to treat, say, beauty, as if the sense of it were identically precipitated in each member of a culture by the same factors; or, even more flagrantly wrong, as if beauty were a universal, a constant across cultures; or as if beauty were a necessary ingredient in everyone's erotism (that is, beauty as a cultural norm, not as a complex, personally-plus-societally-constructed subject worth close scrutiny).

I open at random a volume of Havelock Ellis; he may be quaint when judged by today's styles of writing, but many would agree with his ideas on the dynamics of beauty (especially if the racism and sexism were disguised):

> The fact that the modern European, whose culture may be supposed to have made him especially sensitive to aesthetic beauty, is yet able to find beauty even among the women of savage races serves to illustrate the statement already made that, whatever modifying influences may have to be admitted, beauty is to a large extent an objective matter. The existence of this objective element in beauty is confirmed by the fact that it is sometimes found that the men of the lower races admire European women more than women of their own race. There is reason to believe that it is among the more intelligent men of lower race—that is to say those whose aesthetic feelings are more developed—that the admiration for white women is most likely to be found. (1936:1:153).

What a fascinating piece of ethnologica; you can sometimes read reports today in anthropologic and psychoanalytic journals (also in movie fan magazines) with comparable tacit assumptions. Remarkable: the anthropologists make the same assumptions as their culture-bound colleagues. Only if you read these ethnographic reports on beauty, spanning half a century, will you believe that the observations reported, including those written recently, tell us no more about erotic excitement than this one from Ellis. Even when giving details, the authors do not tell of individuals' subjective experiences but rather of customs, myths, rituals, ideals of beauty, and the like.

In contrast, H.'s field notes impressed me even before we met because they let one know what his friends really experienced, both as they were talking to him and regarding the events they were describing to him. And he recognized how a precise detail, as does a shard in a kitchen midden, congeals vast aspects of the culture invisible to the casual, "objective" observer. Why do thinkers in some schools of anthropology still scorn such data? (It would be too bad if, as I suspect, precise description of erotic behavior remains unacceptable in anthropologic circles because there are those who, even in these liberated days, find the descriptions pornographic. Their shame for having such impulses would in that way guide them to their roles as watchdogs of orthodoxy.[9] How many symposia on erotics have been held at meetings of the American Anthropological Association?[10])

H: It is remarkable, in retrospect, to read chapter 2 and compare its cultural/structural themes with the material of our individual case studies. Here is truly an experience—experience-far and experience-near accounts—that illuminates. We have no independent test of reliability or validity to check for in comparing these data, for I produced both accounts. There is, however, the fact that S. participated as well in our case studies, and the additional fact that chapter 2 was written well before these case materials were put together. Nonetheless, the degree of correspondence between studies of the sexual meaning system, and individual "sex talk" in our interviews, underlines the synergistic nature of the two different perspectives. Sapir (Singer 1961:63–64) called this "theoretical reversibility" in culture and personality.

This sex discourse cannot predict the precise meanings of someone's erotic excitement or the direction of their masculinity/femininity. For those sensibilities or aesthetics (Stoller 1985a: chapter 2) are highly personal, multilayered, and probably contingent on situations too. Culture can provide normative boundaries, guidelines, rules, and goals for subjective self-representation, evocation, discourse: and through these social mechanisms its image contributes to the creation of erotic excitement and gender meanings. But "no culture is ever operative except through and in human beings," even Kroeber (1948:464) admitted. A fact is not a fact unless it's first a fantasy, Stoller says.

Between the social facts of culture and the psychologic events of someone's fantasies and scripts lie desires. A desire—as Foucault (1980) and Ricoeur (1970) have scolded Freud [S: And as Freud always knew]—is socially and historically determined by language and culture. A balance, a synchrony exists, between what is necessary and what is desired or between desire and possibility. What was at one time necessity for Kalutwo, namely ritualized homosexuality, has now become (aberrant) desire. He has failed as a masculine person, his own scripts say and his peers are quick to conclude, especially Weiyu. But he succeeds when fantasizing exploits with boys. In this failure we see a challenge to the Sambia folk theory of transitional same-sex behavior and a challenge to those who believe this form of sexual contact is merely an act of ritual, of domination, of power.[11] The Sambia would find such reductionism amusing. As Dover suggested of homoerotic relationships among the Ancient Greeks, many needs and complex functions are satisfied in "homosexual eros" (Dover 1978: 203). We have written of this elsewhere (Herdt 1984; Stoller and Herdt 1985).

Problems in understanding and explaining erotics take on a special character across cultural boundaries because of the very nature of different attitudes associated with talking about sex. Here our Sambia findings raise two issues that impinge on our material from the complementary perspectives of psychoanalysis and psychologic anthropology. First, how much are our Sambia case studies determined by the mode of discourse I (we) created in the village? We anticipated this question in chapter 3; we should further examine it by comparing Sambia with other societies. Second, how deeply do our interpreters experience these erotics and gender meanings? Are similarities between them a function of social roles? Does a cultural self—a set of learned scripts about the I/me for Sambia—create these meanings? Or is there a deeper universal self, an *anlage* on which culture is overlain?

The first point concerns whether or not sex discourse is restricted to western culture, and is, as it were, privatized and individualized—Foucault's (1980) critique of Freud's repression hypothesis bears on this. Foucault is wrong. There is too much repression, secrecy, guilt to say that the meanings of sex talk among Sambia differ radically from us.[12] But whether such discourse is more widespread remains to be seen. It is too much to argue for a universality of discourse, for this would ignore great structural differences between, for instance, hunters-and-gatherers and horticultural societies.[13] We should ask also whether any and all sex talk counts in our analysis—public and private, and in ritual or myth—and if so how we should weight their signs in each domain. Clearly, the Sambia have concerns about gender and erotic experience; we did not have to import these from the West. But did we—first H. and then S.—influence this Sambia talk?

Yes. Like all ethnographers we influenced this talk about sex: its form was dialogic "inbetweenness" (to use Tedlock's term). Its emergent qualities made our talk special; they spoke to us: we spoke back. Such dialogues, in the whole corpus on sex antagonism and gender in Melanesia, are extremely rare, as Fitz Poole and I showed (Herdt and Poole 1982). Indeed, to my knowledge, ours (H. and S.) is the only work of its kind: you get to see what we asked and were told, and in this way, the context and distortions are clear. This is not the case in ethnography, where a fact can now be a fact without a prior fantasy (question), or, indeed, a prior society, among the historical structuralists.[14]

Beyond Melanesia, however, a far-reaching and in my view underappreciated understanding of the role of culture in sex discourse and therefore in cross-cultural studies of sex was long ago provided by Mead. The privacy of sex raises problems with which only psychoanalysts have tried to reckon. As Mead said:

> One characteristic of human sex behavior is the insistence on privacy. This privacy may be of many types; it may only be a demand that others who share the same dwelling may not be able to observe and there may be no objection to nonparticipants hearing what is going on . . . . In most human societies sex relations are conducted as to exclude witnesses other than couples or individuals who are engaged in comparable activities. . . . The presence of unobservable areas of sex activity presents certain barriers to research which are difficult to overcome. (1961:1434–5)

That no one ever sees sex but only hears about it* is as much a problem for anthropologists today as it was for Kinsey.

Humans, Mead suggested, are shy about their sexual activity, unlikely to discuss it with strangers. Or friends. Or relatives. Or their analysts. Even among our enlightened selves, we know, many American couples avoid discussing sex, or avoid teaching their children about sex; the situation is probably similar among some "primitives." But this is not the *main* point: certain Amazonian Indians, for instance, are enthusiastic sex talkers, their ethnographer, Gregor, tells us. Yet these Mehinaku talk about sex in stories that are distant from their intimate experience: in ribald tales, in popular sexual myths,

---

*Or at least until Masters and Johnson came along, and they saw only its signs, not the minds, of their experiments' actors.

and comparing good sex with good food, often more by men, and more often in the men's house. Their discourse, which seems so open, delivers them from their experience by referring to cultural tales and exploits: stories about stories of sex (Gregor 1985:16–17, 71–72). This does not really challenge the personal and private nature of sex talk.

We agree with Mead that such intimate matters are intimate communications. Sambia appear to agree. They could discuss sex but not just with anyone and not just at the drop of a hat. Specialists can appreciate this by comparing the Sambia data to those collected from other New Guinea societies.

The Hua of New Guinea, as Meigs describes, provide a closer example of culturally-patterned talk that bears comparison.

> While the simultaneous existence of inhibited and uninhibited styles of talking about sex is undoubtedly universal, the distribution of these styles to various contexts in cultures varies. In North American culture the uninhibited expression is most obviously appropriate in such all-male contexts as locker rooms, barracks, and bars. By contrast, the comparable context in Hua culture, the men's house, is consonant only with a relatively inhibited style, or so I was told. Talk about sex that I would regard as uninhibited is permitted in Hua informal social groups including both males and females. In Western society "mixed company" represents precisely the context in which talk about sex is generally more inhibited. (1984:96)

Here we have a nice commentary on the existence of sex talk in another New Guinea society. But again, when Meigs says "or so I was told," we wonder by whom? And why? The Sambia situation differs from that of Hua, for Sambia men often discuss sex with men in ribald ways: this is a feature of their relatedness. Other New Guinea examples could be cited, and Knauft has made a very similar observation on the Gebusi of New Guinea.[15]

My point is not that the content or situations of such sex talk are identical, but that, in New Guinea, one or another such form is common. Too common to be ignored, but alas, the ethnography of such sex talk is almost unknown. And I suspect that it is better reported for New Guinea than other culture areas.[16] For instance: ethnographic reports on same-sex erotic contacts are notoriously deficient, and one must be skeptical in evaluating them, Mead (1961), Read (1980), and others have suggested. Indeed, a whole book that I edited was concerned with establishing the facts and fictions of ritualized homosexuality in Melanesia, and given the uneven quality of sex talk ethnography about homosexuality among anthropologists, I understand critics' dissatisfactions with our field.[17]

But to return to the Sambia, here is S.'s assessment.

S: Our interpreters, after some puzzlement, had no trouble understanding Herdt's desire to get into their heads. These people, who are so outward-directed—how to hunt, how to war, how to placate malevolent spirits, how to observe and cheat on taboos, how to garden, how to maneuver in the jungle: skills not enhanced by one's desire to know oneself, to get to the root of one's own motivations, to reduce self-deception—were far more than just informants on masculine development, customs, and myths. Though they never heard of such a thing, they were able easily, with H., to search themselves for answers to questions about meaning. And as, over the years, the probing became deeper and more psychodynamic, some Sambia had no trouble moving with curiosity into realms of the mind they not only had never seen in themselves or others but for which their culture has no concepts or intimations. Moondi's insights are an example of such. By the time I joined the interviews, H.'s friends were so easy about and interested in the process of investigating their minds that this, perhaps more than anything else, made the meetings feel as familiar as working at home. In creating such an ambience, did H. so transmute natural modes in which Sambia communicate that he distorted the situation and things they said? Did he, that is, merely move the confessional clinical gaze (Foucault 1973) into the Village? We think not: his mode of interviewing was designed in culturally appropriate ways that were innovations on, but did not revolutionize, Sambia communication.

H: Nonetheless, Foucault has made us more cautious, lest, like psychiatrists with patients, we not respect the natives' privacy, extracting from them their guilty secrets. Malinowski may not have thought that wanting to study the natives' vision of their world made him their confessor. Malinowski and Freud differed in their self-consciousness about this, because while Freud saw that patients confessed to him, he also felt that he must confess to himself how little he knew, and how much of what he knew depended on understanding himself. And he used the same word—confess—in describing both aspects of the discovery process (Ornston 1982:414). (By contrast, we see little of Foucault in his lofty critique of the rest of us; he is, like Malinowski was—in his ethnography, not his diary—a confessor only.) Some communications that make people feel more whole, as with Sakulambei, are cheapened by being labeled confessions. There are admissions that will not be made, no matter what, as with Kalutwo, or that will be made, no matter what, as with Weiyu's condemnation of Kalutwo. There are sensitive and insensitive ways of asking people what they feel and of responding to them. We should be wary that our desire to understand does not make the natives say what they think we want to hear and when they do so, we must be sure that we see this. Yes, clinical ethnography involves confessions; but it requires compassion as well—an important part of understanding how much we have to learn about others' lives. Most of all it requires a respectful empathy.

This brings us back to my first point: that sex talk is not institutionalized in some cultures or is missing in others, whereas private or informal talk is there but was never studied. It is unclear whether the anthropologists who claim the former have not in fact been the ones responsible for the latter. This dilemma may account for the impoverished material on erotics in anthropology, whereas data on normative gender codes and roles are now voluminous.[18] No doubt some anthropologists are prudish,[19] but this does not explain the problem. That is caused, rather, by ignoring a whole world of culture—subjectivity. When we open the leading college textbooks[20] on human sexuality to find that the "cross-cultural chapter" trots out Malinowski on the Trobriands and Mead on New Guinea—we cannot help but be impressed by the lack in ethnographic studies of erotism and the failure of contemporary cultural anthropology to enlighten her sister disciplines (Herdt 1987c).

This failure can be explained mainly by anthropology's disregard for the individual. Aside from the core group of culture and personality workers (Spiro 1986:279–281), problems of subjectivity, of self and personhood, were historically ignored; and hence behaviors and meanings of erotics and gender were as well. This absence is still present though transmuted. Though one can say that "anthropology thrives on a tension between the construction of theory and the practice of ethnography,"[21] the tension is less due to paradigm changes and more to fads that avoid study of subjectivity in anthropology. The fact is, the participant-observation epistemology has not fundamentally changed (chapter 1), though fads come and go. The informal and intimate study of the person—and nothing else—yields an understanding of gender sensibilities and erotic aesthetics. And these sensibilities are, as Sontag (1982:106) has said in another context, the most "perishable aspect of a culture." Excluding the person has harmed not only studies of sex and gender but anthropology at large, which is so prone, Spiro (1986) has complained, to an "ethnographic particularism" that tends to the "strange customs of exotic peoples." We find this an unsatisfactory future for anthropology. Moreover, it is not merely ethnography but the writing process that excludes the individual.[22] For anthropology to establish itself at the center of studies on erotics and gender in humans requires our reclaiming the whole person as a source of intrapsychic and interpersonal meanings.

When, therefore, we turn to the second issue on selfhood, similar research aims and problems arise. Is the self a constant, a given, an *anlage* across cultures?[23] Or is it merely a cultural construct through and within which normative meanings and random behaviors of individuals are expressed? Do we seek variation, local adaptation, or do we seek universals and the nomothetics of understanding how the self is related to and regulates erotic excitement, body imagery, developmental goals, and related gender phenomena (Stoller 1979; 1985a)? Though S. and I. disagree somewhat on the interpretation of these matters, we agree that each culture provides for a self and that the experience of the I/me can be charted in its details, through clinical ethnography. When Mead, in *Male and Female* (1949), discussed the aims of ethnographic writing, she focused on the *differences* between human groups as the key to understanding human nature and gender.[24] This heritage seems to have influenced the anthropology of sex more than she might have anticipated.

Locating the causes of sexual excitement and gender in personhood and self provides a stronger heuristic bridge into deeper meanings of our Sambia material. Gender is supposedly constructed so that "sexuality cannot be abstracted from its surrounding social layers" (Ross and Rapp 1981:54). And yet this is what Freud and psychoanalytic studies try to do. When we say gender is constructed, do we mean in its architectural entirety? When S. (1985a, ch. 2) argues that erotic tastes are made and not born, does he mean this literally? Sambia erotism is surely constituted via familial dynamics as well as the dramatic rituals of its society, which creates cultural and gender discontinuity in males, a point to which we shall return. Concomitantly, this poses fundamental difficulties in understanding selfhood among the Sambia. Here we must confront the surface and depth, fix and fluidity, of Sambia subjectivity. Shall we agree with Geertz (1973:363) that these "problems, being existential, are universal; [while] their solutions, being human, are diverse"?

It is too easy to take any number of issues from our Sambia dialogues—on semen beliefs, images of pollution, the erotics of fellatio—and conclude that the erotism and gender of Sambia are *unique,* either absolutely ("They only do it like that in the South") or conditionally ("You, too, can be President [if you try hard enough]"). Epistemologic relativism (Spiro 1986) of this kind is seductive, but we can get caught in its webs. To say, by comparison, that the Balinese self is submerged in collective conceptions of "person," "time," and "conduct,"[25] not only leaves the comparative student of selfhood with the (probably) insoluble task of finding the same webs of meaning in other cultures. It also ignores the similarities in all kinds of spiders. The universalists, including the ghostbusters (the term is Shweder's [1984]), find this unacceptable, so they look beyond collective symbols for screens and symptoms, as Freud[26] often did, to discover underlying psychic meanings: hair=penis, blood-letting=castration, ritual initiation=Oedipal resolution. The usual stuff. On the other hand, the relativists have ignored this challenge. In our search for links between Sambia and other human societies we are also tempted to these facile unconscious meanings. They help get us beyond the impasse of relativism, whereby an irreconcilable dichotomy between Sambia and western selfhood and erotics thwarts comparison.[27]

The dilemma posed by forays of psychoanalysts into the study of erotics and gender in nonwestern cultures is this: though they were often the only thinkers interested in deeper manifestations of erotics and gender, they tended to pathologize the phenomena outside the West. What deviated from the norms that analysts considered the "average expectable environment" were treated as pathologic, LeVine (in press) has suggested. This not only begs the question of a value-laden construct such as average environment, it also tends to ignore the role of culture and meaning systems in allowing for more adaptive variation in social environments than Freud, for instance, imagined when he wrote the *Three Essays on Sexuality.*[28]

Kakar takes up this problem of psychoanalytic formulations of his own culture, India. He notes that where Freud's work on neurosis* was designed for evaluating individuals, the diagnostic labels were soon applied to communities, even civilizations. "Predictably, nonwestern cultures were bunched more at the neurotic end of the spectrum while *their* soul doctors, the shamans, were evaluated as frankly psychotic" (Kakar 1985:441). When they have written of India, Kakar complains, analysts found "oral fixation and oral dependence had never been quite surmounted and the resolution of Oedipal complex has

---

*The same point would apply to erotic neuroses too.

never been quite accepted."[29] Further, a 1981 psychoanalytic commentary sees Indian behavior as

> the result of intense libidinal gratification throughout the oral, anal
> and phallic exhibitionistic phases . . . with stringent constraints
> on aggression. . . . This specific sequence requires strong defen-
> sive measures, particularly against sadism and favors reaction for-
> mation. . . . There is a pull to oral fixation. . . . Oral eroticism
> is seen in a cultural emphasis on generosity, especially around food,
> institutionalized dependency, totalism.[30]

It gets worse. No wonder Malinowski[31] railed against this reduction
of culture and selfhood to the unconscious. This kind of clinical ethnography is far from what we have in mind. But it is a far cry from
the marvellous works of Kakar himself, who is much more culturally
sensitive. Stoller and I want to understand unconscious forces and
development too but in a more reasoned, experience-near manner.

The nature of sex talk in culture is forever shaped by fantasy systems that lie somewhat apart from the time/space world of the behavioral environment. Experiences felt, reprocessed, and re-pre-
sented to self and to others are no longer experiences or memories
but compromises, symbolic limbos of development. Anthropologists
who ignore this history are crippled in their assessment of the meaning of sex talk *across the lifespan.* How critical this point is in a culture, such as Sambia, with such strong developmental discontinuity
in the lifespan. Cohler (1982:217) writes: "This focus upon a developmentally shared fantasy world, rather than the time/space world,
differentiates psychoanalytic accounts from all other accounts of human development."

Anthropology's best reason for using clinical techniques and concepts is to understand and interpret the deep but nontherapy relationships we form in the field. Questionnaires, quantitative measures,
projective tests, normative observational samples and controls help
systematize the data flooding us. But it is the ethnographer's personality, behavior, and communications that underlie the use of those
measures, their acceptance by the natives, the responses we get to
them, and how we interpret them. We can never calibrate this instrument: the ethnographer's or the clinician's personality. All information must be transformed; the bottom line, as Devereux (1967:xviii)
said, is that *all this means that*: the final act of interpreting is done
in the ethnographer's biased, meaning-laden head. And it is communicated via the biased, meaning-laden heads of our interpreters.
How do they present to us when talking in private? Are they con-

cerned to express normative attitudes? If their several identities are in conflict (e.g., Weiyu's position as Kalutwo's kinsman versus W. being an adult warrior and cult member), how do they in their communications handle the conflict? Such clinical issues were ignored in the past because reports homogenized groups (e.g., "all men" includes Weiyu and Kalutwo). But the new attention to the descriptions of selfhood in experience-near, person-centered ethnography, shows an advance in thinking about them.

LeVine (1982:296 ff.) suggests there are three key "domains" of self that can be understood cross-culturally: routine occasions, public occasions, and autobiographic occasions. Each domain implies a context for questions and a related set of internal scripts, social roles, and discourse rules. I have worked in all three modes, yet in our case studies above (because they came at the end of two and a half years' work), I focus mainly on the autobiographic, our sex talk. This focus restricts the data we present and influences how people revealed themselves to us. We see, for instance, not Penjukwi the typical wife/mother/woman, but P. as the object of our unique discourse, with her own values and ideas communicated somewhat idiosyncratically. She tells us she believes other women have orgasms like her, but she is unsure of this. She is not terribly interested to find out, for it was we who asked *her* what she felt. It would be easy to misrepresent what she said. Had we instead presented more interviews on women's rituals or institutional activities, one might have gotten a different picture of both Penjukwi and Sambia society. Still, there are enough routine and public occasions present in our discussions, particularly with Tali and Weiyu (chapter 5), to compare the quality and substance of our communications and differences between men and women, in relation to the autobiographic texts of others. This interplay between public routine and private dialogues that provides the greatest potential for psychodynamic discovery[32] relevant to the ethnography of gender.

Here is a puzzle in normative male selfhood and gender: in everyday conversation Sambia men stress the masculine, vital, phallic quality of themselves and their male institutions. Yet one can go beyond the surface of the idioms with which men speak of these things and of their environment. On doing so, I found in private talk and in the tacit meanings within their beliefs, that the most compelling and ritually useful elements for creating masculinity are fertile, prolific, quiet, steady—what men perceive to be (and privately accept as being) feminine. These two sides of male gender attitudes reflect the contradictions of their development, which begins in the women's world and ends in the men's. Tali and Weiyu hint of this. Sakulambei and Imano exemplify it.

The point emerges more fully in the spectacular myth of parthenogenesis with which I concluded *Guardians of the Flutes* (1981:ch. 8). On the surface, the secret myth-telling among the men seems to confirm the preeminence of masculinity in their inner worlds. It does so by denying the primordial presence of females in the storied beginnings of Sambia society and by interweaving the first acts of homosexual fellatio that dominate every boy's late childhood and adolescence with the rise of the family, ritual custom, and society. Closer examination, however, shows that in the myth-telling, men feel frantic to keep women at a distance to deny the discordance between male public talk and secret myth and the shame that surrounds the setting of ritual. The ways men use their myths, plus their homosexual and heterosexual practices in creating and maintaining masculinity, belie the public ideology of the male cult: at its heart the myth speaks of men's deepest doubts that they are fully male. One's maleness and masculinity will fade away without ruthless, ritual defenses to preserve them. These findings of an earlier study that was clinically informed must make us cautious: many male ethnographers of Melanesia looked only at surface behavior and cultural ideology and misread ritual discourse as pertaining to domestic and private life without any changes necessary. Paralleling this public symbolic system—the ritual cults and signs that anthropologists had taken to be pure assertions of masculinity—is a more complex mental world.[33]

We have already argued that our interpreters went beyond normative social roles in communicating with us. Moondi's erotic daydreams, Kalutwo's strange ideas about his maleness, Saku's pain over his hermaphrodism are examples of such discordance. My house provided people a place to say odd and secret things in odd ways. To the extent that interpreters are aberrant, we should interpret their behavior accordingly. Cautiously. Yet, we also saw people privately expressing their conformity to public norms: Weiyu and Tali's defense of ritual customs, Penjukwi's reaction to S.'s tattoo question, Moondi's fantasies, Kalutwo's avoidance of discussing the pederastic rumor about him, and Weiyu's outrage at Kalutwo are examples of such. Nor can we yet tell the extent to which these normative or aberrant attitudes will eventually go public, stay quiet, be accepted or rejected by others. Only further study will reveal that. Still, being present in members of the community, such attitudes are a part of village life, whether latent or manifest, so they may eventually work their way into the culture of public symbols.[34]

And further: when I ask Moondi, Weiyu, or Penjukwi—who (unlike the aberrant Kalutwo and Sakulambei) have no need to avoid discussing sex—what they feel, am I not encouraging unprecedented conversations? Will their enthusiasms transcend their normative comportment in public? Yes, no doubt: such behavior is of course constrained as a function of social controls and public censorship.[35] Their responses must be seen in relation to what normative people usually did and said in my previous fieldwork, before our interviews. But such data are still data; there are no nondata. Such responses are as much a response of Sambia culture as anything; only, interpreting them requires understanding what is normative or not in different situations.

With the issue of normativeness and aberrance in the discourse of clinical ethnography we reach a hoary problem indeed: what bearing do such materials have on an anthropologist's representations of a public, shared ideology, social action, or culture, as in Durkheim's collective consciousness? What can the microscopic study of an eccentric or even an abnormal self tell us about the social world of normal others? In the vintage culture and personality works of the 1930s, 1940s, and 1950s, this problem was circumvented or muddled. One reads, for instance, the rich and finely textured "autobiographies" of Alorese by Cora DuBois (1944) with appreciation; the "interpretations" by Abram Kardiner that follow them seem impoverished and misguided at times. This great pothole in social theory, though stated now more sophisticatedly, is present in responses to the works of Obeyesekere and Crapanzano, the latter of whom Geertz has scolded for misreading his clinical ethnography of *Tuhami* as "culture."[36] Another reviewer has in the same way[37] chided Spiro's secondary-source reinterpretation of Trobriand culture, which rediscovered the missing oedipal complex.

These are particular instances of a more general problem: nothing in recent years has interested psychologic anthropology more than the issue of what is shared in a culture.[38] There was a time when "culture" indicated that traditional societies shared the same motives, values, rules; or that they enacted roles in the same ways; or that they performed customary practices in the same way. Patterns of culture were relative and adaptively meaningful (e.g., the doctrine of cultural relativism). This fiction was based on another fiction: that personality is isomorphic with culture. Therefore: the same thought, attitudes, biases, stereotypes, feelings, etc. In this model, it was difficult to deal with what seemed—to Westerners—pathologic: warfare, cannibalism, suicide, trance states. How can what is normative in a society be pathologic? Can a society be sick? After World War II subtle shifts occurred.* Questions were asked in a different way. Not, "What do they all share in?" but, "How much—at what levels of awareness and behavior—is shared?" Wallace, Edgerton, Schwartz, and D'Andrade among others have reviewed these problems well.[39]

In asking how much is shared, we must define sharing: correlation; equivalence; identification; association; similarity? At what level: institutional or individual? Conscious; unconscious; nonconscious (ideology)? What links exist between sharing cognitions versus affects? Can a people share in a concept (e.g., soul) and yet still feel differently about it as individuals? Is cultural knowledge uniformly distributed in a society—across age, sex, social status, ritual and other distinctions? (Probably not.[40]) People may believe in a custom, yet react emotionally to it privately in different ways, as you have seen. How much of the variance in their emotional reactions is explained by normative role attitudes (e.g., "Men should control their women and avoid too much sex," Weiyu and Tali say). How much variance results from personality differences across normative roles? (Imano is comfortable with women and enjoys frequent sex with them.) Avoiding clinical methods in gender studies hinders our understanding such issues.

Since social roles influence people's identities in private, might not their gender stereotypes do so too? Of course: stereotypes of masculinity and femininity come through our tapes in many places. Such images, idealized role models, and rule-sets are present in our narrative texts, not just in how people act—via social roles—but in how they feel and think. Important clues come from peoples' attributions about others: "All men think of drinking tree sap when screwing their wives" (Weiyu and Tali) or "All women feel *imbimboogu* when breastfeeding (Penjukwi). How do they know? Can we trust their assertions? Those questions require answers that are context-dependent (do they trust us on this matter?) and quantitatively contingent (we need more cases, perhaps a standardized questionnaire with a large enough n if we want to generalize). Knowing of this cultural influence on gender discourse, however, is different from agreeing—with Malinowski or now with Geertz—that cultural stereotypes[†] speak, rather than the individuals who express them. For in failing to recognize that nor-

---

*Nazi Germany, as much as anything, embarrassed this intellectual position. Anthropology was shocked.

†Cultural images ("man," "woman," "shaman") in myth or narratives, idioms or idiomatic sayings, proverbs, jokes, riddles, art, ritual, social roles, dream theories, etiquette, television commercials, psychologic tests, aesthetic styles, etc.

mative views can be combined with or replaced by private (idiosyncratic) ones—and nowhere as much as in sex talk—these scholars ignored the historical origins of stereotypes, ignored the creative element in cultures, forgot that people make errors (forget customs, magical formulas, etc.), react to their own traditions (rebellions) or those of others (cargo cults), make revolutions, and sometimes change things just for the hell of it. Stereotypes come from minds, not machines.

Example: Kalutwo. K. reveals, as no other Sambia could, the distinctive features of the rubbish man.* But that label is meaningless unless we understand its dynamics: what created him, why does he dislike hunting, why can he not bear women? Another man, Imano—nearly as rubbishy—is as normatively heterosexual (perhaps more so) as others, nor has he ever engaged in adult homosexual acts; yet both men are aberrant. Kalutwo's life reveals the critical points in the male developmental cycle that must be hurdled to attain adult masculine personhood. His failures to do so, to make the normative transitions, indicate his aberrance; but they are *not* that aberrance: that is produced by his motives, goals, fantasies. Kalutwo's communications also express normative beliefs about sex with women: he is terrified they will drain him of semen (maleness, existence). But in acting on this belief to an extreme, he has failed at marriage and his self has failed the men. Should we see his use of that belief as conscious or unconscious rationalization? We guess that the form of his semen depletion fear is shared by other men. Therefore, if we can understand its origin and conscious experience in Kalutwo, we shall understand better what makes normative Sambia masculinity. And that will clarify what energizes marriage, fatherhood, ritual, warfare, and much else. Kalutwo is a guide to a shifting but important current of Sambia culture.

But let us examine the aberrant further by using, this time, a fundamental dynamic of sexual excitement: fetishism. The concept has an odd history—of erotism in psychoanalysis and animism in religious anthropology.[41] Though fetishism is a perversion and its extremes psychopathologic, in fact, Man—(all?) humans—have a touch of this dynamic in the secrets of their erotism (Stoller 1979). Sambia are no different, as you sense in reading chapter 2 and find confirmed in Kalutwo's case study.

---

*In fifty years of New Guinea culture there are no other studies of rubbish men, though specialists frequently use that folk category. That, in itself, is a comment on New Guinea anthropology.

S: Let us say that a fetish* is either a nonhuman object someone animates with human attributes (e.g., a stone worshipped as a god, a shoe more exciting than the woman wearing it) or a part of a human that, in being admired more than the whole person, dehumanizes the person (e.g., women's ankles are craved and the women as individuals ignored). The fetish is factitious, an invention that lies between the human and the nonhuman. Fetishists are collectors (those people who humanize the nonhuman and thereby find passion where philistines see only utility).

Heterosexual Sambia men are as fascinated and erotically excited by the form of boys' mouths as are heterosexual men in our society by women's breasts. In both cultures, a particular anatomic structure has been fetishized; that is, it has been focused on with such intensity that it is more important than the person whose attribute it is. The person is—sometimes a bit, sometimes a lot—dehumanized, of interest for the moment mostly as a contraption to which the desired tissue or organ is attached and even then not for the part's physiologic functions but only for its visual or tactile effect in provoking fantasies.

Thus, Sambia bachelors use these same mechanisms of fetishizing anatomy in their strong erotic fixation on the configuration of prepubertal boys' mouths. H.'s understanding of the dynamics of fetishism allowed him to collect data that thereby illuminated work on gender and erotics. Only an ethnographer allowed to watch the most secret parts of Sambia initiation would know that the boys' mouths are fetishized and then be positioned to also ask why (Herdt 1981; 1987c). And you would have to allow "why" into your research to see how this aesthetic regarding mouths is connected to something that seems far removed, such as the warfare that was the outstanding reality of traditional Sambia society and that structured the selection of a boy's homosexual partners from hostile villages.

To return to our discussion of normativeness, there is the Mind— the Universal Mind that, supposedly, is independent of and the essence of the lifelong mental experiences that we all have all day long and that are so much less heroic than (sound the trumpets): the Mind is made up of innumerable fragments: mouths, breasts, beatings, postures, smells, decorations, taboos, music, genitals, symbols, humiliation, invasions, anxiety, danger, masquerades, foolishness, disgust,

---

*Fetishism is very rare in women; in fact, many perversions are found only in men. Can we get this clinical puzzle to excite those who believe in the Universal Mind?

hope, the dorsal but never the ventral surface of the left (much more than the right) earlobe. And people's shared or idiosyncratic ideas and fantasies about what excitement is and how it* should be expressed. There is no excitement in the absence of these particularities and therefore no such *thing* as excitement without these events. Sexual excitement *is* these experiences; it is not an abstraction but an emotion, a tangible body response. Excitement has no form, no structure, no presence, no existence except in these particularities. The *word* or *idea* "excitement" is, of course, not a perceived body state: words, and ideas are not excitement. There is no nonexcited excitement—that is not an excitement, a felt experience, though all states we call "excitement" share certain qualities or they would not be excitement but, perhaps, potatoes or elephants.

Fetishism therefore permits us to repeat and emphasize our point that fundamentals of erotic experience can be communicated across cultures while other aspects of the same experience may be difficult if not impossible to transmit. Few women ethnographers, even with a man from a most exotic place, would misread an erection despite their professors teaching them that the signs of erotic excitement are culture-bound. What may be unknown and far from universal, however, is what stimuli set off the excitement and why those stimuli set off the excitement and why those stimuli, for that man, are erotic. Too often, if the reasons why seem obvious, it is because they match our experience, not because we really know the reasons.

"I could show you many famous books on anthropology with minute details about pottery and such subjects, which do not even mention what position is normally adopted in coitus. Yet I should think that the man in the street will agree with me if I say that the sexual life of a human being is nearly as important as the chips of stone that fall off when he makes an axe," says Roheim (1932: 21). Do ethnographers still fail to get these data sixty years after Roheim because gender identity or sexual excitement are not important enough for them to study? The suspicious analyst thinks there may be other motives, other reasons why. Why ("why, 'why,'" you cry) has anthropology excluded these data and these questions?

H: Used properly, the longitudinal case study can focus our understanding of culture. My narrative sketches prefacing our chapters place each person in relation to his or her interpretations of Sambia nar-

---

*There really is no "it," the purified, spiritualized, noncorporeal essence of excitement, but for the sake of simple sentences, "it" is the needed word.

rative roles and psychosocial development. We proceeded across a spectrum from the normative side—Moondi, Tali, Weiyu and (in most respects) Penjukwi—to the aberrant—Imano and Sakulambei —and on out to the abnormal (Kalutwo). You may not agree with these assessments. Could you truly disagree—and reinterpret—without our detailed communications? The aberrant person, though unnormative and therefore not representative of the mass, also provides in his or her aberrance important clues for understanding normative behavior and experience.

We cannot shake off the feeling that ethnographers avoid methods of the sort we used in our interviews because they feel they are not interested in or able to study unconscious factors. The domain of psychoanalysis. Many anthropologists, from Kroeber to Victor Turner and Geertz, have voiced such reservations. They also may believe that clinical techniques are not really crucial in doing "standard" participant-observation. Let us review this one last time.

Our field interviews were not primarily concerned with unconscious forces. We believe that the study of conscious experience is itself a challenge, one still awaiting ethnography. The subjectivity of cultural beliefs, rules, and ideas at different levels of understanding and how particular cultural actors put them into use in social and private life is little known in comparative ethnography. We are only beginning to fathom the range of states of awareness covered by "dreaming," "daydreaming," "trancing," "desire," or "motivation" in nonwestern culture. The unfolding of awareness, morality, and acquiring rules and concepts from childhood on, including individuals' adjustments to these phenomena are scarcely known, for example, in New Guinea. The links between social roles and the personal expression of emotions are also vague and only now being studied across cultures.[42] Such problems require an understanding of *conscious* experience, and it would be some time before one needed to start tackling the unconscious.

Not that unconscious forces do not shape behavior. How else do we explain Weiyu's and Penjukwi's slips of the tongue (e.g., inverting gender pronouns)? How do we explain Moondi's avoiding discussing "quiet" men? Is resistance to self-insight (his identifying his father with desired homosexual partners) not useful here? Can we not use the concept "transference" in understanding Kalutwo's reactions better? Are not Weiyu's bodily and emotional resistances to and difficulties with translating for Kalutwo (evident to us and perhaps to him subliminally too) a key to understanding Kalutwo, or masculinity, or male–male social interaction, or translating? And of course unconscious forces motivate the ethnographer as well; unless corrected, they distort research.

The value of studying individuals' conscious experience of their institutions, beliefs, and attitudes lies in the microscopic analysis of how they internally represent these elements; how those representations contain assumptions or rules otherwise missed by an outsider; how they feel about these elements and the extent to which their feelings are hidden or expressed in public and are shared by others; why they have faith in ideas or attitudes even when other beliefs seem to contradict them or cause them anxiety or shame; or how they avoid being aware of such contradictions, or, when they are aware, how they manage to cope with their intrapsychic or interpersonal conflicts.[43]

The interplay between inner experience and public behavior is central to these issues. Though anthropologists have made much progress in studying native ideas in this process, conventional ethnographies less adequately touch on natives' feelings and fantasies. Indeed, Geertz (1968) has argued that these forms of experience—even conscious—are difficult if not impossible for ethnographers to reach. We believe our case studies support a different view. I recognize that our data are conditional and that the conceptual steps that would relate them to an analysis of social practices and symbolic forms (like ritual) have still to be worked out. But these interpretive problems (which I shall not tackle here) seem solvable. Another benefit of our view is that, in believing one can collect subjective data, ethnographers will try harder to do so. That will lead us to pay more attention to our *interpreters'* concerns; to their questions about how life is lived in other places, including that of the ethnographer. By so doing, we return to the final problem we wish to examine: the effect of the fieldworker on the process of clinical ethnography.

TRANSFERENCE IN CLINICAL ETHNOGRAPHY

We should not fear using clinical methods and aberrant case studies in studying culture. As long as observations and interpretations are open to public view, readers can decide if we relied too heavily on such or extrapolated inappropriately from them to the normative. But that, of course, is the same fear we should have of all ethnographic reports. (Perhaps ethnographers at first avoid odd people because they fear natives will think the ethnographers odd too. Or identify the outsider with the odd person he interviews. What a pity if such fears stifle research.) If studies of aberrants do nothing more than sharpen our understanding of the normative they add a lot.

Clinicians should remember that they handle the normative/aberrant spectrum less frontally than anthropologists through the use of the term "appropriate." This oft-used and ambiguous word has subliminal connotations that may block research, particularly when class or ethnicity are relevant factors. Our use of "appropriate" is just as deceptive, for I share in the normative cultural system of Sambia, as I did not five years earlier.[44]

Deciphering the normative from the idiosyncratic in my interpreters' behavior and experience becomes easier by taking the long view. I could collect observations and do interviews over the years; compare a person's ideas and feelings in many different ways to see their full manifestations; I could take my time to absorb, interpret, and thereby extend the ethnography. Such long involvement with the individuals interviewed above has, however, had two other consequences, one not expected.

These long-term case studies have led me first to better understand the range of experience in my interpreters, including their unconscious feelings and defenses. My understanding is limited. But I do feel I know enough about my friends' personalities and psychodynamics to assess the normativeness of certain unconscious feelings. Saku's sense of self is so steeped in his shamanic role that his selfhood is merged with that role, and I believe he is unconscious of how much he defends himself and denies his past through that identity. These defensive identity feelings are aberrant, compared to other shamans. Another example: Moondi's erotic attachments to boys and to his fiancée typify his development and are also normative for Sambia men. These examples only show the presence of such unconscious factors; they do not explain their origins or functions in the individual or in Sambia culture. That explanation would require much more.* But I had expected that.

Second, by talking intimately with people for so long I created in them unconscious responses to myself, which I had not foreseen. They and I communicated (consciously, subliminally, unconsciously) at sufficient depth that they experienced new things in themselves. Insight. Sometimes they wanted this insight (e.g., Moondi) and some-

---

*Nor do we know, on finding similar psychodynamic functions, whether these unconscious factors would be the same for Sambia and Westerners. (Which Westerners? Men or women, children or adults, black or white, rich or poor?)

times not (e.g., Kalutwo). I, being the agent who stimulated these feelings, also awakened in them old conflicts. People resisted insight into that process; Moondi (e.g., his hesitation to describe his fellators' sexually exciting traits), Kalutwo (e.g., his exclusive homosexual orientation), Penjukwi (e.g., her anger over S.'s tattoo-probe, which she avoided), and Weiyu (e.g., his anger at Kalutwo, with whom he could not let himself identify), all showed resistance to knowing more. How typical is such resistance in Sambia culture? And what is being resisted: the questions at hand? Telling me more? Knowing more? (Or all of these avoidances?) In short, I became someone important inside these people, a person, similar to others in their pasts they had needed, from whom they expected feelings (consciously, unconsciously) that may have had little to do with the person I was. Transference. I had not expected that when first doing ethnography. I was naive.

Of all the dynamics of a long-term intercultural research relationship, those of transference and countertransference are the most crucial and the least understood.[45] Ethnographers who cannot draw on these concepts are crippled, their work shaped by forces they do not see. Would they be able to understand Kalutwo's need to be with me even when he cannot say what he wants? K.'s passive-dependent resistance is not a thing in itself; neither is his fear of what I or Weiyu would do were he to have told us what he wants erotically from boys. K.'s behavior is a transference reaction to what he feels I will do, say, or think. How much of Moondi's openness and cooperativeness is also transference? Or Saku's inability to discuss his body? Or his and Penjukwi's use of the term "master" for S.? A clinical ethnography without transference will not be clinical; in fact, it may not be much of an ethnography. [S: It cannot even occur; transference is always there, though rarely recognized.]

The same holds for the ethnographer's countertransference reactions (see Epilogue). Here, especially, we help our research along by observing ourselves. Reality-oriented feelings and ideas that do not spring from unmet needs (e.g., internal objects) filter through our behavior all day. But it takes clinical experience—prefield—to know what part of my annoyance and frustration toward Kalutwo is sensible and necessary for the relationship and what part is my countertransference to K. Knowing such differences shifts behavior, sharpens observations, and makes for different interpretations.*

Devereux (1967; 1978) has suggested that the troubling areas in an ethnographer's response to culture—those that distress him or her

---

*All responses are not countertransference though. See the following.

most—often contain the potential for theoretic insights. Yet, by their nature—distress—we shun them. That the natives do or do not suffer from discussing such areas is also significant. Whatever the area— shame, sexuality, cannibalism, psychosis—such ethnographer reflectiveness offers clues about what it is like (consciously, unconsciously) for the natives to experience these same issues. We cannot afford to ignore or avoid those clues through intellectualizations like "culture shock" or "reverse culture shock" (as examined in chapter 1).

Prolonged interviewing introduces greater transference/countertransference elements in research, at home or abroad. Interpreting these influences becomes a part of interpreting our own and our translators' identities as reviewed above, for instance, in the way people use stereotypes about sexual partners or women (e.g., Moondi in chapter 4), quiet men (i.e., Imano in chapter 8), "true men" or rubbish men (e.g., in chapters 5 and 9). To understand these stereotypes we are safest combining their meaning in private reports with observations of their use by the same people in public, to create a fuller picture. But so far, I have referred to indigenous stereotypes and images. What happens to this transference process when the ethnographer introduces foreign concepts into the conversation?

Example: we used "fantasy" to indicate daydreams in our interviews. (At times, though, "fantasy" also covered "mental images," "scripts," and "free association," concepts we shall not discuss now.) By introducing this concept to interpreters we change them. One must be alert to the consequences. I saw no harmful effects. [S: That depends on who defines "harmful."] But we do know that Moondi— now more aware of his imagery—may change what he does, says, or thinks. Obviously the appropriateness of our use of "fantasy" hinges on how well we understand Sambia culture, language, the interview context, and the person. Quite a lot. Ethnographers working closely with someone a long time will be able to use—and trust in—such concepts and resulting data and then link those to interpretations of culture and experience at large. Readers will want demonstrations of the alien concepts being used in context, to evaluate their meaning.

Some anthropologists may be uneasy using ideas like "fantasy". But remember that many anthropologic concepts, e.g., "soul," "trance," "omen," "self" are as laden with western connotations as is "fantasy," though only recently have we questioned their cross-cultural validity. Clinical ethnography, if it does nothing else, can help us think more carefully about such heuristic terms.

We do not work alone, of course, and we should be remiss not to thank our language/culture interpreters and indicate the importance of understanding their transference responses too. Weiyu's has been dealt with, perhaps more than he really cared for. Whiting and his colleagues (1966:156) indicated the tasks and potential bias of the *ethnographer* here. More recently, Crapanzano's[46] remarkable Moroccan case study has opened up more far-reaching implications of transference/countertransference issues in the interpreters' situation.

When western concepts are imported from other cultures we become more aware also of the specificity of transference responses. Not "Sambia fantasy," but "Moondi's fantasy" (on Tuesday afternoon, when his father was sick his mother gone to tend his father, M. moving into heterosexual relationships, sitting with me as S. looked on). A new concept embodies no necessary stereotypes, connotations, or meanings; thus, a person's responses to it are particularly revealing of his/her inner needs at the time. Thus, in this example of imported concepts, we must raise two other problems: how do they imply trust, and what is the truth-value of such material?

Trust is not truth. People may trust us—in degrees—but still not relate the truth, i.e., give us an account narrative. It is no news that people's communications are not courtroom testimony. Yet ethnographers seldom report that natives forget, misunderstand, have contradictory views, make slips, unwittingly mix information from one mode of discourse to another, etc. Truth is not a thing; it is many experiences buried in all these tactics, as is untruth. Trusting may yield more accurate forms of what our interpreters feel, at a particular moment, to be true about something. Do we show if or how they change their opinions? Trust limits distortions, which may never disappear, only fade. Someone's truth may not be drawn within black and white boundaries. And certain issues (e.g., Saku's hermaphrotism) may hold such power that only time—patience—will bring trust and truth (but not "the truth").

How do these private meanings relate to norms and institutions of a culture? What difference does it make, a structuralist might argue, if people disguise a lie: those untruths do not fundamentally affect the interpretation of social relationships or the unconscious structure of Mind (e.g., dualism as a principle of social structure). I would not be too sure. Whether or not Sakulambei trusts me does not change the existence of shamanism as an institution or a symbolic category in Sambia culture, but it does change how I interpret the relevant beliefs, rules, behaviors, experience. The depth of my knowledge aids my interpretations and colors my view. Perhaps certain structuralists believe they are more objective with primitives. We don't think so.

Our interviews show that when the interpreters trust us, they give us more information, but that is not "the truth;" the information we receive is modified by our interest, sincerity, boredom, hostility. (Granting this, the ethnographer must still make an interpretation that goes beyond the natives' view.) Trust shows itself in many voices. When Tali told us in private of ritual cult practices, for instance, was he speaking for himself or as a representative of the ritual cult? Does he share his private views only or what he thinks Weiyu or ourselves expect to hear? (What does he expect himself to think and feel?[47]) In chapter 5 we have a glimpse of this complex talk. What we cannot see, though, are the years of similar dialogues that came before; the background knowledge to which it refers in a Tali/Weiyu/Herdt discourse that is simultaneously public/private/secret and then again something more: a gestalt of our increasing intersubjective understanding as a group of three. (S. changed this group talk, and he challenged Tali's view, which I had never done.) So much background is needed to interpret these dialogues that the ethnographer draws back in dismay at trying to present them. And yet we did. Clinical ethnography will require creative researchers.

Because our interviews are not public talk or secret ritual talk but occur in an ambience of special private discourse, the nature of trust and transference responses to the fieldworker requires attention. We ensured privacy, asking others to leave the house. (Unprecedented, except in ritual talk viz. the uninitiated.) People were often remunerated: how did that change what they said? Knowing that what they said would remain confidential changed their talk. (Would Sakulambei have agreed to open his painful history to me otherwise?) Each such tactic changes trust, creates different transference responses. This private interviewing style is pretty far removed from conventional participant-observation. In short, as Bourguignon (1979: 87) put it, "Anthropologists have often argued that studying alien, 'primitive' societies made it possible to be a good deal more 'objective' than studying one's own society." By the end of her life, Mead[48] had wavered but never really defected from this view, and yet, she more than anyone, forced us to consider its limitations. Like Freud[49] before her, she was a captive of an old scientific ideology. That view is out of place in clinical ethnography; let us seek creative solutions to the lived contradiction: participate but observe. S. and I disagree somewhat on this matter: the explanation of our difference will bring us to the end of this chapter.

S: I am still not sure why H. has fussed so hard over this participant-observation: were I an ethnographer, I would want to be intimate and yet not family. When used in analytic treatment, participant-observation assures the patient of our closest, most intense attention without the threat of personal entanglements and therefore undue influence (as is inherent in transference). It is an attitude unlike that present in other therapies, for the analyst's desire is to hear—everything, were it possible—but not to coerce: not even with love, for coercion by love too often requires corrupt love. The analyst promises nothing but to listen, and when we do it well, our patients are heard as they never have been before, down to subjective levels they scarcely could imagine. It takes a peculiar personality, however, to practice this analysis: the capacity to merge and yet be fully separate in the same instant. To walk into the fire and not be burned. I don't see why this must be seen as "contradiction lived."

H: This view departs from mine in two ways. First (the least important) is that S. here conflates my criticism of the ideology of fieldwork with what ethnographers actually do. Generally, I agree that we can be involved and still detached in fieldwork. Were this not possible, we would remain only tourists or we would all go native. Yet, the old rhetorical uses of participant-observation ignore the fact that each researcher implements this approach in different ways, dependent not only on situations but our personalities and research interests as well. Nonetheless, that approach is held to be, in some ideal sense, a uniform method that is independent of the idiosyncrasies. That rhetorical uniformity is, for me, a fiction. Second, and more important, psychoanalysts do not do participant-observation, which is based primarily in normative interactions with natives in *their* social world. S. recognizes this by saying, "The analyst promises nothing but to listen," which is not a normative interaction (who, in our world, converses with us by only listening, aside from God, except those in privileged positions of authority, assessment, treatment?[50]). It is a corruption of the already corrupt notion to refer to analytic therapy as participant-observation. [S: You've convinced me.] And likewise for clinical ethnography: we need a different paradigm for the interactions and discourses that occur in our case studies above. Nonetheless, no ethnographer—even in private interviews—could only listen, because others, feeling this to be bizarre, would make tracks.

We see in our difference of opinion a major contrast between the narrative styles of analysis and ethnography. Where the analyst is primarily concerned with the patients' private feelings and fantasies, the ethnographer is concerned mainly to use these as a way to better understand what shapes cultural institutions and public behavior. The difficulty with clinical ethnography is that it *is* concerned with idio-syncracy, but it must also be culturally based. I am distressed that some analysts, psychiatrists, and clinicians—sixty years after Freud's death—continue to ignore cultural factors in their writing (not to mention their treatment and training). There are some exceptions, but the failure of analysis to take culture seriously and the fact that psychoanalytic anthropology came from outside analysis and has not affected it much, remain disturbing signs of its culture-bound design. No one has argued more intelligently or forcefully for a sophisticated union of psychoanalysis and anthropology than LeVine.[51] His careful work reveals the great possibilities inherent in cross-cultural clinical method, a promise of much to come.

We reach an end when we confront the problems and potentials of clinical ethnography. It is neither traditional analysis nor conventional anthropology; it calls for a new intellectual ground. S. is unique: we should not generalize from his ability to reach beyond psycho-analysis to engage the Other in New Guinea. In fact, S.'s trip to New Guinea—aberrant for an analyst—must be seen as a sign that he does not fit the analytic mode in the same way as his colleagues. My friends sense this, though they had not the words to say it fully. In the Epilogue we shall consider finally how analytic supervision under this psychoanalyst influenced this particular clinical ethnographer in the early years of his adventures in Paradise.

EPILOGUE:
Training Clinical Ethnographers

H: How shall we train people to be clinical ethnographers? What skills should be taught and training experiences provided, before the field? What role will the supervisor play in the process? Here are some reflections.

Anthropologists who would do clinical ethnography should learn, as do clinicians in other disciplines, that oneself is the primary instrument. Seminars, books, theories, practicums, internships, and the like help. But they cannot substitute for the personality trained for empathy, self-knowledge, and skill in observing and interviewing. The ethnographer is the instrument; all else is technology. Yet to improve the instrument, we hope at least that students are trained in elementary techniques of interviewing. There are plenty of books on that subject, but they are no substitute for experience.

For training Ph.D. students in anthropology, we do not think it practical that they undergo treatment. Nor is psychoanalytic training indicated. To lay a psychoanalysis onto four years of undergraduate work and three years of graduate training is too much.[1] Analytic training, despite its rewards, may diffuse students' focus in the field. (Postdoctoral analytic training is another matter.) But reading in analysis and participation in seminars on analysis could widen horizons. What else might help? Seminars on counseling and interpersonal relationships, courses in interviewing techniques with practical experience, introductory psychiatry courses in medical schools, etc. The more supervised experience, the better.

To let the reader know I apply the same standards to myself, let me briefly consider how clinical training has affected my ethnography. What did it do to me to return to the Sambia, after receiving my Ph.D., each time loaded not only with more ethnographic knowl-

381

edge but also with the clinical perspectives learned with the psychiatrist/analyst S.? This question is not easy to approach, for, as far as I know, it has never before been studied; we are in unfamiliar territory (Herdt and Stoller 1987). I shall, therefore, only skim the subject (and in doing so, anticipate the last section wherein I examine a shadowy presence crucial to field technique: how does the ethnographer study intimate matters without harming interpreters or information?).

What is different in my ethnography since 1974? First, the obvious: Sambia society shifted significantly. My interpreters changed and aged. And I, as expected of any ethnographer, grew into my profession. But though a system (in this case ethnographer-observing-interpreters-observing-ethnographer) may alter, some elements do so faster or more significantly than others. For me, postgraduate professional change was influenced most by working with S. To show how requires examples.

I brought to New Guinea the conviction that my research required closeness and trust with Sambia. Though I generally opened up my life to my interpreters as indicated above, and I had successes, there were also holes and weaknesses, even failures* in my work, as I concluded in Kalutwo's case study.

Transference issues were involved. Nilutwo's transference to me will indicate the limits of my predoctoral fieldwork (1974–1976) before supervision with a clinician helped change it into clinical ethnography. As noted above, Nilutwo was, in 1974, a troubled married man in his early thirties. He was a renowned womanizer and cassowary hunter. I began working with N. on his hunting activities, which involved his dreaming for prophetic omens. Soon, though, we were sitting daily for an hour or more, my listening to N. tell his previous night's dreams. N. was a prolific reporter of dreams, sometimes recounting two and three different long dream sequences from a night. He was intense, needy, and affectionate, but also broody, fragile, jealous, vindictive, and a bit paranoid. In a word: neurotic. After a few weeks he began to report seeing me in his dreams. I knew that this communicated closer rapport with me. I encouraged and supported his reports and had him interpret his dreams, (as far as he

---

*Perhaps failure isn't the right term; perhaps it is. Not failure *only* in the sense of material I didn't, or did not want to, or could not, collect (e.g., not being conscious that certain phenomena are "data"). Yet failure is the right word when we consciously back off, psychologically, morally, or politically, knowing that we can or should investigate certain matters that we do not.

could). I would ask questions when he finished talking. But I never interpreted his experiences for him. (I did do that, sometimes, later, in 1979.) I encouraged his associating to the dream images. His flair for this mode increased; soon, I often could not distinguish what was dream thought or secondary elaboration. And I appeared even more in his dreams, just as he came to rely on our talking sessions for cathartic release more than ever. I began to be concerned, in 1976—a while before leaving for home—that he was becoming too attached to me. (This later led to discussions between S. and me on the nature of transference and the risks of its flowering under the influence of a naive listener-interrogator-researcher-unwitting-quasi-therapist.)

Yet I did not then know how to deal with my anxiety. I had helped promote Nilutwo's transference to me, had allowed him to be closer to me and discuss subjects (like daydreams) he never discussed with anyone else. But I didn't know what to *do* with that transference. And toward the end I wondered if it was good for him: should we have engaged in this talking—which amounted to a supportive psychotherapy of sorts? (For instance, more than once we discussed his adulterous behavior and how he wanted help in getting out of the trouble it brought him.) In my position as white, powerful, possessions-rich (e.g., tennis shoes), geographically mobile, educated researcher, the power distributions of common friendship were as swamped as in a psychoanalysis.

Looking back over Nilutwo's materials, I realize that I dealt with my anxiety in a way that seems unhelpful now. When he finished a dream report and silence grew, I asked him for a *cultural* interpretation of his dreams. In other words, I referred him back to his own adult cultural symbol system—asking him, in effect, to provide an idealized interpretation of his experience. Anthropologists have often studied the manifest content or native interpretation system of dreams. That approach fits well in New Guinea cultures, the dream interpretation codes of which tend to project the experience (e.g., anxieties) outside of the dreamer onto externalized superego figures (e.g., ghosts).[2] The problem is that when I was uneasy I unconsciously accommodated myself to this cultural defense mechanism referring his *private* experiences to *public* symbols and norms.[3] This dampened his florid associations and made him distance himself from the transference, thus allowing us to be more comfortable.[4] (On the other hand, to have given him depth interpretations without being a competent psychoanalyst and without wrapping him in the safety of formal therapy would have put him at great risk.)

This example shows a bit of my early interview style. What effects of S.'s and my working directly together can be indicated in later fieldwork?

A second example: Kalutwo. My empathy for his rubbish man characteristics and ambivalence to me was low. But once we entered this new phase of clinical research, I became fascinated with his life history. I had told myself that avoiding him was simply a lack of interest. But supervision (which, like therapy, can be a deeper, inner-active process than being given facts and tactics by one's supervisor) revealed this to be a compound of my hostility and anxiety (i.e., coun-tertransference). Now I realize how, like my male friends in the vil-lage, I had reacted to K. with contempt, in part as defense against anxiety he caused me.

By 1979 I also was sensitive to theory that relates sexual excite-ment and hostility, the result of working with S. This part of my clin-ical training culminated in discussions we had at UCLA about Sam-bia gender identity in 1978, before my leaving for the field. It even went on in New Guinea, supported by S.'s visit.

So I then began serious, lively interviewing with K., and I knew that my anxiety had distanced me from him. I had learned from S. more about the various forms of hostility, one of which was in myself: like Sambia men, I was threatened by K.'s unmasculine traits and so was amused at their jokes (a tactic that helped us avoid denying our unacceptable identifications with him). By 1979, more insightful, I saw through this defensive reaction to its cruelty: I had learned not only to recognize that anxiety in myself and to see how to reach for insight in understanding its source, but—the great bonus for one's data collecting (i.e., ethnography)—to use it as a clue to compre-hending the other men's hostility. (A nontrivial understanding, be-cause such clues improve one's search for the dynamics underlying myth, ritual, initiation, erotics, and even war.) Before clinical train-ing at UCLA, I had not known how to proceed toward insight; now it still surprises me to have been hostile like that. (As with other un-consciously motivated reactions, that surprise indicates I can still re-peat that hostility, but now it is easily dissipated, for it is within conscious control.) Anthropology can be done without insight only at the expense of such distortions.

Example three, from fieldwork in 1979: I have returned to the vil-lage after two and a half years' absence. The ritual cult is deterio-rating: In the last initiations (1977) the men did not uniformly nose-bleed boys as they've always done. The elders and ritual leaders are losing their grip. One morning, not long after I arrive, I am in my house with Tali, Weiyu, and other men, who are discussing the scandalous behavior of an eleven-year-old boy. He was initiated in 1977, making him a first-stage initiate. I know him and his family. The men are rubbishing the boy because he was recently caught in sex play with a girl, behavior so astonishing no one knows even *how* to punish him (another sign of the men's deteriorating control). The men generalize from this boy's behavior to all the new initiates—how they are weak, unmanly, and irresponsible—as the cult falls apart ("it's a sign of the times"). Even my friend Moondi, usually moderate in such matters, condemns the boy. So do I; and here is the heart of my example.

As the men related the incident my response changed from shock (to think the society has so deteriorated) to condemnation. I sympathized with the men, found myself feeling hostile to the boy. I joined with the men, righteously identified with their moral outrage—which only increased when an impudent young initiate, who happened along, thumbed his nose at the elders, adding that "One day, up on top there (i.e., heaven), Jesus will condemn the elders" for their sins (e.g., the initiation customs). I was as angry as the other men at this youngster's rhetorical imitation of a local evangelist's preachings (a New Guinean from outside the tribe). As the rhetoric heated up (only five minutes had passed during this whole episode), I suddenly stopped, struck that I, the ethnographer, was hostile to these boys. My sympathies were with the men in this divided camp of old versus young. So I questioned my motives and was ashamed.

Why was I hostile? Obviously I identified with the men, their ritual customs, and experiences of ritual we had shared in years past. My role and status were also tied to those events: not only inside the village but outside, through my work. Reflecting on my feelings I halted. I became—had to become—an observer of myself as well as a participant-observer. My behavior was not to be denied or covered up: it was what had to be explained. My motivations, conscious and unconscious, contributed to my understanding Sambia men and their rituals; but that is another story. Clinical training, especially S.'s supervision of those of my interests concerned with hostility, changed that moment of fieldwork. My point is this: rather than merely acting and reacting, I also reflected. Understanding the dynamics of Sambia ritual, generational relationships, erotics, and authority lies as much in my subjective response that moment as anything one might otherwise learn in Sambia life.

Example four: a reluctant informant. A man I have known for years—Gorutndun—had always refused me an interview. He was married, over thirty, gregarious, well liked. He was in a position of authority, too, which he opportunistically mined. I knew from gossip and my own impressions that despite his marriage and fatherhood he continued to have sex with boys. He seemed, that is, genuinely to like sex with both women and boys, and he defied custom by his persisting homosexual activities. He was not stigmatized like Kalutwo, though, for he was married and a swashbuckler, with achievements K. lacked. He being that kind of bisexual, then, I had long hoped to talk with G., wanting to understand his family history and gender dynamics as another male case study in my research. But despite every cordial move, I could not lure him to talk with me.

Before S.'s supervision, my response to G.'s reluctance would have been annoyance or, more insightful, to worry over what in myself prevented Gorutndun's talking with me. Now I could think further: I felt that G. avoided me to avoid that part of himself that I most wanted to understand. In other words, he feared looking inside, wanted no insight. And in this sense, at least, it is correct to say that he resisted me because he felt (perhaps from stories about my interviewing others) that I might probe areas he didn't want to probe. I saw his posture that way, accepted it, and did not hassle myself for not interviewing him. A shift occurred. We were cordial, but my cordiality had a resonance—an ease never there before. Two years later (1981) I asked him for an interview, which he granted. We discussed this bisexuality. It was no big deal. I was grateful to him and to myself for having the patience to see things through.

Final example: Weiyu's misogyny. Weiyu is my closest Sambia friend. We have seen him as an interpreter; I know his family intimately, know his wife, and helped him in his payment of bride wealth in 1974. Over the years he and his wife have fought a lot, as you know. Added to this is what one might call Weiyu's culturally characterologic misogyny, his feeling that aside from being objects to screw and produce babies, women are dirty, worthless, dangerous, and capable of corrupting and ruining men. Even years ago Weiyu and his beautiful wife would regularly argue and brawl. Villagers intervened but failed to calm them down; friends like Tali even pressed Weiyu to stop exploding; I talked to him too, several times scolding him for his hardness. He ignored us all.

Over the years he, like other Sambia men, also derided women: chauvinist jokes, locker-room talk, and dirty stories. My reactions were of two sorts. On the one hand, I found it distressing to see how men treated women: nothing bothered me then or now as much about

Sambia life as this misogyny. On the other hand, because in the mid-1970s I spent 90% of my time with males, had superficial contacts with females, and needed the men's material and psychologic support—not to mention friendship—I not only abided their antifemale joking but, in a latent way, reinforced it, often by eliciting material (beliefs, idioms, stories) about women, which aroused their jokes. (Again, as with the Kalutwo jokes, these putdowns kept men from being uncomfortable talking about women.) I chuckled or laughed sometimes, too, though often as not I stood back aloof. They seemed not to care, except, perhaps, for Weiyu, who knew from my negative responses how I felt. ("White man's strange morals"?)

This situation came full circle in a 1983 trip to Sambia. I thought that by then—Weiyu was almost thirty—he would mellow out. Yet the marital chaos was fierce as ever. It surprised me: he had not grown beyond his earlier misogyny, as do other men, at least somewhat, with the passing of time and arrival of children. And this pained me. They still had dreadful fights and Weiyu would break into bitter episodes in my hut of foully cursing his wife.

During this same time I had steadily worked more and more with women. Penjukwi had had the courage to talk seriously with me and had also made me for several years aware of the victims' side of the men's jokes about women. She showed me male/female relations through new eyes and ears. And we became friends, caught in grief over Nilutwo's death. And though the sexual antagonism of traditional Sambia culture had softened, I saw more than ever the men's power plays and abuses of women. The pathos of Sambia sexual culture.

Thus I changed: now more clinically adept and self-aware I found Weiyu's behavior hard to accept. His and other men's put-downs of women appealed not at all to me. I saw Weiyu as an extreme example of a character pattern that had this bitter outcome. The phallicness of his war-leader stance was not Sambia culture in the abstract, but, rather, a cold, rigid essence of the idealized masculinity of that tradition. I saw, too, that his wife sometimes created conflicts, as he did. I saw the games in which they entangled each other. I saw the other victims. I saw Weiyu become harder and less a friend to his men friends and to me. My increased identification with Sambia women made me understand the terrible reality of the men's jokes.

What, in regard to this last vignette, has changed in me? Hadn't I always understood Weiyu or the men's misogyny? Hadn't I always empathized with the women? Not quite. Part of me had resisted fully seeing my friend's feeling toward women and Sambia women's plight. I just presumed Weiyu's was a prolonged adolescence, to be out-grown. But it is not. And I resisted knowing Sambia women deeply: the combination of my personality, my American cultural orienta-tion, and an old-fashioned professional androcentric disregard for fe-males as culture-bearers served to intellectualize my reactions. But when congenial supervision met inner possibilities, I was more ready to understand Sambia women. I know Penjukwi as I could not have in 1974.

So I began to learn better, for instance, of the women's desire for erotic fulfillment in their marriages and their yearning to have their achievements as economic producers and mothers recognized. This understanding results from my valuing seeing men and women as individuals; from knowing that as individuals they differ in conform-ing to the cultural ideals ethnographers purport to have witnessed; and from my knowing that I, the ethnographer, sometimes selectively see what I want to see and interpret it according to how well I know myself. I was lucky—and wise—to return to these people enough over the years to observe them, as individuals, changing or frozen, just as the rest of the world is changing. This understanding of my counter-transference I also learned in part from S.

The ability and desire to probe and understand our countertrans-ference reactions is, to me, a hallmark of psychoanalysis and clinical ethnography. This may not require Freud's near obsession [S.: ??] with self-analysis (Becker 1973:102ff.), yet to others it might seem so. In anthropology those who have known this are few in number, but, they have made fine contributions to the study of culture. The diffi-culty is that the object of reflection—culture—and the lens of re-flection—the ethnographer—must be revealed within the same text; and of such achievements one thinks of Lévi-Strauss' *Tristes Tro-piques*, Read's *The High Valley*, and, close to anthropology, Doi's *Anat-omy of Dependence*, and Kakar's *Shamans, Mystics, and Doctors*. Most recently, however, a virtually unprecedented account of countertrans-ference in the construction of clinical ethnography is provided by Kracke (1987). Here is a rich new field of discovery awaiting us, though its mining will be plagued with unforeseeable and unprecedented training issues.

S: From the scientist's godly perch, H. is no more correct to sym-pathize with the cursed women than earlier when he dimly saw their viewpoint. Science is not sympathy. For we cannot argue that there is a final, essential level of truth the researcher on human behavior can attain. To know more is never to know enough. All is always interpretation.

So when he works better with the women. H. will have to go back and reinterpret his work on the men, and that will shift his perspectives on the women; *ad infinitum.* In the meanwhile he keeps changing inside. And then he becomes excited by the ideas of other colleagues—different sorts of psychoanalysts, antianalysts, molecular biologists, limbic lobists, Marxists, Marists, eschatologists, I Chingists, ethnomethodologists, neoplatonists, and phthisists. The hints, data, belief systems, truths—the interpretations—never end, always change.

To say the obvious, the same holds for the psychoanalyst. And in his or her role as supervisor, the analyst—in this case, I—is equally influenced by the ethnographer (or his students or patients), as useful a subject of study as the one we have just aired but too lengthy for consideration here.

Nonetheless, we would be foolishly even-handed not to repeat this last time our idea that ethnography is improved when the ethnographer (just as the medical clinician), by listening well—with what Freud called a "closely hovering attention"[5]—allows his interpreters to communicate better. That there is no bottom to the individual mind need not scare us off. Nor should we fear—as researchers—that by immersing ourselves deeply in individuals we shall ruin the great philosophic effort that searches for laws ruling particular events.

These five examples are the first that came to mind for H. We want to stress to readers that there are numberless more: these intersubjective and subjective processes go on all day long. The point is not that there is something special about H., or me, or this supervision, special though it may be; nor that H. is wise or foolish, insightful or blind, wrong or right. The same basic processes occur in us all, in all research, all the time. All supervision included. What we have added is simply another piece: an ethnography of supervision.

Some readers may see H.'s responses to supervision not as movements toward insight but as confusions due to meddling. Others may see in this book something even worse: exhibitionism, narcissism, sadomasochism, whatever.[6] But remember, the point is not that clinical supervision can strengthen one's ethnography—that cannot be proven with optimistic vignettes—but that *any* supervision (or our personality, not to mention the time of day, the weather, our mood of the moment, our religious beliefs, or our "'inexplicable" liking or disliking of an interpreter) changes the ethnography; we are simply showing again that these effects *are* ethnography, not artifacts to be denied. Or hidden.* If that makes the ethnographer's job harder, messier, more demanding of better and different training, and requires a capacity to study and understand oneself, then that's just too damn bad. As with the practice of psychoanalysis, ethnography—the process of working in one's head, not the morally easy hardships of malaria, lousy food, leeches, itches, rotten weather, hostile natives, exhaustion and fear—should not be done to spare the ethnographer.

H: We guess there are students in anthropology, sociology, psychology and the like who would use clinical skills more and better if only they could learn to trust themselves as one of the sources of understanding others. As Devereux argued in *From Anxiety to Method*, the basic datum in our disciplines is what happens within the observer. This statement is complex, yet there is no magic in it. To use oneself to measure others involves no more than hard work, commitment, an odd personality, formal training, good supervision, insight, worldly experience, and the desire to do clinical ethnography. Some students have the potential; it will become manifest in the right student when there is encouragement and a good role model, as in the supervision. Is not my ethnography more sensitive to interpersonal issues because of S.'s supervision? The answer lies not in our opinions: only more and better ethnographies will allow us to make such assessments.

Students have options in selecting their training. One course in interviewing will help refine one's sensitivity to other people. Where such courses do not exist, other opportunities can be found. Perhaps we should rethink training for the Ph.D. in Anthropology which, in this regard, resembles psychoanalysis: good work requires good technique (Foulks 1977:16), which is a function of one's relationship to others.

For students who wish to develop better field research skills we should allow more time in their training for supervised fieldwork at home before beginning their Ph.D. project abroad. Training in some of these skills (e.g., interviewing techniques) is available in a few anthropology departments in the United States. However, Departments of Psychiatry are not providing the kind of cultural training we need.[8] We must be innovative and activist in developing better training programs.

A final point regarding training: we need—in respect to all the

*H: However, my uneasiness at times with the autobiography here and above is a sign of my professional socialization that we should not truly disclose our insides in publications.[7]

above—better supervision in anthropology. My guess—as an observer of anthropology departments and as a teacher—is that Ph.D. students aren't as afraid of working closely with interpreters as they are of talking to their professors about talking with the natives. Some advisors may still adhere to the sink or swim philosophy critiqued in chapter 1. They may feel it is unnecessary to teach interviewing skills. This would be a pity. They may also be overly concerned with professional boundaries, or be concerned to discuss with students an area in which they themselves are weak. And anthropology does attract the idiosyncratic; who else transplant themselves in this way among aliens?[9] If comfortable with natives, the student may encounter difficulty working intimately with others at home; yet clinical training requires such intimacy. Avoiding such training means people will not see what you are like, or what you do or do not know, or how skilled you are in communicating. The end comes full circle when the student's professors, too, do not have clinical training or skills, and, beyond teaching these subjects, resist knowing themselves what they do not want to know. We do not need a Freud to tell us that this situation will produce unwanted side-effects. Let us hope for another generation of ethnographers who will find clinical ethnography of enough value to overcome these problems.

ETHICAL ISSUES

Does clinical ethnography bring special risks to the ethnographer or the natives? Are we placing additional burdens on young adults' already strained heads in not only sending them to alien places but asking them to get inside their interpreters? The particular answers depend on the personality of the researcher and the circumstances of the research. Still, there are obvious pros and cons.[10]

First, a simple distinction: there is a difference between doing casual interviewing and intensive prolonged talking with individuals. For the latter, care and discretion should be taken in selecting clinical ethnographers. Only someone who is psychologically healthy should go to the field [S: It is not that simple; and what is "psychologically healthy"?]; but only those who are demonstrably skilled at home in one-on-one interactions should do clinical ethnography.[11]

Second, the great risk in ethnographic training is for clinical issues *never* to be dealt with. (1) We cannot know what stresses students will be exposed to, but at least we should let them know something about how to recognize and cope with stress (2) without being undone by their own conflicts, guilt, or exploitation of others in the field. (3)

Being trained to recognize anxiety—particularly disturbing experiences—is a powerful advantage to students. Rather than reacting, they can act. To repeat: what we find most disturbing in another culture is often precisely what is important to study, not avoid. Whatever the substance of these disturbances—cargo cult beliefs, homicide, dreams, whatever—such anxieties felt by a healthy researcher probably point to experiences disturbing in one way or other to the natives. (4) The ideologic baggage of culture shock in anthropology indicates our awareness that we are not adequately handling all the reality we are responsible for recording. (5) The shroud surrounding deep intimacy with the natives—for example, sexual relationships*—and the shadows that make going native so sinful indicate that our training procedures can be improved. These points underline that faulty fieldwork training at present perpetuates the risk of the past. What a pity if our shame at being subjective prevented us from knowing more when we easily could.

Nonetheless, anthropology is too injudicious when, in not giving ethnographers clinical skills, it places certain interpreters at risk. Though it may well be true that "they will live out most of their lives without our creative intervention" (M. Strathern 1981:684), we do not know what the effects of our intervention will be for the rest of their lives.

S: It is unclear, when, because of trusting feelings generated in a relationship, one person may decently, honorably, or legally take advantage of another: the concept of undue influence arises. In ethnography, as long as we seem alien to our interpreters, they may be protected by their suspicions and their lack of love for us. Even so, their envy and awe of the power that accompanies our visible technology, money, capacity to escape their environment when we wish, our education and knowledge, and our other emanations of superiority can endanger them. But they are especially susceptible when they respect and love us.

We presume many ethnographers know of these effects and recognize their power in eliciting information. We feel it is useful, nonetheless, to point explicitly to the problem of undue influence, because it may greatly tempt the ethnographer. It is considered rape to seduce

*It is astounding but understandable that in the whole ethnographic literature I know best—Melanesia—there is not one sentence on an ethnographer's sexual feelings for (let alone involvements with) the natives. (Exclude Malinowski's diaries since he could not rise from the grave to agree to their publication, even though, I am told, they were highly edited by others regarding this sexual content.)

or otherwise inveigle into sexual intercourse people too uninformed to know the consequence of what they are willing to do: children below a certain age, mental defectives, and those rendered incompetent by mental illness. So must the ethnographer not take (nonerotic—as well as erotic) advantage of his vulnerable subjects in order to gain advantage.

As in supervising medical students, clinical psychology predoctorals, social workers, psychiatric residents, and psychoanalytic candidates, graduate schools can choose and train ethnographers to be trusted intimates of those they study, without freezing into pseudoscientific obsessive-compulsivity or broiling to a crisp in hysterical mystical unions with their savages. Either of these extremes is unethical (not to say indicative of poor research), since the ethnographer's work is grossly distorted by his or her neurosis (countertransference).* Why should ethnographers not be bound to that fundamental ethic of the physician: *Primam non nocere*?

This stance means the student will feel, after training, that he or she will not harm others with the information they confide. The ethnographer, so removed from the university, cannot be supervised or monitored in any real sense. Working thus alone, how are we to train students in knowing the difference between a true conviction and a conviction used to rationalize things that harm? There are no simple answers to this problem, but we do have indicators we can follow.[12] First, there are tape recordings, case and field notes that can be shared with supervisors and others. Second, there is the fact of interpreters working with someone a long time. While this is no absolute assurance that the ethnographer was trusted, it is a sign of being able to work intensely with people (who, in general, will not continue talking to those they do not trust, no matter how much they are materially reimbursed). Third, there is the student's presence in the material, which offers a gauge for evaluation by others.[†] Finally, there are the communications with supervisors—letters from the field, discussions and review of material at home.

H. knows—it was latent till made manifest in supervision with me—that aspects of ethnography resemble the risks and rewards of psychoanalysis, a domain wherein patients' well-being must come first. Once that awareness is part of the ethnographer's flesh, one is free.

---

*We should not be too severe. Probably, comparable to what happened in some of the psychoanalytic pioneers, new findings and great ideas sometimes flap out of crazy ethnographers' heads: we do not need many calm, insightful people; they are often unimaginative.

†Though we depend on others to be honest in reports we can do little when someone fabricates material.

Then it is easy to ask about and explore virtually anything, knowing the information will not be used for harm: a historical, political, philosophic, ethical, and moral stand on individual freedom;[13] to be free enough inside ourself to listen so well that we finally hear. Then, when we are with others, we shall be allowed to begin to experience what they know and, beyond that, what they dare not know they know.

When we have it, our interpreters—the ethnographer's subjects and the therapist's patients—are no less able to sense this openness than can our friends. The resulting mutuality will be fine, the beginning of the end of the hatred—the refusal to listen—that still poisons most human endeavors. Including anthropology and psychoanalysis.

S. and H: You see, clinical ethnography can be done most anywhere you stick your nose. That's pretty much how it was with us. S. was to drop in on H. at the village for a few days. Yet here we are, years later, concluding a book we never intended to do, still exploring, agreeing and disagreeing. A few more visits and we would add more case studies; a better view of women, the children, the elderly; a description of the dissolution of a culture; an ethnography of supervision; more on tourists, patrol officers, and missionaries; a picture of what our doing clinical ethnography did to us; and how our clinical interventions (e.g., the coming of insight into one's motives) affect a culture and its people.

If, by doing that, others would know that clinical ethnography has to be done everywhere, then they could easily do it better. Our success will occur when we become passé.

Let us end with this: the discourse in anthropology between ethnographer and interpreters and in psychoanalysis between doctor and patient must be opened to closer scrutiny. And if we in these disciplines cannot do it, who will?

APPENDIX:

The Editing Process

S: In the introduction we examined the value of using subjectivity to learn about culture via others' subjectivity. We face another aspect of this problem in the interviews in this book: how data are infiltrated by a different subjectivity—the process of editing. When the reader reads our words, what stands between what occurred and the conclusions we draw? When we were there talking with our Sambia friends, what was happening in them and what in us that no machine can capture? How are our data thereby flawed and what are the consequences of that impairment for those who would be scientific? Our book is a study of these questions; but at this point, let us suffice with a description of the editing process that starts when the tape begins to run and ends with the published words.

One speaks. The tape does not pick up the words with their original fidelity. Some are muffled, some are overridden when more than one person talks, some are hard to retrieve if a participant sits rather far from the machine. Batteries or tape run out without our being aware. The tape ends, and we notice but lose a sentence or two every time because the process of recording stops a few moments before the tape stops. Tapes disappear in harsh living and traveling conditions (this did not happen to us). Conversation is lost when a cassette is turned onto the second side or a new one installed.

The tapes arrive home safely. H. now listens and translates onto new tapes in English. Will he miss anything due to fatigue or unconscious slips? What is the relationship between the Sambia or Pidgin spoken and the words he chooses for the English translation? (This problem was faced continuously during the interviews when Sambia was being translated to Pidgin and when H. translated and summarized in English for S.) How well—months and years later, when trying

395

to recapture exactly what was happening—do we recall the setting, the looks on people's faces, the other forms of communication that so much shape and change the meanings of words? How (in 1979) does S.'s memory (age 54 in 1979 and in a different relationship to the participants from H.) compare with H.'s (age 31 then, talking with friends he has known for several years)?

H: It may interest the reader to know I transcribed in two ways: by dictation and by writing. Most of the tapes were transcribed by listening word-for-word to the tapes, while simultaneously dictating literal translation (with punctuation, intonation remarks, etc.) onto another tape from which a secretary typed to produce a text. Some of the last tapes I transcribed by listening and writing down dialogue word-for-word in longhand. It is boring. But checking my transcriptions I find that dictating throws in more errors (slips, gaps), and the translation is much rougher than when I write it. On the other hand, the dictated text preserves better the Sambia flavor. An hour of original dialogue took about ten hours (depending on the speaker, situation, etc.) to translate, but one cannot work continuously: I am numb after four or five hours. We suffer, but not as much as the linguists. Healey (1964:19) reports that it took seventy hours to transcribe an hour of text phonemically and "to obtain a fairly accurate free translation." (He says he and his translator could only bear three hours a day.) "Fairly accurate" is all I can claim for my translations; will I think that in twenty years?

S: Now H. delivers the tapes to secretaries for transcription. This transcribing work is hard: boring, wearing. (Even H.'s tapes—his translations, not the originals—are occasionally hard to make out.) What about secretaries transposing words, leaving out fragments, misperceiving words, making slips?

Let us call the product of the above labors our "raw material." What do we do to it? From here on, the reader is completely at our mercy. We could invent conversations that never occurred, report nuances we know were not present or nuances we sensed but that other observers would deny were there. (See Stoller and Geertsma [1963] on clinicians' inability to agree on what they observe.) What if pieces were removed to win arguments rather than because they are repetitive, or garbled, or—in the mass—would bore the reader into giving up reading?

Most people would despair if confronted, in a book bought for amusement or education, with raw typescript. It is our task to edit the material to make it coherent and lively and to add commentary, hoping we can restore the experience to one that simulates, for the reader, what we believe happened.* That removes the words we publish from the category of data; they are now only approximations of the original.[†] (The professional reader's defense against this is the presence of our original tapes, but who will go to the effort of retracing our steps; and if you do so, you have only the verbal/aural parts of the interviews. That portion is hardly enough. Though we do not know how to solve this problem, we illustrate it with a fragment in chapter 4 to show, by example, how we did this first-stage editing: see pp. 107–108).

Once we have in place, for better or worse, the replication/simulation of interviews, we must not then fool the reader: whenever we narrate, speculate, hypothesize, and conclude, we shall somehow announce our tentativeness.

And what about style? All writing has its style, even that alleged to be pure reporting. Which style should be used? How does style get created when there are two authors?

Writing is editing (Moraitus 1981). (So, of course, is conversing, thinking, remembering, daydreaming and other forms of fantasizing.) Even choosing not to edit is to edit. And if the task is to take written typescripts and try to make them (force them to) evoke a situation where speech and presence are the vehicles of communication, then we are into creative work, perhaps comparable to that of the artist but with different constraints of honesty imposed. (Ours are more severe, though we are not necessarily less corrupt.) We must even imagine how to keep readers interested, as when we decide to throw away a piece that concerns us but would be too picayune or esoteric for the audience we imagine.

All right: we do our writing and, on each submitting a piece to the other, we force on ourselves another level of editing—framing—in our effort to agree on that we shall allow to stand.

H: Here the problem of aptness in style (formal, informal) and the

---

*May I call this true fiction? All nonfiction is fiction. All fiction is nonfiction fictionalized to hide that it is nonfiction(?). Mailer (1980:33): "No writer of serious consideration is ever honest except for those rare moments—for which we keep writing—when we become, bless us, not dishonest for an instant. . . . We are all dishonest, we exaggerate, we distort, we use our tricks, we invent. After all, it is almost impossible even writing at one's very best to come near the truth." Is this quote one of those instants; or is the liar lying?

[†]Analytic colleagues look puzzled or disbelieving when I say that no one has ever yet presented the data on which so much of analytic theory depends. Their reaction is even less benign when I say there has never been a psychoanalytic report—Freud's included—that is clinically accurate. (See Gill 1982; Gill and Hoffman 1982.)

choice of idioms and colloquialisms enters. If informal style, we select apt constructions for awkward ones (e.g., "let's look at" instead of "it is time to examine"). Knowing the cultural/personal load of Sambia idioms, I choose American idioms that best match the corresponding meanings in Sambia/Pidgin (e.g., Sambia "shame" for the English "ashamed," the former more powerful; English "encircles" or "fences in" for Sambia "encircle with a fence" in the sense of protecting or hemming someone in). We (H. and S.) then must decide on the appropriateness of colloquialisms: S. inserts these at places that seem awkward or wrong to me, so I remove them or suggest substitutes for them. What concerns me is not just literalness in the translation but metaphoric appropriateness. (How do you measure appropriateness?) Does our American sexual slang "screwing" cover the Sambia term, which literally says "to shoot into"? I agree with S., so the word stands. But others (the reader does not see) are changed; and some changes are so subtle that even New Guinea specialists might miss them: editings of editing without warning signs to readers. So our Americanness is always there. Again, we are concerned that as *clinical* ethnographers our clinical language style not usurp the ethnography, which must faithfully reflect the subtle meanings of the moment. Most anthropologists will regard such nuances as important but not germane to normative, institutional-oriented ethnographies. But in our work they are crucial.

S: When we have a first draft, we do it again; and again and as often as necessary till we are satisfied. That draft we submit to a publisher; which firm publishes the book helps determine its contents, too. The publisher sends the manuscript to one or more professional referees to evaluate the book. The referee gives his/her opinions, which may be sent to us for incorporation. When the manuscript is accepted, an editor (supposedly) goes over every word and mark, making suggestions of greater or lesser import and at times thereby introducing a ghostly new presence into the material. We get that feedback; on which suggestions do we agree? Then the copy editor intervenes, in some places to help and some to be bossy. And at the end of the production process are the several bouts of proofreading, which result (one hopes) in only a few more changes.

If photographs are used, verisimilitude brings dozens more distortions, from type of film used (e.g., color or black-and-white, ASA number) and camera technique (e.g., make and type of box and of lens, aperture, f-stop) to time of day, framing of the scene, or blurring for dramatic effect. These are all acts of editing, the greatest of which is, perhaps, one's decision even to take a picture. Then comes the gross editing, once the film is developed (and, by the way, which laboratory shall we use?) of choosing the shots that best illustrate our points, or of cropping, or of quality of reproduction, or placement in the text, or how many pictures to use.

And then there are attention-transformers like dust jackets, forewords, indexes, covers—hard and soft, printing type, paper used.

All that work, all that editing, all that struggle to be clear, all that strain toward accuracy. Yet we shall still be defeated, by one reader more and by another less, by our very words, syntax, even punctuation, devices that, in stirring up multiple meanings we tried to avoid, make the reader believe something we did not say. And a skeptical or angry or friendly or inexperienced or experienced or psychotic or uneducated or prejudiced or intelligent or sensitive or knowledgeable reader may understand exactly what we are saying and decide that, nonetheless, what we are saying hides rather than exposes the truth. Each page is a Rorschach card.

Another problem that infuences the editing is that of confidentiality. In order to underline the great ethical issues involved, I separate this discussion here from the more mundane matters just reviewed. In both psychoanalysis and ethnography there are, of course, innumerable situations in which our subjects are not jeopardized by what they tell us. But ethnographers know as well as analysts that they could put their informants at risk; to prevent that, one must use disguises and deletions, devices against which readers may have no defense. In the balance between scientific integrity and protecting one's subjects, our society and our consciences demand that subjects come first*—if they are our own people. How close to that decency should the ethnography of alien cultures come? In the case of the Sambia, it is not enough to tell them that we plan to release our findings to strangers. For, obviously, they cannot imagine the process of placing a book into public hands and the uncounted ways in which information can disseminate without limitation. Should ethnographers abide by the standards of informed consent applied to physicians in the United States? To do so might end the practice of ethnography. (Were the same ethical concerns enforced for newspapers, magazines, radio, and TV, these media would also shut down. And so would the First Amendment to our Constitution.)

Only a person who has never written for publication would think

---

*Which, if there were no others, is a reason why analysts can never present their data—only anecdotes; and no one knows better than an analyst how critical can be each word, each inflection, each gesture, each pause: anything left out can skew the report.

these issues of writing and editing—suffered but not publicly discussed—are trivial in research (though most who do write decide then not to mention the matter). For us, the absence of stated concern among psychoanalysts, psychiatrists, and anthropologists (and sociologists, psychologists, and historians) makes it unsafe to accept anyone's descriptions in the way we usually can in the physical sciences. The differences between the latter and our disciplines are not just those of appropriate measuring instruments but the failure of our kind of researchers to admit that *they* are the primary instrument, which puts them splat in the middle of the field to be examined.

Why punish our reader with this review of the publishing process? Because we believe that many colleagues forget and their audiences do not realize that each of these steps is as much a part of the research as the original encounters with "the culture." At the heart of this book is the idea that "the data" are in an unending state of change from the instant they first pass into the researcher's mind (that is, are perceived) until, transformed by writing and publishing, the reader incorporates them. Since a search for accuracy—for even a truth— can be disrupted at *any* step in the process, we want *all* to be legitimized as methodology.

Being an analyst, I am distressed that these issues are not acknowledged whenever analysts write up their clinical data. In the absence of research to find the effects of editing on the observations reported from treatment, I must insist that psychoanalysis today has no unique, acceptable database. (It could when analysts realize we do not yet.) It is physically painful for me to read one more analyst's bragging—repeated dozens of times a year in our literature—about "our science" (Stoller 1985b). Well, "science" is only a word. Our concern is not with labels but with our desires *to trust that what is reported actually occurred*. For me (but not for the dictionary, where even reading, writing, boxing, and theology are sciences, leaving therefore the question what in human endeavor is *not*), that is an essence of science; and there is a well-tested system—called "scientific method"—for protecting the trust we put in people who are reporting experiences. (The issue here is not one of discovery but of confirmation, for the scientific method is not necessarily suited for making discoveries. Discovery comes from exploration [first in our mind, then in the world], which, depending on the problem, may or may not benefit from scientific method.)

What I am discussing, then, is trust, and this long description of the problems of editing is an aspect of the principal subject of this book, which is about trust. In what ways are the statements made by a researcher connected to his or her original observations? Because researchers are inevitably and manifoldly biased, their audience deserves every possible defense against these distorting tendencies. Therefore, though this is a book on ethnography, we feel that our concerns about researchers' subjectivity apply as well for all who would study behavior. Whenever research aims at understanding human behavior, researchers' personalities—idiosyncracies, styles, neurotic conflicts, cultural background, biology, social status, education, etc., etc.—become part of the data.

NOTES

Preface

1. "Why is so much anthropological writing so antiseptic, so devoid of anything that brings a people to life? There they are, pinned like butterflies in a glass case, with the difference, however, that one often cannot tell what color these specimens are; and we are never shown them in flight, never see them soar or die except in generalities. The reason for this lies in the aims of anthropology, whose concern with the particular is incidental to an understanding of the general" (Read 1965:ix).

2. LeVine (1982:220 ff.) suggested collaboration between a behavioral scientist of the host culture and one from the outside.

3. Devereux (1967, 1978); LeVine (1982:292–293); and Sullivan (1937).

4. H: Over the years I have come to realize that psychoanalysts must practice analysis and anthropologists ethnography, whether in New Guinea, Chicago or wherever, or else the strength in such fields evaporates, the practitioners transmuted.

5. La Barre (1978:70) lists a number of such teams. Also Singer (1961:65): "The culture and personality approach thus requires an alternating and almost simultaneous use of two different perspectives—that of culture and that of the individual person. The approach necessarily requires either a close collaboration between an anthropologist and a psychologist or, as in Sapir's case, the capacity for bifocal vision."

Introduction

1. DuBois (1944), Lewis (1965); reviewed in Langness and Frank (1981).

2. Especially the vintage Geertz (1973) and his lecture on anti-antirelativism (Geertz 1984), for a statement of the issues.

3. The term comes especially from Marcus and Cushman's (1982) review.

4. Especially the Shweder and LeVine (1984) volume, and Shweder's (1984) rethinking of the critical problems in cultural perspective.

5. H: Since Malinowski, the professional ethnographer has had to spend from one to two years or more in one place for his colleagues to feel comfortable that his reports are trustworthy. But certain ethnographic classics, we know, have often

403

come from intermittent or brief episodes of field work (e.g., Lévi-Strauss 1969; Radcliffe-Brown 1922) and some classical papers derive from just a few days' or a week's visit, and yet priceless data were collected (e.g., Elkin 1953; Read 1954).

6. One can also read the early work of Sapir (1937), Mead (1949, ch. 2; reviewed in our chapter 1), and even Benedict (1934) as illustrative of the point; but for contemporary and extraordinary demonstrations of the perspective, Crapanzano (1980) and Kracke (1987).

7. Sapir's (1938) classic essay is "Why Anthropology Needs the Psychiatrist"; see also the discussion in chapter 1.

8. Psychoanalysis is a very blurred microscope, but our enemies are wrong in attacking not only our microscopy but the idea of a microscope.

9. Again, the basic insight comes from Devereux's (1967) text, which, in spite of follow-up comments from LeVine (1982) on this same point, is still largely ignored (Kracke and Herdt 1987).

1. Clinical Ethnography

1. Stocking (1980:285). And Habermas (1971:228): "Thus psychoanalytic hermeneutics, unlike the cultural sciences, aims not at the understanding of symbolic structures in general. Rather, the act of understanding to which it leads is self-reflection."

2. Reviewed in Marcus and Cushman (1982); Singer (1980).

3. For instance: how do we—in the profession—reconcile the very different images and interpretations of the same culture? Viz. Bennett's (1946) classic paper on Pueblo ethnography; Lewis (1951) on Tepotzlan; and Feil (1978) and Meggitt (1974) on the Enga. (Reviewed in Agar 1980; Bourguignon 1979.)

4. "It began as the observer moved from the mission compound or from the rocking chair on the front porch of some inn or the office of a colonial administrator to the place where the people actually lived" (Mead 1977:4).

5. Leach(1958); Stocking (1974); Young (1979).

6. For Boas (see Stocking (1968), Benedict (1934), and Mead (1939), there was the "Science of Culture" and the "Science of Man"; for Radcliffe-Brown (1952) it was the "Science of Society"; and for Malinowski (1926) it was the "Science of Custom."

7. It is perhaps no accident that much of the earliest anthropology developed in museums, and that museums are ". . . cultural institutions in the 'marked' sense of the word. For museums . . . metaphorize ethnographic specimens and data by analyzing and preserving them, making them necessary to our own refinement although they belong to some other culture. The totem poles, Egyptian mummies, arrowheads and other relics in our museums are 'culture' in two senses: they are simultaneously products of their makers and of anthropology, which is 'cultural' in the narrow sense . . . . In this light it is scarcely astonishing that Ishi, the last surviving Yahi Indian in California, spent the years after his surrender living in a museum" (Wagner 1975:27–28).

8. "The anthropologist's laboratories are primarily primitive societies, small isolated groups of people who because of their geographical or historical isolation have remained outside of the mainstream of history . . ." (Mead 1949:23).

9. The ethnomethodologists have provided a partial repositioning of this model, minus cultural and personal intentionality (Giddens 1976:40).

10. Malinowski (1922:22); Leach (1954, 1961b, 1976) for a similar view. Stocking (1983) insightfully reviews this trend.

11. Cf., for example, Giddens (1976), Hallpike (1973), Harris (1979).

12. Malinowski (1922, 1927; but see 1935) and Radcliffe-Brown (1922:viii–ix).

13. Barnes (1967:197–199; Hymes (1974); James (1973). Asad (1973:17): "The colonial power structure made the object of anthropological study accessible and safe—because of it sustained physical proximity between the observing European and living non-European became a practical possibility. It made possible the kind of human intimacy on which anthropological fieldwork is based, but ensured that intimacy should be one-sided and provisional."

14. Reviewed in M. Strathern (1988).

15. We do not perform experiments. Even the useful idea of a "natural experiment" fudges the term "experiment." As Geertz (1973:23) says: "The famous studies purporting to show that the Oedipus complex was backwards in the Trobriands, sex roles were upside down in Tchambuli, and the Pueblo Indians lacked aggression (it is characteristic that they were all negative—'but not in the south'), are, whatever their empirical validity may or may not be, not 'scientifically tested and approved' hypotheses. They are interpretations, or misinterpretations, like any others, arrived at in the same way as any others, and the attempt to invest them with the authority of physical experimentation is but methodological sleight of hand."

16. For instance, Briggs (1970), Dumont (1978), Levy (1973), and Read (1965).

17. Indeed, Geertz's *The Religion of Java* (1960:7) opens with this statement: "But it seems to me that one of the characteristics of ethnographic reporting. . . is that the ethnographer is able to get out of the way of his data, to make himself translucent so that the reader can see for himself something of what the facts look like and so judge the ethnographer's summaries and generalizations in terms of the ethnographer's actual perceptions." Do facts speak for themselves, as Durkheim thought? How could one judge the "actual" perceptions of someone without knowing that someone? Here we see a somewhat more positivist Geertz speaking than that of his "thick description" essay (1973). Marcus and Cushman (1982) and others have critiqued this stance, but in cultural, not psychologic, terms.

18. Casagrande (1960), Freilich (1972), Golde (1970), and others.

19. LeVine (1982) and Schneider (1968:1–8) for discussion.

20. LeVine (1982:237–240, 285–304). Also Crapanzano (1980); Herdt (1981: chapter 2); Obeyesekere (1981).

21. Herdt (1987d) on this aspect of Sambia dreaming.

22. At all levels of awareness. We know, however, that powerfully felt mental states, with their inevitable conviction, may never, no matter how well conscious knowledge is brought to consciousness, reach insight regarding the effects of economic, political, or other social forces—the avalanche of history—that shape the individual's subjective sense of self with all its dynamics.

23. As a conceptual framework in its time, notwithstanding its costs or benefits.

24. Herdt (1981:328), borrowed from Wallace (1969). In having joined the critics of the so-called "privacy theories of meaning," Geertz has not, either in early (1966) or later (1976) writings, addressed the problem of how private meaning relates to the public; what role the individual plays in related cultural transformations; how anthropologists can know about the "experience near" (Kohut 1971); or what reliability symbolic interpretations have.

25. "Ethnographic findings are not privileged, just particular: another country heard from. To regard them as anything more (*or anything else*) than that distorts both them and their implications . . . " (Geertz 1973:23).

26. Are these tactics the result of our lack of real understanding, our ignorance of the vernacular (Owusu 1978)? How do—and will—natives react when they read our texts? Not too well, Tedlock (1983) argues.

27. Sapir (1938). We might have begun with Sapir's (1949:574) far-reaching advice: "Instead, therefore, of arguing from a supposed objectivity [uniformity] of culture to the problem of individual variation, we shall, for certain kinds of analysis, have to proceed in the opposite direction. We shall have to operate as though we knew nothing about culture but were interested in analyzing as well as we could what a given number of human beings accustomed to live with each other actually think and do in their day to day relationships."

28. LeVine's (1982) treatment of the subject, to repeat, is the essential text.

29. *Reports of the Cambridge Expeditions to the Torres Straits* (1901–1933).

30. See Herdt (1984) for a review of the dizzying assortment of styles, flavors, depth and breadth and fantasy in Melanesianists' accounts of ritualized homosexuality in Melanesia since the 1860s.

31. The Oxford English dictionary generously defines ethnography as the "scientific descriptions of nations or races of men, their customs, habits and differences."

32. "In his *Elementary Forms of the Religious Life* Durkeim subjects other theorists of religion to remorseless criticism, but not the writers about the Australian Aboriginals on which he bases his own. So elementary a precaution applies also to our own monographs, which we take far too much on trust" (Evans-Pritchard 1962:176). Inevitably, of course, Evans-Pritchard's criticism has been turned back on his own work (Read 1980:183).

33. Turnbull on the Ituri (1961).

34. Turnbull on the Ik (1972).

35. Lévi-Strauss (1969).

36. Freud (1913).

37. Hallpike (1977).

38. Fortune (1932).

39. Benedict (1946).

40. Malinowski (1927).

41. Benedict (1934).

42. Geertz (1966).

43. Briggs (1970).

44. Mead on Arapesh (1935).

45. Gluckman (1969); Rappaport (1968).

46. Thomas (1959).

47. Lanternari (1963).

48. Mead on Mundugumor (1935).

49. Mead on Tchambuli (1935).

50. Heider (1976).

51. Meggitt (1964).

52. Malinowski (1922); Mead (1949).

53. Roheim (1932).

54. Victor Turner (1968).

55. Lévi-Strauss (1967).

56. Radcliffe-Brown (1952).

57. Leach (1961a).

58. Geertz (1973).

59. For example, Sontag's (1966) "The anthropologist as Hero"; and see also Hymes (1974) and Bohannan (1979).

60. Mead (1970:328) believed that some of this criticism stemmed from the small world of anthropology, which involves colleagues who are "real or fictive husbands, lovers, friends, parents, or children . . . . The violence of some of the internecine in-fighting that goes on within anthropological circles can be explained by the incestuous overtones of such intense relationships. Anthropologists of my generation still regard all other anthropologists, including those whom they have never met, as kin, toward whom one may express all the ambivalence generated by close family ties and toward whom one is totally obligated to provide succor *in extremis*. As the profession grows so much larger, this sense of kinship becomes harder to establish and it may be that it will survive only in the extraordinary bad manners of anthropological reviewers who will imitate their elders' style without recognizing that that style was accompanied by the kind of unquestioning willingness to help appropriate to those who regard themselves as members of one large family."

61. Reviewed in Agar (1980), Bourguignon (1979), Devereux (1967). See Murray (1979) on the especially problematic case of Castaneda's works.

62. By 1953, Fortes could write: "What Crooke foresaw in 1910 has come to pass, and it is no longer possible for the amateur, however gifted, to make a contribution of theoretical value in social anthropology" (Fortes 1974:433). Lay ethnographers in Melanesia, whether missionaries (e.g., Chalmers 1903; Leenhardt 1979), administrators (e.g., Murray 1912), patrol officers (e.g., Sinclair 1966), aside from the government anthropologists, have made contributions, though their theoretic value is open to debate.

63. For example, Agar's (1980:43) discussion of the classic Lewis/Redfield controversy.

64. This omission is reviewed most recently in Kracke (1987).

65. Thankfully, in some work (e.g., Crapanzano 1980; Dumont 1978; Herdt 1981; Parsons 1969; Reisman 1977) this trend is changing. But these accounts make only partial use of ethnographer experience in theory building. No Freud has yet appeared.

66. "I have asked leading anthropologists who espouse this 'before and after' view of fieldwork why they have not written on the subject themselves. . . . The response I received was culturally standardized: 'Yes, I suppose I thought about it when I was young. I kept diaries, perhaps some day, but you know there are really other things which are more important' (Rabinow 1977:4). Also Freilich (1977:27, n.17).

67. This may seem bold, but if one compares the ethnographic reports of, say, Malinowski (1929), Mead (1930), and F. E. Williams (1936), where the author is clearly at the scene and sometimes even in the text, with those of Radcliffe-Brown (1922), Evans-Pritchard (1937), or Fortes (1945), where they are absent, the difference is striking. This absence fills transitional period works (Clay 1975), Geertz (1966), Hogbin (1970), Kelly (1977), Leach (1961a), Meggitt (1965), Munn (1973), Newman (1965), Rappaport (1968), A. Strathern (1972), Wagner (1972), and Young (1971).

68. J. D. Watson (1968).

69. Haddon (1924), though obscure, is close to Malinowski's ideal methodologic stance.

70. Kracke (1980); LeVine (1982); Parsons (1969).

71. Reviewed in Edgerton and Langness (1974). Also Clifford and Marcus (1986), and Read (1986).

72. Crapanzano (1980), Kracke (1987), S. LeVine (1981), and Obeyesekere (1981) are fine exceptions.

73. DuBois (1944). Bourguignon (1979:97) claims that the DuBois work made data available for the first time on the natives as people. But were these people "typical" Alorese? See our discussion in "Part Two: Interviews."

74. For examples, Casagrande (1960), Freilich (1977), Golde (1970), Kimball and Watson (1972).

75. Malinowski's (1967) diary was published posthumously by his widow. (Did he have that in mind?) Also Mead (1977).

76. In her last work, Mead (1977:12) pointed out that even in her letters, "There were limits that I myself imposed. This collection might also be called 'what I told my friends it was like to do fieldwork.' I did not tell them all of it by any means." Some of her richest material is contained in her appendices (see especially Mead 1956:Appendix I, and 1949:22–47). "I remember a sharp-tongued and very sophisticated old cousin of my mother's commenting that she preferred the appendices to the text of my books. 'They really tell you something,' she said" (1977:14).

77. Mead (1949) and Geertz (1973) are surprisingly alike in this view.

78. Here we can agree with Malinowski (1926).

79. We shall not enter here into technical questions about semantics, pragmatics, and cultural knowledge (but see Keesing 1979); we leave it to others more qualified to wrestle with problems in defining the theory of meaning. But we wish to state that our interest goes beyond word meaning, which is why we emphasize subjectivity (including the unspoken) and not just that of expressed social behavior. Better still, in Tyler's (1978) idiom, we want to describe both the said and the unsaid. In studying meaning systems this subjectivity includes one's own empathy and resonances of the other's unsaid, as well as words in relation to things (reference), words in relation to words (sense), and words in relation to deeds (function).

80. Cf. Foucault (1980).

81. Herdt (1981); Herdt and Stoller (1985); Stoller and Herdt (1982, 1985).

82. Cf. LeVine (1982:185–248); also Devereux (1980a:72–90); Parin et al. 1980:372–388.

83. Erikson (1958); cf. Levy (1973) and Ricoeur's (1977) essay on psychoanalytic proof.

84. Mead (1952:343, emphasis mine). See Agar's (1980) extended critique.

85. Chapple (1952:342). Freilich (1977:12–13, n.11) shows clearly Boas's strong influence on creating this attitude.

86. "The mystique of field work—the magical properties of the term, the mysterious aspects of the work involved, the wonderful transformations that occur through living and working 'in the field'—never disappears" (Freilich 1977:15).

87. See also Chapple (1952:341–342) and Freilich (1977:15–16 ff.).

88. Cf. Spiro's (1986) critique of relativism here and its effects upon anthropology.

89. Chapple (1952) was groaning about this years ago.

90. "Anthropology, a new science, welcomed the stranger. As a science which

accepted the psychic unity of mankind, anthropology was kinder to women, to those who came from distant disciplines, to members of minority groups in general (with American Indians assuming a special position as both the victims of injustice and the carriers of a precious and vanishing knowledge), to the 'overmature,' the idiosyncratic, and the capriciously gifted or experienced, to refugees from political or religious oppression" (Mead 1960a:5).

91. Barzun (1981:34) has singled out anthropology as an example of deleterious change in American university teaching: "Moreover, in the new ambulant university, what might have been fresh and engrossing was presented in its least engaging form, that of the specialist: not anthropology as a distinctive way of looking at peoples and nations, with examples of general import, but accumulated detail about a tribe the instructor had lived with—and apparently could not get away from."

92. "In her study of life histories of eminent scientists, Roe (1953) found that anthropologists and psychologists early showed considerable concern about social relations; open rebelliousness in the family was usual among the former, and occurred only slightly less in the latter. . . . Biologists and physicists, on the other hand, had neither rebelliousness nor family difficulties and developed ways of life with less personal interaction. All the scientists stood somewhat apart from life, in contrast to successful businessmen" (Powdermaker 1966:20). In other words: "Why should a contented and satisfied person think of standing outside his or any other society and studying it?" (Ibid.).

93. Mead had definite and old-fashioned ideas about women in the field. Thus: women "are more personally lonely" but also "more easily live as part of the households of others" in villages; and they are "handicapped either by an inadequate knowledge of the equipment they need to use" (e.g., typewriters) "or by a kind of reversed masculine protest that makes them resent the fact that they should have to use . . . monkey wrenches"; and "women alone in the field are more likely to be preoccupied with present or future personal relationships than are men"; they are "more personally vulnerable in the field . . . more likely to become rundown, ill, or depressed or to break off their fieldwork prematurely." And more: Mead (1970:325).

94. One professor advises his students to go to an area they'll like, regardless of their topical interest, because if they're miserable they'll wind up doing bad research no matter what subject they study.

95. Mead (1972:221) writes of her and Fortune's decision to work near Bateson in the late 1920s: "We knew that Gregory was back on the Sepik—and why, Reo demanded, should he, and not we, have that magnificent culture?"

96. "I went to New Guinea to experience a world entirely different from anything I had known before—different both in its overt features and in the reality that its residents construct" (Barth 1975:5).

97. Few anthropologists have written about this subject, though Mead (1970:317–321; 1977) is again a welcome exception. It is a constant source of informal conversation when anthropologists gather; yet few of the authors in an important work (Long-term Field Research in Social Anthropology, Foster et al. 1979) discuss their personal reasons for going back to do restudies. The authors, in concluding, couch their collective experience in restrained terms: "Not only is it a pleasure to renew acquaintances, to see the genuine pleasure of those who welcome the anthropologist back . . . but psychologically reentry is easier than shifting to a totally different society. . . . The return is also reaffirmation of concern and

interest in the people with whom we work and gives new validation to our right to learn" (Foster et al. 1979:330–331).

98. "Anthropology affords me an intellectual satisfaction: it rejoins at one extreme the history of the world, and at the other the history of myself, and it unveils the shared motivation of one and the other at the same moment. In suggesting Man as the object of my studies, anthropology dispelled all my doubts . . . set at rest, what is more, the anxious, and destructive curiosity of which I have written above: I was guaranteed, that is to say, a more or less inexhaustible supply of matter for reflection, in the diversity of human manners, customs, and institutions. My life and my character were reconciled" (Lévi-Strauss 1969:62).

99. "In not going to the field armed with prefigured questionnaires (which find only what they are shaped to find), culture-bound hypotheses (one is motivated to verify), models (based on what verbal analogies), and problems (whose?), anthropological fieldwork is more like the naturalism of the clinical method. Beyond the hypothesis that human beings can communicate about themselves if only one listens and watches, how much does one really know beyond a vague perception of his own somehow universal humanity? But from this he must constantly delete his own cultural presuppositions, as the clinician must constantly subtract his personal countertransference distortions" (La Barre 1978:276).

100. Watson (1972).

101. For example, Whittaker et al. 1975.

102. See Spradley (1979, 1980) for numerous and varied schemas of types of observations, interviewing, etc., mainly drawn from urban ethnographic work in America. The more complex a society, the more exact we can be in the micro-analysis and classification of situations and descriptive modes, which may say more about natives studying their own society than it does about ethnographic methodology.

103. See Agar's (1980) important discussion of ways of thinking about ethnographic techniques, which has many examples from urban research.

104. "The investigator's professional training should enable him to realize that what is more important than the ceremonial or bureaucratic delays of the administration is its power to prevent him from doing any work at all in its territory" (Barnes 1967:198).

105. On New Guinea, see Lawrence (1971); Read (1984); Reay (1964); Rodman (1979); M. Strathern (1972).

106. Barnes (1967:203–294) notes how anthropologists can stress to authorities "those aspects that seem innocuous" about their research, rather than the controversial ones. And further: "I well remember the surprise with which a District Officer greeted my naive remark that I was studying him too, and I think was more circumspect thereafter." (Also Mead 1977:13–14.) In Third World countries like Papua New Guinea, anthropologists rarely write about these touchy problems lest research be denied them later. Though tactful, this self-imposed censorship is undesirable, resulting in areas of incomplete research.

107. For example, Robin's (1982) valuable but highly critical review of missionary activity in one part of Papua New Guinea.

108. In Papua New Guinea today the government grants research visas to foreign anthropologists only after having received permission from local people and authorities. Ideally, then, an ethnographer will only work among friendly (or at least not hostile) people. It does not always turn out that way. One young anthropologist was allowed in but could not contact even whole villages for two

months: everyone vanished at his approach. For all the difficulties, he eventually did fieldwork; to my knowledge, however, in his publications he has not ever described the initial traumas.

109. For an example typical of many textbooks, see Edgerton and Langness (1974:35).

110. "As Zempleni appropriately reminds us, ethnographers are 'spies' par excellence. They are, indeed, professional detectors of secrets" (Schwimmer 1980:45).

111. Foster et al. (1979:331).

112. For example, Spradley (1980). Also Oberg's (1954) classic essay. There are many allusions to culture shock used—vis-à-vis our implicit ideology—however: see, for example, Agar's (1980:50–53) review; and Wagner (1975:7) on "anthropologist shock."

113. I have heard the term on television, and Toffler's pop book, *Future Shock*, plays on it. My optometrist (a middle-aged white American man) told me the following story: "Several years ago I was in Berlin having dinner with a German (male) friend. A beautiful woman entered the restaurant, escorted to the next table. She wore furs and a sleek dress—she was a sensation. But when she removed her cloak I could see her hairy underarms. I was instantly turned off. I told my friend, who said it turned him on (he was visibly titillated). Now that's culture shock!"

114. See Oberg's (1970:6, 10–12) discussion, which cites DuBois, who credits Ruth Benedict with the invention.

115. Typically, "culture shock" is put in quotation marks or with citations to authorities. In his widely cited textbook example (which undergraduate students love), Chagnon (1968:4) anticipates excited passages by pleading: "My first day in the field illustrated to me what my teachers meant when they spoke of culture shock. I looked up and gasped when I saw a dozen burly, naked, filthy, hideous men staring at us down the shafts of their drawn arrows! Immense wads of green tobacco were stuck between their lower teeth and lips making them look even more hideous and strands of green slime dripped or hung from their noses. We arrived at the village while the men were blowing a hallucinogenic drug up their noses. One of the side effects of the drug is a runny nose. . . . Then the stench of the decaying vegetation and filth struck me. I was horrified. What sort of welcome was this for a person who came here to live with you and learn your way of life, to become friends with you?" (Chagnon 1968:5).

116. As members of the same cultural tradition we do not have to change much or change the urban culture, which is a part of our own, is less alien, "more natural, more human." But more than this, its symbolic image is different from that of the changeless tribal order. Warner (1941:787) said it forty years ago: the anthropologist studies "the development of the personality and its maintenance of its equilibrium in the social system. . . . The urban sociologist has tended to emphasize the study of social change and social organization. . . . From the anthropologist's point of view, the smaller and larger towns where the social tradition has been little disturbed and the ways of life are more harmonious and better integrated have perhaps been neglected by the sociologist. The selection of communities to be studied by anthropologists was determined by criteria which accented harmonious adjustment, high integration, and well-organized social relations."

117. Oberg (1972:85–86) states: "I have known individuals who claimed that they had never experienced culture shock. Close examination revealed that many

of them never really lived in a different culture from their own but withdrew into a self-centered cocoon and associated only with their fellow countrymen. Missionaries also survive well over long periods in alien societies. Here the lesson is quite clear. A missionary's objective is to persuade the people to give up their religious beliefs and to adopt his belief and value system. The best adjusted individuals whom I have met in strange lands have been individuals with a strong 'missionary' motive in religion, science, or welfare programs. If one lacks this motivation, the best he can do is understand another culture and to become aware of the nature of his psychological adjustment to it."

118. "Culture shock" can be used as a way to discovery, as Meintel (1973) notes. The Japanese analyst Doi, for instance, notes how he began to realize the psychocultural significance of the concept of *amae* from his "culture shock" in America (Doi 1973).

119. Perhaps Mead knew this better than anyone, which is why she scolded Malinowski's detractors with such enthusiasm (Mead 1970:324n.). More soberly, Young (1971:12) writes: "In Malinowski's defense, it must be said that innovating as he did the social anthropologists' role of participant-observer, he was without the psychological security afforded by existing precedents." But in this regard see as well Spiro's (1982) probing questions regarding Malinowski's view of the father in Trobriand Society, which involves Malinowski's own projections from his personal and cultural background (Herdt 1985).

120. A textbook example: "Thus the first task of the ethnographer is to *learn the culture* of the group he is studying; in this respect, his task is similar to that of a child born into the group, for both must discover the categories and plans shared by other group members" (Bock 1969:325).

121. For an exposure of this elitism see Crapanzano (1980); cf. Lévi-Strauss (1969).

122. When first on patrol in Sambia territory, I was mistaken for a government patrol officer. Not until I could prove otherwise—through friends' testimonies or my actions—could I shake off the first layer of distrust. And I was never trusted elsewhere as in my village. Sometimes people thought me a missionary (a mistake dispelled when I smoked my pipe in public, for they believed missionaries do not smoke). No one ever took me for a spy or a tax collector, the bane of ethnographers (Barnes 1967).

123. One young married couple in the Highlands found they had too little privacy. So they invented the fiction that their culture required them to eat—as a ritual—in private. And the natives were not allowed inside their house after dark. (See also the anecdote in Edgerton and Langness 1974:24.)

124. While I lived in Australia a foreign student conducted a strictly behavioral study on time and motion in an Aboriginal settlement. He sat atop a tractor and observed people's movements from a distance for a few months. Apart from the theoretic problems with his study, he angered the anthropologic community by his lack of involvement with the natives; was he biased by a lack of direct interaction? His study matched his personal style: he was uncomfortable interacting with people at home.

125. See Hayano (1982), Herdt (1982c), and Poole (1982a) for examples of how New Guineans, who previously lacked alcohol, learned to drink and not drink from foreigners, including anthropologists.

126. Discussed in Herdt (1981:332–337).

127. Even hermeneuts, sensitive to the issue of seeing our material in an interpretive light, are still saddled with "the informant" (Rabinow 1977:151).

128. Geertz (1973) uses this analogy.

129. Foucault (1973) refers to a similar clinical process as "the gaze."

130. For example, Aberle (1951), Dubois (1944), La Farge (1929), Mead (1960b), and Turner (1960).

131. See Watson's (1960) "key informant" portrait on this point.

132. See Spradley (1979:46–54) on "the good informant."

133. DuBois (1944:441) reports transference in a key informant's dream report, and then she states (without further comment): "I doubt that this dream is authentic." How did she reach that conclusion? More important: how did she arrive at the point of having such a rich relationship that she received dreams and could doubt the authenticity of one?

134. Mead (1960b:189) states: "I've always given pseudonyms to informants." Sometimes whole societies—like the Sambia—have been given pseudonyms (e.g., Davenport 1965; Devereux 1951; Messenger 1969).

135. Thoughtfully reviewed in Tedlock's (1983) work.

136. See Herdt and Stoller (1987).

137. Of Malinowski's diaries, Forge (1972:294) writes that they are "not about the Trobriand Islanders and what Malinowski thought about them nor even about Malinowski. They are a partial record of the struggle that affects every anthropologist in the field: a struggle to retain a sense of his own identity as an individual and as a member of a culture."

138. After noting risks in "a high degree of participant observation," Bock (1969:319) states: "Another is the danger of 'going native' to the extent of refusing to reveal any information about the group studied: and it is obvious that anthropological science could not progress if this always happened."

139. Perhaps the most infamous example is Frank Hamilton Cushing, who is alleged to have gone native with the Zuni Indians a hundred years ago (Gronewald 1972:33).

140. Vogt (1979:33).

141. "Visitors from outside this closed circle of attention [village] are both a temptation and an interruption. Letters from home wrench one's thoughts and feelings inappropriately away" (Mead 1977:7).

142. Mead (1970:324n.), commenting on a fieldwork symposium in the 1960s, was astonished at how ethnographers "testified—I can find no better word for it—to their boredom with, aversion to, or sentimental regard for members of primitive or urban proletarian communities. One does not go to a primitive community to satisfy one's demands for sophisticated twentieth-century conversation or to find personal relationship missed among one's peers." I agree; also, though I have heard a researcher describe a society studied as "very boring," I do not believe this: boredom is inside oneself.

2. *Sambia Sexual Culture*

1. Mead: "But so far, in seeking to make anthropological accounts useful to the sophisticated reader, who may be psychiatrist or biologist or geologist, judge or pediatrician or banker or mother of five children, we have tried to do only two things: either to convey that some aspect of human behavior could be organized

differently—such as adolescence, or a proneness to heavy drinking, or a sensitivity to art—or to convey the extent to which cultures differ from one another" (1949:31). A generation later Geertz's (1973) essay on thick description awakened the social sciences again to the place of anthropology in the Academy through a similar but fresher rhetoric.

2. See Herdt (1977, 1980, 1981, 1982a, 1982b); and Stoller and Herdt (1982). After one has written a few set pieces they fade into each other: we plagiarize ourselves and make straw men that respond to the straw men of other disciplines (M. Strathern 1981). These false creatures are as important as the original observations.

3. What is a fact in ethnography? Where do data end and interpretations begin? Geertz (1973) has written eloquently of this problem (cf. Marcus and Fisher 1986).

4. These cultural categories cross-cut various symbolic domains and social arenas, such as taboos (*kumaaku*), ritual (*pweiyu*), food sharing, myth, etc. One certainly could abstract from action and rhetoric the normative and metaphoric operations of these categories (cf. Wagner 1967, 1972). As I indicate below, sexual interaction is a conscious though not always marked frame for acting and speaking among Sambia, but I cannot here provide a description of all its manifestations.

5. See Herdt 1981 for conceptual models. This chapter considers mainly the male viewpoint, and it is not meant to be a complete cultural analysis, by any means.

6. Sambia tend to treat and think of semen as an energy force, in individuals and society, that may be compared, by direct analogy, to Freud's concept of libido. The analogy is apt in several ways: this energy force circulates through others (e.g., as subjects), who may be taken in (e.g., as objects) via semen or its equivalents (mother's milk); and it can be dammed up or released—the imagery of the hydraulic model is apt (but cf. Heider 1979:78–79, who thinks otherwise). Translated in Freudian lingo, Federn (1952) would contrast subject-libido (energy available to self qua subject) and object-libido (energy available for investment in objects). Technically, I think, semen as a symbol among Sambia is used narcissistically (object libido invested in ego is narcissistic libido) in self/other interactions.

7. My use of the terms *commodity* and *fetishization* is not a homology with Marx's usage, which was tied, of course, to the specific analysis of capitalist production, characterized by the production of commodities that emerge in a market economy. By analogy, though, these terms are useful for my analysis. Marx argued that the results of human activity transform resources into items of use-value, which are assigned an exchange value by society; the worker's time is overshadowed by the supreme importance attached to the commodity, a process through which the capitalist extracts surplus labor as profit. The Sambia, however, acknowledge semen as a result of social relationships of production (e.g., as in marriage bonds), and they tend also to stress the importance of semen as a fluid that can transform resources into more useful reproductive items or characteristics (e.g., babies, warrior strength). Nonetheless, the way that men value semen as a circulating commodity has a mystifying effect on these social relationships of production: they deny women's essential part in the reproductive process and claim final biologic development in boys is achieved only through insemination. This mystification of the total reproductive process thus enables men to extract from others the resources needed to sustain and expand themselves and their clans and to control the related scarce resources in relation to women. Finally, I do not im-

ply by use of these terms that other Melanesian groups, or even all societies with ritualized homosexuality, use semen as a key resource in the same way as Sambia, or that they value it as a commodity in their systems of circulation in order to reproduce social entities. Elements or fluids such as semen and blood clearly have variable significance in Melanesian societies; our separable analyses of them must, in a sense, renegotiate their meaning in each cultural system.

8. For instance, Sambia men do not use *duvuno* in reference to masturbation, their term for which means "peeling away the glans from penis." Genital rubbing, in the limited sense (not necessarily erotic) of stimulation of the genitals, occurs; I have seen children do it, boys sometimes do it to bachelors (to produce erections for fellatio), and men sometimes report doing it to themselves in preparation for coitus with their wives. But what they *mean* is self-stimulation *without ejaculation*. This conceptual distinction is important and should not be misunderstood: spilling one's seed not only makes no sense to Sambia, it does not seem erotically exciting for them. Their fantasy life and erotic scripting have no place for it.

9. Sambia have invented an art we could call *semenology*: they are fascinated with the forms, textures, and tastes of semen, which they discuss frequently, like wine tasters. Among boys, a fellated's penis size is not accorded much importance, whereas his seminal fluid, amount of flow, etc., is. (Privately and unconsciously, though, penis size is sometimes important.) Among women, the situation seems the reverse: a man's penis size (and sexual prowess) is important—women prefer men with big penises—whereas semenology is less significant, or so say men.

10. Sexual behavior in the imagery of dreams is viewed as erotic play: wet dreams are pleasurable but wasteful erotic play with spirits, who may wish to harm the dreamer. Breast-feeding, even though women say they experience *imbimboogu*, is not ever conceived of as erotic play by women, as far as I know, though breast-feeding is apparently a common image and form of scripting for *men's* erotic daydreams (vis-à-vis fellatio performed on them).

11. However, there is ambiguity here, since a woman who lives in another hamlet (her husband's) long enough becomes after death a ghost or hamlet spirit who may haunt there, rather than returning to her natal hamlet or clan territory. Even so, the souls of females are not a subject in which men place much interest.

12. Cf. the Great Papuan Plateau societies, especially Kaluli (Schieffelin 1976:127f. 1982), which have institutionalized such beliefs about homosexual insemination (see also Kelly 1976; Sørum 1982). On the individual level, Sambia boys report fantasies and beliefs that make it clear that identification is a part of their homoerotic experience, including, for instance, notions that incorporating a fellated's semen may bestow his personality traits.

3. Interviewing Sambia

1. See especially Dubois's (1944) classic on life-histories. For recent statements of the best psychocultural biographic work in context, see Levy (1973) and Crapanzano (1980).

2. Which Freud (1900:122n.2) sensed in translating dreams between different languages. Devereux's thoughts of thirty years ago still hold: "What is particularly needed is a system of psychotherapy based not on the content of any particular culture—as the psychotherapy described in my book *Reality and Dream* (1951) was based . . . but on an understanding of the nature of Culture per se: on an insight into the meaning of cultural categories, which, as the French sociological–eth-

nological school of Durkheim and Mauss stressed long ago, are identical with the great fundamental categories of human thought. This culturally neutral—or metacultural—psychotherapy is still in the making. . . . " (1980a:90).

3. I am dismayed that many colleagues still use the terms "masculine" and "feminine" as if they were self-evident or identical experiential entities across cultures. Since gender concepts are based in part on psychodynamic (especially ego) traits, learned behaviors and attitudes that are culturally relative to the society, historical period, and status-context factors (age, sex, class) being measured, the reader should know about the baseline sample of Sambia on which the piecemeal interpretations below were made. Especially since, like virtually all anthropologists working on gender in New Guinea, I have not used random or control samples. Between 1974 and 1979, I interviewed at length (not just observed) the following people on issues directly concerning masculinity and femininity, as these framed our 1979 work: two uninitiated boys, about six years old (several casual private interviews); 45 first- and second-stage initiates, each interviewed over a three-month period before and after an initiation, using a formal interview schedule (about ten of these or other initiates were seen in private open-ended interviews between five and twenty times each, between 1974–1976); five bachelors and young married men each casually interviewed between two and five times; five adult women shamans interviewed formally between two and five times each (including Moondi's mother, seen several times more); two male elders, casually or more formally interviewed between five and about twenty times each; one female elder formally interviewed several times; Nilutwo, who was seen about 230 hours over a two and a half year period, 1974–1979 (see Herdt 1981); two "gentle" men (including Imano) and two extremely masculine men, seen about ten times each, in 1979; four newly initiated boys and several older initiates (previously seen and interviewed for follow-up studies), privately interviewed in 1979; a handful of bachelors interviewed in Port Moresby in 1979 (see Herdt 1982c); and in-depth studies of Moondi, Weiyu, Sakulambei, Kalutwo, and Penjukwi, each seen between about 30 and 100 hours. Note that I have not included Tali, whom I have seen primarily to understand ritual matters; even though I have frequently interviewed him privately on gender issues, his materials raise other problems of interpretation because, in various ways, Tali saw himself as a spokesman for the ritual cult in much more self-conscious ways than do others. Thus dogma and ritual rhetoric more fully permeate his material. The above interview data also do not include other interviews on subjects such as ritual, warfare, social organization, etc. In 1981, 1983, 1985, and 1988 I returned to New Guinea and conducted additional follow-up studies of Weiyu, Moondi, Sakulambei, Kalutwo, Penjukwi, Imano, and a few others. These data are not included; but they have helped sharpen my views of these people and clarified some of the interpretations presented here.

4. Didn't the best of the culture and personality theorists (reviewed in Honigmann [1967]) do ethnographic accounts of these same phenomena? Why have we forgotten them (Spiro 1979, 1986)? And have we really advanced so far as it might seem (LeVine 1982:ch.19)? Yes and no. Yes, these newer interpretive accounts offer more of the native's *conscious experience* and emic concepts of identity, selfhood, etc. (e.g., Crapanzano 1980; Herdt 1981; Obeyesekere 1981), whereas older accounts tended to offer normative descriptions of modal personality, or anecdotal ethnographic accounts (e.g., Malinowski 1927; Mead 1935) to validate etic constructs (e.g., temperament) of local conceptions of personality. Levy (1973) on Tahitians is clearly the remarkable exception to this tradition in the 1970s. Today

we wonder where anthropologic studies of "self," "gender," and "personhood" are headed, toward experience-near and clinical accounts of lives.

5. Herdt (1987a) details this argument.

6. See Read's (1955) classic essay.

7. Langness (1981:25); Read (1965); Watson (1964).

8. Reviewed in Herdt (1982a); and see Barth (1975), Poole (1982b), M. Strathern (1988).

9. Sambia almost never describe their *actual* sexual experience with anyone but me, and that is only because I ask about it. Men's locker-room banter is another matter. Sexual partners (homosexual and heterosexual) do so only very rarely; most never do.

10. Which is why adultery is so hard to study, unless people are caught in the act (Malinowski 1926). Adultery is a great problem in the cross-cultural study of sexuality for this reason (see Gregor 1985).

11. Ignoring secret intelligence activities (Shils 1956) and the new secret sophisticates—the computer whizzes—who speak to each other via classified information across continents. Should the secrecy of the therapist's office also be excluded (reviewed in Foucault 1973; and from the margins by Malcolm 1984)? And what of the mafia, street gangs, radical political groups, subversives, Wall Street bankers, academic tenure committees, and famous chefs? None of these examples, however, suggests the religious and supernatural overtones of New Guinea secret societies.

12. See Schwimmer's (1980) important review.

13. See, in this context, Nauta's (1972) idea of "potential meaning" that represents new syntheses of meaning.

14. I subliminally reinforced my friends to discuss sensitive subjects like sex by my curiosity. Beyond that, however, they talked of what interested them.

15. See Crapanzano's (1980) procedures and discussions of this problem area.

16. Some anthropologists have said to me, "Well, of course; what you got were individual statements, filtered through normative cultural modes (attitudes, values, beliefs) of what people expected they should say to you." I respond, "Yes, but only in part." When people sit with you for hours and discuss their lives, they do so through the only way they know possible—their language and culture; they must innovate in order to keep the dialogue going, if nothing else (Tedlock 1983; Wagner 1972). They also respond to the special understanding you have jointly constructed—ethnographic interviewing—that makes their narratives meaningful to you and the situation. Those statements reflect both their culture and their experience.

4. Moondi's Erotism

1. I taught Moondi meanings and operations of "fantasy" and "free association" and began exploring—but haven't yet succeeded in using—the idea of "insight." This work is mentioned later. The guided imagery techniques I use are a form of active imagination I learned from Marielle Fuller at UCLA. In all I did guided imagery about ten times over five months, using it to uncover feelings and experiences M. associated with childhood or early initiation (against which he had memory blocks). I also used it to explore latent aspects of his sexual fantasies and symbolic behavior (e.g., surrounding the ritual flutes: see Herdt 1982a).

2. We shall mention these issues in chapter 11, but a word about them here

will clarify what I mean. People who talk and share feelings over time tend to identify with one another, and, as for example with friends, tend to transfer needs to the other, in the hope of getting comfort and guidance. We might say that these feelings are therapeutic when they lessen our anxiety and help us to feel more at ease with the other. Many relationships have these therapeutic aspects but are not therapy. That is how I see my relationships with everyone in these case studies. Moondi, however, has had a more therapy-like relationship since he began doing guided imagery with me in 1979. There are difficulties and risks in such cross-cultural therapy; I shall describe them elsewhere. For now, what matters is that, after seven years, I felt I could use guided imagery to help M. work through mild anxieties and emotional blocks on several occasions when it was appropriate. I also gave him advice, especially concerning his impending move to the city, where I could provide information that he lacked. Eventually I provided him with lo-gistical and financial help in making his move, which was successful.

3. Moondi is pretty well balanced. Yet he has suffered nightmares, as many Sambia men do, and he is wary of his environment. It was difficult to do guided imagery with him at first because of the fears he found inside.

4. See Herdt (1987c) for a profile of her.

5. See Herdt (1982a:69–71) on Moondi's self report.

6. People who go crazy (*abrumbru*) tear off their clothes to expose themselves to others (cf. Herdt 1986); Sambia regard this as totally ridiculous.

7. This ceremony ends the third-stage initiation, which means the end of cer-tain taboos for Weiyu. It was then appropriate for him to inseminate boys as a fellated. Moondi was one of those boys.

8. Incest rules apply here, as in heterosexual relationships: all sex is forbid-den with all patrilineal kinsmen and frowned on with all other kin, matrilateral and patrilateral, as well as with one's hamlet age-mates and ritual sponsor; both affines, especially one's brother-in-law, are appropriate homosexual partners. Weiyu is vaguely related by adoption to Moondi, and since they grew up in the same village, that proximity further relates them and makes sex inappropriate between them. Wieyu's *public* reserve that day of the night of their homosexual activity probably stemmed from their kinship and their seniors. The great majority of ho-mosexual contacts are promiscuous and Sambia males culturally regard them that way. Some boys do form sexual liaisons with bachelors for a few weeks—an in-teresting formative pattern in male gender identity development (see chapters 7 and 9).

9. The day before S. arrived, Moondi's father left on a long trading expedition over the mountains. He went to exchange salt bars for dried fish at a lowland place Sambia fear, for it is swampy, has many snakes, and is believed inhabited by ma-levolent forms of sickness and evil spirits. For someone to fall sick there, which he did, is a bad omen. So M.'s mother went to him and performed healing cere-monies. He was soon better, eventually to return weak but healthy to the village.

10. It is immoral and shameful for a betrothed couple to interact directly. Talking or arguing in public is especially bad, for this familiarity signifies the couple are already acting like spouses—implying they have begun sexual intercourse. Moondi is too sexually moral, respectful of elders, passive, and who knows what else to do that.

11. An extraordinary fantasy since Sambia husbands and wives never sleep together, much less in the same bed. (They have no platform beds.) He tells this daydream confidently and without hesitation, expressing a well-rehearsed wish.

It may derive from rumors—I heard them—that down the valley [S: where missionaries brought the Word as well as square houses with tin roofs], several men sleep all night in bed with their wives. Most Sambia men say such behavior would be wrong and dangerous to maleness.

12. Since pacification (c. 1965) many social changes have occurred, including change in dress and the sexual code. One of the first changes was the uncovering of young women's breasts. Traditionally, maidens, like all young initiates, had to hide themselves and avoid all sexually eligible men. Since the early 1970s, young women have changed in this. It seems strange to me that this custom disappeared so rapidly, to be replaced by women wearing Western blouses. Was it that the taboo on women's breasts was fragile? Older married women, however, could always go nude from the waist up, and some still do. This subject is complex and cannot be discussed here, but we can infer that erotic hiding and excitement were always associated with the face and breasts—the breasts themselves associated with many overt and subtle features of Sambia symbolism. Moondi, thus, is not expected to see women's breasts, especially those of his fiancée. Yet while some things change, things also remain the same. Some young women still hide their breasts in this way. And, ironically, the cycle is repeating itself: the effect of the missionaries is now for most women to wear clothes, so that their breasts are now more covered than ever.

13. He is dodging here. He had once hidden on the edge of a garden, to steal a glance at her face. She turned toward him, and, realizing he was staring at her from a distance, she smiled. That is the smile that delights but also embarrasses him. [S: So much for the primitive, the simple savage; for the impossibility of understanding across cultures, the worthlessness of empathy and the pointlessness of intimate communications in ethnography.] What does that smile mean? Does it communicate desire? What complex mix of her fantasies and memories is in that desire of hers? That this woman, who is to be his wife, looks at him with desire, fills him with marvelous sensations.

14. Initiated boys, bachelors, and adult men—all say they do not masturbate *to ejaculate*. It is the ejaculation outcome that may help clarify the confusion, since we Westerners assume masturbation leads to orgasm. (Is this distinction not useful?) There is a ritual injunction, whose truth no man denies, not to waste one's semen (Herdt 1980). Only if necessary to arouse himself before penetrating a boy's mouth will a bachelor play with his own penis. (I have no evidence that women masturbate to orgasm. I believe my key woman informant, Penjukwi, who says they do not.) Sambia children often touch their genitals, but I do not know if this is erotic. Sambia suppress the general subject as vigilantly as any other aspect of sexuality on which I questioned them. Is this true elsewhere in New Guinea? Is this not a subject for ethnography? Do ethnographers need a Freud to tell them children and adults have erotic lives and that erotism drives and shapes culture and experience in places besides New York and Kiriwina? Will someone please study this?

15. Extracted in part from Stoller, *Observing the Erotic Imagination* (1985:112–114).

5. *Tali and Weiyu on Ritual and Erotics*

1. I was the handiest source of money and influence to Sambia then. In Weiyu's case, I chipped in (without being asked) $4.00 (Australian), and some food as

wedding gifts to his wife's family in 1974. He was appreciative, but I recently discovered he forgot. No harm. He's given me a lot over the years, which cannot be repaid.

2. Looking back, I see that my closest friends are all unusual in some respects; for instance, Weiyu and Moondi are both *bomwalyu* (men living in hamlets that are not their fathers'); Nilutwo was a neurotic dreamer; Sakulambei is a strange mixture of hermaphrodism and shamanism; Penjukwi is far more verbal and independent than most women; even people like Kanteilo (my aging sponsor), Chemgalo (Weiyu's stepfather, who before his death loved to sit around my house in his old age), Kwinko (my cook), and Kambo (my best initiate-informant)—are all verbal, gregarious, and more reflective than most Sambia. I subliminally selected them, grew close to them, because they matched traits in me. And remember: anthropologists are, themselves, marginal people (or "marginal natives," Freilich 1977): misfits. Isn't that why many tend to have key informants who are marginal in *their* own societies, such as Turner's (1960) "Muchona the hornet"? Is it methodologically wrong to have unusual informants in interpreting the usual in a culture? There are cross-checks, of course: we know and observe many other people in many social situations. But as Schwartz (1978) asks, how do we define, at this primitive stage of ethnographic theory, the usual center of a culture? It doesn't exist; we are far better describing what we really experience, not what we imagine ideally exists (the dull reality of the perfection-seeking structuralists, who have made flawless formal arrangements out of messy, but more believable, human action).

3. Strange legends survive from that time, telling how the dying man was still strong enough to wound one of his assailants; how the dead man's body was thrown in a bog and rose to the surface; how the skull (on which revenge-sorcery could be performed) mysteriously disappeared; and of strange misfortunes befalling the murderers after their death. Even in death Weiyu's father exercised great power.

4. Chemgalo, a tall, skinny man, who is tough as nails, became the first convert, in old age, to a local mission. His mission membership is the main reason he never remarried. The fact that he was the first to be missionized points again to unusual influences in Weiyu's development.

5. Weiyu's wife is his step-sister's daughter, who was, like him, reared in Nilangu. This closeness gave their marriage incestuous overtones, but Sambia pay little notice, since such close marriages are well known.

6. I thought Weiyu would mellow out, but in 1981 the chaos still persisted (see the Epilogue). It surprised and pained me. Weiyu and his wife were often at odds or not speaking. He has grown closer to his son (who is at initiation age). He talks of taking another wife, and his antics in trying to marry Penjukwi still continue (see chapter 6). Along with Moondi and others, I had tried to help him and his wife to get along, but to no avail. On working more with women (1979, 1981), I found Weiyu's misogyny harder to accept than ever. I now realized from women's viewpoint how terrible were the situations into which men like Weiyu put their wives. I changed: I found Weiyu's behavior harder to accept, though I knew some of it was of his wife's making. His jokes about women were no longer funny: I knew their side.

7. Since 1975, when working with Weiyu and Tali, I have paid the equivalent (in cash and tradegoods) of full-time local wages. They worked with me full days many times, though we usually worked in mutually-agreed-on times convenient

for us all. I compensated them for time they could have spent in other productive ways; but they both continued gardening and hunting, though on a reduced scale. (This work did not seem to affect their family's food supply much, since their wives do most of the daily gardening, and they supplemented their meat supply with foods I gave them or they purchased with cash from tradestores.)

Did I introduce a class-system into the village in this way? I don't think so, but I did exacerbate economic change already in progress. Both Tali and Weiyu used their resources to help pay school fees of children in their extended families and in contributing to kinsmen's marriage exchanges, which are changing due to local inflation. I tried to compensate for lopsidedness in this resource-flow by employing a number of people from different villages (Nilutwo, Moondi, etc.), by giving food and occasional cash gifts to others who were simply supporters or friends, by helping several other boys through school, by contributing to villagewide feasts from time-to-time, and by giving away a wide range of small gifts (pots, blankets, knives, etc.) to various families over the years. This strategy has equalized wealth in the village, I believe; but it has also contributed to a longer-term disparity I had not originally anticipated in the overall wealth of the village vis-à-vis others in the tribe.

8. Nilutwo was first sketched in Herdt 1981, chapter 5, and is discussed further here in chapter 6. In 1979 I worked with N. in January and February as I had in past years. Then I returned to the States. In March, Nilutwo suffered his fall, as I learned on returning in May. Meanwhile he had been suffering, hospitalized, carried back to the village in horrid pain, and had had weeks to sour himself and his friends with the agony of dying.

9. Herdt (1982a). We want to underline our awareness that H. previously, and H. and S. here, *have* created and then reinforced an extraordinary social experience in our talk sessions. We know that our discourse with Weiyu and Tali is special in that way; this intimate talk now concerns us as much as the traditions of Sambia society. We only wish others would acknowledge more exactly the same: see chapter 11.

10. See Herdt (1981) for a description of this technique.

6. Penjukwi: Portrait of a Woman

1. P's step-father was an *aambei-wutnyi* like Imano (chapter 8). He was not so quiet that he didn't fight with P.'s mother, but since I knew him only vaguely, I cannot say much about him otherwise. Years later, in 1979, he hung himself after it came out that he was discovered in adultery with a woman in the village. Apparently he was overcome with shame. And while adultery is very shameful and men have been known to commit (or attempt) suicide out of shame, such an extreme response is rare. When the news came of the suicide, Weiyu, who happened to be with me at the moment, turned and said: "He was an *aambei-wutnyi*. What other kind of *man* would hang himself!" (especially, in Weiyu's view, over adultery). P. felt sorry that this happened and did mourn—for a day or two—but she felt no great loss.

2. Yanduwaiko could play both sides of the fence—government and locals— but in private he clearly placed his loyalties with the Sambia vis-à-vis others. He once mentioned to me (in 1979) at the patrol post that the "government doesn't care about much except itself," meaning that he realized he and just about everything else was expendable compared to the central bureaucracy.

3. When I first entered the Valley (1974), there were no women speaking Pidgin. (P.'s aunt was living at the patrol post.) By 1979, P. and several other women were able to converse somewhat in Pidgin, but, shamed by the men, they rarely did. By 1981, several more women were speaking it, and they were becoming bolder.

4. Moondi attended this bush school. When it closed he was sent elsewhere to a larger and more sophisticated school. (See chapter 4.)

5. It has never been clear what P.'s father did during all this fighting. Did he stand by and watch or merely shout curses? Was he in complicity with Kanteilo? We'll probably never know. But no Sambia father, or brothers, or her uncle would ever have stood for this abduction. In past times, a war would have started over it. Unfortunately, P. had no real defenders at that moment.

6. P. is, by character, an affectionate person (a character trait shared by other Sambia women and men). In their first months, P. was angry and bitter at Nilutwo. He tried to assuage her as best as possible, and in time P. made the best of the situation. But another dynamic may have added to P's feeling affectionate: N.'s ambivalence. N. was constantly torn between ambivalent feelings of all kinds, and he was, therefore, malleable: given to pleasing others. Penjukwi—being so different (nonambivalent—assertive but cordial)—complemented N. in this regard and, in fact, probably made many of the practial, day-to-day decisions in running the family. (For which N. was grateful, though he never said this in words, only showed it in actions, like providing meat for the family from his hunting.) After their children were born, P. was stuck with N. for good, since female-initiated divorce is extremely rare among Sambia. Consequently, when N. got into trouble (e.g., adultery attempts), P. stood by him, for it was really the best way to deal with such problems—over the long haul. After N.'s accident, though, his death was imminent. P. could be affectionate in a very different way: saying goodbye. Feeling between the spouses is a very complex thing in Sambia land, not so different from us.

7. Here is a letter that came later from Penjukwi, dated December 25, 1979. (It took four months to arrive.) Her younger brother (who has some schooling) was the scribe. It is the first letter I had ever gotten from her. Since we left in July, I had waited, fearing the worst, but she seemed to be all right.

"Dear Gilbert:

"Oh, yes, Gilbert, thank you very much for your letter which I have received, and I am happy about. I am all right but I am very sorry that my man [husband] is dead and you, as if you were my father, have sent me some money. [I sent her K5.00, about $7.50.] That has come to me, and I am really happy about that. I am happy to get your letter, and I am right now visiting in Kwoli [hamlet], where I have received your letter.

Well, at the time that my husband died [shortly after we left], nothing came up and happened to me until they removed the ghost* and some women cried and hit†me. But now I am all right.

---

*At death, everyone becomes a malevolent spirit and must eventually be driven from the hamlet through rites and incantations for a week.

†The antifeminist impulse in women is not restricted to our folks. However badly they may be treated, if the society has a dependable traditional structure, most of its beneficiaries will accept some aggression in exchange for stability (safety).

The time that I got your letter I was very pleased because all of my money you had given me from before I had long finished, and I was very worried about that, and you sent me some.

So that's how it is, since you asked me: are you all right? Yes I am here, and I am all right. Nothing [bad] has come up for me. Suppose some trouble comes up for me at Nilangu hamlet. . . . All right, I will go back to my place [Kwoli, where she was born and where her mother now lives]. But I am staying with Tali at Nilangu. You asked me before and I am with him. And you sent a picture, and I'd really like another one. The picture when you and I both stood up and they took it, and I'd like you to send that when you send another letter. I have to get some grass thatching for my brother [classificatory brother] at Kwoli, who he is writing this letter for me to you. I don't know at whatever time really you will come back, and so I am asking you. You must tell us; I've already heard that you're there in America, and I am very pleased to get your letter. Gilbert, good morning."

Your friend,
Penjukwi"

7. Sakulambei: A Hermaphrodite's Secret

1. This syndrome, identified in the work of Imperato-McGinley et al. (1974) on the Dominican Republic, is a biologic disorder that causes ambiguous-looking external genitals. The ambiguity is striking enough that certain individuals are mis-categorized and assigned to the female sex. Later, at puberty, through the action of normal circulating testosterone, further androgenization of the genitals leads to shifts or changes in sex role categorization and self-perception. The issues are reviewed, with respect to Sambia data, in Herdt and Davidson (1988).

2. Saku asked to serve as my cook, and at the time I had no reason to say no, since I was not working with him. He did so for about two months. In retrospect, I regret doing this, for it complicated my relationship with him. House servants can be interpreters (Kwinko was), but Saku is more fragile, and employment introduced distortion. (Has this aspect of field relationships been studied?)

3. Both Nilutwo (see Herdt 1981) and Saku formed stronger transference relationships to me than did others; my studying their dreams played its part. Both had strong needs to talk with me, but Saku, despite his hermaphrodism, was the more psychologically healthy of the two. (Nilutwo had a short psychosis in his teens, attempted rape, and engaged in horrible arguments.) Kalutwo, I feel, was more aberrant than either Saku or Nilutwo, but I never really studied his dreams. Kalutwo was so desperate for a person to attach to that he did not need dream reporting to generate a transference.

4. I finished my case study of Saku in 1981 after seven years of interviews. The old woman (and his sister) with whom I talked confirmed that at birth he was labeled a hermaphrodite but marked "male," because his glans was just visible, protruding from the top of his scrotal area.

5. Sambia believed that further growth of the male hermaphrodites' penes and retarded secondary sex traits such as facial hair occur around puberty. They therefore assign these people to the male sex in anticipation of the later male features. (cf. Imperato-McGinley et al. 1974). Saku's development confirms these views.

6. Mon and another Pundei clan brother (also still living) conspired to kill

Weiyu's father (see chapter 5); Mon masterminded it. Still, Saku, whose mother was a biologic sister to Weiyu's mother, and Weiyu, are the closest of friends. Neither has much love for Mon.

7. Saku's sister is married and has children. His older brother, however, left for the coast in 1967, while still a second-stage initiate. He has never returned to the valley, never married, and has had only vague contacts through letters with Saku and others. Since I have never seen the brother, and his social development is definitely strange, Saku's brother must remain another puzzle in an already strange story.

8. Probably an imaginary playmate, now his symbolic double.

9. Weiyu is often present in Herdt (1981), where Saku is absent; but see Herdt (1987c).

10. Saku told me he just did not want his nose to bleed, and it did not. His nose never was bled. Now, as a married man, it is appropriate that Saku regularly nosebled himself, but he says that it is needless and he'll have no part of it (see Herdt 1982c). Saku says his uncle (a member of a clan with somewhat different ritual practice) never nosebled himself either. Saku uses that to rationalize his behavior. Perhaps the selfhood of a Sambia hermaphrodite is to too fragile (his body boundaries too tenuous) to let loose anything as precious as blood. And perhaps these hermaphrodites accept more femininity in core identity and so need not so clearly mark their maleness by bloodletting.

11. Saku felt compelled to present himself to me in this way, lying if necessary to say, in essence, "I am different but still masculine and don't need the semen other males need." Saku's sexual behavior belied that intellectualization: older men say he was an expert fellator. Since he was chameleonic (as I shall describe later), he may have felt this so as to identify with men when alone, perhaps to prove that he was, in that sense, more masculine than other men.

12. Many initiates have said they tried to get Saku to screw them out of curiosity to see what his genitals looked like. Saku was probably wise to avoid them: Sambia initiates are inveterate gossips, not above humiliating him. Saku is extraordinarily careful always to cover his genitals.

13. Weiyu says Saku continued to suck older males even on the Coast, in the early 1970s, well after his puberty; that is aberrant. Saku confirmed this report. Further, he quit being a fellator mainly because his sexual partners no longer felt comfortable screwing such an advanced youth.

14. Sambia is a racially mixed population, with both Papuan and New Guinea elements. This mixture probably results from the original migrants coming from the Papuan Lowlands but moving into Highland populations.

15. Why do ethnographers seldom describe the physical appearance of their interpreters or friends? Do we ethnographers select key interpreters who not only match our personalities, but (as with some of our friends) also resemble us physically? Would such a prototype be especially true of same-sex interpreters?

16. In 1974–1976, Sa. had no facial hair. By 1979 he had some small growth on his upper-lips, which he does not shave off.

17. At the time, jokes were being made that Saku's penis had finally—inexplicably—grown enough to copulate with women. The men said it would be fruitless and that the woman would spit on him. The women said his wife must be crazy or immature and that she'd soon grow bored with a man without much of a penis. What none reckoned on was Saku's intelligence. He has arranged his life to make

his wife as happy as possible. And, a dynamic in their marriage, his wife somewhat fears Saku's shamanic powers. By 1979 the marriage was still in good order.

18. The final secret of Saku's shamanism—still unexplained by him to me— is that his familiars are real and in control of him: Saku's bedrock.

19. Staring directly into someone else—when not engaged in sexual looking or in a trance (as a shaman) is bizarre to Sambia. But because it was S.—white-haired friend/boss of H., a western doctor—it was permitted. By Saku saying S. was not a ghost, he tells us that no one but a ghost would do what S. did (e.g., in a dream), but that it was okay, not bad. In denying S. is a ghost, Saku also rejects weirder interpretations (i.e., S. is a ghost-like figure, in the cargo cultist sense), at least for us, since he is being pressed by us (authorities) for his opinion.

20. I have disguised Gronemann's true identity. Though we have to omit some and disguise other details about him, our presentation of Gronemann fits Saku's experience and others' reports of what happened.

8. Imano—Considerate Masculinity

1. In the United States we equate (or at least we used to) age with experience and social influence. Sambia do too. Though Tali and Imano are peers, no one equates them: Imano is socially insignificant compared to Tali, largely because Imano looks and acts younger, lighter, less weighted-down with responsibilities.

2. Infant mortality (through malaria, pneumonia, malnutrition, etc.) is high among New Guinea Highlanders, running perhaps—there are no reliable data— as high as 50 percent in some areas some years among Sambia.

3. For more precise cultural descriptions of the following aspects of Sambia gender distinctions, see Herdt (1981; 1987c).

4. Except that Sakulambei is so aberrant (even beyond being biologically intersexed) that he should be considered differently. I have heard women refer to Sakulambei as *aambei-wutnyi;* though what really counts is that he is *kwoluaatm-wol* (male pseudohermaphrodite). As we saw, Saku is pretty successful, except that he has no children (he is probably sterile), for he is married, has property and social power, and is a top-ranking shaman. He is tough, a fighter too, attributes that make people refer to him as "strong," and he is called a "strong shaman." He does not seem, socially at least, to fit the *aambei-wutnyi* category. Nonetheless, he does subliminally: he likes women, likes to sit and gossip, is caring and nurturant in his shamanistic role. Furthermore, he actively resists doing critical male rituals (e.g., self-nosebleeding). Saku is thus one of those people who fit no category easily (see chapter 7)—a reminder that we should not forget that models are *about* but not the *same* as social reality.

5. See Mead's (1935:225–230) wonderful characterizations of what she called "mild" men in Mundugumor society on the Sepik.

6. See, for example, Moondi's father, who has produced many offspring. Obviously men who like women and enjoy sex with them will—all things being equal— produce many children (cf. Chowning 1980). Being prolific reproductively is something Sambia admire, regardless of what else comes with the package. No amount of heroic deeds or battle scars can make up for lack of progeny, which is why full masculine personhood requires prowess and many children. So here is an attribute of *aambei-wutnyi* that is (subliminally) read as intensely masculine.

7. Effeminate (see Stoller 1975a) is different, a caricature of women that ex-

aggerates stereotyped feminine qualities. Effeminacy implies gender aberrance. I know of no effeminate Sambia. *Aambei-wutnyi* men do not live out that hostile exhibition. They are comfortable being, in a few important ways, more feminine than masculine.

8. Again, we can't assume that males and females show the same behavioral acts or traits from society to society, that these are seen in all places as masculine and feminine, or are experienced everywhere as the same. Ethnographers: let us please be more specific about how we use "masculine" and "feminine."

9. These category terms all refer only to males, not females. Women use the generic nouns *wogaanyu* and *wusaatu*, never *aambei-wutnyi*, in reference to each other's weak or inappropriate social performance.

10. Caveat: Sambia have been at peace for years. With warfare gone, in everyone and in all situations much of the force behind gender differentiation has diminished. Perhaps *aambei-wutnyi* would have been pushed further, have had more demanded of them in masculine performance, or else have been treated more shabbily, before pacification. We ethnographers may be underrating such social changes on gender role behavior (see Faithorn 1976; Feil 1978; and perhaps Mead fifty years ago: see Gewertz 1983).

11. Reliability and validity are aspects of all scientific data. What about ethnography? Seldom, except in glaring cases (e.g., Castaneda: see DeMille 1976; Murray 1979), is this issue discussed, though the Samoan case created great controversy (Freeman 1983). When we deal with an *n* of 1, we need to think hard on what we expect in reliability and validity (cf. chapter 11), especially since full information in our work is impossible. As long as someone is living, our constructions of his or her experience are incomplete and interminable (Freud 1937). The same basic issue but transmuted applies to the study of cultures too.

12. Weiyu's behavior differed when interpreting for these two men. He was more anxious with Kalutwo, more comfortable with Imano. He was more interested, relaxed, spontaneous, in direct eye contact, and easy in translating with Imano, but with Kalutwo tense, bored, slumped, frustrated, with bad or no eye contact, making verbal slips, and finding it difficult to translate questions or answers. For years Weiyu has translated for me with many people; thus, this just described difference isn't an artifact of his closer relationship to Imano than to Kalutwo. Here, the translator's behavior is a kind of projective test to be studied, over time, like the ethnographer's own subjectivity (chapter 10).

13. Of Imano's three biologic brothers, the eldest is a weak shaman, another *aambei-wutnyi*, who has two wives and many children; the second is more of a fighter, has an acid-sharp tongue, three wives and many children; the youngest (an agemate of Weiyu) also is quiet and gentle; he obviously likes women, and is newly wed with two children.

14. In local idiom, such a person's speech style is called *nuvuchelu*, which refers to a mouth so stuffed with betel-nut that one's speech is slurred. Precisely what caused this condition is hard to say, but it is rare. (It made one self-conscious.)

15. I knew Imano's mother before she died in 1980; then in her seventies, she was a wonderful old lady, proud and generous. Her generosity was renowned, so much so that her nickname meant "mother of the hamlet." She also had extensive gardening and sorcery magic, and she was unquestionably the most important woman elder in Nilangu, for she did the key ritual teachings for girls.

16. A major clue that Imano's father's gender identity was different from other men's. Moreover, by the time Imano arrived, his father was middle-aged. Age may

have further diminished his father's male attachments and desire to spend time in all-male company, as it does in older men today: here is certainly an important sib-position factor in Imano's masculine development.

17. Westerners may find this hard to believe, but it is commonly stated among Sambia (as elsewhere in New Guinea). When people are breast-fed (or have access to the breast) till they are three or four, they remember. There are no great discontinuities, such as secretiveness, in this domain: children see breast-feeding all the time. Those memories are filtered, screened, and reinterpreted over the years, but they survive in consciousness.

18. Of the various things boys and men have said of their responses to the first homosexual teachings, no other has ever said he (silently) laughed at them. Most boys, from my observations of ritual, are scared and confused. When Imano said this he broke into guffaws.

19. Sambia homosexuality is structured to be promiscuous. Yet Imano's relationship with the older youth was that of lovers. In previous writings I never used this term, but rather "partners," "contacts," or "liaisons," feeling that our notion "lover" (one who is in a romantic love affair) distorted the indiscriminate, promiscuous, bump-and-grind quality of homosexual intercourse among Sambia. What Imano described is different: it was *enduring*, lasting about three months; *intense*, for they had sex just about every other night; *caring*, for they slept together, shared food, hunted together, and Imano was protected by the youth; and, for Imano, *exclusive*, for he had sex with no other man during this time or afterward. (He did continue having sporadic sexual contacts with this youth for several years after.) You could see this attachment between Sambia males only when someone was confortable in the way Imano was.

20. For a comparison of the behavior and experiences of secret nosebleeding among men, see Herdt (1982b). Developmentally, such rituals as nosebleeding— done both in collective situations and private ones—are identity-contexts, providing the ethnographer with important clues about variations in the person's fantasy, life-history, and dynamics.

21. Why *overly* self-conscious? ("Overly" means: he laughed, giggled, and hid his face [men do not do that] when first disicussing that he had sex with his wife, that he wanted to please her, and that he was letting us know of it.) Did this self-consciousness reflect a sense of aberrant erotism? I think not. For example, he was just as embarrassed to talk of his nosebleeding and of having been a fellator. (Other men are also self-conscious in these sensitive areas, but less so. And they grow out of it after adolescence.) Imano was also unlike other Sambia men in finding women marvelously exciting to possess, while not needing to be like them (e.g., by competing with, fearing, or imitating them); he does not wish to be like his wife. Thus: where other men have no such respect for women, he is overly self-conscious.

22. Masculinity, like other patterns in Sambia culture and personality, is changing, particularly in relation to western experience (Herdt 1987c). Imano has been to the coast. Is this quirk—giving money to his wives—a result of that? It probably influenced him. But, to repeat, other men don't do this, not even other returned coastal migrants. Details in gender differences like this one should make us careful about claiming that western contact is the sole instigator of change in traditional culture, or that when western intrusion occurs, it changes everyone the same way.

23. Which "him," the gender researcher wonders? Imano ten years ago? The "true" Imano self now? Or is this just a performance for friends? Or is it all of

these? Interpretation: Imano's spontaneity makes me think this is genuine excitement, which he allows us to see because he is comfortable. Hypothesis: the only other person who sees this excitement is his wife.

24. Reference to Turner's (1964) important paper on individual and collective symbolism (reviewed in Herdt 1981, Appendix A). The reader should know that S. and I have had this conversation, in one form or another, before; we seem to suffer the same quirk in talking like this, whether it's in New Guinea, UCLA, or some Washington restaurant.

9. *Kalutwo: Portrait of a Misfit*

1. Some of this biographic material is reprinted from Herdt (1980).

2. Out of my total research population (about 150 males I can profile), only four or five adult men are known to engage in homosexual fellatio regularly (not merely on the sly and occasionally) done by (never to) boys, even though, being married, the behavior is socially inappropriate and morally wrong. These men, however, are also less deviant because they are married and have children. In addition, several older men resemble K. slightly in having failed at marriage and in being quiet, conservative, unobstructive. (One, mentally retarded, has never married and engages only in homosexual activities.) I doubt if these men, on closer examination, would look like K.

3. Half the Sambia men by 1980 between age fifteen and forty-five have worked on the coast for a year or more, usually on plantations. This is a sort of rite of passage in that coastal experience has become a substitute for warrior and ritual activities. About 25% of them speak Pidgin, only some of whom are fluent. (Women do not work on the coast, and few speak Pidgin.) Many return wearing one or another western garment, usually as status symbols. Though K. differs in these regards, he is not considered deviant on these grounds.

4. By chance I was first introduced in 1974 to K. by a local missionary. The memory stands out because he told me in English that K. was one of the strange people in the Valley: he was a "strange man" with a "weak handshake," who had an "oddly close relationship to his sister." He added that K. was one of the few Sambia he didn't care for. (Deviance theorists: I dismissed the missionary's view until, years later, Sambia repeated similar views long enough that they finally sank in. In this case I believe the missionary reached his opinion independently of the natives.)

5. He usually arrived early in my house, sometimes to spend as much as two hours before interview time. In part this was because he was not doing much garden work; he had lots of time to kill.

6. Weiyu pledged himself to confidentiality, as had I, but K. knew this wasn't good enough in a tiny hamlet. In collaborative work with others (relatives, friends), I also had to be careful not to violate K.'s trust.

7. See the next chapter, where we take up problems of the interpreter's presence and reactions in more detail. Some anthropologists think ethnographic dialogue is hindered by our not being able to speak directly to the native in the vernacular. I agree. Particularly in clinical ethnography—the one-to-one sustained dialogue of a case study—third parties, even mutually trusted translators, shift the interviewing dynamics. But another dimension of the interpreter's presence also plays a part that might be overlooked: the third party provides a legitimate

reason for the native not to reveal more than is wanted of him or herself. K., who is inherently untrusting, must have known (I asked him, but he could never directly respond) that he could not completely trust Weiyu. And so he avoided certain subjects: for instance, in working on his sexual daydreams, he could talk about the scenario but would leave out exactly what he felt.

8. So it goes in a society organized by sexual polarity: women—and ultimately men (e.g., K.)—suffer the costs. (His older sister was already married and away making a family of her own. Her husband had a cordial relationship with K. and his mother, but he died prematurely.)

9. This man—Gorutndun—is Imano's age (early thirties), married, has children, is well liked, gregarious, and in a position of some authority. I knew him for years and was friendly with him, but he steadfastly refused to be interviewed until 1981. He described then how he had always liked sex with boys as fellators and women as well. (See Epilogue.) My hunch is that this bi-erotic behavior in adulthood occurs quietly among a few men, but because it is wrong, they, like Gorutndun, are loathe to discuss it.

Incidentally, if there are any who believe anthropologists get informants to say anything if well bribed, they should know of Gorutndun, Kalutwo, and others of my acquaintance: when people fear examining their own behavior—want no insight—no amount of bribery can persuade them until they trust. See Epilogue.

10. The only reliable data I have on this adult erotic role-switching comes from Nilutwo, Penjukwi's husband. He once told me how an older bachelor had tried to switch roles with him (N. was a fellator) and suck him off. N. was frightened and fled. This bachelor was Zaito, an insane man. On mentioning it, N. laughed and spoke of the act as crazy, by a crazy man. However, it occurred before the onset of Zaito's psychotic episodes. Even so, the crazy attribution indicates how Sambia regard this inversion. I have heard fleeting rumors of attempted inversion by two other men. The details of these incidents are too complex to describe here.

11. Like other regular interpreters I paid K. with money, trade goods, and food. These items cannot be discounted as motivation. But they are not enough to make someone work unless he or she wants to (as we find with K., Sakulambei, and the reluctant interpreters mentioned previously). One hears stories of fieldworkers who buy information in New Guinea, such as paying the equivalent of ten cents to many dollars per myth or folktale that people bring them. That may occur. (I never did that.) My point is that such stories concern superficial, depersonalized information: sit someone down for a few hours, ask questions they don't like, and watch them run. No amount of money will induce answers (not even lies, if an interviewer persists) an interpreter refuses to give.

12. This contrast between "primary" and "secondary" shamans as different developmental tracks and character structure formations will be taken up elsewhere. It compares with Spiro's (1968a) distinction between the psychocultural patterns of men versus women shamans' callings in Burma but differs in that I here suggest different motivations among members of the male sex. In both Spiro's and my case, though, I believe that only a psychodynamic approach will lead us to discoveries in a field overly dominated by cultural relativism (cf. Price-Williams 1975; Peters and Price-Williams 1980) or reductionistic Freudian pathologizing.

13. This statement is only roughly correct. Every hamlet desires shamans; in general, the more, the better (but recall Weiyu's father). If this social desirability is what S. meant, then I was wrong. But if—as I suspect—he was asking me if

anyone in *particular* desired K. to be a shaman, then the answer is still no—his sister included. (Note how different Saku's situation is in this regard.) A lot of qualifications for a "simple" question.

14. S: H.'s translation of these conversations with K. was the only one hard for me to edit: untranslated words, literal translations so that the meaning is incomprehensible, persisting with Pidgin and unable to break free into English, loss of narrative sense, quite a mess. Here is an example that comes up about this point.

H: [*Pause.*] You say that you feel happy when that—

H: Kalutwo breaks in, in Sambia, louder than my talk, and he continues to talk for about thirty seconds here. And Weiyu asks him some questions. This goes on for about a minute, then the tape switches—there's no translation here. Apparently we must have reached an impasse, but I don't know why it wasn't recorded. A slight break and then we continue in another line of the interviewing.

H: Now, what was the first time when he was big or, a little bigger or a little smaller, when he started to think about [fantasize about] the faces of initiates, about when he could start to copulate with them. Was that when he was a *choowinuka* or *imbutu* or what? [*Weiyu translates to K. who clears his throat again. The tape switches.*]

W: It was at that time, then. [He was an *imbutu*.]

S: My first editing of H.'s translation takes, on the average, one half-hour per typed page of transcription. When my first is typed, I read and touch it up: two and a half hours on the second round for thirty-six pages for this piece. H. goes over that version, and then I go over his. Just to be clear and accurate.

H: During the past month, I had grown increasingly exasperated with K. Though he came regularly to work, he was evasive. My frustration, and our impasse, places Weiyu in an uncomfortable position. He never avoided translating for K. Yet, as the interviews became more intense, they were more trying for him, and he lost all enthusiasm for working with K. I was aware of this pressure on W. and tried to help him. In retrospect, I did not realize how uncomfortable he was and how much hostility toward K. (and hence, for me, since I continued the work) he had bottled up. (See chapter 10.)

10. *The Interpreter's Discomfort*

1. Evans-Pritchard (1956). Cf. also Whiting et al., (1966:156–159). Today, there are many and more fancy texts on the problem (Marcus and Fisher 1986; Geertz 1988; Tedlock 1983).

2. Today, in a shrinking postcolonialist world, some of these corrupted are now political leaders, the new cultural spokesmen—interpreters—who must approve foreign research visas in their countries.

3. Naroll (1970) argues that the ethnographer's ability to work in the vernacular is the key factor influencing the quality of our reports.

4. In Melanesia, there are two broad types of languages: Austronesian (or "Melanesian") languages, and non-Austronesian ("Papuan") languages. New Guinea's non-Austronesian languages are among the world's most difficult tongues. Most of them are unwritten and unrecorded; they must be learned *in situ*. Experienced

linguists, working full-time on language, have spent years learning single languages like Fore, Binamurian, or Baruya. And Eunice Pike, a noted linguist, once described the Anga language family (to which Sambia belongs) as one of the most complex in the world. When it takes five years and more to achieve competence, ethnographers cannot succeed (there are exceptions, e.g., Andrew Strathern, given enough time). Thus, many New Guinea ethnographies are constructed from materials collected in Pidgin or Motu (see Bateson 1944; Mead 1939; and Tuzin 1976:xxxiv for discussion). Probably ninety percent or more of all fieldworkers in New Guinea have used interpreters in some capacity, more or less (usually more). Nonetheless, this aspect of the hermeneutics of ethnography has been ignored (Langness 1976:100 ff.).

5. The reasons for this disengagement are pretty simple: you need only credit a technical aid once; and anthropologists are supposed to be experts working from direct, sensory experience, in the vernacular: why make a big deal out of facts that give contrary impressions. Nowhere is this message clearer than in Mead's ethnographies (e.g., 1935), as opposed to her more technical discussions (e.g., 1939; 1949; 1956).

6. Though there are allusions galore to this aspect of field methodology, from Boas (1920), Malinowski (1922; and especially 1935), Mead (1939), and on up to the present (e.g., Paul 1953; Pelto and Pelto 1973; Whiting et al. 1966:157), rarely has the interpreter's role been rigorously explicated (but see Crapanzano [1980], Owusu [1978], and Powdermaker [1966] for nice exceptions). Werner and Campbell (1970) have written on the general problem in anthropology; the other social sciences have generally ignored it (cf. e.g., Burgess 1982).

7. In the Melanesian literature, Mead's *The Mountain Arapesh* ([1968], see especially pp. 19–20), though a psychologic account, is an early and valuable exception.

8. I did little interpreting using Penjukwi in 1979. But when I returned in 1981 and worked more with women, she was crucial as my woman interpreter throughout. S. and I also used Moondi, but on a smaller scale.

9. For instance, Sambia use words with meanings completely different from dictionary glosses (such as those in the Standard Pidgin dictionaries). For a few days (in 1974) I was constantly confused because women used *sisa* (sister) to refer to two brothers (male siblings), when it formally applies only to siblings of the opposite sex. (This usage reflects a native identification in their own kinship system.)

10. This is a more serious source of distortion of the native view, which only the ethnographer's cultural and linguistic knowledge can correct. Examples: my interpreters would use Pidgin *"spirit"* or *"tebari"* (corruption of *tewel*) to gloss soul (*koogu*), shadow (*wakoogu-nambelu*), spirit familiar (*nemulyu*), and even thought (*koontu*, which can also be used pragmatically as a marker for "self"); or "growim" to cover: to expand, to get big, to make someone or something big, or to psychologically separate from someone (see Herdt 1982b). I feel that the semantic complexities of New Guinea cultures have been seriously underplayed due to such translation generalities.

11. I did not do this systematically at first but simply sat around talking about the ambience and working conditions of my house. Later, in 1979, we talked about how they felt after a particular interpreting session. I have always discouraged Weiyu and Moondi from publicly discussing an informant's private communications in public, even at my house, unless we were alone, and even then I discouraged them from talking about others in my work, for that tended to gossipy in-

terchanges. Public matters were another story. I did systematically work with Moondi to develop formal interview procedures (on tape) for studying boy-initiates' cognitive and ritual variation in two sets of interviews in 1975.

12. I know now that I made Weiyu be patient. He is, by nature, impetuous, like Moondi: quick to argue and to move toward adventure (e.g., a ritual, a trip) when wisdom counseled otherwise. Both Weiyu and Moondi have changed in this regard over the years due to age, social maturing, or, in Moondi's case, schooling.

13. S. is my mentor, a role model with whom I consciously identify (ego-ideal). This identification is deeper, because I sometimes see him in dreams (transference object). I feel that he has not only taught me but also helped me learn to stay honest in my research.

14. "The investigator himself has strong motivation to overlook the interpreter's faults. If he admits that the interpreter often makes mistakes, this amounts to admitting that much of his laboriously collected data may be unreliable or that much more checking than he had hoped to do is required to establish facts conclusively" (Whiting et al. 1966:156).

15. "No outsider could understand these multiple roles and Chinese intricacies. . . . It was not the American kind of loyalty-duplicity; in America the emotions were different somehow, perhaps thinner. Here you lead a crypto-emotional life. . . . You had no personal rights, but on the other hand, the claims of feeling were more fully acknowledged" (Bellow 1982:80).

16. Weiyu is being extreme here, showing some idiosyncracy. If I were to generalize (and it is difficult to do so on this topic) there are differences, based on three factors, in men's abilities and desire to discuss sex: generation, personality, and situation. (1) Some older men are reluctant to discuss sex due to older, more conservative, cultural values. (Very old men are too, because it is beneath their dignity, in a sense.) Weiyu's generation has been exposed to and acculturated by western attitudes toward sex. In this regard, Weiyu is an example of those wage-labor migrants who have been to the coast and tasted a more promiscuous life. (2) But even in the subset of Weiyu's peers who will have coastal experience, some are still prudish and reluctant to describe sexual exploits—not in public, which almost never occurs—but in private with peers. Weiyu is here again an extreme. (Don Juan complex? See chapter 5.) (3) Even when talking in private, in the club-house, older men feel shame if sex with their wives comes up, though they will, when alone with their cronies, brag and joke to some extent about sexual exploits. Younger men friends—in part because of my influence—do this more easily than their seniors. All this information is needed to set in context that remark of Weiyu's. Here again the difference between normative and idiosyncratic behavior requires attention to variance in the population with which one is working.

17. See Herdt (1981: ch. 8) and Stoller and Herdt (1982).

18. After this session we were to have seen Sakulambei. He never showed, as we noted in chapter 8. But in the minutes following our interview with W., we happened to have taped our private talk which compared them. An excerpt of that tape follows:

H: This interpreting is just . . . this is teaching me how tremendously exhausting this is. I am exhausted. I feel like I have walked five miles with Kalutwo. Yesterday the feeling was the same way. That was especially—even more so, that was far more emotional to me—than the session with Sakulambei. Yet both were the same: three hours.

S: The two interviews were similar in the intensity of the resistance, but Saku was resistant because of a post-infancy-early-childhood-reality-traumatic-experience. Kalutwo's resistance also comes from early childhood [abandoned and denied by his father] but has a different structure inside, a fundamental damage to early character structure development. But you get resistance from both. Yesterday was really tough as hell, but it was child's play compared to this.

H: Two heavy resistances, yet as you compare the two of them, it's remarkable that this man, a hermaphrodite, has the more normative sense of masculinity. Saku had the maternal uncle and his mother and father, so Saku must have got enough love from his maternal uncle whom he adored.

S: Of course. When I say to him, "Come in your greatest finery," he's proud. I would not know what to say to this guy K. . . . "get a shave?" There is no way that he would ever come looking different. But all I had to do was say it to Saku. He has the resources. This guy K., there is nothing you could say to him that would make him stand up and be a real person. The only real person is passive/resistance hopelessness. It's the only thing he's got, his only gimmick. Too bad.

11. Summing Up: Clinical Ethnography of Sambia Erotics and Gender

1. Herdt (1981, 1987c); Stoller and Herdt (1982).

2. Kohut (1971), made popular in anthropology by Geertz (1976).

3. S: Once, thinking the new generation of ethnographers—beneficiaries of our modern sexual freedom—could do it, I felt I had an antidote to the pretty useless ethnographic literature on sexual excitement: have them write up the realities of the excitements in which they personally participated with the subjects of their field studies. It did not work out. I can only guess why.

4. Doi (1973); Kakar (1985).

5. "The Other must matter in one's own self-constitution; he must not simply be an object of scientific or quasi-scientific scrutiny" (Crapanzano 1980:141).

6. Sapir (1938:9–10); cf. Singer (1961:61–65).

7. "One can predict too few of the people too much of the time" (Shweder 1979:268).

8. S: I suppose certain positions (schools) in anthropology [H: and psychoanalysis] are really metaphysical. Structuralists are Idealists, and grubbers like H. and me, with our love of the detail, are Nominalists. Were I an ethnographer, I would not seriously believe in Culture but in cultures. My belief is visceral and starts literally in the body: the ideal apple is no apple. The ideal sound is silent, beyond the sounds we experience. The ideal lizard has no legs, because the ideal leg is no leg. Then the ideal tennis has no net, and the ideal ideal has no existence:

> I swear, I swear
> I do not see
> How what is not
> Can be, can be.

9. Mead (1961) hinted of and cautioned against the same possible bias in ethnographies of sexual behavior long ago.

10. None. See note 3 above.

11. Creed (1984). Cf. Knauft (1987).

12. Foucault (1980) is critiqued in Herdt (n.d.).
13. See for example, Friedl (1975).
14. Example:

"If culture is as anthropologists claim a meaningful order, still, in action meanings are always at risk. They are risked, for example, by reference to things (i.e., in extension). Things not only have their own *raison d'être*, independently of what people may make of them, they are inevitably disproportionate to the sense of the signs by which they are apprehended. Things are contextually more particular than signs and potentially more general. They are more particular insofar as signs are meaning-classes, not bound as concepts to any particular referent (or stimulus-free). Things are thus related to their signs as empirical tokens to cultural types. Yet things are more general than signs inasmuch as they present more priorities (more reality) than the distinctions and values attended to by signs. Culture is therefore a gamble played with nature, in the course of which, wittingly or unwittingly—I paraphrase Marc Bloch—the old names that are still on everyone's lips acquire connotations that are far removed from their original meaning." (Sahlins 1985:ix)

To rescue us from such islands of Culture in the dark stream of post-structuralist theory we are going to need sturdy lifeboats.

15. See especially Knauft (1987). The most accessible review of the literature, though slanted to institutionalized homosexuality, is Herdt (1984). See also Herdt and Poole (1982), Mead (1961), Read (1986), and Whiting (1941). Far-reaching revisions will stem from M. Strathern's monumental *The Gender of the Gift* (1988).

16. This could be credited, in part, to Mead's (1935, 1949, 1961) ever-popular presence; and it is now being sustained by the important work of many excellent fieldworkers (reviewed in M. Strathern, 1988).

17. See, for instance, the divergent reviews of Adam (1986), Carrier (1980), Murray (1984), and Rubin (1975).

18. Monographs and journals, too numerous to list, are notable in one respect that supports my contention: none of the major journals on sexuality has much anthropologic input, and rare are the anthropologists who sit on their editorial boards.

19. Mead (1961) and Carrier (1980) use this argument.

20. See Katchadourian and Lunde (1980), which was, I am told, the largest selling text on human sexuality.

21. Atkinson (1982:249); cf. M. Strathern (1981).

22. "Because of the overwhelming concern of early anthropologists to establish culture or society as a legitimate focus for inquiry, the existence of the individual was usually suppressed in professional ethnographic writing" (Marcus and Cushman 1982:32).

"We are constantly under the gun to produce ethnographies, critical essays, theoretical treatises, and reviews, most of which are judged according to the theoretical contributions they make to the science of anthropology. This epistemological process of extracting the etic from the emic is scientific method par excellence and is an engrained structure in our system of scientific evaluation. And yet, how do we know that the data from which etic categories are extracted reflect the social reality of the people under study? Owusu (1978) has suggested that many classic works on African societies are fundamentally flawed, for they are based on misinterpretations of the data. In my own work (P. Stoller 1980:419), I have called attention to how what Whitehead called 'perceptual delusion' unwittingly creates ethnographic fiction (1980:419)" (P. Stoller 1982:1–2).

23. Moerman (1979) makes this argument. Cf. Shweder and Bourne (1984).

24. See Mead (1949:31); cf. Geertz (1984), who provides a modern interpretive functional relativism, which Spiro (1986) criticizes as ethnographic particularism.

25. Geertz (1966). Cf. the insightful Hallowell (1967).

26. Beginning with *Totem and Taboo* (1913).

27. Kakar's (1983) work on India is helpful here.

28. Freud (1905); see also Stoller (1975b); cf. Davidson (1987); Kakar (1985); Obeyesekere (1981).

29. Kakar (1985:442) quoting Silvan (1981:97).

30. *Ibid.*

31. Malinowski's complaint, in response to Ernest Jones' response to M.'s Trobriand work (published in an analytic journal!), was that the unconscious was always the cause, the culture the effect. "The universal occurrence of the Oedipus complex is being assumed, as if it existed independently of the type of culture, of the social organization and of the concomitant ideas" (Malinowski 1927:126). Malinowski's own "myth" of the absent Oedipal complex in the Trobriands has been exhaustively critiqued by Spiro, who draws attention to the "uncritical acceptance of the finding" (1982:179): a point that also touches on the mystification of fieldwork discussed in chapter 1. Spiro is reviewed in Herdt (1985).

32. Freud's insights from dream interpretation apply here to the meanings of erotics in cultural discourse and in private interviews: "At the same time, however, I should like to utter an express warning against overestimating the importance of symbols in dream interpretation, against restricting the work of translating dreams merely to translating symbols and against abandoning the technique of making use of the dreamer's association. The two techniques of dream-interpretation must be complementary to each other; *but both in practice and in theory the first place continues to be held by the procedure which I began by describing and which attributes the decisive significance to the comments made by the dreamer*" (1900:395, my emphasis).

33. The manifestations of this mental world are most recently reviewed in Herdt (1987c). I find increasing attention paid to the problem (Herdt and Poole 1982; M. Strathern 1988; Tuzin 1982).

34. Obeyesekere (1981) more than anyone has examined the problems of transformation of private or psychologic symbols into public shared knowledge. Cf. Wagner (1975) for a nonpsychologic view of the problem in Melanesia and more generally.

35. This aspect of the issue of discourse accounts and social/ritual controls is studied in initiates' experience, in Herdt (1987a).

36. See Crapanzano (1980), chastised in public lectures by Geertz (1988).

37. See especially Weiner (1985).

38. Reviewed in Bourguignon (1979:75–115), LeVine (1982), Schwartz (1978); cf. Marcus and Fischer (1986).

39. Wallace (1969); D'Andrade (1986); Edgerton (1985); Schwartz (1978).

40. See Keesing (1979, 1982); Pelto and Pelto (1973).

41. Reviewed in Herdt (1982a).

42. See Shweder and LeVine (eds. 1984); White and Kirkpatrick (1985).
43. See especially LeVine's (1982) seminal work on psychoanalytically oriented ethnography. Cf. Parin, Morganthaler, and Parin-Matthey (1980).
44. Most novice ethnographers cannot rely on intuitions about appropriateness. They are not knowledgeable enough, which is actually an advantage: the wisdom of knowing that one is ignorant. Because of our inability to introspect and resonate in foreign settings, classical psychoanalysis there is probably impossible. (See Brody 1980; Foulks 1977: Haldipur 1980; Littlewood 1980; Spiegel 1976.)
45. But see Parson's early work (1969).
46. Crapanzano (1980:146) remarks of his translator: "He gave me distance and protected me from direct and immediate contact and from the fears and pleasures of contact."
47. See chapter 5, and Herdt (1981: Appendix A).
48. "Through the use of such techniques—and the training of students to use these techniques reliably and confidently—the ethnographic monograph came to contain a large body of ordered information which was reasonably independent of observer bias, whether that bias was owing to ethnocentricity, temperamental preferences, research interests or applied aims" (Mead 1977:3–4).
49. "No one since has contributed as much as Freud to breaking the charm of *facts* and opening up the empire of *meaning*. Yet Freud continues to include all of his discourses in the same positivist framework which they destroy" (Ricoeur 1979:326).
50. See Doi (in press), on the analysis of psychoanalysis.
51. LeVine (1982:ix): "In my view, there is no need for more theory in this field unless it is accompanied by a sturdier method of data collection. Methodology has been the central problem of culture and personality research, its greatest stumbling block, and it claims the most searching scrutiny."

Epilogue: Training Clinical Ethnographers

1. Precisely which clinical training will work for Ph.D. students is not clear, but a psychoanalysis is not the answer. It is lengthy and expensive. [S: And unnecessary and at the wrong time. And, analysis does not work well when one seeks it primarily for training rather than primarily for inner needs.] While others (Agar 1980:42 *n.* lists them, and cf. LeVine 1982) have advocated analytic training, the advice has made no great impact (Pelto and Pelto 1973). Given the difficulties, one is tempted to throw up his hands and say, "Here are your cultural biases; for the rest of it, go to a shrink" (Agar 1980:42). That is not necessarily prescribed: read on.
2. See Tuzin (1975), who demonstrated this in his study of Ilahita Arapesh.
3. See Herdt (1981:142–144) on Nilutwo's dreaming.
4. Cf. Herdt (1987d) for an attempt to see Nilutwo's dreaming in the context of Sambian and Freudian dream theory.
5. Malcolm's (1984:18) quote concerns an analyst who is: "following Freud's directive to listen with 'closely hovering attention' in order to put himself in a position to make use of everything he is told for the purposes of recognizing the concealed unconscious material."
6. H: Perhaps nothing in a footnote, or our work, or the opinions of colleagues and friends will change such views. But as an anthropologist, I am aware enough of the culture of anthropology and of cultural rules regarding scholarly writing in

America, to be warned about this point. Such opinions, too, are culturally shaped: what Americans may regard as exuberant performance, Europeans will see as exhibitionism. (See Bateson 1972. Though remember the response to Freud's *The Interpretation of Dreams*, so long ago.)

7. The word "truly" is a necessary redundancy, because, to use today's jargon, the genre conventions and tropes of ethnography have seemed to change. Now, to be in vogue, one should self-confess without truly disclosing oneself (which would be gauche). Crapanzano (1980) and Kracke (1987) are exceptions to this. Many writing in the interpretative ethnography field (Clifford and Marcus 1985) are not: their sense of disclosure is, if I recall Umberto Eco's medieval metaphor correctly, more like viewing a tapestry from its underside.

8. A recent review of education in cultural psychiatry (Moffic et al. 1987) shows this.

9. Again: Powdermaker (1966).

10. Recent issues of the *American Anthropological Association Newsletter* discuss the ethical sides of fictitious cases.

11. Some advocate "clinical anthropology"—anthropologists doing psychotherapy and making interventions—which raises issues beyond our purview here, for we did not try for treatment. I cannot see, however, that anthropologists differ from psychologists in requiring extended and supervised clinical training in formal and supervised settings before doing treatment anywhere. (See *Open Forum: Clinical Anthropology*, 1980–81.)

12. H: Warwick (1980) suggests that the key to ethical training in social science is the building of professional responsibility in students. I would add that such responsibility is internalized when the student believes there are no pat or impersonal solutions to ethical dilemmas in fieldwork; so care and patience are wonderful assistance always in these situations.

13. Not Hegel's history. Our view of mental life is the opposite of Hegel's tub-thumping idealism: "In Hegel's philosophy, history has a purpose. It is the march of Mind toward freedom. The chief barrier to freedom is the fact that Mind does not understand that it is a unity ['Mind' here is probably the same 'Self' that is being promoted these days] and as such, master of its destiny. Instead, the individual minds of human beings—which are all really manifestations of Mind—see themselves as separate, and often opposed, entities. From this comes the alienation and unhappiness that exists in this world" (P. Singer 1980). (As Popper 1971 knows, such sentiments argue for a unitary viewpoint by all people: totalitarianism.)

BIBLIOGRAPHY

Aberle, David F. 1951. *The Psychosocial Analysis of a Hopi Life-History*. Berkeley: University of California Press

Adam, Barry D. 1986. Age, Structure, and Sexuality: Reflections on the Anthropological Evidence on Homosexual Relations. In E. Blackwood, ed., *Anthropology and Homosexual Behavior*, pp. 19–34. New York: Harrington Park Press.

Agar, Michael H. 1980. *The Professional Stranger*. New York: Academic Press.

—— 1982. Toward an Ethnographic Language. *American Anthropologist* 84:779–795.

Alland, Alexander Jr. 1970. *Adaptation in Cultural Evolution*. New York: Columbia University Press.

Allen, Michael R. 1967. *Male Cults and Secret Initiations in Melanesia*. Melbourne: Melbourne University Press.

Ardener, Edwin. 1975. Belief and the Problem of Women [and] the 'Problem' Revised. In S. Ardener, ed., *Perceiving Women*, pp. 1–27. London: Malaby Press.

Asad, T., ed. 1973. Introduction. *Anthropology and the Colonial Encounter*, pp. 9–19. New York: Humanities Press.

Ashley-Montagu, M. F. 1937. *Coming into Being Among the Australian Aborigines*. London: Routledge.

Atkinson, Jane M. 1982. Anthropology. *Signs* 8:236–258.

Barnes, J. A. 1967. Some Ethical Problems in Modern Field Work. In D. G. Jongmans and P. C. W. Gutkind, eds., *Anthropologists in the Field*, pp. 193–213. Assen: VanGorum.

Barth, Frederik. 1974. On Responsibility to Humanity. *Current Anthropology* 15:99–102.

—— 1975. *Ritual and Knowledge Among the Baktaman of New Guinea*. New Haven: Yale University Press.

Barzun, Jacques. 1981. The Wasteland of American Education. *The New York Review of Books*, 28(17):34–36.

Bateson, Gregory. 1942 (1972). Experiments in Thinking About Observed Ethnological Material. *Steps to an Ecology of Mind*, pp. 73–87. New York: Ballantine Books.

—— 1944. Pidgin English and Cross-Cultural Communication. *Transactions of the New York Academy of Science*, Series 2, 6:137–141.

439

——1949. Bali: The Value System of a Steady State. In M. Fortes, ed., *Social Structure: Essays Presented to A. R. Radcliffe-Brown*, pp. 35–53. Oxford: Clarendon Press.

——1958. *Naven*. 2d ed. Stanford: Stanford University Press.

——1972. *Steps to an Ecology of Mind*. San Francisco: Chandler and Sharp.

——1976. Some Components of Socialization for Trance. In T. Schwartz, ed., *Socialization as Cultural Communication*, pp. 51–63. Berkeley: University of California Press.

——1978. Toward a Theory of Cultural Coherence: Comment. *Anthropological Quarterly* 51:77–78.

Bateson, Gregory and Margaret Mead. 1942. *Balinese Character: A Photographic Analysis*. Special Publications of the New York Academy of Sciences, vol. 2.

Becker, Ernest. 1973. *The Denial of Death*. New York: Free Press.

Bellow, Saul. 1982. *The Dean's December*. New York: Pocket Books.

Benedict, Ruth. 1934. *Patterns of Culture*. Boston: Houghton Mifflin.

——1938. Continuities and Discontinuities in Cultural Conditioning. *Psychiatry* 1:161–167.

——1946. *The Chrysanthemum and the Sword*. Boston: Houghton Mifflin.

Bennett, John W. 1946. The Interpretation of Pueblo Culture: A Question of Values. *Southwestern Journal of Anthropology* 2:361–374.

Berndt, Ronald Murray. 1965. The Kamano, Usurufa, Jate and Fore of the Eastern Highlands. In P. Lawrence and M. J. Meggitt, eds., *Gods, Ghosts, and Men in Melanesia*, pp. 78–104. Melbourne: Melbourne University Press.

Bertrand, William and Charles Kleymeyer. 1977. Misapplied Cross-Cultural Research: A Case Study of an Ill Fated Family Planning Research Project. In M. Stacey, M. Reid, C. Heath, and R. Dingwall, eds., *Health and the Division of Labor*, pp. 215–236. New York: Prodist.

Bettelheim, Bruno. 1955. *Symbolic Wounds, Puberty Rites and the Envious Male*. New York: Collier Books.

——1984. *Freud and Man's Soul*. New York: Vintage Books.

Blackwood, Beatrice. 1979. *Kukukuku of the Upper Watut*. C. R. Hallpike, ed. Oxford: Pitt-Rivers Museum.

Blackwood, Evelyn, ed. 1986. *Anthropology and Homosexual Behavior*. New York: Harrington Park Press.

Boas, Franz. 1920. The Method of Ethnology. *American Anthropologist* 22:311–321.

Bock, Philip K. 1969. *Modern Cultural Anthropology: An Introduction*. New York: Knopf.

Bohannan, Paul. 1979. You Can't Do Nothing. *American Anthropologist* 82:508–524.

Bowen, Elenore S. (pseudonym). 1954. *Return to Laughter*. New York: Doubleday, Natural History Press.

Bourguignon, Erika. 1979. *Psychological Anthropology*. New York: Holt, Rinehart, and Winston.

Briggs, Jean L. 1970. *Never in Anger: Portrait of an Eskimo Family*. Cambridge: Harvard University Press.

Brody, Eugene B. 1980. The Relevance of Cultural Anthropology for Psychoanalysis. *The Academy Forum* 24:7–10.

Brown, Paula. 1978. *Highland Peoples of New Guinea*. Cambridge: Cambridge University Press.

Brown, Paula and Georgeda Buchbinder. 1976. Introduction. In P. Brown and

G. Buchbinder, eds., *Man and Woman in the New Guinea Highlands*, pp. 1–12. Washington, D.C.: American Anthropological Association.

Brown, Penelope and S. Levinson. 1978. Universals in Language Usage: Politeness Phenomena. In E. N. Goody, ed., *Questions and Politeness*, pp. 56–189. Cambridge: Cambridge University Press.

Burgess, Robert G., ed. 1982. *Field Research: A Sourcebook and Field Manual*. London: Allen and Unwin.

Carrier, Joseph. 1980. Homosexual Behavior in Cross-Cultural Perspective. In J. Marmor, ed., *Sexual Inversion*, pp. 100–122. New York: Basic Books.

Casagrande, Joseph B., ed. 1960. *In the Company of Man: Twenty Portraits of Anthropological Informants*. New York: Harper.

Chagnon, Napoleon A. 1968. *Yanomamo: The Fierce People*. New York: Holt, Rinehart, and Winston.

Chalmers, James Rev. 1903. Notes on the Bugilia, British New Guinea. *Journal of the Royal Anthropological Institute* 33:108–110.

Chapple, Eliot D. 1952. The Training of the Professional Anthropologist: Social Anthropology and Applied Anthropology. *American Anthropologist* 54:340–342.

Chodorow, Nancy. 1978. *The Reproduction of Mothering*. Berkeley: University of California Press.

Chowning, Ann. 1980. Culture and Biology Among the Sengseng of New Britain. *Journal of Polynesian Society* 89:7–31.

Clay, Brenda. 1975. *Pinikindu*. Chicago: University of Chicago Press.

Clifford, James. 1986. Introduction: Partial Truths. In J. Clifford and G. Marcus, eds., *Writing Culture*, pp. 1–26. Berkeley: University of California Press.

Clifford, James and George Marcus, eds. 1986. *Writing Culture*. Berkeley: University of California Press.

Cohler, Bertram. 1982. Personal Narrative and Life Course. In B. Baltes and O. G. Brim, Jr., eds., *Life-Span Development and Behavior*, 44:205–241. New York: Academic Press.

Cole, Michael. 1975. An Ethnographic Psychology of Cognition. In R. W. Brislin, ed., *Cross-Cultural Perspectives on Learning*, pp. 157–174. New York: Wiley.

Collier, Jane F. and Michelle Z. Rosaldo. 1981. Politics and Gender in Simple Societies. In S. B. Ortner and H. Whitehead, eds., *Sexual Meanings*, pp. 275–329. Cambridge: Cambridge University Press.

Counts, Dorothy, A. 1980. Fighting Back is not the Way: Suicide and the Women of Kaliai. *American Ethnologist* 7:332–351.

Crapanzano, Vincent. 1980. *Tuhami: Portrait of a Moroccan*. Chicago: University of Chicago Press.

——1986. "Hermes' Dilemma: The Masking of Subversion in Ethnographic Description. In J. Clifford and G. Marcus, eds., *Writing Culture*, pp. 51–76. Berkeley: University of California Press.

Creed, Gerald W. 1984. Sexual Subordination: Institutionalized Homosexuality and Social Control in Melanesia. *Ethnology* 23:157–176.

D'Andrade, Roy G. 1986. Three Scientific World Views and the Covering Law Model. In D. W. Fiske and R. A. Shweder, eds., *Metatheory in Social Science*, pp. 19–41. Chicago: University of Chicago Press.

Davenport, William H. 1965. Sexual Patterns and Their Regulation in a Society of the Southwest Pacific. In F. A. Beach, ed., *Sex and Behavior*, pp. 164–207. New York: Wiley.

Davidson, Arnold I. 1987. How to Do the History of Psychoanalysis: A Reading of

Freud's Three Essays on the Theory of Psychoanalysis. *Critical Inquiry*, 14:252–277.

DeMille, Richard. 1976. *Castaneda's Journey: The Power and the Allegory*. Santa Barbara: Capra.

Devereux, George. 1937. Institutionalized Homosexuality of the Mohave Indians. *Human Biology* 9:498–527.

—— 1951. *Reality and Dream: The Psychotherapy of a Plains Indian*. New York: International Universities Press.

—— 1957a. The Awarding of a Penis as a Compensation for Rape. *International Journal of Psycho-Analysis* 38:398–401.

—— 1957b. Dream Learning and Individual Ritual Differences in Mohave Shamanism. *American Anthropologist* 59:1036–1045.

—— 1967. *From Anxiety to Method in the Behavioral Sciences*. The Hague: Mouton.

—— 1978. The Works of George Devereux. In G. D. Spindler, ed., *The Making of Psychological Anthropology*, pp. 364–406. Berkeley: University of California Press.

—— 1980a. Normal and Abnormal. *Basic Problems of Ethno-psychiatry*, pp. 3–71. Chicago: University of Chicago Press.

—— 1980b. *Basic Problems of Ethno-psychiatry*. Trans. B. M. Gulati and G. Devereux. Chicago: University of Chicago Press.

Doi, Takeo. 1973. *The Anatomy of Dependence*. Tokyo: Kodansha International.

—— In press. The Cultural Assumptions of Psychoanalysis. In J. Stigler et al., eds., *Cultural Psychology*. New York: Cambridge University Press.

Douglas, M. 1966. *Purity and Danger*. London: Routledge & Kegan Paul.

—— 1970. *Natural Symbols*. New York: Pantheon Books.

Dover, Kenneth J. 1978. *Greek Homosexuality*. Cambridge, Mass.: Harvard University Press.

Dubois, Cora. 1944. *The People of Alor. A Socio-Psychological Study of an East Indian Island*. Minneapolis: University of Minnesota Press.

Dumont, Jean-Paul. 1978. *The Headman and I*. Austin: University of Texas Press.

Durkheim, Émile. 1965. (English trans. orig. 1915). *The Elementary Forms of the Religious Life*. Trans. J. W. Swain. New York: The Free Press.

Edgerton, Robert B. 1985. *Rules, Exceptions, and Social Order*. Berkeley: University of California Press.

Edgerton, Robert B. and L. L. Langness. 1974. *Methods and Styles in the Study of Culture*. San Francisco: Chandler and Sharp.

Edsall, John T. 1981. Two Aspects of Scientific Responsibility. *Science* 212:11–14.

Elkin, A. P. 1953. Delayed Exchange in Wabag Sub-District, Central Highlands of New Guinea. *Oceania* 33:161–201.

Ellis, Havelock. 1910 (1936). *Studies in the Psychology of Sex*, vol. I. New York: Random House.

Epstein, T. Scarlett. 1979. Mysore Villages Revisited. In G. M. Foster et al., eds., *Long-Term Field Research in Social Anthropology*, pp. 209–226. New York: Academic Press.

Erikson, Erik. 1958. The Nature of Clinical Evidence. *Daedalus* 87:65–87.

Evans-Pritchard, E. E. 1937. *Witchcraft, Oracles, and Magic Among the Azande*. Oxford: Oxford University Press.

—— 1956. *Nuer Religion*. Oxford: Clarendon Press.

—— 1962. *Social Anthropology and Other Essays*. New York: Free Press.

Faithorn, Elizabeth. 1975. The Concept of Pollution Among the Kafe of Papua New

Guinea. In R. R. Reiter, ed., *Toward an Anthropology of Women*, pp. 127–140. New York: Monthly Review Press.

——1976. Women as Persons: Aspects of Female Life and Male-Female Relations Among the Kafe. In P. Brown and G. Buchbinder, eds., *Man and Woman in the New Guinea Highlands*, pp. 86–95. Washington, D.C.: American Anthropological Association.

Federn, Paul. 1952. *Ego Psychology and the Psychoses.* New York: Basic Books.

Feil, Daryl K. 1978. Women and Men in the Enga Tee. *American Ethnologist* 5:263–279.

Firth, Raymond. 1981. Spiritual Aroma: Religion and Politics. Distinguished Lecture for 1980. *American Anthropologist* 83:582–605.

Forge, Anthony. 1972. The Lonely Anthropologist. In S. Kimball and J. B. Watson, eds., *Crossing Cultural Boundaries*, pp. 292–297. San Francisco: Chandler.

Fortes, Meyer. 1945. *The Dynamics of Clanship Among the Tallensi.* Oxford University Press for the International African Institute.

——1974. Social Anthropology at Cambridge since 1900. In R. Darnell, ed., *Readings in the History of Anthropology*, pp. 426–439. London: Harper & Row.

Fortune, Reo F. 1932. *Sorcerers of Dobu.* London: George Routledge.

——1939. Arapesh Warfare. *American Anthropologist* 41:22–41.

——1947. The Rules of Relationship Behavior in One Variety of Primitive Warfare. *Man* 47:108–110.

Foster, George M. 1969. *Applied Anthropology.* Boston: Little, Brown.

Foster, George M., Elizabeth Colson, Thayer Scudder, and Robert V. Kemper. 1979. Conclusion: The Long-term Study in Perspective. In G. M. Foster et al., eds., *Long-Term Field Research in Social Anthropology* pp. 323–348. New York: Academic Press.

Foucault, Michel. 1973. *The Birth of the Clinic.* Trans. A. M. S. Smith. New York: Pantheon Books.

——1980. *The History of Sexuality.* Trans. R. Hurley. New York: Pantheon Books.

Foulks, Edward F. 1977. Anthropology and Psychiatry: A New Blending of an Old Relationship. In E.F. Foulks et al., eds., *Current Perspectives in Cultural Psychiatry*, pp. 5–18. New York: Spectrum.

Frake, Charles O. 1969. Notes on Queries in Ethnography. In S. A. Tyler, ed., *Cognitive Anthropology*, pp. 123–137. New York: Holt, Rinehart and Winston.

Freeman, J. Derek. 1970. Human Nature and Culture. In D. Slayer, ed, *Man and the New Biology*, pp. 50–75. Canberra, Australia: Australian National University Press.

——1983. *Margaret Mead and Samoa.* Cambridge: Harvard University Press.

Freilich, Morris, ed. 1977. *Marginal Natives: Anthropologists at Work.* New York: Schenkman.

Freud, A. 1965. *Normality and Pathologoy in Childhood.* New York: International Universities Press.

Freud, Sigmund. *Standard Edition of the Complete Psychological Works of Sigmund Freud.* 24 vols. James Strachey, ed. and tr. London: Hogarth Press, 1953–1974; New York: Macmillan.

——1900. *The Interpretation of Dreams.* In *Standard Edition* 4–5:339–627.

——1905. *Three Essays on the Theory of Sexuality.* In *Standard Edition* 7:125–245.

——1913. *Totem and Taboo.* In *Standard Edition* 13:ix–162.

——1926. The Question of Lay Analysis. In *Standard Edition* 20:183–250.

——1927. The Future of an Illusion. In *Standard Edition* 21:3–57.

——1937(1938). Analysis Terminable and Interminable. In *Standard Edition* 23:211–253.

Friedl, Ernestine. 1975. *Men and Women in Cross-Cultural Perspective.* New York: Holt, Rinehart and Winston.

Garfinkel, Harold. 1967. *Studies in Ethnomethodology.* Englewood Cliffs, N.J.: Prentice-Hall.

Geertz, Clifford. 1960. *The Religion of Java.* Chicago: University of Chicago Press.

——1966. *Person, Time and Conduct in Bali: An Essay in Cultural Analysis.* Yale Southeast Asia Program, Cultural Report No. 14. New Haven: Yale University Press.

——1968. *Islam Observed.* New Haven: Yale University Press.

——1973. Thick Description: Toward An Interpretive Theory of Cultures. In *The Interpretation of Cultures: Selected Essays by C. Geertz*, pp. 3–30. New York: Basic Books.

——1976. From the Native's Point of View: On the Nature of Anthropological Understanding. In K. Basso and H. Selby, eds. *Meaning in Anthropology*, pp. 221–237. Albuquerque, N.M.: School for American Research and University of New Mexico Press.

——1983. *Local Knowledge.* New York: Basic Books.

——1984. Distinguished Lecture: Anti Anti-Relativism. *American Anthropologist* 86:263–278.

——1988. *Works and Lives.* Stanford: Stanford University Press.

Gell, Alfred. 1975. *Metamorphosis of the Cassowaries.* London: Athlone Press.

Gewertz, Deborah. 1982. Deviance Unplaced: The Story of Kaviwon Reconsidered. In F. J. P. Poole and G. H. Herdt, eds., *Sexual Antagonism, Gender, and Social Change in Papua New Guinea, Social Analysis* 12:29–35.

——1983. *Sepik River Societies.* New Haven: Yale University Press.

Giddens, Anthony. 1976. *New Rules of Sociological Method: A Positive Critique of Interpretive Sociologies.* New York: Basic Books.

Gill, Merton M. 1982. *Analysis of Transference*, vol. 1. New York: International Universities Press.

Gill, Merton M. and I. Z. Hoffman. 1982. *Analysis of Transference*, vol. 2. New York: International Universities Press.

Gladwin, Thomas. 1953. The Role of Man and Woman on Truk: A Problem in Personality and Culture. *Transactions of the New York Academy of Science:* 305–309.

Glasse, R. M. and M. J. Meggitt. 1969. *Pigs, Pearlshells, and Women.* Englewood Cliffs, N.J.: Prentice-Hall.

Gluckman, Max. 1967. Introduction. In A. L. Epstein, ed., *The Craft of Social Anthropology*, pp. xi–xx. London: Tavistock Publications.

——1969 (1956). The License in Ritual. In *Custom and Conflict in Africa*, pp. 109–136. New York: Barnes and Noble.

Goffman, Erving. 1974. *Frame Analysis.* Cambridge: Harvard University Press.

Godelier, Maurice. 1982. Social Hierarchies Among the Baruya of New Guinea. In A. Strathern, ed., *Inequality in New Guinea Highland Societies*, pp. 3–34. Cambridge: Cambridge University Press.

——1986. *The Production of Great Men.* Trans. R. Swyer. Cambridge: Cambridge University Press.

Golde, Peggy, ed. 1970. *Women in the Field.* Chicago: Aldine.

Gregor, Thomas. 1985. *Anxious Pleasures*. Chicago: University of Chicago Press.

Gronewald, Sylvia. 1972. Did Frank Hamilton Cushing Go Native? In S. T. Kimball and J. B. Watson, eds., *Crossing Cultural Boundaries*, pp. 33–50. San Francisco: Chandler.

Gutkind, Peter. 1967. Orientation and Research Methods in African Urban Studies. In D. G. Jongmans and P. Gutkind, eds., *Anthropologists in the Field*. Assen: Van Gorcum.

Habermas, Jurgen. 1971. *Knowledge and Human Interests*. Trans. J. J. Shapiro. Boston: Beacon Press.

Haddon, Alfred Cort. 1901. *Headhunters: Black, White, and Brown*. London: Methuen.

——1924. Introduction. In J. Holmes, *Primitive New Guinea*, pp. i–xii. London: Macmillan.

Haldipur, C. V. 1980. The Idea of "Cultural" Psychiatry: A Comment on the Foundations of Cultural Psychiatry. *Comprehensive Psychiatry* 21:206–211.

Hallowell, A. Irving. 1967. The Self and Its Behavior Environment. In *Culture and Experience*, pp. 75–110. New York: Schocken Books.

Hallpike, C. R. Fundamentalist Interpretations of Primitive Man. *Man* 8:451–470.

Harris, Marvin. 1964. *The Nature of Cultural Things*. New York: Random House.

Hayano, David M. 1982. Models for Alcohol Use and Drunkenness Among the Awa, Eastern Highlands. In M. Marshall, ed., *Through a Glass Darkly: Beer and Modernization in Papua, New Guinea*, pp. 217–226. Port Moresby: Institute of Applied Social and Economic Research.

Healey, Alan. 1964. *Handling Unsophisticated Linguistic Informants*. Series A, Occasional Papers No. 3. Canberra: Linguistic Circle of Canberra Publications.

Heider, Karl. 1976. Dani Sexuality: A Low Energy System. *Man* 11:188–201.

——1979. *Grand Valley Dani: Peaceful Warriors*. New York: Holt, Rinehart and Winston.

Herdt, Gilbert H. 1977. The Shaman's 'Calling' Among the Sambia of New Guinea. *Journal de la Société des Océanistes* (special issue) 33:153–167.

——1980. Semen Depletion and the Sense of Maleness. *Ethnopsychiatrica* 3:79–116.

——1981. *Guardians of the Flutes*. New York: McGraw-Hill.

——1982a. Fetish and Fantasy in Sambia Initiation. In G. Herdt, ed., *Rituals of Manhood: Male Initiation in Papua New Guinea*, pp. 48–98. Berkeley: University of California Press.

——1982b. Sambia Nose-Bleeding Rites and Male Proximity to Women. *Ethos* 10(3):189–231.

——1982c. Uses and Abuses of Alcohol and the Urban Adjustment of Sambia Masculine Identity. In M. Marshall, ed., *Through A Glass Darkly: Beer and Modernization in Papua New Guinea*, pp. 227–241. Port Moresby: Institute of Applied Social and Economic Research.

——1984. Ritualized Homosexual Behavior in the Male Cults of Melanesia, 1862–1983: An Introduction. In G. Herdt, ed., *Ritualized Homosexuality in Melanesia*, pp. 1–82. Berkeley: University of California Press.

——1985. Review: *Oedipus in the Trobriands*, by Melford Spiro. In *American Anthropologist* 87:205–207.

——1986. Madness and Sexuality in the New Guinea Highlands. *Social Research* (special issue on Sexuality and Madness) 53:349–368.

——1987a. The Accountability of Sambia Initiates. In L. L. Langness and

T. E. Hays, eds., *Anthropology in the High Valleys: Essays in Honor of K. E. Read*, pp. 237–282. Novato, Calif.: Chandler and Sharp.

——1987b. Homosexuality. In *The Encyclopedia of Religion*, 6:445–452 (15 vols.). New York: Macmillan.

——1987c. *The Sambia: Ritual and Gender in New Guinea*. New York: Holt, Rinehart and Winston.

——1987d. Selfhood and Discourse in Sambia Dream Sharing. In B. Tedlock, ed., *Dreaming: Anthropological and Psychological Interpretations*. Albuquerque: School for American Research and University of New Mexico Press.

——1987e. Transitional Objects in Sambia Initiation Rites. *Ethos* 15:40–57.

——1988. The Ethnographer's Choices. In G. N. Appell and T. N. Madan, eds., *Choice and Morality in Anthropological Perspective*, pp. 159–192. Albany, N.Y.: State University of New York Press.

——n.d. Sexual Repression, Social Control, and Gender Hierarchy in Sambia Culture. In Barbara Miller, ed., *Gender Hierarchies*. New York: Wenner-Gren Foundation for Anthropological Research.

Herdt, G. and J. Davidson. 1988. The Sambia "Turnim-Man": Sociocultural and Clinical Aspects of Gender Formation in Male Pseudohermaphrodites with 5-Alpha Reductase Deficiency in Papua New Guinea. *Archives of Sexual Behavior* 17(1):33–56.

Herdt, Gilbert H. and Fitz John P. Poole. 1982. Sexual Antagonism: The Intellectual History of a Concept in the Anthropology of Melanesia. In F. J. P. Poole and G. H. Herdt, eds., "Sexual Antagonism," Gender, and Social Change in Papua New Guinea. *Social Analysis* (special issue) 12:3–28.

Herdt, Gilbert H. and Robert J. Stoller. 1985. Sakulambei—A Hermaphrodite's Secret: An Example of Clinical Ethnography. *Psychoanalytic Study of Society* 11:117–158.

——1987. The Effect of Supervision on the Practice of Ethnography. In H. P. Duerr, ed, *Die wilde Seele Zur Ethnopsychoanalyse von Georges Devereux*. Frankfurt: Suhrkamp, pp. 177–199.

Herdt, Gilbert H., ed. 1982. *Rituals of Manhood: Male Initiation in New Guinea*. Berkeley: University of California Press.

——1984. *Ritualized Homosexuality in Melanesia*. Berkeley: University of California Press.

Hogbin, Ian. 1970. *The Island of Menstruating Men*. Scranton, Pa: Chandler.

Honigmann, John Joseph. 1967. *Personality in Culture*. New York: Harper and Row.

Hymes, Dell. 1974. *Reinventing Anthropology*. New York: Vintage Books.

Imperato-McGinley, Julianne, J. Guerrero, T. Gautier, et al. 1974. Steroid 5-Alpha Reductase Deficiency in Man: An Inherited Form of Male Pseudo-Hermaphroditism. *Science* 186:1213–1243.

Kaberry, Phyllis. 1957. Malinowski's Contribution to Field-Work Methods and the Writing of Ethnography. In R. Firth, ed., *Man and Culture*, pp. 71–91. New York: Humanities Press.

Kakar, Sudhir. 1983. *Shamans, Mystics and Doctors*. Boston: Beacon.

——1985. Psychoanalysis and Non-Western Cultures. *International Review of Psycho-Analysis* 12:441–448.

——1986. Psychotherapy and Culture: Healing in the Indian Culture. In M. I. White and S. Pollak, eds., *The Cultural Transition*, pp. 9–23. Boston: Routledge & Kegan Paul.

Kardiner, Abram. 1939. *The Individual and His Society*. New York: Columbia University Press.

—— 1945. *The Psychological Frontiers of Society*. New York: Columbia University Press.

Katchadourian, Herant A. and Donald T. Lunde. 1980. *Fundamentals of Human Sexuality*. 3rd edition. New York: Holt, Rinehart, and Winston.

Keesing, Roger M. 1979. Linguistic Knowledge and Cultural Knowledge: Some Doubts and Speculations. *American Anthropologist* 81:14–36.

—— 1982. Introduction. In G. H. Herdt, ed., *Rituals of Manhood*, pp. 1–43. Berkeley: University of California Press.

Kelly, Raymond. 1976. Witchcraft and Sexual Relations: An Exploration in the Social and Semantic Implications of a Structure of Belief. In P. Brown and G. Buchbinder, eds., *Man and Woman in the New Guinea Highlands*, pp. 36–53. Washington, D.C.: American Anthropological Association.

—— 1977. *Etoro Social Structure*. Ann Arbor: University of Michigan Press.

Kiki, Albert M. 1968. *Kiki: Ten Thousand Years in a Lifetime*. New York: Praeger.

Kimball Solon Toothaker and James Bennett Watson, eds. 1972. *Crossing Cultural Boundaries: The Anthropological Experience*. San Francisco: Chandler.

Kluckhohn, Clyde et al. 1945. *The Personal Document in History, Anthropology, and Sociology*. New York: Social Science Research Council Bulletin, no. 53, pp. 79–174.

Kleinman, Arthur. 1980. *Patients and Healers in the Context of Culture*. Berkeley: University of California Press.

Knauft, Bruce M. 1987. Homosexuality in Melanesia. *Journal of Psychoanalytic Anthropology* 10:155–191.

Koch, Klaus-F. 1974. *War and Peace in Jalemo*. Cambridge: Harvard University Press.

Kohut, Heinz. 1971. *The Analysis of the Self*. New York: International Universities Press.

Kracke, Waud H. 1980. Amazonian Interviews: Dreams of a Bereaved Father. *The Annual of Psychoanalysis* 8:249–267.

—— 1987. Encounter with Other Cultures: Psychological and Epistemological Aspects. *Ethos* 15:58–81.

Kracke, Waud and Gilbert Herdt. 1987. Introduction. In *Interpretation in Psychoanalytic Anthropology*. Special issue of *Ethos* 15:3–7.

Kroeber, Alfred L. 1948. *Anthropology*. Rev. ed. New York: Harcourt, Brace.

La Barre, Weston. 1978. The Clinic and the Field. In G. D. Spindler, ed., *The Making of Psychological Anthropology*, pp. 259–299. Berkeley: University of California.

La Farge, Oliver. 1929. *Laughing Boy*. Boston: Houghton Mifflin.

Langer, Suzanne K. 1951. *Philosophy in a New Key*. New York: Mentor Books.

—— 1967. *Mind: An Essay on Human Feeling*. Baltimore: Johns Hopkins University Press.

Langness, L. L. 1967. Sexual Antagonism in the New Guinea Highlands: A Bena Bena Example. *Oceania* 37:161–177.

—— 1976. Discussion. In P. Brown and G. Buchbinder, eds., *Man and Woman in the New Guinea Highlands*, pp. 96–106. Washington, D.C.: American Anthropological Association.

—— 1981. Child Abuse and Cultural Values: The Case of New Guinea. In Jill E.

Corbin, ed., *Child Abuse and Neglect: Cross-Cultural Perspectives*, pp. 13–34. Berkeley: University of California Press.

Langness, L. L. and Gelya Frank. 1981. *Lives*. Navato: Chandler & Sharp.

Lanternari, Vittorio. 1963. *The Religions of the Oppressed*. Trans. L. Sergis. New York: Knopf.

Lawrence, Peter. 1965–66. The Garia of the Madang District. *Anthropological Forum* 1:371–392.

Leach, E. R. 1954. *Political Systems of Highland Burma*. London: G. Bell.

—— 1958. The Epistemological Background of Malinowski's Empiricism. In R. Firth, ed., *Man and Culture*, pp. 119–137. New York: Humanities Press.

—— 1961a. *Pul Eliya*. Cambridge: Cambridge University Press.

—— 1961b. Two Essays Concerning the Symbolic Representation of Time. In *Rethinking Anthropology*, pp. 124–136. London: Athlone Press.

—— 1966. Virgin Birth. *Proceedings of the Royal Anthropological Institute for Great Britain and Northern Ireland for 1965*, pp. 39–50.

—— 1976. *Culture and Communication*. Cambridge: Cambridge University Press.

Leenhardt, Maurice. 1979. *Do Kamo*. Trans. B. M. Gulati. Chicago: University of Chicago Press.

Levine, F. J. 1979. On the Clinical Application of Heinz Kohut's Psychology of the Self. *Journal of the Philadelphia Association for Psychoanalysis* 6:1–19.

LeVine, Robert A. 1966. Outsider's Judgments: An Ethnographic Approach to Group Differences in Personality. *Southwestern Journal of Anthropology* 22:101–116.

—— 1982. (1973). *Culture, Behavior and Personality*. 2d ed. New York: Aldine.

—— In press. Beyond the Average Expected Environment of Psychoanalysis: Cross-Cultural Evidence on Mother–Child Interaction. In J. Stigler, R. Shweder, and G. Herdt, eds., *Cultural Psychology*. New York: Cambridge University Press.

LeVine, Sarah. 1981. Dreams of the Informant About the Researcher: Some Difficulties Inherent in the Research Relationship. *Ethos* 9:276–293.

Lévi-Strauss, Claude. 1949. *Les Structures Elémentaires de la Parenté*. Paris: Presses Universitaires de France.

—— 1963. *Totemism*. Trans. R. Needham. Boston: Beacon Press.

—— 1966. *The Savage Mind*. Chicago: University of Chicago Press.

—— 1967. *Structural Anthropology*. Trans. C. Jacobson and B. G. Schoepf. Garden City, N.Y.: Anchor Books.

—— 1969. *Tristes Tropiques*. Trans. J. Russell. New York: Atheneum.

Levy, Robert I. 1973. *The Tahitians*. Chicago: University of Chicago Press.

Lewis, Oscar. 1951. *Life in a Mexican Village*. Urbana: University of Illinois Press.

—— 1965. *La Vida: A Puerto Rican Family in the Culture of Poverty—San Juan and New York*. New York: Vintage Books.

Lindenbaum, Shirley. 1972. Sorcerers, Ghosts, and Polluting Women: An Analysis of Religious Belief and Population Control. *Ethnology* 11:241–253.

—— 1979. *Kuru Sorcery*. Palo Alto: Mayfield.

Lipuma, E. 1981. Cosmology and Economy Among the Maring of Highland New Guinea. *Oceania* 51:266–285.

Littlewood, Roland. 1980. Anthropology and Psychiatry—An Alternative Approach. *British Journal of Medical Psychology* 53:213–225.

MacCannel, Dean. 1976. *The Tourist*. New York: Schocken.

McDowell, Nancy. 1980. The Oceanic Ethnography of Margaret Mead. *American Anthropologist* 82:278–303.

Mahapatra, S. B. and M. Hamilton. 1974. Examinations for Foreign Psychiatrists: Problems of Language. *British Journal of Medical Education* 8:271–274.

Mailer, Norman. 1980. *New York Times Book Review,* May 11.

Malcolm, Janet. 1984. The Patient Is Always Right. *New York Review of Books.* December 20:13–18.

——1985. *In the Freud Archives.* New York: Vintage Books.

Malcolm, L. A. 1969. Determination of the Growth Curve of the Kukukuku People of New Guinea From Dental Eruption in Children and Adult Height. *Archaelogy and Physical Anthropology in Oceania* 4:72–78.

——1970. Growth, Malnutrition and Mortality of the Infant and Toddler in the Asai Valley of the New Guinea Highlands. *American Journal of Clinical Nutrition* 23:1090–1095.

Malinowski, Bronislau. 1913. *The Family Among the Australian Aborigines.* London: University of London Press.

——1922. *Argonauts of the Western Pacific.* New York: E. P. Dutton.

——1926. *Crime and Custom in Savage Society.* Totowa, NJ: Littlefield, Adams.

——1927. *Sex and Repression in Savage Society.* Cleveland: Meridian Books.

——1929. *The Sexual Life of Savages in North-Western Melanesia.* New York: Harcourt, Brace and World.

——1935. *Coral Gardens and Their Magic.* 2 vols. London: Allen and Unwin.

——1954. (1948). *Magic, Science and Religion, and Other Essays.* Garden City, N.Y.: Doubleday Anchor Books.

——1967. *A Diary in the Strict Sense of the Term.* London: Routledge and Kegan Paul.

Marcos, Luis R. 1979. Effects of Interpreters on the Evaluation of Psychopathology in Non-English-Speaking Patients. *American Journal of Psychiatry* 136:171–174.

Marcus, George and D. Cushman. 1982. Ethnographies as Texts. *Annual Review of Anthropology* 11:25–69.

Marcus, George and Michael Fisher. 1986. *Anthropology as Cultural Critique.* Chicago: University of Chicago Press.

Marx, Karl. 1977. The Fetishism of Commodities and the Secret Thereof. In J. L. Dolgin, David Dolgin, S. Kemnitzer, and David M. Schneider. eds., *Symbolic Anthropology: A Reader in the Study of Symbols and Meanings,* pp. 245–253. New York: Columbia University Press.

Mead, Margaret. 1930 (1968). *Growing Up in New Guinea.* New York: Dell.

——1935. *Sex and Temperament in Three Primitive Societies.* New York: Morrow.

——1939. Native Languages as Field Work Tools. *American Anthropologist* 41:189–206.

——1949. *Male and Female: A Study of the Sexes in a Changing World.* New York: Morrow.

——1952. The Training of the Cultural Anthropologist. *American Anthropologist* 54:343–346.

——1956. *New Lives for Old, Cultural Transformation: Manus 1928–53.* New York: Morrow.

——1960a. Introduction. In M. Mead and R. Bunzel, eds. *The Golden Age of Anthropology,* pp. 1–12. New York: Braziller.

——1960b. Weaver of the Border. In J. B. Casagrande, ed., *In the Company of Man* pp. 176–210. New York: Harper.

——1961. Cultural Determinants of Sexual Behavior. In W. C. Young, ed., *Sex and Internal Secretions,* pp. 1433–79. Baltimore: Williams and Wilkins.

——1962. Retrospect and Prospects. In *Anthropology and Human Behavior*, pp. 115–149. Washington, D.C.: Anthropological Society of Washington.

——1968 (1940). *The Mountain Arapesh*. Garden City, N.Y.: Natural History Press.

——1970. Field Work in the Pacific Islands, 1925–1967. In Peggy Golde, ed., *Women in the Field*, pp. 293–331. Chicago: Aldine.

——1972. *Blackberry Winter: My Early Years*. New York: Morrow.

——1977. *Letters From the Field 1925–1975*. New York: Harper Colophone Books.

Mead, Margaret and Ruth Bunzel, eds. 1960. *The Golden Age of Anthropology*. New York: Braziller.

Meggitt, Mervyn. 1964. Male–Female Relationships in the Highlands of Australian New Guinea, in New Guinea: The Central Highlands. *American Anthropologist* 66 (part 2): 204–224.

——1965. *Desert People*. Chicago: University of Chicago Press.

——1974. Pigs Are Our Hearts. *Oceania* 44:165–203.

——1977. *Blood Is Their Argument*. Palo Alto, Calif.: Mayfield.

——1979. Reflections Occasioned by Continuing Anthropological Field Research Among the Enga of Papua New Guinea. In G. M. Foster, et al., *Long-Term Field Research in Social Anthropology*, pp. 107–125. New York: Academic Press.

Meigs, Anna. 1976. Male Pregnancy and the Reduction of Sexual Opposition in a New Guinea Highlands Society. *Ethnology* 25:393–407.

——1984. *Food, Sex, and Pollution: A New Guinea Religion*. New Brunswick: Rutgers University Press.

Meintel, Deidre A. 1973. Strangers, Homecomers, and Ordinary Men. *Anthropological Quarterly* 46:47–58.

Messenger, John C. 1969. *Inis Beag: Isle of Ireland*. New York: Holt, Rinehart, and Winston.

Milgram, Stanley. 1974. *Obedience to Authority: An Experimental View*. London: Tavistock.

Minol, Bernard. 1981. A Review of the Manus Sections of Letters From the Field 1925–1975, by Margaret Mead. *Research in Melanesia* 5:43–45.

Moerman, Daniel E. 1979. Anthropology of Symbolic Healing. *Cultural Anthropology* 20:59–80.

Moffic, H. Steven, Ernest A. Kendrick, James W. Lomax, and Kelly Reid. 1987. Education in Cultural Psychiatry in the United States. *Transcultural Psychiatric Research Review* 24:167–188.

Moraitis, G. 1981. The Psychoanalytic Study of the Editing Process: Its Application in the Interpretation of a Historical Document. *Annual of Psychoanalysis*: 237–263.

Muensterberger, Werner. 1974. Introduction. In *Children of the Desert*, by G. Roheim, pp. ix–xix. New York: Basic Books.

Munn, Nancy. 1973. *Walbiri Iconography: Graphic Representation and Cultural Symbolism in a Central Australian Society*. Ithaca: Cornell University Press.

Murray, J. H. P. 1912. *Papua or British New Guinea*. London: T. Fisher Unwin.

Murray, Stephen O. 1979. The Scientific Reception of Castaneda. *Contributions in Sociology* 8:189–196.

——1982. The Dissolution of "Classical Ethnoscience." *Journal of the History of the Behavioral Sciences* 18:163–175.

——1984. *Social Theory, Homosexual Realities*. New York: Gai Sabre Monographs.

Murphy, Jane M. and Alexander H. Leighton. 1965. *Approaches to Cross-Cultural Psychiatry*. Ithaca: Cornell University Press.

Murphy, Robert F. 1959. Social Structure and Sex Antagonism. *Southwestern Journal of Anthropology* 15:89–98.

Murphy, Yolanda and Robert F. Murphy. 1974. *Women of the Forest.* New York: Columbia University Press.

Nabokov, Peter. 1967. *Two Leggings: The Making of a Crow Warrior.* New York: Crowell.

Nader, Laura. 1970. From Anguish to Exultation. In P. Golde, ed., *Women in the Field,* pp. 97–116. Chicago: Aldine.

Naroll, Raoul. 1970. Data Quality in Cross-Cultural Surveys. In R. Naroll and R. Cohen, eds., *A Handbook of Method in Cultural Anthropology,* pp. 990–1003. New York: Columbia University Press.

Nauta, Doede. 1972. *The Meaning of Information.* Gravenhage: Mouton.

Newman, Phillip. 1964. Religious Belief and Ritual in a New Guinea Society. *American Anthropologist* 66 (part 2):257–272.

—— 1965. *Knowing the Gururumba.* New York: Holt, Rinehart and Winston.

Niles, J. 1950. The Kuman of the Chimbu Region, Central Highlands, New Guinea. *Oceania* 21:25–65.

Oberg, Kalvero. 1954. Culture Shock. *The Bobbs-Merrill Reprint Series in the Social Sciences,* no. A-329.

—— 1972. Contrasts in Field Work on Three Continents. In S. T. Kimball and J. B. Watson, eds., *Crossing Cultural Boundaries,* pp. 74–86. San Francisco: Chandler.

Obeyesekere, Gananath. 1981. *Medusa's Hair.* Chicago: University of Chicago Press.

Open Forum. 1981. Open Forum: Clinical Anthropology. *Medical Anthropology Newsletter* 12.

Ornston, D. 1982. Strachey's Influence: A Preliminary Influence. *International Journal of Psycho-Analysis* 63:409–426.

Ortner, Sherry and Harriet Whitehead, eds. 1981. *Sexual Meanings.* Cambridge: Cambridge University Press.

Owusu, Maxwell. 1978. Ethnography of Africa: The Usefulness of the Useless. *American Anthropologist* 80:310–334.

Panoff, M. 1968. The Notion of the Double-Self Among the Maenge. *Journal of Polymer Science* 77:275–295.

Parin, Paul, F. Morgenthaler, and G. Parin-Matthey. 1980. *Fear Thy Neighbors as Thyself.* Trans. Patricia Klamerth. Chicago: University of Chicago Press.

Parkinson, Richard. 1907. *Dreissig Jahre in der Sudsee: Land und Leute, sitten und Gebrauche in Bismarck Archipel und auf den deutschen Salmoninseln.* Stuttgart: Strecker and Schroder.

Parsons, Anne. 1969. On Psychoanalytic Training for Research Purposes. *Belief, Magic, and Anomie: Essays in Psychological Anthropology,* pp. 334–357. New York: Free Press.

Paul, Benjamin D. 1953. Inteview Techniques and Field Relationships. In A. L. Kroeber, ed., *Anthropology Today,* pp. 430–451. Chicago: University of Chicago Press.

Pelto, Pertti J. and Gretel H. Pelto. 1973. Ethnography: The Fieldwork Enterprise. In J. J. Honigmann, ed., *Handbook of Social and Cultural Anthropology,* pp. 241–288. Chicago: Rand-McNally.

Peters, Larry and Douglass Price-Williams. 1980. Towards An Experiential Analysis of Shamanism. *American Ethnologist* 7:397–418.

Pettit, Philip. 1977. *The Concept of Structuralism: A Critical Analysis*. Berkeley: University of California Press.

Piers, Gerhart and Milton B. Singer. 1953. *Shame and Guilt*. New York: Norton.

Polanyi, Michael. 1966. *The Tacit Dimension*. Garden City, N.Y.: Doubleday Anchor Books.

Poole, Fitz John P. 1981. Transforming "Natural" Women: Female Ritual Leaders and Gender Ideology Among Bimin-Kuskusmin. In S. B. Ortner and H. Whitehead, eds., *Sexual Meanings*, pp. 116–165. New York: Cambridge University Press.

—— 1982a. Cultural Significance of "Drunken Comportment" in a Non-Drinking Society: The Bimin-Kuskusmin of the West Sepik. In M. Marshall, ed., *Through A Glass Darkly: Beer and Modernization in Papua New Guinea*, pp. 189–210. Port Moresby: Institute of Applied Social and Economic Research.

—— 1982b. The Ritual Forging of Identity: Aspects of Person and Self in Bimin-Kuskusmin Male Initiation. In G. Herdt, ed., *Rituals of Manhood: Male Initiation in Papua New Guinea*, pp. 100–154. Berkeley: University of California Press.

Popper, Karl R. 1971. *The Open Society and Its Enemies*. Vol. 2: *Hegel and Marx*. Princeton: Princeton University Press.

Powdermaker, Hortense. 1966. *Stranger and Friend*. New York: Norton.

Price-Williams, Douglass. 1975. *Explorations in Cross-Cultural Psychology*. San Francisco: Chandler and Sharp.

Rabinow, Paul. 1977. *Reflections on Fieldwork in Morocco*. Berkeley: University of California Press.

Radcliffe-Brown, A. R. 1922. *The Andaman Islanders*. Cambridge: Cambridge University Press.

—— 1939. Taboo. Reprinted in *Structure and Function in Primitive Society*, pp. 133–152. London: Oxford University Press.

—— 1952. *Structure and Function in Primitive Society*. London: Oxford University Press.

Rappaport, Roy. 1968. *Pigs for the Ancestors*. New Haven: Yale University Press.

—— 1971. Ritual, Sanctity, and Cybernetics. *American Anthropologist* 73:59–76.

Read, K. E. 1951. The Gahuku-Gama of the Central Highlands, New Guinea. *South Pacific* 5:154–164.

—— 1952. Nama Cult of the Central Highlands, New Guinea. *Oceania* 23:1–25.

—— 1954. Cultures of the Central Highlands. *Southwestern Journal of Anthropology* 10:1–43.

—— 1955. Morality and the Concept of the Person Among the Gahuku-Gama. *Oceania* 25:233–282.

—— 1959. Leadership and Consensus in a New Guinea Society. *American Anthropologist* 61:425–436.

—— 1965. *The High Valley*. London: Allen Unwin.

—— 1980. *Other Voices*. Navato, Calif.: Chandler and Sharp.

—— 1984. The Nama Cult Recalled. In G. Herdt, ed., *Ritualized Homosexuality in Melanesia*, pp. 248–291. Berkeley: University of California Press.

—— 1986. *Return to the High Valley*. Berkeley: University of California Press.

Reay, Marie. 1959. *The Kuma*. Melbourne: Melbourne University Press.

—— 1964. Present-day Politics in the New Guinea Highlands. *American Anthropologist* 66:240–256.

—— 1966. Women in Traditional Society. In E. K. Fisk, ed., *New Guinea on the Threshold*, pp. 166–184. Canberra: Australian National University Press.

Redfield, Robert. 1930. *Tapoztlan, A Mexican Village.* Chicago: University of Chicago Press.

Reisman, Paul. 1977. *Freedom in Fulani Social Life.* Chicago: University of Chicago Press.

Reports. 1904–1935. *Reports of the Cambridge Expedition to the Torres Straits.* 6 vols. Cambridge: Cambridge University Press.

Ricoeur, Paul. 1970. *Freud and Philosophy: An Essay on Interpretation.* New Haven: Yale University Press.

—— 1977. The Question of Proof in Freud's Psychoanalytic Writings. *Journal of the American Psychoanalytic Association* 25:835–871.

—— 1978. Can There be a Scientific Concept of Ideology? In J. Bien, ed., *Phenomenology and the Social Sciences: A Dialogue,* pp. 44–59. The Hague: Martins Nijhoff.

—— 1979. Psychoanalysis and the Movement of Contemporary Culture. In P. Rabinow and William M. Sullivan, eds., *Interpretive Social Science,* pp. 301–339. Berkeley: University of California Press.

Rivers, W. H. R. 1914. *The History of Melanesian Society.* 2 vols. Cambridge: Cambridge University Press.

Robin, Robert. 1982. Revival Movements in the Southern Highlands Province of Papua New Guinea. *Oceania* 52:320–343.

Rodman, Margaret. 1979. Introduction. In M. Rodman and M. Cooper, eds., *The Pacification of Melanesia,* pp. 1–23. Ann Arbor: University of Michigan Press.

Roe, Anne. 1953. A Psychological Study of Eminent Psychologists and Anthropologists, and a Comparison with Biological and Physical Scientists. *Psychological Monographs* (American Psychological Association), no. 352:1–55.

Róheim, Geza. 1926. *Social Anthropology, A Psycho-Analytic Study and A History of Australian Totemism.* New York: Boni and Liveright.

—— 1932. Psychoanalysis of Primitive Culture Types. *International Journal of Psycho-Analysis* 13:1–224.

—— 1974. *Children of the Desert.* W. Muensterberger, ed. New York: Basic Books.

Rosaldo, Michelle Z. 1980. The Use and Abuse of Anthropology: Reflections on Feminism and Cross-Cultural Understanding. *Signs* 5:389–417.

Rosaldo, Michelle Z. and Louise Lamphere. 1974. Introduction. In M. Z. Rosaldo and L. Lamphere, eds., *Woman, Culture and Society,* pp. 1–15. Stanford: Stanford University Press.

Ross, Ellen and Rayna Rapp. 1981. Sex and Society: A Research Note From Social History and Anthropology. *Comparative Studies in Society and History* 23:51–72.

Rossi, Alice, ed. 1985. *Gender and the Life Course.* New York: Aldine.

Roustang, F. 1982. *Dire Mastery.* Baltimore and London: Johns Hopkins University Press.

Royal Anthropological Institute of Great Britain and Ireland. 1951. *Notes and Queries in Anthropology.* London: Routledge and Kegan Paul.

Rubin, Gayle. 1975. The Traffic in Women: Notes on the "Political Economy" of Sex. In Rayna R. Reiter, ed., *Toward an Anthropology of Women,* pp. 157–210. New York: Monthly Review Press.

Runciman, W. G. 1983. *A Treatise on Social Theory.* Vol. I: *The Methodology of Social Theory.* Cambridge: Cambridge University Press.

Sahlins, Marshall. 1963. Poor Man, Rich Man, Big Man, Chief. *Comparative Studies in Society and History* 5:205–213.

——1985. *Islands of History*. Chicago: University of Chicago Press.

Sapir, Edward. 1937. The Contribution of Psychiatry to an Understanding of Behavior in Society. *American Journal of Sociology* 42:862–870.

——1938. Why Cultural Anthropology Needs the Psychiatrist. *Psychiatry* 1:7–12.

——1949. *Selected Writings of Edward Sapir in Language, Culture, and Personality*, D. G. Mandelbaum, ed. Berkeley: University of California Press.

Schafer, Roy. 1976. *A New Language for Psychoanalysis*. New Haven: Yale University Press.

Schieffelin, E. L. 1976. *The Sorrow of the Lonely and the Burning of the Dancers*. New York: St. Martin's Press.

——1977. The Unseen Influence: Tranced Mediums as Historical Innovators. *Journal de la Société des Océanistes* 56–57:169–178.

——1982. The Bau'a Ceremonial Hunting Lodge: An Alternative to Initiation. In G. Herdt, ed., *Rituals of Manhood: Male Initiation in Papua New Guinea*, pp. 155–200. Berkeley: University of California Press.

Schneider, David M. 1968. *American Kinship: A Cultural Account*. Englewood Cliffs, N.J.: Prentice-Hall.

Schwartz, Theodore. 1973. Cult and Context: The Paranoid Ethos in Melanesia. *Ethos* 1:153–174.

——1978. Where Is the Culture? Personality as the Distributive Locus of Culture. In George Spindler, ed., *The Making of Psychological Anthropology*, pp. 419–441. Berkeley: University of California Press.

Schwimmer, Eric. 1980. Power, Silence and Secrecy. *Toronto Semiotic Circle, Monograph No. 2*. Toronto: Victoria University.

Seligman, C. G. 1910. *The Melanesians of British New Guinea*. Cambridge: Cambridge University Press.

Serpenti, L. 1984. The Ritual Meaning of Homosexuality and Pedophilia Among the Kimam-Papuans of South Irian Jaya. In G. Herdt, ed., *Ritualized Homosexuality in Melanesia*, pp. 292–317. Berkeley: University of California Press.

Shils, Edward. 1956. *The Torment of Secrecy*. Glencoe: The Free Press.

Shostak, Marjorie. 1981. *Nisa: the Life and Words of a !Kung Woman*. New York: Vintage Books.

Shweder, Richard A. 1979. Rethinking Culture and Personality Theory: Part I. *Ethos* 7:255–278.

——1984. Anthropology's Romantic Rebellion Against the Enlightenment, or There's More to Thinking than Reason and Evidence. In R. Shweder and R. LeVine eds., *Culture Theory*, pp. 27–66. New York: Cambridge University Press.

Shweder, Richard and E. J. Bourne. 1984. Does the Concept of the Person Vary Cross-Culturally? In *Culture Theory*, pp. 158–199. New York: Cambridge University Press.

Shweder, Richard A. and Robert A. LeVine., eds. 1984. *Culture Theory*. New York: Cambridge University Press.

Silvan, M. 1981. Reply to Alan Roland's Paper on "Psychoanalytic Perspectives on Personality Development in India. *International Review of Psycho-Analysis* 8:93–99.

Simmel, George. 1950. *The Sociology of George Simmel*, Kurt H. Wolff, ed. and trans. Glencoe, Ill: Free Press.

Sinclair, James P. 1966. *Behind the Ranges*. Melbourne: Melbourne University Press.

Singer, Milton. 1961. A Survey of Culture and Personality Theory and Research.

In Bert Kaplan, ed., *Studying Personality Cross-Culturally*, pp. 9–90. New York: Harper and Row.

—— 1980. Signs of the Self: An Exploration in Semiotic Anthropology. *American Anthropologist* 82:485–507.

Singer, Peter. 1980. Dictator Marx? *New York Review of Books*, September 25, pp. 62–66.

Sontag, Susan. 1966. *Against Interpretation*. New York: Farrar, Straus, Giroux.

—— 1982. *A Susan Sontag Reader*. London: Penguin Books.

Sørum, A. 1982. The Seeds of Power: Patterns in Bedamini Male Initiation. *Social Analysis* 10:42–62.

—— 1984. Growth and Decay: Bedamini Notions of Sexuality. In G. Herdt, ed., *Ritualized Homosexuality in Melanesia*, pp. 318–336. Berkeley: University of California Press.

Spiegel, John P. 1976. Cultural Aspects of Transference and Countertransference Revisited. *Journal of the American Academy of Psychoanalysis* 4:447–467.

Spindler, George D. 1970. *Being an Anthropologist: Fieldwork in Eleven Cultures*. New York: Holt, Rinehart, and Winston.

Spiro, Melford E. 1964. Religion and the Irrational. In J. Helm, ed., *Symposium on New Approaches to the Study of Religion*, pp. 102–115. Seattle: American Ethnological Society and University of Washington Press.

—— 1968a. *Burmese Supernaturalism*. Englewood Cliffs, New Jersey: Prentice-Hall.

—— 1968b. Virgin Birth, Parthenogenesis, and Physiological Paternity: An Essay in Cultural Interpretation. *Man* 3:242–261.

—— 1979. Whatever Happened to the Id? *American Anthropologist* 81:5–13.

—— 1982. *Oedipus in the Trobriands*. Chicago: University of Chicago Press.

—— 1986. Cultural Relativism and the Future of Anthropology. *Cultural Anthropology* 1:259–286.

Spradley, James P. 1979. *The Ethnographic Interview*. New York: Holt, Rinehart, and Winston.

—— 1980. *Participant Observation*. New York: Holt, Rinehart, and Winston.

Spradley, James P. and David McCurdy. 1972. *The Cultural Experience*. Chicago: Science Research Associates.

Stein, Howard F. 1982. The Ethnographic Mode of Teaching Clinical Behavioral Science. In N. J. Chrisman and T. W. Maretzki, eds., *Clinically Applied Anthropology*, pp. 61–82. Boston: Reidel.

Stephen, Michele, ed. 1987. *Sorcerer and Witch in Melanesia*. New Brunswick: Rutgers University Press.

Stocking, George W., Jr. 1968. *Race, Culture, and Evolution: Essays in the History of Anthropology*. New York: Free Press.

—— 1974. Empathy and Antipathy in the Heart of Darkness. In R. Darnell, ed., *Readings in the History of Anthropology*, pp. 281–287. London: Harper and Row.

—— 1980. Innovation in the Malinowskian Mode: An Essay Review of Long-term Field Research in Social Anthropology. *Journal of the History of the Behavioral Sciences*. 16:281–286.

—— 1983. The Ethnographer's Magic: Fieldwork in British Anthropology from Tylor to Malinowski. In *Observers Observed: History of Anthropology*, 1:70–120. Madison: University of Wisconsin Press.

Stoller, Paul. 1982. Beatitudes, Beasts, and Anthropological Burdens. *Medical Anthropology News*. 13:1–10.

Stoller, Robert J. 1968. *Sex and Gender*, vol. 1. New York: Science House.
—— 1973. *Splitting*. New York: Quadrangle.
—— 1975a. *Perversion*. New York: Pantheon.
—— 1975b. *Sex and Gender*, vol. 2. London: Hogarth.
—— 1979. *Sexual Excitement*. New York: Pantheon.
—— 1985a. *Observing the Erotic Imagination*. New Haven: Yale University Press.
—— 1985b. *Presentations of Gender*. New Haven: Yale University Press.
Stoller, Robert J. and R. H. Geertsma. 1963. The Consistency of Psychiatrists' Clinical Judgments. *Journal of Nervous and Mental Disease*. 137:58–66.
Stoller, Robert J. and Gilbert Herdt. 1982. The Development of Masculinity: A Cross-Cultural Contribution. *Journal of the American Psychoanalytic Association*. 30:29–59.
—— 1985. Theories of Origins of Homosexuality: A Cross:cultural Look. *Archives of General Psychiatry* 42:399–404.
Strathern, Andrew J. 1969. Descent and Alliance in the New Guinea Highlands: Some Problems of Comparison. *Proceedings of the Royal Anthropology Institute of Great Britain and Ireland for 1968*, pp. 37–52.
—— 1972. *One Father, One Blood*. Canberra: Australian National University Press.
Strathern, Marilyn. 1972. *Women in Between*. London: Seminar Press.
—— 1978. The Achievement of Sex: Paradoxes in Hagen Gender-thinking. In E. C. Schwimmer, ed., *The Yearbook of Symbolic Anthropology*, pp. 171–202. London: C. Hurst.
—— 1980. No Nature, No Culture: The Hagen Case. In C. P. MacCormack and M. Strathern, eds., *Nature, Culture, and Gender*, pp. 174–222. Cambridge: Cambridge University Press.
—— 1981. Culture in a Netbag. The Manufacture of a Subdiscipline in Anthropology. *Man* 16:665–88.
—— 1988. *The Gender of the Gift*. Berkeley: University of California Press.
Sullivan, Harry S. 1937. A Note on the Implications of Psychiatry, the Study of Interpersonal Relations, for Investigations in the Social Sciences. *American Journal of Sociology* 42:848–861.
Taylor, Charles. 1985. The Person. In M. Carrothers, S. Collins, and S. Lukes, eds., *The Category of the Person*, pp. 257–281. New York: Cambridge University Press.
Tedlock, Dennis. 1983. *The Spoken Word and the Work of Interpretation*. Philadelphia: University of Pennsylvania Press.
Thomas, Elizabeth Marshall. 1959. *The Harmless People*. New York: Knopf.
Turnbull, Colin. 1961. *The Forest People*. New York: Simon and Schuster.
—— 1972. *The Mountain People*. New York: Simon & Schuster.
Turner, Victor. 1960. Muchona the Hornet. In J. B. Casagrande, ed., *In the Company of Man*. New York: Harper.
—— 1964. Symbols in Ndembu Ritual. In M. Gluckman, ed., *Closed Systems and Open Minds: The Limits of Naiveté in Social Anthropology*, pp. 20–51. Chicago:Aldine.
—— 1967. Betwixt and Between: The Liminal Period in Rites de Passage. In *The Forest of Symbols*, pp. 93–111. Ithaca, N.Y.: Cornell University Press.
—— 1968. Mukanda: The Politics of a Non-Political Ritual. In M. Schwartz et al., eds., *Local-Level Politics*, pp. 135–150. Chicago: Aldine.
—— 1978. Encounter with Freud: The Making of a Comparative Symbologist. In

George D. Spindler, ed., *The Making of Psychological Anthropology*, pp. 58–583. Berkeley: University of California Press.

Tuzin, Donald F. 1975. The Breath of a Ghost: Dreams of the Fear of the Dead. *Ethos* 3:555–578.

——1976. *The Ilahita Arapesh*. Berkeley: University of California Press.

——1980. *The Voice of the Tamberan: Truth and Illusion in Ilahita Arapesh Religion.* Berkeley: University of California Press.

——1982. Ritual Violence Among the Ilahita Arapesh: The Dynamics of Moral and Religious Uncertainty. In G. Herdt, ed., *Rituals of Manhood: Male Initiation in Papua New Guinea*, pp. 321–355. Berkeley: University of California Press.

Tyler, Stephen A. 1978. *The Said and the Unsaid: Mind, Meaning, and Culture*. New York: Academic Press.

Vogt, Evon Z. 1979. The Harvard Chiapas Project: 1957–1975. In G. M. Foster et al., eds., *Long-Term Field Research in Social Anthropology*, pp. 279–301.

Wagner, Roy. 1967. *The Curse of Souw: Principles of Daribi Clan Definition and Alliance*. Chicago: University of Chicago Press.

——1972. *Habu: the Innovation of Meaning in Daribi Religion*. Chicago: University of Chicago Press.

——1975. *The Invention of Culture*. Englewood Cliffs, N.J.: Prentice-Hall.

Warner, W. Lloyd. 1941. Social Anthropology and the Modern Community. *American Journal of Sociology* 46:785–796.

Wallace, Anthony F. C. 1969. *Culture and Personality*. 2d ed. New York: Random House.

Warwick, Donald P. 1980. *The Teaching of Ethics in the Social Sciences*. Hastings-on-Hudson, N.Y.: The Hastings Center.

Watson, James B. 1960. A New Guinea Opening Man. In J. B. Casagrande, ed., *In the Company of Man*, pp. 127–173. New York: Harper.

——1964. Anthropology in the New Guinea Highlands. In J. B. Watson, ed., *New Guinea: The Central Highlands, American Anthropologist* (special Issue) 66, 4 (part 2): 1–19.

——1972. Epilogue: In Search of Intimacy. In S. T. Kimball and J. B. Watson, eds., *Crossing Cultural Boundaries*, pp. 299–302. San Francisco: Chandler.

Watson, James D. 1968. *The Double Helix*. New York: New American Library.

Weiner, Annette B. 1978. The Reproductive Model in Trobriand Society. In J. Specht and P. White, eds., *Trade and Exchange in Oceania and Australia. Mankind* (special issue) 11:150–174.

——1980. Reproduction: A Replacement for Reciprocity. *American Ethnologist* 7:71–85.

——1985. Oedipus and Ancestors. *American Ethnologist* 12:758–762.

Werner, Oswald and Donald T. Campbell. 1970. Translating, Working Through Interpreters, and the Problem of Decentering. In R. Naroll and R. Cohen, eds., *A Handbook of Method in Cultural Anthropology*. Chicago: Rand-McNally.

White, Geoffrey M. and J. Kirkpatrick, eds. 1985. *Persons, Self, and Experience*. Berkeley: University of California Press.

Whiting, John W. M. 1941. *Becoming Kwoma*. New Haven: Yale University Press.

Whiting, J. W. M., I. L. Child, and W. W. Lambert, et al. 1966. *Field Guide for the Study of Socialization*. Six Cultures Series, vol. 1. New York: Wiley.

Williams, F. E. 1936. *Papuans of the Trans-Fly*. Oxford: Clarendon Press.

——1940. *Drama of Orokolo*. Oxford: Oxford University Press.

Wittaker, J. L., N. G. Gash, J. F. Hokey, and R. C. Lacey. 1975. *Documents and Readings in New Guinea History: Prehistory to 1889*. Brisbane: Jacaranda Press.

Young, Michael N. 1971. *Fighting with Food*. Canberra: Australian National University Press.

——1979. *The Ethnography of Malinowski*. London: Routledge & Kegan Paul.

Zwigman, Charles. 1973. The Nostalgic Phenomenon and Its Exploitation. In C. Zwingman and M. Fister-Ammende, eds., *Uprooting and After*, pp. 19–47. New York: Springer-Verlag.

Index

Aatmwunu (full adult manhood), 57; *see also* Initiation; Masculinization
Aberle, D., 413*n*130
Adam, B., 126, 434*n*17
Adultery, 65, 72, 75, 417*n*10
Affinal ties, 75, 76, 79, 80, 83
Agar, M., 404*n*3, 407*n*61, 408*n*84, 410*n*103, 411*n*212, 436*n*1
Alland, A., 22
Analysts, *see* Psychoanalysts
Anthropology, vii-viii, 3-4, 26-27, 88, 137, 351, 352, 360, 407*n*7, 434*n*14, 434*n*22; cultural, 18-19; Mead on, 407*n*60, 408*n*90; women as, 408-9*n*90, 409*n*93
Asad, T., 405*n*13
Ashley-Montagu, M. F., 82
Atkinson, J. M., 1, 2, 434*n*21

Bachelors, 57, 58, 67, 71, 131-32; *see also* Initiation
Bamboo flutes, 58
Barnes, J. A., 405*n*13, 410*n*106, 412*n*122
Barth, F., 26, 57, 409*n*96, 417*n*8
Barzun, J. 409*n*91
Bateson, G., 25, 88*n*, 150, 151, 430*n*4, 435-36*n*6
Becker, E., 388
Bellow, S., 432*n*15
Benedict, R., 20, 21, 24, 404*n*6, 406*nn*39, 41
Bennett, J. W., 404*n*3

Berndt, R. M., 82
Bettelheim, B., 82
Bisexuality, 58, 126; *see also* Homosexuality
Blackwood, B., 26
Blackwood, E., 2
Blood revenge, 130
Boas, F. 20, 431*n*6
Bock, P. K., 412*n*120, 413*n*138
Bohannan, P., 407*n*59
Bourguignon, E., 377, 404*n*3, 407*n*61, 408*n*73, 435*n*38
Bowen, E. S., 19
Breast-feeding, 68, 137, 427*n*17; and orgasm, 72, 415*n*10; *see also* Penjukwi; Tali; Weiyu
Breast milk: biological growth, 65; strength, 66-67, semen transformation, 66, 68, 76-77; *see also* Tree sap
Briggs, J. 405*n*16, 406*n*43
Brody, E. B., 436*n*44
Brown, P., 246
Burgess, R. G., 431*n*6

Carrier, J., 2, 353, 434*nn*17, 19
Casagrande, J. B., 405*n*18, 408*n*74
Cassowary meat, 67
Chagnon, N. A., 411*n*115
Chalmers, Rev. J., 407*n*62
Chapple, E. D., 32, 408*nn*85, 87, 89
Charisma, 8*n*

Chemonyi (as erotic play), *see* Erotic play
Children, 93, 108*n*; discipline of, 251*n*
Chodorow, N., 1
Chowning, A., 425*n*6
Classical ethnography, 28; *see also* Ethnography
Clay, B., 407*n*67
Clifford, J., 5; and G. Marcus, 5, 28, 408*n*71, 437*n*7
Clinical ethnographers: ethics, 391-94; training, of 32-36, 381-94; *see also* Transference
Clinical ethnography, xiii, 1, 10, 15-52, 352-53; Durkheim's collective consciousness, 366; ethics, 244, 245, 391-94; global perspectives, 31; repeated observations in, 31; shared culture, 366-67; situational perspectives, 31; training of, 32-36, 381-94; transference in, 372-79; trust, 30, 244; *see also* Anthropology; Ethnography; Methodology; Participant-observation
Cohler, B., 363
Cole, M., 28
Collier, J. F. and M. Z. Rosaldo, 63
Commodity, sexual and reproductive fluids, 82, 414*n*7; Marxist sense of, 60; *see also* Semen value
Communication, 7, 96; complexity of, 92-93; intimate, 7, 49-50; Melanesia, 97-98
Conception, *see* Procreation
Confederacies, 55
Countertransference, 6, 287*n*, 328, 374, 375, 388, 393; *see also* Transference
Crapanzano, V., 366, 404*n*6, 405*n*20, 408*n*72, 412*n*121, 415*n*1, 416*n*4, 417*n*15, 431*n*6, 433*n*5, 435*n*36, 437*n*7; on hermeneutics, 24, 29, 407*n*65; on transference/counter-transference, 376, 436*n*46
Creed, G. W., 433*n*11
Cult, *see* Initiation; Ritual cult
Cult house (and shamans), 214
Cultural anthropology, *see* Anthropology
Cultural relativism, 33, 40, 362, 366
Culture, 2, 366; and experience

principles, 23, "public culture," 168-69
Culture shock, 4, 38-43, 375, 411*nn*112, 115-18

D'Andrade, R., 367
Davenport, W. H., 413*n*134
Daydreams, *see* Fantasy
DeMille, R., 426*n*11
Detachment, 50-51
Devereux, G., 5, 23, 28, 30, 31, 87-88, 320, 345, 363, 374-75, 390, 403*n*3, 404*n*9, 407*n*61, 408*n*82, 413*n*134
Dialogues, 87, 349-50, 428*n*7; *see also* Interviewing; Sex talk
Disengagement, 431*n*5
Division of labor, 55
Divorce, 64
Doi, T., 388, 412*n*118, 433*n*4, 436*n*50
Douglas, M., 82
Dover, K. J., 356
Dreams, 92, 97, 415*n*2; cultural interpretations, 383; Freud, 435*n*32; wet, 60, 72, 104, 415*n*10; *see also* Fantasy
Dubois, C., 19, 366, 403*n*1, 408*n*73, 413*n*133, 415*n*1
Dumont, J.-P., 405*n*16, 407*n*65
Durkheim, E., 366, 406*n*32

Edgerton, R. B. and L. L. Langness, 32-33, 38, 367, 408*n*71, 411*n*109, 412*n*123
Editing process, 395-401; confidentiality, 399; as methodology, 400; style, 397-98; trust, 400-1; *see also* Ethnography
Effeminacy, 425*n*7
Ego, 91
Elkin, A. P., 26, 403-4*n*5
Ellis, H., 354-55
Epstein, T. S., 44
Erikson, E., 408*n*83
Erotic looking, 239*n*; Moondi on, 107-11
Erotic play (*chemonyi*), 61-62, 70-71, 72, 77, 83, 415*n*10; defined, 61-62; direct sexual transactions, 70; indirect sexual transactions, 77; life-

cycle changes, 71; *see also* Homoerotism

Erotics, vii, viii, 1, 2; defined, 1, 2; and gender, 353-72

Erotism, 170, 273, 285; cross cultural study of, 349, 350, 352, 356, 362; *see also* Erotics; Moondi

Ethics, 244, 245, 391-94

Ethnographer, xi-xii, 28-29, 50, 51; intervention by, 200; observer bias, 16-17, 27; personal characteristics of, 199, 363

Ethnography, viii, xiii, 2, 4, 15, 20, 25-29, 88, 405*n*17; classical, 15, 28; conscious/unconscious experience, 372-73; criticisms of, 27; defined, 27-28, 406*n*31; editing process, 395-401; emergence of, 15; experimental, 2, 3, 5, 9*n*, 405*n*15; field report, 15, 25, 27; process, 17, 25; science, 20; styles, 19, 28; subjectivity, 9, 16; supervision, 389, 391; *see also* Clinical ethnography; Ethnographer

Ethnoscience, 3, 24

Evans-Pritchard, E. E., 21, 26, 88, 323*n*, 406*n*32, 407*n*67, 430*n*1

Experience, private, 6, 97; conscious/unconscious, 372-73, 416*n*4

Experimental ethnography, *see* Ethnography

Faithorn, E., 60, 426*n*10

Fantasy, 116*n*, 118*n*, 363, 375, 417*n*1; *see also* Dreams

Federn, P., 414*n*6

Feil, D. K., 404*n*3, 426*n*10

Fellatio, 62, 71, 72, 73, 77, 137, 428*n*2, 429*n*10; erotic reversal, 285; homosexual inseminations, 62, 65, 66, 67, 69, 74-75, 76, 79-80; homosexual teaching of, 57-58, 427*n*18; pederastic, 73, 283, 284, 285; *see also* Breast-feeding; Homosexuality; Semen; Taboos

Females: attitudes towards, 55-56; menarche, 56, menstrual hut, 57; *tingu* (menstrual blood organ), 56, 64; *see also* Feminization; Women

Feminization, 95, 152, 416*n*3; *see also* Penjukwi

Fetishism, 126-27, 263, 368-69, 370, 414*n*7

Field life, 48-52; adjustment to, 51-52; communication, 49-50; data collection, 48; living arrangements, 48; participant observation, 50; respect, 50

Fieldwork: changes between 1920-1970, 33-34; criticisms against, 17; entry, 36-38; identity problems, 43-44; informant, 44-48; training for, 32-36; *see also* Culture shock; Field life; Participant-observation

Firth, R., 19, 83

Flutes, bamboo, 58

Forge, A., 47, 80, 413*n*137

Fortes, M., 407*n*62

Fortune, R. F., 26, 406*n*38

Foster, G. M., 38-39

Foster, G. M. et al., 409-10*n*97, 411*n*111

Foucault, M., 355-56, 359, 408*n*80, 413*n*129, 417*n*11, 434*n*12

Foulks, E. F., 390, 436*n*44

Free association, 116*n*, 417*n*1

Freeman, J. D., 426*n*11

Freilich, M., 17, 405*n*18, 407*n*66, 408*nn*74, 85-86, 420*n*2

Freud, S., 7*n*, 91, 350, 356, 359, 361, 362, 377, 388, 389, 406*n*36, 414*n*6, 415-16*n*2, 426*n*11

Friedl, E., 434*n*13

Functionalism, 21, 22, 23

Geertz, C., 20, 29, 88, 361, 366, 372, 406*n*42, 407*nn*58, 67, 408*n*77, 413*n*128, 430*n*1, 433*n*2, 435*nn*24-25, 36; the ethnography, 17, 405*n*17, 406*n*25, 413-14*n*1, 414*n*3; ethnoscience, 24; experimentation and the oedipal complex, 405*n*15; "privacy theories of meaning," 405*n*24; relativism, 403*n*2

Gell, A., 72, 82

Gender, viii, 1, 2, 56, 63-64, 93; attitudes, 56; definition, 2; differentiation, 63-64; identity, vii, 1-2, 89, 353-54, 361, 416*n*3; stereotypes, 367-68; study of, 353, 355, 362; theoretical treatment of, 2;

see also Erotics; Feminization; Masculinization

"Gentle" man (*aambei-wutnyi*), 112-13, 246, 247, 248; compared with rubbish man, 249; *see also* Imano

Gewertz, D., 426n10

Giddens, A., 404n9, 405n11

Gill, M. M., 397n; and I. Z. Hoffman, 397n

Glasse, R. M. and M. J. Meggitt, 82

Gluckman, M., 29, 406n45

Godelier, M. 54

Goffman, E., 98

Golde, P., 405n18, 408n74

Gorutndun (Sambia man), 385-86, 429n9

Gregor, T., 358, 417n10

Gronewald, S., 413n139

Growth, biological, 65-66, 73; *see also* Semen

Habermas, J. 404n1

Haddon, A. C., 26, 408n69

Haldipur, C. V., 436n44

Hallowell, A. I., 435n25

Hallpike, C. R., 405n11, 406n37

Hamlets, 55

Harris, M., 29, 405n11

Hayano, D. M., 412n125

Healey, A., 326, 328, 396

Heider, K., 406n50, 414n6

Herdt, G. H., 10, 126, 133, 246, 405n21, 406n30, 408n81, 412nn119, 126; 414nn2, 5, 417nn5, 8, 418nn4, 5, 6, 421nn8, 9, 10, 423n3, 428n1, 432n17, 433n1, 434n15, 435nn31, 33, 35, 41, 436nn4, 47; erotic play, 42, 61; gender and personhood, 93, 94, 175n, 416n3; gender research, vii, viii, 1, 2, 360, 425n3; guided imagery, 417n1; informants, 37n, 45-46, 339; initiation, 57, 58, 105, 251; language, 431n10; parthenogenesis, 97, 365; Sambia sexual culture, 53, 56, 190, 356, 419n14, 424n10; semen transactions, 70, 71, 73, 76; semen valuation, 59, 60, 63, 65, 66, 67, 82; shamanism, 69, 213, 214; trees, genderization of, 68

Herdt, G. and J. Davidson, 423n1; and F. J. P. Poole, 56, 81, 357, 434n15, 435n33; and R. J. Stoller, 2, 10, 380, 408n81, 413n136

Hermaphroditism, 203, 315, 318, 423nn1, 4-5; *see also* Sakulambei; Sex typing; Shamanism

Heterosexuality, 58, 62, 73, 96-97, 118, 126; heteroerotic play, 71; relationship to homosexuality, 58-59, 72, 126-27; transition to, 58

Hogbin, I., 407n67

Holism, 21

Homoerotism, 62, 70, 71, 72, 75, 120, 126; homoerotic play, 62, 70, 71; *see also* Fellatio; Homosexuality

Homosexual behavior, 1, 74, 83-84, 428n2; *see also* Fellatio; Homoerotism; Homosexuality

Homosexuality, 57-58, 62, 65, 70, 71, 74, 75, 76, 84, 320, 418n8, 427n19; insemination, 65, 69, 415n12; *see also* Fellatio; Homoerotism; Kalutwo; Semen transactions

Honigmann, J. J., 416n4

Human Relations Area Files, 26

Hymes, D., 405n13

Iaamoonaalyu (tree mother's milk), 68; *see also* Breast milk

Id, 91

Idealism, Hegelian, 437n13

Imano ("gentle" man), 246-78; biographical sketch, 246-53; erotism, 254-78; foreplay, 273; tree sap, 263-64, 266-67

Imbimboogu (orgasm), *see* Orgasm

Imperato-McGinley, J., et al., 423n5

Informant, 44-48, 331n; ideal, 46; as interpreter, 46-47; role of, 45; *see also* Interpreter; Tali; Weiyu

Initiation, 56, 96; fifth stage (*taiketnyi*), 57, 68; first stage (*moku*), 56-57; fourth stage (*nuposha*), 57; second stage (*imbutu*), 57; sixth stage (*moondangu*), 57, 68; third stage (*ipmangwi*), 57, 58, 418n8

Insemination, *see* Erotic play; Procreation; Semen

Insight, 417n1

Intermarriage, 80, *see also* Marriage
Interpretive anthropology, 4, 16, 22-25; *see also* Anthropology; Interpreter
Interviewing, 10, 23, 98-100, 360, 384; dialogues, 87; obstacles, 197, 198; passive-aggressive, 345; resistance in, 112, 113, 288, 339-40; transference, 197, 199; translation problems, 88; *see also* Communication; Ethics
Interpreter, 46-48, 301, 323-46, 350, 428n7; bias, 282; compared with translator, 323n; Moondi (Sambia man), 325, 326, 327; personal characteristics of, 324; role of 47; Weiyu (Sambia man), 325-46

Jerungdu (strength), 55, 213n; *see also* Semen; Strength

Kakar, S., 362, 388, 433n4, 435n29-30
Kalutwo (Sambia man), 279-322, 384; biographical sketch, 279-85; erotic dreams, 289-92; first-stage initiation, 286-89; homosexual behavior, 280, 284, 305, 306; semen organ, 312-17, 319; shamanism, 303-12, 315
Kardiner, A., 3, 35
Katchadourian, H. A. and D. T. Lunde, 434n20
Keesing, R. M., 408n79, 435n40
Kelly, R., 75, 407n67, 415n12
Keriku-keriku (semen organ), 56, 332n; *see also* Kalutwo
Kimball, S. T. and J. B. Watson, 408n74
Kluckhohn, C. et al., 3
Knauft, B. M., 433n11, 434n15
Kohut, H., 4, 405n24, 433n2
Kracke, W. H., 388, 404n6, 407n64, 408nn70, 72, 437n7
Kracke, W. and G. Herdt, 404n9
Kroeber, A. L., 355, 371
Kwoli hamlet, 153
Kwoluaatmwol ("turnim-man"), 203; *see also* Hermaphroditism
Kwooluku (shamanism), *see* Shamanism

La Barre, W., 403n5, 410n99
La Farge, O., 19, 413n130
Langness, L. L., 56, 82, 417n7, 430-31n4
Langness, L. L. and G. Frank, 403n1
Language, semantics, 144n, 375, 431n10; Melanesia, 430n4; sexual metaphors, 60-61
Lanternari, V., 406n47
Leach, E. R., 29, 78, 82, 404n5, 405n10, 407nn57, 67
Leenhardt, M., 407n62
LeVine, R. A., 1, 5, 21, 88, 362, 379, 403nn2, 3, 404n9, 406n28, 408nn70, 82, 416n4, 435n38, 436nn1, 42, 51; "inter-cultural research relationship," 25; methodology, 436n51; person-centered ethnography, 4, 23, 405nn19-20, 88; self, domains of, 364
LeVine, S., 408n72
Levi-Straus, C., 21, 27, 84, 388, 406nn35, 55, 410n98, 412n121
Levy, R. I., 318, 405n16, 408n83, 415n1, 416n4
Lewis, O., 403n1
Lindenbaum, S., 8, 54, 82
Littlewood, R., 436n44
Lululai ("head-man"), 153

MacCannel, D., 37n
Mailer, N., 397n
Malcolm, J., 417n11, 436n5
Males: adulthood, 56, 57; initiation, 56-57; semen organ, 56; *see also* Masculinization
Malinowski, B., 1, 23, 82, 359, 405nn10, 12, 406nn40, 52, 407n67, 408n78, 416n4, 417n10, 431n6; culture shock, 42-43; diaries, 6, 403n5, 408n75; the ethnography, 26, 27, 29, 404n6; fieldwork, 19, 20, 352; methodology, 15, 21, 22; oedipal complex, 363, 435n31
Marcos, L. R., 324-25
Marcus, G. and D. Cushman, 25, 403n3, 404n2, 405n17, 434n22
Marcus, G. and M. Fisher, 414n3, 430n1
Marriage, 54-55, 57, 63, 64, 79, 84,

117*n*, 120*n*, 156*n*, 158; *see also* Penjukwi; Semen value

Marx, Karl, 60, 414*n*7

Marxism, and commodities, 23, 60

Masculinization, 56-57, 65, 66, 94, 251, 365, 416*n*3; initiation system, 56-57; secret cult, 56, 57

"Master," 161-62

Masturbation, 58, 60, 121, 274, 415*n*8, 419*n*14

Mead, M., 2, 60, 82, 345, 404*n*6, 406*nn*44, 48, 49, 407*n*67, 408*nn*75, 77, 409*n*95, 410*n*106, 412*n*119, 413*nn*1, 134, 142, 416*n*4, 430-31*n*4, 433*n*9, 434*n*, 435*n*, the ethnography, 21, 22, 24, 27, 377; fieldwork, 19-20, 36-37, 50, 404*n*8, 408*n*76; fieldwork training, 32, 33-34, 436*n*48; "gentle" males, 246, 248, 425*n*5; sexual privacy as barriers to research, 357, 358, 361, 433*n*9; women as anthropologists, 408-9*n*90, 409*n*93; and R. Bunzel, 33-34

Meggitt, M., 60, 82, 404*n*3, 406*n*51, 407*n*67

Meigs, A., 59, 73, 82, 358

Meintel, D. A., 412*n*118

Melanesia, fieldwork in, 25-26; language, 430

Menarche, 56, 95, 96, 122

Menstrual blood, 60; *tingu* (menstrual blood organ), 56, 64

Menstrual hut, 57; Messenger, J. C., 413*n*134

Methodology, ix, 21-22, 111-12, 150, 292, 400, 410*nn*99, 102, 436*n*51; *see also* Clinical ethnography; Participant-observation

Misogyny, 130, 386-87, 420*n*6, see also Weiyu

Moerman, D. E., 435*n*23

Moffic, S., et al., 437*n*8

Mon (Sambia man), 203-4

Moondi (Sambia bachelor), 101-27; biographic sketch, 101-6; erotic daydreams, 116-25; erotic looking, 107-11; on "gentle" males, 112; homoerotism v. heteroerotism, 118-19, 120; incest taboos, 114-15

Moraitis, G., 397

Munn, N., 407*n*67

Murray, J. H. P., 407*n*62

Murray, S. O., 2, 426*n*11

Nabokov, P., 28

Nader, L., 32, 33

Narangu (shaman cult house), 214

Naroll, R., 430*n*3

Narratives, *see* Sex talk; Talk

Nauta, D., 417*n*13

Newman, P., 82, 407*n*67

Nilutwo (Sambia man), 156-60, 218*n*, 219*n*, 383-83; biographical sketch, 156-157

Nonexperimental ethnography, 2

Nose-bleeding, 384, 424*n*10, 427*n*20

Numelyu (spirit familiars), *see* Spirit familiars

Oberg, K., 39-40, 411*nn*112, 114, 411-12*n*117

Obeyesekere, G., 366, 405*n*20, 408*n*72, 416*n*4, 435*n*34

Objectivity/subjectivity dichotomy, 3

Observer bias, 16-17, 27; *see also* Ethnographer; Ethnography

Oedipal complex, 362, 435*n*31

Open Forum, 437*n*11

Orgasm (*imbimboogu*), 61, 70, 137, 144*n*; *see also* Breast-feeding; Penjukwi

Ornston, D., 359

Ortner, S. and H. Whitehead, 1

Owusu, M., 406*n*26, 431*n*6, 434-35*n*22

Pandanus nuts, 65, 68; *see also* Growth; Tree sap

Panoff, M., 82

Parin, P., F. Morgenthaler, and G. Parin-Matthey, 408*n*82, 436*n*43

Parsons, A., 407*n*65, 408*n*70, 436*n*45

Parthenogenesis, myth of, 97, 365

Participant-observation, 15, 16, 17, 18-22, 24, 25, 27, 29, 34, 35-36, 56, 371, 377-78, 385, 413*n*138; degrees of, 35-36; principles of, 18-22; *see also* Clinical ethnography; Methodology; Subjectivity

Patrilineality, 54, 78-79

Paul, B., 431*n*6
Pelto, P. J. and G. H. Pelto, 431*n*6, 435*n*40, 436*n*1
Penjukwi (Sambia woman), 135, 136*n*137, 152-201, 387, 388; biographical sketch, 152-60; erotic dreams, 172-92; fellatio, 189-90; orgasm, 160-71, 175; tattoos, 192-95
Person-centered ethnography, LeVine on, 4, 23, 88, 405*n*19-20
Personhood, 69, 77, 93, 94-95, 98; *see also* Feminization; Masculinization; Self; Thought
Pettit, P., 84
Philosophic behaviorism, and Geertz, 24
Phratries, 55
Polygyny, 63
Poole, F. J. P., 82, 412*n*125, 417*n*8
Popper, K. R., 437*n*13
Positivism, 89, 351-52
Powdermaker, H., 17, 45, 409*n*92, 431*n*6, 437*n*9
Price-Williams, D., 304, 429*n*12
Procreation, 62-65, 72, 73, 83, 332*n*, 425*n*6
Productive work, 63; *see also* Procreation
Psychoanalysis, viii, xi-xiii, 3, 5-6, 8, 9, 16, 90-02, 351, 352, 362, 404*n*7
Psychoanalyst, *see* Psychoanalysis
Psychodynamic process, 5

Rabinow, P., 407*n*66, 413*n*127
Radcliffe-Brown, A. R., 20, 21, 22, 403-4*nn*5-6, 405*n*12, 407*nn*56, 67
Rappaport, R., 406*n*45, 407*n*67
Read, K. E., 2, 18, 28, 57, 64, 82, 246, 358, 388, 403-4*n*5, 405*n*16, 406*n*32, 408*n*71, 417*n*6, 434*n*15
Reay, M., 82
Reisman, P. 45, 407*n*65
Relativism, *see* Cultural relativism
Religion, 83, 155, 406*n*32; *see also* Spirituality
Reports of the Cambridge Expeditions to the Torres Straits (1901–1933), 406*n*29
Ricoeur, P., 17, 356, 408*n*83, 436*n*49

Ritual cult, deterioration of, 365, 384-85
Rituals, 55, 93, 96, 121-22, 146*n*, 365; *see also* Secrecy; Taboos
Rivers, W. H. R., 26
Robin, R., 410*n*107
Roe, A., 409*n*92
Róheim, G., 121, 370, 406*n*53
Rosaldo, M. Z. and L. Lamphere, 1
Ross, E. and R. Rapp, 361
Rossi, A., 1
Rubbish man, 246, 247-48, 368; compared with "gentle" man, 249; Kalutwo as, 281
Runciman, W. G., 7

Sacred and profane, 61, 96
Sahlins, M., 246, 434*n*14
Sakulambei (hermaphrodite), 202-45; biographical sketch, 202-10; dreams, prophetic, 205, 211-18; hermaphroditism, 202, 203, 221, 225-32; sexual exploitation of, 232-43; shamanism, 218-29
Sambia culture: division of labor, 55; dress codes, 419*n*12; ethnographic sketch, 54-84; gender relationships, 55-56, 64, 65-66, 93, 99; semen value, cultural ideas of, 59-69; semen value, social transactions, 69-81; social change, 98, 426*n*10; social organization and economy, 54-55, 420*n*7; traditionalism, 280
Sapir, E., 25, 29, 352, 404*n*6-7, 406*n*27, 433*n*6
Schieffelin, E. L., 69, 415*n*12
Schneider, D. M., 405*n*19
Schwartz, T., 367, 420*n*2, 435*n*38
Schwimmer, E., 411*n*110, 417*n*12
Secrecy, 96-97, 168-69; male cults, 56, 57, 74, 365; myth-telling, 365; whispering, 138*n*; *see also* Rituals; Taboos
Self, 90-92, 95-96, 350, 360, 361, 364; *see also* Personhood; Psychoanalysis; Thought
Seligman, C. G., 26
Semen, 53, 58-59, 414*n*6; biological growth, 65-66; cycle of, 67; depletion, 62, 67, 141; political

power of, 76; procreation, 62-65; replenishment, 67, 77; scarce commodity, 60, 62, 75, 80, 83, 414n7; spirit familiars, 69; spirituality, 68-69; strength, 66-68; transactions, 69-81; transformer compared with transmitter, 59; value of, 59-81
Semenology, 415n9
Semen organ, 56, 332n; *see also* Kalutwo
Semen transactions, 70-81, 84; delayed exchange, 79-81; direct, 70-76; indirect, 76-81
Semen value: cultural ideas, 59-69; defined, 59-60; social transactions, 69-81; *see also* Marriage
Serpenti, L., 75
Seventh-Day Adventists, 155
Sex (*duvuno*), defined, 2, 60, 65, 415n8
Sex assignment, *see* Sex typing
Sex talk, 356-57, 358, 360, 363, 432n16; *see also* Ethnography
Sex typing, 56, 203, 423n5; *see also* Hermaphroditism
Sexual and reproductive fluids, 63-64, 81-82; *see also* Menstrual blood; Semen
Sexual behavior: conflict in, 72-73; forms of, 58; reciprocity in, 61, 71; *see also* Heterosexuality; Homosexuality
Sexual culture, 53-84
Sexual excitement, 169-71, 370; *see also* Fetishism; Stoller, R. J.
Sexual intercourse, 56, 60, 65; *see also* Erotic play; Erotism; Marriage
Sexual metaphors, 60-61
Sexual taboos, *see* Taboos
Shamanism, 203, 205, 208, 213, 216n, 303, 304, 311n, 429nn12, 13; *see also* Dreams; Shamans
Shamans, 57, 216n; *see also* Kalutwo; Sakulambei; Shamanism
Shame (*wungulu*), 97, 108n, 338
Shils, E., 417n11
Shostak, M., 2
Shweder, R. A., 29, 362, 403n4, 433n7
Shweder, R. and E. J. Bourne, 435n23

Shweder, R. A. and R. A. Levine, 403n4, 436n42
Silvan, M., 435n29
Sinclair, J. P., 407n62
Singer, M., 355, 403n5, 433n6
Singer, P., 437n13
Social change, *see* Sambia culture
Social Darwinism, 20, 46
Social organization, *see* Sambia culture
Social reproduction, 64, 77, 81
Sontag, S., 45, 360, 407n59
Sørum, A., 75, 415n12
Soul (*Koogu*), 68, 96
Spiegel, J. P., 436n44
Spirit familiars (*numelyu*), 68, 69, 204, 222n
Spirituality, 68-69, 73
Spiro, M. E., 82, 352, 360-62, 408n88, 412n119, 416n4, 429n12, 435n24
Spradley, J. P., 410n102, 411n112, 413n132
Stephen, M., 94
Stocking, G. W., Jr., 404n6, 405n10
Stoller, P., 434-35n22
Stoller, R. J., viii, 92, 170n, 350, 353, 355, 361, 368, 400, 419n15, 425-26n7, 435n28
Stoller, R. J. and R. H. Geertsma, 396
Stoller, R. J. and G. Herdt, 2, 10, 127, 356, 408n81, 414n2, 432n17, 433n1
Strathern, A. J., 82, 407n67
Strathern, M., 1, 82, 392, 405n14, 414n2, 417n8, 434nn15, 21, 435n
Strength (*jerungdu*), 66-68, 73, 74; *see also* Semen
Subjectivity, 1, 2-3, 4, 7, 8, 16, 30, 51, 89, 119, 123n, 346, 360, 395-401; *see also* Ethnography; Methodology; Participant-observation; Self
Suicide, 421n1
Sullivan, H. S., 403n3
Superego, 91

Taboos: avoidance, 56, 110; incest, 70, 114-15, 418n8; postpartum, 66, 138, 257; sexual, 2, 56, 70, 126, 285
Tali (informant), 128-51; biographical sketch, 128, 130-33, 134; orgasm and

breast-feeding, 138-41; tree sap, 141-50; wife-stealing, 134-37
Talk, 23-24; *see also* Sex talk
Tattoos, 195*n*; *see also* Penjukwi
Taylor, C., 7
Tedlock, D., 5, 87, 406*n*26, 413*n*135, 417*n*16, 430*n*1
Theory of meaning, 408*n*79
Therapy, cross-cultural, 417*n*2
Thompson, E. M., 406*n*46
Thought (*Koontu*), 69, 95-96, 97, 118, 143; *see also* Personhood; Self
Tingu, see Menstrual blood
Transference, 197, 199, 212, 287*n*, 319-20, 382, 383; in clinical ethnography, 372-79
Translator, 317-18, 323; *see also* Informant; Interpreter; Interviewing
Tree sap, 68, 77-79, 141, 142*n*; *see also* Semen transactions; Tali; Weiyu
Trust, 30, 196-97, 244, 400-1, 429*n*9; compared with truth, 376-77
Turnbull, C., 406*n*33-34
Turner, V., 276, 346, 406*n*54, 413*n*130, 420*n*2, 428*n*24
Tuzin, D. F., 74, 97, 430-31*n*4, 435*n*33, 436*n*2
Tyler, S. A., 408*n*79

Vogt, E. Z., 413*n*140

Wagner, R., 82, 404*n*7, 407*n*67, 411*n*112, 414*n*4, 417*n*16, 435*n*34

Wallace, A. F. C., 367, 405*n*24
Warfare, 55, 81, 93-94, 98
Warner, W. L., 411*n*116
Warwick, D. P., 437*n*12
Watson, J. B., 246, 410*n*100, 413*n*131, 417*n*7
Watson, J. D., 407*n*68
Weiner, A. B., 82, 435*n*37
Weiyu (Sambia man), 128-51, biographic sketch, 128-30, 133, 134; as interpreter, 325-46; orgasm and breast-feeding, 138-41; tree sap, 141-50; wife-stealing, 134-37
Werner, O. and D. T. Campbell, 431*n*6
White, G. M. and J. Kirkpatrick, 436*n*42
Whiting, J. W. M., 434*n*15
Whiting, J. W. M., I. L. Child, W. W. Lambert et al., 325, 376, 430*n*1, 431*n*6, 432*n*14
Wife-stealing, 134-37; *see also* Marriage
Williams, F. E., 26, 57, 73, 407*n*67
Wittaker, J. L., N. G. Gash, J. F. Hokey, and R. C. Lacey, 26, 410*n*101
Women, 388, 422*n*; as commodities, 72, 80; secret cults, 56, 168-69; suppression of, 162*n*; *see also* Females; Feminization; Gender identity; Penjukwi

Young, M. N., 404*n*5, 407*n*67, 412*n*119
Yumalo (Sambia man), 204-5